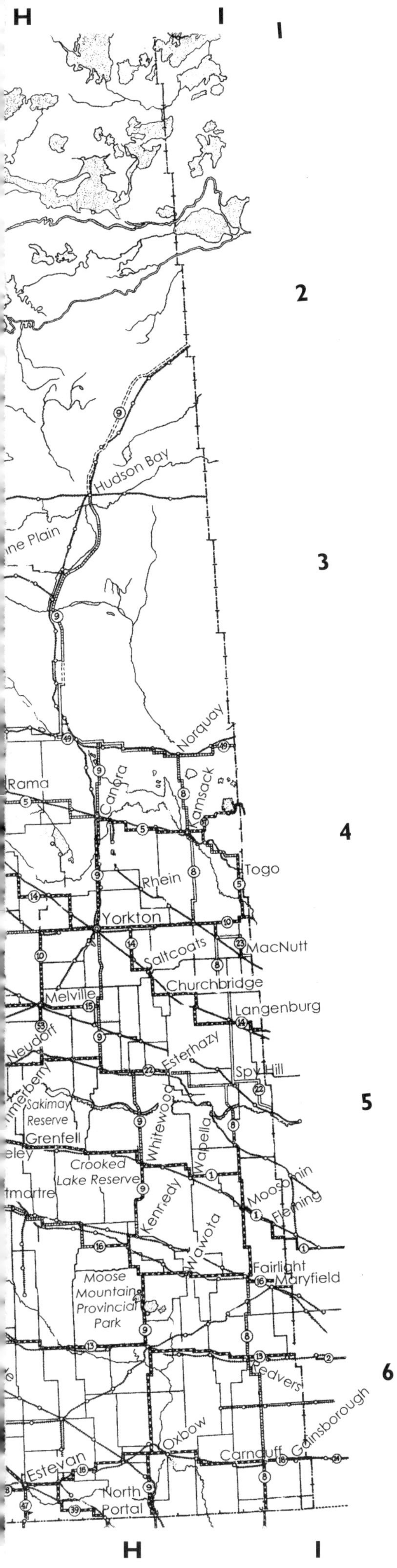

HOME TOWNS OF SASK

Admiral B6
Ahtahkakoop (Sandy Lake Reserve) D2
Allan D4
Alsask D4
Aneroid C6
Asquith C3
Assiniboia E6
Avonlea E5
Aylsham G2

Balcarres G5
Battleford B3
Beechy B5
Belle Plaine E5
Bengough E6
Bethune E5
Big River C3
Biggar C3
Birch Hills E2
Bladworth D4
Blaine Lake D3
Blucher D3
Borden C3

Cabri B5
Canora H4
Canwood D2
Carlyle H6
Carnduff I6
Carrot River G2
Central Butte D5
Chamberlain E5
Chelan G3
Churchbridge I5
Climax B6
Colonsay E4
Condie F5
Corinne F5
Craik E4
Craven F5
Creelman G6
Crooked Lake Reserve H5
Cudworth E5
Cupar F5

Debden D2
Delisle C4
Dinsmore B4
Divide A6
Dodsland B4
Domremy E3
Drake F4
Duck Lake D3
Dunblane D4
Dundurn D4
Dysart F5

Eastend B6
Elfros G4
Esterhazy H5
Estevan H6
Eston B4
Ettington D6

Fairlight I6
Fielding C3
Fillmore G6
Fleming I5
Flin Flon I1
Floral D3
Foam Lake G4
Fort Qu'Appelle G5
Frobisher H6
Froude G6

Gainsborough I6
Goodsoil A1
Gravelbourg D6
Grenfell . .
Gull Lake .

Hafford . .
Harris . . . .
Hazlet B5
Hearne E5
Herbert C5
Holdfast E5
Hudson Bay H3
Humboldt F3

Indian Head G5

Jansen F4

Kamsack I4
Kelvington G3
Kennedy H5
Kerrobert A4
Kindersley A4
Kinistino E3

La Ronge E0
Lac La Ronge E0
Lac Pelletier C6
Lafleche D6
Laird D3
Landis B3
Lang F6
Langenburg I5
Lanigan F4
Lashburn A2
Leask D2
Liberty E4
Lloydminster A2
Loon Lake A1
Lucky Lake C5
Lumsden F5
Luseland A3

MacNutt I4
Major A4
Manor H6
Maple Creek A6
Maryfield I6
Meadow Lake B1
Melaval D6
Melfort F3
Melville H5
Mervin B2
Meskanaw E3
Milestone F6
Montmartre G5
Moose Jaw E5
Moose Mountain H6
Moosomin I5
Mortlach D5
Muskeg Lake Reserve D3
Naicam F3
Neilburg A3
Neudorf G5
Neville C6
Nipawin F2
Nokomis F4
Norquay H4
North Battleford B3
North Portal H6

Odessa G5
Ogema F6
Osler D3
Oungre G6
Oxbow H6

Paddockwood E2
Paradise Hill A2
Pense F5
Piapot Reserve F5
. . . . . A5

Prince Albert E2
Prud'homme E3
Punnichy F4

Quill Lake F3

Radville F6
Rama H4
Red Pheasant Reserve E3
Redvers I6
Regina F5
Rhein H4
Rosetown B4
Rosthern D3
Rouleau F5

Sakimay Reserve H5
Saltcoats H4
Sandy Lake Reserve (Ahtahkakoop) D2
Saskatoon D3
Sceptre A5
Scott B3
Sedley F5
Semans F4
Shackleton B5
Shaunavon B6
Shellbrook D2
Silton F5
Sintaluta G5
Snowden F2
Speers C3
Spy Hill I5
Star City G3
Strasbourg F4
Summerberry G5
Sutherland D3
Swift Current C5

Tisdale G3
Togo I4
Tuberose B5

Unity A3

Val Marie C6
Vanguard C6
Vibank G5
Vonda D3

Wadena G4
Wakaw E3
Waldheim D3
Wapella I5
Warman D3
Waskesiu D1
Watrous E4
Watson F3
Wawota H6
Webb B5
Weyburn G6
Whitewood H5
Wilcox F5
Wilkie B3
Wolseley G5
Wynyard F4

Yellow Grass F6
Yorkton H4
Young E4

Zealandia C4
Zehner F5

Source: Saskatchewan Archives Board

SASKATCHEWAN SPORTS LEGENDS

One Hundred Years of Athletic Distinction

John Chaput

Johnson Gorman Publishers

 (continued on page 328)

PUBLISHED BY
Johnson Gorman Publishers
Distributed in Canada and the USA by
Fitzhenry & Whiteside Limited
195 Allstate Parkway
Markham ON Canada L3R 4T8

CREDITS
Cover design by Kal Barteski, iDeaMonsters, Winnipeg
Text design by John and Evelyn Chaput
Front cover images, top, left to right, courtesy of Gene Suignard, Frank and Margaret Puhl, Ron Estay, Bogetti-Smith Photography (www.bogetti.com), Andrew Klaver Photography and Scott Paper Ltd., Jim Hunter.
Front cover images, bottom, left to right, courtesy of Claus Andersen, Saskatoon *StarPhoenix* (2, 4 and 5), Gerry Thomas, Regina *Leader-Post,* Saskatoon Public Library Local History Room.
Back cover images, top, left to right, courtesy of Saskatchewan Baseball Hall of Fame (1, 2 and 4), Saskatchewan Sports Hall of Fame and Museum, and Yorkton Sports Hall of Fame and Museum.
Back cover images, bottom, left to right, courtesy of: Indian Head Rural Sports Hall of Fame, Joe Daley, Saskatchewan Baseball Hall of Fame (3 and 6), Lyle Helland, and Saskatchewan Sports Hall of Fame and Museum.
Author photo: Evelyn Chaput.

ACKNOWLEGEMENTS
Financial support provided by the Alberta Foundation for the Arts,
a beneficiary of the Lottery Fund of the Government of Alberta.

Alberta Foundation for the Arts

NATIONAL LIBRARY OF CANADA CATALOGUING IN PUBLICATION
Chaput, John, 1955–
Saskatchewan sports legends : 100 years of athletic distinction / John Chaput.
Includes bibliographical references and index.
ISBN 0-921835-72-8
1. Sports—Saskatchewan—History. I. Title.
GV697.A1C425 2004   796'.097124   C2004-902685-2

5 4 3 2 1

PRINTED IN CANADA

CONTENTS

ACKNOWLEDGEMENTS

IF YOU ENJOY THIS BOOK, THE CONTRIBUTIONS AND HELP PROVIDED BY THE PEOPLE LISTED HERE MADE IT possible. If you don't, it's my fault; they sure gave me enough to work with.

My sincere gratitude is extended to:

My publisher, Dennis Johnson. Thanks for initiating the project and for not complaining when the manuscript was late.

Everyone I interviewed: Roger Aldag, Red Berenson, Jan Betker, Johnny Bower, Murray Brace, Garnet Campbell, Ed Chynoweth, Wendel Clark, Joe Daley, Darrell Davis, Lorne Davis, Ray Elgaard, Bernie Federko, Sylvia Fedoruk, Norm Fieldgate, Rick Folk, Norm Fong, Emile Francis, Terry Harper, Bill Hay, Lorne Henning, Billy Hicke, Dale Hoganson, Brad Hornung, Gordie Howe, Jim Hunter, Dale Isaac, Diane Jones Konihowski, Daisy Junor, Bobby Jurasin, Lynn Kanuka, John Konihowski, Ron Lancaster, Patti Lank, Catriona Le May Doan, Rueben Mayes, Deb McCormick, Joan McCusker, Mick McGeough, Bernadette McIntyre, Jack McLeod, Bryan Murray, Bert Olmstead, Vera Pezer, Ned Powers, Metro Prystai, Terry Puhl, George Reed, Ernie Richardson, Dave Ridgway, John Rittinger, Roy Romanow, Terry Ruskowski, Fred Sasakamoose, Tom Shepherd, Gregg Sheppard, Stacy Singer, Kathy Thiele, Tim Tisdale, Bryan Trottier, the late Bob Turner, Ted Urness, Charlie Wickenheiser, Hayley Wickenheiser, Brian Williams. Some of you ended up on the literary equivalent of the cutting-room floor, but your insight expanded my knowledge and is very much appreciated. Some of you also contributed terrific photographs for which I am doubly grateful.

Gordie Howe again, for providing the Foreword during a time of great personal trial. Del Reddy and Aaron Howard at Power Play International were also a great help.

Some dedicated people who keep history alive: Dale West, Jacqueline Campbell and Sheila Kelly at the Saskatchewan Sports Hall of Fame and Museum; Tim Novak of the Saskatchewan Archives Board; Jean Nelson at Athol Murray College of Notre Dame; Dave and Jane Shury of the Saskatchewan Baseball Hall of Fame in Battleford; Ken McCabe of the Indian Head Rural Sports Hall of Fame; Don Hilsendager of the North Battleford Sports Hall of Fame and Museum; Vern Pachal and Don Pfeiffer at the Yorkton Sports Hall of Fame; Hugh Henry of the Swift Current Museum; Bill Smiley of the Prince Albert Historical Society; Don and Elva Turner of the Turner Curling Museum in Weyburn; Barb Silvester at the Moose Jaw Public Library; Craig Campbell of the Hockey Hall of Fame; and, Andrea Earl of the Manitoba Sports Hall of Fame.

Some newspaper people who were especially helpful: Cam Hutchinson, Bob Florence and Doug McConachie of the *Saskatoon StarPhoenix*; Rob Clark of the *Moose Jaw Times-Herald;* Roy Antal of the *Regina Leader-Post;* Keith Solomon of the North Battleford *News-Optimist* and Anne Sandeson of the *Wadena News.* Most of all, Gregg Drinnan, a great mentor and friend, who contributed some priceless background material and proofread the manuscript.

Robin Wilson of Whitewater Communications and photographer Andrew Klaver for the photographs of Team Schmirler and to people who contributed other photos, research and resource material: Paul Dojack, Billy Warwick, Doug Maxwell, Dick Irvin, Joey Weinmeister, Lyle Helland, Chick Baker, Alex McFadyen, Ernie Iluk, Herb Pinder Jr., Greg Prpich, Gene Suignard, Marv Kereluke, Don Turner, Tom Schmidt, Jay Mah, Eric Zweig and Bill Argan.

Blair Stonechild and Solomon Ratt of First Nations University for their help with Saskatchewan history and Cree spelling, respectively.

Whoever I have inadvertently omitted.

Finally, my wife Evelyn. Thanks for the transcribing, proofreading, coffee and constructive criticism.

FOREWORD

A LOT OF PEOPLE REALLY DON'T UNDERSTAND SASKATCHEWAN. I remember a train ride about 40 years ago, when I was travelling from Calgary to Regina, and I heard people snickering. It was some Americans, laughing that they hadn't seen a tree yet. They didn't realize what the prairie is all about.

He can still drive it, and Howe!

No, there weren't many trees outside the cities then, but if you watched closely you could see an antelope. Even someone who has lived a lifetime in the bush, who hasn't seen anything past the next tree or the next bluff, would come here and marvel at how you can see the weather coming for two days. That's a big help, you know, when you're on some place like Lac La Ronge and the wind blows up a little cold.

I grew up in Saskatoon, but it wasn't until after I became a professional hockey player and came home in the offseason that I really got to see a lot of Saskatchewan—Prince Albert, Regina, Moose Jaw and dozens of small towns in between. I was received very well all around the province, especially when I travelled with the Bentley brothers to play baseball and softball. That was easy; if you wanted to get some attention, go eat with the Bentleys from Delisle, they were so popular. Fishing also took me to a lot of places I had never seen before, like La Ronge and Waskesiu. I'll never forget boating on Saskatchewan's lakes with the clean water, the tall trees and those big fish!

Our sports were definitely shaped by our surroundings. Soccer was very popular when I was in school. Honestly, you can put a soccer field almost anywhere you want in the province, and you wouldn't have to do much grooming other than to put in the goals. It was the same way with baseball and football; maybe we didn't have the best equipment, but we didn't have to look far for a place to play.

As for golf, it is amazing how many courses have been built, especially with the scarcity of trees we had back then. I was a lucky kid because I got to work a couple of summers at the Waskesiu golf course and get some golfing in on that exciting course with all those trees and animals. There are few courses like that south of the tree line, and it amazes me that our golfers are as good as they are with the short season they have.

But Saskatchewan people aren't much for excuses. It's funny that one excuse I hear from some kids now is that Mom and Dad don't come to see them play hockey. My father was a very hard-working individual, and my mother didn't get around too well, so the first time they saw me play in Saskatoon was when the East Side played the West Side. The second time was when I was engraved with the Red Wings emblem, and we played an exhibition game in my home town. I had a bet with my coach for that game. He said I wouldn't score a goal. He was right. I scored five.

When kids are very small and can't get around, they definitely need their parents' help. As for me, I had to walk or skate down the road to my next game. I think the best thing I had going for me was King George School. It had good ice, always available if we wished to help ourselves to it.

What helped me a great deal when I became a teenager was that I was playing hockey with a lot of others that would finally make it to the big time. I was the beneficiary of stiff competition that made me a better hockey player. That love of competition is something you'll find deep in the heart of all great Saskatchewan athletes. We believe we can be as good as anyone, and we'll prove it by going up against the best we can find, whatever the situation or the obstacles.

Some of our best curlers have come from the cities, like Regina's Richardsons and Saskatoon's Joyce McKee

Gordie Howe (back row) wearing lucky No. 13 with the Bruins midget team in Saskatoon, about 1942

and Rick Folk. Others like Garnet Campbell and Sandra Schmirler have proved that champions can also emerge from small towns like Avonlea and Biggar. The Saskatchewan Roughriders remain competitive and stable in the smallest market in the CFL. George Genereux became an Olympic gold medal winner in trapshooting when he was still a high school student. My fishing buddy Johnny Bower was 35 years old when he played his second full NHL season, but he went on to win four Stanley Cups and a place in the Hockey Hall of Fame. Hayley Wickenheiser's love of hockey has led to a lifetime of playing against boys, older women, and finally men in her drive to improve her skills, and she has never looked out of place on the rink. Finally, there are countless swimmers, track and field stars, speed skaters, and participants in virtually every sport who have become champions and world-class athletes through hard work and the desire to compete.

That is what has to be understood about Saskatchewan and prairie people. The land goes on and on, the winters are brutal, and it's a long way to the nearest town, city or game. Yet we insist on being as much a part of Canada, and the world, as anyone or anyplace else.

I am so proud that Saskatchewan was my home. If there's one thing I'd want to say on the occasion of the provincial centennial, I guess I would be like a coach and say, "Don't change a thing. Keep working on the same lines." When the time came for me and my wife Colleen to raise our family, we had to do what was best for our children, and that meant settling in Detroit. To all of you who have remained in Saskatchewan, I say, "Well done. You have made it a beautiful and popular place."

Best wishes,

Mr. Hockey

Gordon Howe

PREFACE

"OUR BIGGEST EXPORT HAS NOT BEEN WHEAT, IT'S BEEN PEOPLE."

So Sylvia Fedoruk told me in one of 65 interviews conducted for this book. Saskatchewan celebrates its 100th year as a Canadian province in 2005, and few people have been so vitally involved with Saskatchewan as Sylvia Fedoruk. She was born and raised in Canora, left the province during the Second World War, returned to become a pioneer in cancer-fighting radiation physics and interrupted her retirement to serve as Lieutenant-Governor from 1988 to 1994.

Sylvia Fedoruk, 1947

She has spent many of her 70-plus years in Saskatchewan as an enthusiastic and accomplished athlete, an Olympic hopeful in the javelin and discus until she threw out her right shoulder in 1948, a terrific shortstop in softball, and third on Joyce McKee's team that won the first two Canadian women's curling championships in 1960 and '61.

Fedoruk has witnessed the exodus, the steady flow of young people leaving the province to pursue professional opportunities. That has been especially true in sports, where our hockey players head to the NHL, our football players no longer go to the Roughriders except by chance, and our best amateur athletes must move to larger cities for the better facilities and coaching they will have there.

We understand the situation, accept it, and maintain the connection. When they achieve their success, we share in their joy and satisfaction. Usually, they acknowledge their roots, and our affection and appreciation for them grows all the more.

Yet, no matter how many of them leave Saskatchewan, others take their place. This province that can't sustain a population of even one million people keeps churning out Olympic gold medallists, NHL stars, major-league baseball players, you name it.

This is not a small book. I believe the quality of people and achievements contained on these pages are a chronicle worthy of any Canadian province, any American state. After spending two years researching, writing, and rewriting this material, I only have this to say:

I apologize for everything that had to be left out.

Saskatchewan Sports Legends is not meant to be a comprehensive history so much as a collection of facts and stories about the most interesting athletes to emerge from, or compete in, Saskatchewan. Some people will be disappointed at the exclusion of certain parties, to which I can only say Saskatchewan's living skies may hold infinite space, but this book's covers cannot.

INDIANS AND OTHER HUMAN BEINGS

In some official circles, it is policy to refer to people of First Nations ancestry as "Aboriginal" people. It's short, it's not as unwieldy as "First Nations people" and it doesn't carry the baggage of old labels like "Indian" or "native." This book's manuscript began with "Aboriginal" as its *mot juste*, with a capital A as preferred by First Nations University in Regina.

Then the author spent many hours on the telephone and in the company of Fred Sasakamoose, who never used anything but "Indian" to comfortably and proudly identify himself, his family and his people. Finally, there was coffee with David Acoose, grandson of Paul Acoose, Saskatchewan's first nationally recognized star athlete.

"Indian is fine with me, that's what I've always called myself," David said. "Heck, Indian, First Nations, indigenous, it doesn't matter. Just don't call me Aboriginal. To me, Aboriginals are native people who live in Australia. I'm not Australian, I'm Canadian, a Canadian Indian."

If David Acoose isn't comfortable being called "Aboriginal," I'm sure not going to refer to his *omosôma* as one, thank you.

Likewise, George Reed, who in his time has seen North American people of his race popularly referred to as coloured, Negro, black, Afro-American and African-American (though rarely, thank God, Afro- or African-*Canadian)*, is just fine being black. So, in my experience, is every athlete of that race I've encountered.

Since political correctness trembles with every passing breeze but good character stands resolute, the terms "Indian" and "black" are commonly used in this book out of respect for the people of good character who use them to describe themselves.

This is a book about sports and the lives of the people in them. Nearly all of them were adults at the time of their achievements. Mature language and subjects may be included.

–John Chaput

"Goddammit, guys . . . you mean we spent the afternoon talking God when we could have been talking hockey?"
–Rev. Athol Murray, 1971

Dedicated to Evelyn, who married me on September 1, 1979—the 74th anniversary of the establishment of Saskatchewan as a province—and who helped me make a home here.

Alex Decoteau breezes to the finish line in one of his road race victories

1905–1919

First Steps

ARRIVALS

July 9, 1905: Clarence Campbell, NHL president (1946–77), Fleming.
January 22, 1908: Sinclair Ross, writer, Shellbrook.
September 20, 1908: Ernest Manning, Alberta premier (1943–68), Carnduff.
August 7, 1909: Dorothy MacKenzie Walton, badminton player, Swift Current.
September 10, 1910: Harry Thode, nuclear scientist, Dundurn.
August 31, 1911: Gas Eichel, boxer, Condie.
July 17, 1912: Art Linkletter, television personality, Moose Jaw.
October 13, 1912: Max Bell, newspaper publisher, Regina.
July 16, 1913: Woodrow Lloyd, premier (1961–64), Webb.
July 31, 1913: Bryan Hextall Sr., hockey player, Grenfell.
March 13, 1914: W.O. Mitchell, author, Weyburn.
January 23, 1915: Noel MacDonald, basketball player, Mortlach.
November 30, 1915: Henry Taube, chemist (Nobel laureate 1983), Neudorf.
February 23, 1916: George Abel, hockey player, Melville.
March 5, 1916: Phyllis Dewar, swimmer, Moose Jaw.
May 25, 1916: Brian Dickson, Supreme Court of Canada chief justice (1984–90), Yorkton.
September 3, 1916: Doug Bentley, hockey player, Delisle.
May 24, 1917: Ross Thatcher, premier (1964–71), Neville.
November 17, 1917: Roderick Neil "Scotty" Munro, hockey coach/executive, Shackleton.
January 22, 1918: Elmer Lach, hockey player, Nokomis.
February 22, 1918: Sid Abel, hockey player, Melville.
November 26, 1918: Ossie Herlen, boxer, Star City.
July 10, 1919: Mary Baker, softball/baseball player, Regina.

DEPARTURES

October 30, 1917: Alex Wuttunee Decoteau, runner, 29.
August 14, 1918: Lyman "Hick" Abbott, hockey player, 25.
August 24, 1918: Harry MacKenzie, hockey player, 25.
November 2, 1918: Hugh Cairns, soccer player, 21.

SASKATCHEWAN'S FIRST ATHLETES WERE THE INDIGENOUS PEOPLE WHO LIVED HERE CENTURIES BEFORE anyone of European descent saw the prairie. There was nothing of what we know today as "organized sport," however, until white Canadians—most notably the men of the North-West Mounted Police— entered the Saskatchewan and Assiniboia sections of the North-West Territories, the sections that in 1905 would form the province of Saskatchewan.

Many of the policemen were of British descent and engaged in the pastimes of the "mother country." Diaries record cricket matches being played at Fort Walsh (near what is now Maple Creek) as early as October 1876, the year after the garrison was built, and spreading as far north as Prince Albert within 20 years. "Football" in the nineteenth century referred exclusively to soccer, which picked up popularity among both the police and the indigenous population. Apparently, the locals caught on quickly; in an early game at Fort Walsh between Indians and Mounties, one of the latter lowered his shoulder into his opponent. The Indian tumbled to the ground and, knowing a foul when he received one, rose with knife in hand. Immediately the Mountie sprinted back to the fort. Peace was soon restored, and the game resumed.

Baseball, an American invention, also got off to an early start with the first recorded game taking place outside Fort Battleford on May 31, 1879, as the side captained by Richard Wyld defeated his brother Robert's team 18–15. The *Saskatchewan Herald* singled out the play at first base of a Mr. Scott; this was Walter Scott, who 26 years later would become the first premier of Saskatchewan. In the interim, Scott would distinguish himself as the editor of the *Regina Leader* and as a pitcher on baseball teams in Regina and Moose Jaw.

The 1888 Regina baseball team with Walter Scott standing at the extreme right

By 1895 baseball's popularity had spread to the extent that the championship for the North-West Territories was held August 1, 1895, at the Regina Exhibition. Moosomin downed Regina in a battle of teams that were bolstered by outside help, but Moose Jaw, whose players slept overnight in Regina in tents rather than risk missing their games because of a late train, toppled Moosomin 10–8 in the final. The champions' lineup included the ubiquitous Walter Scott at second base and left fielder George Tuxford, who would rise to the rank of Brigadier General in the First World War.

Rugby was not so quick to gain acceptance. Apparently, Mounties didn't even play rugby among themselves until 1886. Once the CPR was completed, challenges between distant towns and cities became feasible, and the Regina NWMP team travelled to Winnipeg to face that city's Mounties amid considerable hoopla. Facing a team from beyond its community for the first time in 11 years, the Winnipeg force romped 39–4. Regina salvaged its pride by defeating the Mounted Infantry and also squeezed in some cricket.

Altogether, the excursion was a grand success except for the matter of one fellow who deserted the Regina company.

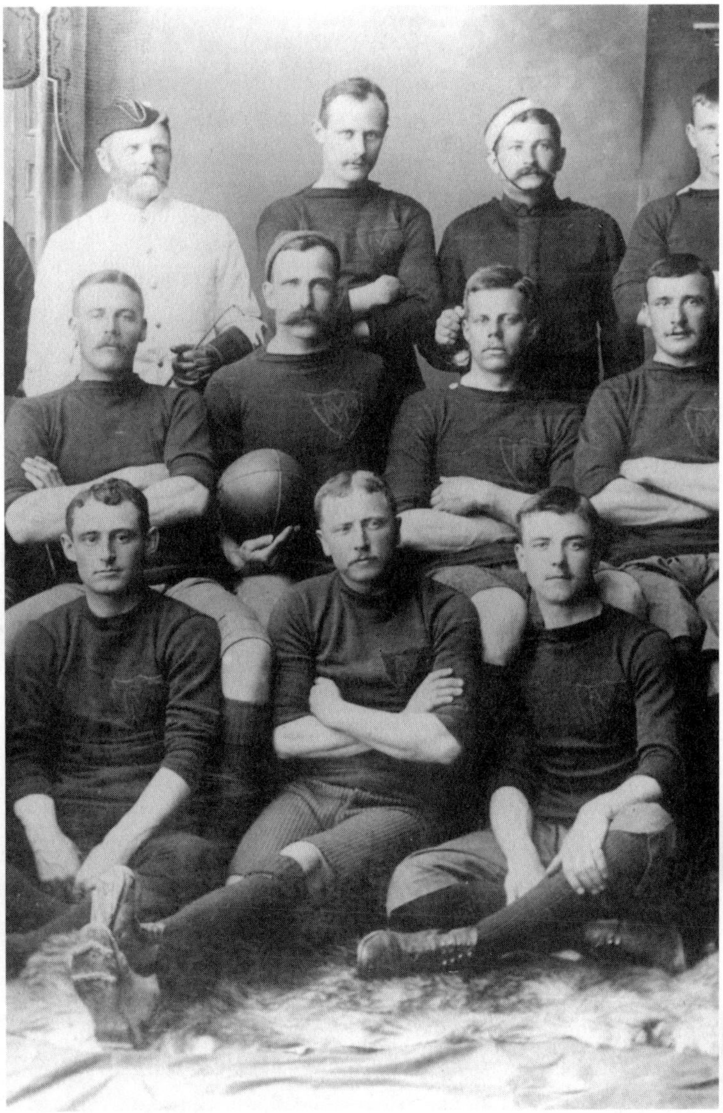

North-West Mounted Police rugby players, 1891

THE PROVINCE'S FIRST YEAR: 1905

From a sporting perspective, the historic year of 1905 got off to a roaring start when the First Territorial Bonspiel—renamed the Regina Bonspiel in future years—began January 16 under the auspices of the Assiniboia branch of the Royal Caledonian Curling Club. With 43 teams and 172 curlers taking part, only Winnipeg boasted a larger bonspiel on the continent. D.R. Anderson defeated G. Hill 12–4 in an all-Sintaluta final to win the Grand Challenge.

Regina Capitals claimed the territorial senior hockey championship, winning all 12 of their games and outscoring their opponents 84–24. Seeking a higher level of competition, the team applied for membership in the Manitoba Hockey League in the summer of 1905 but was denied.

Cricket rivalled baseball for popularity in the summertime. Every edition of the *Regina Leader* included a cricket report, but baseball news was sporadic. Regina's cricket squad thrashed Foxleigh 159–85 in a single-inning match and defeated the Mounted Police by 10 wickets on consecutive June weekends.

The highlight of the baseball season was a mid-September visit to Regina by the Winnipeg Maroons, who topped Regina 4–0 and 6–2 in a pair of exhibitions.

IN HIS OWN WORDS: CARL BATTELL

Carl Battell (1893–1988) was one of Saskatchewan's first home-grown hockey players. He was born in Moose Jaw 11 years after his father settled there in 1882. Carl would play at the highest levels of amateur hockey with teams in Moose Jaw and Regina. He also skipped the Saskatchewan men's curling champions in the 1932 Brier. The following is excerpted from an interview he gave the author for the Moose Jaw Times-Herald *in 1977:*

We played in a little rink that is situated where the Natatorium is now. That rink just had a canvas roof on it at first. They weren't able to complete it for the first year. There weren't any accidents caused by that, but the snow would get on the roof, and they would have to bump it off with long poles.

The game was played much differently. The defencemen were set up differently, for one thing. We were called point and cover point. I played point and was positioned right in front of the goalkeeper with Pallie Pascoe in front of me playing cover point. We played with seven men then. The rover, he was just all over the ice. You couldn't be ahead of the puck; you had to be alongside the puck or behind it, and you couldn't pass forward. Otherwise you were offside. There were no lines on the rink except for the goal crease—no such thing as blue lines.

The point and cover point weren't expected to rush with the puck either but often just flip it down the ice. There was quite a bit of that. I remember before I even played senior hockey that when we played on the street we would practise shooting the puck as high as we could. Once we got indoors, the lighting wasn't as good, and you'd shoot the puck high in the air and it would bounce right down in front of the goal, or even go straight in the goal! We would count on the goalie losing sight of it. Sometimes I scored on those shots, at least occasionally.

Equipment was much different. We never used to wear shoulder pads or anything like that, just shin pads and gloves. There was no such thing as a goaltender's mask. The goalies didn't have a catching glove like they do now, just a little bit of padding in the gloves with both hands the same.

Carl Battell (top) and Pallie Pascoe, Moose Jaw 1907

THE FIRST ATHLETIC STAR: PAUL ACOOSE

Competitive sport was blossoming throughout Saskatchewan, but it had yet to produce an individual or team that would capture the attention of sports enthusiasts beyond its borders. Greatness finally emerged in 1908 when Paul Acoose of the Sakimay Reserve near Grenfell began to run competitively.

Acoose was descended from a line of legendary Saulteaux runners. His grandfather, Qwewitch (also known as Roll of Thunder or Flying Deer), was an exceptional buffalo hunter who lived to the age of 105. In his youth he would shoot arrows on the run while the rest of the party rode on horseback.

Flying Bird, son of Qwewitch, was born around the middle of the 19th century. In time he would become chief of the Sakimay band and, as most Indians were pressured to do once Canadian authority took over the North-West, adopted a new name: Samuel Acoose. Once when the band was short on food, Chief Samuel spotted nine elk and chased them on foot for two days, from Moose Mountain to the Hudson's Bay Company post on Crooked Lake Reserve, a run of about 150 kilometres. Upon reaching the post Samuel stocked up on ammunition, dashed back to the herd, killed it and brought the meat home. Samuel almost achieved Qwewitch's longevity, succumbing at 102.

Paul Acoose achieved manhood at a time when a new order had taken over his homeland, one that viewed running as an exercise in competitive entertainment, not as a means of subsistence. By the age of 25, Paul had been winning races at Grenfell sports days for at least six years but was unknown beyond the Qu'Appelle Valley. Then, on Victoria Day of 1908, a field featuring the province's best runners descended on Summerberry for a five-mile race. Acoose left them all in his wake, finishing in less than 28 minutes. About six weeks later, on Dominion Day, Acoose made a shambles of virtually the same group of runners in a 10½-mile cross-country race at Regina, covering a muddy course in 1 hour 4 minutes 6 seconds—eight minutes ahead of the runner-up.

Acoose entered several races in Winnipeg over the course of the summer, losing at one mile but recording impressive triumphs at three and five miles over rough courses. When he coasted to another five-mile victory in 27 minutes 34 seconds at Winnipeg's Labour Day race, speculation rose as to whether he could challenge Tom Longboat, the Ontario Onondaga who was one of the world's finest marathoners. Suspected of being professional for some time, Longboat openly shed his amateur status after the 1908 Olympics. Acoose himself turned pro in April of 1909, placing himself under the management of William Patterson, future Premier and Lieutenant-Governor of Saskatchewan.

Paul Acoose

Acoose made his pro debut May 17, 1909, in a 15-mile match race at the Winnipeg Arena against England's Fred Appleby, the world champion and record-holder at that distance. The indoor track was 160 yards long, 11 circuits to a mile. Appleby immediately took the lead and maintained it for the first seven miles, averaging 5 minutes 21 seconds per mile with Acoose unflinchingly a couple of strides behind him. Acoose assumed the lead on the eighth mile, which he ran in 4:59, and followed it with a 4:45 that put him right back where he had been—a couple of strides behind Appleby but now with a 158-yard lead. Acoose won by 24 seconds in 1 hour 22 minutes 22 seconds, setting a new world record. Pandemonium erupted as "the redskin was swarmed around by the wildly enthusiastic mobs," according to the *Manitoba Free Press*.

A rematch the following week became a fiasco when someone threw tacks on the track. Acoose had to withdraw when the tacks pierced his moccasins. Appleby and his thick-soled running shoes claimed an uncontested but repugnant victory.

Acoose had only two more significant races in 1909, losing a 15-miler in Winnipeg to Fred Meadows of Guelph and running 12 miles in 1:03:12 to beat a two-man relay team in Victoria, B.C. The indoor season of 1910 held great promise, including a showdown with Longboat himself. A match race scheduled for March 10 in Toronto was postponed when Longboat became ill. Acoose rerouted himself to New York for a 20-mile contest against a seven-man international field at Madison Square Garden on March 15 and finished second.

At last, on March 30, 1910, in Toronto's Riverdale rink, Acoose and Longboat met in what promoters billed as "The Redskin Running Championship of the World." (Not that making hundreds of left turns around the same oval was any Indian's idea of *running*, but this was the promoters talking.) As a race, it did not amount to much. Longboat dropped out after the tenth mile of the 12-mile course. Acoose literally ran him off the track.

It was to be his last significant race. Paul Acoose had grown disenchanted with professional running; perhaps he also recognized that the sport was rapidly losing its appeal. He disliked travel and urban living and longed for the quiet existence he had enjoyed around the Qu'Appelle Valley. Less than two years after becoming a professional, Acoose retired from his sport with $500 in his pocket—only a fraction of his winnings but a good stake for a young farmer in 1910.

Paul Acoose returned to the Sakimay Reserve and remained there until his death in 1978 at the age of 95, an esteemed member of both the Grenfell and Sakimay communities.

The Regina Capitals lacrosse team poses for the camera prior to its two-game Minto Cup championship series in May of 1909. Regina, liberally stocked with players from other provinces, travelled to Vancouver to meet the defending champions from New Westminster, B.C., in a two-game series. The Capitals lost both games, 6–4 and 12–2, and ceased to be a force in lacrosse as most of its best players went to other teams. Regina's best player was the man seated fourth from left: Edouard "Newsy" Lalonde, who would return to Saskatchewan in 1922 as a hockey star with the Saskatoon Crescents.

The 1910–11 Prince Albert Mintos; Rusty Crawford is seated second from left

THE FIRST PRO HOCKEY STAR: RUSTY CRAWFORD

PROFESSIONALISM CREPT STEADILY INTO HOCKEY as the first decade of the twentieth century progressed. Russell "Rusty" Crawford was lured to Saskatchewan to play for the newly formed Prince Albert Mintos in 1909–10. Details and statistics of this season are minimal; Crawford, a left winger who stood 5-foot-11 and weighed 165 pounds, is credited with four goals in three regular season games and one tally in four playoff contests.

Still classified as amateurs while teams tried to establish semi-professional hockey in Alberta and northern Saskatchewan cities, the Mintos became the focus of controversy in February of 1911 when the *Toronto Globe* reported that the team was professional. Crawford and goaltender Bunk Leach were indeed getting paid, and Crawford returned a handsome dividend in his second season with 26 goals in seven games. Officially declared professional after an investigation by the Amateur Athletic Union of Canada, the Mintos were granted the opportunity to challenge for the Stanley Cup. Prince Albert travelled to Winnipeg for a two-game, total-goals series against the Port Arthur (Ont.) Bearcats to determine who would face the Ottawa Senators for the Cup. Port Arthur won both games by 6–3 scores and the privilege of being clobbered 13–4 in its sudden-death showdown with Ottawa. Crawford was a key figure in the first loss, taking five penalties and witnessing three Bearcats goals from the penalty box.

Crawford and Leach joined the Saskatoon Hoo-Hoos (oh yes, they did) for the 1911–12 season. The Hoo-Hoos joined forces with another team shortly before the end of the season to form the Saskatoon Wholesalers and make a stronger challenge for the Cup. Full of confidence, the Wholesalers faced the same Port Arthur Bearcats in Winnipeg for another two-game series and got pulverized 11–1. Rebounding to win the second match 5–1 was small consolation.

Crawford headed back east in 1912 to join the Quebec Bulldogs of the National Hockey Association, forerunner to the NHL. He was at his peak from the 1913–14 through 1916–17 seasons, his 62 goals and 175 penalty minutes in 80 games proving him to be a good offensive player and one of the game's roughest characters.

Crawford spent the NHL's first two seasons (1917–19) with the Ottawa Senators and Toronto Arenas, then returned to Saskatoon for four seasons with the Crescents, the first two as an amateur and the others in the major professional Western Canada Hockey League. He played four seasons in his 40s with the Minneapolis Millers of the American Hockey Association, where on one occasion the players of that league tried to get him thrown out. Apparently, it had something to do with the old geezer injuring three opponents . . . in one game!

REAL PROFESSIONAL BASEBALL UNDER THE PRAIRIE SUN

For all the sometimes thrilling, sometimes rollicking, always tenuous history of professional baseball in Saskatchewan, there has been only one period when the province was included in the realm of sanctioned organized baseball. That was from 1909–21 (excluding the war years of 1914–18) when Moose Jaw, Regina and Saskatoon fielded teams in the Western Canada League, a member of the National Association of Professional Baseball Leagues, the official administrative body of minor-league baseball. Leagues within the National Association sphere enjoyed the benefits of standardized business procedures, limited player control, roster and salary limits, and official classification. The lowest level of professional ball was set at D; the highest, during the Teens and Twenties, was Double-A.

Saskatchewan entered minor league baseball because of the failures of leagues on its borders. The Western Canada League began with four Alberta teams in 1907 but wasn't stable enough to play another season in 1908—a year in which Winnipeg, a well-seasoned city of five Northern League campaigns, found itself in limbo when that Class D loop expired. A new Western Canada League, stretching from Edmonton to Winnipeg, began operations in 1909. All eight teams, including the Moose Jaw Robin Hoods and the Regina Bonepilers (yes, Bonepilers) lasted the entire season.

Although the Medicine Hat Mad Hatters and the Bonepilers had financial problems, the 1910 season began with the same eight teams playing a split season. On July 20, six days after the end of the first half, the Mad Hatters transferred to Saskatoon. The next day, the Berrypickers—you can look it up—drew 3,000 spectators to the Hub City's first official pro ballgame and prevailed 4–2 over the Winnipeg Maroons.

Depending on which source you trust, either the Edmonton Eskimos or Calgary Cowboys were declared league champions. (*The Encyclopedia of Minor League Baseball*, a thoroughly researched reference book and the source of the standings shown on these pages, reports in its Second Edition that the Eskimos and Cowboys were eventually named co-champions.) More historically significant is the case of Richard Brookins, who was driven out of organized baseball because of his skin colour and someone's spiteful desire for revenge. Brookins was one of several light-complexioned blacks who played minor-league ball between 1900 and 1920, usually on teams that tried to pass them off as Indians or Cubans. Unlike most of his kind who were chased out of "white" baseball in a matter of weeks, Brookins actually built up a decent professional resumé, spending 1905 and '06 with Green Bay of the Wisconsin Association and 1908 with Fargo of the Northern League. In 1910 he was the Bonepilers' first baseman.

Lethbridge Miners owner Benton Hatch was livid when Regina acquired a player through Miners manager Chester Cox, who was on the verge of being fired. When Regina rejected Hatch's demand to return the player, Hatch threatened to arrange that "that nigger did not play anymore." The following day Medicine Hat protested a Regina victory on the grounds that Brookins was ineligible. League president C.J. Eckstrom of . . . hmmmm . . . Lethbridge referred the matter to National Association headquarters, which deferred the matter right back to Eckstrom, who, without explanation, upheld the protest.

Whether Brookins was partially of African descent is unproven. An Edmonton newspaper reported his demise with the headline "Alleged Negro has been declared ineligible to play in the Western Canada League." In a 2002 book review, Brookins was redefined as an "apparent African-American." "Blacklisted" seems

Western Canada League game at Dominion Park in Regina, 1913

most appropriate. Brookins never appeared in a National Association league after 1910.

Regina finished dead last (26–69) and was about $1,500 in debt, prompting the league to take over the franchise, then rescind it. Lethbridge also dropped out, leaving the Western Canada League with six teams for 1911. Moose Jaw ran away with the pennant behind the batting of 18-year-old Michigander "Jake" Fournier, who hit .377 and scored a league-leading 106 runs. One year later, Fournier began a major-league career in which he would post a .313 lifetime average over 15 seasons.

Eckstrom found a new way to stick it to Saskatchewan in 1912: eliminate its teams altogether. Eckstrom, who had the leverage as president to pull off a unilateral power play, decreed the league would operate with only four Alberta teams. Happily for those who savour just desserts, Eckstrom's all-Alberta league was an unmitigated disaster, and the Western Canada League was reborn in 1913 under new management with three teams in Alberta and three in Saskatchewan. (Winnipeg rejoined the reborn Class C Northern League.) Saskatoon's team was now the Quakers (named after the religious denomination, not the Quaker Oats company) and Regina's the Red Sox while Moose Jaw remained the Robin Hoods. All three merited distinction in 1913. Saskatoon won the first half of the split-season schedule. Moose Jaw posted the league's best overall record at 68–35, won the second half and beat the Quakers 4–2 in the best-of-seven playoff. (Well, maybe. The last game was protested and ordered replayed by President Frank Gray of Edmonton, but the Robin Hoods' players had dispersed and the team refused to abide by Gray's decision. First the playoff title was awarded to the Quakers; then it was to be shared by both teams. *The Encyclopedia of Minor League Baseball* lists Moose Jaw as the champion.) Regina, deeper in the cellar than your great-grandmother's fruit preserves, included on its roster outfielder Ken Williams, who moved up to Cincinnati in 1915 and stuck in the major leagues until 1929, mostly with the St. Louis Browns. In 1913, however, Williams was overshadowed in his home province by batting champion Roy Mills (.362) of Saskatoon; Fred Weed of the Robin Hoods, league leader in runs (90) and hits (146); and Moose Jaw pitchers Bob Steele (190 strikeouts) and James Concannon (13–3).

At least in 1914, the Red Sox boasted a batting champion in Hap Morse (.344) but the Quakers rode the pitching arm of Sam Beer (23–7) to triumph in a hard-fought four-team pennant race. This, a season

WESTERN CANADA LEAGUE

1909 Standings
Class D

	W	L	Pct.	GB
Medicine Hat	68	33	.673	
Winnipeg	66	38	.635	3½
Calgary	56	44	.560	11½
Lethbridge	51	46	.526	15
Moose Jaw	50	50	.500	17½
Regina	42	53	.442	23
Brandon	37	67	.356	32½
Edmonton	28	67	.295	37

1910 Standings
Class D, split season

	W	L	Pct.	GB
Calgary s1	68	29	.701	
Edmonton s2	61	32	.656	5
Moose Jaw	49	44	.527	17
Winnipeg	53	50	.515	18
M.Hat/Saskatoon	45	47	.489	20½
Lethbridge	40	53	.430	26½
Brandon	41	59	.410	28½
Regina	26	69	.274	42

- Medicine Hat franchise transferred to Saskatoon July 20.
- s1, s2: Calgary and Edmonton won first and second halves, respectively, of split season. Teams declared co-champions.

1911 Standings
Class D

	W	L	Pct.	GB
Moose Jaw	83	28	.748	
Calgary	64	36	.640	13½
Edmonton	52	51	.505	27
Winnipeg	51	52	.495	28
Saskatoon	37	71	.343	44½
Brandon	25	74	.253	54

1912
No Saskatchewan teams.

1913 Standings
Class D, split season

	W	L	Pct.	GB
Moose Jaw s2	68	35	.660	
Saskatoon s1	63	37	.630	3½
Medicine Hat	59	46	.562	10
Calgary	51	56	.477	19
Edmonton	39	57	.406	25½
Regina	29	78	.276	41

- s1, s2: Saskatoon and Moose Jaw won first and second halves, respectively, of split season.
- Playoff: Moose Jaw defeated Saskatoon 4 games to 2.

1914 Standings
Class D

	W	L	Pct.	GB
Saskatoon	71	52	.577	
Moose Jaw	63	52	.548	4
Regina	67	57	.540	4½
Medicine Hat	61	53	.535	5½
Edmonton	53	57	.482	11½
Calgary	37	81	.314	31½

1915–18
League suspended operations.

played nine decades ago, is the pinnacle of professional baseball in the province. Saskatoon opened the season in a new ballpark, the original Cairns Field (though not yet named so), jammed with 6,500 ecstatic fans who watched the Quakers defeat Regina 6–4. Saskatchewan's teams finished 1–2–3 in the standings and enjoyed bountiful attendance until midsummer, when war broke out in Europe, and Canada became involved as a member of the British Empire.

It was announced on November 11, 1914, that the Western Canada League would not play a 1915 schedule. In fact, the league would not resume operations until 1919 and even then would sustain its existence for only three more seasons. *(See 1920–29.)*

1914–15: ALLAN CUP CHAMPIONS IN REGINA AND MELVILLE

The Stanley Cup had been emblematic of hockey supremacy since 1893, but the onset of professionalism led to a new trophy, the Allan Cup, for Canada's national amateur senior champions in 1909. Winnipeg teams held the trophy from 1910–11 through 1912–13, but that season Dick Irvin, star of the defending champion Monarchs, began the season with another team and rendered himself ineligible for Allan Cup play. Suddenly, the Winnipeg dynasty was vulnerable.

Regina boasted an excellent senior team in the Victorias. Austin Creswell supplied superior goaltending, and offensive firepower came from rover Fred Wilson (he of rugby kicking fame), deaf-mute centre Walter Moliski, left wing Frank Mastel and right wing Lyman "Hick" Abbott. Regina went 17–4 in league play but barely survived the two-game, total-goal southern playoff against Melville, winning 7–6 when Abbott's pass from behind the net went in off a skate of Melville defenceman Bob McCutcheon with two minutes to go.

After trampling Battleford and Wolseley for the provincial title, the Victorias downed the Edmonton Dominions 5–2 in Moose Jaw to earn their one-game challenge against the Monarchs on March 13 in Winnipeg. Abbott scored twice in the opening 12 minutes, and Regina captured the Allan Cup by a 5–4 score made deceptively close by two last-minute Monarch goals.

A team from Grand'Mère, Que., poised to challenge the Allan Cup holders, simply travelled further west when the Monarchs lost. Grand'Mère grabbed a 3–0 lead in the early going of the first contest, but Regina responded with six straight goals, won the game 6–4 and the series 10–5.

Abbott enlisted in the army when the Great War broke out and was an infantry captain on the French battlefields by 1916. He was decorated with the Military Cross but died of wounds suffered in battle on August 14, 1918, at the age of 25. The Abbott Memorial Cup was named in his honour and presented to the Western Canadian junior hockey champion until the 1970s. After a brief spell as the prize for the Western Tier 2 junior champion, the Abbott Cup was honourably retired and placed in the Hockey Hall of Fame.

While the Victorias were winning and defending their national title, hardware salesman Goldie Smith was busy padding the roster of his Melville team. Smith had moved to Melville from Russell, Man., in 1913 with hockey players "Moose" Callin, Sid Moynes, and Gordon Mullins. Smith spent so much money importing players from Manitoba and Ontario that the team was called the Millionaires. Rivals became agitated when Smith recruited brothers Bill and Harry MacKenzie from Kenora, Ont., in 1914. When Melville defeated Prince Albert 9–8 and 6–5 in the provincial final, the Mintos protested the Millionaires' use of "illegal imports." The Saskatchewan Amateur Hockey Association denied the protest, but the Ontario Hockey Association raised the same complaint and instructed its champion, the Toronto Victorias, not to challenge for the Allan Cup. Hardly awed by the OHA's authority, the Victorias ventured west for a two-game, total-goal series. Fans thrilled to an 8–8 tie in the opener, then enjoyed a 7–3 Millionaires victory.

Melville had, on the ice anyway, cemented its grip on the Allan Cup by overcoming Regina in league play, earning the Saskatchewan championship, and beating the best of the East. Possession being nine points of the law, the Millionaires also had the trophy in their hands and accepted the Winnipeg Monarchs' challenge to defend it. In hindsight, this proved Melville's undoing. With Irvin legally back on their roster, the Monarchs prevailed 7–6 in the two-game series and reclaimed the Allan Cup.

Afterwards, the newly formed Canadian Amateur Hockey Association absolved the Millionaires of any

The 1914–15 Melville Millionaires. Top row, from left: Bill MacKenzie, "Moose" Callin, Bob McCutcheon (captain), Gordie Mullins, Harry MacKenzie. Bottom row: D'Arcy Smith, H. Thompson, Sid "Speed" Moynes, Mel Hepburn (stickboy), Harold Brown, Bill Ross.

wrongdoing because residency rules had not taken effect until midseason, when all the Millionaires had settled into Melville. In a convoluted decision, however, the CAHA also ruled that only the Winnipeg Monarchs would be recognized as champions because they held the trophy at season's end—this despite the Allan Cup's status as a challenge trophy. (Precedent for multiple winners existed with none other than the Stanley Cup, a challenge trophy itself until 1912. In a 12-winter span from 1896–1907, there were six seasons when two teams were recognized as distinct champions.)

Goldie Smith had enlisted in the army and was in no position to fight the CAHA's decision. He survived a German gas attack to return to Melville, resume his business and hockey interests, and battle the CAHA to recognize the 1914–15 Millionaires as legitimate champions. It wasn't until 1933 that Smith prevailed and his team's name was engraved on the Allan Cup. (To this day, though, there are still many sources that list only the Winnipeg Monarchs as 1914–15 champions.)

Sadly, Harry MacKenzie—Melville's star and the man Smith regarded as the best hockey player he had ever seen—was long dead, killed in the Great War.

ALEX DECOTEAU: THE LONG RUN CUT SHORT

Alex Decoteau was born December 20, 1887, on the Red Pheasant Reserve near North Battleford. The family name was probably an approximation of "Dakota" implemented by Christian authorities in the aftermath of the North-West Rebellion. Alex's father Pierre was a Cree warrior with Poundmaker's forces at the Battle of Fish Creek on May 2, 1885. Pierre was murdered in 1891 while looking for horses, and David Latta, a young officer of the North-West Mounted Police, was dispatched to investigate the crime.

Alex Decoteau

Latta married Alex's sister and moved to Edmonton to open a blacksmith and machine shop. Alex followed in 1909 at the age of 22 and, at his sister's urging, resumed what he had done at the Battleford Indian Industrial School: enter races. He finished second in his first effort, a one-mile race at Fort Saskatchewan, Alta., on May 24, 1909. Decoteau won a pair of five-mile contests in June, the latter in 28 minutes 41.6 seconds. Later that summer he improved that to a Western Canadian record time of 26:34.4.

He worked only briefly at his brother-in-law's business and joined the Edmonton police force in 1909 to become Canada's first law enforcement officer from its First Nations population. Decoteau, also one of the first motorcycle policemen in the country, was promoted to sergeant in 1914 and placed in charge of Edmonton's Station No. 4.

His athletic achievements kept pace with his pro-

HUGH CAIRNS: THE SINGULAR TRIBUTE

Hugh Cairns

English-born Hugh Cairns moved to Saskatoon in 1911 as a 14-year-old. The pinnacle of his sports achievement was to play on the St. Thomas soccer team that won the 1915 city league championship. Cairns never accomplished anything further on a playing field because he volunteered for the Canadian Expeditionary Force that summer.

Cairns was within 10 days of surviving the Great War. His demise, however, was so exceptional—"a superhuman effort," in the words of Canadian commander Gen. Arthur Currie—that he was posthumously awarded the Victoria Cross, the highest honour a Canadian soldier can receive. The citation reads:

For most conspicuous bravery before Valenciennes on 1st November, 1918, when a machine gun opened on his platoon. Without a moment's hesitation Sergeant Cairns seized a Lewis gun and single-handed in the face of direct fire, rushed the post, killed the crew of five, and captured the gun. Later, when the line was held up by machine-gun fire, he again rushed forward, killing 12 enemy and capturing 18 and two guns. Subsequently when the advance was held up by machine-guns and field guns, although wounded, he led a small party to outflank them, killing many, forcing about 50 to surrender, and capturing all the guns. After consolidation he went with a battle patrol to exploit Marly and forced 60 enemy to surrender. Whilst disarming this party he was severely wounded. Nevertheless he opened fire and inflicted heavy losses. Finally he was rushed by about 20 enemy and collapsed from weakness and loss of blood. Throughout the operation he showed the highest degree of valour, and his leadership greatly contributed to the success of the attack. He died on 2 November from his wounds.

Cairns was not reckless so much as audacious. He had pulled off a similarly brazen manoeuvre as a private in June 1917 when he captured a German machine-gun emplacement and single-handedly held off an enemy advance for an hour and a half. He suffered 13 shrapnel wounds in his back but returned to action two weeks later and earned, in the military tradition of profound understatement, a Distinguished Conduct Medal.

Saskatoon honoured Cairns in 1921 with a life-size marble statue atop a 12-foot granite base. Cairns is not shown in military dress but in sweatshirt and shorts, his right foot resting atop a soccer ball—a reminder of what he left behind and would never enjoy again. Carved on the base are the names of 75 others who had played soccer in Saskatoon and sacrificed their lives on European battlefields. Many, like Cairns, had served in the South Saskatchewan 46th Overseas "Suicide Battalion" that suffered 4,917 casualties—1,433 dead and 3,484 wounded, 91.5 percent of its roll—in 28 months of duty.

fessional success. In 1910 he won the Fort Saskatchewan 10-miler by eight minutes and swept four events (half-, one-, two- and five-mile) in a Dominion Day meet at Lethbridge. The great Tom Longboat visited Fort Saskatchewan in 1911 for a cross-country race and boasted, "When this race starts, I'll be over that hill there and that's the last you'll see of me." Wrong. Decoteau left Longboat a distant second.

Decoteau ran 10 miles in 59:59 to qualify for the 1912 Olympic trials in Montreal, where he cramped up and dropped out of the 10,000 metres but recovered to win the 5,000. He finished eighth in the Olympic 5,000 final at Stockholm. Another Olympiad beckoned four years hence but war cancelled it.

Decoteau resigned from the Edmonton police force in 1916 and joined the army. While undergoing military training in England, he won several races, usually entering them in his childhood fashion of running to the venue. On one occasion he discovered upon arrival that he had run to a bicycle race, so he borrowed a two-wheeler and won that competition, too.

Decoteau served with the 202nd Sportsman's Battalion and the Edmonton 49th Battalion. He was killed in action by a sniper's bullet on October 30, 1917, during the Battle of Passchendaele Ridge and is buried at a military cemetery in Ypres, Belgium.

Cree tradition dictates that an individual's spirit will wander the earth without rest until given a proper burial. In August of 1985, relatives, friends, Red Pheasant band council members, Indian war veterans and honour guards representing the Edmonton Police Force and the Canadian Armed Forces attended a Cree burial service to bring Alex Decoteau's spirit home to the Red Pheasant Reserve.

1919: PIFFLES AND HIS PALS TRAMPLE EVERYBODY

Neil "Piffles" Taylor was a four-year-old when his family moved from Ontario to Yellow Grass in 1899. He joined the Regina Rugby Club as a teenager in 1913, split time between the intermediate and senior squads for two years, and in 1915 became the big team's full-time quarterback. The Rugby Club established itself as the mightiest outfit this side of the Great Lakes with Western titles from 1912–15 and a 19-game winning streak dating back to the start of the 1913 regular season. Fred Wilson was a sensational punter and runner; in a 1913 game against Saskatoon he twice broke free for 50-yard gains. Playing coach Fred Ritter was renowned for his leadership and for playing through pain in an era when substitution was rare or non-existent. Al Urquhart had been around since the formation of the team in 1910, and Hick Abbott of hockey fame was mature beyond his years.

War did what no opponent could. It broke up the Regina Rugby Club. There were no playoffs in 1916, and no seasons at all in 1917 and 1918 as Canada's young men answered the enlistment call with the same enthusiasm as an opening kickoff. Some 42,000 volunteers from Saskatchewan joined the ranks; more than 13,200 were wounded; 4,389 were killed, among them Abbott and fellow rugby players Tommy Blair, Bob Boucher, Clarence Dale, Howie Longworthy, Howard Pawley, Jimmy Scott, Punk Thompson and Sam Taylor, Piffles' brother, a pilot who was shot down over France. Piffles himself lost an eye and was taken prisoner but survived and returned home.

Bone-crunching tackles on the gridiron were child's play after years of dodging bullets and shrapnel in muddy trenches. Taylor, fitted with a glass eye that popped out at least once on the playing field, was back at quarterback, Wilson and his legs were as good as ever, Urquhart was rejuvenated, Jerry Crapper and Tare Rennebohm were just coming into their prime. It was time for a bit of fun, which amounted to making life miserable for everyone else who took the field. Just let the scores tell the story:

Piffles Taylor

Regina 40, Moose Jaw Millers 6.
Regina 36, Moose Jaw Millers 1.
Regina 30, University of Saskatchewan 0.
Regina 45, University of Saskatchewan 0.
Regina 29, Saskatoon Quakers 0.

Regina 12, Winnipeg Victorias 0.
Regina 13, Calgary Canucks 1.

Winnipeg, like Regina, was entirely manned by tough war veterans, but the Victorias enjoyed an average 30-pound weight advantage. Regina's advantages in the Western semi-final on November 1 were home field and their growing sense of invincibility. The issue was settled in the first quarter when the Victorias fumbled a pair of Wilson's punts deep in their own end and Regina capitalized on both for tries (or touchdowns, then worth five points) and a 10–0 lead. Wilson was the hero again two weeks later on a muddy Calgary field as his deep punting and the downfield coverage of Crapper, Nels Newbatt and Allan Wetmore gave Regina the upper hand in field position. The Canadian Rugby Union kept the Grey Cup an all-East affair, so another Western title was as far as Regina could go. With the new decade, Piffles Taylor raised fan interest even higher by leading a new football team, the Regina Boat Club, into the sporting wars—which promised to be as entertaining as the real ones were horrific.

ALSO DURING THESE YEARS

- Winnipeg was declared the winner of a lacrosse game on July 7, 1906, when the visiting Regina team abandoned the field in the second half. Winkler of Regina had a cut above his nose stitched by a doctor, and McGregor was gashed above an eye, both in the first half. A melee broke out among players and spectators in the second half after Regina's McDougall broke the nose of Winnipeg's Milan. Regina, trailing 2–1, walked off when its demand to replace Winnipeg referee Toddy Wasdale was rejected.

- Qu'Appelle Shamrock Football Club won the Saskatchewan Shield provincial soccer championship in 1907 with a 1–0 victory over Grenfell before 500 spectators at Summerberry.

- A free-for-all broke out in Regina between soccer and baseball players on June 12, 1908. Ballplayers from the city league were practising and their ball kept rolling on to the pitch until one of the Victorias threw it far away from both fields. Peacemakers contained the brawl until city police and Mounties arrived. The Victorias went on to defeat Pense 3–0 in the soccer game.

- A touring men's basketball team from Moose Jaw posted victories in Lethbridge, Banff, Calgary, Edmonton and Saskatoon in January 1914.

- Birch Hills and Melfort of the North Saskatchewan League played to a 22-inning 1–1 tie on July 19, 1919, in the longest baseball game in Saskatchewan history. Herby Bird, a Metis, of Birch Hills and Jerry Cummings of Melfort did all the pitching.

Cal Bricker is usually included among Saskatchewan's greatest early athletes. Not here.

Bricker was a magnificent athlete, a gallant soldier, and a bastion of the Grenfell community for more than 40 years, from setting up his dentistry clinic in 1919 to his death in 1963. As an athlete, he won bronze medals in the running long and triple jumps in the 1908 Olympics and a silver medal in the 1912 Olympic long jump.

All that, however, was accomplished while Bricker was a student at the University of Toronto. He was born in Listowel, Ont., and did not move west until after the First World War.

He was never a Saskatchewan athlete.

Ethel Catherwood practises the high jump in her home town of Saskatoon

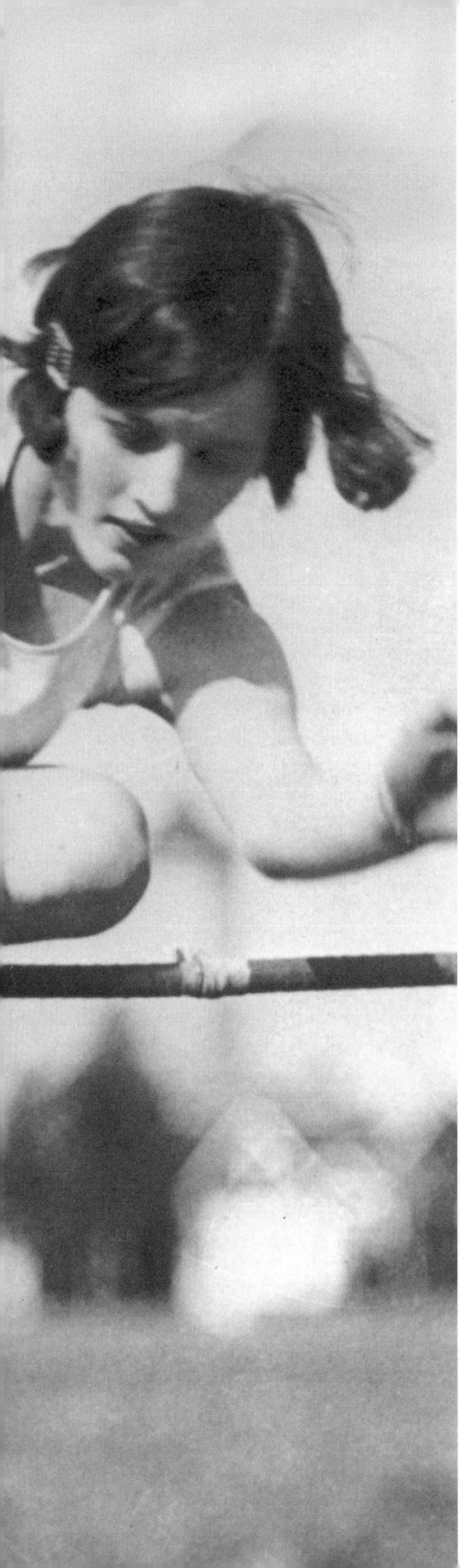

1920–1929

Golden Years

ARRIVALS

March 1, 1920: Max Bentley, hockey player, Delisle.
April 16, 1920: Ken Charlton, football player, Regina.
May 5, 1920: Bill Hunter, sports entrepreneur, Saskatoon.
August 11, 1920: Chuck Rayner, hockey player, Sutherland.
January 6, 1921: Hazen Argue, politician, Moose Jaw.
April 26, 1922: Jeanne Sauvé, governor-general (1984–90), Prud'homme.
September 27, 1922: Frank Germann, multi-sport athlete, Qu'Appelle.
October 25, 1922: Sully Glasser, football player, Regina.
December 3, 1922: Eli Mandel, poet/writer, Estevan.
March 23, 1923: Arnie Weinmeister, football player, Rhein.
May 6, 1923: Harry Watson, hockey player, Saskatoon.
January 1, 1924: Arleene Johnson Noga, softball/baseball player, Ogema.
November 8, 1924: Johnny Bower, hockey player, Prince Albert.
December 20, 1924: Bob Adams, decathlete/coach, Alsask.
February 11, 1926: Leslie Nielsen, actor, Regina.
May 3, 1926: Matt Baldwin, curler, Blucher.
September 4, 1926: Bert Olmstead, hockey player, Sceptre.
September 11, 1926: Art McKay, painter, Nipawin.
September 13, 1926: Emile Francis, hockey player/executive, North Battleford.
October 9, 1926: Al Rollins, hockey player, Vanguard.
October 29, 1926: Jon Vickers, opera singer, Prince Albert.
January 11, 1927: Garnet Campbell, curler, Avonlea.
January 25, 1927: Fern Flaman, hockey player, Dysart.
January 26, 1927: Richard Downey, scientist/developer of canola, Saskatoon.
May 5, 1927: Sylvia Fedoruk, physicist/athlete/lieutenant-governor (1988–94), Canora.
July 20, 1927: Jack Horner, politician, Blaine Lake.
November 7, 1927: Metro Prystai, hockey player, Yorkton.
March 31, 1928: Gordie Howe, hockey player, Floral.
October 1, 1928: Jim Pattison, entrepreneur, Luseland.
October 2, 1928: Arnold Richardson, curler, Estevan.
January 2, 1929: Allan Sapp, painter, Red Pheasant Reserve.
February 12, 1929: Philip Kives, entrepreneur/founder of K-Tel, Oungre.
April 18, 1929: Adam Faul, boxer, Regina.
November 18, 1929: Pat Lawson, multi-sport athlete, Saskatoon.

Prosperity came to Saskatchewan and the people came with it. Where 91,000 people lived in 1901, ten times that number would live by the end of the Twenties. Harvests averaging over 200 million bushels, never seen before, would not be seen again for an entire generation.

Sports boomed along with the population and the economy. Saskatoon and Regina were part of a genuine major professional hockey league, the equal of the NHL during its brief existence. The name *Regina Pats* joined the ranks of Canadian junior hockey *and* football champions. A curling rink from Yellow Grass upset the Manitoba champion to take part in the first Brier.

Most notable of all were a pair of Olympic gold-medal triumphs that serve as appropriate bookends for the Twenties. Earl Thomson and Ethel Catherwood together symbolized the ultimate in athletic achievement, then diverged to reflect the best and worst consequences of athletic fame.

EARL THOMSON: YANKEE CANADIAN DANDY

Earl Thomson was born in Birch Hills, near Prince Albert, in 1895 but moved with his family to Long Beach, Calif., when he was eight years old. He was nearly killed at the age of 14 when he was hit point-blank in the chest by a shotgun that went off accidentally. A four-hour operation was performed to patch the gaping wound, but Thomson's prognosis was summed up in the surgeon's question the next morning: "What time did the young lad die?"

Earl Thomson

Much to the surgeon's surprise, Thomson had survived the night and would make a full recovery. It took two years, but once healed, Thomson threw his body into baseball, football, swimming and especially hurdling. He took his sports so seriously that he would tie his legs to the foot of his bed at night to prevent himself from curling up and possibly cramping. Thomson made the track team at the University of Southern California as a freshman and was the first man in the world to break 15 seconds in the 110-yard high hurdles. He transferred to Dartmouth University in Hanover, N.H., but soon left the Ivy League school to enlist as an observer trainee in Canada's Royal Flying Corps at Beamsville, Ont. Thomson competed for the base team and once won a Royal Air Force meet in nearby Toronto single-handedly with five victories and a second-place showing. Obliged to hurry back to the base, Thomson missed the trophy presentations and had to pick up his gold medal and six cups later—three decades later, in 1948, from a cousin who had them in his safekeeping.

Thomson completed his training and was commissioned in September 1918, weeks before the war's end and too late to see action. After being discharged he returned to Dartmouth and in 1919 ran the 120-yard hurdles in 14.4 seconds to shatter the world record. American officials dreamed of a medal sweep in the 1920 Olympic 110-metre hurdles by Thomson, Harold Barron and Fred Murray until Thomson told them he wouldn't compete for the United States but for the country of his birth. Thomson easily qualified at the Olympic trials in Montreal and went to Antwerp as a Canadian.

Heats were necessary to trim the field of 26 entrants to the six who would contest the final. Thomson and Barron were matched in one heat of the quarterfinals, where only the top two from each race would advance. Thomson finished a comfortable second, easing up to protect a pulled thigh muscle.

Thomson (far left) clears the last hurdle en route to a gold-medal finish at the 1920 Olympics

Some Canadians grumbled that he was going to let the Americans win. In separate semi-finals, Thomson and Barron equalled the Olympic record of 15 seconds flat. The stage was set for a neck-and-neck final.

And so it was . . . for half the race. The field broke cleanly, and Barron had a slight edge at the third hurdle. Thomson, however, emphasized form over quickness and had spent years training himself to jump the hurdles with a minimum of clearance and wasted effort. He took over the lead at 50 metres and increased it at each hurdle, breaking the tape in a new world record of 14.8 seconds, leaving Barron and Murray in his wake at 15.1 and 15.2 seconds respectively.

No one since 1920 has won the Olympic men's high hurdles by so large a margin.

Thomson graduated from Dartmouth and coached there and at West Virginia and Yale before starting a 37-year (1927–63) tenure as head coach of the Naval Academy at Annapolis, Md. There he guided the Midshipmen to a 154–70–2 record in dual meets and the NCAA championship in 1945. He remained a superlative coach despite encroaching deafness that ultimately left him reliant on lip reading to converse with people.

THE WESTERN CANADA LEAGUE TAKES ITS LAST CUTS

Baseball's Western Canada League rose from the dead much like Lazarus: long enough to show its face and then vanish forever. Whereas 43 minor leagues operated under the National Association umbrella in 1914, only 14 tried to make a go of it five summers later when the able-bodied young men who had survived military service were discharged. The WCL, which had been on hiatus from 1915–18, took advantage of the shortage to get reclassified from D to C and, for the 1920 and 1921 seasons, all the way up to B. That would be the end of the league, however. An unusually wet summer led to poor attendance in Regina and Moose Jaw, and both teams disbanded before season's end. Teams in Calgary, Edmonton and Winnipeg split off to join other leagues in 1922, leaving the Saskatoon Quakers geographically isolated and forced to fold. Saskatchewan's first foray into true "Organized Baseball," and its last, was over.

While it lasted, there were some high points. Saskatoon won a dramatic best-of-nine playoff for the 1919 title in a four-team WCL that included the Regina Senators, Moose Jaw Millers and first-half champion Winnipeg Maroons. Key victories for the

WESTERN CANADA LEAGUE

1919 Standings
Class C, split season

	W	L	Pct.	GB
Saskatoon s2	69	34	.670	
Winnipeg s1	54	47	.535	14
Regina	43	60	.417	26
Moose Jaw	38	63	.376	30

- s1, s2: Winnipeg and Saskatoon won first and second-halves, respectively, of split season.
- Playoff: Saskatoon defeated Winnipeg 5 games to 3.

1920 Standings
Class B, split season

	W	L	Pct.	GB
Calgary s2	73	39	.652	
Regina s1	72	41	.637	1½
Moose Jaw	56	57	.496	17½
Winnipeg	53	57	.482	19
Saskatoon	44	72	.386	31
Edmonton	39	73	.348	34

- s1, s2: Regina and Calgary won first and second halves, respectively, of split season.
- Playoff: Calgary defeated Regina 5 games to 4.

1921 Standings
Class B, split season

	W	L	Pct.	GB
Calgary s1	70	39	.642	
Winnipeg s2	72	42	.632	½
Saskatoon	57	59	.491	16½
Edmonton	51	60	.459	20
x–Regina	37	43	.463	–
x–Moose Jaw	21	65	.244	–

- x: Regina and Moose Jaw suspended operations August 10.
- s1, s2: Calgary and Winnipeg won first and second halves of split season.
- Playoff: Calgary defeated Winnipeg 4–2, 1 tie.

Quakers were an 18-inning 3–0 decision in Game 5, a 14-inning 3–2 squeaker in Game 7 and finally a comfortable 10–3 romp to clinch the series in eight games.

Alberta re-entered the picture in 1920 with the inclusion of the Edmonton Senators and Calgary Bronchos, who duelled to the wire with Regina for league supremacy and won a quirky best-of-nine championship series. Herman Pillette tossed a two-hitter, a three-hitter and won another game in relief as the Senators took four of the first five games, including the first three in Regina. Needing only one more victory, the Senators totally collapsed as Calgary reeled off 8–4, 11–3, 15–5 and 17–9 beatings to take the championship.

Moose Jaw's last team included a future big-leaguer, shortstop Mark Koenig. He lasted 12 years (1925–36) in the majors and gained immortality as the starting shortstop on the 1927 New York Yankees, one of the greatest teams ever assembled. Koenig batted .279 lifetime and .285 for the '27 Bronx Bombers, which must have been quite a surprise to his former teammates on the '21 Millers. He hit a paltry .202 for them.

Barnstorming baseball teams, often starring Satchel Paige and other greats of the Negro Leagues, made regular excursions through Saskatchewan until the '60s.

Ex-major leaguers could be spotted occasionally as well, most notably members of the Chicago White Sox who were banned from Organized Baseball for their roles in the 1919 World Series gambling scandal. Sometimes these "Black Sox" assumed aliases to hide their identities, but Hap Felsch was right out in the open as the 35-year-old playing manager of the 1927 Regina Balmorals, who spent most of the summer chasing tournament money.

On July 23, with $600 at stake, Felsch went 7-for-9 and scored five runs as Regina crushed Ponteix 17–0 and Sherwood, N.D., 8–1 in the last two games. Two weeks later, the Balmorals took the self-proclaimed provincial semi-pro championship series from the Rosetown Goose Lakers four games to two. In the four boxscores from that series published in the Leader, Felsch was 10-for-13 with three homers and two doubles.

No one accused him of throwing games.

BIG TIME: THE WESTERN CANADA HOCKEY LEAGUE

Senior hockey surged to the forefront again in 1919, catapulted by a Canadian Amateur Hockey Association ruling that any professionals who had seen military service in the war were automatically reinstated as amateurs. Regina benefited immensely from this when Dick Irvin was lured to the city to play for the Victorias. With Irvin in Regina and Rusty Crawford toiling for the Saskatoon Crescents, some wondered just how "amateur" the provincial senior hockey scene truly was. Eligibility regulations were creatively interpreted or openly flouted, and small towns complained about the unfair advantage large cities enjoyed when they could afford to slip money under the table to thinly disguised professionals. Moose Jaw, whose key acquisition was goaltender Hal Winkler from Winnipeg, won the 1919–20 provincial senior title. One year later Regina prevailed as Irvin scored twice in a 4–3 victory over Saskatoon in the final game, but the amateurism controversy had boiled over to the point that the University of Saskatchewan Huskies were dispatched to represent the province in the Allan Cup.

Meanwhile, events in Alberta and British Columbia were about to solve Saskatchewan's amateur/professional dilemma. Frank Patrick, owner of the Vancouver Millionaires of the professional Pacific Coast Hockey Association, accused the Alberta Big Four league in 1920 of being professional. Patrick and his brother Lester, owner of the PCHA's Victoria Cougars, were running a three-team league on the West Coast and eager to expand. Frank Patrick won his battle to prove the Big Four wasn't amateur, causing the Alberta league to turn professional in 1920–21. The big-city franchises, the Edmonton Eskimos and Calgary Tigers, enjoyed too large a competitive advantage over other Alberta centres in the Big Four and recruited the Saskatoon Crescents to form the Western Canada Hockey League on November 9, 1921. Nine days later, the Regina Capitals made it a four-team arrangement and the WCHL, playing seven-man hockey, joined the National Hockey League and the PCHA as the sport's third elite professional loop.

While the WCHL would last only five years, there is no denying its stature as a first-rate hockey institution. Many of its stars like Irvin, Bill Cook, Eddie Shore, George Hainsworth, Frank Fredrickson, Frank Boucher, George Hay, Duke Keats and Harry Oliver shifted to the National Hockey League with scarcely a change in stride when the NHL assumed its major-league monopoly in 1926. In fact, six of the NHL's top 10 scorers in 1926–27 were newcomers from the dissolved Western league: scoring champion Cook, runner-up Irvin, Fredrickson in fourth place, Boucher tied for sixth, and Oliver sharing ninth place with Keats.

George Hay

WESTERN CANADA HOCKEY LEAGUE

1921–22 Standings

	W	L	T	GF	GA	P
Edmonton a	15	9	1	118	76	31
Regina a	14	10	1	94	78	29
Calgary	14	10	0	75	62	28
Saskatoon t	5	19	0	67	137	10

- a: Additional game played to decide first place after Edmonton and Regina tied with 29 points apiece; Edmonton won 11–2. Result included in standings and statistics.
- t: Transferred to Moose Jaw for last four home games of season.

Scoring Leaders

	G	A	P
Duke Keats, E	31	24	55
Ty Arbour, E	27	6	33
Joe Simpson, E	21	12	33
George Hay, R	21	11	32
Barney Stanley, C	26	5	31
Dick Irvin, R	21	7	28

- Playoffs: Regina defeated Calgary 2–1 in two-game, total-goals semi-final. Regina defeated Edmonton 3–2 in two-game, total-goals semi-final.
- Stanley Cup Elimination: PCHA champion Vancouver defeated Regina 5–2 in two-game, total-goals series.

WESTERN CANADA HOCKEY LEAGUE/ PACIFIC COAST HOCKEY ASSOCIATION

1922–23 Standings

WCHL	W	L	T	GF	GA	P
Edmonton	19	10	1	112	90	39
Regina	16	14	0	93	97	32
Calgary	12	18	0	91	106	24
Saskatoon	8	20	2	91	125	18

PCHA	W	L	T	GF	GA	P
Vancouver	17	12	1	116	88	35
Victoria	16	14	0	94	85	32
Seattle	15	15	0	100	106	30

Scoring Leaders

	G	A	P
Frank Fredrickson, Vic	39	16	55
Art Gagne, E	22	21	43
Mickey MacKay, Vcr	28	12	40
Duke Keats, E	24	13	37
George Hay, R	28	8	36
Newsy Lalonde, S	30	4	34
Harry Oliver, C	25	7	32
Lloyd Cook, Vcr	19	11	30

- WCHL final: Edmonton defeated Regina 4–3 in two-game, total-goals series.
- PCHA final: Vancouver defeated Victoria 5–3 in two-game, total-goals series.
- Stanley Cup Elimination: NHL champion Ottawa Senators defeated PCHA champion Vancouver 3–1 in best-of-five series..
- Stanley Cup Final: Ottawa defeated Edmonton 2–0 in best-of-three series.

WCHL/PCHA

1923–24 Standings

WCHL	W	L	T	GF	GA	P
Calgary	18	11	1	83	71	37
Regina	17	11	2	83	67	36
Saskatoon	15	12	3	91	73	33
Edmonton	11	15	4	69	81	26

PCHA	W	L	T	GF	GA	P
Seattle	14	16	0	84	99	28
Vancouver	13	16	1	87	80	27
Victoria	11	18	1	78	103	23

Scoring Leaders

	G	A	P
Bill Cook, S	26	14	40
Harry Oliver, C	22	12	34
Art Duncan, Vcr	21	10	31
George Hay, R	20	11	31
Duke Keats, E	19	12	31
Frank Fredrickson, Vic	19	8	27
Barney Stanley, R	15	11	26
Mickey MacKay, Vcr	21	4	25

- WCHL Final: Calgary defeated Regina 4–2 in two-game, total-goals series.
- PCHA Final: Vancouver defeated Seattle 4–3 in two-game, total-goals series.
- Stanley Cup Elimination: Calgary defeated Vancouver 2–1 in best-of-three series to earn berth in Stanley Cup final.
- NHL champion Montreal Canadiens defeated Vancouver 2–1 in best-of-three series.
- Stanley Cup Final: Montreal defeated Calgary 2–0 in best-of-three series.

Written accounts testify that the WCHL was just as fast, intense and mean as the NHL ever was. With starters expected to play 40 to 50 minutes and only five substitutes on the bench, conditioning and efficient skating were vital factors. Small rosters also left no room for enforcers, so individuals had to fend for, and defend, themselves, especially veteran stars like Dick Irvin.

"That Irvin was a pretty cool customer," Carl Battell, a teammate of Irvin on the Capitals, said in 1977. "One time we were playing Victoria, whose star player was Frank Fredrickson. He and Dick had kind of a feud going, and in this game Fredrickson was back in his own end. Dick took a shot and when he followed through just kept his stick out in front of him. After the game Fredrickson took off his sweater in the dressing room, and there was this long mark running from his stomach almost up to his chin.

"Another time we were playing the Tigers in Calgary. They had this guy Cully Wilson who had a reputation for nicking guys with his stick. There was a lot more of that then than you have nowadays. Anyway, this one time he nicked Dick and got a penalty. A minute or so later there was a faceoff right in front of the penalty box where Wilson was sitting, and Dick gave him a two-hander right across the face with his stick, right across the mush with the flat of the blade. They had to escort Irvin out of the rink that night."

Attendance was healthy, thanks in great part to competitive parity, the infrequency of contests and maybe, just maybe, the prospect of mayhem. It was reported that in 1923–24, teams averaged from 3,000 to 5,500 fans per game. Schedules ranging from 24 to 30 games over three months worked out to one home game every week or two. Teams were uncommonly competitive and always provided terrific battles for league and playoff championships.

Saskatoon's franchise was owned by Bob Pinder, who reacted to fan apathy for his last-place team by moving the Crescents to Moose Jaw on February 9, 1922, for the last weeks of the season. Prudently, Pinder did not surrender control of the franchise. In the meantime, the 24-game 1921–22 season almost ended in a three-way tie as Regina and Edmonton mustered 29 points to Calgary's 28. In hindsight, there seems no compelling reason (other than a crowded

The 1924–25 Saskatoon Crescents. From left: Laurie Scott, Harry Cameron, Newsy Lalonde, Leo Reise, Phil Stevens, George Hainsworth, Fred Gordon, Corb Denneny, Leo Bourgault, Bill Cook, Bun Cook.

house of paying customers) for the one-game tiebreaker to decide first place, since the league playoff was to be a two-game total-goals affair with each team getting one home date. The Eskimos breezed to an 11–2 decision that made them the first WCHL regular-season champions.

Then things got serious. Regina buckled down and held the Eskimos to a 1–1 tie in the playoff opener. Back home, the Capitals got first-period goals from Amby Moran and Irvin to win the game 2–1, win the series 3–2, and go on to face the Vancouver Millionaires in another two-game showdown with a Stanley Cup final berth on the line. Stanley Cup opportunities were nothing new to the Pacific Coast Hockey Association or its champion, the Millionaires; the PCHA, under the sharp direction of the Patricks, had been in existence since 1911 and challenging for the Cup since 1914. Vancouver was heavily favoured to defeat Regina, but the Capitals shocked the Millionaires' home-town crowd of 11,000 with a 2–1 upset on goals by Irvin and Ernie Anderson. A record turnout for a Saskatchewan sporting event of 6,803 fans jammed Exhibition Stadium in anticipation of another Capitals upset two nights later, but Art Duncan's hat trick paced a 4–0 Vancouver victory and 5–2 series decision.

The Patrick brothers, impressed by the Capitals and the new league's fan support, arranged for the PCHA to play an interlocking schedule with the WCHL for the 1922–23 campaign. Seven-man hockey, almost extinct anyway, was abandoned in favour of the six-man game. Pinder moved the Crescents back to Saskatoon and got the publicity he needed by pulling off a trade with the NHL's Montreal Canadiens that startled the entire country. Saskatoon acquired Edouard "Newsy" Lalonde, the most prolific scorer in all of hockey, from the Montreal Canadiens, in exchange for $3,500 and the rights to a tiny forward, Aurel Joliat, who would quickly become a star but at the time was virtually unknown.

Lalonde had scored 415 goals at the highest levels of competition since 1905 and had been a fixture with the Canadiens since their first season of 1909–10. Well past his prime at 36, he became the Crescents' prime scoring threat with 30 goals. Also notorious as a brawler, Lalonde engaged in a bloody battle with Red McCusker that left the Capitals' goaltender out of commission until the following season. Despite the spirit and scoring punch Lalonde injected, the Crescents finished a distant last among the four teams. Edmonton and Regina staged a playoff rematch that was forced to overtime when two games produced a 3–3 deadlock. Capitals netminder Bill Laird gallantly held the fort as the home-town Eskimos dominated the sudden-death action. At 10:35 of the second extra period Regina defenceman "Puss" Traub (his real name was Percy) tripped Calgary forward Ty Arbour right in front of the Regina goal. Edmonton was awarded a penalty shot. At the time, that entailed an unimpeded shot from a spot 36 feet in front of the net with the netminder positioned one foot ahead of the goal line.

WESTERN CANADA HOCKEY LEAGUE

1924–25 Standings

	W	L	T	GF	GA	P
Calgary	17	11	0	96	80	34
Saskatoon	16	11	1	102	75	33
Victoria	16	12	0	84	63	32
Edmonton	14	13	1	97	109	29
Vancouver	12	16	0	91	102	24
Regina	8	20	0	82	123	16

Scoring Leaders

	G	A	P
Duke Keats, E	23	9	32
Bill Cook, S	22	10	32
Frank Fredrickson, Vic	22	8	30
Frank Boucher, Van	16	12	28
Archie Briden, E	17	6	23
George Hay, R	16	6	22

- Playoffs: Victoria defeated Saskatoon 6–4 in two-game, total-goals semi-final. Victoria defeated Calgary 3–1 in two-game, total-goals final.
- Stanley Cup Final: Victoria defeated NHL champion Montreal Canadiens 3–1 in best-of-five series.

WESTERN HOCKEY LEAGUE

1925–26 Standings

	W	L	T	GF	GA	P
Edmonton	19	11	0	94	77	38
Saskatoon	18	11	1	93	64	37
Victoria	15	11	4	68	53	34
Portland	12	16	2	84	110	26
Calgary	10	17	3	71	80	23
Vancouver	10	18	2	64	90	22

Scoring Leaders

	G	A	P
Bill Cook, S	31	13	44
Dick Irvin, P	31	5	36
Art Gagne, E	21	11	32
Corb Denneny, S	17	15	32
George Hay, P	19	12	31
Duke Keats, E	20	10	30
Harry Oliver, C	13	12	25
Frank Fredrickson, Vic	16	8	24

- Playoffs: Victoria defeated Saskatoon 4–3 in two-game, total-goals semi-final. Victoria defeated Edmonton 5–3 in two-game,total-goals final.
- Stanley Cup Final: NHL champion Montreal Maroons defeated Victoria 3–1 in best-of-five series.

Duke Keats fired the puck past Laird and the Eskimos won the WCHL championship.

While Regina recorded another second-place finish in 1923–24, Saskatoon cast off its role as WCHL doormat and posted a 15–13–2 record that fell three points short of catching the Capitals. Newsy Lalonde's production plummeted from 30 to 10 goals, but Pinder had filled the roster with eight other Eastern recruits, all of whom had the NHL in their past or future. Most notable among them were goal tender George Hainsworth and centre Bill Cook. Hainsworth, 28, was already an 11-year veteran of senior hockey in Kitchener (or Berlin, as the city was called until 1916). Hainsworth would spend three seasons in Saskatoon, then 11 years with the Canadiens and Toronto Maple Leafs and set the NHL record for career shutouts with 94. Terry Sawchuk eventually surpassed that with 103, but if all major-league shutouts were taken into consideration, the 10 Hainsworth recorded in Saskatoon would make him the all-time leader with 104.

Cook won the scoring race twice in his four years with the Crescents. Although he didn't reach the NHL until he was 30, he won two scoring championships as captain of the New York Rangers and led them to the Stanley Cup twice. Saskatoon finally made the playoffs in 1924–25 when his brother, Fred "Bun" Cook, joined him. The WCHL took on a new look that season with the demise of the Seattle Metropolitans, which prompted the Patricks to simply fold the PCHA and shift the Vancouver and Victoria franchises to the WCHL. Victoria beat Saskatoon in both the 1924–25 and '25–26 semi-finals.

As for the Regina Capitals, they went from radiance to non-existence faster than silent film stars confronted with talkies. After three straight second-place finishes and some breathtaking near-misses in the playoffs, Regina plummeted to 8–20–0 in 1924–25. Frank Patrick took advantage of the team's sudden turn in fortune to buy the Capitals from Wes Champ for $25,000 and move the team to Portland, Ore., where they became the Rosebuds. (The American component prompted the league to drop "Canada" from its name and become the Western Hockey League for the 1925–26 season.)

Rather than resurrect the PCHA, the Patricks set their sights East, where the NHL had made its first forays into the U.S. with the Boston Bruins and New York Americans. Anticipating further NHL expansion south of the border, the Patricks began negotiations that would bear fruit in the summer of 1926. Frank Patrick's Portland Rosebuds were purchased by Frederic McLaughlin and relocated in Chicago as the NHL's Black Hawks. Lester Patrick's Victoria Cougars were sold off and became the core of the new

Detroit Falcons (later Cougars, later Red Wings). Both brothers set themselves up as brokers for player transactions between WHL and NHL teams as Calgary, Edmonton and Saskatoon quickly saw the futility of trying to continue as a three-city operation. Lester even managed to step in as general manager and coach of the Rangers when the owner fired Conn Smythe before the season started.

There would be nothing remotely like the original WCHL in Saskatchewan again. Saskatoon would have a run as a minor-league franchise, and senior hockey would come and go on a semi-pro basis in several communities, but the WCHL was genuinely major-league in calibre and scope. It can be argued that the Patricks killed pro hockey in Saskatchewan by snatching the Capitals out of Regina and orchestrating the WHL's demise, but when the end came in 1926, the Great Depression and the Dust Bowl were a few short years away. With the economic conditions that lay ahead and the financial pressures of maintaining a small hockey league over that much geography, the league was doomed regardless.

SASKATCHEWAN'S FIRST MAJOR LEAGUE BALLPLAYER: MEL KERR

JOHN MELVILLE KERR (1903–1980) WAS BORN IN Souris, Man., but his family moved to and from and back to Saskatoon when he was a child. Settling down at 15, Kerr would shine in baseball, track and field, football, basketball and tennis. At 18 he posted a .361 batting average in the city baseball league and won a three-mile steeplechase. In 1922 the 19-year-old batted .440 for the Fifth Battalion baseball squad and won the individual title at the provincial track and field championships. (Kerr's partners on a University of Saskatchewan sprint relay team that year were Vern DeGeer, who became a longtime sports columnist with the *Montreal Gazette*; Jimmy Skinner, who coached the Detroit Red Wings to the 1955 Stanley Cup; and Colborne McEown, who became a vice-president at the U of S.)

Mel Kerr

Kerr was most dazzling on the gridiron as a halfback, leading Saskwanis to the Western Canada junior football championship. He scored seven touchdowns, including one on a 115-yard kickoff return, in a 64–0 manhandling of North Battleford.

Little is known of Kerr's basketball prowess, but it is recorded that he scored 21 of YMCA's 38 points in the opening game of their 1923 Saskatoon senior season, so evidently he had game, in whatever fashion they played it 80 years ago. Later that year he upped his baseball batting average to .481, scored two touchdowns as Saskwanis beat Calgary YMCA for another Western junior football title, repeated as Saskatchewan individual track and field champion and won the first of two consecutive city men's singles tennis championships.

Kerr signed a pro baseball contract with the National League's Chicago Cubs in January of 1925 and was assigned to the Saginaw Aces of the Michigan-Ontario League, where he batted .283 with 31 doubles and 21 stolen bases to earn a mid-September promotion to the Cubs.

Chicago trailed the Boston Braves 8–4 in the second game of a doubleheader at Wrigley Field on September 16, 1925, when Cubs pinch-hitter Tommy Griffith singled to lead off the bottom of the ninth. Manager George Gibson, a Canadian from London, Ont., inserted Kerr as a pinch-runner. Kerr came around to score as the Cubs rallied for two runs, but that was the ballgame as the Braves prevailed 8–6.

And that was it for Mel Kerr's major-league career. He never made another appearance in the major leagues. Like Moonlight Graham in W.P. Kinsella's *Shoeless Joe* and its movie spawn, *Field of Dreams*, Kerr got on the field but never got to bat in the bigs.

Jack Reddick (right), Soldier Jones and referee Lou Marsh pose before 1924 fight

JACK REDDICK: TAKING ON TOO MUCH TOO SOON

Jack Reddick of Moose Jaw was already Canadian middleweight boxing champion in June 1924 when he added the national light-heavyweight title with an eighth-round knockout of Horace "Soldier" Jones in Toronto. Hungry for a shot at the big time, Reddick had forced himself through a 1923 schedule that was downright inhumane: 19 fights that lasted 148 rounds.

Reddick was game but ill-advised in his choice of opponents after the Jones fight. "Paralyzing Paul" Berlenbach, world champion a year later, kayoed Reddick in the eighth round of a slugfest in New York's Madison Square Garden. On April 24, 1925, in Toronto, Reddick lost a 10-round decision to Harry Greb, "The Human Windmill," renowned for his viciousness and as the only man who ever defeated Gene Tunney.

"I knew that I had no business in there with a champion like Greb," Reddick said, "but I will not have any man say that I am yellow. Now, I guess that they will let me go along and fight the second- and third-raters I should be fighting for a year or two yet."

Reddick got to coast on his laurels for two months, not two years, losing twice on points before hanging up his gloves with a record of 41 wins, 9 losses, 3 draws and 6 no-decisions.

Beattie Ramsey (centre) scores for Canada at the 1924 Winter Olympics in Chamonix, France

BEATTIE, CAGEY AND MUSH: AMATEUR HOCKEY HEROES

As had been hoped, the formation of the WCHL cleared the amateur hockey picture on the prairies, although it took some time for senior hockey to recover. Only two teams, the Regina Victorias and Indian Head Chiefs, took to the ice in 1921–22, with the Victorias going all the way to the Allan Cup final, where the Toronto Granites, featuring Saskatchewan expatriate Beattie Ramsey, prevailed 13–2 in a two-game, total-goals series. Ramsey, who was born near Lumsden, was a fighter pilot in the First World War and a hockey star at the University of Toronto. He was also with the Granites when they represented Canada at the first Winter Olympics in Chamonix, France, in 1924 and waltzed to the gold medal by outscoring their opponents 88–3. Ramsey later played briefly with the Toronto Maple Leafs before returning to Saskatchewan, where he would coach the Prince Albert Mintos in the '30s and help re-establish the Regina Pats in the '40s.

Al Ritchie would experience a lot of football heartbreak as the manager and sometimes coach of the Roughriders, but in 1925 he would enjoy the taste of total victory in those dual roles with the Regina Pats. Sil Acaster was still around to supply plenty of scoring punch along with diminutive Ken Doraty. Johnny Gottselig was literally a tower of strength on defence, equally adept at breaking up opposing rushes as he was at carrying the puck. Ike Morrison, a late arrival from Moose Jaw, provided depth at forward.

By the time the Pats had advanced past two more opponents and reached the best-of-three national final against Toronto Aura Lee at Toronto Arena Gardens, Doraty and Morrison were suffering from colds, and Acaster was wearing a head bandage to protect a wound suffered in the Western final. Nevertheless, Regina managed a 2–1 victory on Frank Ingram's overtime goal. Doraty was the centre of attention in the second game, first when he and Aura Lee forward Shrimp McPherson came to blows and sparked a bench-clearing brawl. Policemen had to bring the players under control and the donnybrook ended with Doraty and McPherson—the smallest man on each team—apologizing to each other and laughing in the penalty box. Doraty was also the offensive star with two goals in a 5–2 romp that gave the Pats and the province of Saskatchewan their first Memorial Cup triumph.

Doraty and Gottselig were both born beyond Saskatchewan, Doraty in Stittsville, Ont., and Gottselig in Odessa, Russia (now Ukraine). Both moved to Saskatchewan in their childhood and would gain fame in the National Hockey League. Doraty was the smallest player in NHL history, weighing as little as 128 pounds although he could bloat all the way up to 133. Gottselig would be converted to left wing and play 16 NHL seasons, all of them with the Black Hawks as a teammate of Harold "Mush" March.

March, a tightly wound 5-foot-5 and 154 pounds, had been the scoring star of the Regina Falcons until the team combined with the Pats to form a new club, the Monarchs, for the 1927–28 season. Putting the Queen City's best players together left all Western opposition in the dust, especially with March making life miserable for goaltenders. Heading into Toronto for the best-of-three Memorial Cup series against the Ottawa Gunners, March had 42 goals in 13 games!

Ottawa, led by future NHL great Syd Howe, had a substantially bigger squad and tried to overwhelm the Monarchs with an intimidating physical game in the opener at Arena Gardens. It didn't work—certainly not on March, who scored all four goals in Regina's 4–3 victory. March was held to one goal in Ottawa's 2–1 victory in Game 2, but he and Art Dowie netted two apiece as the Monarchs ran away with the rubber match, and the Memorial Cup, 7–1.

1924–25 Regina Pats, Memorial Cup champions. Top row, from left: Frank Ingram, Bert Dowie, Jack Cunning, Stan Fuller, Ken Doraty. Front row: Jack Cranstoun, Sil Acaster, Al Ritchie, Ike Morrison, Jack Crapper. Inset: Johnny Gottselig.

JUNIOR FOOTBALL: DEMOCRACY AND DYNAMITE

There has never been, and probably never will be, another football team like Saskwanis, a Saskatoon junior contingent that was the scourge of the province for three years (1921–23) before disappearing forever. Named for a YMCA boys club, Saskwanis was the ultimate in non-authoritarian organization. It didn't have a real coach. Vern DeGeer acted as captain on the field, but off-field decisions were made by the team as a whole. Saskwanis could run off five minutes' worth of plays in total silence and equally total precision. The team went undefeated in 1921 and 1922 to reign as Western Canadian champions. Defeat didn't come until the Western final of 1923 at the hands of Winnipeg St. John's, after which Saskwanis, most of its players having exhausted their junior eligibility, disbanded.

Junior football in the West lived with the same lack of recognition as its senior counterpart. Saskwanis didn't play for the Canadian title because that privilege was reserved for Eastern teams until 1925, when the Regina Pats were allowed to challenge the Montreal Amateur Athletic Association. Montreal was hard pressed to prevail 6–4, but the West couldn't get back in the national final until 1928, when the same Pats went up against the St. Thomas (Ont.) Tigers.

The 1928 Pats boasted a fearsome quartet of halfbacks in Gordon Arnott, Johnny Achtzener, Saul Bloomfield and "Dynamite" Eddie James. At 19, the 185-pound James was skilled beyond his years, the prime beneficiary of Pats coach and Roughriders manager Al Ritchie's decision to have the teams practise together. Ritchie placed five of the juniors, including

The 1922 Saskwanis junior football team

James and Bloomfield, on the Roughriders' roster for the Grey Cup game December 1, and James proved to be Regina's best player in the 30–0 loss to the Hamilton Tigers. Bloomfield had missed most of the Pats' games when he left for Kingston to attend Queen's University, but he was able to rejoin his mates for the national championship games in Ontario.

St. Thomas got the jump on the Pats with a first-quarter touchdown (then worth five points) on a fumble recovery after a lateral from Achtzener to James went awry. Regina trailed 6–2 with three minutes to go when Bloomfield pulled off the play of the game on a fake onside kick from the Tigers' 15-yard line. Bloomfield converted the touchdown and added a single after James intercepted a St. Thomas pass.

Despite trailing for most of the game, Regina inside wing Bill Traynor insisted the bigger, hard-running Pats were destined to vanquish the Tigers. "They couldn't stop our ball carriers," Traynor related under a byline in the *Regina Daily Post*. "They had more of their men carried off Saturday than they ever dreamed of. 'Dynamite' carried three and four with him every time he broke through." Traynor also boasted openly that the Pats covered $365 in bets in St. Thomas.

THE FIRST BRIER: YELLOW GRASS FOR THE WEST

Saskatchewan had something at the first Brier that British Columbia, Alberta, and even the mighty curling power of Manitoba didn't have: a participating team. Skip Ozzie Barkwell, third Pete Wilken, second Hector Hay and lead Alf Hill of Yellow Grass travelled to Toronto in 1927 to compete in the first national men's championship, though not as the result of a rigidly structured series of playdowns. There were several odd details involved in determining the field for the '27 Brier, not the least of which was that Barkwell and his crew didn't have to prove they were the best team in Saskatchewan.

It was Winnipeg curler George Cameron who envisaged an event that would crown a national champion. Bringing it to fruition when he first proposed the idea in 1924 was fraught with difficulty. Curling had no nationwide governing body and would lack one until the formation of the Dominion Curling Association in 1935. That handicap was overcome when the Macdonald Company agreed to sponsor the event and name it after Brier, one of its brands of tobacco. It would be held in Toronto, the most accessible city in Canada by rail, and would feature a round-robin format to decide the winner.

So far, so good. Then it got silly.

Despite Cameron's trail-blazing role, most of the organizers were Easterners. They decided to limit the field to eight teams. There would be one apiece from Nova Scotia, New Brunswick, Quebec and Ontario—no, two apiece from Quebec and Ontario, because the cities of Montreal and Toronto were granted their own spots in the field. Wait, make that three from Ontario because the province was just so gosh-darn big that it wasn't fair to grant it only one representative (not counting Toronto). So, to this point, the field would consist of, from east to west, Nova Scotia, New Brunswick, the province of Quebec, Montreal, Ontario, Toronto and Northern Ontario.

One spot remained, and rather than assign it to Prince Edward Island, the organizers magnanimously put it up for grabs among the prairie provinces. Little did it matter that the three provinces boasting most of the nation's competitive curlers happened to be Manitoba, Saskatchewan and Alberta. They wouldn't be able to enter their own teams until 1928. (British Columbia and P.E.I. didn't join the fold until 1936.) For 1927, each of the three was to hold a tournament that would include only teams that placed in the top eight of the provincial bonspiel's grand aggregate event.

In Saskatchewan, Joe Dundas of Moose Jaw won the Regina Men's Bonspiel that served as the SCA Bonspiel. Dundas, however, chose not to enter the tournament for the Brier. Neither did anyone else except Barkwell's men from Yellow Grass, so they won by default.

Next on the schedule was the three-team Western championship in Winnipeg. Not so fast—the Henry Trimble quartet of Lacombe didn't care for the stipulation that the Alberta representative would have to pay its own way to Winnipeg, so it elected to stay at home. (The same condition applied to Saskatchewan, which probably accounts for some of the teams that did not oppose Barkwell.) Now the Western championship would be a best-of-three affair between

Western Canada's first Brier representatives: (from left) Alf Hill, Hector Hay, Pete Wilken and Ozzie Barkwell of Yellow Grass

Barkwell and home-town favourite Jimmy Congalton, whose third, Howard Wood, would become one of Manitoba's most accomplished curlers. Winnipeg's expectations of routine victory evaporated as the Yellow Grass men swept the first two games 11–10 and 12–9, the latter essentially decided by Barkwell's big six in the third end.

Unlike this era's major championships that are stretched out over eight days, feature 10-end games and culminate in playoffs, the '27 Brier ran off its seven round-robin draws in three days from Tuesday, March 1 to Thursday, March 3, and was the only national competition to employ 14-end games. For Barkwell, Wilken, Hay and Hill, there was another, more significant novelty: it was their first experience on artificial ice. Furthermore, they were venturing into territory where the aggressive hitting game common to Western curlers was virtually unknown and certainly unwelcome.

"We tried to play our brand of game once," Alf Hill recalled in 1969. "The other team—Sarnia (Ontario) I think it was—were laying six and Ozzie just got fed up with it all. He decided he was going to open things up, so he asked Pete to throw a hot one. Pete threw, and seeing as there were no partitions between the sheets of ice, it took me about five minutes to gather up the rocks from two sheets over. We were the most unpopular sons of guns in Ontario for a while."

Barkwell and his mates almost won both their Tuesday games, yielding a steal of two in the 14th end to lose 13–12 to Ontario before downing Montreal 13–8. Wednesday's decisions were all clean cut, 17–15 and 11–9 decisions over Toronto and Northern Ontario and a 12–9 loss to Nova Scotia. When the sun rose on the final day, Nova Scotia led the Brier with a 4–1 record, followed by Western Canada and New Brunswick at 3–2.

Thursday's morning draw began to unfold perfectly for Barkwell. Nova Scotia, skipped by Murray Macneill, trailed Montreal 8–0 after five ends. Meanwhile, in the game that would break the second-place tie, Western Canada gradually pulled away from New Brunswick to lead 11–4 after 10 ends. Nowadays it is natural for the losing team to remove their gloves and concede the game when victory seems out of reach. No such practice existed then, primarily because the imperfections of early icemaking made big comebacks possible. Case in point: In this very draw Nova Scotia ran off 11 straight points to lead

11–8 after 11. Back on Barkwell's sheet, New Brunswick staged a more sudden turnaround:

Western Canada 101 202 110 3 02 0❑—(13)

New Brunswick 010 020 001 0 50 3❑—(12)

At least Barkwell had the hammer and a lead, if not momentum, coming home. He had three rocks in play, but Macneill had a guarded shot rock when it came time for Barkwell's last shot. A successful draw or tapback would bring at least one point and a victory; a clean miss would force a 15th end. Perhaps a third possibility—missing to the inside and promoting New Brunswick's guard for a steal of two—didn't occur to Barkwell until after it happened, which it did. New Brunswick 14, Western Canada 13. And Nova Scotia 13, Montreal 9. Suddenly, Barkwell was eliminated from contention.

An 11–9 loss to Quebec dropped Western Canada to 3–4 and fourth place, behind Nova Scotia (6–1), New Brunswick (5–2) and Toronto (4–3). The men from Yellow Grass expressed the opinion that the games should have been 12 ends long, which had become the standard out West, and in 1928 the Brier did shorten its games to that length. Had 12-enders been the norm in 1927, Barkwell's rink would have gone 5–2 . . . but Nova Scotia would have gone undefeated.

THE ROUGHRIDERS PAVE THE ROAD TO HELL

DENIED THE OPPORTUNITY TO PLAY FOR THE national championship, burdened with a $500 deficit (imagine, a deficit expressed in only two zeroes), and hampered by an unappealing facility, the Regina Rugby Club resolved to reverse its fortunes in 1928. The field at Park Hughes was shifted to a nearby space adjoining it and Park De Young, thus providing more seating and space for fans to park beside the field and watch games from their cars. Sporadic opposition of previous seasons was overcome with the formation of a three-team league comprising the Moose Jaw Maroons, Winnipeg Tammany Hall and the Roughriders. (Regina had taken up "Roughriders" in earnest in 1924 when Ottawa's team, called the "Rough Riders" since the 19th century, briefly renamed itself the Senators.)

Al Ritchie (right) and friends pose for photographers before a Grey Cup game

To spark fan interest in the home opener, Roughriders president Emmett McCusker boarded an aeroplane the evening before the game for a publicity stunt in which he would drop balloons carrying free tickets to the game. That balloons tend not to plummet but to float on air seemed to escape the originator of the idea. (As God is his witness, he thought this turkey would fly.) When McCusker released the balloons, people gathered on Regina streets watched them glide horizontally eastward—far, far past the city limits, beyond the blue horizon to rural parts unknown, their cargo rendered worthless in the hands of farmers occupied with harvesting a bumper crop.

On the field, the Roughriders were far more

efficient, winning all six league games and whipping Winnipeg St. John's 12–1 for a third straight Western championship that, along with a 17-game winning streak, convinced the CRU to let Regina play for the Grey Cup on December 1. Given nearly a month to prepare, the Roughriders arranged an exhibition game in Calgary on November 10—a good idea, but in the course of winning 32–10 Fred Wilson, Regina's superb kicker since 1911, suffered a broken ankle. For the Grey Cup, the Roughriders bolstered themselves with Eddie James and four other junior stars while the Hamilton Tigers enjoyed a weight advantage that averaged 15 pounds per man. James and quarterback Fritz Sandstrom were the most visible Roughriders, James for his hard running and the helmetless, blonde Sandstrom for the blood that kept running down his face after he had been kicked in the head. Hamilton, held to a 6–0 lead at the half, pulled away to win 30–0.

Regina made it back to the big game in 1929—behind James' two touchdowns in a 15–8 victory over Calgary in the Western final—with an even smaller squad to face the same Hamilton Tigers in frigid conditions. Again, the first half was a battle, with Hamilton holding a 2–1 edge and a decided advantage on the line of scrimmage. Regina was effective with the new weapon of the forward pass, however, especially when thrown by left-handed snapback (centre) Jersey Campbell. (Rules of the day put few restrictions on who could attempt a forward pass.) Regina was coming on strong in the third quarter when Saul Bloomfield, the hero of the Pats' 1928 junior triumph, fumbled a punt that the Tigers recovered and ran in 35 yards for a touchdown and a 9–3 lead. That proved decisive as Hamilton prevailed 14–3.

Regina had achieved respectability on the national stage, to be sure, but the Grey Cup was still out of reach. Furthermore, the bitter cold in Hamilton kept attendance down to a mere 1,906. With meagre gate receipts, the Roughriders took a $1,400 loss on their Eastern trip.

JIM TRIFUNOV: ROLL OVER AND TRY AGAIN

EVERY MORNING, IN THE BRIGHT DEWY SUMMER and the dark blizzards of winter, little Jim Trifunov would fill his bags with newspapers and deliver *The Morning Leader* to hundreds of homes, up and down the streets of Regina, six to eight miles of walking his route making his legs strong, six to eight miles of carrying newspapers building up his arms and torso. It was all Trifunov could do to remain in school but still help support his mother and three sisters since his father died in 1913 when Jim was 10 years old. The family had emigrated from Serbia only three years earlier.

Grown to his full height of only 5-foot-5 at 19, Trifunov joined the YMCA Boxing and Wrestling Club. The head man at the YMCA club was one of the biggest in the city in both size and reputation, Sgt. Dan Matheson of the Regina City Police. Matheson, silver medallist in the heavyweight division at the 1921 Canadian wrestling championships, also coached many of the YMCA's wrestlers and organized the boxing and wrestling cards that kept the sports financially viable. Matheson, despite the combined load of his police work and his YMCA duties, won three straight national heavyweight championships (1923–25) and another in 1931.

Never an Olympian, Matheson was consoled by the success of YMCA products like Trifunov, Earl McCready and Vern Pettigrew. Trifunov, essentially self-coached, needed only one year of Matheson's encouragement and guidance to earn a national title at 56 kilos (123 pounds) and held on to it as carefully as he did his paper route money, reigning as Canadian champ for nine of 10 years (1923–30, '32) and simultaneously holding the 134-pound title in 1926. Nothing held greater prestige than the Olympics, of course, and Trifunov was selected to represent Canada at the 1924 Games in Paris.

He was dominating his opening bout with Englishman H.E. Sansum when the Swedish referee suddenly declared Trifunov the loser on a rolling fall—an astonishing ruling as the Canadian team had been told that a rolling fall could not count as a pin. A newspaper account after the Olympics recounted the incident:

> *He was having all the best of it with Sansum, a Britisher, when the referee decided that his opponent had scored a rolling fall and held up his hand as the victor. The crowd "booed" the decision, for*

the Canadian had merely bounced off the mat as the pair fell and was immediately on top of his man. Moreover it had been decided that referees must count to "2" before awarding a rolling fall, but the referee was a Swede who did not understand this ruling and could not be made to understand it.

Judge J.A. Jackson of Lethbridge, a witness to the fiasco, produced one of the most poignant sports quotes of the decade: "The Olympic Games are attended by the world's best athletes and judged by the world's worst officials."

Trifunov hoped for retribution at the 1928 Olympics but, even with his string of national titles, was left off the team. The Canadian Olympic Association told him he could compete only if he paid his own way to Amsterdam.

Far from rich, Trifunov was so well-liked at the *Morning Leader*, where he now had an office job, that the employees there raised the money to get him to the Netherlands. Trifunov responded with a bronze medal to purge the bitterness of his 1924 disqualification.

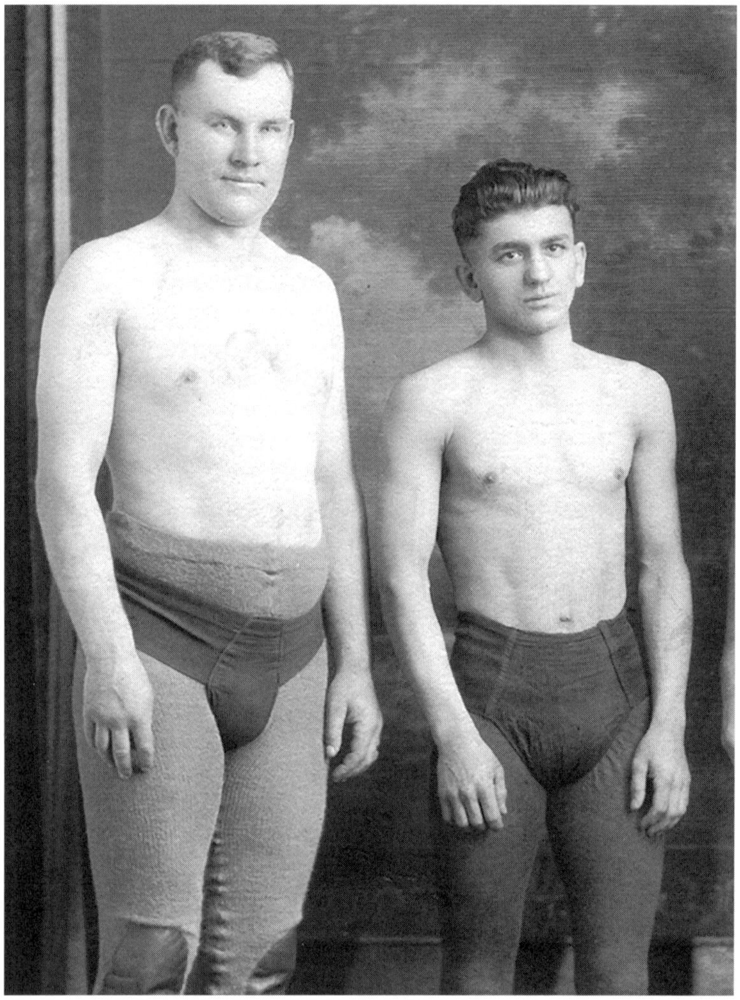

Dan Matheson and Jim Trifunov

Two years later, Trifunov won gold at the British Empire Games. He made it to another Olympiad in 1932 before retiring from competition and would attend three more as Canada's wrestling coach in 1952, '56 and '60.

ETHEL CATHERWOOD: GILDING THE LILY

SHE DREW NOTICE BECAUSE SHE WAS A SENSATIONAL natural athlete, but she held everyone's attention because she was drop-dead gorgeous. In the space of six years Ethel Catherwood went from an unspoiled high school girl to a national outcast; in between she was an incomparable high jumper, the world record-setter and the first female Olympic champion in that discipline.

Ethel was born April 28, 1908, in Hannah, S.D. Her family moved to Scott, about 160 kilometres west of Saskatoon, shortly after her second birthday. Ethel enjoyed and excelled at most everything she tried, but she had a special knack for the high jump, which she practised in the backyard of the home she shared with her parents and eight siblings.

At 16, Ethel received the family trait that would prove to be her greatest blessing and curse: her height. According to a 1928 feature in the *Saskatoon Morning Star*, her best jump as a 15-year-old had been 4 feet 2 inches. Then, like the rest of her siblings, she sprouted; in her case, six inches to her adult height of 5-foot-10. She was also developing the ideal look of the Flapper era: bobbed hair, sparkling eyes, trim figure and long, slim legs. Standing almost a head taller than most women of her time, she would be impossible not to notice—

just as it would have been impossible for her not to notice the effect her beauty had on men.

Her agility and co-ordination were not at all diminished by the growth spurt. Her personal best shot up to 4 feet 10 inches. Challenged by her father to do even better at 17, she reportedly cleared 5 feet 4 inches in the backyard. Joseph Catherwood knew his daughter had athletic talent, but how much? Who knew? It was 1925, and the previous year's men's Olympic champion had cleared 6 feet 6 inches. Women, however, were barred from all Olympic competition except swimming and archery. Women's track and field standards were a mystery to Joseph Catherwood.

Ethel's athletic career might have sputtered to an obscure end had it not been for a family decision in the summer of 1925 to move to Saskatoon so she, two younger brothers and a sister could pursue higher education. Ethel had completed Grade 11 at Champagne School in Scott and would enter Bedford Road Collegiate as a senior student and star on the basketball, skating, hockey, baseball and, of course, track and field teams. At a meet in the fall of 1925, she set records in the 50-, 75- and 100-yard dashes, won the long jump with a leap of 14 feet 6 inches and set another record in the high jump at an even 5 feet. No one took special notice of the last figure—with the notable exception of Joe Griffiths, one-time football star and now Physical Director at the University of Saskatchewan. He knew the height was either a typographical error, an incorrect measurement, or sensational. If it was for real, it was better than the existing Canadian record and almost equal to the world mark. Griffiths went to the Catherwood home the next day and spoke to Joseph. Soon Ethel arrived home from school.

"I was almost struck dumb with amazement when I saw this tall beautiful girl walk in through the house," Griffiths related in a newspaper article. "I asked her if she would get into her track suit and show me a jump or two in a pit they had in the back yard. I immediately saw the report in the paper was quite true."

Griffiths volunteered to coach Ethel with a goal of placing her on the 1928 Canadian Olympic team if the International Olympic Committee proceeded with its controversial plan to add some women's track and field events to the schedule in Amsterdam. Ethel and her parents accepted, and in the spring of 1926 she began her first formal athletic training. Within two weeks she was bettering the world record in practice with her scissors kick. Griffiths tried to teach her the roll technique, but it produced no improvement and was soon abandoned. Griffiths scheduled her first test for August 31 at the U of S with a goal both lofty and achievable: the Canadian record of 4 feet 9½ inches. Griffiths requested the local branch of the Amateur Athletic Union to sanction the meet, which would make any records achieved official. Catherwood did her part, rising 4 feet 11¾ inches, almost duplicating her high school championship effort.

Ethel Catherwood, 1925

Joe Griffiths

Six days later, on Labour Day at the provincial championships in Regina, Griffiths cut his protégé loose. Catherwood easily made the first official 5-foot jump by a Canadian woman, and Griffiths quickly asked officials to raise the bar to 5 feet 3 inches, a good 1½ inches above the world record set five weeks earlier by Phyllis Green of England. Catherwood cleared the bar on her first attempt. When she touched down the 1,500 spectators exploded in cheers. Official remeasurement showed the bar had sagged, reducing the official height to 5 feet 2⁷⁄₁₆ inches. No matter; Saskatchewan and Canada had a world record holder.

With the 1926 season over, there was plenty of time to build up anticipation for her next major appearance. Catherwood made her debut on the national stage August 13, 1927, at the University of Toronto. It was the first Canadian women's track and field championships, conducted under the auspices of the newly formed Canadian Women's Amateur Athletic Federation. Catherwood, representing the Saskatoon BPOE (Benevolent and Protective Order of Elks), sailed an eighth of an inch over 5 feet, which was hailed as a Canadian record. (Her Regina jump would not be officially recognized until December 1927.) In the throwing events, which she had been practising only three months, Catherwood threw the javelin a record 114 feet 7 inches and placed third in the discus. She remained in Toronto and was the sensation of the Canadian National Exhibition meet on September 3, clearing 5 feet 2 inches before 15,000 spectators.

Sports writers fell over themselves to proclaim the arrival of the Dominion's new star. She was "as white as a lily and as retiring as a morning glory," not to mention "a dream in repose and a sweetheart in action." One scribe tried to usurp her residency by calling her "Toronto's sweetheart," but the nickname that permanently attached itself to her was "The Saskatoon Lily." With feminine participation in the Olympics finally confirmed, Catherwood settled in Toronto to train at the Parkdale Ladies Athletic Club. She and her sister Ginger found work in the brokerage firm of millionaire Teddy Oke, who hired Walter Knox to take over Ethel's coaching.

Five thousand people attended the Olympic trials July 2, 1928, in Halifax for what might have been Catherwood's finest athletic performance. First she hurled the javelin 118 feet 8 inches, surpassing her own record. (Exactly *why* the javelin was included in trials for an Olympics that didn't include a women's javelin throw is a mystery.) Then she delivered her *pièce de résistance*, a clean high jump of exactly 5 feet 3 inches, measured and remeasured, an improvement on her own world record and a clear message to Phyllis Green, who had recently cleared 5 feet 2½ inches.

At Amsterdam, Catherwood stayed away from the stadium and trained until August 5, the last day of track and field competition. There was a new favourite, Carolina Gisolf of the host Netherlands, who had broken Catherwood's world record with a jump of 5 feet 3¼ inches. Cool, drizzly weather settled on Amsterdam in the morning for the qualifying round, where 23 women cleared 4 feet 6 inches to advance to the afternoon final.

Although Catherwood was facing the ultimate international field in her first competition outside of Canada, she proceeded as calmly as if she was back at a Saskatoon high school meet. She kept her sweatsuit on for her opening jumps and didn't remove it until she missed on her first attempt at an even 5 feet. She stripped down to her shirt and shorts just before the second try, smiled and cleared the bar with ease.

Mildred Wiley of the United States and Gisolf were the only other women to succeed at 5 feet. Unlike them, Catherwood had no teammates to assist her between jumps because only competitors were allowed on the infield. She kept warm between jumps by wrapping herself in a large red Hudson Bay blanket but might have stiffened in the chilly conditions were it not for the return of a favour. Days earlier, Belgian runners in the women's 800-metre run had no one to massage them. Canadian team manager Alexandrine Gibb and a chaperone volunteered their services. Now the Belgian high jumpers, long since eliminated, kept Catherwood carefully tucked in her blanket and cleaned her spikes between jumps.

The three remaining jumpers all cleared 5 feet 1¼ inches, and the bar was raised to 5-foot-3. Catherwood, as she had on every attempt, smiled before beginning her run at the bar. Her first attempt was good. Gisolf and Wiley failed on all three of theirs. Catherwood was the Olympic gold medallist. As had occurred two years earlier in Regina, the remeasurement lowered the official height, in this case to 5 feet 2 9/16 inches. Gisolf beat Wiley in a jump-off for the silver medal.

Catherwood left Amsterdam with tangible proof of her greatness as an athlete and an ever-increasing sense of her desirability as a woman. Before the Games had even begun, she was unofficially proclaimed the Prettiest Athlete, or Beauty Queen, of the Olympics. Not that there was a process to bestowing these titles—reporters (male, of course) simply thought it was worth watching the ladies practise and telling the public who had the prettiest faces and shapeliest figures. Catherwood was overwhelmingly the consensus choice of the American and European writers. (You can scan microfilm until you go blind, but you'll never discover whether Earl Thomson or any other man was chosen the most handsome athlete of the 1920 Games.) There were reports of motion picture studios offering Catherwood contracts. "I'd rather gulp poison than try my hand at motion pictures," was her response to the rumours.

Hundreds greeted Catherwood at the Saskatoon railway station upon her return home September 5, and thousands turned out for Ethel Catherwood Day on September 28. The Board of Trade, the City and several service clubs collected $3,000 and presented the money in a trust fund for Ethel to continue her education in piano studies. During the presentation the crowd surged forward. Elementary school children crowded the platform and surrounded Catherwood as she expressed her gratitude.

Manager Ross Brown with Ethel Catherwood

Ethel Catherwood, 20 years old, had reached the pinnacle of her athletic success, her popularity and perhaps her happiness. Before another Olympiad presented itself, she would transform from icon to outcast.

She returned to Toronto with her sister Ginger in October 1928 and entered the Royal Conservatory. Music training went badly, so she switched to secretarial studies at a business college. Her 1929 athletic

The Saskatoon Lily

season ended before it started when she suffered a spike injury. Catherwood tasted victory in the high jump and javelin at the 1930 British Empire Games in Hamilton, but her height (5 feet 1¾ inches) and distance (111 feet 5¾ inches) didn't match 1928 standards. She slipped further in 1931, clearing only 4 feet 10½ inches to win the Ontario championship, then settling for third place at 4-foot-9½ in the nationals at Wetaskiwin, Alta.—the first time in her life she didn't win a high-jump competition. It was said that Catherwood was troubled by an injury that she had aggravated on the train ride from Toronto.

Yet it was scandal, not injury, that drove Catherwood away from competition. In December of 1931, it was revealed that she had been secretly married for two years. On January 2, 1932, she announced her intention to obtain a Nevada divorce and to marry an American—pretty tame stuff by 21st-century norms but outrageous in the '30s. Catherwood admitted that she married Toronto bank clerk James McLaren, whom she had met shortly before departing for the Amsterdam Olympics, on November 25, 1929. They kept the marriage secret, she said, "because he had endangered his job with the Bank of Toronto by violating its rule against matrimony on the part of its younger officers." According to Catherwood—or, as she was now called, Mrs. James McLaren or "Miss Catherwood," with heavy emphasis on the quotation marks—the couple never lived together.

While the world's press virtually drooled over her in Amsterdam, she captured the attention of Byron Mitchell—former Toronto resident, manager of the American eight-man rowing crew that won the gold medal, and member of a socially prominent San Francisco family. Mitchell courted the secretly married darling of Canada with little fanfare until reporters sniffed out the marriage. Catherwood did not express a shred of shame or regret, only a profession of love for Mitchell. She did not budge from her path, even when the consequences of her intended divorce were made clear. Canadian courts would not recognize the legality of a Nevada divorce; if she returned to Canada to compete for a berth on the 1932 Olympic team, she would certainly be arrested for bigamy.

"My attorneys have studied the laws of both nations, and I have decided to marry Mitchell and keep out of trouble by keeping out of Canada," she declared. And so she did. Ethel Catherwood, or Mrs. James McLaren, obtained her divorce in Reno, Nev., on July 5, 1932, and became Mrs. Byron Mitchell. She willingly faded into obscurity in California. Athletics would hold no more attraction for her.

Whether Ethel Catherwood lived happily ever after is a mystery; no evidence suggests that she did. She was divorced from Byron Mitchell in 1960 and returned to office work as a statistical stenographer in San Francisco. She made a rare public appearance in 1965 on the CBC television show *Flashback* that disappointed the national audience; she remembered little of her glory days and did not acknowledge anyone who had assisted her progress. When contacted by a *Toronto Star* reporter in 1977, Catherwood said she had given away all her trophies and mementos, including her gold medal to her sister. "I have no interest whatsoever in sport, and I just wish some Canadian girl would jump 17 feet so that all you people up there would leave me alone," she insisted.

Catherwood delivered her ultimate rebuff in 1980 when Ottawa columnist Earl McRae telephoned her regarding an article for *Today* magazine. In perhaps the most memorable non-interview of McRae's career, Catherwood snapped, "Look, cut the crap. Let's get to the nitty-gritty. What do you want?" McRae asked Catherwood if she would like to meet Debbie Brill, Canada's high-jump medal hopeful for the Moscow Olympics (which had not been boycotted yet), as part of a story he was writing.

"First off," she replied, "I am not a Canadian. I never was a Canadian. I'm an American and always have been."

But that day in Amsterdam, the gold medal, the maple leaf on her shirt . . . "It was an unfortunate period of my life. I was never an athlete. I was a natural. It was no big thing. I went, I did it, and quite frankly, I'm sick and tired of the whole thing. I haven't thought about it in years, and I don't want to think about it. Okay?"

Ethel Catherwood's final years were spent in Grass Valley, Calif., battling bone cancer. She died September 26, 1987, in a sadly triumphant way, leaving the world on her own terms, so withdrawn into her seclusion that the Saskatoon *StarPhoenix* didn't learn of her passing until the following January.

ALSO IN THIS DECADE

- Pete Parker of Regina called the play-by-play of the first game of the WCHL final on March 14, 1923, between the Regina Capitals and the Edmonton Eskimos on Regina radio station CKCK. This has been touted as the first complete broadcast of a hockey game. In April 2004, however, Toronto hockey writer Eric Zweig published an article on early radio coverage that summarized his findings and those of fellow researcher Larry Robertson. Zweig discovered the first partial broadcast to be an OHA intermediate contest between North Toronto and Midland by Norman Albert of Toronto station CFCA on February 8, 1923. Albert also handled the first call of an NHL game, the third period between the Ottawa Senators and Toronto St. Pats on February 14. A senior game in Winnipeg between the Falcons and Port Arthur was broadcast on local radio in its entirety on February 22, 20 days before Parker's debut.

- Saskatoon high school student Jim Hogg ran the mile in 4 minutes 52.4 seconds in 1924, setting a Western Canada junior record that would stand for 25 years.

- Jackie Lewis won the Canadian professional bantamweight (118 pounds) boxing title in 1925 before a home-town crowd in Regina. Lewis outpointed champion Vic Foley of Vancouver 5–4 with six rounds even.

- Stanley Glover of Saskatoon, who had led the Nutana Marksmanship Team to three national marksmanship titles from 1924–26, won a bronze medal in the 1928 Olympics as part of the Canadian 4x400 relay team. Glover later took up curling and won the Saskatchewan Tankard men's championship in 1943.

Regina Dales and Montreal Westmount (with "W" on shirts) contest the 1938 Canadian junior football championship on Montreal's icy field

1930–1939

Hard Times

ARRIVALS

August 4, 1931: Ernie Richardson, curler, Stoughton.
October 3, 1931: Glenn Hall, hockey player, Humboldt.
January 12, 1932: Norm Fieldgate, football player, Regina.
February 24, 1932: John Vernon, actor, Zehner.
August 31, 1932: Allan Fotheringham, humorist, Hearne.
September 19, 1932: Bob Pickering, curler, Regina.
November 25, 1932: Bill Clarke, football player/curler, Regina.
April 6, 1933: Barb Stone Turnbull Danaher, golfer, Saskatoon.
June 19, 1933: Robin Hahn, equestrian, Regina.
October 29, 1933: Joyce McKee, curler, Asquith.
March 16, 1934: Ray Hnatyshyn, governor-general (1990–94), Saskatoon.
October 4, 1934: Rudy Wiebe, writer, Speedwell.
October 22, 1934: Gerry James, football/hockey player, Regina.
March 1, 1935: George Genereux, shooter, Saskatoon.
December 7, 1936: Larry Dumelie, football player, Lafleche.
June 24, 1937: Ted Urness, football player, Regina.
October 14, 1938: Lee Morrison, curler/softball player, Regina.
January 13, 1939: Vera Pezer, curler, Melfort.
February 24, 1939: Wayne Shaw, football player, Bladworth.
August 12, 1939: Roy Romanow, premier (1991–2000), Saskatoon.

DEPARTURES

March 23, 1938: Walter Scott, first premier (1905–16), 70.
April 13, 1938: Grey Owl (Archie Belaney), conservationist, 49.

THE DIRTY THIRTIES. THE DUST BOWL. DROUGHT. THE GREAT DEPRESSION.

Hockey, football and other sports took a back seat to a team effort called Survival. Appropriately, the decade's major sporting tales involve struggle.

Earl McCready's game, wrestling, was all about struggle.

The Regina Roughriders ached to win a Grey Cup but couldn't.

Gas Eichel overcame childhood illnesses to become a champion boxer.

Rowers from the Regina Boat Club trained in archaic equipment under trying circumstances, yet still achieved amazing victories.

And young Paul Dojack took a bunch of wayward boys, made them into athletes, and took them on a chaotic ride to a national football title.

EARL McCREADY: HANDLING BIG MEN WITH EASE

HE WAS BORN IN ONTARIO IN 1908, MOVED TO Milestone when he was 2½ and grew up on a farm near Ogema. As a 14-year-old with a healthy interest in girls, Earl McCready was at a disadvantage compared to the older, bigger boys in the district.

"All the dances ended up in fights," he recalled 60 years later. "One day I happened to read an advertisement that said, 'Handle Big Men With Ease,' and I sent away for it."

He received six pamphlets written by Frank Gotch, one of the greatest of professional wrestlers. McCready practised the lessons religiously, sometimes by himself, sometimes putting holds on the farm horses. For some, this would be a good way to get kicked into intensive care, but McCready was a clever fellow and something of a horse himself. By the age of 17 he stood over six feet tall and tipped the scales at 220 pounds. He moved to Regina and joined the YMCA to box and wrestle, although his purpose in moving was to attend normal school and advance his education.

McCready fulfilled his ambition in a most unexpected fashion. He travelled to Vancouver for the 1926 Canadian wrestling championships, where his semi-final opponent was American champion and one-time Olympian Charlie Strach. Luckily for McCready, who had one year of local experience, he was unaware of Strach's background.

"Had I known that, I would have been intimidated and ended up flat on my belly, but I knew so little that I went head-to-head with him. I got my foot under him, backed him off and grabbed his ankle. I just held him there for six minutes. We had to go to an extension (extra time) and I won the decision."

Earl McCready

After McCready earned one more victory for the first of his four Canadian amateur championships, Strach and two other Americans who attended Oklahoma A&M (Agricultural & Mechanical) University approached the strapping 18-year-old about coming to their school. McCready jumped at the opportunity. He would make the Dean's List. He would earn his football letter as an offensive guard. And he would wrestle. Boy, would he wrestle!

Freshmen were barred from National Collegiate

Athletic Association (NCAA) competition, so McCready contented himself in 1927 with another Canadian title. He made it three straight in 1928 and collected his first NCAA championship when he pinned Ralph Freese of Kansas in 19 seconds (including the referee's three-second count)—still an NCAA record for the fastest fall in a final. McCready attended the 1928 Olympics in Amsterdam as Canada's freestyle heavyweight (and opening ceremonies flag-bearer) but was eliminated in his first match. He repeated as NCAA champ in 1929. Then came 1930, when he literally won everything in sight: his third straight NCAA title; the U.S. Amateur Athletic Union championship; his fourth Canadian championship; and the gold medal at the first British Empire Games in Hamilton, Ont., where he again served as Canadian flag-bearer.

Most incredibly, in capturing all those honours against elite competition, McCready went through the year undefeated and won every match by a fall, *not once letting the issue go to a decision!*

McCready had conquered every level of amateur wrestling save for the Olympics. He would have to forgo that challenge to earn a living as the Great Depression crept over North America and good money beckoned from the pro ranks. Whereas professional wrestling today is a thoroughly rehearsed spectacle, it was still a sport then. McCready quickly rose to the upper echelons of wrestling and grappled with the likes of Strangler Lewis and Jim Londos, whom he challenged twice (unsuccessfully) for the world title. The British Empire championship was McCready's after he took it from Jack Taylor in 1933. McCready held it for seven years although there was one occasion in 1935 when Yvon Robert Sr., of Montreal nearly took it from him. "We wrestled for 2 hours 30 minutes, and it ended up in a draw," McCready said. "I don't know who stopped it. Some people who were there said they wouldn't let dogs fight on that long. Women were crying and men were swearing."

McCready's greatest pleasure came from his world travels. As Empire champion he defended his title in England, Australia, New Zealand and South Africa. He escaped with bruises when the car he was driving was hit by a train in 1942. A year later he contracted diabetes. He continued to wrestle until 1957, spending most of the '50s as a popular attraction with Stu Hart's fledgling Stampede Wrestling venture.

McCready settled down in Edmonds, Wash., and operated a massage and sauna spa. Before his death in 1983, he was elected to seven Halls of Fame: Canada Sports, Saskatchewan Sports, Oklahoma, Wrestling Canada, U.S. Wrestling, pro wrestling and Stampede Wrestling.

1930 REGINA PATS: YOU'RE SO DEFENSIVE!

To crush another team's Memorial Cup dream is one thing, but to not even let them score is like pouring acid on the dream's remnants. That's just about how the Regina Pats treated their opponents en route to the 1930 Memorial Cup final. To win the provincial final, Regina had to outscore the Wilkie Outlaws in a two-game series, which the Pats did to the tune of 6–1. Wilkie's only goal came at the 3:02 mark of the second game's third period.

At least the Outlaws accomplished what the Alberta and Manitoba champions couldn't: a goal. At two-game, total-goals series in Winnipeg, the Pats blanked the Calgary Canadians 6–0 in the Western semi-final and the Elmwood Millionaires 8–0 in the final. Part of the Pats' strength may have come from coach Al Ritchie's preference to make his best players defencemen. Ritchie's rearguards were Frank "Buzz" Boll and Gordon "Red" Pettinger, who would both go on to notable NHL careers, like Johnny Gottselig of the 1925 Pats, as forwards. Playing defence for Ritchie didn't tie a player to his own end; Boll and Pettinger were the team's best puck-handlers and had each scored two of the Pats' six goals against Calgary. At 175 and 166 pounds respectively, Pettinger and Boll were also two of the biggest players on a team that averaged a mere 146 pounds and relied on speed to wear out the opposition.

The big news after the opener of the Memorial Cup final in Winnipeg wasn't the Pats' 3–1 victory but the goal they surrendered to the West Toronto Athletic Club. Regina goaltender Ken Campbell was beaten at 7:50 of the third period, ending a shutout streak of 304 minutes 48 seconds! West Toronto threatened to extend the series to the three-game limit when it grabbed a 2–0 lead in the second game. Clarence Acaster and Pettinger tied it early in the third period, and the score remained that way until the final minute of regulation play, when Pettinger and Ken Moore charged out of their zone on a two-man rush. Pettinger passed to Moore, who was forced to the boards and fired the puck from a sharp angle. West Toronto goaltender Ron Geddes kicked it out, but Moore tipped it right back into the goal mouth, circled the net and jammed the puck home for the winning goal with 40 seconds to go.

That sensational play—think of it as a wraparound where the player wraps himself, not the puck, around the net—by the 130-pound Moore gave Regina its third Memorial Cup triumph in six seasons. It would be 44 years until the Pats (not to mention all of Saskatchewan) would claim a fourth Canadian junior championship. They would come close in 1933 by reaching the national final, only to lose a pair of 2–1 decisions (the second in overtime) to the Newmarket (Ont.) Redmen. Three years later the Saskatoon Wesleys were in similar circumstances but fell 5–1 and 4–2 to the West Toronto Nationals.

Gord Pettinger

1930 (& '31 & '32 & '34) 'RIDERS: BLACK DAYS AT THE GREY CUP

ROOTS OF WESTERN ALIENATION, PART 27D: Regina Roughriders broke out new colours of red and black in 1930 but didn't change their domination of Western football, winning all eight of their games by a combined score of 99–12. Although Dynamite Eddie James had moved to Winnipeg, captain and halfback Greg Grassick had charge of a squad that was resolute on defence and becoming ever more sophisticated on offence as it continued to master the forward pass. When the Roughriders boarded the train for the Grey Cup, they were actually an even-money bet for the big game. The Eastern champion, Toronto Balmy Beach of the Ontario Rugby Football Union, was a surprise winner over the Hamilton Tigers of the Big Four.

En route to Toronto, the Roughriders discovered that the Canadian Rugby Union was banning the forward pass because the ORFU had not used it. The Big Four and the Western Interprovincial Football Union had. The CRU claimed its rules had always stipulated that the forward pass could only be used in games where both teams were accustomed to its use, which was the first the Roughriders had heard about it. Regina filed an appeal that was given as much consideration as the jury's recommendation for mercy at the trial of Louis Riel. Regina also objected, to no avail, to the all-Ontario officiating crew of three men, one of them a former Balmy Beach coach.

Balmy Beach led 10–0 at halftime, but Regina rallied in the third quarter on Fred Brown's touchdown—the first ever scored by a Western team in the Grey Cup—and Saul Bloomfield's single. Trailing 10–6 in the fourth quarter, Regina marched to the Toronto 10-yard line to set up one of Canadian football's most memorable plays to that point. Bloomfield attempted a short onside kick (a tactic not at all uncommon in those days), only to have his punt blocked by Ted Reeve, who had spent most of the game on the bench with a dislocated shoulder. Balmy Beach marched downfield for a single that made the final score 11–6.

Naturally, the CRU made the forward pass legal across the country the following year. Regina, picking up on a national trend, recruited its first American import, Curt Schave, a North Dakota halfback who joined the Roughriders for $200 a month and free rent. Despite the onset of the Great Depression, gate receipts had provided the Roughriders with enough money to spend for a good purpose. Reportedly, they covered all bases on footwear for the Grey Cup game in Toronto against the Montreal Winged Wheelers. Anticipating a soft field, the Roughriders shelled out $67 to have a bootmaker remove all their hard cleats and replace them with leather ones. When a blizzard struck the night before the contest and froze the field, Fred Wilson telephoned an order for a set of canvas lacrosse shoes to be delivered to Varsity Stadium, which they were—but to the wrong dressing room! Montreal appropriated the runners, Regina skidded around on leather cleats, and the Winged Wheelers breezed to a 22–0 decision that included the Grey Cup's first touchdown pass, a 24-yarder from Warren Stevens to Kenny Grant.

From a Regina point of view, the Roughriders had lost the last two Grey Cups on gamesmanship and bad luck. In 1932 the team made its fifth straight appearance in the national final and for once would have to admit that it lost entirely on its own merit. Regina gave the Hamilton Tigers a 25–0 lead on three first-quarter fumbles (two by Schave on kickoff returns), a safety touch caused by a snap over the punter's head, a 20-yard interception return for a touchdown, a third-quarter fumble from scrimmage, and a third-quarter fumbled punt that the Tigers retrieved and took to the end zone. In a fourth quarter that was all garbage time, the Roughriders managed a touchdown to make the final score 25–6. In five straight visits to the national final, Regina had lost by 30, 11, 5, 22 and 19 points. Such misfortune couldn't last forever, and didn't. Winnipeg won the 1933 Western final 11–1 and kept Regina from reaching the Grey Cup game.

Regina's Star Coach

By JIMMY THOMPSON

Grassick became coach in 1934, and the Roughriders splurged on five imports: Steve Adkins, Walter Olson and Bob Walker of North Dakota, Ralph Pierce of South Dakota and Paul Kirk of Minnesota. Olson and Adkins put on an aerial display such as had never been seen before in the West. Against Saskatoon they teamed up for three touchdown passes in the last nine minutes; that day Olson was 12-for-17 for 210 yards passing with Adkins making eight of the receptions. Against Moose Jaw in October, Olson was an eye-popping 17-for-24 for 460 yards, with Adkins making 11 catches for 231 yards. Olson's one-game passing yardage would remain a regular-season team record until Kent Austin had a 492-yard game in 1989; Adkins' receiving yards stood until Chris DeFrance collected 260 in a 1983 contest. Again the Roughriders ventured east with high hopes but sabotaged their own ambitions against the Sarnia Imperials, this time with a pair of costly fumbles on punt returns. Olson ran for a one-yard touchdown and threw to Adkins for another while Johnny Achtzener contributed a blocked punt deep in the Imperials' end. Sarnia prevailed 20–12 to make Regina winless in seven Grey Cups since 1922. The Roughriders embarked on an altogether different frustration, an era of 31 years in which they would reach the big game only once.

PHYLLIS DEWAR: MOOSE JAW MERMAID

CRESCENT PARK ADORNS THE EASTERN EDGE OF downtown Moose Jaw, a short block from Main Street. In the summertime you can sit on a bench and watch elegant swans float effortlessly along Serpentine Creek. In the late 1920s and early '30s, the elegance was there in the form of young Phyllis Dewar.

Encouraged by her mother's love for the water, Dewar learned to swim when she was four years old and practically made a second home for herself around Crescent Park, not far from the Canadian Pacific Railway station that was her father's home base as a conductor. She competed on the boys relay team at Alexandra School because there was no competitive school swimming for girls. In 1928, 12-year-old Phyllis outsprinted her older sister Dora to win the half-mile race at the Watrous Provincial meet on Lake Manitou. Because Phyllis had already won the 100-yard race, the strength of her finishing kick was no surprise. Her combination of speed and endurance, on the other hand, was exceptional. She dominated Saskatchewan women's swimming from 1931–33.

Desirous of a berth on the Canadian team that would compete in the 1934 British Empire Games in London, England, Dewar was doubly motivated when national team coach Tom Walker of Toronto dismissed her potential as good for someone from Saskatchewan "but not of national calibre." She and Dora pitched a tent at the Moose Jaw Aquatic Club and trained twice a day, mornings and afternoons, four to six hours daily. Phyllis would lie on a board and propel herself half a mile with nothing but leg kicks, an exercise that Australians copied when they shot to the top of the swimming world in the '50s. Not only did Dewar make the team and prove herself "of national calibre," she was the star of the Games themselves with four gold medals, a feat that brought her the Velma Springstead Award as Canada's outstanding female athlete of 1934. Dewar won the 100- and 440-yard freestyle in 1 minute 3.3 seconds and 5:45.6 respectively. She was also on the 400-yard freestyle and 300-yard medley relay teams, the latter including 100-metre breaststroke silver medallist Phyllis Haslam of Saskatoon. Upon returning to Canada, Dewar won the prestigious Barker Trophy one-mile race at Toronto, covering the distance in 29 minutes 41 seconds on a Lake Ontario course so cold that 24 competitors dropped out.

Phyllis Dewar

Entirely self-trained to this point, Dewar moved to Vancouver so that she could swim year-round and receive some coaching. The effort paid off at the 1935 Canadian championships in Winnipeg. She broke her Empire records in the 100 (1:03.2) and 440 (5:32.4), then swam the mile in world record time (23:32), setting Canadian records for 1,000 (13:38) and 1,500 yards (20:40) along the way.

Dewar was naturally touted as a medal prospect for the 1936 Olympics, but she came down with influenza in Berlin and was unable to reach the finals. Her last triumph was a gold medal as part of the Canadian 440-yard freestyle relay team at the 1938 British Empire Games in Sydney, Australia.

Uncomfortable with publicity and old for competitive swimming at 22, Dewar happily bowed out of the limelight. She enlisted in the Royal Canadian Navy early in the Second World War and while stationed in Halifax met Lieut. Murray Lowery. They married in 1943 and had four children, whom Phyllis was left to raise alone when Murray was killed in an automobile accident in 1954. Despondent and in sinking health, Phyllis died in 1961, only 45 years old. The Olympic-sized outdoor swimming pool on the southeast edge of Crescent Park is named after her.

1933–34 SASKATOON QUAKERS: LOSERS AND WORLD CHAMPIONS

The Saskatoon Quakers lost the 1933 Allan Cup final to the Moncton Hawks and got a world championship out of it. When the Hawks couldn't afford to make the trip to Milan, Italy, for the 1934 world hockey championship, the Quakers accepted the privilege of representing Canada.

Saskatoon had to play only four games in Milan. First, Ab Welsh and Bert Scharfe had three goals apiece in a 9–0 victory over France.

Scharfe and Tony Rogers each scored a pair as Germany fell 6–0.

Welsh tallied in regulation, and Cliff Lake netted the overtime winner in a 2–1 semi-final decision over Switzerland.

Lake and Jim Dewey connected as the Quakers came from behind to beat the U.S. 2–1 for the gold medal.

Overall, the Quakers went 43–5–3 and drew more than 350,000 spectators on the tour.

REGINA BOAT CLUB: STAYING AFLOAT

MANITOBA HAS 100,000 LAKES AND HAS NEVER had the decency to offer even one of them as a gift to its neighbours. Talk about greedy . . .

This is why, when the Regina Boat Club was formed in 1907, it made do with picturesque but shallow Wascana Lake, conveniently located on what were then the southeast outskirts of Regina. The lake, created in 1883 by damming Pile o'Bones Creek, was used only for sailing. The activity was so popular that the RBC's 120 members erected a picturesque two-storey boathouse on the north shore in 1910.

Then came a literal whirlwind of change. On June 30, 1912, the Regina Cyclone blew the RBC's boathouse, boats and dock to bits. As a new boathouse was built on the lake's southwest corner, sailing was de-emphasized in favour of general aquatics. The mortgage on the first boathouse was paid off in 1915, just as nearly every male member of the RBC was on his way, or about to go, to war.

Workboats and four-oared shells were acquired after the war, but the RBC was sidetracked in 1920–21 by its senior football team that, even with Piffles Taylor at quarterback, couldn't displace the Regina Rugby Club (Roughriders) from its championship perch.

Still, the Regina Boat Club was getting serious about rowing. It achieved its first noteworthy victory at the 1920 North Western International Rowing Association regatta at Winnipeg in the four-man workboat race and took the eights at the 1923 NWIRA at Port Arthur, Ont. Membership swelled to 400 by the close of the decade even though the club would attend only two more NWIRA events. Then in 1930, as in 1912, the club was brought to a standstill, this time by the provincial government's make-work project on the Albert Street Bridge. In addition to extending the bridge at least 10 times longer than the creek it crossed, the provincial government had Wascana Lake drained and dredged. Water would not fill the lake again until 1933.

RBC captain Harry Duckett wasted no time getting himself and his fellow rowers in shape for a return to NWIRA competition. Duckett was training the men in a new technique called the "Regina Style" that made traditional strokes seem lazy in comparison. It required a hard catch, a fast and heavy pull, and a brief layback. It yielded a minimum of 35 to 36 strokes per minute as opposed to the norm of 32. Fine and dandy, if you're in the boat for a minute, but rowers had to tax their muscles, lungs and hearts for considerably longer than that. Success with the Regina Style demanded quickness, strength, timing and, above all, stamina. It was put to the test at the 1934 NWIRA regatta in Winnipeg.

Regina entered two crews in the workboat four and one in the junior four-man shell. (At the time, a rowing "junior" didn't designate age but that an individual had not yet won at a specific level of competition.) First came the workboat race for the Machin Cup. The RBC foursome of George Holmes, Mal Dott, Elwood Henning and Struan Complin shocked their Winnipeg hosts by maintaining their seemingly frantic style in perfect rhythm from start to finish. Their time of 5 minutes 57 seconds shattered the event record, set by the 1923 RBC team, by 13 seconds but was only slightly ahead of the runner-up—Regina's other crew of Arnold Miller, Ted Lydiard, Cam Weaver and Ted Sharpe! Minneapolis finished a distant third and the Minnesotans, in payment of a pre-race wager, handed Holmes' winning crew the shirts off their backs.

There was little expectation of a Regina victory in the junior four-man shell and no possibility of a record. The NWIRA all-time best of 7:07 had been set with the current; this race would be run against it. Duckett, in the bow seat, called upon his mates to start at a suicidal 48 strokes. In less than 20 seconds, they had broken from the six-shell field to gain open water. Regina adjusted its pace to 35 strokes, upped it to 40 for its finishing kick, and crossed the line in an improbable 7:10, four boat lengths ahead of Fort William, Ont. Duckett collapsed in exhaustion and needed 10 minutes to recover.

Innovation wasn't limited to technique. When Wascana Lake was overrun with weeds in the spring of 1935, the rowers stowed their oars and chopped through the water with poles connected to steel bands whose edges were lined with razor blades. Each stroke sent more greenery floating toward the shore and added to the masochistic joy of training. (Among the few things heavier than water is water mixed with a tangle of weeds.) That year, Regina's four crews at the NWIRA in Minneapolis won three races and finished second in the other. As the Depression continued and club members argued over the expense of inter-city competition, the RBC had to limit its NWIRA contingent to one (winning) team in 1936 and 1937. Practice, when there was water in Wascana Lake in those Dust Bowl years, consisted largely of cutting weeds. When the lake was dry, rowing machines were put to use.

Nevertheless, five RBC men and one shell made their way to St. Catharines, Ont., in 1938 for the most prestigious rowing event in the nation, the Royal Canadian Henley Regatta. Bud Gladwell earned a third-place finish in the junior 140-pound single sculls. Duckett, Newt Hughes, Jack Peart and Dick Priest shared one cheap motel room and, with little money left over to eat, at least had hunger's fringe benefit of easily making weight for the 150-pound junior fours.

Another peculiar advantage for the Regina men was the composition of the 1⅓-mile course on Martindale Pond: 100 percent water, no weeds. Duckett, Hughes, Peart and Priest cut through the course like it was air, leaving their nearest pursuers, the West Side Rowing Club of Buffalo, N.Y., eight lengths in their wake. Four thousand spectators whooped it up for the underdogs who were so lightly regarded that they hadn't even been listed in the Henley program.

As winners of the junior race, the RBC earned automatic entry in the 150-pound senior fours, where it would face the 1936 Henley champions from St. Catharines, the '36 Olympic silver medallists from Buffalo West Side and the Argonaut Rowing Club from Toronto. All three Eastern crews boasted sleek new shells. Regina had "Dad Stemshorn," named after a beloved veteran member of the RBC. Dad Stemshorn (the boat, not the man) was a wide, heavy craft that had run aground two years earlier and required replacement of half its bow by Regina cabinet maker Bob "Gloomy" Newton.

Argonaut rowers looked over the relic from yesteryear before the race and disparaged it as "a prairie tub." They got to inspect the bow from another perspective when they crossed the finish line in second place, two lengths behind the upstarts in the prairie tub. Duckett, Hughes, Peart and Priest were instantly acclaimed as Olympic prospects, but war pushed the next Olympiad back to 1948. Their moment of glory really was a moment.

GAS EICHEL: HE WOULDN'T BE COUNTED OUT

Gaston "Gas" Eichel had to make a comeback just to get started in life. He was born in Condie in 1911 and moved with his family to Regina and later Froude. By the time he was 13 he had been through rheumatic fever and St. Vitus' Dance (facial and upper-body seizures) and was warned that he could never play sports and would probably require constant care for the rest of life. The prognosis proved to be incorrect. At 15, he went north to work in a lumber camp, then tried his hand at commercial ice fishing. With willing spirit but weak flesh, Eichel wore himself out and had to return to the family farm at Froude.

His epiphany came in 1928, shortly before his 17th birthday, in the form of an advertisement for a correspondence course in physical conditioning. Eichel would rise every morning at 4 o'clock to do his exercises, then his farm chores. His body grew to a muscular 195 pounds, but he was still jinxed in his attempts to forge a career. In 1931 he applied for a homestead in the northern Saskatchewan village of Chelan, but with the Depression taking hold and money scarce, he couldn't follow through on it. That same year he tried his hand at boxing for the first time and registered a no-decision.

Gas Eichel

Eichel found a job in 1933 as a caretaker and boxing instructor at a Regina gym, for which he received 25 cents a day and a place to sleep. It was better than nothing, which a great many men in the Great Depression were stuck with, but the arrangement took its toll on Eichel. His weight plummeted to 160 pounds. The one bright side of that awful consequence was that for a while Eichel found himself at the perfect weight for his amateur boxing fortunes. At 195 pounds he was a heavyweight with inadequate power for that division. At 160 pounds he was technically a middleweight but medically malnourished. At or near the light-heavyweight limit of 175 pounds, he was a tall, lean fighter with excellent reach, defence and counterpunching ability. Eichel fought three bouts in 1933 and won them all. He took on better opponents in 1934 and captured both the Saskatchewan and Alberta titles, losing only at the trials for the British Empire Games.

Training for seven bouts and losing all that weight exhausted Eichel. His doctor ordered him to take an indefinite rest, which Eichel interpreted to mean "brief." He cut back to only three fights—two wins and a draw—and added the Canadian light-heavyweight title to his laurels. Best of all, his personal life finally took a turn for the better as he married Janet McDiarmid and rented a farm near his bride's home town of Indian Head, which he would make his own home for the rest of his life. While maintaining his Saskatchewan title through the end of the decade, he attended the 1936 Olympic trials (where he suffered his last defeat) and won a spot on the Canadian team for the 1938 British Empire Games. Unfortunately, the '38 Games were in Sydney, Australia. Eichel would have had to pay his own passage and couldn't afford it.

Aside from that, life was treating Gas Eichel well. He was a line inspector for a power company when war broke out. Eichel enlisted in the air force in June of

1940 and proved himself a valuable military man even when his nemesis, medical maladies, hindered his performance. At first assigned to the movement of troops to Europe and rising to the position of permanent ship's warrant officer on the *Queen Elizabeth*, Eichel volunteered for a transfer to air crew in 1943. His physical examination revealed a heart murmur, and Eichel was transferred all the way back to the home front. At war's end he was Station Warrant Officer at the Royal Canadian Air Force post at Souris, Man.

Eichel continued to box in the military, though not with the frequency of his pre-war prime. Undefeated in 15 bouts in 1938–39, he fought only seven times over the course of the war, culminating in 1945 with victory in the No. 2 Command RCAF Golden Gloves tournament. He was forced to retire from boxing shortly after the war because of a back injury suffered in a traffic accident.

And he lived happily . . . not ever after but long enough and prosperously enough to make up for some of the misfortune heaped upon him in his youth. Eichel continued to farm, ran his own gas development company, and became a respected and admired community leader in Indian Head.

Eichel retired in 1958, his energy not sapped so much by any health concerns as by the death of Janet, whose marriage to him 23 years earlier truly marked a turning point in his life. Gas lived on until 2001.

In his amateur boxing career, Gas Eichel fought 47 times. He won 41 (including all 28 bouts after 1936), lost 3, drew 1, and had 2 no-decisions. Not the strongest man in the ring, he knocked out only 12 of his opponents. Appropriately, he was never knocked out—neither by any punch a boxer delivered nor by anything life threw at him.

NOEL MACDONALD: GRAD QUEEN

Noel MacDonald was born in Mortlach and moved at an early age to Moose Jaw, where she was a fourth-grade playmate of Phyllis Dewar. Then her family moved again, to Edmonton, where Noel grew tall and athletic. Topping out at 5-foot-10½, she was the second-tallest girl in the entire Edmonton school system. She hoped to become a dietitian or mathematics teacher, but the MacDonald family couldn't afford to send her to university on her father's hourly salary of 25 cents as a grain elevator agent. Instead, Noel set out on a business career and played basketball with the Edmonton Gradettes, the feeder club for the world-renowned Edmonton Grads senior women's team.

MacDonald spent 1½ years with the Gradettes and was promoted to the Grads in 1933 as an 18-year-old. She spent her first season as a starting forward and backup centre and the next six as Edmonton's first-string centre, leading scorer and undisputed star even though she did not waver from the Grads' disciplined team approach. MacDonald's career average of 13.8 points per game was the best in Grads history, which spanned the years 1915–40. While 13.8 may not seem special today, it was huge for its era; after the Grads started keeping statistics in 1922, the average score of their games was 48–20. The Grads were talented, hard-working and experienced enough to exploit every advantage, as MacDonald explained:

> *None of the girls smoked nor do I know of any of them drinking while on the team. . . . When a challenging team came to town, one of the first things we made a point of finding out was how many and who smoked. If a number of them did, we always could relax a little because we knew we could run them into the ground by halftime.*

In 1938, when the Grads swept all opposition en route to the Canadian title and staved off four challenges for the Underwood Trophy as North American champs, MacDonald was named Canada's outstanding female athlete and received the Velma Springstead Award.

Two games illustrate the quality of MacDonald's all-around skill. As a Grads rookie she was assigned one night to guard Alberta Williams, a three-time All-American centre an inch taller than MacDonald. Asked to neutralize Williams so that the other Grads could concentrate on scoring, MacDonald held the Tulsa star to a mere four points—and poured in 20 of her own.

Her other great moment came in a best-of-five Underwood Trophy series against Eldorado, Ark., which had won the first game 44–40 and held a 35–31 lead in the last minute of the second contest. Rules of the day called for a jump ball at midcourt following each basket. An Edmonton field goal cut the margin to two. MacDonald, who had played the full game without substitution, cleanly won the subsequent tip, worked a give-and-go with a teammate and nailed a 20-foot shot from in front of the basket to tie the score. Another cleanly won jump ball and flurry of passes set up MacDonald for one of her favourite shots, a running release, but again from long range. Time expired as the ball found net for a 37–35 victory. MacDonald collapsed in utter exhaustion, unable to comprehend why she couldn't stop crying even after an assistant coach had carried her to the dressing room.

Noel MacDonald

The Grads won the next two games and, as they always did from 1923 until disbanding in 1940, retained the Underwood Trophy. (The Grads' record with MacDonald at centre was 51–5 in the Underwood series and 125–7 overall.)

MacDonald married hockey player Harry Robertson and left the Grads in 1939. Robertson became a successful petroleum exploration executive with Imperial Oil, and the family became well travelled. Noel got to teach and coach basketball in Estevan for a short spell. She also spent 11 years working as a secretary at Esso Near East in Libya.

DOROTHY WALTON: RACQUETS BOSS

Dorothy Walton did not become world badminton champion until she was 30, not at all bad for someone who didn't take up the game competitively until she was 24.

She was born Dorothy MacKenzie in 1909, the daughter of a prosperous Swift Current merchant. She earned Bachelor's and Master's degrees in economics at the University of Saskatchewan, where she captained the women's basketball, field hockey and swimming teams, and won top individual honours in diving and track and field. A precocious tennis player as far back as high school, she won 54 singles, doubles and mixed doubles titles at local, provincial and regional tournaments from 1924–31. As a U of S senior in 1930 she swept singles and doubles championships for Western universities, Saskatchewan, and Western Canada.

She discovered badminton in Regina while working as secretary to a provincial cabinet minister but didn't have the opportunity to play it seriously. Marriage to William Walton in 1932 took her to Toronto, where her son John was born a year later. In 1934 she returned to tennis competition and would spend the rest of the decade consistently ranked between fourth and sixth among Canadian women. Walton also took to the badminton court and began an inexorable climb to the sport's summit. She was a Toronto finalist and Canadian semi-finalist in 1934; city and Ontario champion, and national finalist in 1935; and queen of an ever-expanding territory—Toronto, Ontario, Canada, plus winner of the United States open, several major American tournaments, and doubles titles in most of those—in 1936, '37 and '38.

Walton did not defend her Canadian badminton titles in 1939 so that she could compete in the All-England tournament that was recognized as the championship of the world. She accustomed herself to the European style of play by entering, and winning, a preliminary tournament in Surrey. In the All-England, Walton's gradual mastery of her competition was obvious in her 8–11, 11–7, 11–0 semi-final victory over defending champion Daphne Young. A decisive 11–4, 11–5 final win over Diana Doveton made Walton world champion.

The All-England championship wouldn't be contested again until 1947 because of the war, which left Walton as the reigning but virtually untested world champion. She cleaned up Canadian and American competition in 1940, when she was named Canada's outstanding female athlete (and runner-up for the Lou Marsh Trophy as the nation's best athlete of any gender for the second straight year), but the sport went into competitive mothballs after that. Walton's post-1940 badminton resumé is bluntly brief: entry and victory in one invitational tournament in each of 1945 and '46, Ontario champion and Canadian runner-up in 1947.

While the Second World War brought a premature end to Walton's badminton dominance, it did allow her to establish an outstanding career in volunteer work and public service. From the Wartime Prices and Trade Board she moved on to Consumers' Association of Canada, eventually rising to the presidency of that watchdog agency.

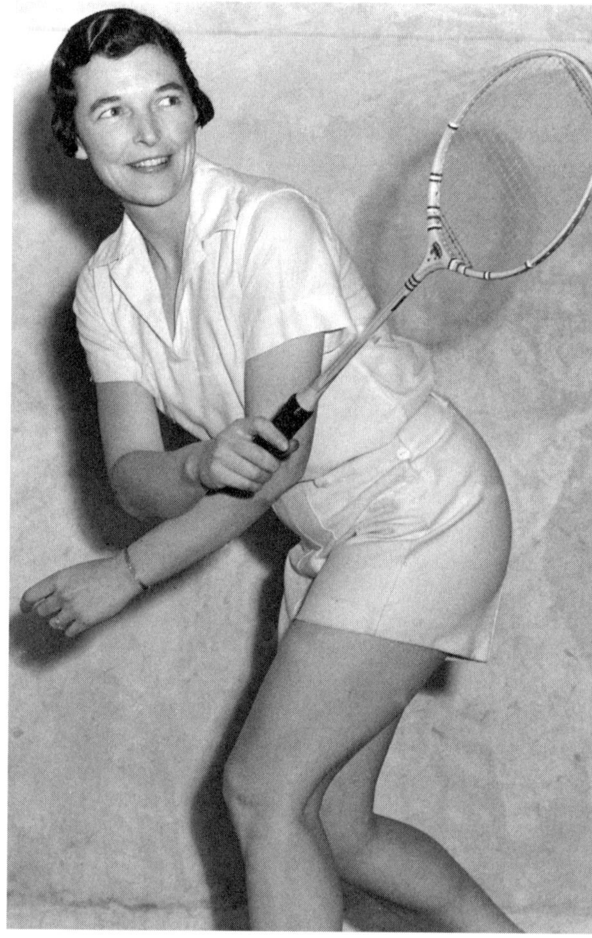

Dorothy Walton

1938 REGINA DALES: THIS TRAIN IS BOUND FOR GLORY

On the corner of 14th Avenue and Broad Street in Regina there once stood Dales Tea House, where one autumn day in 1929 owner Mah Park said in a fatherly way to a neighbourhood teenager: *"Dojack, I'm sick and tired of you kids hanging out in here all the time! I'm tired of calling the police every day! Why don't you go and play in the school playgrounds?"* Although his own father had died that year, Paul Dojack recognized the tone of a well-meaning adult who was being pushed to the limit of his tolerance. Paul's Czech father had moved the family to Regina from Winnipeg to establish a retail music business. Now the economy was falling apart, and 15-year-old Paul and his pals were just a bunch of petty thieves hanging out in local restaurants. Killing time on playgrounds would at least spare his widowed mother the aggravation of visits from the police.

Dojack split his gang into two sides, the Mice and Rats, and began playing football. Eventually, he formed the Dales Athletic Club, sponsored by Mah Park—who preferred the role of benefactor to that of shoplifting victim—and other local businessmen. When the city of Regina organized a juvenile league in 1931, it took on eight teams and 160 players to immediately become the largest rugby football league in Canada. Dojack led the Dales to an undefeated season, declared his team provincial champions and challenged the Young Men's Hebrew Association of Winnipeg to an interprovincial match. The Dales stopped in Portage la Prairie en route to Winnipeg and won an exhibition game 11–7 but suffered five injuries in the process. With no substitutes available the next day in Winnipeg, the Dales fell 19–3 to the YMHA.

Determined to stay together as they passed the age limit for juveniles, the Dales moved up to junior foot-

Paul Dojack in 1931

ball in 1933 and took their lumps from the Regina Pats, Moose Jaw Maroons and Saskatoon Hilltops. One year later, they earned their first official provincial championship. The following year, Dojack was permanently forced to the sidelines with a broken collarbone and a neck injury but remained with the Dales, assuming the role of secretary-treasurer in 1936 and coach in 1937.

Both seasons brought provincial titles to the Dales, and the latter brought the added bonus of another interprovincial match with the Winnipeg YMHA, this time at Regina's Park deYoung before an Armistice Day crowd of 2,000 fans. The Hebrews, as the YMHA team was called, broke out to a 6–0 lead, but a touchdown by Doug Potts and field goal by Toar Springstein gave Regina an 8–6 lead at the half. Lax officiating had opened the way to some rough play, and the second half promised to be a hard-fought battle. And so it was: with seven minutes to play and the Dales ahead 34–6, the game degenerated into fistfights, some of them involving spectators, and the officials called the game.

The Canadian Rugby Union did not stage or sanction any national championship because of the cost involved—remember, there was a depression going on, and on—but Dojack challenged the Eastern champions anyway and scraped together the cash to take the Dales to Ontario, where the Hamilton Italo-Canadians whipped them 27–2.

By 1938, Dojack was 24 going on 50 in terms of street smarts. Somehow he had kept the Dales from going broke after the 1937 trip to Hamilton, and they responded with another Saskatchewan championship and another Armistice Day showdown against the Hebrews, this time in Winnipeg. Springstein's 10-yard field goal stood up for a 3–1 Dales victory in frigid conditions.

"Toar" Springstein (whose real first name was Clarence) was not the Dales' only standout, but he was easily their most visible. Standing 6-foot-4 and weighing about 250 pounds, he was an intimidating blocker on offence, a good placekicker, and a fearsome linebacker. Dojack kept Springstein off the line of scrimmage on defence so he wouldn't be double-teamed, and the big fellow was quick enough to plug most holes punched through the Dales' defensive line.

Dojack, eager to claim a national crown even if the CRU wouldn't sanction it, challenged Montreal Westmount, which had won the Eastern title on November 21. He didn't want to bankrupt the Dales, though, so he insisted on a guarantee of 50 percent of the gate receipts. Westmount balked. Dojack invited the Montrealers west. They declined. No game.

But wait! On the evening of Wednesday, November 30, Westmount offered the Dales the first $920 (which happened to be the Dales' estimated train fare) of the gate receipts, plus 60 percent of everything beyond that, for a game in Montreal. Wonderful! It was a deal. Oh, by the way, there was one catch: the game had to be the coming Saturday, December 3. All Dojack had to do was round up his players overnight, get them on an eastbound train the next morning, make the two-day trip, arrive in

Toar Springstein

Dales' funds. The cheque was checked, and it bounced higher than a place-kick off a crossbar. No tickets, said a CPR functionary.

Now what? The Dales executive met behind closed doors with Dojack, CPR ticket agent Jim Duncan, and a bottle or two of consolation. If only someone higher up could let them have the tickets on credit.

Who was the highest-up person in the CPR? That would be President Sir Edward Beatty.

Where did he live? He was toughing out the Depression in a private suite at the Waldorf-Astoria in New York City.

What time was it in New York? About 1:00 A.M.

Would a phone call help? Couldn't hurt.

President Sir Edward, roused from a sound slumber, authorized a credit note for the tickets and warned Mr. Duncan never to call him at that hour—if ever—again.

Great! Now all Dojack and the executive had to do was collect all the Dales' gear, get it loaded on the train, contact the players who hadn't been reached yet, and send everything and everyone off on the 8:25. By 8 o'clock they were four players short. Food donated for the journey (a box of apples and a carton of oranges) was carried aboard. By 8:25 flying wing Pete Vyvyan and substitute Wayne Pyne were still absent. Sympathetic engineers and conductors avoided looking at the clock. Pyne sprinted to the train at 8:30; he'd been pulling a night shift. Roughriders coach Dean Griffing, who would serve as one of the game officials, boarded the train. Finally, just as Dojack was being told the train would have to pull out,

Montreal on Saturday morning and play that afternoon.

(Funny, but you just don't find Eastern teams being put in this kind of predicament. . . .)

Phone calls were initiated to start rounding up the players. Dojack made a beeline for the train station and negotiated a deposit for 20 round-trip tickets on a train departing Thursday for Montreal at 8:25 A.M. Dojack wrote a cheque for the amount to be drawn from the Dales' account.

Apparently, someone at the Canadian Pacific Railway was familiar with the general state of the

Vyvyan arrived in his army uniform, apologetic but explaining that, without the written leave he had obtained from his commanding officer, he could have been arrested for desertion.

The Dales arrived in Montreal bleary-eyed and squishy-tailed at 10 o'clock Saturday morning, collapsed en masse into their two rooms at the Queen's Hotel for a four-hour nap, and arrived at the Westmount Grounds to find 2,200 spectators surrounding a field of dark ice. Regina's cleats couldn't grip the frozen turf. Duncan borrowed some money from a Montreal CPR agent and hurried to a sporting goods store to buy 18 pairs of running shoes.

At least the Dales had one thing going for them: the windy, frigid conditions were similar to those encountered in Winnipeg against the Hebrews. Patience, they had learned in that game, positively was a virtue. Montreal got the upper hand with a pair of first-quarter rouges and held leads of 2–0, 3–1 and 3–2 at the quarters. Regina's Dan Capraru began the fourth quarter with a mighty punt from the Westmount 30-yard line that went deep into the end zone and produced a rouge to tie the game 3–3. Westmount tried to take advantage of the wind, but Capraru answered every wind-aided punt with a boomer of his own while his teammates held Montreal runbacks to zero or negative yardage.

Flying wing (that's a position, not a pose) Pete Vyvyan

Finally, with two minutes to play, the Dales broke through for a blocked punt and recovered on the Westmount 20. Two plays later, Capraru punted the ball through the end zone for a single. Westmount's desperation forward pass was intercepted, and the Dales triumphed 4–3.

Dojack, who at halftime had made an appeal for money to Regina fans listening to the game on the radio, got the players back to the hotel and treated them to a steak dinner. As the meal wound up, 40 minutes before the team was due back on the train, the hotel manager entered the dining room to inform Dojack that money had indeed arrived from Regina, enough to pay for the rooms, the steak dinner, the debt to Jim Duncan's CPR associate, and all sundry expenses. There was even $8 left over.

Griffing snatched the money from the manager's hand. "I'll see you on the train!" he told Dojack.

In fact, Dojack next saw Griffing on the station platform, a large case of beer under each arm, running at full tilt to reach the train that was starting to pull out with the Dales all aboard. Griffing's hat flew

Coach Paul Dojack (far right) on the bench during a Dales game; Dan Capraru is third from right

off his head, but he entered the passenger car and, with Dojack's help, breathlessly settled into a seat.

"But Dean," Dojack said, "we haven't any money to buy food!"

Griffing produced a bottle opener from his coat.

"Who needs food," he replied, "when you've just won a Canadian championship?"

ALSO IN THIS DECADE

- Walter Martin, son of Saskatchewan premier William Martin (1916–22), was Canada's top-ranked male tennis player from 1933–35. He remains the only Saskatchewan-developed tennis player to have represented Canada in the Davis Cup. Martin played one singles and one doubles match, losing both, in the 1934 zone semi-finals against the United States.

- Wrestler Vern Pettigrew of Regina would have been a medallist at the 1936 Summer Olympics but for a debatable ruling in the fifth round of matches. Judges disqualified him for an illegal hold and awarded a victory to Gösta Jönsson of Sweden, eliminating Pettigrew and placing him fourth in the featherweight (136½-pound) class. Jönsson took the bronze medal. George Chiga, also of Regina, placed eighth in the heavyweight division. Pettigrew retired from competition in 1940, undefeated in Canada, with five national championships to his credit.

- North Battleford Beavers boasted a senior hockey powerhouse in 1936–37. The lineup included three future NHLers: brothers George and Vivian "Squee" Allen of Kerrobert and defenceman Vic Myles of Fairlight. (Myles, who played one NHL season with the New York Rangers, was built like

George Chiga and Vern Pettigrew

Vic Myles

Clark Gillies, only wider.) North Battleford reached the Allan Cup final and extended it to the five-game limit before succumbing to the Sudbury Tigers, after which the Beavers, bankrupt, folded.

■ Ossie Herlen, born in Star City and raised in Saskatoon, won the 1938 Saskatchewan and Canadian amateur welterweight (147-pound) boxing championships at the age of 19. Herlen continued to box after enlisting in the air force and compiled a record of 27 wins (15 by knockout), 5 losses and 1 draw in 33 fights. Herlen was killed in action June 9, 1944.

Ogema product Arleene Johnson tears into a pitch for the Muskegon Lassies during an All-American Girls Professional Baseball League game

1940–1949

War Games

ARRIVALS

April 22, 1940: Sheila Rowan, curler/softball player, Young.
September 30, 1940: Harry Jerome, sprinter, Prince Albert.
November 11, 1940: Henry Dorsch, football player, Weyburn.
December 13, 1940: Ken Mitchell, author/playwright, Moose Jaw.
February 20, 1941: Buffy Sainte-Marie, singer/composer, Piapot Reserve.
August 11, 1941: Dale West, football player, Cabri.
October 25, 1941: Gordon Tootoosis, actor, Poundmaker Reserve.
September 2, 1942: Joe Fafard, sculptor, Ste. Marthe.
July 2, 1943: Alan Ford, football player/executive, Regina.
October 3, 1943: Courtney Milne, photographer, Saskatoon.
July 5, 1944: Grant Devine, premier (1982–91), Regina.
September 6, 1944: Gord Barwell, football player, Saskatoon.
October 25, 1944: Gord Garvie, wrestler, Saskatoon.
October 17, 1945: Dave Cutler, football player, Biggar.
August 30, 1946: Irene Haworth Lacy, gymnast, Nipawin.
April 27, 1947: Keith Magnuson, hockey player, Saskatoon.
May 24, 1948: Lorna Crozier, poet, Swift Current.
August 19, 1948: Susan Jacks, singer, Saskatoon.

DEPARTURES

June 9, 1944: Ossie Herlen, boxer, 25.
September 27, 1944: Wally McLeod, RCAF's top fighter pilot, 28.
March 1, 1945: Claude Warwick, boxer, 22.
March 24, 1945: Walter Murray, educator, 78.

Young men went to war in Europe again, many of them torn from the sporting ranks, their places taken by even younger men who weren't eligible for military service. When the United States finally entered the fray, the dilution of professional baseball compelled a major-league team owner to start a new league composed entirely of *women* ballplayers—and Saskatchewan became a prime provider of womanpower. Mary Baker of Regina and Arleene Johnson of Ogema were among those who became stars of the All-American Girls Professional Baseball League.

Two men with Saskatchewan birthplaces—Ed Bahr of Rouleau and Ralph Buxton of Weyburn—became major-league baseball players. Several others became outstanding boxers, but the best of them, Claude Warwick, was killed before he could achieve true greatness.

In the village of Wilcox, a unique priest named Athol Murray defied convention and poverty to build an educational institution that would use athletics as one of its character-building pillars. Notre Dame was also a stopping point for Bill Hunter, sports entrepreneur extraordinaire.

1940–41 Regina Rangers: Junior-Aged Seniors

It had been 26 years since the Melville Millionaires won the Allan Cup, and no Saskatchewan team had won it since. Amateur hockey was in disarray as men entered military service, but the South Saskatchewan Senior Hockey League produced competitive hockey in 1940–41 with teams in Moose Jaw, Regina, Saskatoon, Yorkton and Flin Flon. The Regina Rangers pulled away from the tightly bunched standings of early January with a 13-game unbeaten streak.

Youth distinguished the Rangers from their opponents. Many teams were pressed for players, but this club, an affiliate of the New York Rangers, relied on junior-aged players to lead the way. Goaltender "Sugar" Jim Henry, a Manitoban, was 20. So was defenceman Garth Boesch of Milestone (via Notre Dame College).

The top scoring line of centre Scotty Cameron of Prince Albert, left-winger Frank Mario of Esterhazy and right-winger Grant Warwick of Regina started the season as 19-year-olds. Whether the kids would stand up to playoff pressure remained to be seen.

Regina swept the SSSHL semi-final against Flin Flon with three one-goal victories: Boesch scored the winner in the 2–1 opener; Mario tallied twice in a 4–3 decision; and Warwick netted a hat trick, including the series-winner with nine minutes to go, in the 5–4 finale. Yorkton forced the league final to the five-game limit, with Cameron's two goals and two assists pacing a narrow 5–4 triumph in Game 5.

Regina travelled to Port Arthur (now part of Thunder Bay) to begin Allan Cup playdowns and split the first two games of the best-of-five series. Back in Regina, the Rangers trailed 3–2 with seven minutes left in the third period when Warwick took the puck behind his own net, bolted up the ice, split the defence and deked Port Arthur netminder Jake Nash to tie the game. Regina scored twice in the 10-minute overtime to win 5–3 and followed with a 3–2 decision to win the series.

Saskatoon was the neutral venue for the opener between the Rangers and Lethbridge Maple Leafs. Mario scored the only goal 35 seconds into the third period when he lofted the puck from centre ice over the lights and into the darkness near the roof, from where the puck descended and fell behind Lethbridge goalie Andy Young. (No, they don't score 'em like that anymore.) Regina took the series in four games.

Henry's playoff goals-against average to this point was a splendid 2.35, but the Sydney Millionaires came west and trounced the Rangers 8–6 and 8–3 to begin the best-of-five national final. Rangers coach Fred Metcalfe urged his team to "go out gloriously" in Saskatoon and at least avert a sweep. The response was inspired defensive hockey and a 1–1 tie that was halted after a 10-minute overtime. Regina survived but could win the Allan Cup only by winning three straight.

Back on home ice, the Rangers got three points apiece from Warwick, Mario and Cameron to win 5–4. Then in Game 5 came a moment unique in hockey history. Cameron scored at 9:15 of the second period to put the Rangers ahead 2–0. On the ensuing faceoff, Warwick headed straight for the Sydney defence, inter-

Regina Rangers' high-scoring line of Grant Warwick, Scotty Cameron and Frank Mario

cepted the puck in full flight and snapped a quick shot for an unassisted goal at 9:17—*two seconds* after Cameron's. Regina held on for a 3–2 decision and completed the comeback by stopping the Millionaires 3–0 on Henry's third shutout of the playoffs. It was odd that the Regina Rangers won the best-of-five final in six games. It is odder still that they remain Saskatchewan's last Allan Cup champions.

NOTRE DAME, WHERE A PÈRE BUILT A FULL HOUSE

NOT ONLY IS TRUTH STRANGER THAN FICTION, it can be a lot more colourful. Witness Athol Murray, whose life and character would be taken as a fictitious creation if it weren't for the legacy he left behind. He was a priest who sampled the vices of tobacco and alcohol as frequently as he practised charity. His adherence to the second commandment, the one about not taking the Lord thy God's name in vain, was pretty goddam lax. Away from the altar, he looked more like a cab driver or a tradesman in the flannel shirts, scarves or buffalo coat he was prone to wear over his clerical collar. He meddled in politics, miffed that for decade after decade the province was in the power of the Co-Operative Commonwealth Federation (later renamed the New Democratic Party), whose socialist policies in his opinion were tantamount to goddam communism, even if that Tommy Douglas fella had his heart in the right place.

Don Metz, 1934 Hounds hockey team

Père Murray (virtually everyone called him Père) radiated character and was a character. Yet he was real. Go to Wilcox and there stands the college that he built from a ramshackle little high school into a bustling, prestigious institution.

Murray was born in 1892 in Toronto and in 1918 was ordained a secular priest, unattached to any religious order. As biographer Jack Gorman succinctly put it, "His unharnessed individualism would have prevented his taking the oath of obedience." Murray was assigned to the Regina archdiocese in 1923 under the guidance of Archbishop Olivier Mathieu, a kindred spirit who believed strongly in classical education and liberal thinking. Upon his arrival Murray found the city embroiled in an incident involving a group of Protestant boys who had broken into Holy Rosary Cathedral and made off with a booty of candy, cigarettes and soda that had been earmarked for church bazaars. The boys' families were willing to contribute $1,000 to the church to head off burglary charges; Catholic parishioners pressured the Redemptorist priests who ran Holy Rosary to prosecute the boys in retaliation for years of anti-Catholic propaganda. Murray intervened. No charges were filed and the money was declined. Murray then asked the reprieved youngsters to join him in forming an athletic club along the lines of the Argonaut Rowing Club back in his native Toronto, one that would engage in football, hockey, baseball and lacrosse, that would be open to Protestants, Catholics or anyone else because religion wouldn't figure in the club at all. Throughout the 1920s and early '30s the Argos were all over the Regina athletic scene, open to anyone who abided by the motto that was taken from the original Argonaut club: "Pull together."

Murray's inspirational and organizational skills were so fruitful that he was made director of all boys' activities in the archdiocese in 1925. Shortly afterward, he heard rumours that he was about to be reassigned to Toronto. Murray begged Archbishop Mathieu to appoint him to the small town of Wilcox, 30 miles away, where the pastor was dying of tuberculosis. When the time came for Murray to assume his new role, he arrived in a run-down touring car filled with 15 of his Argos, one of whom was Catholic, who had come along to help Père and to play baseball with him. Many of them enrolled at Notre Dame, a parochial school operated by the Sisters of St. Louis out of a two-storey house.

Sports, especially hockey, became as much a part of life around Notre Dame as it had around Holy Rosary Cathedral. Profane as his speech sometimes was, Murray could not bring himself to bellow anything stronger at hockey practice than, "Skate, you hounds!" The school's teams became known as the Hounds and, like the Argos had done in Regina, eagerly sought the best competition they could find. Brothers Nick and Don Metz, a couple of Wilcox boys, would go on from Notre Dame to long careers with the Toronto Maple Leafs. Garth Boesch of Milestone went from the Hounds to the Regina Rangers before serving in the Royal Canadian Air Force in the Second World War; he was a defenceman on the Maple Leafs when they became the first team to win three straight Stanley Cups in 1947, '48 and '49. Boys who attended Notre Dame could be sure of three things: good hockey, a good education and uncertainty about everything else. Those who could pay the $18 monthly room and board did; those who couldn't were told not to worry about it. Creditors were kept at bay while Murray tirelessly wrote letters, telephoned, and made personal calls in search of benefactors.

Regardless of Notre Dame's bank balance, Murray's love of sports and his faith in athletics as a character-building endeavour inspired him to attract promising young athletes to Wilcox. Frank Germann, in 1936 a 13-year-old boy in Rouleau, was taken aback one day while giving his confession to the well-known priest.

"Bless me, Father, for I have sinned . . ."

"Hold it, Frank! Have you ever thought of coming to Notre Dame?"

"We can't afford it."

"At Notre Dame we don't let money worry us. Pay what you can. God will take care of the rest."

Germann became a student, outstanding hockey and baseball player, teacher, coach, high school principal, and professor of English literature—all at Notre Dame. He is currently, in his eighth decade of involvement with the school, director of the alumni's national chapter.

Murray chose as Notre Dame's motto *"Luctor et emergo* (I struggle and I emerge)." The decade of the 1940s was a struggle for survival. It was miraculous enough to struggle through the Great Depression, only to emerge into a wartime economy that couldn't make allowances for privately run schools, rich or poor. Notre Dame was poor—not that there was any shame in poverty, but this wasn't anything like St. Michael's in Toronto or Loyola in Montreal.

"I grew up in Hazlet and loved sports," says Jack McLeod, a future NHLer and Olympic hockey coach. "My dad and I were both keen on me getting an education, but we didn't have much cash lying around. We drove to Wilcox to meet Father Murray, and Père said, 'Forget about the money, just send the kid here.' This would be about 1945.

"We lived in boxcars. That's what our accommodation was for two years while I was there. Notre Dame didn't have its own rink at the time but Wilcox did, an older arena with a very low ceiling. In fact, you could reach up and knock out a light with your stick if you weren't careful.

"Frank Germann was my coach in junior, my second year, and he was a great guy. Frank was teaching, and he played all the sports: intermediate hockey, baseball, football, lacrosse. He was a wonderful athlete and coach. He certainly put me in the right mode."

Ex-Hound Garth Boesch, Leafs defenceman

Germann and McLeod teamed up in 1946–47 at two levels. First they were coach and 16-year-old player on the team that finished third in the strong Saskatchewan Junior Hockey League dominated that season by Metro Prystai and the Moose Jaw Canucks. Then they became teammates when, at Murray's urging, the 24-year-old Germann and several over-20 students pursuing their university Arts degrees joined the juniors to enter the SAHA intermediate championships. First the Hounds had to visit the Swift Current Indians for a best-of-three series. When Notre Dame prevailed 2–1, the Indians were so impressed that they invited the Hounds to make Swift Current their home rink for the balance of the playoffs. The invitation was accepted, and the relocated Hounds, with Germann supervising their studies by day, proceeded to eliminate the Gravelbourg Black Cats, Flin Flon Bombers and Prince Albert Regents for the Saskatchewan title. Notre Dame then bounced the Winnipeg Alouettes before losing

Frank Germann (far left) rallies the Hounds Intermediate squad as Jack McLeod (beside Germann) and Père Murray (wearing scarf) listen along with the rest of the players

the Western final to Coleman, Alta. Perhaps the Hounds were worn out by then, having played 23 games in 33 days.

The decades to come would bring financial stability and international prestige to Notre Dame. Still, its charm rested in Père and the efforts he would inspire from his boys. His archetypal pep talk was delivered in two parts in 1950 when the junior Hounds were scheduled to visit the Regina Pats but on the verge of forfeiting, or at best dressing a minimum of players, because of a measles outbreak at Notre Dame. Père tore through the dormitory shacks and roused the sick players from their beds, reminding them of the humiliation they would suffer if they failed to appear for a game against their arch-rivals.

"Goddammit, gang, this is Notre Dame! We can't lie down just because we have the measles. We've got to get up and fight the Pats!"

That night in Regina, the Hounds, prodded and inspired by their spiritual leader, charged on to the Exhibition Stadium ice and played a game such as no Pats team had ever seen from a Notre Dame squad.

The score was 9–0. For the Pats. After the second period.

Père burst in to the dressing room and, finding his players' tails between their legs and their heads between their knees, demanded that they show some spirit, skate harder, forecheck, backcheck . . .

"And goddammit it, boys, if you can't beat 'em, at least give 'em the measles!"

THE SCRAPPIEST WARWICK OF THEM ALL

There were the three hockey-playing brothers: Grant, Billy and Dick Warwick, all of them tough and rambunctious. There was their sister Millie Warwick McAuley, herself a hustling third baseman with the Rockford Peaches of the All-American Girls Professional Baseball League. Then there was Claude, who might have been the best athlete of the family, who might have been the best boxer Canada has ever produced, who instead is the forgotten Warwick because the good die young.

Grant and Billy, considered small for the NHL at almost 5-foot-8 and 150 pounds apiece, made Claude look tiny at 5-foot-4 and his early fighting weight of 126 pounds. Hard training and diligent coaching by Ken Goff at the Regina Boxing Club produced incalculable punching power, though. In 1941 Claude earned the Canadian amateur featherweight title by winning four bouts at the national championships in Vancouver, the last a clean knockout of British Columbia infantryman Jim Lowe that put the soldier in the hospital with a concussion. Warwick stayed in Vancouver an extra day for reassurance that Lowe would recover, which he did. The champion was named the tournament's most popular boxer and most accomplished boxer. A mere 18 years old, he had won 29 consecutive fights.

Warwick enlisted in the Royal Canadian Navy and, while training in Regina, played on the football team that almost upset the Winnipeg Blue Bombers in the Western final on November 9, 1942. The Blue Bombers, expecting nothing more than an easy tune-up for the Grey Cup game, held a comfortable 10–0 lead midway through the fourth quarter on their slippery home field when Warwick, the smallest man on the field, took a lateral on a punt return and flew 50 yards down the sideline for a touchdown. His five-point score and the ensuing convert made it 10–6. A minute later, Regina halfback Bill Orban heaved a long pass downfield. Just as Warwick was about to gather it in and head for another major, Ches McCance of the Blue Bombers tipped the ball away with a desperate leap. Reprieved, Winnipeg tightened its defence and held on for a 13–6 victory.

Claude was the most clean-cut of the Warwick boys. In high school he worked as a page at the Saskatchewan Legislature. His friendliness and good humour outside the ring won him many friends and the romantic attention of Jessie Balfour of Lumsden, a young widow who had lost her husband to tuberculosis.

"Jessie and Claude were so much in love," recalls Billy

Claude Warwick

Claude Warwick stands over the fallen Jim Lowe in their featherweight title fight of 1941

Warwick, "just perfect for each other, and our mother thought the world of her. Once in 1944, Claude was home in Regina on leave, and he and Jess were walking down 11th Avenue, past Royal Billiards and the Capitol Theatre. Jess was a tall woman, half a head taller than Claude, and these three young Mounted Police recruits saw them walking arm in arm. 'What are you going to do with that little shaver?' one of them said to her. Well, Claude tore right into them, knocked out one guy with his right hand, and the other two took off like bats out of hell.

"Eighteen years later, 1962, my brothers Grant and Dick and I were operating Warwick's, a restaurant and nightclub in Edmonton. This gentleman came up to me and said he was one of the three Mounties that Claude tore into on 11th Avenue, and he wanted me to know that when they discovered it was Claude Warwick who'd knocked one of them out, they were the proudest guys in the barracks."

Claude would taste no more football glory, but his ring exploits continued in the armed services. Victory followed victory as he squared off against sailors, soldiers and airmen on boxing cards at military bases and in city auditoriums. Warwick turned professional in 1943, although as a serviceman he was still restricted to bouts arranged through official Navy channels. He moved up to the lightweight division, where the limit was 135 pounds. Warwick not only remained undefeated but, despite fighting in low weight divisions where contests are usually sent to judges for decisions, made a habit of knocking out opponents. He dispatched Baby Face Bouchard, a Navy fighter with a long professional record in Montreal and New York, in less than two minutes. Warwick's power, especially from his left hand, was devastating. He emulated the punching style of his hero, world heavyweight champion Joe Louis, using timing and leverage to turn a short hook into a pulverizing blow.

"Over and over again, I sat close to his corner and would bellow him on," Athol Murray once wrote. "I loved him, and I loved his all-out effort. Cool, clear-seeing, he always distanced his man perfectly to the jaw. When he struck his full-strength blow, all his strength and his reserve of strength went into one smashing muscular explosion. Claude Warwick was a winner."

In fact, he won 50 of 51 bouts, the only blemish on his record being a draw from early in his amateur days. As the Second World War turned decisively in the Allies' favour in 1945, Warwick's prospects for a successful and lucrative professional career were excellent. Mike Jacobs, a prominent New York matchmaker who promoted many of Louis's fights, was eager for the war to end so that Louis and Warwick could be discharged.

Late on the Saturday afternoon of February 17, 1945, Able Seaman Claude Warwick, stationed near Sydney, N.S., hurried to catch a bus that would take him into town to meet Jessie. The coming weeks would be exciting. On the 26th Claude would fight Mickey Paul of Boston, ranked in the Top Ten of pro lightweights, in Sydney. Then, on March 5 in the same city, Jessie and Claude were to be married.

Claude barely caught the bus in time. More sailors and one airman boarded at other stops. A 65-year-old woman was the last person to get on the bus, intending to ride only a quarter of a mile to do some shopping. The driver guided his vehicle across the railroad tracks at the Sydney River crossing, either oblivious to the train that was approaching or certain he could get clear of it. Instead, the train struck the rear of the bus, knocked it into the air and dragged it 100 feet (30 metres) along the rails. The woman was killed. Claude was unconscious and taken to hospital, where he was immediately declared in critical condition with a fractured skull. Twelve other servicemen were injured but would survive their wounds. The driver suffered lacerations on his forehead.

Able Seaman Claude Warwick

Claude Warwick never regained consciousness. He was flown to Montreal in the hope that a brain surgeon at the Montreal Neurological Institute might save him, but the damage was too great. He died March 1 with his mother, his fiancée and his brother Grant at his bedside.

"He was the uncrowned lightweight champion of the world," said Jack Fox, Claude's professional manager.

Had he lived, Claude Warwick might very well have joined the pantheon of great post-war boxers, inevitably moving up in weight to take on the likes of Rocky Graziano, Tony Zale, Jake LaMotta and Sugar Ray Robinson.

No one will ever know if he would have beaten any of them.

No one will ever know if any of them would have beaten him.

THE (NOT-QUITE) ALL-AMERICAN GIRLS BASEBALL LEAGUE

Canada was well into its fourth year of participation in the Second World War by the spring of 1943, but the United States was merely in its second year of a wartime footing. Many of major league baseball's stars and regulars had enlisted or been drafted, leaving team owners with players deemed too young, too old, or unfit for military duty. The minor leagues were decimated. One owner, Phil Wrigley of the Chicago Cubs, sought to fill some of the sporting vacuum with a baseball league composed entirely of women players. The All-American Girls Professional Baseball League played exclusively in the American Midwest, making diehard fans of women, children, farmers, factory workers, and others who were confined to the home front. More than just a successful wartime diversion, the AAGPBL continued to flourish until 1954.

Millie McAuley

Most of the players were recruited from elite softball ranks throughout the United States and Canada. In this regard, the league was not "All-American." More than 600 women played in the AAGPBL in its 12 seasons, and although some sketchy record-keeping has brought about a number of different estimates, the most reliable reports put the Canadian contingent at 63 players. Saskatchewan was easily the biggest supplier of Canadian players with 25: Janet Anderson Perkin of Bethune; Thelma Grambo Hundeby of Domremy; Hazel Measner of Holdfast; Terry Donahue of Melaval; June Emerson, Ann Surkowski and Lee Surkowski Delmonico, all of Moose Jaw; Elsie Wingrove Earl of North Portal; Arleene Johnson Noga of Ogema; Velma Abbott, Mary Baker, Catherine Bennett, Elizabeth Berthiaume, Julie Dusanko, Gene George, Margaret Jones Davis, Christine Jewett, Daisy Junor, Ruby Knezovich, Ethel McCreary, Betty Petryna, Millie Warwick McAuley, and Agnes Zurowski Holmes, all of Regina; and, Muriel Coben and Lucella MacLean Ross of Saskatoon.

The AAGPBL established stringent aesthetic and lifestyle standards. Players had to be not only superior athletes but exhibit ladylike behaviour, comportment and appearance—even if it was impractical. Back home, uniforms had been a utilitarian item; however shapely one's legs might be, they had all the elegance of balloon animals when covered by long woollen stockings similar to those worn by hockey players. Bulky and hot, yes, but they protected thighs from the dreaded "strawberries"—huge patches of skin scraped off by sliding on hard infields. In the AAGPBL, which would also become known as the "Glamour League," uniforms featured one-piece mini-dresses that left about two-thirds of the thighs exposed. It was visually appealing, especially for men who hadn't seen skirts that short since the '20s and wouldn't again until the '60s—although the abrasions, bruises and bandages some players sported on their legs didn't invite comparisons to Betty Grable or Rita Hayworth.

All players had to take lessons in grooming, etiquette and posture. Makeup and hairstyles had to be applied or touched up before any public appearance on or off the field. Smoking, drinking and social carousing were forbidden. In short, what had been an informal activity back home became a regimented job. Considered in the context of the times, however, the restrictions were reasonable and the standards not only good business but welcome training for many of the individuals. Furthermore, the Glamour League paid its players well: $75 to $125 a week for most, on a par with male baseball players in the high minor leagues and better than a typical young American or Canadian male labourer.

Teams enjoyed fabulous fan and community support in their towns, lived in comfortable homes and played before thousands of spectators nearly every day over a five-month schedule. Road trips tended to be brief by baseball standards, with teams generally playing one week at home and the next on the road.

Mary Baker was one of the AAGPBL's genuine star attractions, a nine-year veteran catcher with exceptional baseball instinct, fiery competitiveness and sex

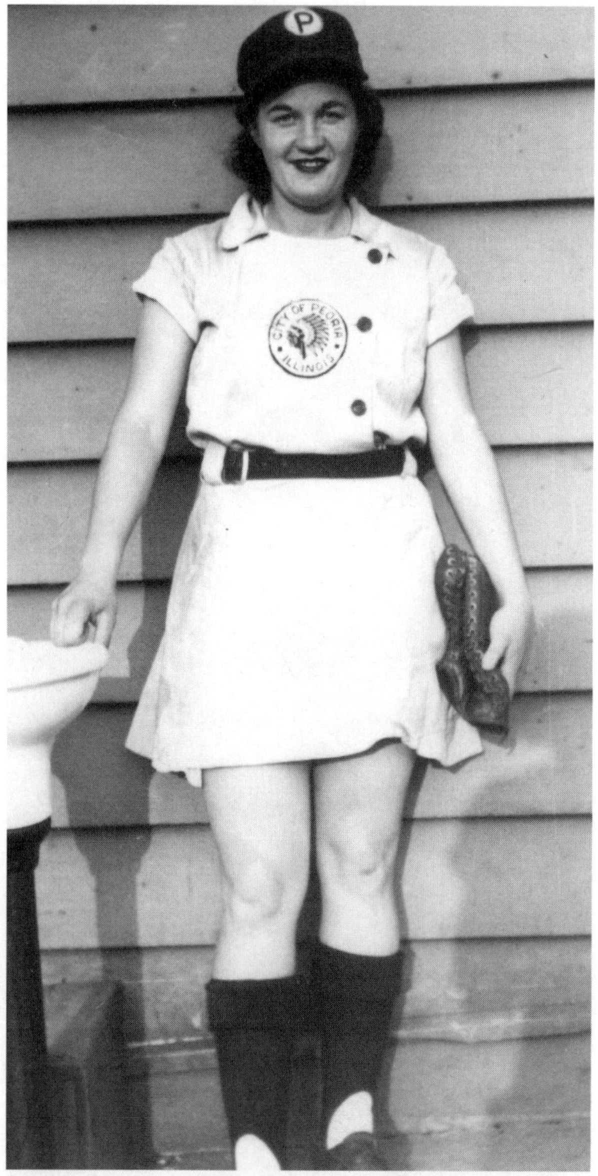

BEFORE: Terry Donahue in the bulky but practical uniform of the 1942 Moose Jaw Royals (left). AFTER: Donahue with hair and make-up done, ready to display—and sacrifice—her thighs for the Peoria Redwings.

appeal. At 5-foot-5 and 133 pounds, with smouldering dark eyes and a coy smile, she was every inch the glamorous lady the AAGPBL sought to convey as the perfect blend of athleticism and femininity. Well, not quite *every* inch—her fingers, battered and broken from decades of foul tips, were a gnarled assortment of bumps and angles that she generally tried to conceal from photographers. Her nickname "Bonnie"—bestowed by a public-address announcer of Scottish descent at a Chicago softball tournament in 1939—was so appropriate that throughout her career she was as likely to be called Bonnie Baker as Mary Baker.

Born Mary Geraldine George in Regina, she advanced only as far as Grade 8 before leaving Wetmore School. She became a star catcher for the Army & Navy Bombers softball team, who won provincial championships in 1940 and '41 while attracting up to 2,500 spectators for big games at Regina's downtown Central Park. When she found out the salary level of the newly formed AAGPBL, she was ready to leave town on the next train.

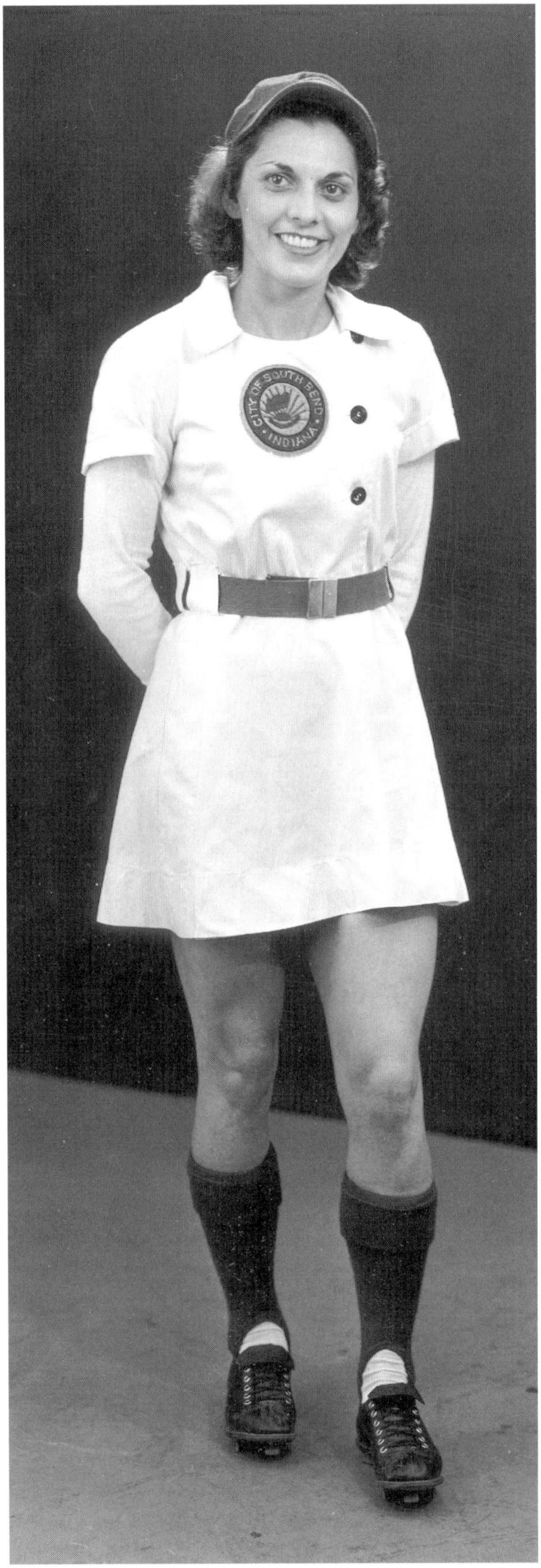

Mary Baker

"My first contract was for $150 a week, and it was like $3 million to me," she said in a 1987 interview. "I left here making $17 a week at the Army & Navy department store.

"They held me up as what they were trying to portray, an all-American girl."

Sisters Ruby and Daisy Knezovich grew up in the same Regina east-end neighbourhood as Baker and her sister, Gene (later Gene McFaul). Daisy, under her married name of Junor, was also Baker's teammate on the South Bend (Ind.) Blue Sox from 1946–49 and remembers plenty of gritty substance behind Baker's image.

"She had no fear at all," Junor says. "She would literally climb the backstop to catch a foul ball. And she had pizzazz. When she strutted from the plate to the pitcher's mound, she'd walk with a wiggle. Everybody would whoop and holler and give her the gears. But she was a crowd pleaser. She loved it."

Away from the public eye, Baker was a daunting poker player and a prodigious consumer of cigarettes and Coca-Cola. Her friends knew that when Baker suggested they "take off" that she was about to raise the stakes and clean out a rival poker player. Withstanding the rigors of a marathon card game on top of her baseball schedule was routine, in part because she was reportedly fuelled by up to 24 bottles of Coke a day. Stories of her Coke consumption—like her habit of leaving a bottle open at her bedside and drinking the lukewarm contents when she awoke—sound incredible but are verified by teammates.

Baker's career batting average of .235 was more than respectable in a league so defensively dominant that in two seasons not a single regular managed to hit .300. She stole 506 bases—94 in one season—and drew 404 walks while striking out only 210 times. Baker also had the distinction of serving as the AAGPBL's only female full-time manager in 1950, when she was traded to the Muskegon Lassies just before the team was moved across Michigan to Kalamazoo. Baker led the team out of the basement and into fourth place (of eight teams) in the final standings, but after the campaign the league barred female managers because the majority of owners considered the notion to be undignified.

Arleene Johnson was born and raised in Ogema with an appetite for softball, curling and bowling.

As a 20-year-old in 1944, she went to Regina to try out for the Meadows Diamonds softball team. Not only did she make the team as its third baseman, but after only her third game she was recruited by AAGBPL scout Hub Bishop for the Glamour League's 1945 baseball campaign. Johnson took care of immediate business by posting the Diamonds' best batting average en route to the Senior A Girls Inter-city Softball League championship. A year later she was in the AAGPBL, where she would stay four seasons. Johnson became known as the "Iron Lady" for her durability, especially when she played in all 112 games of both the 1946 and '47 seasons for the Muskegon Lassies. Her defensive play at the hot corner was both reliable and sensational. On one occasion a ground ball took a bad hop and Johnson leaped to spear the ball with her bare hand and throw the batter out; pitcher Diane Sams went on to throw a perfect game before 7,000 spectators. Johnson returned to Regina after the 1948 season to marry and raise a family. Returning to the softball diamond, she played on nine more provincial and five Western champions.

Daisy Knezovich was another multi-talented athlete, excelling in track and basketball long before she turned to the diamond. She passed on the AAGPBL's early years so that she could marry and, as Daisy Junor, won a provincial softball title in 1945 with the Regina Aces. She spent the next three years in the Glamour League as an outfielder, mostly with the South Bend (Ind.) Blue Sox, and started a fourth season before choosing to settle down back in Regina. Junor found new sports to conquer, making the provincial team for the Western 5-pin Bowling Championships three times and winning one Saskatchewan senior women's title in golf.

Janet Perkin played only the 1946 season in the AAGPBL, partly because she didn't like the daily grind of games and travel, partly because she didn't want to ruin her pitching arm. The league changed something essential about its game virtually every year, from pitching motions (underhand to sidearm to overhand) to basepath lengths to the size of the ball. Perkin got out with a healthy right arm, which she would use to skip Saskatchewan women's curling championship rinks in 1953, '59 and '64.

As progressive as the AAGPBL was in providing opportunity and recognition for its athletes, their fame was largely regional. Few people back in Saskatchewan were aware of their exploits in the Glamour League. Once gone from the Glamour League, fans in Green Bay and Muskegon and Rockford heard nothing more of their former heroines.

Daisy Junor

Baker, Johnson (now Noga), Junor and other surviving AAGPBL veterans in Saskatchewan drew a smattering of attention in 1988 when the National Baseball Hall of Fame in Cooperstown, N.Y., recognized the league and its players with a permanent exhibit. When the movie *A League of Their Own* was released in 1992 with an all-star cast including Tom Hanks, Geena Davis and Madonna, every AAGPBL star became a celebrity all over again. Baker, in retirement after 25 years of managing the Wheat City Curling Club, enjoyed the sudden attention after raising her daughter Maureen, nicknamed "Chick," in an atmosphere of friends, family and peaceful obscurity.

"Growing up with Chick, we used to play with Mary's memorabilia not knowing the significance of what we were playing with," said Bonnie Pugsley, Baker's niece. "She let us play with her glove, her baseballs; we used to peek in her trunk and we would find her uniform.

"So I knew she was a phenomenal baseball player, but she never told us anything about it. She was very humble about her celebrity until the movie came out. Then finally she came out of her shell and started to share her story."

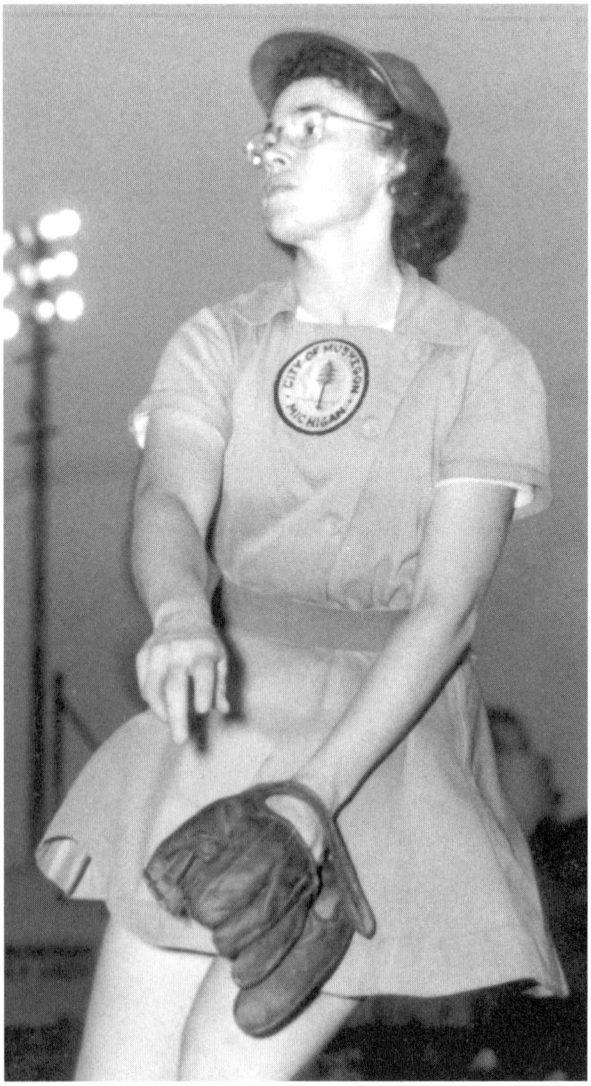

Arleene Johnson Noga

Baker drew special notice for the parallels between herself and Davis's lead character, Dottie Hinson. In fact, no one in the movie is supposed to be a direct portrayal of any individual associated with the league. The characters and their situations are, with occasional flights of fancy, composites of actual players and events. However, Bonnie Baker's influence on the creation of Dottie Hinson is obvious enough: Dottie is a catcher, a player of all-around skill, beautiful, sassy, and is playing while her husband is in military service. On the other hand, Bonnie Baker was not a six-foot-tall American farm girl who bolted from her team when her husband returned from war, nor did she (or anyone else) catch a foul ball while doing the splits.

There is some of Mary Baker in Dottie Hinson. More important, there is a lot of every AAGPBL player in *A League of Their Own*. Thanks to them, there was a movie. Thanks to the movie, Noga, Junor and many like them still receive and accommodate autograph requests every month from fans all over North America.

(Postscript: On July 10, 2004, in conjunction with Ogema's summer fair, the venerable grandstand at the main ball diamond was renamed the Arleene Johnson Noga Heritage Grandstand. Noga was honoured at a ceremony before the first game of a fastball tournament and completed the festivities by throwing out the first ball from the pitcher's rubber. She hummed a strike, waist-high, across the black of the plate.)

BASEBALL'S BIGS BECKON BAHR, BUXTON

Among the men whose military duty interrupted, delayed or wiped out a promising professional baseball career was Ed Bahr of Rouleau. Tall and lanky (6-foot-1½, 172 pounds), Bahr was only 18 when he was signed by the New York Yankees. Control problems, which would bedevil the righthander all through his playing days, manifested themselves in his second season when he went 14–9 for Big Springs of the Texas–New Mexico League but walked 154 batters in 191 innings. Still, he moved up the minor-league ladder until he enlisted in the Canadian military and missed three baseball seasons (1942–44). Upon his return he was placed on the Yankees' top farm team in Kansas City, posted a 12–9 record, and enticed the Pittsburgh Pirates to acquire him and place him on their major-league roster in 1946.

Bahr's rookie season in the National League (8–6, 2.63 ERA in 137 innings) was excellent when considered within the framework of the '46 Pirates team that went 63–91. Pittsburgh manager Frank Frisch used Bahr in mop-up relief early in the season, and didn't give him a start until May 24 against the Philadelphia Phillies, when Bahr scattered eight hits and two walks for a 10–2 victory. Another highlight was a 10–5 decision over the New York Giants on June 7 in which Bahr's bat accounted for a triple, a single, and two runs batted in. Despite Bahr's competence,

Frisch dropped him from the rotation when several rainouts disrupted Pittsburgh's schedule. Bahr finished the season shuttling between relief and starting assignments.

He was used in similar fashion in 1947 but for only 83 innings on the last-place Pirates. His wildness returned, and with it came a permanent demotion to the minors. There was some consolation, however, in departing the lowly Pirates to win American Association pennants with Indianapolis in 1948 and St. Paul in 1949.

Another Saskatchewan-born pitcher, righthander Ralph Buxton, enjoyed his second stint in the majors in 1949—11 years after his first! Buxton was born in Weyburn but as a boy moved with his family to Long Beach, Calif. Relying primarily on a screwball, he had a five-game fling with the American League's Philadelphia Athletics in 1938 before settling down with the Oakland Oaks of the Pacific Coast League in 1940. The PCL was a unique minor league, featuring seasons more than 200 games long. Salaries and the quality of life were both so good that the lure of the majors was somewhat dimmed. Buxton was a mainstay of the Oaks' staff for nine seasons and might never have returned to The Show but for the circumstances of 1948. First, his work out of the bullpen was vital to Oakland winning its first PCL pennant in 21 years. Second, when Oaks manager Casey Stengel was hired by the New York Yankees a year later, he remembered that work. Buxton was used in 14 games as Stengel led the Yankees to the first of five straight pennants.

MOOSE JAW CANUCKS: MAD ABOUT METRO

Moose Jaw made its first appearance in a Memorial Cup final in 1945, snapping a nine-year skid since a Saskatchewan team (the '36 Saskatoon Wesleys) had been the Western representative. Coach Roy Bentley had a talented and solid group in the Canucks, starting with his 17-year-old son Bev in goal, Bert Olmstead on defence and Metro Prystai at centre. Moose Jaw was a sizzling 14–2 in the regular season and a positively explosive 15–1 in the playoffs. The St. Michael's College Majors, featuring future Toronto Maple Leafs stalwarts Jimmy Thomson and Gus Mortson on defence, and Tod Sloan up front, provided the Memorial Cup opposition.

Toronto was also contesting, and winning, the Stanley Cup in 1945 while the Canucks were meeting St. Mike's, and the NHL final between the Maple Leafs and Detroit Red Wings provided a surprise for the Canucks. Moose Jaw had acquired the junior rights to right-winger Gerry Couture, a former star with the Saskatoon Quakers and, in 1945, a medical student at the University of Saskatchewan. Couture played four playoff games for the Canucks, contributing four goals and three assists, then returned to Saskatoon to write his exams. Much to the Canucks' surprise, he showed up in Toronto—with the Red Wings! Although there was considerable talk of him rejoining the Canucks for the Memorial Cup showdown, he never did.

Bert Olmstead, 1945

That Couture could have swung the series in the Canucks' favour is unlikely. Moose Jaw won only the second game (5–3 on two third-period goals by Mark Marquess); St. Mike's prevailed 7–4, 6–3, 4–3 and 7–2 in the others.

Gerry 'Doc' Couture

Moose Jaw had begun a junior dynasty that would rule Saskatchewan for five seasons. The best team of the lot may have been the 1945–46 edition that featured Emile "the Cat" Francis between the pipes. Moose Jaw steamrolled through the province, averaging nine goals a game while winning all 18 regular-season and seven playoff games, but came out flat in the interprovincial playdowns and lost its best-of-seven series to the Edmonton Canadians in five games.

Olmstead and Francis turned pro in the 1946–47 season, but Prystai was still on hand to turn in a truly exceptional performance: the Saskatchewan Junior Hockey League scoring championship with 71 points (including 32 goals) in only 22 games, a league-high 14 points in six playoff games, and a nation-leading 26 points in 15 Memorial Cup elimination and final games. Altogether, in 43 contests, Prystai tallied 46 goals and 65 assists for 111 points. His performance, combined with his modesty and Ukrainian ancestry, made Prystai immensely popular in Moose Jaw, where on at least one occasion the Metropolitan department store only turned on part of its main sign so that it would read METRO.

Prystai and the Canucks enjoyed perhaps the finest moment in the team's history in the Abbott Cup final against the Brandon Elks, who won Game 5 on their home ice to take a 3–1 series lead with one game tied. The Canucks returned home to a rousing reception at the train station, won Games 6 and 7 in Moose Jaw, and prevailed 6–4 in the tiebreaking Game 8 at Regina.

Metro Prystai accepts the Abbott Cup for 1947 from SAHA president Cliff Henderson; Moose Jaw radio announcer Art Henderson is second from left and Ted Ruddin of the Canucks executive is at far right

Home ice, at least in a regional sense, was on the Canucks' side in the Memorial Cup final with games scheduled for Winnipeg, Moose Jaw and Regina. St. Michael's College again represented the East, setting up a rematch of the 1945 final. Prystai and goaltender Bev Bentley were the only holdovers from that Canucks team, while St. Mike's boasted a new but far more imposing lineup led by Red Kelly, Fleming Mackell and Ed Sandford. Moose Jaw was hopelessly outclassed 12–3 at Winnipeg, 6–1 at Moose Jaw and 8–1 at Regina in a game that was terminated with nearly seven minutes to play in the third period when spectators littered the ice with bottles and other projectiles.

"It started with a delayed penalty the ref was going to call on me," Prystai recalled 56 years later. "The play might have gone on about half a minute or so. When we finally touched the puck, he blew the whistle and threw me off—which I deserved, but some people thought I hadn't done anything. They were throwing stuff on the ice, dangerous stuff, bottles and everything. A lot of players were hiding under the nets, not so much us but the St. Michael's team.

"Red Kelly, my good friend that I later roomed with for a few years in Detroit, would talk about that game. He thought the fans were a little rough there, especially on them. We had just come through that tough series with Brandon, and St. Mike's had a heck of a team. They just whomped us."

CAHA vice-president Al Pickard announced over the public address system that the game would be forfeited if the barrage did not stop. Ultimately, the ice was cleared four times and half an hour passed before the game was awarded to St. Mike's. Three nights later at Game 4 in Regina, attendance plummeted from 5,959 to 2,186 and the Majors eked out a 3–2 decision. It was enough to end a series that would be remembered not for the Majors' domination or the end of Prystai's junior career but for the time Regina fans branded themselves as unruly hooligans. Luckily, the city would not have to endure another Memorial Cup embarrassment like that . . . until 1980.

BILL HUNTER: BORN TO BE WILD

Maybe it was the Notre Dame background that set Bill Hunter on such a perplexing business path. Women's softball, senior hockey, curling, junior hockey, professional hockey, North Battleford, Regina, Saskatoon, Moose Jaw, Yorkton, Edmonton—no sooner would he achieve success at one endeavour in one city than he'd pack up, move on and start on something else. It was as if he considered the Notre Dame motto of "Struggle and Emerge" to be a self-regenerating perpetual cycle.

His struggle was every Saskatchewan and Alberta sports fan's delight. He poured his heart, soul and money into every project he undertook. He was sincerely grandiose, not so much full of himself as full of belief in himself and in the people of the prairies to achieve greatness.

Indeed, Bill Hunter's first association with an athlete was exceptional. He was barely old enough for grade school when he would spend free afternoons chasing down the javelin and discus for Ethel Catherwood at her workouts. As a high school student at Saskatoon's Nutana Collegiate, he literally drove himself to exhaustion, and kidney failure, by

Bill Hunter in full oratorical delivery

Mel Hill

trying to play and organize every sport he could. After recovering, Hunter decided to complete his education at Notre Dame, where he could study and get involved in sports without yielding to his compulsion to be the driving force behind everything. His parents, taken by surprise, came to visit him at Wilcox and meet the famous Père Murray who had taken their son Bill under his care.

"Marion," the priest told Bill's mother, "you've got not a bad little bastard at all for a son here."

Hunter helped with the management of Hounds sports teams, completed his Grade 11 and 12, and enlisted in the army as the Second World War erupted. After basic training, his leadership and organizational skills backfired on him when he was kept at home to train new recruits. Disenchanted, he went AWOL and remained a malcontent until his father Jack got an old friend, Lieutenant-Colonel Pallie Pascoe, to arrange Bill's transfer to the air force, where he saw combat duty as a bomber and fighter pilot.

Returning home in 1944, he got his first civilian job as a news and sports reporter with Saskatoon radio station CFQC. He loved the work but not the pay ($85 a month) and became a travelling sales representative for General Foods before happening upon his first entrepreneurial opportunity: a North Battleford sporting-goods store whose owner wanted to retire. In addition to operating the business, Hunter managed and coached a juvenile hockey team, and made his first foray into sports ownership by forming the North Battleford Bombers women's softball club. The Bombers almost took the 1946 provincial championship, forcing the Saskatoon Ramblers to the limit in their best-of-three series. Ramblers shortstop Sylvia Fedoruk denied North Battleford the winning run with a sensational fielding play in the ninth inning, and Saskatoon went on to win 1–0 in 17 innings before 6,000 fans.

In the summer of '46, Hunter sold his North Battleford interests and acquired a piece of the Regina Capitals senior hockey team, whose performance on the ice and at the box office had been dreadful. To make the Caps contenders and gate attractions, he snatched up recognizable names, most notably goaltender Emile Francis, who had just completed his junior eligibility with the Moose Jaw Canucks and whom the Chicago Black Hawks assumed would obediently join them.

"I went to the Black Hawks training camp which was held in Regina," Francis remembers. "In those days you didn't sign your contract before you reported; they waited until they got you there. I had figured out what I could make with them, and it came to about $3,000. Suddenly, who should contact me but Bill Hunter. He said the first thing he was going to do was sign me. I told him that was impossible because I was going to turn pro, but he said he'd give me an offer I couldn't turn down: $500 to sign the amateur card and $5,000 for the season.

"This was huge for an amateur! I was in the Black Hawks' camp for two weeks before (Chicago general manager) Bill Tobin called me in to sign. He offered me $500 to sign the pro contract, $3,000 to play in the minors and an additional $2,000 if I made the Black Hawks. I told him I could do better playing amateur hockey.

" 'WHAT?' he hollered. He was shocked. I repeated myself, and while he didn't call me a liar, he made it plain that he thought I was deceiving him. He said they wouldn't pay a penny more, so I told him I'd be checking out of the hotel in 15 minutes. I packed my bags, called Bill Hunter and that afternoon I signed with Regina."

Francis played 32 games for Regina before Tobin, desperate for a goaltender, agreed to pay Hunter $10,000 for his netminder's contract. Tobin still got the best of the deal, because he never actually sent Hunter the money.

Other stars that Hunter lured to the Capitals included ex-NHLers Sweeney Schriner, Mel Hill and Gus Kyle. Regina would reach the 1949 Allan Cup final, but Hunter was already gone, having sold his Capitals interest to try duplicating his rebuilding feat in Saskatoon as general manager of the Quakers. He would also take a turn as coach, which led to his nickname of "Wild Bill," bestowed by Dave Dryburgh of the *Leader-Post* for Hunter's excitable nature on the bench, particularly during brawls. Hunter made the mistake of actually joining in a melee until he was knocked unconscious and cut for seven stitches—not from a punch but by slipping and smacking his head on the ice.

Bill Dunbar (second from right) poses with one of his prizes after winning the 1949 Saskatoon car spiel with the Pringle brothers and substitute sweeper Lou Fusse (right)

It was while managing the Quakers that one of Hunter's money-making schemes made a huge impact on the Canadian sporting scene. Scotty Moir of Nipawin had pioneered the concept of the car spiel. Curling bonspiels tended to be of little interest to anyone beyond the competitors until Moir upped the ante by making the first prize four new automobiles. Suddenly, every top-notch foursome converged on Nipawin to give the car spiel the most competitive field of any curling event, the Brier included.

Hunter took the idea and magnified it: natural ice to artificial ice, small city to big city, big field to enormous field. As he put it in his autobiography, "I did a little figuring—128 rinks at $200 a rink. Not bad. A gross of $25,000 and change. Plus ticket and concessions sales. I thought I should be able to run things at a profit." (Yeah, and if you jump off the University Bridge in July, you should be able to get wet.) Besides making big money for the Quakers, the Saskatoon car spiel helped turn curling into a real spectator sport and a more competitive one. Curlers became much more serious about their play when cars and cash supplanted trophies as the incentive.

Unhappy with reporting to a board, Hunter departed for new opportunities in 1951. He went to Medicine Hat, returned briefly to Saskatchewan a few years later, and headed back to Edmonton. There he enjoyed some of his grandest hockey achievements—as president and general manager of the junior Oil Kings, as a co-founder of what we now know as the Western Hockey League, and as a co-founder of the Edmonton Oilers and the World Hockey Association.

Hunter's last great endeavour, the most audacious, was his 1983 crusade to obtain the St. Louis Blues and transfer the NHL franchise to Saskatoon. His greatest asset—his ability to turn an unlikely proposition into reality—led to him almost pulling it off. He had the season-ticket pledges, he had the investors, he had the deal worked out with the Blues. The only thing he couldn't get was the necessary approval of the NHL's governors for the sale of the franchise.

Which is just as well. What might have been Hunter's greatest shortcoming—his lack of emphasis on long-range consequences as he pursued an immediate goal—didn't alert him to spiralling salaries and other costs of maintaining an NHL franchise. Logic insists that if the Winnipeg Jets and Quebec Nordiques couldn't survive, neither could a team in Saskatoon.

SASKATOON LIONS SPEED SKATING: OVAL TEAM

Eleanor Powley and Clarence Downey's competitive speed skating days were essentially behind them by 1942. Powley had been Saskatchewan's most accomplished competitor as far back as the 1920s. Downey was renowned for his barrel jumping prowess, winning four straight Western Canadian championships from 1937–40.

Interest in speed skating in Saskatoon had dwindled, and they wanted to revive it, so they joined forces with Albert Hardy, Harold Gillies and other devotees of the long blades, called themselves the Saskatoon Speed Skating Club, and petitioned the Saskatoon Playgrounds Association for winter playground space. The SPA provided three outdoor rinks.

The club put an ad in the *StarPhoenix* inviting children aged 10 to 18 to come out on Saturday mornings and try the sport. Within a year there were 250 participants. It was time to organize a local meet. A sponsor was sought. The local Lions club agreed to foot the bill. By 1945 the program was so popular that the sponsorship became permanent, and the club was renamed the Saskatoon Lions Speed Skating Club.

Downey, determined to produce skaters of national calibre, secured enough funding to take a small team to the 1947 Canadian championships in Sudbury. There Craig Mackay won the senior men's three-mile race and secured a berth on the 1948 Olympic team. Another Lions racer, Pat Lawson, had a tremendous meet, winning the women's 220-, 440- and 880-yard races. Luckily for Lawson, this was the era when the International Olympic Committee was protecting her gender from the dangers of competition. (Exertion, perspiration, over-excitement, the vapours . . .) Olympic speed skating was not opened up to women until 1960 and has been allowed to continue ever since as frail flowers like Catriona Le May Doan take their lives into their hands with every lacing of their skates.

Mackay had the speed, endurance and attitude essential to his sport in the '40s. Most races, outdoors and indoors, were conducted in packs of four or more skaters, much like today's short-track competitions. Good sportsmanship had its place, and that place was off the track. On the oval, establishing and fighting for position was not a polite exercise.

At one Canadian championship, Mackay responded to an opponent's habit of cutting inside him by grabbing the fellow's hips and pushing him into a snowbank. (Apparently, Mackay had learned nothing about strategic elbow placement from his childhood shinny games with Gordie Howe.) One fistfight later, both skaters were given a year's suspension.

Accustomed to frigid, often windy conditions in Saskatoon, Mackay found the ice unusually soft at St. Moritz, Switzerland. He still did remarkably well for an Olympic rookie, placing 14th of 40 in the 5,000 metres and 13th of 27 in the 10,000. Mackay also entered the 500 but fell and did not finish.

Wally Boschuk (hand on ice) leads a race with Craig Mackay (left) and Eugene Hearn in hot pursuit

Back in Saskatoon, a new oval, one-sixth of a mile around, launched the Lions on a permanent course of achievement. Mackay lived on a Norwegian farm for a year to receive European training and earned two top-10 finishes at the 1950 world championships. He made another Olympic trip to Oslo in 1952, entered four events and posted finishes ranging from 15th to 24th. Another Lions skater, Johnny Sands, represented Canada at the 1956 Games in Cortina D'Ampezzo,

Italy, and at Squaw Valley, Calif., in 1960. At the latter, women competed for the first time. Naturally, Canada was represented by a Saskatoon Lion, Peggy Robb. Bob Hodges made it to the 1968 and '72 Winter Games.

In between those two Olympiads, Saskatoon played host to the 1971 Canada Winter Games. As the speed skating races were being contested, a two-month-old Cat was in her cradle . . .

DOREEN DREDGE: SOCK IT TO 'EM

BACK IN 1925, JOE GRIFFITHS DISCOVERED ETHEL Catherwood by reading the results of a local track meet. Twenty-two years later, he encountered another high-jumping prodigy, this time before his very eyes at the provincial championships in Saskatoon. Doreen Dredge, born in Wadena and living in nearby Kelvington, stood 5-foot-7½, had red hair and cherubic cheeks. Athletically, she was head and shoulders above the competition, clearing 4 feet 10½ inches . . . with no coach . . . using the archaic scissors jump . . . in her stocking feet.

"Jumping in sock feet was normal for most country girls at the high school meets," Doreen Dredge Wolff recalled decades later. "Mr. Griffiths believed I could do better with spikes. . . . He took me to the store to get them and kept telling me I could be another Ethel Catherwood."

For a little while, Dredge did follow the path of the Saskatoon Lily. After two weeks of Griffiths' tutelage, Dredge set a world junior record of 5 feet 1⅝ inches at the 1947 Canadian championships in Edmonton, where she also won the long jump with a leap of 16 feet 2½ inches.

At the Olympic trials the following year, she cleared 5 feet 3 inches to tie Catherwood's Canadian high-jump record that was still on the books. Dredge was the only Saskatchewan athlete of 25 in the Canadian track and field contingent and easily the youngest. Her teammates threw a birthday party for her when she turned 17 on the ocean voyage to London, England.

The weather in London also evoked Catherwood's triumph in Amsterdam 20 years earlier. It was cold with a steady drizzle, and with 30 competitors to weed out, more than an hour could pass between an individual's jumps. Dredge was at the further disadvantage of employing the scissors jump because she hadn't had time to master the more effective Western roll.

In spite of that, Dredge finished in a three-way tie for fourth and was officially placed fifth on the basis of missed jumps. Her best clearance of 5 feet 2¼ inches was one inch behind the bronze medallist.

Doreen Dredge

Fame and scandal had left Catherwood a bitter recluse. Dredge's spell in the spotlight was exceptionally brief. She stopped competing after the Olympics and devoted herself to education, first as a student, then as a teacher in Pipestone Valley, Watrous and Liberty, where she met Bernard Wolff. They married in 1955 and still live in Liberty, near their three children and nine grandchildren.

Joe Griffiths was wrong. Doreen Dredge Wolff was not another Ethel Catherwood.

Lucky girl.

Wayne Stephenson with his teammates on the 1949 St. Louis Black Cardinals

WIMPY STEPHENSON: BARNSTORMING WHITE NEGRO

WAYNE "WIMPY" STEPHENSON WAS A 19-YEAR-old three-year veteran of senior and semi-pro baseball in the summer of 1949. His team that summer was the Swift Current Indians, at least until they went broke. In a last-ditch effort to make money, the Indians played an exhibition against the St. Louis Black Cardinals, a barnstorming Negro team. Swift Current won 2–1 behind Stephenson's two-hit pitching, but after the game the players were told the team had to disband. Stephenson started his job search by crossing the field to the Black Cardinals' dugout.

"You fellows are travelling as a 10-man ball club," he said. "Could you use another chucker? I'm unemployed as of 10 minutes ago."

"Can you be ready to leave at 8:00 A.M. tomorrow?" one of the players replied.

The next morning, Indians ex-manager Jack McLeod spotted something you didn't see on a North American street in 1949: one white face, belonging to his former pitcher, amid a row of blacks behind the windows of a bus. Wimpy Stephenson had integrated a Negro barnstorming baseball team, three years after Jackie Robinson had broken the colour bar of white professional baseball by suiting up with the Montreal Royals.

Stephenson's new team "was on the move constantly, averaging five to seven games a week," he related in a 1999 letter to Saskatchewan Baseball Hall of Fame and Museum director Dave Shury. "Payment occurred after each game, based on a percentage from the gate or tournament winnings less team expenses. The balance was then divided equally."

Players would take turns driving the bus. Stephenson displayed his intimate knowledge of Saskatchewan geography on one turn behind the wheel when, at 4:30 A.M., his short cut through Moose Jaw led to a dead end in a farmer's yard. Making a U-turn woke up more than a dozen turkeys whose sudden excitement in turn woke up an unhappy bunch of ballplayers. The reflexive verbal abuse they laid on Stephenson for the bizarre wake-up call was harsher than anything he would ever hear on the field.

"I never heard the 'N' word nor was I openly ridiculed for being part of a coloured ball club," he wrote of the excursions through Manitoba, Saskatchewan and Alberta. "It seemed to me that the game of baseball was well respected by the fans in all three provinces. The players were admired, the ballgames were affordable and well attended. We usually attended the dances after the ball tournaments. There was a little beer and a little white lightning (homemade vodka)."

Everything went well until mid-September when the team reached the American border en route to a game in Minot, N.D.

"I thought I was fully prepared to carry on barnstorming across the U.S.A. to Florida and eventually end up in Puerto Rico for the winter season. But to my dismay the U.S. Customs officials grabbed me, took my fingerprints and questioned me endlessly. (They said) 'there is no way you will be allowed, as an uninformed 19-year-old, to travel into the Southern states as a white ballplayer on a black ball team. You would be shot or knifed.'

"The questioning process took so long, two hours, that the manager advised me that the bus had to leave in order to make the evening encounter in Minot. I assured them I would meet them come game time. My glove, spikes, leather jacket and suitcase got to the game, but I didn't. I hitchhiked back to Rosetown in blue jeans and a t-shirt."

Stephenson's barnstorming adventure kept him in baseball. A shutout he had pitched for the Black Cardinals in Dauphin, Man., so impressed that city's Red Birds that they recruited him for the 1950 and '51 seasons. Following baseball, Stephenson became a successful realtor in Calgary. His summer of '49 faded into a hazy memory until 1994, when a long-misplaced team picture surfaced among his belongings. Stephenson had 10 copies made of the photo and sent them to his old mates on the St. Louis Black Cardinals. Eight returned with notations that there was no such resident or no such address. Two came back with greetings and thanks from the men who received them.

ALSO IN THIS DECADE

- David Greyeyes-Steele of the Muskeg Lake Reserve joined the Canadian Machine Gun Reinforcement Unit and helped it win the 1942 Canadian Army Overseas soccer championship. That year he was promoted to lieutenant, the first Indian to receive a Canadian military commission. By war's end he was decorated for combat service in North Africa, Italy, France, Germany and Greece.

- Prince Albert dentist Bob Reid won consecutive Saskatchewan men's amateur golf titles in 1941 and '46. The championship hadn't been contested in the intervening years because of the war. Reid, the provincial champion in 1936, would win his fourth and fifth titles in 1950 and '52.

- Adam Faul of Spy Hill was the 1947 light heavyweight and 1948 heavyweight amateur boxing champion of Canada. He fought at the 1948 Olympics in London, won his first bout and lost the second when it was stopped because of a cut over an eye. Faul won 60 of his 64 bouts.

- Bethune-born Frank Longridge won the last of his 29 provincial badminton titles in 1949. Dating back to 1937, Longridge won eight men's titles, 12 men's doubles titles and nine mixed doubles titles.

THE DAY NOBODY BROKE 80

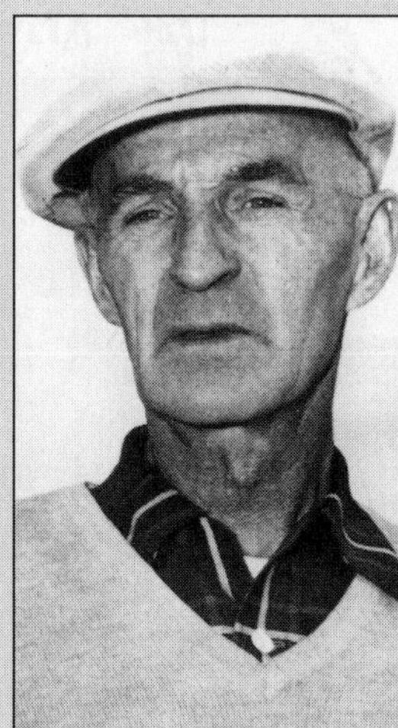

Tom Ross

Tom Ross of Regina won the Saskatchewan Open in 1928, '29, '34 and '38. By the late '40s he seemed long past his prime, especially among young pros who could knock a golf ball considerably higher and farther than he.

On July 2, 1949, though, Ross showed how valuable experience can be. Moose Jaw's Riverside course, site of the one-day, 36-hole Open, was buffeted by winds of 50 miles per hour that took golf shots on trajectories that resembled roller-coaster rides.

Ross, a few days short of his 52nd birthday, kept his shots low and turned in rounds of 82 and 83, respectively 11 and 12 over par and on most days cause for a pro to hang his head in shame. This time, though, 23-over 165 beat the field by two shots and brought Tom Ross his fifth Saskatchewan Open title.

1952 Olympic gold medalist
George Genereux

1950–1959

Fading Glory

ARRIVALS

April 5, 1951: Guy Vanderhaeghe, novelist, Esterhazy.
May 30, 1953: Jim Hunter, skier, Shaunavon.
September 22, 1953: Brian Claypool, rodeo cowboy, Lucky Lake.
October 6, 1953: Roger Aldag, football player, Gull Lake.
February 3, 1954: Dave "Tiger" Williams, hockey player, Weyburn.
May 16, 1954: Dave Williams, astronaut, Saskatoon.
November 29, 1954: Joanne McTaggart, track and field athlete, Regina.
November 6, 1955: Darlene Solie, softball player, Regina.
November 15, 1955: Bob Poley, football player, Saskatoon.
May 12, 1956: Bernie Federko, hockey player, Foam Lake.
July 17, 1956: Bryan Trottier, hockey player, Redvers.
May 25, 1957: Brenda Staniforth, softball player, Lashburn.
June 20, 1957: Mick McGeough, hockey referee, Regina.
September 16, 1957: Arnold Boldt, high jumper, Saskatoon.
January 26, 1959: Cathy Turnbull, speed skater, Regina.

DEPARTURES

December 9, 1956: football players Mel Becket, 27; Mario DeMarco, 30; Ray Syrnyk, 22; Gord Sturtridge, 27.
May 16, 1957: Dick Irvin Sr., hockey player/coach, 64.
December 26, 1958: "Dynamite" Eddie James, football player, 51.

THE '50S IS SASKATCHEWAN'S DECADE OF SELECTIVE NOSTALGIA. TO THIS DAY THERE IS AFFECTION FOR Gordie Howe and the Dobber, Garnet Campbell and the North Battleford baseball Beavers. Yet there are others, fabulous athletes and wonderful people, who are slipping from our collective memory.

When the 50th anniversary of one of the most dramatic Stanley Cup-winning goals, the overtime fluke by Tony Leswick of the Detroit Red Wings, arrived in April 2004, no notice was taken. Every year it is noted that the last Canadian to win the Canadian Open was Pat Fletcher in 1954; who bothers to mention that he was the long-time pro at the Saskatoon Golf and Country Club when he did it? Who remembers Canada's most glorious of world amateur hockey champions, the Penticton Vees, and the Saskatchewan skaters who formed the core of the squad? Who has even heard of Arnie Weinmeister?

If Paul Simon could make "Where have you gone, Joe DiMaggio?" a fitting American lament, Saskatchewan will create one of its own if it doesn't bother to preserve its legacy of athletic greatness:

"Who were you, George Genereux?"

THE 1951 ROUGHRIDERS: A NEW ERA

FRED GRANT'S WORST DECISION HAD NOTHING to do with player selection or on-field strategy. It occurred after the Saskatchewan Roughriders' 1950 season, when they went 7–7 and were humiliated 24–1 by the Edmonton Eskimos in the Western semi-final at Taylor Field. Grant, the head coach, responded to public criticism (of things like player selection and on-field strategy) with a sarcastic open letter.

Punt backwards on first down if you must, but don't knock the fans. Grant was gone, replaced by Harry "Blackjack" Smith.

When team president Don MacDonald followed Grant's ill-advised letter with his own resignation at the team's annual meeting, however, the repercussions were more momentous. Since 1946 the team had been run by a quartet of construction executives known as "The Big Four": MacDonald, Jack Rowand, Stack Tibbitts and Clair Warner. It was time for restructuring. A new constitution established a 14-man executive comprising a president, vice-president, five directors and seven committee chairmen. Active members (who became such by contributing $10) became the community that actually owned the team.

MacDonald had not mismanaged the team; it simply needed more grassroots involvement. In fact, MacDonald was in the process of doing Saskatchewan a great service by procuring the services of Glenn Dobbs, who had starred as a quarterback with the Brooklyn Dodgers and Los Angeles Dons of the All-America Football Conference. Dobbs, also a tremendous punter, figured his football days were finished in 1950 after the NFL absorbed a handful of AAFC teams and let the others die.

MacDonald and oil contractor Charlie Hay, an avid Roughriders supporter, discovered Dobbs' availability through a business contact in Tulsa, where Dobbs had played his college football. Dobbs signed a two-year contract for $12,500 a season and was introduced to his new fans on a February afternoon in Regina, where he discovered the Grand Theatre full to capacity *and* an overflow line of fans a block long standing in four inches of new snow and tem-

Martin Ruby

peratures of 20 below Fahrenheit. "I hadn't seen such enthusiasm since my college days," Dobbs would remember. "Football really is a game of fun and companionship, and if you don't get that out of it, there's no sense being in it."

Glenn Dobbs

Another ex-AAFC product joining the Roughriders in 1951 was two-way tackle Martin Ruby. Ends Jack Russell and Jack Nix and centre Red Ettinger also came aboard as imports. Bill Clarke, a rangy lineman who had starred with the junior Regina Dales and as the Canadian schoolboy curling champion skip of 1950, was another newcomer. So was Bob Sandberg, an ex-Winnipeg Blue Bomber halfback lured out of retirement who had put in enough years of service to be declared a non-import by the Western Interprovincial Football Union.

Local veterans included tackle Toar Springstein and halfback Ken Charlton, game performers but near the end of their careers. Charlton, a product of Central Collegiate and the Regina Dales, had started with the Roughriders but wartime enlistment in the RCAF led to stints with the Blue Bombers and Ottawa Rough Riders before returning to Regina in 1948 to become a perennial Western all-star and, since 1949, captain of the team. Charlton's running mate, Sully Glasser, was a six-year veteran who typically missed the first few games of the football season because he was a superior baseball player.

Dobbs rewarded the fans' enthusiasm in the opening game, played before a near-capacity crowd of 7,700 in a steady downpour. It was too wet to pass and too muddy to run, so Dobbs unleashed his other weapon, the punt. Five times in the third quarter he booted singles to lead the way to an ugly but satisfying 8–1 victory over the Calgary Stampeders. Dobbs passed for 2,313 yards and 28 touchdowns, scored seven touchdowns himself and punted for 20 singles over the course of the season. Saskatchewan carried on to an 8–6 record, the same as Edmonton and Winnipeg but enough to earn first place for the first time since the WIFU was formed in 1936. Saskatchewan squeaked past Edmonton in the best-of-three Western final (11–15, 12–5, 19–18) for its first Grey Cup berth in 17 years.

More than 1,000 fans headed to Toronto on special trains to take in the Grey Cup game against the Ottawa Rough Riders. All the support in the world, however, couldn't heal the injuries that had accumulated. Guard Pete Martin had broken a leg in the regular-season finale. Russell had blown a knee on the last play of the Western final. Dobbs was hobbling with a severe charley horse. Halfback Del Wardien and defensive end Jack Wedley had sprained ankles. Finally, Sandberg, who had been declared a non-import before the season by the WIFU because he had played the requisite four seasons in Winnipeg, was declared ineligible by the Canadian Rugby Union because the four seasons weren't consecutive. Accounts vary as to whether the Roughriders knew all along that Sandberg couldn't have played in the Grey Cup, but he did spend the whole game, in uniform, on the bench. Roughriders president Bob Kramer wanted Sandberg to play regardless of the CRU's decision and was livid when Blackjack Smith refused. Smith was fired after the season.

Given their state of collective health, it was no surprise that the Western 'Riders lost their first national final since 1934. Dobbs launched a pair of towering punt singles for a 2–0 lead in the first quarter, but turnovers and big plays gave Ottawa a 19–2 advantage after 45 minutes. Saskatchewan

George Abel (8) scores against Switzerland in the 1952 Olympics

1952 OLYMPICS: GEORGE ABEL GETS HIS OPPORTUNITY

While Sid Abel became a hockey star, his older brother George stayed in Melville to help their father with their family draying business. (The dray—a heavy, horse-drawn cart—was a practical means of hauling small loads of freight in the Dirty Thirties, when trucks and gas were a luxury.)

Aside from playing with Sid on the 1937–38 Flin Flon Bombers senior team that reached the Allan Cup western final, George's own hockey skills lay dormant. George took over Abel's Cartage, now a trucking business, in 1946 and starred for five seasons with the Melville Millionaires at the modest Intermediate A level.

It wasn't until the winter of 1951–52 that Abel could afford to take time off from his business interests for a serious hockey project. Invited to try out for the Edmonton Mercurys, who were going to represent Canada at the 1952 Winter Olympics in Oslo, Abel made the team and joined it on a whirlwind schedule of 51 games in three months. Abel and his Edmonton teammates almost didn't make it to the Olympics. En route to Oslo for a pre-Olympic exhibition, the team bus skidded off the road, slid down an embankment and struck a tree that saved the bus from plummeting further. Several players were injured. Abel, who turned 36 during the Olympics, played the eight-game round robin with a sore back.

Only a few teams in the field were expected to challenge Canada. Canada passed its first real test easily, downing Czechoslovakia 4–1 after three blowouts. Sweden threw a genuine scare into the Canadians, who would outshoot the Swedes 36–9 but spend most of the game rallying from a 2–0 deficit. Abel led the comeback, setting up Louis Secco for a first-period goal and tallying his own unassisted marker late in the second. Billy Dawe scored with 20 seconds remaining for a 3–2 victory that maintained Canada's perfect record. By crushing Norway 11–2, the Mercurys went into their last game needing only a draw to win the gold medal for Canada and got it, tying the United States 3–3 while outshooting the Americans 58–13. Abel finished the tournament with six goals and six assists for 12 points, tied for second on the team.

Sid Abel was a three-time winner of the Stanley Cup, a beautiful trophy of silver. George got the gold.

scored two fourth-quarter touchdowns, on a third-down pass from Dobbs to Nix and a 10-yard run by Glasser, and raised hopes of a comeback before falling 21–14.

It was a far better showing than the team had managed in its Grey Cup forays of the '20s and '30s, and raised expectations for a new era of glory for the Green and White (colours the team adopted in 1948 after Jack Fyffe of the team executive discovered two sets of uniforms in those colours at a heavily discounted price in a Chicago war surplus store).

Dobbs was named player-coach for 1952. Although he proved to be an ineffective coach as the team fell to 3–13, he would stay one more season and remain as popular as he was in 1951. However brief his stay, those who witnessed his performance remember when Regina was "Dobberville."

Sully Glasser

GEORGE GENEREUX: OLYMPIAN ACHIEVEMENTS

Beware lest you lose the substance by grasping at the shadow. –Aesop.

GEORGE GENEREUX WAS A SASKATCHEWAN HERO. People treated him like one when he won an Olympic gold medal at the age of 17.

Then, his athletic career over, he became a real hero.

As a boy, young George would frequently hunt sharp-tailed grouse with his father, George Sr., a Saskatoon ophthalmologist. Dad taught Junior all he knew, but the boy was eager to improve his marksmanship. Jim Girgulis, a Greek-born trapshooter who had been one of Canada's best, showed young George the fundamentals of the sport and, in years to come, the fine points that defined champions.

Genereux was 13 years old and had one year of trapshooting experience when he achieved his first victory in Winnipeg at the 1948 Midwest International Handicap, an event that drew competitors from Ontario, Manitoba, Minnesota and the Dakotas. He followed that with Man-Sask junior championships in 1948, '49 and '50. His reputation spread in 1951 when he travelled to Vandalia, Ohio, for the Grand American championships, the biggest event on the North American calendar. There Genereux won the North American Junior title by blasting 193 of 200 clay pigeons to tie for first, then 49 of 50 to win the shootoff. Later he won a preliminary handicap with a score of 99x100 and lost a three-way shootoff for a class championship after making 199x200. Returning to Saskatchewan, he collected his fourth straight provincial title with a perfect 100.

Once he had qualified for the 1952 Olympics in Helsinki, Genereux, then 17, also entered the world championships in Oslo that preceded the Games. Pablo Grossi of Argentina took the world title with a 287x300 score while Genereux and Knut Holmqvist of Sweden made 286 apiece. Genereux won the shootoff for the silver medal in his first overseas test. Competitors and officials were impressed that Genereux competed with a single-barrelled shotgun, which some thought would handicap him at the Olympics. Genereux thought otherwise, as he explained in a 1974 letter to a trapshooting historian:

> *Everybody save myself used either an under/over or a double-barrel gun; I used a trap-grade pump which I do not feel put me to any disadvantage at all, since many of us on this continent had been*

used to these guns for doubles for many years. We could use what was equivalent to 'duck loads' in those days, which meant that it was permissible to shoot the old Imperial shell. However, since the birds travelled so fast, it was imperative that one not only be prepared but actually fire both shells off every time, whether or not you hit with your first shot. This meant an awful lot of pounding over a two-day event.

George Genereux at home with some of his trophies

In other words, you—*oof!*—simply braced your—*oof!*—right shoulder for—*oof!*—twice as many—*oof!*—recoils.

Just before the Olympic trapshooting competition started on July 25, Genereux predicted the winning score (not necessarily his) would be 192. One could follow a simple, though demanding, plan to a gold medal if that were so. The 39 marksmen would fire eight rounds of 25 targets, four rounds on Friday and four on Saturday. Eight rounds of 24x25 would total 192x200. Simple as that, if you happen to think that shooting a four-inch disc travelling 70 mph from 16 yards away is simple.

That is almost what Genereux did on the opening day, posting rounds of 24, 24 and 24 before closing with a 23 that put him in third place at 95x100, two hits out of first place. He didn't have the eyes of a nation upon him—in fact, few in Canada had even heard of George Genereux yet—but his mother, Catherine, was among the spectators. Like everything else in the environment, he had to block it out of his mind and concentrate on the targets more rigidly the second day.

He began with a 24 and followed by posting 24 again. While others succumbed to physical and mental fatigue, Genereux posted a perfect 25 in the third round and finished with another 24. His Saturday score was 97x100, his cumulative 192x200. Genereux's prediction was correct! He was in first place, no one could catch him, and Holmqvist of Sweden could only match Genereux's 192 with a perfect closing round of 25.

"Everybody on the grounds knew what the total picture was," Genereux wrote in his 1974 letter. He patiently waited and prepared for a shootoff as Holmqvist proceeded to hit, hit, hit, hit, 5, hit, hit, hit, hit, 10, hit, hit, hit, hit, 15, hit, hit, hit, hit, 20, hit, hit, hit, MISS!

"I can honestly say that I felt a bit sorry for him, but after realizing that my score was now tops and that it could not be beaten, my mood changed rather dramatically." Holmqvist made his last shot for 191 to take the silver medal, one hit ahead of fellow Swede Hans Liljedahl. No one else in the field bettered 188. Genereux was besieged by reporters and left the interviews embarrassed because, rather than talk about himself, he had startled a Toronto reporter by asking if the Detroit Red Wings were really going to stop Gordie Howe from playing baseball for the Saskatoon Gems.

In addition to his gold medal, Genereux was also honoured as Saskatoon's citizen of the year and the recipient of the Lou Marsh Trophy as Canada's athlete of the year, still the only Saskatchewan man to receive that award. Even if someone wanted to debate the athletic merits of trapshooting, there was no doubting Genereux's physical prowess. An imposing 6-foot-3, he was a standout on the baseball field and the hockey rink as well. The Toronto Maple Leafs asked him to move to Ontario and play junior within their organization. No, they were told by George Sr., the boy has his heart set on a career in medicine.

It wasn't a lie, but it wasn't the whole truth either.

Even before George Genereux Jr. had arrived in Helsinki, he knew this was his one and only opportunity at athletic fame. He would never be an Olympian again. He would never play professional hockey or professional baseball or pursue any sport that required a healthy body.

George Genereux, at 17, knew he was condemned to a short, painful life in a degenerating body.

It was early in 1952, months before the Olympics, that he felt stiffness in his back, an ache that was peculiarly out of place for a robust teenager. With his father's connections to doctors at the University of Saskatchewan, the diagnosis was rapid but devastating: ankylosing spondylitis (AS). Outside of medical journals, Genereux's condition was usually reported as rheumatoid arthritis because it has similar symptoms to AS and is more recognizable to the lay community. Ankylosing spondylitis is also a rheumatic disease but attacks primarily the spine and/or pelvis. Its side effects include the considerable pain and stiffness of the joints associated with rheumatoid arthritis.

Athletics, sadly, were out of the question. Following in his father's footsteps in medicine was still appealing, but how could one treat patients in any kind of general or specialized medicine if the physician's body was, from a purely professional standpoint, unreliable? Genereux found a viable, practical and stimulating career path in radiology, particularly in research. His eyes and brain would be able to diagnose, theorize, learn and correlate long after his hands and the rest of his body rendered him unable to administer X-rays.

Genereux graduated with a Bachelor of Science degree from the University of Saskatchewan in 1956 and went to study medicine at McGill University in Montreal. There he struck up a friendship with another renowned Saskatchewan athlete, Montreal Canadiens left-winger Bert Olmstead, and Olmstead's wife Nora.

"Bert would get two tickets for every game, and George would come to quite a few of them with me," Nora said in a 2003 interview. "I doubt that anyone in the Forum knew who he was.

"We had him over for dinner several times. His dad would hunt ducks in Saskatchewan and ship them down, packed in dry ice. George would bring them over to our house, and I'd cook them. Those were some great meals.

"He had the arthritis at the time that we knew him in Montreal. (Bert Olmstead was with the Canadiens until 1958.) He had a cot at his residence, and he told us there were some mornings when he couldn't get out of bed. Then he'd have a spell where he'd be in remission and be okay for a while."

Once in a while Genereux could, within a private circle, demonstrate the keen eye and reflexes that made him an Olympic champion.

"Oh yeah, he could shoot," said Bert Olmstead. "Even as sick as he was, he could beat me, and I was pretty good. I won a provincial trapshooting championship when he wasn't there. We'd go to a fish and game club, sometimes with (Montreal defenceman) Tom Johnson. The only guy on the club I introduced George to was Tom; they'd go shoot together after I left Montreal.

"George never complained about his situation, not once. He'd call us long distance, just to chat, and never mention it, never say a word. Mainly, it was, 'how are *you*?'"

Out of McGill with his medical degree in 1960, he took his radiology training at the University of Minnesota and his pathology back at the U of S before returning to Montreal to work under Dr. Robert Fraser at the Royal Victoria Hospital in 1964. Fraser, one of the world's foremost radiologists, was beginning work on a definitive textbook in the field. Impressed by Genereux's thorough attention to detail, Fraser took him on as a protégé and later as a co-author.

Returning to Saskatoon for good in 1966, Genereux joined the Faculty of Medicine at the U of S and earned a full professorship in eight years. He maintained his association with Dr. Fraser and in 1985

Bert Olmstead

became a co-author of *Diagnosis of Diseases of the Chest*, the textbook project that Fraser had initiated.

"It's one of the best-selling radiology textbooks ever published, the definitive source worldwide and a mandatory reference for residents," says Dr. Stuart Houston, now retired after 32 years in the Department of Diagnostic Radiology at the U of S. "In addition, he was a member of a select world-wide circle called the Fleischner Society. This consisted of the 30 best chest specialists in the world—the *crème de la crème* of pathologists, surgeons, radiologists, physiologists, and so on—and membership was by invitation only.

"The Fleishner Society was on the cutting edge of medical research. They would gather once a year, meet privately for one day to exchange their latest findings, then hold a public symposium the second day to share their knowledge. George was renowned for delivering well-organized summations of this new information and conducting dynamic dialogues with the audience.

"To my mind, his contributions to *Diagnosis of Diseases of the Chest* and his role in the Fleishner Society are successes every bit as outstanding as his Olympic gold medal."

Genereux's moment of glory on the sporting stage was gradually forgotten. One man who experienced it from a Saskatoon perspective and then got to know Genereux as a medical scholar was Roy Romanow, who would become premier of Saskatchewan (1991-2001) and chairman of the Royal Commission on the Future of Health Care in Canada (2002).

"All of a sudden, this just burst on to the news, this Saskatoon boy achieving this Olympic title," says Romanow, who was a few weeks short of 13 when Genereux triumphed in Helsinki. "There was enormous excitement and pride among all of us.

"The Genereux family was very prominent in Saskatoon. I lived on the west side, which was sort of a sociological barrier. Those that lived on the east side, like the Genereuxes, had 'made it,' if I can put it that way. But my wife Eleanore knew George because they were both Nutana Collegiate alumni, and then George married a school friend of mine, so I got to know George quite well.

"He was a fine specimen of a man, a handsome guy. You could see the skill of trapshooting from that look in his eye. I actually saw him shoot once, and it was something, so precise: scanning the sky, shoot, pump, shoot, pump and so on. But he also was ill. He was hunched already, and he had lots of Aspirin sitting there to keep him going. It was a credit to his stamina that he was able to get a medical degree and practise medicine."

Romanow, who acquired a great deal of general medical knowledge while touring Canada as Royal Commissioner, was unfortunately quite familiar with ankylosing spondylitis.

"I have a close personal friend who has exactly the same condition, and in my conversations with him I came to know how painful it was," Romanow says. "George himself was reluctant to talk about it but would on occasion. His neck and back were basically fused. He could not turn his neck independently. He would have to turn his whole body to talk to you.

"His greatest courage was in the way he conducted himself day in, day out, hour after hour, minute after minute, while battling the disease. The medication was nowhere near as sophisticated as it is today in controlling the pain.

"I never heard him grumble. I'm sure there must

> **"His greatest courage was in the way he conducted himself day in, day out, hour after hour, minute after minute, while battling the disease."**
>
> –Roy Romanow on George Genereux

have been times in a family setting and the like where he would obviously be in great pain."

Genereux, whose marriage broke up after 17 years, admitted as much in an interview he gave early in March 1989.

"Yes, I've been frustrated," he told *StarPhoenix* columnist Paul Jackson. "Obviously, it's got me down on occasion. Yet, it's my problem, and I've always said I'd have to deal with it myself, which I have done. Many a night I went to bed telling myself I'd feel better the next day, but it never happened."

Jackson pointed out that Genereux's gold medal, which yielded no commercial reward, could have produced $1 million had it been won in the '80s.

"It would be nice to have a million," Genereux replied, "but I'd rather have my health."

Shortly after that interview, complications from AS and cortisone (prednisone) treatment that had dogged Genereux for three decades became more severe. He was admitted to hospital and underwent abdominal surgery.

When viral pneumonia set in a week later, he was warned that death was imminent. George Genereux spent his final hours telephoning friends to say goodbye and his final minutes in prayer. On the evening of April 10, 1989, the body that betrayed George Genereux finally let him go.

THE BEST FOOTBALL PLAYER EVER BORN IN SASKATCHEWAN

STATISTICALLY? MAYBE GERRY JAMES.

Quality of play over a long career? Probably Roger Aldag.

Achievement at the highest level? Maybe Rueben Mayes.

Maybe not any of them.

No, the most accomplished gridiron great from Saskatchewan has to be Arnie Weinmeister, and he will remain so until someone else born in this province is acclaimed as one of the greatest players of his era in the National Football League and gets elected to the Pro Football Hall of Fame in Canton, Ohio.

Weinmeister spent little time in Saskatchewan. He was born in Rhein (25 kilometres northeast of Yorkton) in 1923, hustled off to Oregon by his parents when he was just a baby, and returned to Saskatchewan only in 1954 and '55 as a member of the British Columbia Lions.

His family was big in every sense: three brothers and four sisters all grew to be at least six feet tall. Arnie himself sprouted to 6-foot-4 and weighed 235 pounds during his professional career, which was a bit late in coming. He was a high school standout in Portland and a promising running back at the University of Washington, but he left school in 1942 to enlist in the U.S. Army. Weinmeister served as a field artillery sergeant with the First Army and then the Third Army, the latter commanded by General George Patton.

Returning to Washington after the Second World War, Weinmeister ran for 140 yards (including one dash of 56 yards) in his first game back with the Huskies. In his second, a blind-side hit tore cartilage in his left knee, putting a premature end to Weinmeister's 1946 season. His straight-ahead speed reduced, he was moved to tackle for his senior year and was impressive enough to be invited to the post-season East–West all-star game. There he was named the game's best lineman, although the reward he cherished was the respect and praise he won from Frank Leahy, a coach of mythical proportions at the University of Notre Dame and the West's head man for the all-star game.

Bursting with confidence, Weinmeister turned pro as a 25-year-old rookie with the New York Yankees of the All-America Football Conference in 1948. When the NFL absorbed the Yankees and the rest of the AAFC in 1950, the New York Giants were compensated for the intrusion into their territory by getting to pick six men off the Yankees' roster. Weinmeister, the AAFC's top rookie in 1948 and an all-star tackle in 1949, was one of them. To welcome him to the new, monopolistic NFL, the Giants sent a letter of congratulations and a contract for $6,400 to his offseason address in Seattle. Weinmeister—a soft-spoken war veteran who had been a card-carrying Teamster since he was 16, with a college degree in economics and a public-relations job with the Rainier Brewery—reported to the Giants' training camp with a return ticket to Seattle, reminded management he had earned $10,000 a year with the Yankees and negotiated a salary of $12,000 for himself. According to published reports, that would rise to $18,000 within two years.

Weinmeister was frequently double-teamed, which actually suited the Umbrella Defence employed by Giants head coach Steve Owen (who would guide the Saskatchewan Roughriders in 1961 and '62) and his young defensive assistant, Tom Landry. Landry's Umbrella Defence spread linebackers across the field

Arnie Weinmeister

and would even drop the ends into pass coverage. Such a scheme could work only with exceptional tackles who would contain the inside running game and rush the quarterback, a responsibility that until then had been relegated to defensive ends. In Weinmeister, the Giants had the game's best tackle. Beside him was Al De Rogatis, excellent in his own right. About the only thing Weinmeister couldn't do was win a championship because his Giants (like his AAFC Yankees) couldn't overcome the powerhouse Cleveland Browns, not even in the 1950 and '51 seasons when the Giants were a combined 19–4–1. Not that Weinmeister didn't try.

"He's Murder Incorporated!" Browns quarterback Otto Graham said of Weinmeister. "He comes through so fast and hits you so hard that you've got to throw the ball in a hurry or get killed. The only way to stop him is to put two men on him, and even then he breaks through too many times."

Quarterbacks and running backs alike became uncomfortably familiar with Weinmeister's "smother" technique of tackling, in which he would wrap his arms around the ball carrier before taking him to the ground so that a pass or lateral was impossible. How often this happened became evident one rainy day when the field became a muddy morass. By game's end no player's number was legible save for the 73 on the clean back of Weinmeister's white jersey. The front of his uniform was as filthy as all the others.

Weinmeister's instinct for reading offensive plays was as impressive as his strength and quickness. On one occasion the Philadelphia Eagles had the ball on the Giants' 4-yard line and sent Steve Van Buren, the Hall of Fame running back, on an end run to De Rogatis' side of the field. It seemed like a good idea at the time, but Weinmeister read the play, shed his blockers and ran down Van Buren for a two-yard loss. Philadelphia didn't score on the drive.

Weinmeister was All-Pro for a fourth straight year in 1953, but six years of double-teams and innumerable tackles took their toll. The Giants told him they probably wouldn't re-sign him for 1954. When Annis Stukus offered him $15,000 to play for the new Canadian franchise in Vancouver, a short flight from Seattle, Weinmeister leaped at the opportunity. Within a week of his signing, the Lions sold 4,000 season tickets. Weinmeister put in two seasons as a play-

Arnie Weinmeister and future Roughriders coach Steve Owen as depicted by Willard Mullin

ing coach for the Lions, then retired from football. A team player in the commercial world as well, he would be elected to several key executive union positions, as high as Director and Vice-President of the 400,000-strong Western Conference of Teamsters.

1950–56: SIX OF SEVEN SCHOOLBOYS FOR SASKATCHEWAN

In 1950 the Canadian Curling Association established a genuine national championship for high school boys. But for an extra-end sudden-death playoff loss in, of all places, Saskatoon, Saskatchewan teams would have won all of the first seven Schoolboy championships.

1950: Skip Bill Clarke of Regina's Scott Collegiate and his crew of Gary Carlson, Ian Innes and Harold Grassie scored deuces in the 11th and 12th ends to beat Manitoba in the decisive game. Saskatchewan won its last six games to top the round robin at 7–2 in the only Schoolboy that featured 12-end games. Clarke, who would play 15 seasons with the Saskatchewan Roughriders, would remain an excellent competitive curler but would never reach the Brier, partially because of knee injuries that hampered his curling delivery and partially because he was trapped in Ernie Richardson's wake.

1951: Gary Thode, Gary Cooper, Orest Hryniuk and Roy Huffsmith of Saskatoon Tech faced Alberta in a last-draw showdown of 7–1 rinks. Down one after eight ends, Thode took three in the ninth and held Alberta to one for a 9–8 victory.

1952: The Thode rink, with Doug Conn succeeding Hryniuk at second, went undefeated to extend its Schoolboy winning streak to 13 games. Highlighting the run was a 17–5 rout of Quebec that included an eight-ender.

1953: At Saskatoon, Donnie Cochrane of Scott Collegiate pushed the province's winning streak to 19 before falling 11–3 to Ontario's Bob Walker. When the two teams tied for first at 8–1, Walker won a tension-filled sudden-death playoff 8–7 with a draw to the four-foot in the extra end.

1954: Saskatoon Tech's Bayne Secord won his first Schoolboy with Don Snider, Stan Austman and Don Brownell, going 8–1 and beating Manitoba 10–7 in a playoff.

1955: Secord, Austman, Merv Mann and Gary Stevenson trounced Prince Edward Island 12–5 when those teams entered the final draw tied for first place

1951 Canadian Schoolboy champions (from left) Roy Huffsmith, Orest Hryniuk, Gary Cooper and Gary Thode enjoy a heroes' welcome upon their return to Saskatoon

Stan Austman makes his dazzling slide to the button after the 1955 Schoolboy

with one loss apiece. After that game, Austman, at the encouragement of three-time Brier champion Ken Watson, slid with a rock in his hand all the way from the hack to the button. It was an eye-popping stunt, athletic on Austman's part and calculated on Watson's to wake up the country to the potential danger of lax regulations. Rules were soon redefined so that shooters clearly had to have their hands off the rocks once they had reached the first hogline.

1956: Regina's Central Collegiate foursome of Bob Hawkins, Ted Clarke, Bruce Beveridge and Dave Williams went 7–2 to force a post-midnight playoff against Wayne Petch of Northern Ontario. Hawkins drew to the button against Petch's counter in the eight-foot for a 9–8 extra-end victory to claim the only national curling title ever decided at 3:40 in the morning.

GUNS 'N' NOSES OUT OF JOINT: THE 1952 ROSETOWN RIOT

To call the events of August 30, 1952, a "riot" is an exaggeration, especially when placed against riots that occurred in Regina and Estevan, where people were actually killed. Still, alliteration will have its day, and "Rosetown Riot" rolls readily off the tongue. In truth, it was just a daylight melee no different from any other that reaches its climax in a prairie kitchen involving a black American armed with a butcher knife, a Cuban with rocks, the homeowner with a shotgun and his son with a rifle. Naturally, because it involved Saskatchewan baseball in the '50s, Emile Francis was in the middle of it.

"It was the Legion Tournament in Rosetown," recalls Francis, then the manager of the North Battleford Beavers, "a one-day deal with $3,000 up for grabs. The tournaments were very important to us because we were always scrambling to have enough money for payday. We had beaten Sceptre in a 16-inning game, a real battle, and now we had to go straight into the next game against the Florida Cubans, an outfit based out of Indian Head."

Beavers catcher Louis Green was on first base in the middle innings when a ball grounded to the Cubans' shortstop.

"Instead of going in sliding to break up the double play," Francis continues, "Louis gave the guy an elbow, and with that there were a couple of punches thrown. Our on-deck hitter, Curtis Tate, wandered towards the mound with his bat in his hand.

"When the Cubans saw that, they made a beeline for their dugout along the first-base side, and in a matter of seconds they all had bats. I was in front of the pitcher's mound, and I hadn't seen Tate come out. I could see all these Cubans coming with baseball bats. I looked to my right and who's standing there but Jack McLeod, and he's got a bat. I said to myself, 'Holy shit, I'm the only guy here who hasn't got a bat.'

"Well, the Cubans ran right past McLeod and me because they knew who they were after: Tate. Tate waited, and then he took a full swing at the closest guy to him and he hit this guy, Leopolda Reyes, right over the head. Then Tate dropped the bat, took off down the third base line and burst through the bleachers. I see three guys chasing him, and I've gotta get going because I can't leave Tate with three guys. So I take off. We're weaving through parked cars, and about a quarter of a mile ahead I can see Tate running like hell down the highway and out of the bush come these two Cubans. They've got bats and I don't. Away I go. I know there's another guy on the loose down there."

Emile Francis: Cat Man

Curtis Tate: Bat Man

A little further up the road, outside the house belonging to Mr. W.H. Craddock, stood his wife, Mrs. W.H. Craddock, blithely hanging laundry on the clothesline. Mrs. W.H. was accustomed to men visiting the house—after all, Mr. W.H. was the local grain elevator agent—but few of those men were so athletic, so dressed in a baseball uniform, so terrified and so coloured as this man who staggered towards her.

"You gotta hide me. They're after me. You gotta hide me," the stranger panted as he lurched into Mrs. Craddock's home. She followed him, perhaps relieved that he was carrying his spiked shoes in his hands; at least the linoleum was safe. When the stranger entered the kitchen and grabbed a large butcher knife, however, Mrs. Craddock dashed to the back of the house, where her daughter was playing with a friend. She told them to hurry to the nearby elevator and get Mr. Craddock to hurry back to the house. Which he did, along with his son.

"Now, I come up to this farmhouse," Francis says, "but Tate's in there with a knife, the Cuban's got a couple of rocks, the husband had grabbed a shotgun, and the kid's grabbed a .22. So I come up a bad last."

How does it go? Rock breaks scissors, scissors cut paper, firearms make everyone drop knife, rocks and baseball bats.

"Shortly thereafter the Mounties came, so peace was sort of restored. They took Tate to jail, and the rest of us went back to the ballpark, where we should never have left, I guess. We finished the game, and I got Tate out of jail.

"Jack McLeod was driving an Oldsmobile that trip, brand new Oldsmobile. His tires were slashed. We don't know who did it."

That evening—while Leopolda Reyes rested at Rosetown Hospital in "fairly good" condition—the Beavers drove to Moose Jaw for a Western Canada

The Florida Cubans after winning the 1952 Indian Head tournament

Baseball League doubleheader the following day. While the car was in radio range of Saskatoon, Francis tuned in CFQC and got an earful from sportscaster Bill Cameron.

"He was a real good guy, Cameron, and he's on about 'Francis and his troublemakers,' how they should take me and my team and run us right out of the country."

The team checked into the Harwood Hotel in Moose Jaw, and Francis had a late supper at the Ambassador Café with Bob Herron, the Beavers' slugging outfielder. At 6-foot-4 and 220 pounds with a dark chocolate complexion, Herron stood out in stark contrast to Francis, who was nine inches shorter, 70 pounds lighter and plainly of the Caucasian persuasion. As they took a leisurely post-meal stroll up Main Street, in no hurry to settle in to the Harwood Hotel for the night, they made a very recognizable duo to the occupants of an eastbound bus.

"The bus stops at a red light," Francis remembers, "and all these heads pop out of the windows. It's the Cubans.

"'Francees, where ees Tate, where ees Tate? We keel heem!' The bus pulls away and big Bob Herron says to me, 'I smell death in the air. I'm going back to my hotel room.'"

Bob Herron (centre): a nose for danger

One day later . . .

"We play the first game of the doubleheader, and Tate goes 5-for-5, hitting them to all fields. There's a break between the two games, and I go down to the railway station and send a telegram to Bill Cameron there at CFQC. It says: 'Dear Bill, if you're going to run Tate out of the country, you'd better do it fast because he just went 5-for-5.' I figure I got the last laugh on him.

"Just before the nightcap's about to start, I'm sitting in the dugout when a boy rides up on his bicycle with a telegram for me.

"It's from Bill Cameron: 'Of those five hits Curtis Tate got, how many are in the hospital?' "

OUTSTANDING PATS: A JUNIOR HOCKEY DYNASTY

The Regina Pats of the 1950s were the most sustained junior dynasty in Saskatchewan's history. Five times (1950, '52, '55, '56 and '58) in nine years the Pats won the Abbott Cup as Western champions and with frustrating monotony found themselves overmatched in the Memorial Cup. Although a farm team of the Montreal Canadiens, the Pats themselves were only the top point in an efficient system.

"The Pats had a terrific organization from the junior team down," Red Berenson recalls. "They had a juvenile team, a midget team, a bantam team and literally leagues of teams that played every Saturday at the Stadium. At the end of the year they picked an all-star team to represent the city in the provincial playoffs, and typically the Pats won every championship. In addition to that, the city had the Parks League organized on outdoor rinks in different parts of town. It was great to be a youngster in Regina in the '50s.

"Playing outdoors wasn't something you complained about; you just did it because you wanted to play, and it was such an important part of your life. The bottom of your earlobes would be peeling all winter. There were nights when you could hardly skate down the ice because the wind was so strong, yet we were all out there having a great time, really not even thinking about the weather."

Rink custodian, whether the facility was Exhibition Stadium or a Parks League rink with a shack, was a powerful position. Boys smart enough to help the custodian shovel snow from the ice or fetch firewood for the potbellied stove would be rewarded with prime ice time. A relationship with the custodian might even prove educational.

Lorne Davis (8); the goalie is Regina product Harvey Bennett

"I played in the Parks League at Rink One, right by Taylor Field," says Lorne Davis. "The caretaker was Ranger Bell, a character from Providence, Rhode Island. He had the real Boston accent, and he'd sit all night and tell us stories that weren't true.

"He lived just across the tracks, on the south side, and he always told us northsiders that we weren't allowed across the tracks because he was in the exclusive end of town. He came up with the most fantastic hockey stories. One was that he wasn't allowed to shoot the puck anymore because he shot it once and it went through the two spires of Holy Rosary Cathedral over on 13th Avenue. He'd tell us his butler was coming to pick him up. And we'd sit there with our mouths open and believe this stuff."

Bill Hay, five years younger than Davis, had the pleasure of hearing Bell's stories after they had been further embellished.

"He'd tell us other rinks had luxurious shacks," Hay remembers. "They had couches to sit on and we were on wooden benches; their stove provided a lot more heat than ours did. He could only shoot the puck north. Shooting south, the pucks would go through the boards, and he kept killing the cows."

Skills were honed outdoors, but the first ambition of a Regina boy was to make a team that would play Saturday in Exhibition Stadium.

"The only time we played indoors was on Saturday," Berenson says. "Games started at 8 o'clock, so I got my mom to wake me up at 5, and I would walk to the rink. I knew how to sneak in through an old window that was loose, and I'd skate for two or three hours with nobody in the building, pitch dark. Then the janitor would come in and turn on the lights.

" 'How did you get in?' he'd say.

" 'The door was open.' "

Red Berenson, Bill Hicke and Terry Harper, 1958

Naturally, boys so passionate about playing hockey were equally passionate about watching it.

"In those days, when I was about 11 years old, they had what was called a pigpen at the very top of the north end of the Ex," remembers Bill Hicke. "It was quite large, held about 300 or 400 people, and all the kids from your class would be right there with you. My favourites on the Caps were Jim Fairburn and Norm Blackett. I met Blackett because my dad was a barber and he cut Blackett's hair. I knew Gus and Bill Kyle because Mom bought all our equipment at Kyles' Sporting Goods. And Mel Hill was there, he could really shoot the puck. I worked for him when I was only 13 years old, sorting bottles on top of the truck."

Hill, though born in Manitoba, had grown up and played junior hockey in Saskatoon, and after a decade of excellent NHL play, settled down in Regina to operate Mel Hill Beverages, a soft drink distributorship. That kind of part-time employment was essential to hockey players even while they were starring with the Pats.

"We worked any kind of day jobs," says Terry Harper. "We had free time away from the rink, and there were lots of businesses who needed casual labour. I would unload boxcars at the Colgate-Palmolive warehouse or the Molson brewery. Molson was a big supporter of the Pats, but we could only handle empty bottles outside the brewery. They couldn't put us inside because we were underage."

Education could be a contentious issue, one that the Pats of the '50s would face from a variety of uncomfortable standpoints. Mike Kartusch, along with Del Wilson the guiding forces of the organization, was a principal in the separate (Catholic) school system and sometimes found himself acting as peacemaker between the club and civic interests. Murray

Red Berenson with the Pee Wee Pats

Armstrong, coach in the early part of the decade, would move on to Denver University, preach the gospel of post-secondary education for hockey players, and openly recruit Saskatchewan players.

"Murray supported further education, but he also did an awful lot for boys that were not going to pursue that route," says Hay. "They'd graduate, play a few years of minor pro, and get a job. He didn't talk only about going to school. If you had the ability to do it, that was okay. But if you had the ability just to play hockey, that was good, too. He made men out of young boys. There were guys who played for the Pats who were drifters, who had difficult homes, and Murray was the stabilizer, a very solid leader for them. He was a grand mentor."

Berenson followed the path of higher education at the University of Michigan.

"My dream obviously was to play for the Pats," Berenson says, "but when I got the chance, at 16, I had already finished high school. I had been moved ahead a couple of times in grade school, so I was only 15 when I started Grade 12 at Scott Collegiate. I took Grade 11 and 12 chemistry during my rookie season just to stay in sync with school and in touch with my friends. The next year I really just hung out, didn't do anything. Hicke and Harper and I spent a lot of time together and took odd jobs when we could.

"I still had two years of junior left when I made up my mind to go to Michigan. Hicke had signed his C-form with Montreal, and the Canadiens were pressuring me to sign one, too. I'd been out of high school for two years, and it didn't make any sense to play two more years of junior. Murray Armstrong was recruiting several of us hard for Denver, but Michigan was stronger academically.

"I knew I was jeopardizing my NHL prospects, no question about it. Sam Pollock told me point blank that I'd never be a pro, that I'd never play in the NHL if I went to school. I was definitely going against the grain. But Bill Hay had gone to Colorado, and I just believed what people told me: if you're going to make it, you'll make it. I listened to a lot of old pros who told me to get an education, that hockey was not what it was cut out to be, there were only six NHL teams, and there was no money in it."

All Pats players were Montreal property. Sometimes the best-of-seven Memorial Cup final looked like a Montreal Canadiens junior intramural tournament, pitting the Habs' top Eastern teens against their best Western prospects. Such was the case in 1950 when the Pats rode the rails eastward to face the Montreal Junior Canadiens, who boasted Dickie Moore and Don Marshall among their stars. Montreal won 8–7, 5–2 and 5–1 before the Pats saved face in Game 4, rallying from a 4–1 deficit to win 7–4 as Davis scored three goals. Montreal ended the series with a 6–3 victory.

Two years later, Pats coach Armstrong boasted a deeper and bigger club. Ed Litzenberger, a Neudorf native, was the captain and star centre, scoring 50 times in 49 league games (including playoffs) and netting both goals in the 2–1 victory over the Fort William Hurricanes that finished the Western final in six games. Another strong forward, Doug Killoh, would go on to an eight-year football career with the Roughriders. Bob Turner was a stellar two-way defenceman, an excellent puckhandler whose offensive skills would be lost in the NHL as Doug Harvey's blue-line partner on the Canadiens.

Too bad the 1952 Eastern reps were the Guelph Biltmores, a New York Rangers affiliate and one of the most awesome junior teams ever assembled. Eight of them—Andy Bathgate, Harry Howell, Dean Prentice, Ron Stewart, Ron Murphy, Lou Fontinato, Bill McCreary and Aldo Guidolin—went on to NHL careers that, put together, accounted for more than

1951–52 Regina Pats: Ed Litzenberger is the captain; coach Murray Armstrong is beside him; Doug Killoh (alternate captain) and Bob Turner flank Armstrong in the second row; the stickboy whose head is barely visible in the middle of the back row is Murray Balfour

7,000 games and 1,400 goals. The Guelph–Regina scores were 8–2, 4–2, 8–2 and 10–2.

"We didn't have a chance," Turner says. "They were a powerhouse."

Like the Brier and the Canadian boxing championships, the 1955 Memorial Cup was played entirely in Regina between the Pats and Toronto Marlboros, whose roster included Shaunavon-born Gary Aldcorn, Regina-born Gerry James and Lanigan-born Bob Baun, not to mention Bob Pulford and Billy Harris. Regina won the opener 3–1, but then it was all Toronto: 5–2, 3–2, 3–2 in overtime and 8–5 in overtime. (The extra sessions were a full 10 minutes.) Regina's stars were Murray Balfour, who forced the Game 4 overtime on a goal with 13 seconds left in regulation, and Hay, who had a hat trick in the finale.

A Pats–Marlies rematch in 1956 also ended in five games, with the Pats earning a 4–4 overtime tie before falling 5–1, 4–2, 6–1 and 7–4. Pulford, who scored 10 goals in the last four games, was supported by future NHLers Baun, Al MacNeil, Carl Brewer, Charlie Burns, Wally Boyer and Lou Angotti. Bryan Whittal had a pair of two-goal games for Regina.

For their last Memorial Cup series of the decade, the 1957–58 Pats went east to visit their old pals the Hull-Ottawa Canadiens. Regina's coach was now Frank Mario. Hicke had torn the SJHL apart with a second straight 50-goal season and won the scoring championship with 54 goals (in 49 games) and 43 assists for 97 points. Berenson had kept pace with a 46–49–95 line. Harper anchored the defence. Jerry Kolb, Gord Wilkie and Gary Butler were an excellent second line. Defenceman Aut Erickson and left-winger Dave Balon were picked up from the Prince Albert Mintos. Hull-Ottawa countered with Ralph Backstrom, Bobby Rousseau, Gilles Tremblay and J.C. Tremblay.

Hicke registered a hat trick in a 4–3 opening win. Backstrom got one and then three as the Canadiens bounced back with 4–2 and 6–2 victories before Regina tied the series with another 4–3 decision, this one in overtime. Finally, the Pats were in the thick of a Memorial Cup final. Not for long, though; Hull-Ottawa took the last two contests 6–3 and 6–1.

That was the end of Hicke's junior career, one of the most sensational of anyone to have worn a Pats jersey. It had begun under unusual circumstances.

"I tried out for the Pats bantams when I was 10, but I didn't make it. My brother John was 12, and he did make it. The next year I made the team, but he didn't. That was the beginning of a long association with the Pats.

"I was always the youngest player on the team until I was a few years into junior. Some of the guys on the Pat bantams were three years older than I was. I was probably the only kid in the history of the Pats organization to have played on their bantam, midget and juvenile teams, and I did all that by the time I was 15.

"I was fortunate to play in the Canadiens organization—and to play in the Pats organization. Let's see, I think the Pats paid us $2.00 after every game, plus we got a Pats jacket. And the years when Murray Armstrong was there, we each got a hat because he represented Biltmore hats. I still have one.

"He gave us a blue blazer every year, too, and I still have two of those. Everybody dressed the same: blazer, navy blue tie, white shirt, grey slacks. We always looked good on the road. We felt like we had class."

PAT FLETCHER: KEEP IT DOWN

After Pat Fletcher won the 1954 Canadian Open at Vancouver's Point Grey course, he revealed that he was using a unique set of golf clubs. Nearly all the irons actually had less loft, by half a club, than the numbers indicated—save for his pitching wedge, a weapon that Fletcher used with unerring efficiency. His 3-iron was really a 2½, his 4-iron a 3½, all the way up to his 8-iron being a 7½. He wasn't comfortable with his 9-iron, so he borrowed an 8-iron (a true one) from fellow Canadian Stan Leonard and used it as his short iron.

Pat Fletcher

"I like to hit 'em low and keep 'em out of the skies, and know that I have an adequate club in my hands," Fletcher explained.

Now, where would he develop that approach? Where else but Saskatchewan, where the wind comes sweeping down the plain and up the fairway and through the trees and across the deep rough?

Fletcher was born in England in 1916 and came to Canada as a four-year-old. He grew up in Victoria, learned the craft of a golf pro, and toiled at several Alberta clubs before settling in at the Saskatoon Golf and Country Club in 1946. Here he thrived not only as a teacher but as a competitor, winning the Saskatchewan Open three times (1947, '48 and '51) and the Canadian Professional Golfers Association championship in 1952. Fletcher was the low Canadian at the 1953 Canadian Open in Scarborough, Ont., finishing fourth as Dave Douglas continued an exasperating streak of non-Canadian champions.

The Canadian Open, which had been contested since 1904, had not produced a winner from its own country since Karl Keffer of Ottawa topped the field

"There was a great team," says Sylvia Fedoruk (front row, second from left) of the 1954 Regina Govins. "That was the best infield I was ever part of." Shortstop Fedoruk handled grounders along with Dot Fitch (right of Fedoruk) at second base, Arleene Noga (far right, first row) at third base and Dot Griggs (behind Noga) at first base. The Govins, so named because they were sponsored by Saskatchewan Government Insurance from 1949–57, won four provincial championships and the Western Canada championship in Calgary in 1954, when this picture was taken. The team (top row, left to right): Laura Malesh, Willie Francis, Gil Strumm, Barry Wenzel, Jean McBoyle; (middle row) Helen Sidaway, Eileen Gates, Marlene McEachern, Joan Schatz, Vern Anthony, Griggs; (front row) Mary Malesh, Fedoruk, Fitch, Helen Roundy, Noga.

in 1914. Since then, some of golf's immortals, like Tommy Armour, Sam Snead (three times apiece), Walter Hagen and Byron Nelson had won the tournament. So had pedestrians like Gene Kunes, C.W. Congdon and Joe Kirkwood. Whether great or merely good, however, none were Canadian.

Fletcher got off to a tremendous start in the '54 Open with a Wednesday opening round of 65, but Bob Rosburg of San Francisco pushed him down to second place with a blistering 63, eight under par. Perhaps Point Grey was insulted, because it tortured the field for the rest of the week. Fletcher and Rosburg carded 70 and 72 respectively on Thursday to share the second-round lead at 5-under 135. On Friday, they gave way to Gord Brydson of Toronto, whose 68 gave him a two-stroke lead going into Saturday's final round. The top four were Brydson at 207, Fletcher at 209, and Rosburg and Bruce Cudd of Portland, Ore., at 210.

Playing with Fletcher in the final group, Brydson maintained a comfortable lead until he took a double-bogey 6 on the ninth hole. Then his approach on the 10th hit the flagstick and caromed off the green, leading to a 7. Fletcher, propelled into a sudden lead, carded a 32 on the back nine that gave him even-par 71 on the day and a four-stroke victory over Brydson and

Bill Welch of Kennewick, Wash. At 4-under 280, Pat Fletcher was the only golfer to beat par for 72 holes.

Fletcher gave way to a Pennsylvania youngster named Arnold Palmer in the '55 Open and left Saskatchewan the following year for the Royal Montreal Golf Club, where he remained until his retirement in 1975. The Canadian Open fell back into the rut of being won by the great (Lee Trevino three times, Greg Norman, Tiger Woods) and the ordinary (Ted Kroll, Bob Gilder, Dudley Hart) of other countries.

Every year Fletcher's name resurfaces as the last Canadian to win our national tournament, the only one to do so in the last 90 years. Rarely is it mentioned that, when Pat Fletcher accomplished the feat, he was a longtime Saskatoon resident.

But he was. Pat Fletcher was as Saskatchewan as Ron Lancaster.

GRANT WARWICK'S PENTICTON VEES: RESTORING CANADA'S PRIDE

Grant Warwick had reached the end of his NHL road in 1952 but had plenty of hockey left in him; 99 points the previous season in Buffalo was proof of that. Far away in Penticton, B.C., his younger brother Dick was badgering him to be the player-coach for that city's senior team, the Vees. Dick had moved from Nanaimo in 1951 when Penticton joined the Okanagan league; he lured middle brother Billy into joining him, and the two were going to open a restaurant. Now Dick wanted Grant to join the enterprise if he could just get his release from the Montreal Canadiens. When word got out it could be had for $2,500, Vees fans pitched in $1,300 of their own money.

More than half the Penticton team had Saskatchewan connections. First there were the Warwicks. Billy, once Grant's wartime teammate in New York, had bounced all over the minors, a deadly shot but at 150 pounds (the same as Grant) considered too small for the NHL. Serious lacerations in Billy's right hand from a 1951 car accident had put his career in jeopardy. Forward Mike Shabaga had been a junior and senior standout in Saskatoon. Jack McIntyre and Jim Fairburn were products of the Regina Parks League. Don Berry was from Burnaby, B.C., but had played junior for the Moose Jaw Canucks. So had defenceman Hal Tarala, a punishing body checker in pro hockey's minor leagues. Backup goaltender Don Moog, whose son Andy would become an NHL star between the pipes, hailed from Regina.

Mike Shabaga

Grant Warwick's impact was immediate. Penticton won the 1952–53 Okanagan league championship and went all the way to the Allan Cup final before bowing to the Kitchener-Waterloo Dutchmen. Naturally, nothing less than the Allan Cup itself would do in 1953–54. Billy enjoyed a sensational regular season with 50 goals and 95 points, both league-leading figures, in 58 games. Come the post-season, Grant possessed the magic touch with 27 goals and 37 assists in 33 games as the Vees teetered constantly on the brink of elimination. First they fell behind 2–1 in the best-of-five OSAHL semi-final against Vernon before winning the last two games and then bouncing Kelowna in a routine 4–1 final.

Then came the Allan Cup playdowns and the incredible comebacks. Down 3–1 with one tied game in the B.C. final against the Nelson Maple Leafs, Penticton rallied to take the best-of-seven in *eight* games. Next, in the Western final against the Winnipeg Maroons, the Vees won only one of the first six games; but three of them were 4–4 overtime ties, so subsequent 3–1 and 5–2 victories gave Penticton *another* eight-game series. The Allan Cup final was comparatively humdrum: after the Sudbury Wolves took three of the first four, Penticton won 6–5 in overtime, 6–4 and 3–2.

En route to winning the Allan Cup, the Vees faced elimination 11 times; in those games, they were 10–0–1. Penticton won on five occasions when a tie would have ended their season. Two games were saved on goals with 17 and 45 seconds remaining respectively.

Without those comebacks, the Vees would have been denied not only the 1954 Allan Cup but the opportunity to represent Canada at the following year's world hockey championship in West Germany. That event took on enormous importance when the Soviet Union made its debut at the 1954 tournament and won the gold medal with a 7–2 rout of the Toronto Lyndhursts, a senior B team. Canada's reaction ranged from catatonic shock to indignant outrage. Bad enough that Canada had suffered a (then) rare loss in international hockey, but this was in the middle of the Cold War to the godless Communists!

What better battleground for a Cold War than a patch of hockey ice? What better commander than the man who tried to sneak his near-deafness past army doctors in 1942? Grant Warwick would wear his country's hockey uniform and win or else. His team no longer represented Penticton; it was playing for all of Canada and he never stopped reminding his players of it.

It's a lost fact in Canadian history that the '55 Vees are to radio as 1972 Team Canada is to television. Mortification over the 1954 defeat paralleled the 7–3 loss to the Soviet national team in Montreal 18 years later, only the Lyndhursts' disaster had a full year to fester in the national hockey ego. Canada was so hungry for retribution that Foster Hewitt went to Germany to do live play-by-play of the 1955 Canada-Soviet game.

Billy Warwick

The format was a simple round robin, with Canada and the Soviets matched in the last game. Canada trounced Poland 8–0, Switzerland 11–1 and Germany 10–1. Grant Warwick wasn't happy with the effort against Germany, chastised the team, and ordered a practice the next morning even though the schedule demanded eight games in 10 days. After crushing Finland 12–0, the Canadians joined the Finns around goaltender Lars Svensson to show their appreciation for his 50-save effort. Billy Warwick poured in six goals in a 12–1 whipping of the United States.

Only Czechoslovakia offered more than token resistance, taking a 3–2 lead into the dressing room after the second period. Bill White, the Vees team physician, and team manager Clem Bird were despondent as their men left the ice. "Grant said later that he (looked into our faces) and saw despair and defeat," White told a reporter. "He multiplied that by all the people in Canada and figured there was no way they would lose that game." Canada scored three unanswered third-period goals to prevail 5–3.

When Sunday, March 6 arrived, Canada and the Soviet Union were both 7–0, but Canada had outscored its opponents 61–6 to the Soviets' 39–8. Canada would win the gold medal with just a tie—as if the Vees were interested in one. This was war; total victory was the objective.

All of Canada listened to Foster Hewitt—as best they could. Hewitt was not seated in his gondola, high above the upper crust of Toronto society in Maple Leaf Gardens, but in the middle of an overflow crowd of 10,000 people in Krefeld. Most of the 2,000 standees were Canadian servicemen stationed in West Germany. In addition, the Vees had won over the home fans since their game against the host team.

Jack McIntyre and Dick Warwick with the World Cup

German hockey had been greatly influenced by Canadian imports in the '30s, so its game included more hitting than other European countries. Accustomed to seeing Swedes, Czechs and Russians respond to body checks as if they had been shot, German fans were impressed when Canadians bounced right up, without complaint, after they were decked. The Vees definitely dished it out, but they could take it, too.

The Russians couldn't take it. Grant Warwick caught Vsevolod Bobrov, the top Soviet scorer, with his head down early in the first period. Down went Bobrov. No penalty. Later Bobrov came tearing down the ice with the puck, head down, straight into defenceman George McAvoy, who sent Bobrov flying. No penalty. Bobrov sat on the ice and waved his arms at the referee. McAvoy stood over Bobrov and waved his arms at the Russian. Laughter filled the arena.

Shabaga scored the only goal of the first period. Billy Warwick and Shabaga widened the lead to 3–0 in the second. Warwick connected again, 32 seconds into the third period, during Canada's only power play of the game. McIntyre set up McAvoy for the last goal two minutes later. Goaltender Ivan McLelland earned his shutout with a busy first period but wasn't worked hard after that. Bobrov never had a shot on goal even though Canada took six minor penalties to the Soviets' one.

In Vancouver, because of the time difference, the game was taking place in the morning. A minister halted his Sabbath service to announce the final score: 5–0.

Back in Krefeld, Grant Warwick could barely stand on his skates as hundreds of soldiers and airmen pounced upon him and his teammates.

"Thank God! We made it!" he bellowed into Foster Hewitt's microphone, his mission accomplished.

"It could have been 10–0. We knew we had them in the first period. Boy, the guys were real great! I never felt like this before. . . ."

Billy Warwick was as exultant as his older brother was relieved.

"We outsmarted them, outskated them, outpassed them and outplayed them, boy . . . This is better than winning the Stanley Cup!"

Dick, Grant and Billy Warwick flash the V for Victory

Canada's hockey honour was restored. The Soviet Union would never hold the world championship trophy again. Oh sure, it won world championships but never that trophy. With their restaurant doing bang-up business, the Warwick brothers hired a silversmith to create a replica of the World Cup. The replica was surreptitiously shipped back to the International Ice Hockey Federation for the next world tournament.

The original remained with the Warwicks and spent years on display when they opened another successful restaurant in Edmonton. Half a century after winning the World Cup, Billy Warwick still has it. Somewhere.

ODE TO AVONLEA: THE CAMPBELLS WIN THE BRIER

SASKATCHEWAN WAS CELEBRATING ITS GOLDEN anniversary as a province and, as a hotbed of curling, was the ideal venue for the Macdonald Brier in 1955. To make it a perfect occasion, all that was required was for Saskatchewan to do something it had never done before—namely, win the darn thing. It had come close the year before, when Garnet Campbell of Avonlea went 8–2. Alberta skip Matt Baldwin (born in Blucher, Sask.) edged Campbell 12–11 in the opening draw and went on to the first of his three Brier triumphs.

For Garnet Campbell, the Brier was as much his own personal quest as it was Saskatchewan's. He had won virtually every curling prize available since an inauspicious introduction to the sport when he was a 13-year-old boy in Avonlea.

"Pa took Gooch and I out to the rink and let us throw some rocks," he remembers. "I never got a rock in the house. It wasn't until I was well into high school, around Grade 11, that I really took up curling. Then Dude would take me to the weekly bonspiels around Moose Jaw; sometimes he'd have to pull me out of school."

If one listened to the Campbells spin tales long enough, you'd swear there were a dozen children in the family. In fact, there were seven, but every boy

Garnet Campbell, also known as Mac

had at least one nickname. In order of birth, there were Verna, Lloyd (Dude), Glen (Sambo), Don (Dobey), Gordon (Gooch), Garnet (Mac or Willie) and Margaret. Dad's name was Alexander, but most people called him Sandy. On some lists, the 1947 Saskatchewan men's curling champion skip is listed as Mac Campbell. It's Garnet. The rest of that rink comprised Glen/Sambo, Lloyd/Dude and Sandy/Alexander/Dad.

"That was the first time my father ever curled with us," Garnet says. "Usually, we'd go all brothers or pick up one of the older guys when we went to Moose Jaw to curl, because Dad had his own friends that he curled with. But we were short a man for playdowns. Don was in the RCMP and didn't want to do anything that might attract attention. He was recently married, and the Mounties didn't allow that back then.

"Lloyd had been skip, but he offered me the job at one of those bonspiels because he thought that nothing seemed to scare me."

The Campbells did all right at the '47 Brier, tying for second but losing the playoff for the runner-up prizes. When the Campbells earned their second Brier berth in 1954, the personnel was Garnet, Don, Glen and Gordon. Winning the provincial championship was a harrowing experience. After splitting the first two games with Glenn Richardson of Saskatoon, Campbell won the rubber match 10–9 on a last-end measurement.

Neither Garnet nor his brothers were going to wilt under pressure. Besides handling playdowns calmly, the Campbells had also distinguished themselves on the car spiel circuit, winning in Rosetown, Swift Current, and at Bill Hunter's big show in Saskatoon. (One of their automobile prizes was raffled off to raise money for a new curling rink in Avonlea.) The Campbells had become an elite team in that they would not defeat themselves; only a superior team, a hot opponent, or peculiar ice conditions would prevent them from winning.

Early draws of the '55 Brier at Regina's Exhibition Stadium went Saskatchewan's way. Except for a sixth-round come-from-behind victory over British Columbia, the Campbells were hardly even challenged. Manitoba also beat all comers, though with considerably more work, and the tournament ultimately boiled down to one game: Manitoba's Reg Forsyth against the Campbells of Saskatchewan, both teams undefeated, on Thursday night.

Garnet (left) and Glen Campbell look on as Manitoba third Glenn Gray signals Matt Baldwin's winning shot in the '54 Brier

Lee Donison

Butch Donison

DONISON BROTHERS GET A GRIP ON WRESTLING TITLES

Brothers Butch and Danny Donison delighted a hometown crowd by pinning their opponents in the finals of the 1955 Canadian wrestling championships in Regina.

Danny won the lightweight (147-pound) gold medal, Butch the featherweight (135-pound) gold and Fred Bennett of Moose Jaw the bantamweight (126-pound) silver medal. The Donisons' national titles were Saskatchewan's first in 15 years.

Butch would become the most accomplished of the Donisons, with 13 provincial championships in seven different weight categories between 1953 and 1967. He didn't win any more national titles but picked up a silver medal as Canada's light-heavyweight at the 1966 British Empire Games in Jamaica.

Danny had six firsts and five seconds in provincials from 1953–68 and added one silver and one bronze medal at national championships.

Eldest brother Lee, meanwhile, was provincial heavyweight wrestling champ from 1953–56 but was even better as a boxer. In fact, by winning four of his seven Saskatchewan boxing titles in that same span, he became the only man in Canadian history to win concurrent provincial boxing and wrestling championships four years in a row.

He won his last provincial boxing title, and his only national title, as a light-heavyweight in 1963.

Ninth-draw action at the 1955 Brier: Garnet Campbell, at the centre of the extreme right sheet of ice, watches one of his shots against Manitoba

Garnet Campbell was virtually perfect. Long before competitions maintained official statistics, reporters kept their own. That night Campbell checked in at 94 percent for his 24 shots. Saskatchewan took control in the third end with the only steal of the game and grabbed a deuce in the sixth after Don nullified three Manitoba counters with a deadly hit-and-roll behind cover in the four-foot. Saskatchewan came home in the 12th end with a 7–6 lead and the hammer. Don's nose hit on a guard initiated a series of draws that forced Garnet to use his last rock to punch out Forsyth's counter on the button. Garnet put hack weight on his out-turn to slip around the long guard with enough force to remove the Manitoba stone and stick around for the point that made the final score 8–6.

Saskatchewan methodically defeated Northern Ontario 9–7 to finish the week unbeaten—which was even more than the people of Saskatchewan had envisioned when they dreamed of the perfect Brier! For years the province had been the national leader in the number of curlers and curling clubs; now, at last, it had not only the most but the best.

Among the enthralled spectators in Exhibition Stadium were a pair of brothers, curling neophytes now inspired to master the game. In four years, Ernie and Sam Richardson—with cousins Arnold and Wes—would take Saskatchewan curling to heights no province had enjoyed.

BACK ON TRACK: BOB ADAMS KINDLES A REBIRTH OF ATHLETICS

BOB ADAMS, AN ALSASK PRODUCT WHO SCRIMPED and saved to put himself through the University of Saskatchewan, started Saskatoon on its way back to track and field excellence. He entered the 1948 Canadian Olympic trials in the pole vault and discus, failed to qualify in either event, and reasoned that his overall competence in all disciplines suited him to the decathlon. Essentially coaching himself, Adams broke the Canadian decathlon record with 6,722 points at the 1952 trials and finished 19th in the Helsinki Olympics. He placed fourth in the pole vault in the 1954 British Empire Games in Vancouver, where he was selected Canadian team captain. When he suffered torn cartilage playing basketball, Adams decided to stop competing and start some serious coaching. Just as he was looking for a project, a prodigy burst on the Saskatoon track scene.

Eleanor Haslam was the star student at Nutana Collegiate, where Adams was employed as a teacher. In 1956, she was a 16-year-old going through Grade 11 with a 97 percent average, 5-foot-7 and 130 pounds, her trim physique buffed by Adams' recommendation that she augment her running workouts with weight training—at that time, a revolutionary concept in women's athletics. In addition to natural speed and a great work ethic, Haslam had what Adams lacked as a decathlete: a rival.

Maureen Rever, in Grade 12 at Luther College in Regina, won the 100-yard dash and long jump at the 1955 Canadian championships and broke national juvenile and open records at distances from 60 yards and up. Records inevitably fall, but her juvenile 100-yard mark of 11.2 seconds didn't last past 1956. Haslam ran the 100 in 11.1 and the 220 in 26.6 to break two of Rever's records. A 24.7 in the 220 put Haslam in a class by herself in the longer sprint. That summer both teenagers qualified for the Olympic team.

Six Canadian women would compete in track and field at Melbourne. Half of them were Saskatchewan teenagers. A third athlete, Margaret George, had taught herself how to throw the javelin and discus and to put the shot on her family farm in Mervin. When she threw the javelin 120½ feet at the 1955 high school championships, she attracted the attention of Joe Griffiths and became his last pupil. George threw the javelin 145 feet 5 inches at the Olympic trials to break the Canadian record by 17 feet.

At Melbourne, Haslam and Rever were eliminated in the heats of the 100 and 200 metres. Both ran well, Haslam covering the distances in 11.9 and 25.3 seconds, Rever in 12.2 and 26.1. George's timetable was thrown out of whack when Canadian officials were late getting her to the stadium, and her best throw was just over 130 feet.

Eleanor Haslam (24) crosses the finish line first in a high school race

Bob Adams and Eleanor Haslam

George placed first at the trials for 1958 British Empire Games to be held in Cardiff but wasn't put on the team. Haslam and Rever did go to Wales and won bronze medals in the sprint relay. Haslam lowered her Canadian record times in the 100- and 220-yard dashes to 10.8 and 24.1 seconds respectively in 1958. Rever enjoyed one more international success with another relay bronze medal at the 1959 Pan-American Games in Chicago.

Haslam focused on the 1960 Olympics in Rome but had to undergo throat surgery a month before the Canadian trials. She was devastated when she failed to qualify in the 100 metres but snapped out of her depression in time to make it in the 200 and 800 before failing to make the Olympic final in either event. Unfortunately, the 400 wasn't added to the women's program until 1964.

"There was no doubt in my mind that she was tailor-made for the women's 400 metres," Adams once said of Haslam. "I'm sure she would have been a world medallist in any 400-metre race if she had ever had a chance to run one. She had the right mix of speed and stamina."

Adams continued teaching and coaching at Nutana, then Aden Bowman. He helped sprinters Stu Cameron and George Short qualify for the 1958 Empire Games and 1960 Olympics, respectively. Adams was head coach of the Canadian athletics team at the 1964 Olympics in Tokyo. Closer to home, his guidance and influence was vital in laying the foundation for track and field success that Saskatoon enjoys to this day.

GERRY JAMES: FEROCIOUS PRECOCIOUSNESS

On September 6, 1958, in a Labour Day Weekend game at Taylor Field, Gerry James of the Winnipeg Blue Bombers caught a short option pass from fellow running back Leo Lewis and was tackled by Jack Hill of the Saskatchewan Roughriders after a six-yard gain. It looked like a routine collision until James remained on the grass with a broken tibia and fibula. Suddenly, one of the most amazing athletic careers in Canada was in jeopardy.

To that point, James had twice been named the best non-import in Canadian pro football, had set the record for points in a season, had twice rushed for more than 1,000 yards in a season and played in two Grey Cup games—despite sitting out the entire 1956 campaign. "Kid Dynamite," the son of "Dynamite" Eddie James, had missed that football season to devote his full energy to playing hockey for the NHL's Toronto Maple Leafs. Gerry James the hockey player was a rock-hard right wing who had won a Memorial Cup with the Leafs' top junior team, the Toronto Marlboros, and played parts of four seasons with the Maple Leafs themselves.

All in all, not a bad résumé for a guy who was just 22 years old.

Applying common frames of reference or athletic stereotypes to Gerry James was a waste of time. He was born in Regina but raised in Winnipeg. A superb athlete in football, hockey and baseball, his school grades averaged in the mid-80s. Working in an era when professional athletes were little more than chattel, James played the Maple Leafs and Blue Bombers organizations off each other so that he was earning double to triple the money of similarly accomplished but older performers.

Uncommonly intelligent and independent-minded, James also had a violent side. On the football field, he was as mean and rough as anyone. On the hockey rink, he could be terrifying. As a Saskatchewan Junior

Hockey League coach in the 1970s and '80s, he would shrug off fights with the remark, "A punch in the mouth never hurt anyone." The subtext to this seemingly callous comment was that wounds from hockey fights rarely resulted in permanent damage. Yet, as a junior in the Ontario Hockey Association, he had broken Marc Rheaume's nose with one punch and sent another opponent to hospital with a concussion from another blow. (Perhaps James was just splitting semantic hairs; technically, neither of those punches landed on the other guy's mouth.)

With the Maple Leafs, James was a penalty-killer and third- or fourth-line forward who got little ice time but could be counted on to play hard and give the team a boost with his physical play. Although few NHL opponents dared to test him in a fistfight, he was still a destructive force. Once he took Chicago's Ken Wharram into the boards and broke Wharram's jaw without drawing a penalty. On another occasion, an open-ice collision left Eddie Shack of the Rangers with a broken nose, a concussion and 25 stitches over his left eye. James was given a high-sticking major, but film revealed that James had kept his stick on the ice and had hit Shack cleanly; some of the facial damage came from Shack's head bouncing off the ice.

As inelegant as James was on skates, he was a gazelle on the gridiron. He joined the Blue Bombers in 1952 as a return specialist. On October 13 of that year, given a chance to play halfback against Saskatchewan, he scored two touchdowns. His 18th birthday was still nine days away. James began to show a penchant for sensational clutch plays in 1953. His 87-yard kickoff return for a touchdown in the second game of the Western Interprovincial Football Union semi-final against Saskatchewan was a lifesaver for the Blue Bombers, instantly turning a 6–1 deficit into a 7–6 lead; Winnipeg would win the game 13–11 and the two-game series 27–25. In the second game of the WIFU best-of-three final against the Edmonton Eskimos, James was used exclusively on punt returns (when no blocking was allowed) and touched the ball only five times: for a 38-yard return, for a 35-yard return, for a nine-yard return, to punt the ball himself for a 70-yard single as time ran out in the first half, and to recover a teammate's fumble.

Winnipeg won 21–17 to even the series at one victory apiece, won the deciding contest and went to the

Gerry James, Winnipeg Blue Bombers

Grey Cup, where the Blue Bombers lost 12–6 to the Hamilton Tiger-Cats. James scored Winnipeg's only touchdown on a one-yard run set up by his own long kickoff return.

When an Outstanding Canadian player award was established for Canadian pro football in 1954, James was its first winner. Most football players his age—20—were toiling in the junior ranks. In 1955 he rushed for 1,205 yards. He missed the 1956 season while abiding by the terms of a two-year hockey con-

Gerry James, Winnipeg Warriors, 1961

tract. He returned in 1957 to run for 1,192 yards, set Western records with 19 touchdowns and 131 points, and won his second Schenley Award as the best Canadian footballer in the country.

James had established himself as a football star on the same elite plane as Jackie Parker, Normie Kwong, Hal Patterson and Sam Etcheverry. Even missing a season, Kid Dynamite accumulated all these credentials by the age of 22, just about when most American stars were finishing college or becoming professional rookies. (Slotback Jason Clermont, the best player to come out of Saskatchewan in recent years, was 24 when named the CFL's top rookie with the B.C. Lions in 2002.)

Hill's bone-breaking tackle in 1958 marked a turning point in James' career. Somewhat slowed, James became Winnipeg's alternate backfield weapon, giving way to Leo Lewis as the primary threat. The injury and the years of double duty wore out his legs prematurely. He was finally given the opportunity to live year-round in Winnipeg in January of 1961 when the Maple Leafs arranged for the Winnipeg Warriors of the senior Western Hockey League to acquire his hockey contract.

James remained with the Blue Bombers through their 1958–62 dynasty when they finished first for five straight years and won five Grey Cups. He was released in 1964, joined the Roughriders for one season and finally retired after another knee injury just as he was turning 29, a veteran of 12 pro football seasons.

Kid Dynamite would become intimately reacquainted with the province of his birth through hockey. He became player-coach of the senior Yorkton Terriers right after the Roughriders released him and won four straight provincial titles. He hung up his skates to coach the senior Terriers from behind the bench for three more years, then turned his attention to junior hockey. James spent two seasons with Yorkton and five with the Melville Millionaires before buying the junior Terriers in 1980.

At each stop, James invariably produced a contending team that would win a playoff series or two but fall short of a Saskatchewan Junior Hockey League title. James achieved a championship in 1984–85 through a ploy that was—depending on one's point of view—brilliant, audacious, outrageous, or just good business. Unhappy with his ice rental arrangement at the Parkland Agriplex for several years, James followed through with a threat to fold the Terriers franchise in the summer of 1984. Just before he did, he sold eight of Yorkton's best players to the Estevan Bruins, who then hired James as their coach. Estevan took the '84–85 league crown while the resurrected Terriers languished in the cellar.

ALSO IN THIS DECADE

- Stan Obodiac of Yorkton and Don Vogan of Moose Jaw won gold medals as the Lethbridge Maple Leafs won the 1951 world hockey championship for Canada. Obodiac, the leading scorer with 12 goals in six games, would spend a quarter-century as the Toronto Maple Leafs' publicist.

- Saskatoon Quakers, with Doug Bentley as player-coach and Gump Worsley in goal, won the 1951–52 Pacific Coast Hockey League championship after finishing second in the regular season. The league was renamed the Western Hockey League the following season.

Gump Worsley

- Two members of the Indian Head Rockets went on to break the colour bar of major league baseball teams. First baseman Tom Alston became the first black man to play for the St. Louis Cardinals in 1954. Infielder Elijah "Pumpsie" Green made it to the big leagues in 1959 with the Boston Red Sox, the last of the original 16 teams to integrate its roster.

- The Saskatoon Gems represented Canada and finished third, behind the United States and Hawaii, at the 1955 Global World Series of Baseball in Milwaukee. Mexico, Japan, Puerto Rico and Spain rounded out the tournament field. The North Battleford Beavers carried Canada's colours in 1956 and were knocked out with two quick losses.

- Saskatchewan Roughriders head coach George Terlep said of rookie Jim Marshall, "He can become the best tackle here since Martin Ruby." Double wrong: Not a tackle and not here. Marshall went south after the 1959 season, played 20 seasons (one for Cleveland, 19 for Minnesota) as an end and set an NFL record for consecutive games played with 282.

- The Saskatoon Adilman Aces won the Canadian women's basketball championship, overcoming a 17-point second-half deficit to beat nine-time defending champion Vancouver Eilers 55–49. Judy Holt led the Aces with 19 points, Lee Fior contributed 16, and Pat Lawson added nine. Vancouver had defeated Saskatoon for the 1955 and '56 titles.

Running back Cookie Gilchrist (91) played only season, 1958, for the Roughriders but gained 1,254 yards. His awesome size (6-foot-3, 250 pounds) and speed complemented an untamed, often undisciplined free spirit. Tolerance for strong-willed, 'uppity' blacks was minimal then; he changed teams eight times in a 14-year pro career in Canada and the U.S.

Merv Moore (top row, second from left) was the only player on the 1922–23 Melville Millionaires who settled in the city, working for 60 years as a pharmacist; when the city built a new arena in 1989, it was named after him, not NHL legend Eddie Shore (seated in front of Moore)

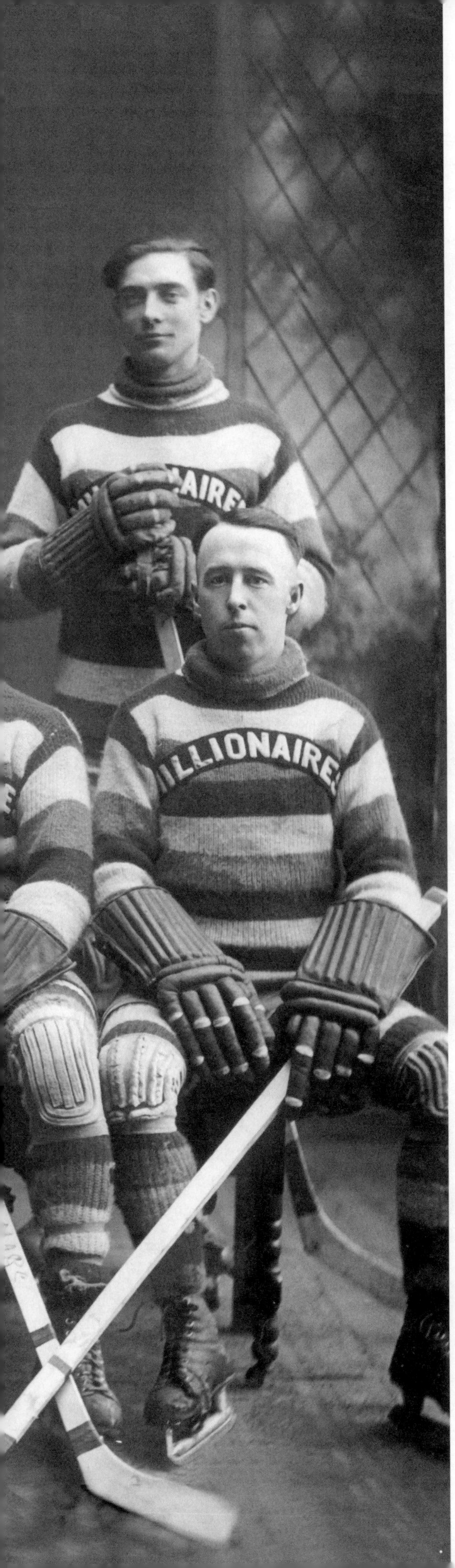

THE NHL

FROM ABEL TO ZOBOROSKY, 434 NATIONAL HOCKEY League players of every size, position and quality have claimed Saskatchewan as their birthplace. Sid Abel emerged from Melville to achieve the sport's ultimate accolade, enshrinement in the Hockey Hall of Fame. Marty Zoborosky of Moose Jaw is the ultimate in obscurity. He played one game with a bad team (Chicago) in a season (1944–45) when the NHL's talent pool was at its shallowest level; his only statistical note is a two-minute visit to the penalty box. There's no apparent record of his birth date, either. How obscure can you get?

On a per-capita basis, this is the source of more NHL players than any other province or, beyond Canada, any country. Excellence abounds whether you base your criteria on quality, quantity or both. Saskatchewan boasts 17 members of the Hockey Hall of Fame, 57 trophy winners and 80 berths on NHL First (42) and Second (38) All-Star teams. Need someone to do the dirty work? Ten flatlanders spent more 2,000 minutes in the penalty box.

More Saskatchewan NHLers were born in Regina than anyplace else, but the greats came from communities large (Saskatoon), small (Humboldt, Lloydminster) and barely visible on the map (Sceptre, Foam Lake, Oxbow). This province is so deep in talent and determination that it can ice a native-born all-star team (page 187) worthy of facing any other province's or country's all-time contingent.

Within this chapter are tales of only some of the Saskatchewan-born men who have provided the NHL with much of its colour and excitement. An appendix on pages 322–327 lists the birthplace and career record of every one of them.

EDDIE SHORE: ONE OF A KIND

Many stories are told about Eddie Shore (Fort Qu'Appelle). The definitive Eddie Shore tale concerns the events of January 2–3, 1929, when the Bruins were scheduled to play a road game against the Montreal Maroons. His taxi, caught in Roaring Twenties gridlock, reached the station just in time for him to see the Bruins' train fading out of sight. Shore inquired into hiring an aeroplane to fly him to Montreal, but a heavy storm between the cities grounded all flights. Undeterred, Shore decided to reach Montreal by automobile over rough roads that wound through the Green Mountains and Adirondacks. A wealthy friend provided his limousine and chauffeur. Shore was picked up at 11:30 P.M., and the 350-mile (570-kilometre) excursion began.

It was an uneventful journey—excluding the sleet, the chauffeur's fear of driving faster than five miles per hour on icy roads, Shore soon taking over the wheel, happening upon an all-night service station and purchasing tire chains just in time to see the storm escalate into a full-scale blizzard, the sleet sticking to the windshield and the wiper freezing to the glass, Shore remedying the visibility problem by removing the top half of the windshield, the resultant discomfort in the limousine, the chains wearing out somewhere in New Hampshire at 5:00 A.M., the reprieve of chancing upon another gas station that sold chains, then ditching the car and pushing it back on the road . . . *four times* . . . crossing the Canadian border, having the second set of chains wear out and fall off at 3:00 P.M., letting the chauffeur drive again (with strict instructions to go at least 12 mph), the chauffeur deep-ditching the car while Shore napped, Shore walking a mile to a farmhouse to commandeer a team of horses (for $8) to extricate the vehicle, and the arrival at the Windsor Hotel at 5:30 in the afternoon, 18 hours after he left Boston.

Shore took a brief snooze and was revived with several dashes of cold water to his face. Once the game began, he got his adrenalin flowing by hammering Montreal's Hooley Smith and drawing a minor penalty. In the second period, Shore took the puck behind his own net, rushed end to end and scored. He took another penalty in the third period. For the night, Shore spent four minutes in the penalty box, 56 on the ice, and none on the bench. The final score was Bruins 1, Maroons 0.

Eddie Shore

Shore was a superb skater and stickhandler, accustomed to vicious attacks from opponents, and quick to retaliate in kind. That warlike approach led him to nearly kill a man on the ice in Boston on December 12, 1933. Mistaking Toronto Maple Leafs forward Irvine "Ace" Bailey for another player who had tripped him, Shore drove his right shoulder into the unsuspecting Bailey's lower back. Bailey fell head-first to the ice, suffered life-threatening injuries, and never played hockey again. One of Shore's first games after a 16-game suspension was the all-star benefit for

Bailey at Maple Leaf Gardens on February 14, 1934. Bailey shook Shore's hand prior to the opening faceoff, and the terrible deed was forgiven—but never forgotten.

Shore's own medical record reportedly included fractures of the back, hip and collarbone, a nose broken 14 times, five fractures of the jaw, more than 900 stitches and, of course, the loss of all his teeth. Shore's left ear was damaged so badly on one occasion that doctors told him it would have to be removed. Instead, Shore found a doctor with a more optimistic prognosis who stitched the ear back in place while Shore, without anaesthetic, watched in a mirror to be sure the job was done properly.

Shore was the first player to receive the Hart Trophy as the NHL's most valuable player four times and is still the only defenceman with that distinction. (Bobby Orr won three Harts.) Shore was named to the First All-Star Team seven times. Late in his NHL career he purchased the Springfield Indians and spent three decades as an eccentric but successful minor-league owner and coach.

Shore was nicknamed "The Edmonton Express" despite spending only one winter in Alberta. He was born in Fort Qu'Appelle in 1902, moved to Cupar at the age of five and played hockey in Melville from 1919–24 at the intermediate and senior levels. Shore played two major-league seasons in the Western Canada Hockey League, one with the Regina Capitals and one with the Edmonton Eskimos before joining the Bruins in 1926.

BUZZ BOLL AND THE BROOKLYN AMERICANS

Frank "Buzz" Boll (Fillmore) was an excellent second-line left-wing for five years with the Maple Leafs, who traded him to the New York Americans in 1939. He stayed with that team through to its demise as the Brooklyn Americans in 1941–42, then finished his NHL career with two seasons in Boston.

The Brooklyn Americans are a noteworthy curiosity because they existed for that one single campaign, the last gasp of a franchise whose owner thought a name change would give them a new fan base. (Continuing to play all their home games in Manhattan's Madison Square Garden indicates how much thought went into this marketing ploy.) Somehow a disproportionate number of Saskatchewan men found themselves with, if not exactly in, Brooklyn: Murray Armstrong, Boll, Jack Church (Kamsack), Norm Larson (Moose Jaw), Chuck Rayner, Earl Robertson (Bengough), Harry Watson and Ralph Wycherly (Saskatoon). That's eight players, or the same number of French-Canadians the Montreal Canadiens used that season.

Boll's Brooklyn jersey, on display in the Saskatchewan Sports Hall of Fame and Museum, is believed to be the only one left in existence.

Buzz Boll

Harold "Mush" March (Silton) could really rise to an occasion. He scored the first goal in the first game ever played at Chicago Stadium (November 21, 1929). He did likewise at Maple Leaf Gardens (November 12, 1931) in Toronto. His biggest goal, on April 10, 1934, was the winner at 10:05 of the second overtime to give Chicago a 1–0 victory over the Detroit Red Wings and the Black Hawks their first Stanley Cup. March was both a football and hockey star as a teenager in Regina despite being only 5-foot-5 and 154 pounds. He went directly from the junior ranks to the NHL and played 17 seasons, all as a right winger, with Chicago.

Mush March

SID ABEL: ABLE AND THEN SOME

Sid Abel

SID ABEL (MELVILLE) WAS A RARITY IN THAT HE established himself as a top-flight NHL star before having his career interrupted by military service and returned to become an even greater player. He was fifth in scoring and the NHL's Second Team All-Star left wing with Detroit in 1941–42. Abel was named captain shortly before his 24th birthday and picked up 13 points in 10 playoff games as the Red Wings won the 1943 Stanley Cup, then spent nearly three years in the Royal Canadian Air Force.

He resumed his captaincy in Detroit, was moved to centre and placed between left-winger Ted Lindsay and rookie right-winger Gordie Howe. The Production Line, as it came to be known, would terrorize the NHL for six seasons.

Abel won the Hart Trophy as the league's MVP in 1949, earned two First Team All-Star selections and enjoyed two more Stanley Cup triumphs before playing out the string in Chicago, where he also coached two seasons. He would coach Detroit for 13 seasons (1957–58 to 1969–70) and reach the finals four times. The Red Wings retired Abel's number 12 in 1995.

Murray Armstrong (Manor) and Gordie Howe are the two Saskatchewan-born hockey players who have had statues erected in their honour. Armstrong's stands on the grounds of the University of Denver in appreciation of his 21 years there as hockey coach. His influence on the game is enormous as an advocate of American college hockey for Canadian boys, who learned that they could acquire a valuable education and still pursue the option of pro hockey. He played for the Regina Pats in his youth and coached them after an eight-season NHL career with the Maple Leafs, Americans and Red Wings. Armstrong won five NCAA titles as Denver's coach and received the Lester Patrick Trophy for outstanding service to hockey in the United States in 1977.

Doug (left) and Max Bentley with the Chicago Black Hawks in 1946

THE BENTLEY BROTHERS: HAWKWARD BEGINNING

Doug and Max Bentley (Delisle) did not take rejection seriously, which allowed them to win three NHL scoring titles within a decade of being alternately rejected by the New York Rangers, Boston Bruins and Montreal Canadiens. Doug, a four-year veteran of senior hockey with the Regina Vics and Moose Jaw Millers, had already been rejected by the Rangers when he travelled to Boston's camp in 1938 with younger brother Max in tow.

Upon their arrival, the Bruins told Doug he was too

small and that the Canadiens held Max's rights. Off they went to Montreal. Max fell ill on the train, was diagnosed with a serious heart condition by the Canadiens' doctor and was advised to give up hockey.

Obviously, the diagnosis was incorrect. Max Bentley, like Doug, would have a Hall of Fame career but also turned into the game's all-time greatest hypochondriac. God knows why.

Returning west, the men of the prolific Bentley clan (six brothers, seven sisters) assured Max his life was not in danger and encouraged him to return to his last place of hockey employment, the Drumheller Miners of the Alberta Senior Hockey League. To make it more fun, five Bentleys spent the season in Drumheller. Doug (22), Max (18) and Reg (14) made up a forward line while Roy (34) and "Scoop" (16, real name Wyatt) played together on defence. Doug and Max had 53 points apiece in 32 games, with Doug adding seven goals in six playoff games and earning an invitation to Chicago's training camp in the fall of 1939. At 5-foot-8 and 145 pounds, he impressed Black Hawks president Bill Tobin as "the first walking ghost I've ever seen" but made the team. Meanwhile, Max went to the Saskatchewan senior league's Saskatoon Quakers and fired 37 goals in 31 games. Doug convinced the Black Hawks to give Max a tryout. Max earned a pro contract although Tobin labelled him "the sickest-looking kid I ever saw," Doug included.

After two seasons of unspectacular results, the Bentleys broke out in 1942–43. Doug led the NHL in goals (32) and points (73) and made the First All-Star Team at left wing. Max was third in the scoring race with 70 points. Brother Reg was brought up to form an all-Bentley line, but he managed only three points in 13 games and never returned to the NHL. Max spent the next two seasons in Calgary with the infantry, which might have cost Doug his best chance at the Stanley Cup. After piling up a league-leading 38 goals and finishing second in scoring with 77 points in 50 games, Doug kept up his pace in the playoffs. His eight goals and four assists in nine games couldn't hold off the Canadiens' four-game sweep in the final, though.

Canadian authorities wouldn't let Doug shuttle across the borders for the rest of the war, so he stayed home. When the Bentleys returned to Chicago in 1945 they were given a new right winger, Bill

Clint "Snuffy" Smith (Assiniboia) played junior hockey in Saskatoon and tore apart the North West league with the Vancouver Lions for three years before joining the Rangers in 1937. He was one of the cleanest players to lace on skates, drawing only 24 penalty minutes (all minors) during his six years with New York and four with Chicago. Smith earned the Lady Byng Trophy in 1938–39 with the Rangers and in 1943–44 with the Black Hawks, when his 49 assists set a single-season record that would be broken by Elmer Lach one year later.

Clint Smith

Roy, Wyatt ("Scoop"), Reg, Doug and Max Bentley of the Drumheller Miners

Mosienko, who at 5-foot-8 and 160 pounds was an inch taller and five pounds heavier than Max. Mosienko's speed and the Bentleys' stickhandling more than compensated for their lack of size. The tiny trio proved unstoppable and quickly became known as the Pony Line. Max skyrocketed to stardom as scoring champion in 1945–46 and '46–47, Hart Trophy winner as the league's most valuable player and First Team all-star centre the first season, Second Team all-star the second.

Mosienko's broken leg suffered in the pre-season NHL all-star game of 1947 led to the breakup of the Pony Line and the Bentley brothers. Chicago, carrying five rookies, opened the season on a six-game losing streak. Tobin had approached Conn Smythe midway through the slump to talk trade and was taken aback by the Toronto owner's offer: five young players, all genuine NHLers, for Max Bentley. Tobin liked the package but gave Max the option to call off the deal. It was a tough call. Toronto was the defending Stanley Cup champion, but Max wasn't eager to be separated from his brother. Doug pointed out that the Maple Leafs, with Syl Apps and Ted Kennedy at centre, wouldn't need to play Max up to 40 minutes a game as the Black Hawks did. Max told Tobin to make the deal.

On November 2, 1947, Chicago traded Max Bentley and Cy Thomas, a forward of little distinction who soon found his way back to the minor leagues, to the Toronto Maple Leafs for an entire five-man unit: defencemen Bob Goldham and Ernie Dickens, left wing Gaye Stewart, centre Gus Bodnar and right wing Bud Poile. There was no questioning the value of the men Smythe sent to Chicago. After the trade, they would play a total of 30 seasons in the six-team NHL.

Max packed his bags and prepared to leave the Chicago apartment he shared with Doug. A telegram for Max arrived from their father, Bill, whom all the brothers addressed as Boss.

VERY DISAPPOINTED TO HEAR THAT YOU

BROKE UP WITH DOUG STOP WORST MISTAKE YOU EVER MADE STOP DON'T EVER COME AROUND ME AGAIN

It would take a few months, but Boss got over his outrage, exacerbated as it was by discovering the news over the radio instead of from his sons. For the time being, Max was doubly troubled by his father's rebuke and the expectations he anticipated in Toronto.

"Who do you think I am, Superman?" he asked Smythe.

"I want you for one specific reason," Smythe replied, "the power play."

Although Max had little affection for his alliterative nickname, "The Dipsy-Doodle Dandy From Delisle," his stickhandling wizardry and playmaking skills were legendary. He also had a tremendous wrist shot that he said came from years of milking cows. Coach Hap Day anchored him on the left point to quarterback the Maple Leafs' power play.

As the third centre, however, Bentley's linemates over the years were Joe Klukay and a cast of thousands. Klukay, a reliable two-way grinder, manned the left wing. An ongoing procession of rookies and journeymen were tried on the right side with little success. Bentley did indeed enjoy a lighter workload but was no longer a threat in the scoring race. He was third in the league with 62 points in 1950–51 but didn't reach 50 points in any of his other five seasons in Toronto. Smythe didn't care. All he coveted was the Stanley Cup and Bentley was instrumental in winning three of them in 1948 (11 points in nine playoff games), 1949 (seven points in nine games) and 1951 (13 points in 11 games).

Back in Chicago, Doug Bentley's record was precisely the opposite. He finished third, then second, then seventh in the scoring race, but the Black Hawks didn't come close to making the playoffs. Doug got out of Chicago in 1951 at the age of 35 to become player-coach of the Saskatoon Quakers, where he spent four seasons. Max left the Maple Leafs midway through the 1952–53 campaign, was sold to New York, and spent 1953–54 with the Rangers. Doug took a hiatus from Saskatoon and joined Max for 20 games of that season. Max returned the favour by playing parts of the next two seasons with the Quakers. Max and Doug finished their NHL careers with 544 and 543 points respectively, placing them fourth and fifth (behind Maurice Richard, Elmer Lach and Milt Schmidt) on the all-time scoring list at the time of their departure.

Max Bentley

Although separated for about half of their time in the NHL, Doug and Max habitually reunited (along with several of their brothers) for baseball season back in Saskatchewan. One of their more enjoyable summers on the diamond was probably 1950, when Doug patrolled centre field and Max handled third base for the Delisle Gems. Max posted the Saskatoon and District Senior League's second-best batting average with .389 in 72 at-bats. The batting champion, at .410 for 83 at bats (with a league-leading 10 stolen bases) was, of course, Doug Bentley.

IN HIS OWN WORDS: ELMER LACH

Elmer Lach (Nokomis) spent 12 years feeding the puck to Rocket Richard. (Nice work if you can get it.) Following are excerpts from an interview the author had with Lach in 1977:

I ATTENDED MY FIRST PROFESSIONAL TRAINING CAMP with Toronto in 1937. Doug Bentley and Harvey Burns were there, too, but we were all small and young at the time, and we didn't last too long. I was never a big hockey player. When I played senior I only weighed around 155 pounds, and when I got to the NHL, my best playing weight was between 162 and 167. I never let my size stop me from being aggressive. I used to rap Doug quite a few times. That was the only style of hockey I knew how to play, though, and I suppose that because of it I ended up getting more than my fair share of injuries.

I came to Moose Jaw in 1938, the year after Doug Bentley left the team. I wasn't a star or anything like that so it wasn't a case of me being expected to come in and take over for the job he did. I was still young and the team had a lot of veterans who were expected to do a big job, which they always did. Even when I was with Regina and Weyburn, I was never much of a goal scorer. I was always more interested in making a pass to set up a goal since we were always taught to look for the open man before working the puck in ourselves for a shot. Almost all of our goals came about by faking a player out of position in order to put someone in the clear.

When I made the move from junior to senior I wasn't thinking of making a career out of playing hockey. Hockey for me was something I could use to help me get a better job. When you played senior hockey, you often used it as something to keep you going through the winter while you worked through the summer months. I had a job with the Robin Hood mill in Moose Jaw when I played with the Millers. It was a standard arrangement because it was the only way you could afford to play. Combining the two incomes, mainly from the job, was all right.

I was always looked after pretty well in Moose Jaw. Cliff Henderson, who owned the team, got me a job reading meters and did me a big favour when I got invited to a tryout with Montreal after the 1939–40 season. First of all, I never even thought I could make the Canadiens, and I was a little reluctant to go because it might have affected my standing in Moose Jaw. The Canadiens were offering me $10,000 for two years which was a good starting salary in 1940, and Cliff reminded me that there was no way I could possibly make that money playing senior hockey.

1939–40 Moose Jaw Millers. Top row: Coach Art Wiebe of Rosthern and centre Elmer Lach of Nokomis

I thought I was taking a chance, but it ended up being the turning point in my life. Montreal was rebuilding that season. Dick Irvin was just moving in as the new coach from Toronto, and the team had a lot of veterans who were getting old that they wanted to replace. I was very fortunate because they brought up nine rookies in that year alone.

My first season was a good one, but I broke my arm in the opening game of 1941–42. We were playing in Detroit and Alex Motter (Melville) tripped me into the boards. The arm broke right at the elbow. That took care of the whole year for me. I didn't play another game. My arm ended up with a permanent little bend in it from that.

Maurice Richard came up to the team the following season. When I came back from the injury, we were put on a line with Toe Blake. I was fortunate, in the right place at the right time, you might say. We always considered Toe Blake to be the stabilizing force on the Punch Line. We called him "The Old Man" because he had been in the league 10 years. He was good for us, kept us consistent and playing both ways, minding our defensive duties.

Toe broke his leg in 1947–48 and retired afterwards, but I kept on playing with the Rocket through to the end of my career. Bert Olmstead, who had played in Moose Jaw with the Canucks, took a turn at left wing after we got him from Chicago, and he was a good replacement. He was a great player both offensively and defensively, so we were able to rely on him to cover up for us when we went on the attack as Toe had. He was also good for being in the right place at the right time, so we always knew where he would be at any given moment.

One of our biggest moments, and I guess one of the funniest, was when we won the Stanley Cup in 1953. We beat Boston in five games with the final game at the Forum. It was 0–0 after three periods so we went into sudden-death overtime. It was only the second minute when the Rocket got the puck to me in the slot. I just let it go without even looking at the net, and I got lucky and it caught a high corner. It was a very emotional moment for both of us, and he was so happy he rushed up and jumped right into me and broke my nose.

CHUCK RAYNER: BONNIE PRINCE CHARLIE

Chuck Rayner (Sutherland) was one of the greatest netminders Saskatchewan ever produced; he just doesn't have the numbers to prove it. In fact, he probably has the most peculiar statistic of any goalie in the Hockey Hall of Fame: 10 seasons, 10 losing records. Yet his skill was so respected that he won the Hart Trophy, only the second netminder to do so, in 1949–50, when he took the Rangers to overtime of the seventh game of the Stanley Cup final against Detroit. He was so heroic in a 2–1 Rangers loss in 1952 that Red Wings goalie Terry Sawchuk skated over to him after the game to express his admiration.

Rayner was a pioneer of handling the puck, frequently leaving the crease and even stickhandling beyond his blue line to start a rush. While playing for the Victoria Navy team in 1942–43, he carried the puck all the way up the ice to fire home the first goal known to have been scored by a goaltender—not as the last player to touch the puck, not on a heave-ho into an empty net but with a real shot past another fully prepared goalie. He almost scored in an NHL game in 1950 when the Maple Leafs pulled their goalie in the last minute and Rayner banked the puck off the boards just wide of the empty Toronto cage. Another Rayner specialty was the pokecheck, which he taught to Johnny Bower, the man who perfected it.

Rayner, the Brooklyn Americans' last goalie, enlisted in the Canadian Navy after the 1941–42 season. Unlike some of the famous netminders of the era (notably, Bill Durnan and Frank McCool), he never had a reputation for being especially nervous, perhaps because his military duty made goaltending seem like a picnic. Rayner made 22 convoy excursions across the Atlantic Ocean, missions in which sailors never knew where or when German U-boats might strike.

Chuck Rayner

TONY LESWICK: MIGHTY MOUSE

Tony Leswick (Humboldt) was the hero of the 1954 Stanley Cup final—nowhere near as big a hero as Doug Harvey was the goat, but it was Leswick who scored in overtime of Game 7, a next-goal-wins-the-Cup scenario that hasn't been repeated since then. Leswick, playing right wing for Detroit, collected a loose puck along the boards in the Montreal zone and unleashed his typically weak wrist shot from 40 feet away.

"You could have caught the puck in your teeth," says Bert Olmstead, who was on the losing side on April 16, 1954.

Harvey, standing 10 feet in front of Canadiens goalie Gerry McNeil, tried to slap the puck down with his left hand, but the puck glanced off his thumb and past McNeil.

"Tony wasn't even watching the puck," says Metro Prystai, Leswick's linemate that night. "He heard the crowd yell, and all of a sudden he turns around and the puck's in the net."

That goal was far from the sum of Leswick's career. He joined the New York Rangers as a 22-year-old left-winger in 1945 and built a reputation as a fearless two-way player. One regular assignment brought him special recognition: checking Maurice Richard.

"On each team there's a bulldozer who is responsible for driving the Rocket out of his zone," Roch Carrier writes in his fanciful biography *Our Life with The Rocket*. "The Rangers count on Tony Leswick." Carrier also includes Leswick among a number of players "who have strong arms and slight talent."

Actually, Leswick scored 113 goals in his six seasons with the Rangers, which in those days took more than "slight" talent. As for being a "bulldozer," Leswick may have had the engine but not the chassis, standing no taller than 5-foot-7 and weighing only 160 pounds.

His best season in New York was 1949–50, when he was voted to the Second All-Star Team and held Richard to one goal as the Rangers upset Montreal in the semi-finals.

When Leswick was traded to Detroit in 1951, the Red Wings moved him to starboard and told him not to worry about scoring goals. (They already had a high-scoring right wing.) As a defensive forward and penalty-killer who took his goals as they came, Leswick was instrumental in Detroit's Stanley Cup victories in 1952, '54 and '55. He went to Chicago, played one season for the Black Hawks, and except for a brief return to Detroit finished his career in the senior Western Hockey League.

Leswick was nicknamed "Mighty Mouse" for his small stature and the enormity of his contributions. He was also a willing scrapper, always fighting against bigger men. Richard was a frequent opponent and on one occasion beat Leswick senseless, but Mighty Mouse always came back for more. In his 11 full seasons in the NHL, Leswick missed only two of 720 games.

Tony Leswick

FERN FLAMAN: BRING 'EM ON, BRING 'EM ALL ON

Few defencemen used their bodies as often and effectively as Fern Flaman (Dysart). He delivered devastating bodychecks, was one the best shot-blockers of his day, and a willing and able battler who exchanged punches with many of the toughest men on ice: Johnny Mariucci, Maurice Richard, Dollard St. Laurent, Glen Skov, Marcel Bonin, Bert Olmstead, Jean Beliveau, Butch Bouchard, Dickie Moore, Jack Evans, Lou Fontinato.

Flaman and left-winger Joe Schmidt (Odessa), fresh-faced juniors from the Regina Abbotts, became 16-year-old professionals when they reported to the Boston Olympics in the fall of 1943. Schmidt got into the only two NHL games of his career in the winter of '43–44 with the Boston Bruins while Flaman played one game with the big club in each of the next two seasons.

Flaman moved up for good in 1947, was traded to Toronto in 1950 and shared in the Maple Leafs' 1951 Stanley Cup triumph. In 1954 he was dealt back to Boston, where he was named to the Second All-Star Team three times.

Flaman went to Providence in 1961 to become a player-coach and in 1970 began a 19-year tenure as coach at Boston University, where he became one of the most successful and respected men in American college hockey. He was inducted into the Hockey Hall of Fame, as a player, in 1990.

Fern Flaman

CLARENCE CAMPBELL: ORGANIZATION MAN

Clarence Campbell (Fleming), president of the NHL from 1946–77, was a distinguished gentleman but never came off as, shall we say, a man of the people. He graduated from the University of Alberta in 1924 at the age of 18 and attended Oxford University as a Rhodes scholar. Returning to Canada, he practised law and refereed hockey on the side. By 1936 he was officiating NHL games.

Campbell enlisted in the army in 1940 and rose from private to lieutenant colonel. He commanded the 4th Armored Division and immediately after the war was a prosecutor at the Nuremberg war trials. In 1946 the NHL hired him as its third president, a position he held for 31 years. As an employee of the owners, he generally acted in their interests more than those of the players. His culpability in the crushing of the players' union movement and the misappropriation of their pension money is an unsavoury episode. In Quebec, he is forever cast as the arch villain in the 1955 drama of the Richard Riot, the stoic anglo-Canadian authority who suspended the Rocket for the playoffs. Campbell was also, however, a major force behind strengthening the Chicago Black Hawks when that franchise was a competitive disaster, a proponent of the intra-league draft that allowed have-nots to claim stronger teams' leftovers, an uncompromising sentinel against gambling, and a thoroughly organized executive who guided the league through four expansions.

"I don't think I met a more knowledgeable, hard-working person in my life than Clarence Campbell," says Emile Francis, who coached and/or managed the Rangers and St. Louis Blues during the last 14 years of Campbell's tenure. "He loved the game of hockey. You could call the NHL office at 10 or 11 at night, and he'd be the only one there to pick up the phone: 'Campbell here.' I can still see him coming into meetings carrying two briefcases and somebody pushing a couple more behind him."

To the general public, Campbell wasn't so much dedicated as aloof.

"He came across that way," Francis admits. "I think he had so many things on his mind and so much work to do that he wasn't given to small talk. I often felt sorry for him. He married his secretary; I guess that was probably the only way she could see him.

"But," says Francis, "I'll tell you a story about the type of man he was:

I'm coaching the Rangers around 1967. We're playing in Chicago, and Pierre Pilote puts his hand on the puck in the crease. Should be an automatic penalty shot, but Bill Friday blows his whistle and points to the faceoff circle beside the net instead.

After the game I mouth off and I say Friday's got no balls and no guts, Friday's a homer, every word in the dictionary and, of course, I was quoted. A couple of days later, I get a call from Campbell; he says I see you're in Montreal in a couple of Saturdays, I'd like to see you in my office. So I go to his office and he's got a file about an inch thick; he opens it up.

"This quote attributed to you—did you say that?" he asks me.

"Yes."

"Did you say this?"

"Yes."

"One thing I'll say for you, you're honest. But if you said those things, you will be fined $500."

I'm looking behind him, and he has an oil painting of Clint Smith, the great Chicago Black Hawks player, with the puck, looking like he's scoring a goal.

I said, "Where did you get that picture from?"

Gordie Howe and Clarence Campbell, 1963

"Why?"

"Because that's me there."

"It is?" He calls his secretary. "Hilda! Bring me the folder for the picture behind me." She brings the folder and he looks at it. "You're right—'Chicago Black Hawks scrimmage, 1947, Clint Smith, Emile Francis.' "

"Well, I've only got one thing to say. I'll give you your 500 bucks. But if you ever retire and you've got no place to put that picture, I'd appreciate having that."

He didn't say a word; never looked up.

"I'll send you the cheque," I said, and I got up and left.

I left New York in 1976 and went to St. Louis. A few years later a guy at the reception desk called me: "I've got a big parcel here for you. Do you want me to bring it up to your office?"

"Yeah, do that."

I took the wrapping apart and there it was, that oil painting, all those years later.

GORDIE HOWE: FLORAL TRIBUTES

GORDIE HOWE (FLORAL) IS THE GREATEST ATHlete who was ever born in, came from or competed in Saskatchewan.

So it's obvious. It still has to be put on the record.

Mr. Hockey's life and career have been chronicled in numerous books. To summarize his story in a few pages here would be an injustice to it. Instead, let us sample some of the more colourful aspects of his decades on the ice.

EARLY ROLE REVERSALS

Howe's first big game was a Saskatoon schools all-star contest in which he tended goal for the West side while a fourth-grader at King George School. The only East player to score on him was Vic Lynn, who became a valuable defensive forward on the Toronto Maple Leafs in the late 1940s as well as the only man to play for every team in the "Original Six."

Harry Watson

BLADE WORK

Howe and his childhood buddies didn't have the money to buy tickets to senior hockey games in Saskatoon. They would rely on the generosity of players to get them in.

"We used to stand outside the Arena on the school side and hope that one of the players would say, 'Here, carry my skates in.' Most players at that time carried the skates instead of putting them in the bag, to be sure they didn't get lost. I must have said the right thing to Ab Welsh this one time because he took me right into the dressing room, and he asked me if I played. I said yes.

" 'What hand are you?'

" 'Right,' I said.

" 'You're in luck,' he said, and he gave me my first new stick. God, I slept with that thing."

Vic Lynn

JUST OUT OF ELEMENTARY, WATSON

"I played on a pickup team against Harry Watson in 1944 when he was with the Number 4 air base in Saskatoon. I got through the defence, and I scored a goal.

" 'Very well done,' Mr. Watson said. 'What's your name?'

" 'Gordon Howe.'

" 'How old are you?'

" 'Fifteen.'

" 'Oh my God, I'll see you in the NHL.' "

ALL-STAR CAST

According to his "fishing buddy," (see *Foreword*) Howe was amazing with a rod and reel, too.

"How he loved to fish!" says Johnny Bower. "Just like when he scored goals, he'd never shoot on the same side twice. He'd throw his rod toward one spot and then the other. He could tell by a little whirl in the water that there's a fish there after something. He started coming up to Waskesiu while I was still in the American league, and he kept coming up after I went to Toronto. In fact, Gordie worked at the golf course for a few years, too, to keep in shape. He was a good golfer, too."

NEAR-DEATH EXPERIENCE

Howe's first season as an NHL star was nearly his last. He finished 1949–50 second in goals (35) and third in the scoring race (68 points). In the first game of the 1950 playoffs on March 28—three days before his 22nd birthday—Howe fell face-first into the boards at Maple Leaf Gardens when Toronto centre Ted Kennedy sidestepped his intended check.

Gordie Howe in his rookie season with Detroit (yes, his face cleared up)

Howe's injuries were dreadful: a broken nose and cheekbone, a serious concussion and, worst of all, swelling around his brain. Surgeons had to drill through his skull to relieve the pressure, and his life was not deemed out of danger until the following day.

Howe began the next season wearing a helmet, which he soon cast off. Obviously, the injury did not affect his play in any way. He played all 70 games and led the NHL in scoring in each of the next four seasons.

Anyone who thought Howe's fall in Toronto would be followed by his retirement was proven correct . . . 30 years later.

HITS AND MYTHS

Train rides played an important part in Howe's hockey education in the 1940s. One of the lessons he learned would be the decisive factor in his spectacular fight on February 1, 1959, when Lou Fontinato of the New York Rangers came gunning for him and Howe mashed Fontinato's nose into a whole new indefinable shape.

"We used to have our own private sleeper when we took the train from Montreal back to Detroit," Howe says. "I would just sit back and listen to the veterans. You would pick up tips on how to protect yourself, how to do all sorts of things. Sid Abel told me one of the best: 'When you start your shift it takes only two seconds to scan the ice and see who you're with and against. Then you're a step ahead because you know what you need and what you're going to do.'

"So when (teammate) Red Kelly and Eddie Shack (of the Rangers) got to fighting that night in New York, we were all just standing there, watching, until I thought, 'Oh-oh, Louie's out here, and he's been trying to get me.' I turned around and sure enough, his gloves were off, his stick was down and he was coming in. I pretended I didn't see him, so when he took a swing at me, I pulled back and that gave me an opportunity to get a shot at the nose."

Several shots, actually. Reporters testified that the sound of Fontinato's nose breaking could be heard from the press box.

"Well, it was all because of what Sid Abel told me. That's why I say to kids, listening can save your career sometimes."

The "Gordie Howe hat trick" of a goal, an assist and a fight is a myth. His destruction of Fontinato is the only all-out battle Howe fought after his near-fatal crash into the boards in 1950—not because Howe was guarding himself against further injury but because no one (except Fontinato) wanted to test the strength of his fists.

WELCOME TO THE NHL

The late Bob Turner spent eight seasons trying to

contain Gordie Howe. What was it like?

"Not fun. My first NHL game was in Detroit. The Canadiens called me up from Shawinigan, put me beside Doug Harvey, and I thought I was the greatest thing since sliced bread. On one of my first shifts, the Red Wings passed it up to Howe, and I ran at that son of a bitch. He brought his elbow up and broke my nose. A broken nose my first game. Blood was just flying, I could see it. I stayed away from him as best I could after that. He was a dirty bugger, and I don't mind saying it."

Bob Turner

ME AND MY SHADOW

"I never had a problem with him," Howe says of Bert Olmstead, the man who checked him for more than a decade. "The thing about him was, if you played a clean game, he played a clean game. If you tried to rough it up, he could be master of that, too. You know, after he retired there were a couple of occasions when I saw him in Toronto at functions, and it was almost as though we had played for the same team. He was an extremely friendly individual."

1952 Saskatoon Gems baseball with Gordie Howe's autograph

POWER HITTER

"Every year Saskatoon would stage a very large baseball tournament around the July 1 holiday weekend at Cairns Field, right downtown on Idylwyld Drive," former premier Roy Romanow recalls. "This involved teams from all over the province: Regina, North Battleford . . . I particularly remember the Colonsay Monarchs and Unity Cardinals as small-town but powerful teams. Gordie was playing for the Saskatoon Gems, and I was a young student and radio announcer working at CJOM.

"I'm sure that time has coloured my recollection of this, but I remember him swatting so many balls out of the park. I know he hit several home runs during the course of the tournament; I might also be thinking of warm-ups, because as youngsters we would watch the players take batting practice. The movements of this outstanding athlete and this effortless crossover from hockey amazed me. The story was circulating that the owners of the Detroit Red Wings were insisting that he drop this summer pastime lest he be injured. It made sense for them, but it sure spoiled our fun. He was a magnificent physical specimen and such a wonderfully talented athlete that he could do almost anything he chose to do."

WHAT DID HE HAVE AGAINST NOSES, ANYWAY?

Notes from a February 1952 Associated Press story: The Rangers want the NHL to do something about Gordie Howe. A few nights ago in New York he allegedly broke Allan Stanley's nose with his stick and Eddie Kullman's nose with his elbow. Emile Francis is probably smarting, too; Howe broke his shutout with a minute and 47 seconds to go as Detroit salvaged a 1–1 tie.

AS GOOD AS HIS WORDS

The city of Saskatoon honoured its most famous export on July 22, 1966, with Gordie Howe Day. Gordie, wife Colleen and their four children were the featured attraction of a full-scale parade through downtown streets. In addition to the cheers of several thousand citizens, Howe enjoyed reuniting with his parents and, for the first time in 18 years, with all three of his brothers and five of his sisters. At a rally following the parade, Howe responded to the speeches that showered him with praise:

"People have been so great and kind to me. . . . I don't think I'll ever get over it. So I just want to say once again, people behind me, thank you for all the kind words. I know if I can live up to even 10 percent of it, I'll be a very happy man. And I hope I never go astray in such a way that some youngster maybe gets into a little trouble and says, 'Howe did it, and I can do it, too.' "

YOU'RE THE TOP

The author's personal favourite statistic involving Gordie Howe: He finished among the NHL's top five scorers for 20 consecutive seasons (1949–50 through 1968–69). His progression in the scoring race from the age of 21 to 40, with T indicating a tie, goes 3, 1, 1, 1, 1, 5, 2, 1, 4, 4, T5, 5, T3, 1, 5, 3, 5, T4, 3, 3. No other athlete in any major team sport has a similar streak in any comparable category.

MAKING NO. 9 NO. 1

Gordie Howe played his first game in the World Hockey Association when he was 45 years old. When the WHA folded six years later, he was seventh on its career scoring list. His line: 419 games, 174 goals, 334 assists, 508 points, 399 penalty minutes.

Remember how George Hainsworth noses ahead of Terry Sawchuk as the all-time shutout leader if you include WCHL games from the 1920s? The same rationale works splendidly with WHA statistics if you want Gordie Howe to be major-league hockey's all-time leading scorer. Add his 174 WHA goals to 801 in the NHL, don't forget to include Wayne Gretzky's 46 WHA tallies along with his subsequent 894, and—*voila!*—Mr. Hockey surpasses The Great One, 975–940. (Include playoff goals and Gretzky prevails by one, 1,072–1,071.)

STRAIGHTEN OUT THE OLD MAN

How do you deal with Gordie Howe when you're the team captain and he's twice your age?

"Well, he was a hard guy to control." Terry Ruskowski says of their time on the WHA's Houston Aeros. "I worked him over once in a while, and he turned out all right."

Terry Ruskowski

But seriously, folks . . .

"All he wanted to do was play hard, have fun and win," says Ruskowski, Howe's teammate from 1974–77. "At 48 he still had that competitive spirit. He was absolutely incredible. There were optional practices where he was the only guy that showed up. He scored one of his milestone goals, his 900th, with a cracked heel. They made a special cast of his heel and put it in his boot. He held off a Phoenix defenceman and with one hand snapped the puck top shelf. All the confetti came down, balloons, big accolades.

"The trainer came up to him and said, "Okay, Gordie, you got your goal, it's time to quit for tonight." He said, "Nah, the game's not over yet. We gotta make sure we win." I'll never forget that.

"We won the Avco Cup my first year in Houston. We lost the final the next year to Winnipeg, and I felt so bad that I was crying in the back of the bus. I was a young kid then. He was the only guy to come back to console me. After that moment Gordie and I were much closer. He knew my desire to win was there. I hated to lose, and he was the same way."

MEXICANS CAN'T SKATE

After retiring from hockey, Howe had plenty of time to work on his golf game. Every summer he would

Gordie Howe shakes hands with Winnipeg Jets (and former Weyburn Red Wings) goalie Joe Daley after the 1978 WHA final. Although the Jets swept the New England Whalers 4-0, you couldn't tell by looking at these two

enjoy taking part in the pro-am of the Greater Hartford Open, a regular stop on the PGA Tour.

"I was very fortunate to play with golfers like Arnold Palmer, Billy Casper, Hubert Green and Lee Trevino. The first year I played, I was there as a 9 handicap."

(Coincidence. It had nothing to do with his number.)

"I had practised, and I was hitting the ball long and straight. Trevino and I were even at about the 11th hole and then he looked at me and said, 'You don't see me scoring goals, do you?' That threw me off a little bit."

APPRECIATION

"He knew every trick in the book; he *invented* every trick in the book," says Bryan Trottier, who starred for the Islanders during Howe's last NHL season, 1979–80, when Howe was 51. "You'd watch him, emulate him, try to read off him as best you could. I was fortunate enough to get to know Gordie, and he's an absolute father of hockey. He treats everyone in the hockey world as if they're family."

EMILE FRANCIS: TRUE GLOVE

Emile Francis (North Battleford)—goalie, infielder, baseball manager, hockey coach and executive—is an incomparable storyteller. This tale concerns the introduction of the trapper (catching glove) to goaltending:

It was while I was with the Moose Jaw Canucks that I got my nickname, "the Cat." Scotty Melville of the Regina *Leader-Post* gave it to me. It went back to baseball, where my strongest asset was my hands, particularly my catching hand, which carried over into goaltending. I took a George McQuinn first baseman's mitt, and I sewed it onto a regular hockey glove so any puck that came up around there was in that mitt to stay. All the goaltenders used at that time was a leather glove with a pad on the back. Not only was that not effective, but when you took shots on your palm it would knock the hell out of your hand.

No one said anything about it while I was playing junior, but they sure did in my first game with Chicago (in 1947). We were playing Detroit, and their coach, Jack Adams, called the referee, King Clancy, over to the bench. I saw Adams pointing at me. I couldn't figure out what was going on.

Clancy skates over and says, "Let me look at your glove." I show it to him and he says, "That's illegal. You can't use it."

"What do you mean, I can't use it? By the rule book it's legal as long as I haven't put on an extra cage. I haven't changed it in any way."

"No, you can't use it."

"Well then, I can't play. I don't use any other glove. I haven't for two years."

There was only one goaltender dressed then, so I knew I couldn't be put out of the game. Clancy let me use the glove, but he told me the Rules Committee would take it up the next day. Finally, they said it was okay, and other goalies started to use it.

A CONVERSATION WITH BERT OLMSTEAD

You were born in Sceptre. Did you live there until you went to Moose Jaw to play junior hockey?

Yup. There would be about 300 people in the village, and most of the kids played baseball and hockey. We would probably push a chair when we were beginning to learn how to skate—on bob skates, with two blades—then you graduated to a hockey stick holding you up, then to playing hockey as soon as you could. I don't think we even had minor hockey then, but as soon as you became old enough you played with the men; the men always looked after you.

Was your family hit hard by the Depression?

We never went without anything. A lot of people said that we grew up on porridge and love. Heck, nobody in the area had any money, so nobody was hit hard. My father did everything. He taught school, he was a carpenter, he owned some land, but I never saw him farm it, just rent it out. He was a pretty smart guy.

Do you fit into the old cliché of playing hockey on sloughs with horse turds?

No, we made our own rink. We fixed the boards, shovelled the snow, wired it with lights to play at night. We had a well in town, and we used to pipe the water over 300 yards to the rink, put it in a barrel and tip it over. We tried to do that after the first snowfall, take ice and snow and pack it down. That would be the foundation for our ice.

You had lights on your outdoor rink?

Yeah, we used to put the big bright bulbs up in front of the visiting team so their goaltender would be hampered by the 250-watt bulbs. It helped us a little bit there, but we got the same treatment when we went away.

Bert Olmstead, 1945

Metro Prystai

Were you an excellent player at an early age, good enough to entertain thoughts of a pro career?

No, not really. I was a good athlete, that's all. It was hard to measure way back then what a good athlete was, based on a sense of the Saturday night radio broadcast or what everyone else said. I would be like thousands of other kids in Saskatchewan or Alberta or anywhere in Canada. You played under the streetlights at night and thought you were somebody out of Toronto, like Charlie Conacher or Joe Primeau, big-name players. We never had any aspirations of chasing a puck for a living. I suppose after you get into junior hockey, that's when people began to take note of you.

How did you get from Sceptre to Moose Jaw?

Back in those days we used to have lots of salesmen come out. A gentleman named George Vogan, who ran the Moose Jaw Canucks, had a bird dog in town who happened to live right across the street from me. George asked this person, Ernie Shields, who the best athlete in town was. Ernie steered him my way. The following year I went to Moose Jaw, played hockey and took my Grade 12 with Metro Prystai at Central Collegiate.

How good a player was Metro?

He was the Wayne Gretzky of junior hockey in our day, Metro was. Smooth, fast, smart, great shot. He wasn't a physical player, but he didn't have to be. I played with Metro later on in Chicago. In 1949–50 (with Bep Guidolin on right wing) we were the second-highest scoring line in the league. Lindsay, Abel and Howe were the only line that was ahead of us, so

AL ROLLINS: TAKING HOME THE TROPHIES

Al Rollins (Vanguard) enjoyed one season of junior hockey with the Moose Jaw Canucks (1942–43) before making his pro debut with the Eastern League's New York Rovers shortly after his 17th birthday. Six seasons with seven minor-league clubs made him a grizzled veteran at 23, and Toronto, knowing Turk Broda was nearing the end of the line, gave the AHL's Cleveland Barons four players and $40,000 in exchange for Rollins.

Unusually tall (6-foot-2) for his position at the time, Rollins had a sensational rookie campaign in 1950–51, playing 40 of Toronto's 70 games and posting a 27–5–8 record with a 1.77 GAA to win the Vezina Trophy. Although Broda, perhaps the best playoff netminder in NHL history, saw more post-season action, Rollins was on the ice when Bill Barilko scored the famous overtime goal that beat Montreal in Game 5 of the final and won the Leafs the Cup.

Barilko's sudden death and a dearth of young talent eroded the Toronto dynasty. Owner Conn Smythe thought a change of goalies might change things and dealt Rollins to the woebegone Black Hawks for Harry Lumley just before the 1952–53 campaign. Rollins proved he wasn't the problem in Toronto: While the Maple Leafs missed the playoffs for only the second time in 23 years, Chicago earned its only post-season berth between 1946 and 1959.

It was the next season, 1953–54, when Rollins would pull off his most singular feat: winning the Hart Trophy with the league's worst team. Chicago's 31 points were 37 behind fifth-place New York, the Black Hawks were outscored 133–242 and five of their 12 victories came on Rollins shutouts. Reporters overlooked Gordie Howe's 81 points and 14-point cushion over Maurice Richard in the scoring race to select Rollins the league's most valuable player.

Rollins' career went into decline after that, presumably from exhaustion. For NHL purposes, he was pretty well done after Chicago acquired Glenn Hall in 1957, but he hung around long enough to enjoy a distinguished exit with the 1966 Allan Cup champion Drumheller Miners.

we weren't too bad. Metro and I were the youngest guys on the Chicago squad. Then the management let Metro go to Detroit and I went to Montreal, and we both thanked them.

Dick Irvin had a reputation as a tough, mean player. Did any of that come through in his coaching?

He was a hard man, hard but square. He knew the game and he knew people, what to expect from a certain player. He was very accurate that way. He could describe every player and compare him to one of the pigeons he used to race. He'd do the same thing with an automobile. He could tell you what kind of automobile you were, and why and what your functions were. He was extraordinary. Generally, he was my kind of guy.

Dick Irvin Sr.

Did Irvin put you on a line with Richard and Lach right away?

Yup. I'd been in Milwaukee for a couple of weeks because Chicago sent me down, and at that time I think it was compulsory to spend two weeks in the minors before they moved you. Of course, my conditioning suffered; I know for a fact that Chicago's conditioning was not equal to Montreal's. When I arrived in Montreal I was half a stride, maybe a full stride, short on my conditioning. After I got in the condition that I was expected to be in, we got along okay.

Elmer Lach

Lorne Davis said you were one of very few people who could actually criticize the Rocket. You roomed with Richard for a while; were you able to tell him when you thought he screwed up?

Absolutely. Why not?

What kind of things might you criticize him for?

Don't take the word "criticize" in its obvious sense. You're doing constructive criticism. If you see a guy slacking, you'd better—well, I would anyway—remind him: come on, I'm busting my ass, you'd better bust yours, too. Nothing wrong with that. Everybody becomes a better hockey player, the team becomes a better team. That's not hard to understand.

The Rocket would have his slack days, too?

Over the course of time. Everyone does, I don't care who you are. Nobody's perfect. The only time he ever got mad or pissed off is because he was playing poorly and was mad at himself. If the team lost and he felt he didn't work hard enough, same thing. He was a little more self-centred about it. That's why he was so bloody good, that's why he scored those 1–0 goals all by himself.

How did your skills, and Richard's, mesh with those of Elmer Lach?

Elmer the Elegant . . . He was tough, a good skater, good goal-scorer. I played with him and Rocket for three years. We played two men on the attack and a trailer, and I was always the trailer. But I learned quite a bit about what to do with the puck from Elmer. Rock, you could pretty well forecast what he was going to do: overpower you with his strength or his speed. Elmer, he could dilly-dally with the puck and do things with it. Elmer, of course, had played with the Rocket all his life, and they were probably the best 1–2 punch ever, bar none. I would be a little behind, I could see what they were doing, I could think with them and move with them. I wasn't unselfish as a hockey player, but I wasn't going to suicide myself just to get a shot at the net. I would figure the play out and get in the right spot, set myself up.

Did you do the same later on the line with Jean Beliveau and Bernie Geoffrion?

They were a little bit more offensive there; I would go in a little farther with them. A lot of Beliveau's goals came out of my corner. He would spot easily. Here's what I mean by that: Some people use the phrase "fighting" for the puck; "get" the puck is what I say. You don't compete for it, you *get* the puck. And

Max Bentley: "flashier, quicker" than Beliveau in stickhandling

I'd tell John, you stay in that spot, the same spot as where I last saw ya. Don't you move from there, because that's where that pellet's coming. Adjusting for who was checking me and how far apart we were, he'd be ready.

Was Beliveau the best stickhandler you ever saw? What about Max Bentley?

Max was flashier. John was smooth, oooh man, was he smooth. Max was a little jerkier, quicker. Being slighter, he couldn't go into the same traffic as John could, so he avoided it.

In 1952–53 Gordie Howe had 49 goals, one away from Richard's single-season record, with his last game against the Canadiens. Do you remember the game?

Oh, absolutely. Before the game Dick Irvin wanted to know who would volunteer to check Howe tonight. I said I would; so did a couple of other guys. I knew who was going to get Howe because I'd played for years against him.

So Irvin says, "You're going to take Howe tonight."

"Fine. What do you want me to do?"

"Go where he goes," Irvin tells me.

Okay, so that's what I did. I recall Gordie going back and talking to Sawchuk when the faceoff was in our end; I'm three feet from Howe.

"What are you doing here?" they asked.

I wouldn't answer. Usually, when you played against someone and talked to 'em, that's bad business. I heard this from boxers: talking to your opposition means you're weak, he's got the better of you. In all my life against Gordie Howe I never, I don't think, said even 50 words to him. I spent 14 seasons in the NHL and most of that time against Detroit, I was playing against Howe. I always accused him of ruining my career because my first instruction was, don't let Howe score. So there's no way you could think offence too much. You made sure you were back, because he was the best hockey player in the league, and probably the toughest, and very smart.

He was notorious for, shall we say, enforcing his body space. How did he deal with you?

I would stay a good stick's length away from him. That's how I'd do it with Mr. Howe. But the secret to dealing with him is to have your centreman get on the puck. Everybody says, "You checked Howe." Well, sure, I'm around him and stuff like that, but the main man on the checking assignment is the centreman. If he gets on the puck early, Howe isn't going to get the puck. If our guy lags, their centre has lots of time to play with Howe, and Howe's got lots of time to manoeuvre.

Over time, all hockey comes down to is repetition, doing the same thing over and over and over, a million times, and you become good. You do the fundamentals well, you're a great hockey player. Gordie Howe, what did he do? Nothing fancy. He played hockey: skate, shoot and check.

You broke the NHL record for assists in a season in 1955–56. Was that a big deal to you?

Yeah, because I knew the record was there. The last game of the season in New York, I needed one assist to break Ted Lindsay's record (of 55). I beat my man to a puck in the corner, John (Beliveau) was in the slot, bang, in the net. Happened that quick.

How do you account for the events of January 4, 1954?

What's that?

You had four goals and four assists in one game. Until Darryl Sittler had his 10-point night, you and Richard shared the record for points in a game with eight.

Oh, yeah. Against Chicago. Doug Harvey came in to the dressing room and said, "Nice season, Bert." They were going in off the post that night. Usually, it never happened that way to me. Al Rollins was in goal for the Blackhawks, and they gave him the Hart Trophy that year—for bravery! Some goaltenders you never have any trouble with; others you couldn't put a pea past 'em. I could score on him.

IN HIS OWN WORDS: FRED SASAKAMOOSE, THE NHL'S FIRST INDIAN

I WAS IN RED FEATHER SCHOOL AND ST. MICHAEL'S College at Duck Lake since I was about seven years old. We went to the midget provincial finals in '48–49 in Weyburn when I was 14, and they beat us out. The year after that we had exactly the same team, and we won the Saskatchewan midget championship. We didn't know we were being scouted. None of us ever thought about going to any higher level.

George Vogan

'Cause at residential school, after you turned 16 years old, you were gone, gone home. I was born in 1933 on the Sandy Lake Reserve, what we now call Ahtahkakoop, and in 1940 I was taken away from my family. I never knew my parents too well. It was tough, tough to be in that school. It was a lot of battles, a lot of scars, a lot of things that had to be dealt with: sexual abuse, physical abuse . . . and our language was taken away from us, we were not allowed to talk our language. It felt like a jail. There was a wire fence there that you could only go so far and that's it. I didn't like it, and I didn't want to stay any longer than I had to. My mother and father were not allowed to come and visit because the priests thought they would take us home, and it was 100 miles from Duck Lake to Sandy Lake Reserve.

The school was like a farm. We had cattle, horses, pigs, chickens, you name it, and we did a lot of work over the years. We used to milk about 70 cows a day, two cows apiece—we'd wake up about 6 o'clock in the morning, be in the barn by 7:00, milk the cows, separate the milk and do the same thing in the evening. That was our chore.

Living conditions were pretty good. We had running water. The thing is, like I said, the abuse and all that. A lot of times, the kids cried every day. There was a lot of punishment. And a lot of discipline, which was good. I mean, there's good things that happened in the residential schools, a lot of good training. I'm not going to say that it was all bad.

Those Catholic priests were French, from Quebec I guess, and they knew quite a bit about hockey. We played a lot of tournaments in the surrounding area, like Rosthern and Laird. But I hated that school, and when I came home in June of 1950, I was glad to be with my parents. I had been away from them for nine years and didn't really know them.

We lived in a tent all summer working for the white farmers, picking roots, picking rocks. I think it was the first part of October, we were cutting and stooking grain in a field near Canwood, 50 cents an acre. I see this car pulled up in the grid road and a couple of guys walking about a quarter-mile away from me. I realize that one of them is Father Chevrier, the administrator from St. Mike's, and the other guy I don't know. My brother and I, we took off. I'm about a hundred yards away while my parents are talking to Father Chevrier and the stranger and then my mother calls to me in our language, in Cree, to join them.

"They've come for you," she tells me.

"Where am I going?"

"To Moose Jaw, to play hockey."

"No, Mom, I'm not going other places, I'm not leaving you again."

"We'll give you the equipment," says Father Chevrier. "We'll buy you new clothes."

"No."

After about an hour we were still sitting there.

"You know," my mother says quietly, "you can try it for two weeks."

"Two weeks," my father says. "You can come back."

"Two weeks," I said, "that's too long." But I agreed. I went to Moose Jaw with George Vogan. He was the stranger. I didn't know where Moose Jaw was. All I knew is that we travelled for maybe seven or eight hours on gravel road. And George took me in to his home. George was the manager of the Moose Jaw Canucks and worked for SGI (Saskatchewan Government Insurance). George had kind of a dream for me, to become the first Indian professional hockey player in Western Canada. George was a good man, very good.

Those two weeks felt strange for me, being among those white kids. After two weeks I was doing pretty good, and I started to deal with them a little bit. But my time was up, so I packed up my clothes and away I went while George was working. He caught up to me in Chamberlain. I had been on the road for about four or five hours, hitchhiking. A car pulled up right beside me.

"Where are you going?"

"I'm going home, George. I don't know if I'm going in the right direction."

George Hunchuk

"Oh, you're going the right way, all right. But, are you hungry?"

"I haven't ate all day."

"Well, let's go to the café."

So that's where he took me, and we started talking.

"A couple more weeks, Freddie, I want to keep you for another two weeks. You'll make the team."

So I went back for two more weeks, and I stayed four years. We played in the Western Canada Junior Hockey League—against Edmonton, Lethbridge, Medicine Hat, Calgary, Regina, Saskatoon and Crowsnest Pass.

There was discrimination, a lot of names I was called. But you learn to brush it off, to accept that. At least I knew that I must be performing well or else they wouldn't be calling me names. I got into a lot of fights, a lot of battles, but that's part of the game. My teammates called me Chief, you know. I didn't mind that. It was acceptable to me, as long as they didn't hurt my pride by calling me some kind of a dirty name.

When I was 18 years old I started having a dream where I was skating side by side with white kids. I was the only Indian in there. I started to realize that these kids are good, but I'm just as good as they are, maybe even better. I've got to work harder to make it to the big time. One morning before the season starts I go to the rink early, about 9 o'clock, and there's a man on the ice all alone—George Hunchuk. He used to play for the Canucks and almost made the

NHL, when there were only six teams. He was a big star in the Western pro league with the Vancouver Canucks. And George Hunchuk, he was jumping around and dancing on his skates, all alone on this ice at 9:00 in the morning, boy, he was just pouring sweat. But he kept his head up and he'd jump sideways and glide and make figure-8s and float on the ice. I really admired that guy. After about 20 minutes he skated up to me.

"Hey, Chief!"

"What?"

"Would you like to skate like me?"

"George, I would give anything to skate like you."

"Well, you be here tomorrow at 9 o'clock."

Mister, I was there at 7 o'clock in the morning, dressed up and ready. He taught me everything, in just that one day.

"Freddie," he told me, "never look at the puck. Never. Feel it on your stick. Always keep your head up. 'Cause when you get to the big time, you put your head down, you're gone. Somebody out there is gonna kill ya."

When I watched how he skated, I knew I could do that. And I skated and I skated. I wanted to be like George Hunchuk. I started running on my skates. I started to dance on my skates. One year later I was invited to go to the Chicago training camp in Petawawa, Ontario, because the Canucks were a farm team of the Black Hawks. I see George and I say, "George, watch me." I performed in front of George and showed him what I'd done in one year with what he taught me. You know what he said? "Freddie, you're better than me." Ain't that funny? That's when I knew that the dream was to look forward, that I was a better hockey player than what I thought. You'll make it if you listen well, work hard and play hard.

My last year of junior hockey, I was voted most valuable player in the Western Canada league. In March, the Regina Pats beat us out in the playoffs, and as I skated off the ice I thought, "I'm going home now, I'm done with junior hockey." We went into the dressing room, all these kids that I played with for years. We were a team. The colour didn't matter. I was one of them. That's how they looked at me, that's how they accepted me. It was a great feeling to have that. That's why I don't discriminate against the white man.

Into the dressing room come George Vogan, the coaches and about six women with a couple of suitcases. They told the players not to take any equipment off, that there would be some presentations. Then George looked at me and read a telegram: Fred Sasakamoose, you report immediately to Chicago Black Hawks. You have a train ticket to Toronto to play on Saturday—*Hockey Night in Canada.*

Fred Sasakamoose, Moose Jaw Canucks

What a feeling. The room was still. Nobody said nothing. Finally, I said, "Why is it me?" Every one of my teammates got up, shook my hand, wished me well, grabbed me, rubbed my head. The women opened the suitcases: two sets of suits, shirts, cufflinks, ties, shoes, everything. A watch. They said, this is for you, Freddie. Because now you're a professional hockey player, you've gotta dress like a pro.

It took me two days to get up there to Toronto. Wow. I walk into Maple Leaf Gardens, into the dressing room, who's sitting there? Bill Mosienko, Bill Gadsby, Lee Fogolin, Al Rollins, Gus Bodnar. Sid Abel's the coach. You couldn't go any higher. It was my dream, the highest level. I had the opportunity to talk to old Foster Hewitt, he was such a great announcer. My mother and dad, they listened to *Hockey Night in Canada* the first game I played, and they told me it was just like watching the game. We made that swing from Toronto to Montreal and then from there to Boston and New York and back to Chicago. We lived on a train. Jump on there after the game, sleep in your berth, get to the next city in the morning and check into the hotel.

Remember the organist in Chicago? I stepped on the ice and he played that song "Indian Love Call," I remember that just like today. They had this Blackhawk logo and me, the real Indian, wearing that sweater. It was something to see, I guess. There were three balconies in that Chicago Stadium, about 18 to 19 thousand people. And what a tremendous feeling you get, you know, in your stomach.

They put me on a line with Bill Mosienko and George Gee. I didn't score no goals, I didn't have no assists. I think I came close to scoring a goal. I don't know now, it's been too long. I played my 11 games, and I went home.

I went as far as North Dakota with Bill Mosienko and from there I took a bus to Moose Jaw. I picked up my car, a 1946 Chev coupe that the Moose Jaw people gave me while I was playing junior hockey. All these weeks I was with the Black Hawks I never received any money; my cheques were being fed to George Vogan, and he put them in an account in Moose Jaw. George gave it all to me and I don't remember how much it was, but it was lots! In Humboldt I bought a new car, a 1954 Dodge De Soto, for $3,900. When I hit Debden, which is about seven miles from my parents' house, I went to the store.

"Gentlemen," I asked, "have you seen my mom or my dad?"

"Who is your dad?"

They didn't know me because all those years I was at the residential school and then Moose Jaw. So I told them who I was. Oh, man. Within about 15 minutes the whole damn town was in that store. They wanted to see Fred Sasakamoose. They'd heard about him. They knew his mom and dad.

Then I drove to the old 24x24 log house that was handmade by my dad. No running water, no electricity, no bedrooms, just one complete room. There was no road, just a wagon trail. It took me an hour to go those seven miles with my new car. Finally, I stop in front of the new house. I was dressed in tie, suit, long coat, and I stayed in my car. My mom stepped out and called back into the house.

"Môniyâs!" White man, she was saying in Cree to my father. This is a white man, come and talk to him.

"Môniyâs!"

I wanted to get out, I wanted to hug Mom. But I wanted to play a little, I wanted to hold back a little longer. My dad came out.

"Môniyâs . . ." Both of them were standing there. It took about a minute, maybe a minute and a half. It seemed like a whole hour. I got out of the car.

"NIKOSIS! NIKOSIS!"

That's all you could hear was her screaming that one word. That's all she knew, that word.

"NIKOSIS! NIKOSIS!" My son! My son!

There was still snow on the ground, but she came out, barefoot, and she hugged me. Then she took me into the house. I looked in the cupboard.

"What you got to wear, mom?"

"Oh, I got an apron, I got a dress."

"How about food in the cupboard?"

"Oh, we got rabbit, we got chicken." Prairie chicken, wild meat.

"Mom, you put your best clothes on, I'm taking you to P.A. You too, Dad."

I load them into that big car, Mom sitting in front, Dad in the back, and we went to town. Filled the car with groceries.

"Mom," I said, "pick out some dress for yourself."

"No, I don't want a dress, I want a print. I want a print where I can sew my own clothes."

"Well, pick it." She picked the best-looking silk she could find. We were gone about four, five hours.

The next day, I said, "Dad, what do you want?"

"I need horses. I need a wagon. I need a sleigh."

"Well, Dad, where you gonna get 'em?"

"At Leask." About 40 miles.

"We'll go there tomorrow."

Out on Muskeg Lake Reserve, George Greyeyes wanted to sell a team of horses with a democrat for $600. I paid for them.

That's when my career fell apart. My parents came home with the horses, Mom and Dad sitting together on the democrat. I had made them happy. I drove home alone, and I stopped in a bar and started to drink. My grandfather saw me.

"Slow down, son," he said to me. "Your body can only take so much, and after that you'll be no good."

I never listened to him. "I'll buy three more of these cars next year," I said. They didn't know how much money I was making. Nobody knew. The truth was, my contract was for $4,600 a season if I stayed with the Black Hawks and between $3,000 and $3,500 for different levels of the minor leagues.

I went into that bar because I thought I'd finished my job when I made my father and mother happy. Then I figured it was my turn to go meet my friends because of all the years that I haven't seen 'em. I was a little tin Jesus, I guess you'd say. Everybody thought, ooh, Freddy's here, the hockey player. That feeling, it really got into my head. I didn't care about my body, I didn't care for nothing else, all I cared was for myself. Before then, I had never got drunk in my life. In Moose Jaw I never even smoked. When I got to the big cities out East, I had a bottle of beer sometimes and that was it.

I drank and I drank for 90 days, three months. By the end of the summer, my vehicle was smashed up, ruined. There were no highways on the reserve, nothing but wagon trails. The car was always touching bottom. The muffler, drive shaft, everything was coming off. Finally, Tommy Ivan, Chicago's general manager, phones me at the hotel in Debden a month before training camp and tells me to run, to get in shape, report in condition because if I don't they'll send me to the minors. So I ran to town and back, seven miles each way, for 30 days straight. Sometimes I'd do a little more, splitting wood and lifting logs.

When I reported to camp in Welland, Ontario, I was 180 pounds, about 10 pounds overweight. Tommy Ivan said you're not bad, but you'll have to take that off. They'd put these all-rubber suits on us, with cuffs on your neck, your wrists and your ankles. They get you on that damn bike and you pedalled and pedalled. But it was good. I was still hanging on when we got to Montreal for our first game. Then Tommy Ivan tells me I'm going to play for the New Westminster Royals. I was really mad and disappointed. After all that hard work that I'd done, I burned myself out because of the one time that I was not listening, when my grandfather told me to look after myself.

Gus Kyle

I went to New Westminster. Then they phoned me up in December and said you're going to the American Hockey League—to Buffalo because we're going to call you up. You know where they shipped me? Chicoutimi, way the hell north of Quebec City. After the playoffs I got married to Loretta. I went to the training camp again, and she went back to her parents' house. I didn't receive one letter from my wife, not even one phone call. I couldn't think well. I wanted to go home. Hockey was not in me anymore. My wife was that important, more important than my career. Management wanted to put me in Buffalo, but I talked them into sending me to Calgary. Then I told Gus Kyle, the coach and general manager of the Stampeders, that I had to get my wife. I took a taxi from Calgary, which was about 700 miles, and got to the house at 4 o'clock in the morning. Loretta woke up when she heard the taxi and opened the window.

"What do you want?"

"I have come for you, my wife."

"No. I am not going."

Then my father-in-law invited me inside. I told him I had signed a contract with the Calgary Stampeders, that I had a house there, that Loretta could move over there with me. She refused. I went to my place and told my dad about it. He said, "Well, son, there's a lot of women . . ." but I never believed that. The next morning, before I went back to Calgary, Loretta told me, "Freddie, it's me or your hockey." And I left. I went back to Calgary that same day.

About a week later the Stampeders were in Saskatoon for a game. A whole bunch of Indians came to watch me. And the most amazing thing happened. My mom walked right out on the ice. She opened the gate—how she even got there, I don't know—and carried out a moose hide jacket.

Oh man, my mother. She was so proud of me that she would do anything. Nobody stopped her. She just walked right to the middle of that bloody ice and covered me up with that jacket, a beaded jacket that she made all by herself! And a tie, a beaded tie with the Black Hawks logo on it. I still got that tie; that's the only thing I got left of my mother that she made for me.

Fred Sasakamoose, 2004, with the tie his mother made

I looked around. "Mom, where's my wife?"

"She didn't want to come."

After the game I tell my roommate, Blinky Boyce, I'm leaving, I'm going home. Blinky was sitting in a chair and phoned up Gus Kyle.

"The Chief is leaving."

It must have been 11:30 or midnight. Gus came in.

"What are you doing, Chief?"

"I'm packing. I'm going home, and nobody's going to stop me."

I walked out. I never said goodbye to my teammates. I just went. There was a taxi downstairs, and I grabbed it and I went home to my wife.

Later, I played in Kamloops for a few years in the Okanagan league. Loretta lived there with me for a couple of seasons, then stayed home. I remember once I was facing off in Kelowna and somebody in the crowd yelled, "Hey, ya squawhumper!" Even the referee stopped and looked in the direction where it came from. It hurt for a while. Yet I learned to shake it off. He was only one bad apple. Finally, I went back to Saskatchewan for good.

A lot of times people ask, if you were to start over again, would you do it differently? And I say, I made the right choice. When my wife told me, "it's either your hockey or it's me," I made the right choice. I love my wife. We'll celebrate our 50th anniversary in July 2005. We have nine children, 39 grandchildren, 17 great-grandchildren. You talk about riches—not in money, I'll never have money. But riches in life, that's me.

I worked hard after my hockey career was over to give something back to kids. I like the good feeling you get when you give your best, and for me now that's when we have Fred Sasakamoose All-Star Week in August for a couple of hundred kids in Saskatoon. I'm hoping someday we can have the Stanley Cup there so the kids could shoot for something, something they could look at and touch, to show that dreams can become reality.

GLENN HALL: HE LOOKED LIKE A REAL 'FIND'

LEO PARKER, GENERAL MANAGER OF THE Humboldt Indians, was in a bind. One of his players had got in trouble off the ice, and coach Don McIntyre had kicked the player off the team. No problem. Only the player's best friend was the goalie, and he was threatening to quit if his buddy wasn't reinstated. Problem. Only five games remained in the 1947–48 season, the Indians' second in the Saskatchewan Junior Hockey League. The goalie wasn't any great shakes, allowing 5.74 goals a game, but he was all the team had. Humboldt, although dead last in the six-team SJHL with a 6–16–1 record, could still make the playoffs.

Indians forward Howard Hall had a lead on a goalie. His younger cousin played on the Humboldt juveniles, but that calibre of hockey was far, far below the SJHL. There weren't any experienced junior net-minders available at this time of year. Parker's options, then, were to go with the untested, 16-year-old Glenn Hall or let the incumbent goalie dictate team decisions. Glenn Hall it was.

Hall's first two games would be against the Saskatoon Quakers, occupants of fourth place and the last playoff spot. Humboldt won both games, 8–4 and 10–5. Next came consecutive contests against the third-place Prince Albert Mintos. Again the Indians took two, 5–2 and 4–3. In the regular-season finale, Humboldt pulverized the Quakers 9–3. Glenn Hall, the untested 16-year-old, had won all five of his games with a goals-against average of 3.40 and taken the Indians into the playoffs against the first-place Moose Jaw Canucks!

"Shaky" Jack McLeod was not about to let some upstart ruin the Canucks' playoff run, though. He poured in three goals and two assists as Moose Jaw won the opener of the best-of-three series 7–3 in Humboldt. Still, there was no denying the potential of the kid goalie, according to the *Moose Jaw Times-Herald:* "A feature of the hard-fought contest was the smart cage work of youthful Glen (sic) Hall of Humboldt. The youngster came through with some spectacular saves in the first and third periods." Down in the Friendly City for Game 2, McLeod flipped his numbers (two goals and three assists) as the Canucks prevailed 8–3. Again, the *Times-Herald* was impressed:

Glenn Hall, Humboldt Indians, 1948

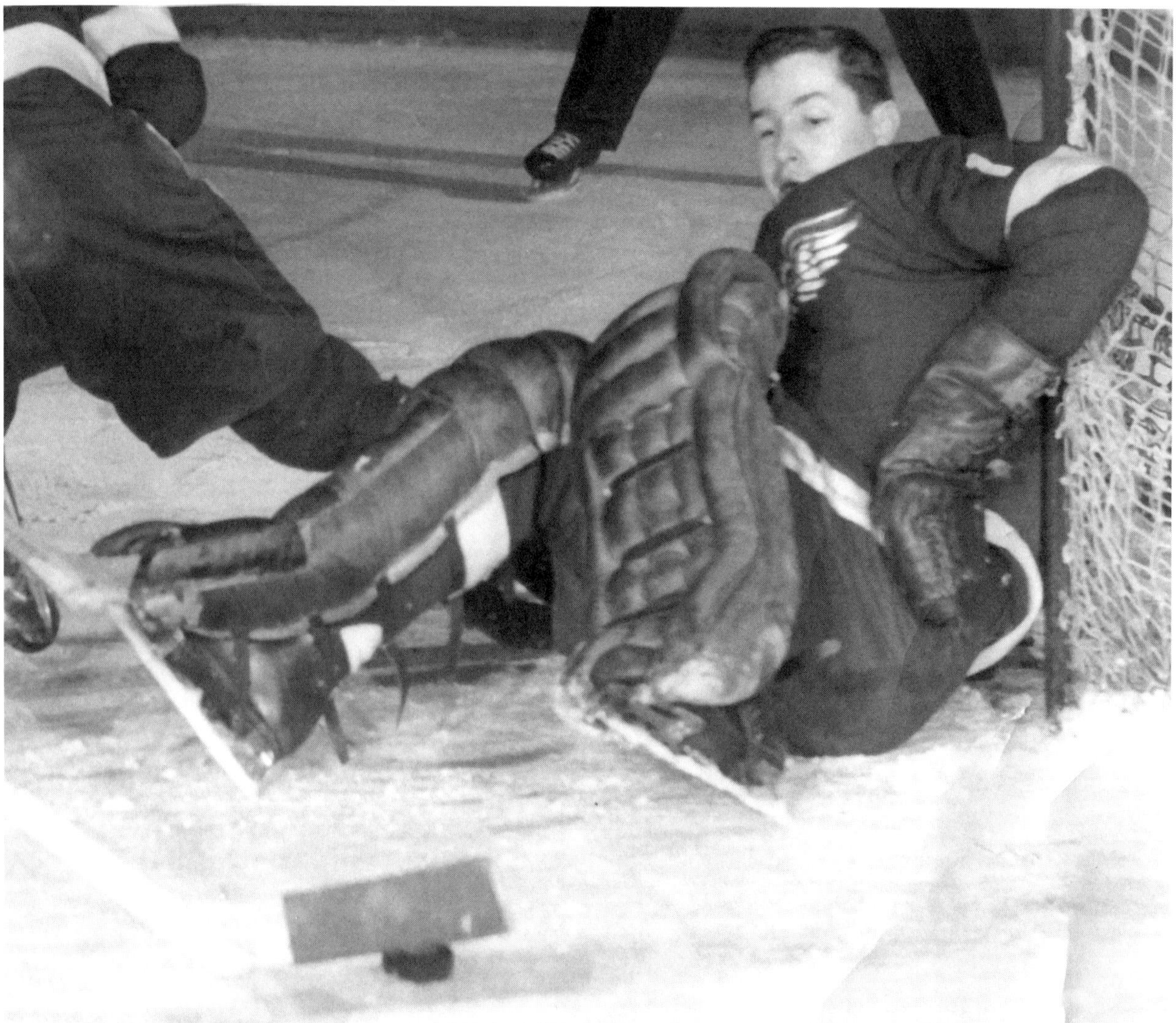

Glenn Hall in his early years with the Detroit Red Wings

"There wasn't much wrong with the way 16-year-old Colin (sic) Hall performed. In fact, he looked like a real 'find'." No doubt about it, Glenn Hall was going to make a name for himself; maybe even his own.

Realignment put Humboldt in the Northern Saskatchewan Junior Hockey League in 1948–49. Hall continued to shine in the Humboldt goal, posting a 3.58 GAA as the Indians finished in second place. That, to Saskatchewan's misfortune, ended his playing days in the province. The Detroit Red Wings, the Indians' parent club, moved Hall to the Windsor Spitfires of the more highly regarded Ontario Hockey Association to get him better prepared for his professional career.

It was in Windsor that Hall began to vomit before games, a habit he would maintain for three decades. His ritual brought him from a state of overexcitement to one of equilibrium, although it didn't always sit well (so to speak) with teammates. Hall's retching prompted Chicago Black Hawks forward Ed Litzenberger (Neudorf) to bestow a nickname that was known only to Hall's teammates during his career: "The Ghoulie."

Rarely is it mentioned that The Ghoulie was, along with Johnny Bower, one of the few great old-time goalies who did not let the job drive him up the wall, as it did Bill Durnan, Jacques Plante and Terry Sawchuk.

"They talk about me throwing up before a game as a weakness," Hall told Dick Irvin Jr. "I've always looked at that as one of the great strengths I had. I didn't take things home with me after a game too much."

Hall developed a new style of goaltending that

evolved from observing Chuck Rayner. Attending Red Wings training camps and playing in Windsor gave Hall opportunities to see NHL games in Detroit. Rayner's many strengths included the ability to turn his stick so that hard shots would fly off to the corners of the rink.

Hall lacked Rayner's arm strength; low shots would virtually go through his stick. He compensated by dropping into the "butterfly" position with his knees on the ice, his lower legs turned diagonally, and his stick blade on the ice. This way, the stick was reinforced by his knees and easily redirected the puck to the corner. Shots out of stick range struck his pads and were quickly smothered. His glove was at the ready for high shots—low shots, too. Jimmy Skinner, his coach at Windsor, didn't care for that.

"What if you let one in?" he asked Hall.

"Talk to me after I let one in."

Hall finished junior hockey as the most valuable player in the OHA and served a four-year minor-league apprenticeship while Sawchuk kept a firm grip on the goaltending job in Detroit. On the two occasions when Sawchuk needed relief, Hall was called up from the Edmonton Flyers and allowed only 12 goals in eight games. Sawchuk was traded to Boston in the summer of 1955 and Hall was sensational in the Red Wings' goal, earning the Calder Trophy his first season and First All-Star Team status the second.

Glenn Hall, Chicago Black Hawks

Three minutes into the second game of the 1957 semi-finals, Boston's Vic Stasiuk unloaded a hard wrist shot that smashed into the right side of Hall's mouth. It took half an hour and 18 stitches before Hall could return to action, but he did, just as he had during the regular season when he was cut for 10 stitches over his right eye and in another game for eight stitches over the left eye. Hall finished the contest, made 30 saves, and the Red Wings prevailed 7–2. He played the rest of the series with blackened eyes and a swollen face, but the Bruins won in five games. Detroit general manager Jack Adams publicly blamed Hall for the loss and called his goaltender "puck-shy." Neither Hall nor Ted Lindsay was saddened when Adams traded them to Chicago that summer.

Puck-shy?

"If you don't think I was familiar with that puck," Hall once said, "then let me tell you exactly what was written on it: Art Ross, patent No. 22656."

In Hall's first season with the Black Hawks, they were outshot in 55 of their 70 games. They missed the playoffs, the only time in his 16 full NHL seasons that he wouldn't compete in the post-season. His GAA swelled from 2.21 to 2.86. He was voted to the First All-Star Team anyway. The Black Hawks got better; in 1960–61 they actually posted a winning record, their first in 15 years, and squared off against the five-time defending Stanley Cup champion Montreal Canadiens in the playoffs.

Chicago managed to split the first two games in Montreal. Game 3 was a classic. Murray Balfour of the Black Hawks scored in the second period. Hall was 36 seconds from a shutout when Henri Richard forced overtime on a power play that was reinforced with a sixth attacker. Doug Harvey put the puck past Hall in the second overtime, but referee Dalton MacArthur immediately disallowed it, ruling that Harvey's stick was too high. Hall's work in the third overtime was astonishing: he stoned Jean Beliveau from point-blank range on a Montreal power play, held his ground when Richard tried to deke him on a breakaway and gloved Claude Provost's shot on another breakaway. Finally, at 12:12 of the third overtime, Balfour connected again with a short backhand on a Black Hawks power play. Montreal coach Toe Blake scooted across the ice and threw a punch at MacArthur, who never worked another NHL game. Blake drew a $2,000 fine.

Hall, who made 53 saves in the triple-overtime thriller, followed it with a 55-save losing effort (5–2) in Game 4 and finished off the Habs with consecutive 3–0 shutouts. He then held Detroit to 10 goals in six games as Chicago won, as of this writing, its last Stanley Cup.

That would be the only championship of Hall's career, but he had another 18 months to go on one of the most incredible achievements in sports history: his streak of 502 consecutive games played in goal. From the opening night of the 1955–56 season to the first period of a contest on November 6, 1962, Hall played every minute of every game. He played every minute of all 50 playoff games in that span, so if the post-season is included Hall's NHL streak is 552 games. Backtrack to the beginning of his first professional season with the Indianapolis Capitols and the only minor-league time he ever missed occurred on those two occasions when he went to Detroit to substitute for Sawchuk. Include the NHL call-ups and the four seasons of minor-league league contests, including playoffs, and Glenn Hall played 881 consecutive games without absenteeism or substitution. Facial gashes couldn't drive him from the crease; he finally removed himself when he let in a weak goal because a sore back hindered his movement.

A general disdain for backchecking among his teammates in Chicago, where Hall spent 10 seasons, limited him to two Vezina Trophies in that city. (He also won it once in St. Louis.) He led the NHL in goals-against average only once but in shutouts six times. Hall was selected to more all-star teams and played in more all-star games than any goaltender in NHL history. He retired with a 2.49 GAA and 84 shutouts, third on the all-time list. While still in the prime of his career, Chicago fans gave Glenn Hall the nickname that many would covet but only he earned: "Mr. Goalie."

Not bad, eh? Mr. Hockey and Mr. Goalie, both from the heart of Saskatchewan.

JOHNNY BOWER: ONE FOR THE AGES

RUMOURS SWIRLED THROUGHOUT JOHNNY BOWER'S career that he was somewhat older than his official birth date of November 8, 1924, suggested. Never mind that he was playing junior hockey in his home town of Prince Albert in 1944–45 when he would have been 20; he just seemed so . . . old. Surely, the rumours have died, for Johnny Bower has passed his 80th birthday with the energy of a man considerably younger, his calendar still full of personal appearances for charitable functions despite undergoing bypass surgery four years ago.

Among his vivid memories is the first pair of goalie pads that he wore in P.A.

"Yes, I was maybe 10 or 11 years of age," Bower recalls. "There was a gang of kids that played hockey together, and one of them, Joe, lived just down the street from me. He was a very handy guy with tools and making things. There was a baby crib mattress being thrown away, so he picked it up and made a pair of pads out of them by cutting the mattress lengthwise and stitching the sides. He left an opening at the bottom for our shoes, because we didn't have skates. We bound them with twine just tight enough to hold them on our legs, and took turns using them. They left lots of rebounds, mind you, but we had lots of fun with 'em."

At different stages of his youth his surname was Kiszkan. Details on this vary in the many articles written about him. Bower prefers not to discuss the change, mentioning only a "separation in the family," but it is clear that he lived a life of poverty with his eight sisters.

"I got my first pair of skates when I was 12 or 13 from Father Delisle of St. Paul's Catholic Church. They were really big for me, probably about size 8s, and I stuffed them with paper. It was difficult to get skates because we didn't have any money at all to buy equipment. When Christmas came I might get a hockey stick. My dad couldn't afford it, but he went across the river and got a branch that looked like a hockey stick and trimmed it down for me. I'll tell you, it was really heavy, but it lasted a long time."

The puzzle of Bower's age stemmed from the

Second World War, when he did lie about his age to enlist in the army as a 15-year-old in 1940.

"When the war broke out a lot of us younger guys joined the reserves in P.A. To us, being a soldier was a big thing; we probably didn't know better. We were just kids. They'd train us to march and to handle rifles. I went overseas around 1943.

"I was going to play hockey at one of the camps, but when I arrived I found out that Turk Broda and pretty well all the pros that played for the Maple Leafs were there on this hockey team. There was just no way, so I turned around.

"I was in England for just a short time. It was very damp, and we had to go through water up to our necks. I came down with arthritis in my back and hands, so they discharged me and sent me home."

So it was that a young man with a four-year military record returned to civilian life with a year of junior eligibility remaining. Suspicious, yes, but entirely legitimate. Bower—"Kiszkan" in team photos and newspaper reports—tended goal for both the junior Black Hawks and the senior Warhawks, most of whom worked at the local munitions works.

"The Warhawks were a proud team," he said. "A lot of former Warhawks had died at Dieppe."

Bower (his surname thereafter) went to Cleveland in 1945 and spent eight years with the Barons of the American Hockey League. He was practically an institution in the city in the early '50s, averaging 42 wins a season and leading the Barons to two championships. A friendly AHL rival was high-scoring Johnny Chad of the Providence Reds, an Albertan by birth who had played junior hockey in Prince Albert and Saskatoon and had enjoyed some NHL time before sacrificing his prime years to the war effort.

"Johnny was the golf pro at Waskesiu Golf Course, and he asked me if I'd like to be an assistant. At that time I didn't like golf at all, but I learned how to play, and I was assistant pro there for four or five years. I started around 1946, and I'd come back every summer. I had a coffee shop, too, and after the golf I decided to do the coffee shop on my own. I worked long hours, but it was only for the summer. A lot of the hockey players came up for golf tournaments, and they'd stop in for coffee and hamburgers—'Bower's Big Boys,' we called 'em."

New York traded Emile Francis and two other players to acquire Bower for the 1953–54 campaign. Accustomed to winning in Providence while the Rangers had made the NHL playoffs only twice in the last 11 years, Bower was hesitant to debut on Broadway. He was a smash success, playing every minute of the 70-game schedule, posting a 2.60 GAA with five shutouts and winning the Calder Trophy as the league's best rookie as the Rangers achieved their best record since 1941–42.

Unfortunately, New York missed the playoffs again and resumed its zany rotation of four netminders, three of them from Saskatchewan, that had begun back in 1952: 1. Chuck Rayner from New York to Saskatoon to retirement; 2. Francis from Cincinnati to New York to Vancouver to Saskatoon; 3. Bower from Cleveland to New York to Vancouver to

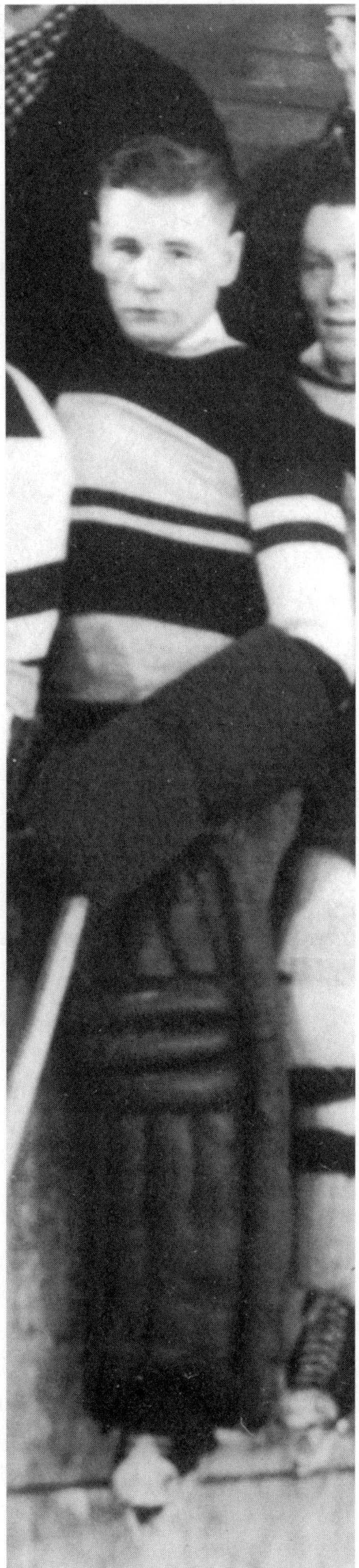

John Kiszkan, P.A. Warhawks, 1945

Rangers goalie Johnny Bower kicks out a shot from Montreal forward Lorne Davis (14)

Providence and back to Cleveland; and, 4. Gump Worsley (of Montreal) from Saskatoon to New York to Vancouver before the Rangers finally settled on him as their goalie.

Still, Bower's New York experience would prove invaluable as the starting point for his signature move as a goaltender.

"That's where I met Charlie Rayner. He had retired, but he watched me closely and was a great help to me because he taught me how to do the poke check, eh? It was very effective for me, one of my best weapons."

Prepared to play out the string in the AHL, Bower was startled when Punch Imlach, veteran AHL coach and new general manager of the Toronto Maple Leafs, drafted him in the summer of 1958. Imlach made himself Toronto's head coach after firing Billy Reay in midseason and soon made Bower the first-string goalie ahead of Ed Chadwick. Bothered by self-doubt because of his age before reporting to Toronto, Bower would spend 11 years with the Maple Leafs, deliver spectacular performances in four Stanley Cup triumphs and earn a place in the Hockey Hall of Fame. He won more professional hockey games than any goaltender before or since: 639 in the regular season (250 in the NHL, 389 in the minors) and 67 in playoffs (35 NHL, 32 minors), 706 overall.

MURRAY BALFOUR: BRAVE WARRIOR OF THE BLACK HAWKS

MURRAY BALFOUR (REGINA) WAS A BRUISER, AN honest digger who took no prisoners as a defenceman with the Regina Pats and a right winger with the Chicago Black Hawks. In Chicago, he was the cornerman and enforcer on the Million Dollar Line for playmaking centre Bill Hay and high-scoring left-winger Bobby Hull. Hay and Balfour were surplus Canadiens' property who were sold to the Black Hawks in 1959.

"Neither of us had very much ice time until around Christmastime," Hay recalls of their rookie season in Chicago. "Then Eric Nesterenko and Ron Murphy were injured, and (coach) Rudy Pilous put Murray and I with Bobby Hull. Bobby was sort of banging around, thinking he could score from behind his own net, and we happened to click. We did what I did in college, which was have a tough guy to work the corners, get the puck to me, I'd fool around with it for a little while, pass it to the left winger and he'd shoot it in the net. I told Bobby, 'Shoot the puck, that's all you gotta do.'

"Murray was a good, good pal, a hard worker. He played tough but clean."

Balfour's second season, 1960–61, was his best. He

Ex-Pats with 1961–62 Chicago Black Hawks: (from left) Bob Turner, Murray Balfour, Bill Hay and publicist Johnny Gottselig

scored 21 goals and had a terrific playoff. His goal in the third overtime of Game 3 was the pivotal moment in the semi-final against Montreal that the Black Hawks won in six games to end the Canadiens' five-year championship reign. Chicago then beat Detroit to capture its third and, to date, last Stanley Cup. Balfour, with five goals and five assists in 11 games, missed the last contest with a broken left arm.

Then Balfour's career went into a baffling decline. The broken arm didn't heal properly and had to be reinforced with an eight-inch steel rod between his wrist and elbow. Abdominal maladies started to trouble him. His production dropped to 15 goals, then 10, then two. His energy gradually diminished. Balfour was traded to Boston, went scoreless in 15 games, and was sent to the minors.

On February 5, 1965, exploratory abdominal surgery revealed that Murray Balfour had inoperable lung cancer. On May 30 he was dead, a chilling testament to cancer's power. He was young, robust (5-foot-9, 175 pounds), so fiercely aggressive that he literally terrified some opponents, avoided the common vices and lived a virtuous life. If cancer could kill Murray Balfour, it could kill anyone.

"It was unbelievable that he died at the age of 28," says Bill Hicke, Balfour's teammate with the Regina Pats (1954–56) and Rochester Americans (1958–59). "He never smoked or drank in his life, and I know that for a fact. I used to go to parties at his parents' house on Winnipeg Street. His dad was a milkman. Murray would have two cases of milk there for the guys that didn't drink, and booze for the guys that did.

"If you ever had a chance to pick a guy to play with you, you'd pick Murray Balfour. He gave 110 percent all the time."

BOB BAUN: ONE GOOD BREAK DESERVES ANOTHER

Bob Baun (Lanigan) moved to Ontario at the age of three and repaid the province of his birth by helping the Toronto Marlboros whip the Regina Pats in consecutive Memorial Cup finals (1955 and '56).

He forever established hockey's standard for grit in the 1964 Stanley Cup final when, in Game 6, he blocked a Gordie Howe shot that fractured his ankle. Baun took a painkilling injection, scored the winning goal in overtime and played Game 7 before finally having a cast put on the leg.

An extremely shrewd businessman and investor, Baun's most selfless moment during a 17-year NHL career may have occurred in 1968 when he was traded to the Red Wings and had a private conversation with Howe. Baun bluntly told Howe he was accepting salaries unworthy of a superstar's stature and was consequently undermining the pay structure of the entire league.

When Baun disclosed he was making more than $90,000, Howe was aghast—not because Baun had never so much as won an individual trophy or made an all-star team, but because Red Wings management had told Howe he was the highest-paid player on the team at $45,000!

Howe and his agent-wife Colleen demanded, and got, a six-figure salary in record time and were forever after more circumspect in their financial dealings.

CLUB DE HOCKEY CANADIEN INC.

2313 ST. CATHERINE ST. WEST · TEL. WELLINGTON 2-6131 · MONTREAL 25, P.Q.

May 22, 1959

Mr. Wm. Hicke,
1433 Royal Street,
Regina, Sask.

Dear Billy:

I have a little favor to ask of you. Perhaps you will remember meeting my sister-in-law, Miss Clara Schmidt, the chief operator of the Bell Telephone Company in Kitchener, at the Stanley Cup party at the Queen Elizabeth Hotel.

She thought that you were just about the nicest young man she had ever met and was surprised that a fellow could have so much charm and still play as tough a game as professional hockey. Miss Schmidt is a spinster, old enough to be your mother, and I don't want you to misunderstand the high regard she has for you.

Yesterday she underwent a very serious operation and although she is dreadfully ill the doctors feel she will recover and I have an idea she would get quite a lift out of a "Get Well" card selected by you and sent to her. The address would be:

Miss Clara Schmidt,
C/o St. Mary's Hospital,
Kitchener, Ontario.

Before I close I must congratulate you on the various awards you gathered in the American Hockey League and to urge you to take the best of care of yourself so that you will return prepared to win new laurels with Canadiens. Your principal job, you will understand, is to take Maurice Richard's place if and when he retires...and that is quite an assignment.

With best wishes, I remain,

Sincerely yours,

Frank J. Selke

FJS:D — Frank J. Selke.

Frank Selke's 1959 letter to Bill Hicke: "take Maurice Richard's place"

BILL HICKE: A BREATHTAKING EXPERIENCE

THERE ARE EXPECTATIONS AND THERE ARE EXPECTATIONS. Bill Hicke (Regina) was EXPECTED to be the next Maurice Richard—by Montreal fans *and* team management. Check out that 1959 letter from Canadiens general manager Frank Selke. No pressure . . .

No one was going to be the next Rocket, but Hicke had the makings of a star when Selke wrote that letter. After consecutive 50-goal seasons with the Regina Pats, Hicke had swept the AHL's major awards in 1958-59 as top rookie, leading scorer (97 points) and most valuable player.

"I had some God-given talents," Hicke says. "One was to know where to be when the puck came out of the corners or from behind the net. And I never had trouble skating. I was always one step ahead of my linemates. The only guys I ever had to push myself to keep up with were Henri Richard and Yvan Cournoyer."

Hicke's first three seasons after Rocket Richard's retirement were good (55 total goals), but not of star quality. Frustration and a knee injury led to a trade request that was granted in December of 1964: to New York for Dick Duff. A different Bill Hicke would toil in the NHL for the next seven years: one who was sick, sick, sick.

"I got pneumonia in training camp in 1965," he remembers. "Then it turned out I had a trillion allergies. And I had asthma, which I never had before."

Of course, Hicke's simple version of the story shouldn't be taken at face value. He didn't have a trillion allergies; he came up positive on only 140 of 180 tests. He also omits the part about lapsing into a coma and flirting with death.

Hicke was the Oakland Seals' second non-goaltender selection (after Bob Baun) in the 1967 expansion draft and began to produce as well as he ever had in Montreal.

"I was leading the West Division in scoring (with 40 points in 52 games)," Hicke says. "Bert Olmstead was our coach, and he played me 30 minutes a game. Then one day at practice I didn't feel well. I couldn't breathe, like from my New York days. I did all the drills and I collapsed. They put me on a pulmonary function monitor in the hospital, and I failed everything. Had I not got sick, I would have had the best year of my life."

Bill Hicke with Rochester, 1958-59

All things considered, Hicke had four decent seasons in Oakland. He finished his career with the Alberta Oilers of the World Hockey Association and returned to Regina, where he became a successful businessman, most notably as proprietor of Kyle's Sporting Goods and part-owner of the Pats. Despite the decades of bad health, Hicke has long been the life of the party wherever he happens to be.

DAVE BALON: NO RESPECT, NO JUSTICE

Dave Balon

Then there's the case of Dave Balon (Wakaw), who got so little respect that he envied Rodney Dangerfield. Balon (rhymes with Malone) hitchhiked from Wakaw in 1955 to attend the junior Prince Albert Mintos' training camp as a 17-year-old uninvited walk-on. He made the team and, with Orland Kurtenbach (Cudworth) as his centre, became the team's star left winger. After three years of up-and-down movement between the New York Rangers and their farm teams, he made it to the NHL for good in 1962 and a year later was shipped to Montreal as part of a blockbuster trade featuring goaltenders Jacques Plante and Gump Worsley.

Life was good in Montreal for a couple of years: 24- and 18-goal seasons, a pair of Stanley Cups, and recognition as a hard-skating, two-way player. His playing time gradually diminished, and he was disappointed when, at 28, he was left unprotected in the 1967 expansion draft and was immediately claimed by the Minnesota North Stars. Re-acquired by the Rangers a year later, Balon enjoyed a career year in 1969–70 with 33 goals, 70 points and a plus-40 rating that ranked fourth in the league.

So what did people call him? Garbage Collector. New York's Bulldog Line of Balon, Walt Tkaczuk and Bill Fairbairn would play tic-tac-toe with the puck, Balon would be left unguarded with a five-foot shot or an easy rebound that he had worked like hell to get, and people called his goals garbage.

"It takes the joy out of scoring," he said once. "This is the way it makes you feel after a while, when people criticize you for scoring. I take a lot of abuse in front of the nets. I have to be in the right spot, I have to anticipate the play."

If 1969–70 was garbage, 1970–71 started off like landfill. Balon reached 29 goals with a four-goal outburst on January 25 and was on course for a 50-goal season. Instead, he managed only seven more, enough for a new high of 36 but a disappointment all the same. Worse, Balon felt his legs losing their strength. Trainers and medical staff couldn't find anything wrong. So what was his real problem?

Balon was traded to Vancouver the following November, produced a 23-goal effort, and was booed out of town a year later when he scored only three times. His last stop was in Quebec of the WHA, where he broke his leg after nine scoreless games, had his no-cut contract voided and had to sue the Nordiques to get his money. Balon left Quebec the way he left Vancouver and New York, with legions of fans, teammates, coaches and executives assuming he was either washed up or dogging it.

Returning to Saskatchewan to coach the Tier 2 junior Humboldt Broncos, he struggled to do simple things like skate on the ice for practice and stand behind the bench during games. Sometimes he would literally coach from the bench, sitting down. His speech was slurred. There were people who drew their own conclusions and spread the word: Dave Balon had become a drunk.

Finally, he went to University Hospital in Saskatoon and underwent a battery of tests. The diagnosis made Dave Balon a justifiably bitter man.

Multiple sclerosis.

He wasn't imagining things, or dogging it or a drunk.

MS.

Balon coached a few more years and operated a paddlewheel boat on Waskesiu Lake until the degenerative disease forced him into a wheelchair. His resentment towards the hockey community that had been cruel to him gradually subsided. At a benefit dinner in the summer of 1996 that left him in tears, Balon was given a specially equipped van with a wheelchair lift. The Canadiens alumni organization, at the instigation of Garry Peters (Regina), paid for the vehicle and fitted it with licence plates that read HABS 20, the number Balon wore as a Stanley Cup champion.

BILL HAY: LEADERSHIP AND VERSATILITY

Bill "Red" Hay (Saskatoon) insists he was not born in Lumsden, as his mother and older brother were, so don't believe the reference books. Hay won the Calder Trophy in 1958–59 with a 55-point season, outshining, among others, teammate Stan Mikita.

That's an interesting photo of Hay posing with the Calder Trophy at the Black Hawks' 1960 training camp. First, there's an elegant crescent-shaped scar on his forehead. Second, how many players with only one season of NHL experience were made an assistant captain in those days? Practically none.

One of hockey's tallest players at 6-foot-3 and 190 pounds, Hay enjoyed setting up goals and was frequently criticized for not shooting enough, as his career totals of 113 goals and 273 assists readily suggest. He began as Bobby Hull's centre and wasn't bothered when a young Phil Esposito took over that assignment. Hay moved around at all three forward positions, killed a lot of penalties and got a share of power-play action.

"I got a lot of ice time. It was quiet ice time, and that's the way I liked it. We won more games than we lost, we always got in the playoffs, we played hard, I enjoyed it very very much. Travelling on the trains and competing against some pretty good talent, it was a good way to spend eight years of your life."

Hay retired from hockey in 1966 but was reluctantly lured back when Chicago threatened to record the first regular-season championship in its 40-year history. He was more interested in getting his other career on track at Bow Valley Energy Ltd. and presumed the Black Hawks would leave him alone if he insisted on a salary figure they surely wouldn't meet.

Bill Hay with Calder Trophy, 1960

"Yes, they did meet it: $45,000, more than twice as much as I made the year before. And not prorated but $45,000 for only 36 games. The thing is, it helped me retire for good. You're in a new job, struggling, learning it, and you remember all the wins from when you were playing hockey. Your mind doesn't go back to the losses or the struggles. It didn't hurt me at all to go back for that half a year. And we walked away with first place, so it was very gratifying."

St. Louis claimed him in the 1967 expansion draft and tried to tempt him with another enormous raise.

"The $300 a month I was getting at Bow Valley was fine with me at that time. Besides, I gave Chicago my word that I wouldn't come out of retirement again."

Hay stuck with Bow Valley until 1990, rising to the position of senior vice-president for drilling operations—presumably with a raise or two along the way. Since then, he has been back in hockey as president of Hockey Canada, president of the Calgary Flames and now chairman of the Hockey Hall of Fame.

He takes pride in the distinction that both his father, Charlie, and he have been inducted into the Saskatchewan Oil and Gas Hall of Fame as well as the Saskatchewan Sports Hall of Fame.

Charlie Hay, U of S goalie, 1923

RED BERENSON: HARD HAT AND A DOUBLE HAT TRICK

RED BERENSON (REGINA) WAS CHRISTENED Gordon, "but no one ever called him Gord or Gordie," says Bill Hicke. The Montreal Canadiens figured he had an obvious attitude problem when he came to the team in 1962. First of all, he reported three years late, having had the audacity to defy their authority and obtain an administration degree at the University of Michigan. Second, he wore . . . *a helmet!*

"Helmets were mandatory in the NCAA," Berenson explains. "I didn't wear one my first 20 games as pro. Then I had a concussion. I didn't say anything to anyone, but I knew I was dizzy and had all kinds of symptoms, so I called my old coach at Michigan and asked him to send up my helmet. I put it on and never took it off. The Canadiens sent me down to Hull-Ottawa the first day after I wore the helmet. They didn't like the idea."

Well, we all know what a progressive approach Montreal coach Toe Blake took to Jacques Plante's mask . . .

"My only answer was, 'I'm just wearing a helmet so I don't have to wear one.' There were a couple of guys in the league that had to—Charlie Burns had a plate in his skull, and Red Kelly fractured his skull and had to wear a helmet. But I was wearing one so that I wouldn't have to; people couldn't understand that. I had just gone to school for four years so I'd have something to fall back on after hockey. I didn't want to lose that.

"I wasn't scared of getting hurt, but I could see that the game was evolving. For example, at Michigan we had chicken wire around the ends and corners. But then you got to the NHL and they had just came out with Plexiglas. Players were getting more head injuries just because they were getting hit into the glass every time they got boarded."

Berenson endured parts of five seasons with the Canadiens and two with the Rangers, hindered by Montreal's overwhelming depth at centre and by injuries in New York. His opportunity finally came in November 1967 when the Rangers traded him to St. Louis. Given lots of ice time by Blues coach Scotty Bowman, Berenson responded with 51 points in 55 games. Stardom came on November 8, 1968, when he scored six goals in an 8–0 victory at Philadelphia—the NHL's first six-goal game in 24 years and the first ever achieved by a player on a visiting team.

"Up to then I might have had only two or three goals, but the team was playing well," Berenson recalls. "The first goal was in the last minute of the first period. I got around Ed Van Impe, made a move (on Flyers goalie Doug Favell) as if I was going to cut in and went the other way. It was a good goal, and I remember saying to myself, 'Thank God I can still

Regina Pats linemates (from left) Bill Hicke, Red Berenson and Joe Lunghamer

score.' I was expected to be one of the leading scorers on the Blues, and your confidence goes up and down with your production.

"Then in the second period I scored four more, and they were all clean-cut goals—a three-on-two break, another breakaway on a pass from Camille Henry, no power play goals, no rebounds, no deflections. I hit the crossbar on another shot. It was unbelievable. It wasn't a one-sided game. We went to the second intermission, and Doug Harvey said, 'This would have been a good game if Red wasn't playing.'

"The stick I was using had tape falling off of it. It was a mess, I don't know if it was broken, but I changed sticks, and the next one felt like a club. I didn't feel comfortable with it. I thought, 'I don't even know if I'll even get the puck to the net with this.' And jeez, if I didn't get the puck going down the wing, and I slapped the puck from the top of the circle and it took off right over Favell's shoulder.

"Scotty wanted me to go back on in the last couple of minutes. The crowd was chanting, 'We want Red, we want Red,' and this was in Philadelphia! I said, 'I don't think so, we've got a shutout going, I don't want to jeopardize that.' Jacques Plante got the shutout for us, and after the game Glenn Hall said, 'Well, at least you were plus tonight.' I was plus-7.

"It's good to have a performance like that, but I don't know whether I deserved to do it at all, even though I was an honest player. It shouldn't be me who has the modern record for six goals, it should be a

Gretzky or Lemieux or Bobby Hull, one of the great goal scorers of our era. But it just happened. I tried not to base my career or my reputation on that game."

Berenson retired after the 1977–78 season. He had 16 career goals and 42 points when he was traded to St. Louis nine days before his 28th birthday; he hung up his skates with 261 goals and 658 points to his credit. Shifting to the coaching ranks, he won the Jack Adams Award as the NHL's outstanding coach with St. Louis in 1981–82. Since 1984 Berenson has been head coach at his alma mater, Michigan, and led the Wolverines to six conference and two national championships.

He is also the answer to the trivia question, "Who is the only Saskatchewan-born man to have played for Team Canada in the 1972 Summit Series against the Soviet Union?" Berenson played two games (the first and fifth) and picked up an assist.

TERRY HARPER: A CAREER ALMOST LOST IN A FLASH

Terry Harper (Regina) spent half of his 18 NHL seasons with the Los Angeles Kings, Detroit Red Wings, St. Louis Blues and Colorado Rockies but is primarily remembered for the first half of his career as a reliable stay-at-home defencemen with Montreal. His knack of forcing attackers away from the net and into the boards played a significant role in the Canadiens' five Stanley Cup victories from 1965–71.

Terry Harper

Harper's lean face belied a tremendously strong body that was hidden underneath his uniform and pads. Also hidden were the scars of a dreadful childhood accident.

"I was burned quite seriously when I was 12," Harper says. "It was late summer, a very hot, 100-degree sort of day. We were burning some trash at a friend's place in his backyard, and I had some gasoline in a jar. I never really got to pour it. The fumes were spilling out of the jar, and it fireballed in front of me. I rolled across the garden and tried to put it out. The fellow whose yard it was, he ran in to the house, got a carpet and wrapped me in it. A neighbour across the street had heard the screaming, and he drove me to Regina General Hospital. There were third-degree burns over 30 percent of my body. It was very painful.

"I had a lot of restriction because of contraction of the skin, like I couldn't straighten one arm and one leg was a little tight. I had skin grafts done later to relieve some of that. Before the accident I was a forward, a very good skater, above all the kids at the rink as far as skill level goes. After that I missed a year having grafts done. I still had skills when I got back to the rink, but I wasn't as dominant. They were short of defencemen, so I said I'll play defence, and once I got started I liked it."

Here's the silver lining to that dark cloud: Between junior seasons with the Regina Pats, Harper was in hospital for new skin grafts when a pretty young nurse caught him sneaking out of his room to go for a walk. Gladys, the nurse, and Terry fell in love and have been happily married since 1960, their three grown children all living within an hour of their Sacramento home.

A strong link between Harper's junior and professional days was John Ferguson, a Vancouver boy who played left wing for the Melville Millionaires. Later the two would be teammates on the Canadiens.

"He was by far the best fighter I ever knew," Harper says. "He never lost a fight that I saw, including in Melville. He was a crazy man then. He took a two-hander at Jerry Kolb. Luckily, Jerry got his stick over his head and Ferguson's stick broke over Jerry's. I knew Fergy might be one to watch out for. When he became a teammate, I loved him. He lived and died to play for the Canadiens. Off the ice he was a super guy—a nice, quiet person, a good family man."

Orland Kurtenbach

Harper, despite his strength, was not in Ferguson's league as a fighter. Orland Kurtenbach, the pride of Cudworth, pounded Harper's face into a bloody mess in a memorable 1965 scrap in Toronto when Kurtenbach was with the Maple Leafs.

"I'd had a fight with him the season before, when he was in Boston. I beat him that time . . ."

Whoa! Terry Harper decisioned Orland Kurtenbach?

"I actually came out on top. That's why I should have been on the watch for him in Toronto. He was waiting for me.

"Now, the thing is, (former Montreal general manager) Frank Selke had once suggested that I take fighting lessons. So he gave me a little bonus, $500, and I went off to summer school at UBC. I still had the $500 when I finished summer school, so I took flying lessons instead; that's where I learned to fly. I didn't really want to be a fighter.

"I paid the price then. Kurtenbach got me."

ACE BAILEY: UNTIMELY END FOR A TRUE TEAM PLAYER

Garnet "Ace" Bailey (Lloydminster) began his decade of NHL service as a sparingly used left wing with the mighty Boston teams of the early '70s. He played on the Stanley Cup winners of 1970 and '72 and scored the winning goal in the first game of the '72 final against New York. After six years with Detroit, Washington and St. Louis, Bailey joined the Edmonton Oilers for their final World Hockey Association campaign and helped young Wayne Gretzky adapt to life in professional hockey.

"I sat beside him in the Bruins dressing room when I was a rookie, so we had a personal relationship," says Gregg Sheppard. "He knew his limitations. He understood he was never going to be a star, but he skated hard, played hard and contributed to the team in his assigned role. He wouldn't be a 30- or 40-goal scorer. He'd play on the third or fourth line, but he filled that role extremely well.

"He was a fun-loving guy who'd give you the shirt off his back. I enjoyed his company. He didn't deserve the way he ended up."

Bailey scouted for the Oilers for 13 years and moved on to the Los Angeles Kings to be their director of pro scouting in 1994. He was bound for Los Angeles from his home in Lynnfield, Mass., on September 11, 2001, aboard United Airlines' Flight 175—the second plane to crash into the World Trade Center in New York.

"I'll tell you this," says Red Berenson, a teammate of Bailey's in Detroit and St. Louis. "If Ace would have sensed any of the imminent danger those passengers faced, he would have tried to stop it. There's no doubt of that in the mind of anyone who knew him. He was that kind of a guy. I think the people on board were reassured that this was a simple change in plans, maybe a simple hijacking or whatever.

"Ace Bailey was a great teammate. Anyone that played with Ace liked his enthusiasm. He was a fierce competitor and an honest player."

Keith Magnuson (Wadena) was proof of Murray Armstrong's faith in the university hockey system, graduating from Denver University with a business degree and numerous honours for his play as a defenceman.

Magnuson bypassed the minors and went straight to the Chicago Black Hawks, where he led the NHL in penalties his first two years and set a single-season record with 291 minutes. All that time in the penalty box distracted people from noticing what an excellent defenceman he was (fifth in plus-minus as a rookie, seventh his third year).

He was never voted to an all-star team in his 10 full seasons with the Black Hawks but was an enormous fan favourite for the all-out energy he put into every shift. Legions of friends and fans were stunned by his death in a car accident on December 15, 2003.

Keith Magnuson

HOMESICK FOR VAL MARIE: BRYAN TROTTIER IN HIS OWN WORDS

I was born in Redvers. I know all the guides and record books say Val Marie, but that's not right. I guess that while I was in Swift Current someone just assumed I was born in Val Marie because I was raised there. Dad moved around quite a bit when I was little, working oil rigs and road construction. We moved back to the ranch when Gramp was getting older, when I was about, oh, six years old. So I was raised in Val Marie, straight south of Swift Current on Highway 4, and stayed there until I was 15.

That picture of me (page 173), I'm just turning 15 and playing for Climax, Val Marie's rival team. We would join forces and kick everybody's butt around C Division in pee wee, bantam and midget hockey. We won every tournament we ever went to. We took the Weyburn pee wee tournament two years in a row, went up to Yorkton and won the bantam tournament, won a midget tournament when we were still a bantam team, won the Saskatchewan midget C provincials twice—just a group of farm kids who had no clue what was going on. Bernie Snyder and I were the only two guys from Val Marie; he's up in Fort McMurray now. Willie Desjardins is coaching the Medicine Hat Tigers. Mike Kirk, I think he's growing garbanzo beans down in southwest Saskatchewan.

We thought we were all gonna make the NHL. That team was really, really stacked—no slugs, not one guy that didn't carry his weight. Willie and I tried out for the Moose Jaw junior B team, and Willie ended up staying there for two or three years. I wanted to play in Moose Jaw real bad; my dad drove me back and forth for a month and then he said, "We can't do this anymore, I'm burning more gas than I can pay for." Harry Barrett, the coach of the Swift Current midget Legionaires, invited me to play for them, and I also played senior with Val Marie. Then I went to midget C provincials with Climax. That season Climax won the provincials again, the Val Marie seniors won their league, and the Legionaires won the big tournament they have in Swift Current. I didn't get to a lot of practices but I sure played a lot of hockey!

The next year I stayed in Swift Current with the

Broncos. I was always homesick. I still get homesick. I'm 48 years old, and I miss my family all the time. I was just a kid, pretty naïve. I sat next to Kelly Pratt in the dressing room, a 19-year-old veteran guy. He was really good. Guys would pick on me a little bit, and he'd stick up for me. About halfway through the season Tiger Williams took me under his wing. He'd take me to the movies, and if he was running around the city, he'd show me around. It was really cool to be hanging around Tiger because he was one of the guns, you know, somebody that everybody knew. I saw how personable he was with people and how he treated kids. Tiger might get a little brash, but he was never rude. I'd take him down to the ranch sometimes for hunting and whatnot. So we were pretty good friends.

My second year in junior, 1973–74, was my springboard season. I played left wing for about two months with Terry Ruskowski, and it was like bing, bing, bing, bing, goal, the way we moved the puck. Then they put Tiger on Terry's line and moved me to centre. I loved playing with Terry, and I emulated him. He was scrappy, very tough, a great leader.

After that season the Islanders drafted me. They told me right away that I wasn't going to the NHL. That was fine. My mom and dad respected the decision. I don't think they wanted me to go to New York right away. They were afraid that their son, who they knew was always homesick, was not going to make it because he'd be 3,000 miles away. That was just way too far for their little boy.

That December I went to the world junior championship in Winnipeg along with Brian Sutter, who was my teammate on the Broncos. It was over the Christmas holiday, we were roommates, and we were both horribly homesick. He's from a farm around Viking, Alberta, and I'm from a farming district. His values are the same as mine. We were young men, but we wanted to be home for Christmas, to be around our brothers and sisters and tease them. We'd sit there and talk, and we'd make each other worse!

The Broncos had moved to Lethbridge that season and Earl Ingarfield was my coach. I've had many dads in my life, and he was one of them. Like Stan Dunn in Swift Current. You put your trust in these people and they don't misuse that. You're like their kids. I knew one of the guys in Lethbridge, Bernie Syrenne,

Bryan Trottier, Climax midgets

SASKATCHEWAN-BORN NHL TROPHY WINNERS

HART TROPHY
(Most Valuable Player)

	Team	Season
Eddie Shore	Boston	1932–33
Eddie Shore	Boston	1934–35
Eddie Shore	Boston	1935–36
Eddie Shore	Boston	1937–38
Elmer Lach	Montreal	1944–45
Max Bentley	Chicago	1945–46
Sid Abel	Detroit	1948–49
Chuck Rayner	NY Rangers	1949–50
Gordie Howe	Detroit	1951–52
Gordie Howe	Detroit	1952–53
Al Rollins	Chicago	1953–54
Gordie Howe	Detroit	1956–57
Gordie Howe	Detroit	1957–58
Gordie Howe	Detroit	1959–60
Gordie Howe	Detroit	1962–63
Bryan Trottier	NY Islanders	1978–79

ART ROSS TROPHY
(Scoring Champion)

See Season Leaders in Points, page 176.

LADY BYNG TROPHY
(Skill & Gentlemanly Play)

	Team	Season
Clint Smith	NY Rangers	1938–39
Max Bentley	Chicago	1942–43
Clint Smith	Chicago	1943–44

VEZINA TROPHY
To 1981: Fewest Goals Against.
Since 1981: Outstanding Goaltender.

	Team	Season
Al Rollins	Toronto	1950–51
Johnny Bower	Toronto	1960–61
Glenn Hall	Chicago	1962–63
Glenn Hall *d	Chicago	1966–67
Glenn Hall *p	St. Louis	1968–69

*d: shared with Denis DeJordy
*p: shared with Jacques Plante

NORRIS TROPHY
(Outstanding Defenceman)

No winners; awarded since 1954.

CALDER TROPHY
(Outstanding Rookie)

	Team	Season
Grant Warwick	NY Rangers	1941–42
Glenn Hall	Detroit	1955–56
Bill Hay	Chicago	1959–60
Bryan Trottier	NY Islanders	1975–76

CONN SMYTHE TROPHY
(Playoff MVP)

	Team	Season
Glenn Hall	St. Louis	1967–68
Bryan Trottier	NY Islanders	1979–80

BILL MASTERTON TROPHY
(Perseverance and Dedication)

	Team	Season
Glenn Resch	Colorado	1981–82
Bob Bourne	Los Angeles	1987–88
Gord Kluzak	Boston	1989–90

KING CLANCY TROPHY
(Leadership and Humanitarianism)

	Team	Season
Bryan Trottier	NY Islanders	1988–89
Kelly Chase	St. Louis	1997–98

JACK ADAMS AWARD
(Outstanding Coach)

	Team	Season
Red Berenson	St. Louis	1980–81
Bob Francis	Phoenix	2001–02

LESTER PATRICK TROPHY
(Service to Hockey in the United States)

1967	Gordie Howe
1970	Eddie Shore
1972	Clarence Campbell
1977	Murray Armstrong
1982	Emile Francis
1988	Keith Allen
1998	Max McNab

from the Climax team that I grew up with. I spent all my free time over at his house, and Dad would drive out to Lethbridge once a week and bunk in with the Syrennes. I was made the Broncos' captain so I had a leadership role—I had to grow up a little bit in that regard. I didn't make it home to Val Marie that whole winter. I didn't see my brothers or sisters except for once when they came to Lethbridge.

That spring, after Lethbridge lost out in the playoffs, I flew down East and stayed with the Islanders for their quarter-final series, the one where they lost the first three games to Pittsburgh but came back to win four straight. I couldn't stay for the semi-final against Philadelphia, though. The Islanders told me I could stay as long as I want, but my dad needed me back home. "We've got calves to get out of the cows, we gotta start working here," he told me, so I got back. But I got to know everybody on the Islanders, and I familiarized myself with Long Island a little bit. When I went back in September I didn't feel like I was alone.

My first training camp I played with a whole bunch of guys, and I didn't get one point in the whole exhibition season—not one goal or an assist or even a penalty—but I hit everybody who had the puck. That's all I did. I chased the puck down, forechecked like a mad dog and backchecked like a mule. I told myself, "I may not get a point here, but I'm going to be seen." I got my body on as many people as I could. All the veterans were like, "You're not going to make it if you keep hitting like that. You're going to get hurt." And I was like, "Maybe, but I'm not going to the minors. I'm going to find out if I'm strong enough *now*." I was so nervous about getting sent to the minors that I was ready to do anything—tape sticks, sharpen skates, whatever I had to do to make the team.

When we started the first game of the regular sea-

SASKATCHEWAN-BORN NHL ALL-STAR TEAM SELECTIONS

GOALTENDER

11 (record): **Glenn Hall**, 7 First Team (record; Det 1956–57, Chi '57–58, '59–60, '62–63, '63–64, '65–66, StL '68–69), 4 Second Team (Det 1955–56, Chi '60–61, '61–62, '66–67).

3: **Chuck Rayner**, 3 Second (NYR 1949–50, 1950–51, 1951–52).

2: **Glenn Resch**, 2 Second (NYI 1975–76, '78–79).

1: **Johnny Bower**, 1 First (Tor 1960–61).

1: **Earl Robertson**, 1 Second (NYA 1938–39).

DEFENCE

8: **Eddie Shore**, 7 First Team (Bos 1930–31, '31–32, '32–33, '34–35, '35–36. '37–38, '38–39), 1 Second Team (Bos 1933–34).

3: **Fern Flaman**, 3 Second (Bos, 1954–55, '56–57, '57–58).

1: **Jim Neilson**, 1 Second (NYR 1967–68).

1: **Brad McCrimmon**, 1 Second (Cgy 1987–88).

LEFT WING

2: **Doug Bentley**, 2 First Team (Chi 1943–44, '46–47).

2: **Clark Gillies**, 2 First (NYI 1977–78, '78–79).

2: **Bert Olmstead**, 2 Second Team (Mtl 1952–53, '55–56).

1: **Sid Abel**, 1 Second (Det 1941–42; also see Abel as centre).

1: **Tony Leswick**, 1 Second (NYR 1949–50).

CENTRE

5: **Elmer Lach**, 3 First Team (Mtl 1944–45, '47–48, '51–52), 2 Second Team (Mtl 1943–44, '45–46).

4: Bryan Trottier, 2 First (NYI 1977–78, '78–79), 2 Second (Mtl '81–82, '83–84)

3: **Sid Abel**, 2 First (Det 1948–49, '49–50), 1 Second (1950–51; also 1- as LW in 1941–42).

2: **Max Bentley**, 1 First (Chi 1945–46), 1 Second (1946–47).

1: **Ed Litzenberger**, 1 Second (Chi 1956–57).

RIGHT WING

21 (record, RW and all positions): **Gordie Howe**, 12 First Team (record, RW and all positions; Det 1950–51, '51–'52, '52–53, '53–54, '56–57, '57–58, '59–60, '62–63, '65–66, '67–68, '68–69, '69–70), 9 Second Team (Det 1949–50, '55–56, '58–59, '59–60, '60–61, '61–62, '63–64, '64–65, '66–67).

3: **Bryan Hextall**, 2 First (NYR 1939–40, '40–41), 1 Second (NYR 1942–43).

1: **Lorne Carr**, 1 First (Tor 1943–44).

1: **Theoren Fleury**, 1 Second (Cgy 1994–95).

ALL-ROOKIE TEAM SELECTIONS (Since 1982–83)

1985–86: **Wendel Clark**, Toronto, LW.

1994–95: **Jeff Friesen**, San Jose, F.

1995–96: **Kyle McLaren**, Boston, D.

Jeff Friesen, Regina Pats

son, I had Clark Gillies on my left wing and Billy Harris on the right. We started racking up some decent numbers, and I kept racking up as many hits as I possibly could. In hindsight, playing with Clark Gillies was a big help because I was bumping everybody, and they probably wanted to knock my head off. But I had big Clark looking over my shoulder, as if he was saying, "Okay, it was a clean hit, part of the game, leave him alone." I was oblivious to it because I just wanted to stay in the league.

That rookie season in the NHL, I kept making hits—and ducking hits. Our players warned me: "Bryan, keep your head up. Protect yourself." I was ducking checks and sliding checks, doing everything I possibly could to keep from getting killed. I was 5-foot-10, 190 pounds, but that wasn't muscle. I was still a little pudgy. I didn't cut back on the body checks until my third year. I stopped being reckless because you realize you can hurt people, and you can get hurt. You have to learn when to bail out, when to slow down. By my third year, I was probably down to 20, 25 hits a game. By the time I was done, I was probably down to two or three.

Trottier, for all his insecurity about making the NHL, was an immediate success. His 63 assists and 95 points in 1975–76 were both rookie records and he was a runaway winner of the Calder Trophy. Trottier topped 100 points six of the next seven seasons. His 1978–79 campaign was a blockbuster: Art Ross Trophy winner with 134 points, plus-minus leader at plus-76, Hart Trophy winner as most valuable player, and his second selection as First Team All-Star centre. All individual honours, save one, would stop there as Wayne Gretzky monopolized awards for most of the next decade. The Islanders embarked on a four-year reign as Stanley Cup champions, with Trottier winning the Conn Smythe Trophy in 1980. He earned two more Stanley Cup rings in 1991 and 1992 as he closed out his playing career with Pittsburgh. In between, he raised some eyebrows when he suited up for the United States in the 1985 Canada Cup after having represented Canada in three previous tournaments.

It was fun to be in a different role in Pittsburgh. I

SASKATCHEWAN-BORN NHL SINGLE-SEASON LEADERS

GOALS

	Team	Season	No.
Bryan Hextall	NY Rangers	1939–40	24
Bryan Hextall	NY Rangers	1940–41	26
Doug Bentley	Chicago	1942–43	33
Doug Bentley	Chicago	1943–44	38
Sid Abel	Detroit	1948–49	28
Gordie Howe	Detroit	1950–51	43
Gordie Howe	Detroit	1951–52	47
Gordie Howe	Detroit	1952–53	49
Gordie Howe	Detroit	1956–57	36
Gordie Howe	Detroit	1962–63	38

ASSISTS

	Team	Season	No.
Clint Smith	Chicago	1943–44	r 49
Elmer Lach	Montreal	1944–45	r 54
Elmer Lach	Montreal	1945–46	34
Doug Bentley	Chicago	1947–48	37
Doug Bentley	Chicago	1948–49	43
Gordie Howe	Detroit	1950–51	43
Elmer Lach	Montreal	1951–52	50
Gordie Howe	Detroit	1952–53	46
Gordie Howe	Detroit	1953–54	48
Bert Olmstead	Montreal	1954–55	48
Bert Olmstead	Montreal	1955–56	r 56
Bryan Trottier	NY Islanders	1977–78	77
Bryan Trottier	NY Islanders	1978–79	87

r: indicates NHL record at the time

R: still stands as NHL record

POINTS (Art Ross Trophy winners)

		Season	G	A	P
Bryan Hextall	NY Rangers	1941–42	24	32	56
Doug Bentley	Chicago	1942–43	33	40	r 73
Elmer Lach	Monteal	1944–45	26	54	80
Max Bentley	Chicago	1945–46	31	30	61
Max Bentley	Chicago	1946–47	29	43	72
Elmer Lach	Monteal	1947–48	30	31	61
Gordie Howe	Detroit	1950–51	43	43	r 86
Gordie Howe	Detroit	1951–52	47	39	r 86
Gordie Howe	Detroit	1952–53	49	46	r 95
Gordie Howe	Detroit	1953–54	33	48	81
Gordie Howe	Detroit	1956–57	44	45	89
Gordie Howe	Detroit	1962–63	38	48	86
Bryan Trottier	NY Islanders	1978–79	47	87	134

PENALTY MINUTES

	Team	Season	No.
Eddie Shore	Boston	1927–28	r 165
Gus Kyle	Boston	1951–52	127
Fern Flaman	Boston	1954–55	150
Keith Magnuson	Chicago	1969–70	213
Keith Magnuson	Chicago	1970–71	r 291
Dave Schultz	Philadelphia	1972–73	259
Dave Schultz	Philadelphia	1973–74	r 348
Dave Schultz	Philadelphia	1974–75	R 472
Dave Schultz	L.A.–Pittsburgh	1977–78	405
Tiger Williams	Toronto	1978–79	298
Tiger Williams	Vancouver	1980–81	343

had Jaromir Jagr, who was a rookie, on my line all through the 1991 playoffs. I got lots of penalties to kill, lots of faceoffs, and a ton of time in the offensive zone with this kid Jagr. I was getting 15 minutes a game and feeling really good about my role. (Coach) Bob Johnson was fantastic, he and (general manager) Craig Patrick were A1-plus. They made me feel really good about my contributions.

As for that Canada Cup, there were a lot of really good articles that explained how I used my native heritage to cross the border and play for the U.S. because I was making my living down there. It seemed the articles that got the most attention, though, were the negative ones. They basically said that I was saying goodbye to Canada. I wasn't. I never once renounced anything of my Canadian heritage that I'm so proud of. All my friends and family recognized what I did, and that's what was important. The ones that didn't understand it, too bad for them.

I'm Métis. My grandfather was from Fort Qu'Appelle, and my grandma is a full-blooded Chippewa down in Montana. Dad's registered down there at Fort Bellnap with the Lost Tribe of the Little Shell Band. They got pushed off all their land and are campaigning hard to get it all back. It's a matter of finding some roots there for all of us. My grandfather and great-grandfather were homesteaders on our ranch so we have a great history—Grandma and Grandpa heading up to Battleford, back down to Pelletier, back across the border, you know, hunting and trapping all the way down there. My grandfather never recognized the border, although he stopped and waved to everybody.

BERNIE FEDERKO: THE INVISIBLE MAN

Bernie Federko

Bernie Federko (Foam Lake) knew he was in demand but not whether he was good enough to play junior hockey.

"There were several SJHL teams that wanted me to try out for Tier 2 junior. My parents wanted me to stay home until I finished high school. I played midget in Foam Lake, but there weren't many midget teams in the area and the level of competition was not very good, so I also played senior in the Fishing Lake Hockey League. I was able to play against men who were bigger and stronger."

Federko's parents gave him permission to attend the training camp of the Western Canada Hockey League's Saskatoon Blades when he was 17, so long as he completed his Grade 12 in the Hub City if he was successful.

"I don't think I realized how good I was or how good I could be until I tried out for the Blades. I didn't have aspirations of making the team right out of midget, but I did, and things just went right on from there."

Federko's first junior season in the WCHL under coach Jack McLeod was a modest success as he recorded 22 goals and 50 points.

"I was always a finesse player in Foam Lake, and if anyone touched me, one of the older guys came in and made sure it didn't happen again. The WCHL was much more physical. I had to learn how to defend myself. Everybody could skate fast. It was a battle all the time.

"Everything was a learning process, plus you were learning systems. Jack was big on that and a great teacher, too. I think I learned more from him than from anybody else about systems and positional play."

Saskatoon finished first in the East Division each of the next two seasons and advanced to the WCHL finals, only to fall in seven games to the New Westminster Bruins each time. Federko had 107 points in 1974–75 and put up eye-popping numbers in '75–76: 72 goals and 115 assists for a record 187 points, and another record 45 points in the playoffs.

"Both years we should have won the league but the biggest thing, the one thing we didn't have, that Jack didn't believe in, was an enforcer or a goon or whatever you want to call him. That was not Shaky's hockey. New West was one of those teams you dreaded playing because it wasn't really hockey. It was survival, for the most part.

"It takes nothing away from (Bruins coach) Ernie McLean because he was very successful as a junior coach. I look at Jack McLeod, and there's something that he doesn't get credit for: he was such a great teacher. You look at the amount of players that came through the Blades organization with Jack coaching. We weren't there just to play junior, we were trying to make careers and lives out of it. Jack was teaching us not just how to win in junior, he was teaching us how to be great pros. I think that says it all."

Despite his exceptional season and expectations of being selected very early in the NHL entry draft, six

ALL-TIME NHL LEADERS AMONG SASKATCHEWAN-BORN PLAYERS

Through 2003–04 season

* indicates active player as of April 2004

GAMES PLAYED

Gordie Howe	1,767
Bryan Trottier	1,279
Brad McCrimmon	1,222
Kelly Buchberger *	1,182
Dave Manson	1,103
Theoren Fleury	1,084
Terry Harper	1,066
Lyle Odelein *	1,029
Jim Neilson	1,023
Brian Propp	1,016

GOALS

Gordie Howe	801
Bryan Trottier	524
Theoren Fleury	455
Brian Propp	425
Bernie Federko	369
Wendel Clark	330
Clark Gillies	319
Brent Ashton	284
Bob Schmautz	271
Red Berenson	261

ASSISTS

Gordie Howe	1,049
Bryan Trottier	901
Bernie Federko	761
Theoren Fleury	633
Brian Propp	579
Ron Greschner	431
Bert Olmstead	421
Barry Pederson	416
Elmer Lach	408
Red Berenson	397

POINTS

Gordie Howe	1,850
Bryan Trottier	1,425
Bernie Federko	1,130
Theoren Fleury	1,088
Brian Propp	1,004
Clark Gillies	697
Red Berenson	658
Barry Pederson	654
Brent Ashton	629
Elmer Lach	623

PENALTY MINUTES

Tiger Williams	R 3,966
Dave Manson	2,792
Jeff Odgers	2,364
Lyle Odelein *	2,336
Garth Butcher	2,302
Kelly Buchberger *	2,297
Dave Schultz	2,294
Laurie Boschman	2,265
Mick Vukota	2,071
Kelly Chase	2,017

DEFENCEMEN—GOALS

Ron Greschner	179
Eddie Shore	105
Dave Manson	102
Brad McCrimmon	81
Wade Redden *	78

DEFENCEMEN—ASSISTS

Ron Greschner	431
Brad McCrimmon	322
Jim Neilson	299
Dave Manson	288
Barry Gibbs	224

DEFENCEMEN—POINTS

Ron Greschner	610
Brad McCrimmon	403
Dave Manson	390
Jim Neilson	368
Wade Redden *	286

TEAMS PLAYED FOR

Brent Ashton	9
Jim McKenzie *	9
Mike Sillinger *	9
Dave Manson	7
Lyle Odelein *	7
Greg Paslawski	7

R: indicates NHL record

DAVE SCHULTZ: HAMMER'S TIME

Dave Schultz (Waldheim) broke Keith Magnuson's NHL penalty record with 348 minutes in 1973–74, then chalked up 472 minutes the following season for a mark that still stands. Those happened to be the same seasons that Philadelphia won the Stanley Cup, and yes, Schultz's brawling had a lot to do with it.

He wanted to be regarded as a real hockey player, not as a goon, and even scored 20 goals one season. However, fighting and fighting alone earned him his place on the Flyers' roster. There was nothing in his junior record that suggested an NHL career, and it was only after "The Hammer" pounded his way through two minor leagues that he hit the big time.

His effectiveness as an intimidator depended on an aura of invincibility that vanished the night he challenged Clark Gillies of the New York Islanders. Gillies nailed The Hammer with three solid rights, and that was the beginning of Schultz's end. He was traded to Los Angeles, then Pittsburgh and finally Buffalo before his time—535 games and 2,294 penalty minutes—was up.

Dave Schultz, 1969, North Battleford Beaver Bruins

teams passed on Federko before the St. Louis Blues took him. Two of his Saskatoon teammates, right-winger Blair Chapman and centre Fred Williams, were selected before he was.

"I'll never forget draft morning. It was done by conference call, very different from the way they do things now. Gerry Ehman, the director of player personnel for the Blues, called to tell me I was their first pick, and, of course, I knew the draft order. I knew that I could play, and I thought should have been No. 1 overall. I was very disappointed, especially when there were two guys from my team that went ahead of me. No disrespect to Blair, but I felt that I was the playmaker and the key to the success of our line. And no disrespect to Fred either, he was a great skater and great penalty killer, but do you draft a penalty killer fourth overall?

"(Blues general manager) Emile Francis was shocked I was available. He had Red Berenson, Garry Unger and Derek Sanderson and didn't even need a centre, but he believed in getting the best player available.

"Two weeks before training camp I broke my foot playing basketball, and I reported to the Blues wearing a cast on my leg. They didn't have room for me anyway, so maybe starting the year in the minors at Kansas City was the best thing that ever happened to me. I got introduced to pro hockey at a different level. Barclay Plager was a great coach, and I was playing a regular shift with Brian Sutter on my left wing."

Federko tore apart the Central league with 69 points in 42 games. He and Sutter were promoted to St. Louis in January of 1977 and remained regular linemates for 11 years. Federko became the great unknown star of the NHL. He had four 100-point seasons, three more in the 90s, and was the first player in history to compile 50 assists for 10 straight years. But St. Louis was not a media hub, nor were the Blues frequently seen on *Hockey Night in Canada*. Election to all-star teams was impossible without media exposure and when even greater stars like Bryan Trottier, Marcel Dionne, Wayne Gretzky, Mario Lemieux and Steve Yzerman were also playing centre.

"I never got an opportunity to go to a Canada Cup tryout. I never got a chance to go and play in a world championship because we almost always made the playoffs, and they used players from the teams that didn't make the playoffs or got knocked out early. The only chance I had was in 1979 when the Blues were way out of it, and I was going to be with the Canadian team in Russia. I broke my wrist in Colorado the last week. So I never got to wear a jersey with Team Canada on it, which is one of the disappointments of my career."

He was still good for 40 assists in the last of his 14 seasons, with Detroit, and retired with 1,130 points in exactly 1,000 games played.

DOUG WICKENHEISER: THE EPITOME OF TRAGEDY

A whole is that which has beginning, middle, and end.
–Aristotle

Doug Wickenheiser's NHL career never really began, didn't have a middle stage. It spent 10 years ending, right from the moment he was made the first overall choice in the 1980 draft by the Montreal Canadiens. Few athletes' lives have been so incomplete, such a powerless struggle against unfulfilled expectations, untapped potential and unfair misfortune. And what was his solace? That he had his health? He was found to have cancer when he was 33. That he had a loving family? A dubious comfort when you die at 37, having witnessed only the first four years of your twin daughters' lives.

In an era of communications shaped by broadcast journalism that unthinkingly labels every death as tragic, Doug Wickenheiser's story fits the definition of tragedy in its classic Aristotelian sense, that of a hero whose downfall is brought about by one flaw in his character, who suffers consequences far worse than he deserves, whose shift in fortune moves us to a sympathetic response. Even though we perceive him as greater than ourselves, we see ourselves embodied in him and feel his pain. Doug Wickenheiser's fatal flaw as a hockey player was that he was shy. He wanted to excel at his sport but was uncomfortable as the centre of attention. When he was transformed from a focal point to a target, his destruction was under way.

Oh, you should have seen him as winter turned to

spring in 1980. He had just turned 18, was tall, handsome and broad-shouldered, 6-foot-1 and 200 pounds. Everybody in Regina called him Wick, as if they all knew him, and in a way they did. In leading the Western Hockey League with 89 goals and 170 points, he was Superman on ice—a smooth skater, brilliant stickhandler, smart playmaker, as tough in the corners as he was in the slot, with a whole arsenal of scoring weapons: wrist shot, backhand, slapper, dekes. This was what had been expected from him for years. Some had anticipated this for a decade.

"Doug first attracted attention when he was only eight years old," says his father, Charlie. "He went to atom tryouts, and the coaches couldn't believe his age; he looked like a pee wee already. He was so good a skater and had such strong legs that when other players tried to check him they'd fall off. There were times when he'd take the puck behind his net, go the length of the ice to score and all the players on the other team would be lying on the ice."

He played bantam hockey when he still had a season of pee wee eligibility remaining. Scoring goals and winning games was fun; being singled out was not.

"He didn't say too much then," Charlie says. "In his later years, if anyone brought up how good he was in his teens or with the Pats, or said anything about him being drafted first, he walked away. He had heard so much of it growing up that either he was embarrassed about it or tired of it."

Wickenheiser's quiet demeanour misled the Pats' executive into thinking he had no interest in junior hockey.

"They thought Doug was going to go to university," says Lorne Davis, who was coaching the Pats when Wickenheiser was having an 88-point season as a 15-year-old with the Tier 2 Regina Pat Blues of the SJHL. "Our executive told me, 'Don't even bother going to see him, because he's not going to play for us.' Well, Doug came to training camp in September of '76; players could still attend camp and be eligible for the NCAA. I said, 'Doug, I'm not putting pressure on you, but if you decide that you want to play for us, you let me know, I'll come around and talk to your mom and dad.'

"About two days before the season started, he says, 'Maybe you should come over.' I signed Doug that night, and Darren Veitch, who the executive also thought was going to go to school, and Greg Dumba, who would be our No. 1 goalie for a while. All three of them I got the same night, and the executive couldn't believe it."

Wickenheiser enjoyed a splendid Tier 1 rookie campaign, repeating his 88-point SJHL performance, but Davis was fired after the season and replaced by Gregg Pilling, who emphasized rough hockey and expected his phenom to play a leading role on the scoresheet—all over it. Wickenheiser never shied away from a battle for the puck, nor would he hesitate to drop his gloves if necessary, but habitual fighting was not to his liking. As it was, his penalty minutes shot up from 49 to 141. His points, however, merely crept from 88 to 94. For the first time, Wickenheiser's inner fear was realized. It wasn't the responsibility of leadership that scared him; it was the fear of letting people down if he didn't succeed. Sure enough, fans and media murmured that he was a big reason for the Pats missing the playoffs.

"Pressure," Charlie says. "It's not good to have that amount of pressure put on you when you're that young. A kid should enjoy the life of sport, shouldn't have to think, 'I have to score two or three goals' every time he puts on the uniform.

"Lorne Davis knew how to deal with Doug; he let him enjoy the game. The next guy put too much pressure on him. The Pats had a poor team, and the pressure built. Then Bryan Murray came."

Pilling was cast off after one season and replaced by Murray, then a relative unknown with a solid resumé climbing the coaching ladder in the Ottawa region. Murray and Pats general manager Bob Strumm assembled a deep roster: Mike Blaisdell, Darren Veitch, Ron Flockhart, Brian Varga, Darren Bobyck, Bill Ansell. Given the captaincy but not an overbearing share of offensive responsibility, Wick scorched the WHL.

"Doug was very talented, a big guy that had a chance to be a star player," Murray says. "As I got to know him, I discovered that he certainly wasn't a rowdy, loud kind of guy; he was very professional.

"We made demands on Doug. I think we were fair. I was able to play guys with him who were, you know, not the top wingers and he really made it a successful line. Doug was the focal point of the team, but the cast of characters around him, the type of style we had, the discipline we demanded of them, helped every-

Darren Veitch (A on sweater) and captain Doug Wickenheiser lead the Pats' victory parade after winning the 1979–80 WHL championship

body and gave them all a chance to be successful."

"I had a great relationship with Doug. He played so well for me."

Regina won the 1979–80 WHL championship handily. Wickenheiser was the league's scoring champion and most valuable player. He was named Canada's outstanding junior player at the Memorial Cup banquet in Regina, his broad smile acknowledging the honour but his eyes constantly cast downward lest he see all the eyes locked on him. His happiness was also stifled by his performance in the tournament, a single goal and four assists in four games as the Pats failed to reach the final game.

Despite that, the buzz would not diminish: Would Wick go first overall in the draft? Three other players were also strong candidates: Denis Savard, a small centre who was eager to continue being a francophone star in Montreal; defenceman Dave Babych of the Portland Winter Hawks; and, defenceman Larry Murphy of the Peterborough Petes. It remained a mystery right up to draft day, June 11, 1980, the beginning—and the beginning of the end—of Doug Wickenheiser's professional life.

"He didn't know," Charlie Wickenheiser says. "He was hoping he'd go No.1. He wanted to play for the Canadiens. They were *the* team at the time, what kid

GORD KLUZAK: OF ALL THE JINXED JOINTS . . .

When defenceman Gord Kluzak (Climax) was selected first overall by Boston in the 1982 draft, the Bruins wanted him to emulate Bobby Orr in the worst way. And he did. Orr had knee surgery 11 times, Kluzak 10.

No one ever tried harder than Kluzak, that's for sure. He was only 18 when the Bruins drafted him, a veteran of two seasons with the Billings Bighorns and a sensation at the 1982 world junior championship in Minnesota, where he was named top defenceman as Canada won the gold medal. Kluzak had a good rookie season—excellent for a teenager, really—and then embarked on a cruel cycle: good season, knee injury, operation, missed season, repeat. After the 1989–90 season, when he got into only eight contests, the NHL awarded him the Masterton Trophy for perseverance and dedication.

Kluzak played his last two games early in the 1990–91 season at the age of 26. Freed from his old full-time job of professional recuperator, he entered Harvard University, achieved an MBA and started a new career with a prominent brokerage firm in Boston. He moonlights as colour commentator on Bruins telecasts.

Gord Kluzak, Billings Bighorns, 1981

wouldn't want play with them? I was a little concerned that they may not play him. I talked with Bryan Murray, and he said that certainly Doug should go to Montreal; at least the cheques wouldn't bounce."

Montreal was financially solvent but in organizational disarray. General manager Sam Pollock had retired in 1979. Head coach Scotty Bowman also left when he wasn't chosen to replace Pollock. Irving Grundman, a shrewd businessman but inexperienced hockey executive, became GM. Claude Ruel succeeded Bowman as coach.

"Ruel didn't want the Canadiens to take Doug," Charlie says. "He wanted Savard."

Wickenheiser started his first NHL season in a dual capacity: healthy scratch and bench warmer. Ruel and others in management trotted out the party line that this was Canadiens tradition, that rookies had to sit, learn and wait—which was a crock of *bleu-blanc-rouge* spit. Fellow forwards Bob Gainey, Doug Jarvis, Guy Lafleur, Doug Risebrough and Mario Tremblay had all taken regular shifts practically upon arrival.

"It's said that it took Lafleur three years to develop," Wickenheiser told the author for a May 1981 *Leader-Post* article, "but it seems they always forget he played all the games for those three years. . . .

"Once we were on the road, and I dressed for a couple of games. We were winning one game something like 8–1, and I still hadn't had a shift yet. I was just kind of thinking, 'Well, if I don't play when we're winning 8–1, when will I play?' "

Wickenheiser did play regularly for two weeks in November when injuries necessitated his presence on the third line. He produced 10 points in six games. His parents were in Montreal to watch the last of that stretch.

"We were down there, and he scored three goals," Charlie recalls. "The next night the Canadiens went to Detroit, and they didn't even dress him."

Wickenheiser played only 41 games, or, as he put it, "I dressed for 41 games—dressed, quote, unquote." He managed seven goals and eight assists for 15 points. Ruel's coaching reign ended in disgrace when the Edmonton Oilers swept Montreal in the opening round of the playoffs. Wickenheiser watched all three games from the press box.

Savard, who publicly declared he would prove

Montreal had made a mistake, recorded 75 points in his first season, five times as many as Wickenheiser. The ex-Pat would improve in subsequent seasons under Bob Berry and Jacques Lemaire, but the merciless Montreal media never let anyone forget that No. 25 was far more Not Denis Savard than he was Doug Wickenheiser. "Not Denis Savard" had 105 points over his first three seasons; Savard had 315. (Not that anyone noticed but Savard was plus-53 in 234 games and Wickenheiser was plus-45 in 175 contests with less than half the ice time.)

"It was terrible what happened to him in Montreal," Davis says. "Doug was a natural scorer and playmaker and everything. They tried to make him into a checker and between that and all the pressure and not being French-Canadian, it had a lasting effect on him."

Wickenheiser's stock plummeted so far by December of 1983 that the Canadiens had to attach two players (Gilbert Delorme and Greg Paslawski) to him to get Perry Turnbull from St. Louis. The change of surroundings was welcome but not enough to rejuvenate Wickenheiser's enthusiasm, even with a warm welcome from Blues general manager Ron Caron, a former Canadiens executive who had pushed for his selection by Montreal three years earlier.

"Ron Caron was a big believer in Doug Wickenheiser," says Bernie Federko, then the Blues' scoring leader. "When Doug got the second opportunity, you could see he had been frustrated his entire career. It was almost to the point where he didn't want to get too close to anybody, and I believe it was from all the pressure he had been through in Montreal.

"He seemed disappointed in himself, almost introverted because of all he had gone through. He really lacked confidence. I don't think he ever got that back. He had a sense of humour, but he was afraid to say anything or do anything.

"You could see the skill that he had. When you're the first pick overall, you have to be good, there's no question about it. We knew that. It was unfortunate because he knew he had the skill. He would show us some things in practice, and we would say, '*Wow*, did you see that?' But he'd get in the game, and he just wouldn't do it, almost like he didn't want to do it. Things finally started to go his way a little bit, and that's when he got that knee injury, just when things were looking good for him. It was like there was a black cloud over him."

Doug Wickenheiser with St. Louis

Who else but a man cursed by fate would suffer a catastrophic injury during a prank involving non-existent animals?

On March 13, 1985, the Blues' veteran players invited their rookies to join them on a snipe hunt.

There really is an animal called a snipe; it's a wading bird. In professional sports, however, the snipe hunt has existed for decades in many guises, few (if any) involving waterfowl. In the Blues' version, which was fairly typical of the genre, snipe were purported to be something like weasels, native to Missouri and tricky little critters to catch. Everyone would drive out to the woods at night and split into groups, leaving the rookies by themselves when local lawmen (who also happened to be friends of the team) arrested them for hunting snipe without a licence. The baffled, handcuffed rookies were hauled before a night court judge (another accomplice) and about to be sentenced to 30 days with the extras from *Deliverance* when the gag was revealed. Pranksters and dupes repaired to a nearby soda pop emporium and a good time was had by all.

Not this time. When the veterans reached the snipe hunting ground, Wickenheiser jumped from the back of the pickup in which he had been riding. He stumbled upon landing and was surprised to see an automobile swerve and skid toward him. It struck his left knee and tore nearly every ligament in the joint. He had been on his way to his best season (23 goals in 68 games) and perhaps a rebirth as a hockey player. It was 10 months before he played again, slower, less mobile and just as frustrated as ever. Wickenheiser played 36 games at the tail end of the 1985–86 season, registering a mere eight goals and 19 points, disturbingly similar to his rookie campaign.

A moment of vindication remained, however. St. Louis reached the Campbell Conference final against the Calgary Flames. Game 6 was a must-win for the Blues, who trailed the series 3–2, but the visiting Flames led the contest 4–1 when the second period ended. In the St. Louis dressing room, head coach Jacques Demers reminded his players of Barclay Plager, a well-liked former player and coach of the Blues who was fighting cancer. Demers implored them to give their all for Plager.

Wickenheiser scored an unassisted power play goal five minutes into the final frame to begin the comeback. Goals were traded midway through the frame and then Paslawski, a product of Kindersley and the Prince Albert Raiders, tallied at 15:49 at 18:52 to tie the score at 5–5 and force overtime. Eight minutes in, Federko stole the puck and took off with Mark Hunter on a two-on-one break. Hunter was stopped by Calgary goalie Mike Vernon, but Wickenheiser pounced on the rebound for the winning goal. The occasion—May 12, 1986—would be remembered as the Monday Night Miracle and Wickenheiser's goal as one of the greatest moments in the franchise's history. It didn't matter that the Flames won Game 7 two nights later in Calgary.

Surgery mended Wickenheiser's left knee but didn't really repair it. He became a hockey gypsy: one last season in St. Louis, one more with the Vancouver Canucks, a game with the New York Rangers, a couple of months with the national team, two partial seasons with the Washington Capitals, stints in Italy, Germany and Austria. In 1992 he married Dianne Prebble, whom he had met in St. Louis. He settled down in the American Midwest and played two seasons in the International Hockey League.

It was in the summer of 1994 that he had a bothersome cyst on his left wrist examined. As unexpectedly as the car that clipped him at the snipe hunt, cancer had crept into Doug Wickenheiser's body. That October the twins were born. He retired from hockey. He fought the cancer. The wrist healed.

"He was happy," Charlie says. "He golfed a lot, but he broke so many clubs. One of the pros he used to golf with said he never saw anybody wrap so many clubs around trees as Doug did."

This young man who silently suffered the slings and arrows of outrageous hockey fortune actually vented his aggravation on the golf course? Why?

"He was relaxed."

Three more years passed. Doug developed a hacking cough. X-rays revealed a puck-sized tumour on his right lung. Again he fought the cancer; this time it had too much of a head start.

He died January 12, 1999.

There were 90 cars in the funeral procession.

"They stopped the commuter train to let the procession go by," Charlie says. "I was told it was the first time anyone had ever seen the train stopped for a funeral.

"The church was overcrowded. Lots of people couldn't get in. All the Blues were there, a lot of NHL players, and a lot of flowers! Gee, every team sent a bouquet.

"On his grave one of his friends stuck one of his broken golf clubs. It's still there. Dianne's dad says that every time he sees that, he has to laugh.

"Doug never brought anybody down. If you ran any of his friends or his teammates down, either he'd say something to you or he'd walk away. If you were a friend or a teammate of his, you were something special."

Not long after his death, a recently built indoor rink in the northwest was renamed the Doug Wickenheiser Arena by the City of Regina—which, fully mindful of an NHL career that felt like one long inexorable decline, still considered him something special.

WENDEL CLARK: A HIT WHEREVER HE WENT

Wendel Clark (Kelvington) broke Saskatchewan's first-draft-pick jinx. Greg Joly (1974), Doug Wickenheiser (1980) and Gord Kluzak (1982) were models of frustration after they left the junior ranks. Clark, a defenceman and occasional left wing with the Saskatoon Blades, topped the draft class of '85 and became the toast of Toronto.

The run-into-everything Tasmanian Devil who gave the Maple Leafs newfound courage wasn't quite so wide-ranging in midget hockey with the Notre Dame Hounds or in junior with the Blades, simply because he had to mind his defensive responsibilities. That didn't lessen the impact of his bodychecks, just his attack zone. When set free on a forward line, as he was at the 1984–85 world hockey championship in Finland, he could strike anyplace. Soviet defenceman Mikhail Tatarinov's last memory of his game against Canada was of looking at the puck as he carried it around his own net. Clark stepped into him with nothing but shoulder and knocked Tatarinov out cold. When Canada needed at least a draw in its last game against the Czech Republic to earn the gold medal, Clark supplied the tying goal.

Planted firmly at left wing in Toronto, Clark was a one-man personification of the Maple Leafs as they were before owner Harold Ballard turned them into a laughingstock. Clark hustled and fought like Tiger Williams, bodychecked like Tim Horton and was a natural goal-scorer like Lanny McDonald. No one knew the quality of Clark's slapshot because he virtually never used it; his wrist shot was so forceful and accurate that he didn't need to bother with the windup of a slapper. During Clark's career only Brett Hull unleashed wrist shots with similar velocity.

Clark's first two seasons produced 71 goals, 498 penalty minutes, and advancement into the second round of the playoffs. Much of his ice time was spent on the Hound Line with fellow Notre Dame alumni Russ Courtnall and Gary Leeman. Beginning in 1987–88, though, the chronic back pain that would plague the rest of his career manifested itself. He missed 213 games over the next five seasons. Cause and effect: the Maple Leafs made the playoffs only one of those seasons and were bounced in five games. With Doug Gilmour added to the mix and a rela-

If looks could kill: Wendel Clark with the Blades

Toronto's Hound Line: Gary Leeman (11), Russ Courtnall (9) and Wendel Clark

tively healthy Clark, Toronto went all the way to the conference finals in 1992 and '93. It's interesting to speculate what Clark might have accomplished had he not charged into every shift like it was Game 7 in May, or if he had left the bashing and battling to his more robust teammates, but Clark considered it his duty.

"Why save it for a big game or for the playoffs?" Clark explains. "This game you're playing right now is the one that counts. You might not be around for the playoffs. You might not make the playoffs if you don't win this game.

"Plus, I was the captain (from 1991–94) and an assistant captain before that. They're counting on me to be the leader. You lead by setting an example, and part of that is taking the body every chance you get. Back off and you're not leading."

Toronto rewarded Clark after his best season (46 goals in 1993–94) by trading him at the peak of his value in a blockbuster deal with the Quebec Nordiques that brought Mats Sundin to the Maple Leafs. A serious concussion added to Clark's medical problems, and while he remained effective for a few more years, teams were reluctant to hold on to him for long. He journeyed from Quebec to the New York Islanders, back to Toronto, then Tampa Bay, Detroit and Chicago before a swan song with the Maple Leafs. He hung up his skates in 2000 with 330 goals in 793 games played over 15 seasons.

SASKATCHEWAN'S ALL-TIME NHL TEAM

We've got the tradition, we've got the players, we've got the attitude. Let's take on the world.

Presenting the all-time Saskatchewan-born team of National Hockey League players, good enough to take on any similar aggregation. So says their coach.

"I will take this team and play against any of the other provinces in Canada, the U.S.A. or Europe," declared Emile "the Cat" Francis after tending to the final roster cuts.

Six veteran hockey men, all born or raised in Saskatchewan, were recruited to select this squad for *Saskatchewan Sports Legends*. In alphabetical order, they are:

Johnny Bower, professional goaltender from 1945 on, NHLer with the New York Rangers and Toronto Maple Leafs from 1953 through 1970, later a scout and goaltending instructor, ever a keen hockey observer.

Lorne Davis, player and coach with the Regina Pats, veteran of four NHL teams, and longtime scout still active in that capacity with the Edmonton Oilers.

Emile Francis, star goalie with the junior Moose Jaw Canucks and senior Regina Capitals, NHL veteran with the Rangers and Chicago Black Hawks, longtime head coach of the Rangers and St. Louis Blues, and executive with the Rangers, Blues and Hartford Whalers.

Bill Hay, junior standout with the Pats, Calder Trophy winner as the NHL's outstanding rookie in 1959–60, eight-year veteran of the Black Hawks, currently chairman of the Hockey Hall of Fame.

Dick Irvin Jr., son of the legendary player and coach and himself affiliated with the NHL for nearly four decades as a broadcaster and author.

Jack McLeod, product of Notre Dame College and the Moose Jaw Canucks, New York Rangers veteran, minor pro and semi-pro in Saskatoon and Moose Jaw, coach of the 1968 Canadian Olympic team and nine-year coach of the WHL's Saskatoon Blades.

Each of these men selected, in order of preference, three goaltenders, six defencemen, three left wingers, three centres, three right wingers and, finally, three more forwards without regard to the position they played. The selectors were also invited to submit their preferences for power-play and penalty-killing units, a "tough guy" and a head coach.

Players had to be born in Saskatchewan and evaluated on the strength of their NHL performance. Bob Baun, Theoren Fleury and Bryan Hextall Sr., who moved away as young children, were eligible. Those born outside the province that shone in Saskatchewan before reaching the NHL—such as Bill Cook, Curtis Joseph and Joe Sakic—were not.

Glenn Hall

Francis, who did not vote for himself as either goaltender or coach, outpolled Sid Abel 4–2 for the coaching job. Because there was no formal process for weighing the various selections, Francis was further enlisted to study the overall vote and make the final call on which players would make the team. It was his decision to employ a 20-man roster of two goaltenders, six defencemen and 12 forwards (divided into four lines).

And here it is:

STARTING SIX

GOALTENDER

Glenn Hall, Humboldt. A near-unanimous choice with five first-place votes, Hall is historically important as the innovator of the butterfly style of goaltending. In an NHL career that spanned 20 years (1952–71), he received a record seven First All-Team selections.

DEFENCEMEN

Eddie Shore, Fort Qu'Appelle. Shore was the most dominant, flamboyant and explosive hockey player of the 1930s. He habitually played over 50 minutes a game, had no equal as a rushing defenceman and was a tower of strength in his own end. He won the Hart Trophy as the NHL's most valuable player four times, still an all-time high for defencemen, and made the First All-Star Team on seven occasions.

Fern Flaman, Dysart. Few could match Flaman for defensive skill and body-checking when he patrolled the blue line for Toronto and Boston in the '50s. "A great hitter," says Bower, who only had to observe Flaman at work from the other end of the ice.

LEFT WING

Doug Bentley, Delisle. Doug put in 12 years with the Chicago Black Hawks, led the NHL in goals twice, assists three times, won a scoring title, and almost single-handedly took his team to the Stanley Cup final in 1944.

Eddie Shore

accurate wrist shot with instantaneous release, tough, durable, strong enough to drag a Zamboni up the Yellowhead Highway against the wind. The only unanimous first-team pick on this squad.

Before we get to the rest of the squad, we have an exclusive interview with Bryan Trottier.

Bryan, you're obviously honoured to be lined up with Gordie Howe. How do you plan to work with him?

"Give him the puck and go to the net. Or I'll come into the corner and pick up a loose puck after he's elbowed a few guys. Let Gordie do all the work."

Sounds like a plan.

Who else do we have here?

GOALTENDER

Chuck Rayner, Sutherland. "Bonnie Prince Charlie" nosed out Johnny Bower for No. 2 goalie in a close decision that might have gone differently if Bower hadn't left himself off his own ballot. Bower has a superior record, but Rayner lost three years to military service after he had established himself in the NHL, so what the hey. Those who want to tout Bower as the master of the poke-check must remember that he learned it from Rayner.

CENTRE

Bryan Trottier, Redvers. Trots piled up 524 goals, 901 assists and 1,425 points while delivering untold thousands of body-checks. In a unique era of sensational centres, he accomplished something only Mark Messier could match: six Stanley Cup rings.

RIGHT WING

Gordie Howe, Floral. Pretty fair player, powerful but fluid stride, ambidextrous, unsurpassed in the corners, deadly

DEFENCEMEN

Bob Baun, Lanigan. Baun was one of those fundamentally perfect defencemen who took the man, forced the play into the corner, cleared the goal mouth, and blocked shots with boring, championship-winning consistency.

Brad McCrimmon, Dodsland. Bravo to the panel for picking this underappreciated blueliner. He could play the offensive catalyst or a stay-at-home role equally well and was a plus-minus machine wherever he went: plus-444 for his 18-year career, including highs of 27 in Boston, 83 in Philadelphia, 48 in Calgary, 39 in Detroit and 21 in Hartford.

Wade Redden, Lloydminster. Barring a comeback by Theoren Fleury, this is the only active player on our roster, and he's just turned 27! Redden has always been a consistent offensive contributor and has become reliable in his own end as well. He was one of the key players for Canada's gold-medal teams at the 1995 and '96 world junior championships.

Ron Greschner, Goodsoil. Greschner potted 179 goals in a 16-year career, all with the Rangers, that was frequently hampered by neck, shoulder, back and foot injuries. He had three 20-goal seasons and topped 50 points five times.

SECOND LINE

LEFT WING

Clark Gillies, Moose Jaw. An obscure stat for a hypothetical team: Of the 304 goals Gillies scored for the Islanders, 92 (or 30 percent) were scored on the power play. Guess who we're planting in the goal mouth, and God help any defenceman who cross-checks him in the back.

CENTRE

Max Bentley, Delisle. Spared the fate of his brother Doug, Max was traded after winning two scoring championships for Chicago and won the Stanley Cup three times in six seasons with Toronto. The finest stickhandler of his day, he was also a terrific power-play specialist at the point. Hmmmm . . .

RIGHT WING

Theoren Fleury, Oxbow. Of course, he's had his problems off the ice. That didn't stop Gretzky from putting him on the 2002 Olympic squad or this panel from recognizing his talent. At 5-foot-6 and 160 pounds, he survived on the ice by

Wade Redden

using his stick the way Gordie Howe used his elbows and piled up 455 goals, 1,088 points and 1,840 penalty minutes in 1,084 games.

THIRD LINE

LEFT WING

Bert Olmstead, Sceptre. He was one of the greatest two-way forwards of the pre-expansion era. Defensively, he would contain the best right-wingers in the game. Offensively, he was a master at digging the puck out of the corners and positional play. Think Bob Gainey with finesse and you've got Bert Olmstead.

CENTRE

Bernie Federko, Foam Lake. He was an invisible institution of the '80s: always picked late in the first round of your hockey pool, always justifying the selection with 90 to 105 points. His consistent productivity was all the more remarkable given the lack of depth and continuity on the Blues.

RIGHT WING

Bryan Hextall Sr., Grenfell. Once upon a time, a 20-goal season was the mark of a genuine scorer. Hextall posted seven such campaigns, six of them in a row, for the Rangers in the '30s and '40s. He was named to three First All-Star Teams.

FOURTH LINE

LEFT WING

Harry Watson, Saskatoon. One of the biggest players of his day (6-foot-1, 207 pounds), Watson relied more on finesse than brawn to score 236 goals. He was a key player throughout the Toronto Maple Leafs dynasty that won four Stanley Cups in five years (1947–49 and 1951). Watson, a heads-up player, retired with all his original teeth intact. In a close call, Francis selected Watson over 1,000-point man Brian Propp and the rambunctious Wendel Clark.

CENTRE

Elmer Lach, Nokomis. In addition to two scoring titles and three First All-Star Team selections, Lach was a huge contributor to three Stanley Cup triumphs in Montreal. Upon retiring in 1954, Lach's 623 career points were second only to Maurice Richard's 651. Francis gave Lach the nod for fourth-line centre over Sid Abel.

Theoren Fleury

RIGHT WING

Lorne Carr, Stoughton. Carr spent seven seasons with the hapless New York Americans and was traded to Toronto in 1941–42, the season the Maple Leafs made history by rallying from a 3–0 deficit in games to win the Stanley Cup final. He was the 11th player to reach the 200-goal plateau, finishing with 204.

And there you are. Put the 18 skaters together, and you have 15,826 games of NHL experience, 4,452 goals, 7,253 assists, 11,705 points and 15,104 penalty minutes. In a 70-game season, based on their average output, they would score 354 goals; in 82 games, it would be 415. That's plenty of firepower for a team so deep in excellent two-way players.

(Incredible but true: No one from Regina made the team.)

If the roster has to be expanded as a contingency for injuries or slumps, we have plenty of talent waiting in the wings. To begin with, Johnny Bower of Prince Albert can step between the pipes. On defence, there are reliable stalwarts Jim Neilson of Big River, Terry Harper of Regina and Bill

Bryan Hextall Sr.

Lorne Carr

Hajt of Borden. At forward, versatile stars like Sid Abel (Melville), Wendel Clark (Kelvington), Red Berenson (Regina), Brian Propp (Lanigan) and Bill Hay (Saskatoon) are ready along with penalty-killer *par excellence* Nick Metz (Wilcox).

Tiger Williams of Weyburn, the only man to get two votes as enforcer, is welcome to come along for moral support, but let's face it, a team with Howe, Shore, Flaman, Gillies, Olmstead and Baun doesn't need a cop.

Now Emile "The Cat," the pride of North Battleford, is sending the boys on to the ice for a brisk skate. If only there was an appropriate opponent for this team to face.

Where, oh where, is the other province celebrating its centennial? Where is Team Alberta?

Bring on Fuhr, Gadsby, Bucyk, Messier, Lanny and all the Sutters you can muster.

Just give Glenn Hall five minutes to visit the bathroom, and we'll be ready to go!

Ernie Richardson leads his cousins and brother through an arch of brooms upon their return to Regina after retaining their world curling title in 1960

1960–1969

Celebrations

ARRIVALS

July 11, 1960: Lynn Kanuka, distance runner, Regina.
July 19, 1960: Jan Betker, curler, Regina.
October 4, 1961: Brad Watson, NHL referee, Regina.
April 3, 1962: Nancy Jewitt-Filteau, judoka, Swift Current.
May 2, 1962: Nancy Harvey, golfer, Swift Current.
May 16, 1962: Barb Shockey-Milanese, swimmer, Saskatoon.
September 23, 1962: Bob Molle, wrestler/football player, Saskatoon.
April 29, 1963: Mike Babcock, hockey coach, Saskatoon.
June 6, 1963: Rueben Mayes, football player, North Battleford.
June 11, 1963: Sandra Schmirler, curler, Biggar.
May 24, 1964: Clayton Gerein, Paralympic athlete, North Battleford.
August 17, 1964: Colin James, guitarist, Regina.
February 16, 1965: Shelley Rhead Skarvan, speed skater, Moose Jaw.
June 8, 1965: Joan McCusker, curler, Yorkton.
September 8, 1965: Marcia Gudereit, curler, Moose Jaw.
June 22, 1966: Mark Dacey, curler, Saskatoon.
August 3, 1966: Brent Butt, comedian, Tisdale.
October 25, 1966: Wendel Clark, hockey player, Kelvington.
June 29, 1968: Theoren Fleury, hockey player, Oxbow.
January 25, 1969: Jeff Thue, wrestler, Regina.

DEPARTURES

January 2, 1961: Vic Krekelewitz, hockey player, 33.
March 9, 1961: Vernon Vaughn, football player, 25.
April 8, 1961: Phyllis Dewar Lowery, swimmer, 45.
January 2, 1962: James Gardiner, premier (1926-29, 1934-35), 78.
May 30, 1965: Murray Balfour, hockey player, 28.
February 22, 1966: Al Ritchie, football and hockey coach, 75.
February 3, 1968: Violet McNaughton, feminist, 88.

Canada adopted Medicare in 1962, 17 years after Saskatchewan introduced it. Athletically, meanwhile, the province led the way as the spawning ground of the best men's and women's teams on the planet, the world's fastest human, Canada's best female gymnasts, a unique Willingdon Cup championship team and, oh yes, a Grey Cup champion.

Ernie Richardson became curling's biggest star as the sport took its first steps towards becoming internationally competitive. With brother Sam at second and cousins Arnold and Wes at third and lead respectively, the Richardsons became the first rink to win the Brier four times—in 1959, 1960, 1962 and 1963. (Mel Perry replaced Wes Richardson at lead in '63.) They followed each of those triumphs with convincing victories in the Scotch Cup, curling's newly established world championship.

Saskatchewan's prestige in the sport was enhanced even further when Saskatoon teams skipped by Joyce McKee went undefeated through the first two Canadian women's championships, the first a head-to-head showdown with the Eastern champion and the next a sweep through a truly national field.

As usual, there were numerous individual and team achievements, particularly in athletics, golf and gymnastics, but the sporting highlight of the decade—if not the entire century—occurred November 26, 1966, when the Saskatchewan Roughriders won the Grey Cup for the first time in its history. On a Green and White dynasty that would endure for a decade and feature many men of great character, two stood above the rest: fullback George Reed and quarterback Ron Lancaster.

Perhaps the most valiant Saskatchewan athletes of the decade, however, are forgotten to the province and the nation. Coach Jack McLeod and a squad of Saskatchewan men formed the heart of the Canadian national hockey team that was assigned the task of going for the gold at the 1968 Winter Olympics. Handicapped by biased officiating and minimal support from Canada's hockey establishment and government, the Nats played their hearts out, only to fall before a Soviet colossus whose excellence wasn't yet appreciated by the rest of Canada's hockey community.

MASTER OF THE HOUSE: ERNIE RICHARDSON IN HIS OWN WORDS

Garnet Campbell was one of my heroes in the curling world. I used to watch him play in the '50s before we started on our fortunate run. Sam and Arnold and I went to watch the 1955 Brier at Exhibition Stadium, and we really enjoyed it. And any time Garnet and Bill Clarke tangled, I was usually there watching, learning their strategies. Each was different. Garnet, he had a softer approach with his team and threw softer weight—when the ice was good, mind you. They could throw it up there when the ice was heavy, too, and a lot of the time it was. Bill's team threw a little more weight, but Bill was a great guy to draw to the four-foot.

When we saw Garnet win the '55 Brier, we weren't good enough to even think about playing in the Canadian championship. My first thought was, "Wouldn't it be nice if we could win this city and get into the southern playdowns?" That would have been a great thrill for us. When we finally did break through, we went all the way, but that was four years later.

Our first big thrill was playing Garnet in 1957 in an event final at the Regina bonspiel. We lost in a tight game. I thought, "Gee whiz, he was the Canadian champ! That's my guy, and we went out there and we played them tough!" They told us after the game, "You guys keep playing like that, you'll be good someday."

They used to say about Garnet that when he made a double, both rocks would just make it through; one would slip through the house, the other would roll to the hack. It wasn't like Sam throwing a double and both rocks hitting the backboards—you know: Bang! Boom! Actually, the Campbells were kind of like the Richardsons in that they were all very good at reading the ice and judging weight, too. They could put a rock pretty well any spot they wanted. I marvelled at that. Garnet would tap the ice in the rings or in front of the house, and the rock was usually within two inches of there when it finished.

I played lead when we started curling in 1953. Wes's older brother, Norman, was skip, but he left for the coast the next year. So there were Arnold and I and Sam. I always thought skipping was sort of exciting,

Harold Worth (left) of Delisle shakes hands with Garnet Campbell. Although Worth played in only three Briers (1953, '56 and '65), he matched Campbell's feat of playing as a second, third and skip.

but I'd never had any experience at it, really. Arnold was probably the best curler on the team, but he didn't want to skip. We took a few beatings, and a lot of it had to do with me not making the good key shots to win games. We won a few little prizes, and in 1958 I told Arnold he should skip. He still didn't want to.

"Just don't put life and death on this," he said to me. "Don't treat it like such a horrible thing if you miss. Just forget about it." So that summer I started to think differently, and I said, "Okay, I'll skip. I'll still go home and have supper; I'm still going down to the beer parlour for a couple of beers after the game, and it's not the end of the world if I miss a rock."

Wes joined our team that winter, and he was probably the best athlete among us. He played hockey and was a good ball pitcher. Sam and Wes could sweep from one end to the other for 12-end games like nothing; they seldom got tired. That made them as good as, if not better than, any other front end in sweeping. Then all of a sudden I started making these key shots in 1959, and by gosh if we didn't win the city and ended up playing one of my curling heroes, Bill Clarke, in the southern final. We happened to beat him in the final game, and from then on we never looked back.

That 1959 southern in Yorkton probably had the most challenging ice conditions I ever encountered. It was held in their old curling club, and like a lot of old clubs then it had some holes in the walls. It was 40 below outside so you can imagine how cold it was in the rink. The ice was swingy and heavy, really difficult. The provincial was back home at the Regina Curling Club. A guy named Don McIntyre was the ice maker at the Regina, one of the best ice makers around, and he told us, "You'd better come down to our club and throw some rocks before you go on to this ice because it's going to be very fast." We were members of the Civil Service club on Broadway Avenue at the time. Well, when we threw our first rocks we were sending them through the house like you wouldn't believe because we were still geared for the heavy ice back in Yorkton. Slowly, we geared ourselves back. We played against Gordon Grimes from Eston, who had represented Saskatchewan the year before, so he was favoured to beat us. We beat him two straight, but it's a good thing we went to the Regina club or he'd have had a big early jump on us.

That was the kind of thing you dealt with in those days. You'd go from ice that was heavy on the outside

Premier Tommy Douglas greets Ernie, Arnold, Sam and Wes at a 1960 reception

and keen in the middle to perfectly keen ice or you'd go to swingy and then straight. I mean, it was a very big variation. We learned how to handle that, and that is probably why we were successful. We weren't any better shooters then most of the top curlers, it's just that we formed a team that played well together, and every member knew the ice. Every shot was taken as a team, but we didn't waste time talking because we were the fastest team on the ice. First of all, Arnold never came down to the other end to discuss the shot. He was always in the hack, he knew what he had to do. Wes and Sam were like skips for all the knowledge they had, but they were in the hack, too. When Bill Clarke played us, we could finish one or two ends before any other games because we were both fast—and club games were just 10 ends. You only played 12-end games in major events like the Brier or playdowns or car spiels.

We were able to play our best as a team when we knew we had to. We really got geared for Alberta. I'll tell you, Arnold, if he was gonna miss, it would be against a lesser team, but he didn't miss many against Alberta. He never had a bad series in the provincials because you had to win two out of three. We all averaged 75 to 85 percent in our shotmaking there. I've told the guys that went out of Saskatchewan since then, "Now, if you play as good as you played to win the Saskatchewan championship, then you have a very good chance of winning the Brier. But unless you do, you won't win." Lately, our teams have played pretty well; some of them are sort of also-rans because they are against some very good teams. Our big thing was that when the going got really tough, we got going good.

You're always keyed up to win at the Brier, nervous. You have to be. That means it's important, and your concentration levels are up. We slept apart from our wives during Brier week, Sam and Wes in one room, Arnold and I in the other. Sam and Wes, they would roll around, wake up looking at each other in the middle of the night. Arnold and I would sleep well, get up in the morning and have a nice big breakfast because I never let the pressure affect my eating or sleeping habits. Some very good curlers needed to party it up a little at night, have a few drinks, and yet they could still perform because that was part of their makeup. I couldn't do that. I had to be dead serious and dead sober.

We never swayed from our routine except for the 1964 Brier in Charlottetown. We accepted an invitation to our host's house for a lobster dinner. If we had been on the ball, we'd have gone over and had a beer and one lobster and gone back to our hotel room. We each had a couple of beers—which is not bad, nothing wrong with that—but we also had two big lobsters apiece, with the rich butter and all. We didn't get a good night's sleep, and we were not sharp against Lyall Dagg (of B.C.) the next morning. (Both teams entered the game with 7–1 records.) In the first end we misplayed a draw to let them steal one, and I knew right away we weren't mentally sharp. Dagg beat us (8–3) fair and square. He probably would have beaten us anyway, but I'm sure it would have been a much better game had we not indulged ourselves the night before. (B.C. finished 9–1, Saskatchewan 8–2.)

Ernie Richardson

I'm still the only skip to have won four Briers, although there have been a few that have won two or three. Someday one of those men, or someone else, will get that fourth championship. (Randy Ferbey of Edmonton got it on March 13, 2005.) I'll be the first one to congratulate him, if I'm still alive because that will be tremendous. It is even more difficult to achieve that feat now than it was when we played. You could figure that there were about four teams to contend with; the Western provinces and sometimes Ontario. Now you get at least six contenders at every Brier, and you can't be sure where they'll come from.

Absolutely, it's tougher to win now, but that goes for every sport—baseball, golf, you name it. There were great players then, and some people would say they were the greatest players that ever played. I'm very happy and honoured to be mentioned in the same breath with men like Russ Howard, Wayne Middaugh, Kevin Martin, Randy Ferbey. I think they're better shotmakers than I was; lots of curlers were. Then again, we played in more difficult times on some very tough ice. We were probably the best team in our era. Maybe we were the best of any era to be able to play on every kind of ice. That's what made us strong—that and being able to come up big when we had to. And that's how you gauge a team—no matter whether it is baseball, hockey or curling—by how it responded under competitive pressure. We were a strong team that could play good when we had to, and we could handle any ice conditions that we played on, usually better than the opposition. I think that's one way to put it—without bragging. I don't want to sound like I'm bragging—I just want to state a fact.

JOYCE McKEE: RULING THE DOMINION

IT'S GOOD TO BE THE KING, BUT IT'S NOT EASY being queen. At least it wasn't 50 years ago.

Today women's curling rocks and rules Saskatchewan. The provincial playdowns are a gripping free-for-all that always produces a contender at the Scott Tournament of Hearts. There is a tradition of excellence embodied in rinks skipped by Sherry Anderson and Jan Betker that goes back to Sandra Schmirler, Michelle Englot (Schneider Ridgway), Sheila Rowan, Marj Mitchell, Vera Pezer and the one who started it all, Joyce McKee.

Yet, in 1954, a woman's existence was scarcely even recognized in the world of 12-foot circles. Asquith-born Joyce McKee learned that when, at 21, she skipped her Saskatoon rink all the way to the provincial championship scheduled for Yorkton. When the weather turned warm and the ice turned mushy, the final game was relocated to the artificial ice of the Caledonian in Regina, future home club of world champions Mitchell and Schmirler. Upon arrival, however, the best women's teams in the province found all sheets occupied by men's club games.

"Certainly, ladies, you can have a sheet of ice for your little game," they were told, "right after we finish ours."

Thus, the 1954 women's provincial final began at 11:00 P.M., and Joyce McKee won her first of eight Saskatchewan championships around 1:30 in the morning—no time for a 21-year-old single lady to be out in the city, to be sure. Had she no shame?

McKee wouldn't win another provincial title in the '50s, but she was already noteworthy for her athleticism. Unlike virtually every other woman who released her rock from the hack, she actually employed a sliding delivery. For a few years, McKee maintaining contact with her stone was as unique within her gender as it was for Stan Austman to show off his hack-to-button placement. Even before she left the hack, though, McKee's delivery resembled another, much taller curler.

"She had a backswing just like Bob Pickering," says Sylvia Fedoruk. "She needed it to get momentum. The takeout game was new to women's curling, and Joyce understood that the slide was essential to controlling takeouts. She was the first female I ever saw slide. It wasn't easy because curlers were looking for the right kind of sole to help them slide smoothly. Joyce experimented with all kinds of things to make her left shoe slippery; I think liquid solder was the first."

Bob Pickering

Joyce McKee pioneering the slide delivery for women in the mid-1950s

Hub City Ladies Curling Fraternity
Jan 25th 1960

Miss-Joyce McKee

Although it has been established, that you are one of Saskatoons Primier Lady Curlers. It has also been established, that you have show very poor sportswomenship. Viz by not taking your club rink into the Saskatoon–Bonspiel. When we had our ladies meeting, you were one of the members. Who wished to have a steady rink of ladies with you throughout the club competition. This was done.

But poor sportswomenship. Has certainly shown. By leaving your club, rink and taking your Provincial Rink into the Bonspiel. This of course is entirely up to you. So you will not have as many of your well wishers from your, associated curlers. In future competition.

Disgusted – Women – Curlers

The semi-literate letter of protest Joyce McKee received after entering her competitive rink in the Saskatoon Ladies Bonspiel

Fedoruk, an accomplished multi-sport athlete, had quit playing competitive sports in 1955 to concentrate on her career in medical radiation physics with the Saskatchewan Cancer Commission. Eventually, she discovered the bustling curling community at the University of Saskatchewan, took up the game, and worked her way up from a neophyte lead to a third in a couple of years. That didn't necessarily mean she was McKee's third, although she frequently was.

"Women didn't have teams for club games in a lot of communities," explains Pezer, later a teammate of McKee and author of *The Stone Age*, a social history of curling in the prairie provinces. "Skips would draw the names of their players. You had to earn your spurs to be a skip. It was even common practice to take a randomly drawn club team into a big city bonspiel. Then teams started becoming more competitive, and one year Joyce decided her competitive team needed practice heading into playdowns."

The year was 1960, and McKee was intent on regaining the provincial title that had eluded her the past five years. When McKee bypassed the skips' draw for the Saskatoon Women's Bonspiel and entered her regular team of Fedoruk, Donna Belding and Muriel Coben, it was as shocking as seeing the bishop's housekeeper sipping sherry on a Sunday. McKee received an anonymous typewritten letter of protest, evidently composed by someone ignorant of syntax, spelling and punctuation *(see above).*

Untroubled, McKee won the bonspiel, the provincial championship and the Western Canada title to qualify for the first Canadian women's championship, a simple two-out-of-three series in Oshawa against Eastern titlist Ruth Smith of Lacolle, Que. McKee dispatched Smith 11–3 and 8–5 and returned home as skip of the best team in the Dominion.

By coincidence, the Dominion grocery chain provided sponsorship of a genuine national women's championship (the "Diamond D") in 1961. McKee and Fedoruk, with a new front end of Barbara McNiven and Rosa McFee, defended the Saskatchewan title and joined the other nine provincial champions in Ottawa for a straight round-robin competition. McKee won all nine of her games. As expected, her toughest games were against Western competition: a 7–6 extra-end decision over Dorothy Thompson of Alberta and a 7–6 victory over Margaret Fuller of British Columbia. Eastern Canada was hoping the Diamond D would serve as a coronation for Emily Woolley of Toronto, long considered the unofficial "queen of women's curling," but the 67-year-old Ontario skip could only manage a 5–4 record and personify the difference between East and West:

Sylvia Fedoruk, Barbara McNiven, Joyce McKee and Rosa McFee wear winners' smiles after going undefeated at the 1961 Dominion 'Diamond D' championship

Simply put, curling was an old ladies' game in Eastern Canada and a young woman's game in the West, one that was emerging in athleticism and strategy. When the old guard met the new in the round robin, Saskatchewan charged to an 8–0 lead after three ends and eased home to a 10–4 victory over Ontario. Woolley proclaimed McKee the best woman curler she had ever seen in her life.

McKee, Fedoruk, McNiven and McFee made it back to the second Diamond D at Regina in 1962 and lost only one game, to Ina Hansen of B.C., but Hansen went undefeated to dethrone the Saskatchewan team. McKee's rink broke up. Janet Perkin of Regina won her third Saskatchewan championship in 1964. McNiven skipped a team (Fay Coben, Florence Hill and Avis Carr) that became the new provincial power with titles in 1965, '66 and '68. No team, however, duplicated McKee's Canadian dominance until 1969—when McKee herself led Pezer, Lee Morrison and Jennifer Falk to the top of the heap.

VERNON VAUGHN: DEDICATED, FORGOTTEN ROUGHRIDER

Vernon Vaughn died March 9, 1961, three weeks after being diagnosed with leukemia. He had played three seasons (1958–60) with the Saskatchewan Roughriders as a two-way end, catching 73 passes for 1,058 yards. The *Leader-Post* story of his death noted that at 6-foot-3, 235 pounds, he was "an excellent blocker and fine pass receiver on offence and was a rugged player on defence."

Vaughn's commitment to the Roughriders was so strong that, at his request, he was buried in his No. 78 jersey. Curiously, the team did not retire it, although it is hard to see how his death was any less tragic than those of the four players who were killed in a 1956 plane crash at Mt. Slesse. Nor did Vaughn's 38 games preclude a tribute; Gord Sturtridge played 62, Mel Becket 45, Mario DeMarco 38 and Ray Syrnyk 24.

Saskatchewan didn't use No. 78 again until 1977. Over the next 12 years it would be worn by 12 players, ranging from excellent (Vince Goldsmith) to forgettable (Scott Virkus). Defensive end James Curry was the last to wear it, in 1989.

It would be nice if the Roughriders gave No. 78 some official status, either by retiring it or by conferring it from time to time on an especially deserving player. Just treat it, one way or another, like it's something special.

Vernon Vaughn did.

Vernon Vaughn

YORKTON TERRIERS, 1961: WORST HOCKEY YEAR IMAGINABLE

Vic Krekelewitz, 33-year-old player-coach of the Yorkton Terriers, was driving his automobile west on Highway 14 the afternoon of January 2, 1961, in the company of two teammates, Adam Twardowsky and Ed Moskell. Blowing snow made for poor visibility and road conditions, but there was a Saskatchewan Senior Hockey League game to be played that night in Saskatoon against the Quakers.

Vic Krekelewitz

They didn't make it. Another car containing a family en route to its home in St. Boniface, Man., collided head-on with Krekelewitz's vehicle near the Highway 35 junction south of Elfros, not quite halfway to the hockey players' destination. Krekelewitz and the adult couple in the eastbound car were killed. Twardowsky and Moskell were both taken to hospital in critical condition with head injuries and broken ankles. The two preschool children travelling with their parents survived.

It wasn't long after Yorkton's other players arrived in Saskatoon that they heard the devastating news. Stranded in the Hub City by the weather, the Terriers decided to play the scheduled game. The Quakers loaned them four players, and Saskatoon won a dispirited, tame contest 7–3.

Twardowsky and Moskell recovered from their injuries. Bill Prystai, Metro's brother, coached the Terriers through the end of the season, but the economics of senior hockey dictated the services of a player-coach. Bill Tyshko, a Winnipeg product who had played junior with the Flin Flon Bombers, was hired to fill Krekelewitz's role for the 1961–62 season.

On December 22, 1961, Bill Tyshko was killed when the car he was driving crashed on Highway 9 just outside Yorkton.

HARRY JEROME: FASTEST MAN ON EARTH

Harry Jerome's time in Saskatchewan was brief but significant. He was born September 30, 1940, in Prince Albert, but his father, a porter on the Canadian National Railway, moved the family to St. Boniface, Man., when Harry was just 11 days old. The family moved again, shortly before his 11th birthday, to Vancouver, where he became a superlative sprinter.

Jerome drew national attention in 1959 with a Canadian record of 21.8 seconds for 220 yards and returned to the province of his birth for the 1960 Olympic trials at Griffiths Stadium in Saskatoon. On the mild evening of July 15, 19-year-old Harry Jerome took his mark for the 100-metre final and poised for the sound of the starter's gun.

He saw Lyn Eaves of Victoria, immediately to his left, budge. Jerome exploded from the starting blocks. He wouldn't remember hearing the gun. Already renowned for his fast start, Jerome hit his stride full of confidence. He virtually flew down the track—the epitome of physical, mental and emotional balance. Eaves and George Short of Saskatoon trailed in Jerome's wake, three strides behind.

Three thousand spectators rose in awe and applauded. Timekeepers huddled with their stopwatches as the audience awaited announcement of the time. Only 24 days earlier, Armin Hary of West Germany had run the first 10-flat to break the world record that had been stuck at 10.1 since 1956. How close was this to the new record?

"The winner, in a world-record time of ten point zero seconds . . ."

Jerome's standing ovation lasted five minutes—30 times longer than it took him to run the race.

Jerome pulled a hamstring in his semi-final at the Olympics and was unable to finish. Two years later his left quadriceps tore away from the femur and surgery was required to rebuild the shredded tissue. Jerome rebounded from that horrific injury to earn a bronze medal at the 1964 Olympics in Tokyo, tie the 100-yard world record of 9.1 seconds at a 1966 meet in Edmonton, win 100-metre gold medals in the 1966 British Empire Games in Jamaica and 1967 Pan-American Games in Winnipeg, and compete in his third Olympics at Mexico City in 1968.

Jerome forged a career in amateur sports governance and relentlessly pursued his favourite causes: the multi-front battle against racial discrimination, economic development in the black community and greater access to athletic facilities and equipment for disadvantaged youth. On December 7, 1982, while riding in a friend's car, he suffered a brain aneurysm and died at the age of 42.

GAIL DALEY AND IRENE HAWORTH: GYM DANDIES

Saskatoon produced two Olympic-calibre gymnasts in the 1960s, Gail Daley and Irene Haworth. Because of financial constraints, only one actually competed at the Games—one more than the Canadian Olympic Association wanted to send. They qualified for the 1964 Olympics at the national trials, only to be told that Canada would send three men and no women to Tokyo because of budget restraints.

"It was one of the few times I was ever disappointed and wondered if all the hours I spent in training were worth it," Gail Daley Bakker later said. "But it turned out to be very satisfying the way Saskatoon rallied around me."

Daley's father initiated a letter-writing campaign while coach Chuck Sebestyen personally contacted amateur sports executives to plead her case. If there was something Sebestyen knew how to make count, it was his time. A firefighter with a lifelong fascination for circus aerialists, Sebestyen got involved in coaching in 1957 when his daughters reported that their gymnastics courses at the local YWCA had too many girls and not enough instructors. Two years later, his daughter Glenna, 7, took second place in the 18-and-under class while Daley, 13, won the junior title and Maureen McDonald topped the seniors at the Alberta championships.

Since then, Saskatoon had played host to the 1961 national championships where Daley topped the country's juniors, Daley and Glenna Sebestyen had won the 1962 senior and junior Canadian titles, and Saskatoon's young women had come through like gangbusters in 1963: Daley, Haworth and McDonald led Canada to the team silver medal at the Pan-American Games in Sao Paolo, Brazil, with Haworth taking silver on the beam and seventh all-around, and Daley bronze on the beam and fifth all-around.

The letter-writing campaign and fundraising got Daley to Tokyo, where she justified the support by achieving personal bests in all her disciplines. Her Olympic prize was an International Gymnastics Federation pin for scoring in the 9s in every event.

Gail Daley

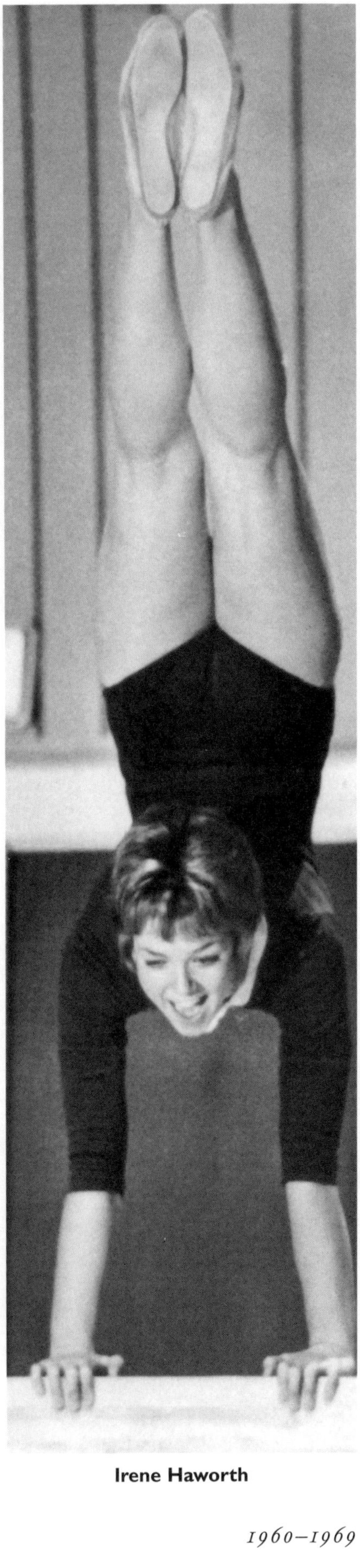

Irene Haworth

(This was a decade before gymnastics officials spewed 10s like beach bums ogling Bo Derek. The average score of a *medal*-winning performance in Tokyo, where there were 86 female competitors, was 9.68.) Daley's performance made her Canada's outstanding female athlete of 1964.

While Haworth was the one left out and Daley the one who reaped the benefit of the Olympic experience, their fortunes went in opposite directions as teammates at Southern Illinois University in Carbondale. Haworth won three individual and the all-around title in the NCAA championships. She also won the gold medal in uneven parallel bars and all-around silver at the 1965 United States Gymnastics Federation championships, denying Daley a clean sweep of the apparatus competitions (uneven bars, vault, beam and floor exercise) and all-around titles. Shortly afterward, Daley blew out her right knee and required reconstructive surgery that basically ended her competitive career.

Haworth carried on to take gold in the beam at the 1966 USGF championships, one of six national team titles (NCAA, USGF and AAU) she helped SIU capture. She also was named All-American, ruled the Canadian women's gymnastics championships, and made her second trip to the worlds in '66. She graduated from SIU in 1967, married, returned to Saskatoon, became a mother, and spent five years teaching physical education and coaching gymnastics at the U of S.

Ray Lougheed pumping iron during a workout in Moose Jaw

RAY LOUGHEED: NO BREAKS FOR THE BRAKEMAN

WORK AS A CPR BRAKEMAN WASN'T ENOUGH TO occupy 19-year-old Ray Lougheed when he moved to Moose Jaw from his native Ontario in 1953.

"I seemed to have energy to burn," he said. "An ordinary job wasn't enough to keep me occupied. I always wanted a challenge."

Lougheed took up wrestling and rigorously applied himself to it. He won the 1954 provincial lightweight (147½-pound) championship, beginning a 14-year string of 10 titles and four runner-up placements. He soon became dominant on the national scene as well, winning the first of six Canadian championships in 1956 and representing the country at the British Empire Games in Cardiff in 1958.

Training was serious business to Lougheed, so serious that he would let nothing interfere with it—not even sleep deprivation.

"There were times I would go maybe three days without sleep," he said. "I'd be doing things on the railway I didn't even know what I was doing. I'd be trying to throw a switch under the train while it was still passing over.

"You just can't find excuses. If you're out to do something, you have to do it, and that's all there is to it, regardless of sleep or no sleep."

Lougheed made the 1960 Olympic team and placed eighth in the 24-man lightweight field at Rome in 1960. He remained one of Canada's best wrestlers throughout the '60s, winning silver medals at the 1966 Commonwealth Games in Jamaica and the 1967 Pan-American Games in Winnipeg.

1964 WILLINGDON CUP: DOWN BY THE RIVERSIDE

SASKATCHEWAN'S SHORT GOLFING SEASON AND SMALL population had handicapped its teams terribly in the annual Willingdon Cup tournament. Since entering the national men's team championship in 1929, Saskatchewan consistently finished near, or even at, the bottom of the standings. A momentous exception occurred in 1950 at the Saskatoon Golf and Country Club, when the host team placed fourth of eight teams—52 strokes behind the winners from Ontario and eight ahead of last-place Nova Scotia.

So, when the 1964 Willingdon Cup came to the Saskatoon Riverside Course, the home-greens advantage wasn't expected to do much for Saskatonians Ed Ross and Jim Scissons and Reginans Keith Rever and Ernie Greenley. True, they were much more familiar with the course than the rest of the field, but what had Saskatchewan ever accomplished before? Besides, they just weren't in a class with Ontario, which boasted Gary Cowan and Nick Weslock, two of the best golfers—amateur or professional—Canada had ever produced.

Then a funny thing happened. Well, the Saskatchewan team found it amusing, anyway.

The wind kicked up on the first day, and kept kicking, at around 30 miles (50 kilometres) per hour. The locals were in their element, so to speak. Rever, armed with a brand new putter, one-putted five greens on the back nine and carded the low round of the day, a two-under-par 68, one shot better than Weslock. Ross matched Cowan's 71. Greenley and Scissons both came in at 77, mediocre on a normal afternoon, but in those conditions almost like shooting par. For the first time in Willingdon Cup history, Saskatchewan held the lead at the midway point of the two-day test at 293, followed by Ontario at 297, Alberta (299), B.C. and Quebec (both 304).

It would be too much to expect the wind to hang around 30 mph for a second straight day and sure enough, it didn't. It gusted to 50. Welcome, fellow Canadians, to real Saskatchewan golf.

Ross turned in a 70 that might have been Willingdon's greatest even-par round ever. Rever followed his superb 68 with a worthy 76. At 141 and 144, Ross and Rever had the best 36-hole scores in the field. Scissons came in at 74 for a 151 total, and Greenley managed another 77 for 154, which was at least three strokes better than the high man on every other team. The final standings weren't even close:

Saskatchewan	293–297–590
Alberta	299–299–598
Ontario	293–307–600
British Columbia	304–312–616
Nova Scotia	305–312–617
Manitoba	307–311–618
Quebec	304–315–619
New Brunswick/P.E.I.	318–320–638

Saskatchewan has not won, or even placed higher than third, in 40 years since then. Still, our men travel to the Willingdon Cup knowing that someday, somewhere, the wind will blow just right, hard enough to intimidate everyone but them but not so hard that the round is postponed.

Saskatchewan's only victorious Willingdon Cup team: the 1964 quartet of (from left) Keith Rever, Ernie Greenley, Ed Ross and Jim Scissons

General manager Ken Preston had picked up three new players for the Saskatchewan Roughriders' 1963 season, but there were no signs of a turnaround in the team's fortunes. Ron Lancaster, who had been relegated to backup duty behind Russ Jackson in Ottawa, was acquired to augment Bob Ptacek, a competent pivot at best. Fullback George Reed and flanker Hugh Campbell, teammates at Washington State University, came on as rookies. Even with the new talent and a solid core of Canadian veterans, the Roughriders barely made it into the playoffs with a 7–7–2 record. When they lost the first game of the two-game Western semi-final 35–9 in Calgary, it looked like 1962 all over again, except that this time the Roughriders were coming back to Taylor Field down 26 points instead of the 25 they trailed by a year earlier. There was no miracle comeback then, and the fans certainly didn't expect one now.

Speers (55 kilometres east of North Battleford) produced the 1962 Saskatchewan and Canadian Schoolboy curling champions: lead David Moore, second Doug MacLeod, third Ed Lukowich and skip Mike Lukowich. The foursome went 10–0 in Halifax. Ed Lukowich went on to become a two-time (1978, 1986) Brier champion—for Alberta. He is now the Athlete Development Director—for USA Curling. You know the brain drain's getting out of hand when it sucks people out of the hacks.

"We hadn't played well in Calgary," Lancaster recalls. "I know I didn't play very well. Everything that could go wrong did go wrong. I don't remember much about it—you forget those games as soon as you can.

"The second game was just the opposite of what you usually see at a sporting event; usually, it's packed at the start, and the crowd thins out as the game goes on. But on that particular day (November 11), it was a Monday night, not the warmest day for a football game. We were trailing by 26, no one gave us a chance to win, and when we came out to play, there weren't that many people in the stands. It wasn't hard to notice. It wasn't noisy like it normally was at Taylor Field."

Perhaps it was the drowsy atmosphere that inspired Bill Clarke to suggest to head coach Bob Shaw that the team try a sleeper play. The audacity of it was unbelievable; after the first play from scrimmage, Ray Purdin didn't return to the huddle but stood right in front of the Calgary bench. Before the Stampeders woke up, Lancaster had broken the huddle, taken the snap and hooked up with Purdin for a 76-yard touchdown. Later in the quarter, Lancaster's 26-yard pass to Ed Buchanan finished off an 85-yard march. Another TD pass, a two-yarder to Dick Cohee as the first half ended, made the game score 19–3 for Saskatchewan and the series score 38–28 for Calgary.

Bill Clarke

As the Roughriders drew closer to the Stampeders in the two-game total, so did the attendance at Taylor Field build towards capacity.

"As the game went on, you noticed more and more people coming in," Lancaster says. "You know, it isn't that far to Taylor Field from most places in Regina. By halftime the place was filling up. By the fourth quarter it was crowded. It got to be very exciting."

Lancaster threw another touchdown pass to Buchanan, this one a screen covering 45 yards. On Saskatchewan's next possession, consecutive gains of 22 and 29 yards by Reed put the ball on the Calgary 10 for Lancaster's fifth touchdown pass of the night and second to Cohee. Saskatchewan led 33–4 on the night and 42–39 in the series! The Roughriders had risen from the dead! It was the Miracle of Taylor Field!

Now they had to stay alive. Shocked out of their stupor, the Stampeders finally accomplished something when quarterback Eagle Day passed to halfback Lovell Coleman for a 60-yard gain that set up Earl Lunsford's touchdown. Calgary was back in the lead, 46–42, and momentum took a U-turn. Lancaster was intercepted, but the Saskatchewan defence stonewalled Coleman on third-and-one at the 'Rider 4-yard line. Calgary lined up for a field goal with three minutes to go, but Larry Robinson missed from 23 yards out. The single made it 47–42, and the 'Riders got the ball on their 25-yard line.

A 44-yard gain on a pass to Cohee, a 31-yard pass interference call against Campbell and a 10-yard off-tackle run by Reed and Saskatchewan was in the end zone, leading the game 39–12 and the series 48–47. For the third time in six tries, the convert failed.

Day drove the Stampeders inside the 'Rider 30. Robinson lined up a 35-yard field goal attempt as the clock approached zero. Again he was wide. Gene Wlasiuk fielded the ball deep in the end zone and hammered a beautiful punt 40 yards downfield. Robinson's attempt to punt it back for a single wobbled 15 yards out of bounds.

Game over. Comeback complete. Pandemonium.

Saskatchewan would lose the Western final in three games to the B.C. Lions, but the "Miracle of Taylor Field" made believers of the fans. Preston kept digging up more skilled players, but the most important move was one of subtraction, not addition.

Gene Wlasiuk (19) who, back in the days before blocking was allowed on punt returns, only *looked* like he was running under people

"Both Ron and I probably would have quit after 1964," Reed once said. "We couldn't have put up with another year if Shaw had still been there."

Shaw's impatience and poor relations with his star players led to his dismissal. His replacement, Eagle Keys, was a man of intimidating presence. As defensive end Don Gerhardt, a Roughrider from 1966–69, put it, Keys "could stare at you through his eyebrows" when he was unhappy with a player. That, however, was simply Keys' way of establishing a serious workplace. Unlike Shaw, he would not humiliate anyone.

"Eagle always treated everyone like men," Reed said. "If he had something to say to you he'd say it to your face. You didn't worry about reading it in the paper or hearing it anywhere else. And if you played poorly, you knew about it. You always knew where you stood with Eagle."

The standings would not show the progress the team was making: seven wins in 1963, nine in '64, eight in '65. Preston was loading the team with the best collection of Canadians the Roughriders would ever boast, nearly all of it produced within the province. Offensive tackle Reggie Whitehouse (a Montreal native) and defensive tackle Ron Atchison had been with the team since 1952, defensive back and fearless punt returner Gene Wlasiuk since '59; linebacker Wayne Shaw, from Notre Dame College via the Saskatoon Hilltops, and centre Ted Urness came aboard in 1961; defensive back Dale West, a standout speed skater and sprinter as a teenager, joined the fold in 1962. Then came wide receiver Gord Barwell from the Saskatoon Hilltops in 1964, do-everything Regina boy Alan Ford from the University of the Pacific and defensive back Ted Dushinski from the Hilltops in '65, and Cliff Shaw, Wayne's younger brother, in '66.

Urness (whose name is properly pronounced with a first-syllable accent, as in "furnace") was part of the second of three generations of Roughriders. His father Al and uncle Fred Goodman played under Al Ritchie. Ted's twin brother Jack and son Mark also wore the Green and White.

Ted, who grew up in Regina and played junior for the Rams, sped his promotion to a starting position by playing college football at the University of Arizona.

"Juniors had to sit two or three years if they were trying to leap into the pros in the '60s. Junior football was quite competitive, but it was still below the calibre you faced in an American college experience. It made quite a difference. I was able to come in to the CFL and start my first year; of course, I was four years older, too."

It has long been a bone of contention with Wayne Shaw that Americans received preferential treatment in salaries and playing time. It took time for him to earn his place in the starting lineup, but he proved his value by being named to the Western all-star team six times. His brother, also a Notre Dame and Hilltop grad who played linebacker, was not so fortunate.

"It was good for me to have Cliff on the team, but it wasn't fair for him," Wayne Shaw said in a 1982 interview. "The worst part of it was that the guy he was trying to beat out of the starting lineup was me."

The best part of it, from a Roughriders perspective, was that they had tremendous depth. Even before Reed, Lancaster and Campbell were acquired in 1963, the imports included defensive end Garner Ekstran and all-star offensive guard Al Benecick, both of whom would be four-time Western all-stars. Benecick had been a tackle but moved over in 1964 to accommodate the tree-like Clyde Brock, who would spend 12 years as George Reed's most frequent lead blocker. The '64 campaign also brought Jim Worden, a tight end with rock-hard shoulders and baby-soft hands, and ball-hungry DB Bob Kosid. Jack Abendschan, a placekicker and guard, solidified the offensive line in 1965, and a year later came a trio of imports: safety Bruce Bennett, linebacker Ken Reed and, most important of all, defensive tackle Ed McQuarters.

Atchison described McQuarters' arrival as "the greatest thing that happened to us" in a 1982 interview. It was one of the best things for Atchison's personal welfare, too.

"We already had the makings of a good team, but he gave us that little extra strength that tipped the scales," Atchison said. "He also gave me three extra years because he took the heat off me. I was double-teamed until he came along, and then they had to double-team him."

Atchison was also fortunate in that his role was rather tightly defined. Keys was, depending on one's point of view, either cautious or paranoid of the trouble the team could get into with the 32-man roster of the day. Ford, who could run, catch, punt, and return kicks, saw that some Roughriders like himself were born versatile while others had versatility thrust upon them.

"Eagle was famous for having about 18 backups," Ford exaggerated in a newspaper interview. "We had maybe four strings of kickers, and we'd have to work on field goals as a unit. Eventually, the third- or fourth-string kicker would drill one off somebody's rear end, and then you'd see all the linemen 'blocking' with their hands protecting their backsides."

Keys' precautions paid off several times, especially in a 1966 game at Winnipeg when Lancaster suffered a sprained ankle and Bennett had to play quarterback.

"When I got to the huddle, Whitehouse told me that if I saw Winnipeg in a certain defensive set, I was supposed to check off and go with a sweep to Reed," Bennett said. "Well, I'd only been in for a couple of plays, and there it was. I called George's number and he took it 70 yards."

Reggie Whitehouse

A penalty put the ball on the Bombers' one-yard line. Bennett called a quarterback sneak and scored a touchdown. On the sidelines, Bennett's teammates asked him why he hadn't given the ball to Reed for the six points.

"My high school coach told me that when you're that close, you should always give the ball to your best back," he deadpanned.

Bennett didn't complete any of his four pass attempts, but the Roughriders managed an 11–11 tie. At season's end they were in first place with a 9–6–1 record and 19 points, two more than the Blue Bombers, their opponents in the best-of-three Western final.

Saskatchewan's biggest playoff heroes would not be Lancaster, Reed or anyone else from the offence. In the opener at Taylor Field, Bob Kosid snuffed out the Blue Bombers' passing attack with two interceptions, including one in the end zone, and several knockdowns. Game 2 was another defensive contest, with the Roughriders holding a 14–12 lead but the home-town Bombers on the march at midfield with five minutes to go. Winnipeg quarterback Ken Ploen dropped back to pass against a 'Rider blitz and was sandwiched between Gerhardt and Ken Reed. The ball popped out of Ploen's grasp and into the hands of McQuarters, who galloped 50 yards for an insurance touchdown that proved necessary when Winnipeg scored late to make the final score 21–19.

For the ninth time in their 56-year history, and the first time in 15 years, the Roughriders were in the Grey Cup. As in 1951, the opponents would be the Ottawa Rough Riders, who boasted an 11–3 regular-season record, a stingy defence and the great Russ Jackson at quarterback. Ottawa was the clear favourite and Saskatchewan the underdog for the national final in Vancouver.

Ed McQuarters

The first half was, as football analysts like to say now, vertical. Jackson unloaded 61- and 85-yard bombs to Whit Tucker for Ottawa's touchdowns. Saskatchewan's first play was a long pass down the sideline from Lancaster to Barwell that gained 46 yards. Lancaster threw two touchdown passes of his own, the first an over-the-top lob to Worden that was designed for a long gain but proved effective on second-and-goal from the 6, and the second a 19-yarder to Ford. Worden's TD had been set up by Dale West's 36-yard interception return to the Ottawa 9, a play that should have been called for pass interference but wasn't.

"I stuck my foot between (Ted) Watkins' legs as he was cutting," Dushinski admitted. "I figured I could make it look like an accident. The refs never caught it. It wasn't

Cliff (left) and Wayne (50) Shaw with their father, Ed, after the 1966 Grey Cup game

legal, but you do what you've got to do."

As the teams reached halftime tied 14–14, the game was shifting from an aerial contest to a ground battle that the Roughriders would win decisively. Ottawa had eight first downs in the first quarter, only four for the rest of the game. Jackson completed only six passes, including the two touchdowns, in 15 attempts all day. On the other side, the Roughriders let George do it. Reed gained 133 yards on 23 carries.

"By the third quarter their linemen and linebackers were hurting or injured," Benecick said. "I recall everyone's eyes in the huddle—Ronnie's, George's, the guys on the line—the extra sense of feeling that we had 'em. It was a physical contest, and we came out on top. We punished 'em."

Campbell broke the tie with a five-yard scoring reception on the first play of the fourth quarter, Lancaster's third touchdown pass. Halfway through the period, with the ball on the Ottawa 31, Lancaster called a trap play. Urness and Abendschan opened a gaping hole and Reed proceeded on an untouched straight line into the end zone. Ottawa tried its favourite trick play—a halfback pass from Ron Stewart back to Jackson—on its next possession, and Gerhardt intercepted it. Ford punted a single to make the final score 29–14.

Portrait of Ron Lancaster by Nicholas de Grandmaison from the Athol Murray College of Notre Dame Museum

Locker-room celebrations were made extra sweet by the knowledge that, to the end, the Roughriders were underdogs. It was discovered that, during the third quarter, television cameras were being set up in Ottawa's room to cover post-game celebrations and victory interviews. Television wasn't the only institution that sold Saskatchewan short. The CFL itself had prematurely stocked each room with cases of what it thought were the appropriate beverages: champagne for the winners, beer for the losers.

"It worked out all right because they had to drag the champagne over to our dressing room," said Ken Reed. "And we kept the beer, too."

When the team returned home to a tumultuous reception at the Regina Armoury, the dignitaries included a positively giddy Lt.-Gov. Robert Leith "Dinny" Hanbidge. After all, as a member of the original 1910 Regina Rugby Club, no one had awaited this achievement longer than he.

GREEN AND WHITE AND BLACK: GEORGE REED IN HIS OWN WORDS

I TOOK A LOT OF PRIDE IN BEING A COMPLETE FOOTBALL player. To be that, you have to do everything well, and when I started out with the Roughriders blocking was probably my weakest point. It was instilled in me that the quarterback needs some time, and if I'm back there, I'm the one that's got to protect him. So I developed the blocking habit and took a lot of pride in it, whether I was blocking for the quarterback or another running back.

One of our pet plays was a sweep off tackle where I was supposed to kick the linebacker out. Nine out of 10 times I was able to complete that. You have to establish a strong running game, and I think that was our trademark. Then Ronnie had time to do things he wanted to do because they couldn't tee off on the pass rush. I got more enjoyment out of pass blocking, protecting Ronnie, than out of run blocking. It was always a challenge to go up against John Helton or Ron Estay or one of those guys. I did enjoy run blocking, don't get me wrong. But patrolling the backfield and picking off people that somebody else missed was my assignment, and I really enjoyed that.

As far as my own running, we had a series between tackles that would allow me to pick where I could go. What I enjoyed about our offensive line was that they would get off the ball so quickly and get right on people. A lot of times I would start out to the right side of the line and wind up clear back on the left. There was one occasion when one of our tackles looked back to see where I was because the play wasn't coming to his side and I ran over him. He said something like, "The play was supposed to be on the other side," and I said, "Well, don't worry about it, all you have to do is block, I'll find the hole."

Then there was a play designed to go either inside the tackle or between the tackle and tight end. Those were probably my bread-and-butter plays. We got into some games the other team knew what we were going to do, and we knew they knew it, but it was up to them to try to stop us. We took pride in doing it anyway.

Once you establish that running game, you say okay, what can we do *off* the running game? And the play-action pass can be devastating. I would carry the football four, five, six times, piling up pretty good yardage, making the first downs. Then Ronnie could put the football in my gut and pull it out—I was still going the same way as if I had the football. That drew the linebackers and some defensive backs for a split-second, made them forget their pass coverage assignment, and that's all it takes to get the pass off.

People would ask me about my workload, carrying the ball 20 to 25 times a game. I don't consider I carried it that much because probably eight of those times I was going for a first down and no more. If I broke it for a big gain, fine, but my concentration was on getting those two or three yards we needed. My job on short yardage was to get the first down; other times I'd do all I could do.

Yeah, there were all those fakes into the line when I didn't have the ball. On those, you're down the same way, but the ball's not in your belly so you're also in a good launching position. You get the chance to put an extra lick on somebody who wasn't expecting it; that was always fun.

Sometimes you didn't do it for fun. Sometimes you'd go straight at someone who had it coming, someone who was throwing cheap shots, dirty shots. One example: We were playing Winnipeg, I had crossed the goal line and, of course, you let up once you're in the end zone. And Grady Cavness just knocked the shit out of me. I'm laying there, thinking, "What? I'm through the goal line, I'm five yards deep in the end zone. Why would anybody take a cheap shot at me?" It's one of those things that kind of sticks in your head—that if you ever get the chance, you owe him one.

So two or three years later we were playing B.C., and Cavness was playing for the Lions now. I went through the line and when I did, I ran over him. Then I kind of backed up and stomped on him again. Someone asked me why I did that and I said I owed him. Cavness understood. He got the message and he got it very clear.

There would be occasions when racial slurs were said on the field or sometimes even from the stands. It never affected my play—not in a negative way. Mentally, I'd be in my little glass cube on Sunday or whenever we played the game. Sometimes I heard the

George Reed protects Ron Lancaster from Edmonton's Ron Estay (55)

name-calling, and I'd let it roll off my back. Sometimes it made me mad, made me more determined to make them pay for it, and with my skill and my offensive line, I could really make them pay. That wouldn't happen often, though. You can't let someone know he's getting inside your head.

What bothered me more than anything was dealing with situations away from the job. On Sunday afternoons and at practice I knew where I was supposed to be, what my responsibilities were, how I was expected to act before, during and after the game or the practice. The rest of the time, though, I didn't know where I fit in or what I was supposed to do. Like, you're not allowed to go and have a beer in this spot. Okay, I understand; am I allowed to go and say hello to this person or not? You know, what do you want me to do? That's the way I felt sometimes, that I could unwittingly get in trouble just for being in the wrong place or talking to the wrong person. I had a lot of problems with that, and I held in a lot of those feelings.

Reed finally spoke up in December of 1967 when he was interviewed by a Toronto Telegram *reporter seeking reaction to accusations of discrimination by Hamilton Tiger-Cats receiver Ted Watkins.*

"There is flagrant discrimination against Negroes in Regina," Reed told the Telegram. *"I have come face-to-face with more racial problems in my five years in Regina than I ever had living in a suburb of Seattle. In the beginning I couldn't find anyone who would rent me an apartment. . . .*

"My five-year-old son, who never knew what discrimination was, is suddenly called names he doesn't understand. My wife has become so defensive that when she leaves the house she's like a coiled cobra that's ready to

George Reed follows Al Benecick (62) into the Montreal defence during a 1966 game at Taylor Field in which Reed ran for 114 yards and three touchdowns in a 44–0 victory

strike at anybody. Regina is like living in the heart of Alabama as far as I'm concerned."

In his off-field job as project manager for Molson Saskatchewan, Reed frequently had to absorb blatant racial insults at public functions.

"Somebody gets filled up with false courage," he told the Telegram, *"and suddenly starts calling me 'Darky' and 'Nigger.' They never say, 'Negro', and I'm proud of being a Negro. It's funny, this never comes from the so-called upper class. It always comes from what you might say is the middle class person."*

I wouldn't retract a word, and I don't regret saying any of it. Maybe those of us who spoke out improved the lot of black CFL players, who were and still are a very small but very visible portion of Canadian residents.

I still remember that apartment-hunting experience vividly. It was my second year with the Roughriders, 1964, and I needed a place for my family to live. I found an advertisement for a furnished apartment, made a phone call, and was told it was vacant. When Angie and I went there and they saw the colour of our skin, suddenly the apartment was rented. We drove back and had some other people, some white people we knew, call about the apartment and check it out. Yes, they were told, they could have the apartment if they wanted it.

As hard as it was to take, it was more difficult to stay silent about it. At first, it was a relief to say my piece and unburden myself. But then there was a backlash. The Regina media were all over me. Reginans who thought their city was just fine were outraged that I had said otherwise. Molson demoted me and almost fired me.

In the future, whenever the matter of racism was put to me, I answered the questions but didn't go into detail. Another thing that was really hard to take after I became well-known, after I'd won the Schenley and made a bunch of all-star teams, is how people started to change towards me. They didn't change towards the problem, they changed towards me. It actually became harder for me after I was accepted for membership at the Wascana Country Club, after I was welcomed into this place and that place, but another black person, whether he was an athlete or not, wasn't accorded the same privilege. That bothered me. It bothered me a lot.

I've never said I hate Canada, I've never said I dislike Canada. What I *have* said is, don't say those problems don't exist. Open your eyes to them, then you're going to have a lot less trouble down the road. You're going to have problems no matter where you go, but the point that I try to get across is that if you recognize the problem, if you talk about it, if you work at it, then you can solve it. I didn't leave Regina because of any dissatisfaction with the city or with my job. Really, I enjoyed most of my time with Molson, and I didn't want to leave Regina. Molson asked me to transfer to Calgary; that's how I wound up here. Otherwise, I'd probably still be in Regina. Yeah, I still love Canada. Canada's my home now. I don't know if I'll stay in Calgary the rest of my life, but I'll be somewhere in Canada.

ESTEVAN BRUINS: THE PUNCH AND SCOTTY SHOW

ESTEVAN DIDN'T LAST LONG AS A MAJOR JUNIOR locale, but it was fun while it lasted. Owner Scotty Munro relocated the Humboldt Indians there in 1957, and in 1971 the team was shifted all the way to New Westminster, B.C., when it was deemed impossible for a community of 9,000 to sustain a WCHL franchise. Estevan still supports its Bruins, though in the economically modest confines of the Tier 2 SJHL.

In the '60s, though, the Bruins were the very model of small-town success. Munro was an entrepreneur cut from the same cloth as Bill Hunter, a man who wasn't shy about coaching the team he owned, who stayed very close to the action when he wasn't coaching, and who happily stirred up whatever commotion would put paying customers in the seats. His right-hand man was Ernie "Punch" McLean, who was a key administrative player in the Bruins' first season of 1957–58 and became coach in 1964.

Munro recognized, from the Montreal Canadiens' NHL success and the Regina Pats' domination of Western junior hockey in the '50s, the necessity of a feeder system. Estevan had a productive pipeline of talent linked to North Battleford, where brothers Mo and Jeep George operated the Beaver Bruins system.

"The Beaver Bruin and Estevan Bruin systems were pretty well identical," says Dale Hoganson, a Bruins defenceman who was born in North Battleford. "We had as many imports, players from out of town, as Estevan did. The expectations were the same as far as what you did on and off the ice; they kept a tight rein on you. Mo and Jeep George coached the same as Scotty and Ernie. They'd break you down if you weren't doing things right, but you'd never leave without getting a pat on the back. They were intimidating, Mo and Jeep. You knew if you made if a mistake; you had a fear of them, but it was a respectful fear. They expected a lot from you and gave you a lot in return."

Lorne Henning, born in Melfort, played in both cities.

"I think I left home when I was 14 to play Junior B in North Battleford," Henning says. "Ernie McLean had scouted me when Melfort won the Midget B provincials down at Notre Dame. That year at North Battleford we played in a senior league, and we were all like 15–16–17 years old, playing against men.

"You really grew up as a person. Ernie had a rule in Estevan: No cars. You had to walk to and from the rink. Whoever had a car got it put up on their wheels, and then they got it back after the season was up. Sometimes coming back from a road game he'd have the bus driver drop us off a mile from the rink so we'd have to walk home and wake up. After a while, you kind of toughened up."

There were worse things than walking a mile in sub-freezing darkness.

"Scotty and Ernie taught the old school values of hard work, fundamentals and authority," says Gregg

North Battleford Beaver Bruins celebrate their 1965–66 Western Canada Midget B championship. Gregg Sheppard is second from left; Jeep George (with hat) is at right

Sheppard. "They ruled with an iron fist. One night we lost in Weyburn, a team we should have beaten, while we were in a battle for first place with Flin Flon. It was a quiet bus ride back to Estevan. We got in at about half past midnight and started to put our gear away when Scotty came running in.

"'Don't hang your equipment up! Put it on!'

"So we went on the ice, and we were skating around with all the lights off in the arena. All we could see in the stands when we first stepped on the ice were two white coffee cups and a couple of cigarettes; Scotty and Ernie smoked. They'd blow the whistle and we'd skate; blow the whistle, change direction. Soon the smokes were out, the coffee cups lay still on the floor, and we were still skating around, skating around until we realized there was nobody there.

"So we went into the dressing room and checked the blackboard: ON THE ICE AT 6:30 A.M. So we were back on the ice at 6:30, before we went to school, and had our regular practice at 1:30 in the afternoon and we thought, 'Boy, this has got to be enough.' Blackboard after practice: ON THE ICE AT 10:00 P.M. We practised for another hour that night. And I'll never forget it, we were standing in the shower and Dale Hoganson said, 'My hands haven't been this clean since I was a baby.' Everybody broke up. I don't remember who we played next, but I do know Scotty and Ernie got 100 percent out of us."

Then there was the time in Flin Flon . . . (Anyone who says he played junior hockey in the '60s, but who doesn't have a Flin Flon story, is lying.)

"Our games with Flin Flon were always promoted with verbal jabs between (Bombers coach Paddy) Ginnell and Ernie and Scotty," Sheppard says. "They put on a show in those days. When we played in Flin Flon, there was a guy just down from our bench who was continually barking at Ernie. Just as the second intermission was ending, Ernie told one of our trainers to bring out a water bucket with a towel in it. Well, it's 30 below in the rink, none of us players has ever towelled down, and he's bringing out a water bucket? He said, 'I'm going to get that guy.'

"Wouldn't you know it, the guy starts barking at him again. Ernie bent down, picked up the bucket to throw it, and the guy jumped back. Ernie hit a lady in a fur coat. Drenched! That was one reason people came to the games, to see what would happen next.

We'd get 2,700 people in that little rink in Estevan, sandwich room only. It was squashed in there."

Estevan won SJHL championships in 1963, '64 and '66 behind the efforts of such players as Joe Watson, Jack Norris, Terry Simpson, Stan Gilbertson, Skip Krake, Ross Lonsberry and Barry Gibbs. Memorial Cup glory eluded the Bruins because Hunter's Edmonton Oil Kings hogged the Western berth for seven straight years (1960–66). It might have been eight, but the provincial structure of Western junior hockey broke down on June 21, 1966, at what became known at the Clear Lake Massacre.

Lorne Henning

The SJHL annual meeting at the Manitoba resort of Clear Lake had to be adjourned minutes after starting because a majority of teams claimed they could not pay their CAHA dues. In fact, the teams, most of them from larger urban centres, were rebelling over the CAHA's control of franchise applications and playoff revenues. The "rebels" reassembled and formed what would be officially called the Canadian Major Junior Hockey League but unofficially called the Outlaw League because it was not sanctioned by the CAHA. Only seven teams rose above the legal and political harangue to take part in the Outlaw League's first season: the Bruins, Pats, Oil Kings, Saskatoon Blades, Moose Jaw Canucks, Weyburn Red Wings and Calgary Buffaloes.

Renamed, expanded, and given the official CAHA stamp of approval, the league entered its second season as the Western Canada Hockey League. Swift Current, Flin Flon, the Brandon Wheat Kings and Winnipeg Jets swelled the ranks to 11 teams. Flin Flon captured first place behind the dynamic duo of Bobby Clarke and Reggie Leach, but the second-place Bruins caught fire in the playoffs, winning four straight from each of the Jets, Pats and Bombers with only one tie in each of the last two series slowing their advance to the Memorial Cup. Estevan then beat the Westfort, Ont., Hurricanes in five games and B.C.'s Penticton Broncos in a four-game sweep to claim the Abbott Cup as Western champions.

It was an Eastern year for the Memorial Cup and, while Munro lobbied for as many neutral-site games as possible, Niagara Falls Flyers owner Hap Emms was just as adamant that all the games be played in their home rink. Emms won the power struggle; all but the second game would be played in Niagara Falls. Game 2, at the Montreal Forum, was memorable for the peculiar sight of both teams taking their warm-ups in identical white uniforms. As affiliates of the Boston Bruins, the only difference was their crests: Estevan wore the same "B" within a wheel as the NHL club, while the Flyers sported the letters "NF" inside a circle. Before the game started, the Flyers were outfitted with the red jerseys of the Montreal Junior Canadiens. Estevan prevailed 4–2 on the scoreboard, its only victory of the series. Niagara Falls proved most inhospitable.

"We had to fight our way into the rink and fight our way out of it," Sheppard remembers. "We needed police escorts. Jimmy Harrison got into a fight in the penalty box near the end of the first game. Some fan got past a policeman and jumped into the penalty box to attack him, and that was a mistake because Jimmy just beat the hell out of the guy."

The fan turned out be the father of Flyers defenceman Rick Thompson, whom Harrison had decisioned in a tussle on the ice minutes earlier. Thompson the elder did indeed pay for his trespass, literally losing his shirt along with some blood, but Estevan suffered more.

"Jimmy broke his hand on the guy's head," remembers Hoganson. "He was our best player, and

1967–68 Estevan Bruins. Alternate captains in front row are Dale Hoganson (left) and Gregg Sheppard; Men in suits are Scotty Munro (left) and Punch McLean; Jim Harrison is far right in the top row; Roy Atcheynum, father of NHL player Blair, is far right in the second row

he had to go the rest of the series with a playing cast on his hand. That eliminated a lot of our offence and some of our intimidation. And we got the dirty end of the stick in some of the games."

Estevan took 11 of 16 minors before the last-minute brawl in the 7–4 opening loss. Niagara Falls won Game 3 by the same 7–4 count. Game 4 was the true heartbreaker. Estevan was assessed 30 of 34 penalties and was outshot 63–31, yet hung in until Tom Webster scored at 12:56 of the second overtime to give Niagara Falls the pivotal 4–3 decision. The series-ending 6–0 contest was a formality. "They had pretty much taken the heart out of us by that time," Sheppard admits.

McLean was proud of his team that barrelled through five playoff series to win the Abbott Cup.

Speaking of which, where *was* the Abbott Cup? Inquiring minds wanted to know, especially those in Regina a year later when the Pats won the West. Would Ernie McLean kindly relinquish the trophy?

Ernie McLean said he could not. The Abbott Cup, he claimed, had disappeared.

Policemen were dispatched to McLean's front door.

Such a timely arrival. The missing trophy, McLean said, had just been discovered in his basement.

THE 1968 OLYMPIC HOCKEY TEAM: NEGLECTED BY HISTORY

I think they were underappreciated at that time, yeah. Today? I think they're forgotten.
–Jack McLeod on the 1968 Olympic team he coached

SASKATCHEWAN HAD DONE ITS PART TO KEEP Canada's hockey pre-eminence alive as long as it could. George Abel was there for the 1952 Edmonton Mercurys; the Warwick brothers and company formed the backbone of the 1955 Penticton Vees; Red Berenson contributed to the 1959 Belleville McFarlands; Jack McLeod helped out the 1961 Trail Smoke Eaters. Inevitably, the Soviet Union asserted its superiority over Canada's amateurs, and countries like Sweden and Czechoslovakia started beating our senior champions.

Father David Bauer, brother of former Boston Bruins star Bobby Bauer, proposed the formation of a permanent national team to the Canadian Amateur Hockey Association in 1962. To secure young talent, the team would be based near a major Canadian university (first in Vancouver, then Winnipeg) and players would receive education and living expenses. Father Bauer's idea was implemented in 1963 and met with middling success at the 1964 Winter Olympics at Innsbruck, Austria. Canada could have taken the gold medal by winning its last game against the Soviets but lost 3–2 and fell into a three-way tie for second place with the Swedes and Czechs. Expecting to receive bronze medals based on the pre-determined tiebreaker of head-to-head goal differential, the Canadians arrived at the presentation ceremony to learn they had been relegated to fourth by a last-minute International Ice Hockey Federation decision to change the tiebreaker to goals differential in *all* games played. Defenceman Marshall Johnston of Birch Hills told Bauer, "Father, your flock was fleeced."

Bauer wanted to relinquish the coaching reins after Innsbruck. In 1965 he travelled to Wilcox to seek a friend's help to enlist the successor he wanted.

"I'm sitting at home in Swift Current, and the phone rings," Jack McLeod recalled in 2003, "and it's Père Murray. He's in his office at Notre Dame with Father Bauer and Al Ritchie, who scouted for the New York Rangers.

"'Jack,' Père says to me, 'you got a plane?'

"'Yeah, Père, I got a plane,' I tell him. (McLeod was both a pilot and salesman of light aircraft.)

"'Get down here.'

"There was a landing strip in Corinne, so I touched down there, got a ride, and met the three of them in Wilcox. I had never met Father Bauer before, but I thought his plan was a good one because it was

Jack McLeod

a pretty tough deal for a senior club to go over there and represent Canada. So I took the job."

McLeod had seen plenty of international hockey with the Smoke Eaters at the '61 and '63 worlds and on a European tour with the Saskatoon Quakers. He also had coaching experience as playing-coach of the Saskatchewan Senior Hockey League's Moose Jaw Pla-Mors.

"One thing that impressed me about the Europeans was their passing," McLeod said. "They'd throw the puck a foot off the ice, and catch it on their blades, just like they had lacrosse sticks, and away they'd go. They were talented. Even when I was coaching the national team, I'd come back to Canada after we'd get beat, and I'd say, 'Hey, look out for those Europeans, I'm tellin' ya.' And they'd say, 'Ah, come on, your national team players, they're all too young, you can't play that well.' Nobody believed me.

"The Russians had a guy in '61 who turned out to be one of their great defencemen, (Alexander) 'Rags' Ragulin. He was just a kid that year, I think about 20 or something. Big! When I first saw this guy at a tournament in Russia, I'm looking up, he's 235 pounds and strong and tough. When he took me into the boards I thought he'd killed me. All the air went out of me, and I was thinking, 'Boy, we're going to the world tournament and I've got to play against this guy?' He would have made it in the NHL very easily, even then. He moved the puck well and could hit."

Canadians didn't appreciate how skilled Europeans, particularly Soviets, were. Canadians didn't appreciate how their team was handicapped, either.

"Remember in 1972 and 1974, how the NHL and WHA teams were crying about the referees? When we used to go to Europe, the referees were worse than that! I'd say something regarding the referees and *we* were the ones who were crying. The refereeing was brutal, I mean just brutal. We got taken a few times over there."

Yugoslavian newspapers railed in protest at the 1966 worlds in Belgrade when three Canadian goals were disallowed in a 2–1 loss to Czechoslovakia that bumped Canada from silver to bronze medals. A year later, the same consequence resulted from a goal waved off for a Canadian being "in the crease" when replays showed him five feet outside it.

With the 1968 Olympics in Grenoble, France, on the horizon, Bauer and McLeod found it harder to attract players to the national team and keep them on it. Expansion in the NHL had doubled the number of big-league jobs. Bobby Orr, a teenager, was on the verge of a six-figure annual salary. The Nats, as they were known, got by on $2,000 a month. Tuition came out of that, as well as living expenses for wives and children for the married men on the squad. Ex-pros like Carl Brewer had to leave the team because only lifelong amateurs were eligible for the Olympics. As the games neared, McLeod was left with a few proud young men willing to put up with the financial hardship, the aggravation, and Canada's general apathy toward their sacrifice.

In a nation of more than 20 million Canadians, Saskatchewan's population of less than 1 million supplied almost half the Olympic team: coach McLeod from Regina via Notre Dame, centre Gary Begg of Moosomin, defenceman and captain Marshall Johnston of Birch Hills, defenceman Ted Hargreaves of Foam Lake, centre Fran Huck of Regina, right wing Morris Mott of Creelman and forwards Gerry and Herb (Jr.) Pinder of Saskatoon. Forward Brian Harper of Regina, Terry's kid brother, would have made the team but for a back injury. Two more defencemen, Barry MacKenzie and Terry O'Malley, would become prominent Saskatchewan citizens later in life as each became president of the renamed Athol Murray College of Notre Dame. Scotty Clark of Saskatoon was the trainer.

Huck, a centre, was perhaps the best hockey player not interested in joining the Montreal Canadiens. Born in December of 1945 in Regina, "The Golden Hawk" had torn apart junior hockey in his last two junior seasons with the Pats, scoring 215 goals (including post-season play with Regina and the Estevan Bruins and Edmonton Oil Kings, who happily picked him up after eliminating the Pats). Huck was on the small side at 5-foot-7 and 165 pounds, but that didn't keep him out of the NHL as much as his determination to get an education—specifically, a law degree—first.

"The big story in those days was that Huck didn't go to Montreal Canadiens right off the bat," according to veteran sportscaster Dale Isaac. "A lot of people say he wasn't necessarily blacklisted but that Montreal frowned upon his choice to play for Father Bauer.

"Fran Huck could control a hockey game all by himself, he was that good. He wasn't big but extremely fast, very adept at stickhandling, a great goal scorer. Fran wasn't any smaller than Theo Fleury; in fact, he might have been a little bit bigger. He wasn't as

The Saskatchewan contingent on Canada's 1968 Olympic team. Standing (from left): Coach Jack McLeod, Brian Harper, Ted Hargreaves, Gary Begg, Fran Huck, Gerry Pinder. Kneeling: Herb Pinder Jr., Morris Mott, Marshall Johnston.

feisty as Fleury, he wasn't that kind of a player, but he had enough talent to play in the NHL, there was no question about that. Very few guys could keep up with him. He had outstanding moves, and he could control the puck while making those moves. That's where he excelled. He could beat people one-on-one, one-on-two, one-on-three, and he could put the puck in the net himself. He was a treat to watch."

Canada's first scheduled opponent at Grenoble was West Germany, but its first test of character came during the pregame warmup when an IIHF official ordered the entire team off the ice in order to check every player's credentials and citizenship. Distracted to the point of scorelessness in the first period, Huck and Johnston set up Ray Cadieux for the icebreaker at 0:09 of the second. Huck added another assist and a goal within 12 minutes as Canada cruised home 6–1.

Then came a shock. Finland, trounced 8–0 by the Soviets on opening day, dumped Canada 5–2. In the '60s, the Finns were considered tournament filler, not quite walkovers but hardly in the class of the Czechs and Swedes. It was an embarrassing defeat for the Nats, who took out their frustration the next day on East Germany. Mott scored four times, Huck had a goal and three assists, and Johnston contributed three helpers in an 11–0 mismatch. Then came the United States, winless and outscored 22–6 in three games. Yet, with only eight shots on goal, the Americans held a 2–1 lead through two periods and had cast a pall over the Nats. Father Bauer, however, had a knack for imbuing his team with inspiration—perhaps divinely so, as Herb Pinder Jr.'s memory suggests:

Here was a team composed basically of eastern Catholics and western Protestants. Father Bauer walked into the dressing room and touched everyone in the room. I could feel the whole room lift as if in a spiritual experience.
–*From* 88 Years of Puck-Chasing In Saskatchewan

Johnston scored the tying goal and assisted on Cadieux's winner within eight minutes. Canada won 3–2 and beat Czechoslovakia by the same score with Huck potting a goal and an assist. Next up was Sweden; a Canadian victory would guarantee a medal. Bauer and McLeod found a more conventional way to motivate the Nats this time, according to Pinder:

The day we played the Swedes, Nancy Greene had just been presented a gold medal and she was a tremendous inspiration to us as she sat on the bench with us during the game. We had gone from the worst feeling during the U.S. game to an emotional high.
–*From* 88 Years of Puck-Chasing In Saskatchewan

Johnston and Gerry Pinder tallied in the first period, and Canada played virtually perfect hockey to beat the Swedes 3–0. All that remained was the game against the Soviets, who had lost 5–4 to Czechoslovakia. If Canada could pull out a victory, it would finish in a first-place tie with the U.S.S.R. and earn the gold medal by virtue of the head-to-head result.

It's hard to say exactly how good the 1968 Soviet team was. Four players—Ragulin, Evgeny Michakov, Vladimir Vikulov and Evgeny Zimin—were on the 1972 team that faced the NHL's best. There was no Valeri Kharlamov or Alexander Yakushev in 1968, but there was the magnificent Anatoli Firsov, whom McLeod called "the best Russian player I ever saw." Canada's 1972 team put up a brave and ultimately victorious battle with people named Esposito, Dryden, Savard, Mahovlich, Clarke, Park, Cournoyer and, the unlikeliest hero of them all, Henderson. In comparison, the Nats had the aforementioned Saskatchewan connection and a few young men who would later kick around the NHL for a few years, grinders like Danny O'Shea, Bill MacMillan, Brian Glennie and the goalies, Ken Broderick and Wayne Stephenson.

It just goes to show that even the most valiant of efforts can be forgotten if it doesn't achieve victory. To give the Nats their props 36 years after the fact, they were excellent hockey players. To give the Soviets their props, they were great, yet the Nats had them on the ropes for most of the first two periods. Canada killed off consecutive first-period power plays and got one of its own, only to have the lightning-fast Firsov grab a loose puck at centre ice and beat Broderick on a breakaway. Still Canada pressed the attack, outshooting the Soviets 12–5 in the second period and 19–16 through 40 minutes.

"They got one in the second period," McLeod said. "One of our defencemen tripped over a broken stick. Down he goes, and their guy (Michakov) skates right in and makes it 2–0. Huck had hit a goalpost, and Gerry Pinder hit a goalpost. Things just didn't go our way that game."

Broderick was beaten three times in the third period, the Soviets won 5–0 and Canada slipped to third place, one point behind Czechoslovakia. Because the bronze medal was not gold, most Canadians looked upon the result as a disappointment. When the country pulled out of "amateur" international competition in 1969, the Nats were relegated to Canada's collective unconscious as a noble but futile failure.

Some might prefer to remember them as Olympic medallists.

ALSO IN THIS DECADE

- Julien Audette, a Radville-born Regina resident, broke all eight national soaring records (distance to goal and return, distance to goal, absolute altitude, gain of height, 100- 200- and 300-kilometre triangle, and free distance) between 1958 and 1964 and at one point held six of them simultaneously. He became the first Canadian to soar above 30,000 feet on April 1, 1961, when he took his Scheizer 1–2–3G glider to an altitude of 30,630 feet (9,336 metres). Audette broke the free-distance record of 332 miles on April 22, 1962, with a glide of 375 miles (604 km) from Pincher Creek, Alta., to a landing just east of Moose Jaw.

- Phil Lederhouse of Prince Albert carded an 89 at the Saskatoon Golf and Country Club on September 17, 1962, to beat by two strokes the world record for best score by a blind golfer on a championship course. That same year he carded rounds of 100 and 96 to become the first man to break 200 in the history of the Canadian blind golfers championship. Lederhouse earned 17 provincial, 16 Western and five national titles after taking up the sport in 1950 at the age of 34.

- Baseball pitcher Satchel Paige made a barnstorming stop in North Battleford in 1963, 32 years after his first recorded appearance in Saskatchewan. Paige, who was kept out of the major leagues until 1948 because of their no-blacks policy, was a frequent visitor to the province over the decades.

- Bowlers Anton "Red" Glasser and Joe Most of Regina won the men's doubles at the 1964 Canadian 10-pin championships. Glasser also took the 1962 national singles title.

- Marion Taylor of Saskatoon won the 1962 and 1964 women's singles finals at the Canadian five-pin bowling championships. She would go on to add Canadian titles with two Saskatoon teams (1967 and '72) and a mixed squad (1973).

- Balfour Tech of Regina, coached by Gord Currie, won six consecutive provincial 4A football championships (1960–65). In 1966, the year Currie turned his full coaching attention to the junior Regina Rams, Notre Dame won the 4A crown with a 1–0 overtime decision over Saskatoon Bedford Road.

- Joe Ferguson played two seasons (1965–66) with Kindersley of the North Saskatchewan Baseball League. In 43 games with the Klippers he hit .404 with 14 home runs and 40 runs batted in. Ferguson put in 14 major-league seasons (1970–83), most notably with the Los Angeles Dodgers. Other NSBL alumni who reached The Show were: Jerry Nymen of the 1963 Neilburg Monarchs (1968–70 White Sox, Padres); outfielder Roger Freed of the '65 Monarchs (1970–79, five teams); pitcher Bill Campbell of the '66 Monarchs (1973–87, Twins, Red Sox and five others); pitcher Bob McClure of the 1972 Eston Ramblers (1975–92, Brewers and five others); and, Gorman Heimueller of the '74 Ramblers (1983–84 Athletics).

Red Glasser

- Wrestler Gord Garvie of the University of Saskatchewan represented Canada at the 1968 Olympic Games in Mexico City. Garvie, a perennial football all-star as well as a champion wrestler at the U of S, was named the Huskies' athlete-of-the-year for four consecutive years.

- Saskatoon Merchants won Saskatchewan's first national men's softball championship in 1969. Saskatoon beat Hull, Que., 7–0 in the final behind the pitching of Pete Zacharias, the winning pitcher in four of Saskatoon's five victories.

- Ed George and his son Ron, both of Regina, helped the Canadian team win all the international team prizes at the prestigious Bisley Shoot in Bisley, England.

Terry Puhl awaits a pitch during his heyday as a Houston Astros outfielder

1970–1979

Emergence

ARRIVALS

December 23, 1970: Catriona Le May Doan, speed skater, Saskatoon.
April 17, 1973: Gene Makowsky, football player, Saskatoon.
January 8, 1974: Deb McCormick, curler, Saskatoon.
August 5, 1976: Jeff Friesen, hockey player, Meadow Lake.
October 26, 1976: Jeremy Wotherspoon, speed skater, Humboldt.
April 12, 1977: Stacy Singer, baton twirler, Regina.
April 19, 1977: Dana Antal, hockey player, Saskatoon.
June 12, 1977: Wade Redden, hockey player, Lloydminster.
January 22, 1978: Kelly Bechard, hockey player, Sedley.
April 19, 1978: Scott Schultz, football player, Moose Jaw.
May 24, 1978: Jason Clermont, football player, Regina.
August 12, 1978: Hayley Wickenheiser, hockey player, Shaunavon.
January 16, 1979: Brenden Morrow, hockey player, Carlyle.
September 15, 1979: Patrick Marleau, hockey player, Aneroid.
December 17, 1979: Colleen Sostorics, hockey player, Kennedy.

DEPARTURES

May 19, 1971: Earl Thomson, hurdler, 76.
July 23, 1971: Ross Thatcher, premier (1964–71), 54.
December 19, 1971: Rusty Crawford, hockey player, 86.
April 7, 1972: Woodrow Lloyd, premier (1961–64), 58.
November 24, 1972: Doug Bentley, hockey player, 66.
December 15, 1975: Athol "Père" Murray, educator, 83.
April 30, 1978: Paul Acoose, distance runner, 95.
May 22, 1979: Brian Claypool, rodeo cowboy, 25.
August 16, 1979: John Diefenbaker, prime minister (1957–63), 83.

It was time for Saskatchewan to achieve, or reclaim, prominence in new areas.

Saskatoon, home of the first Canadian women's curling champion, took a six-year stranglehold on the title. In the middle of this reign, the most illustrious team to hold the national title showed what consequences can occur when men don't give women the respect they deserve.

Junior hockey's Regina Pats, with a team that could outscore and outpunch its opponents, broke the province's 44-year run of frustration in the Memorial Cup. In football, a regular-season Saskatchewan Roughriders dynasty was foiled by three heartbreaking post-season defeats.

Toronto joined Montreal as a major-league baseball city, but Saskatchewan was Canada's producer of big-league ballplayers: Reggie Cleveland, Dave Pagan and Terry Puhl.

In athletics, Arnold Boldt opened countless eyes to the abilities of handicapped athletes while pentathlete Diane Jones Konihowski embarked on a colourful career full of setbacks, triumphs and controversy.

Clark Gillies, powerful left winger and reluctant enforcer of the Pats

WOMEN'S CURLING: SIX STRAIGHT FOR SASKATOON

Saskatoon treated the Canadian women's curling championship in the 1970s the way the House of Windsor treats the Crown jewels: like its own. Occasionally, the crown changed hands, but it was kept within the family.

Joyce McKee ruled the rings when the decade began as the defending champion from 1969 but was bounced in the 1970 northern playdowns by Dorenda Schoenhals, who went on with Cheryl Stirton, Linda Burnham and Joan Anderson to take the national title. McKee's rink shuffled personnel; Vera Pezer became skip, Sheila Rowan came aboard as third, McKee dropped to second and Lee Morrison shifted from second to lead. With Pezer calling the shots, the team became the first to win three straight national tournaments in 1971, '72 and '73. When Pezer abdicated by retiring from the sport after the third title, another Saskatoon quartet of Emily Farnham, Linda Saunders, Pat McBeath and Donna Collins assumed the crown in 1974.

So, of the 12 Canadian women's championships Saskatchewan has won, half were won in the dynastic hot streak of 1969–74. Pezer's rink is celebrated for its three-year reign, but the six-year dominance by Saskatoon is equally impressive.

"Part of our success was that we always had these excellent teams in the city pressuring us," Pezer says. "We always had good rivalries going with Dorenda Schoenhals and Emily Farnham."

There were several close calls for the various Saskatchewan champs, most notably Schoenhals' in 1970. After shooting to first place with victories in her first seven games, she was seemingly within grasp of clinching the title in Draw 8 with a 6–4 lead over Manitoba's Glenda Buhr through seven ends. Then Buhr stole four points to win 9–6. Schoenhals also lost her last game to end up in a three-way tie for first at 7–2 but rallied to win the tiebreakers 8–6 over B.C.'s Donna Clark and 8–4 over Buhr.

Pezer followed a similar script to her first national title as a skip in 1971 with two tiebreaker victories after a three-way first-place tie, but she was fortunate to reach that tiebreaker. Alberta's Kay Baldwin had first place virtually locked up when she trounced Pezer 11–4 in Draw 7 but lost her last two round-robin games to also-rans Quebec and Prince Edward Island. Saskatchewan needed an extra end to down B.C. 10–7 in the first tiebreaker but hammered Alberta 9–2 in the final.

Macdonald Tobacco lent its sponsorship to the championship in 1972 and renamed it the "Lassie." The scheduling remained the same, however. With a field of 10 provincial representatives, there were exactly nine round-robin draws: two each on Monday, Tuesday and Thursday, and three on Wednesday. Without any byes, the competition was a test of endurance as well as skill—and few teams were as physically fit as Saskatchewan's.

"We were probably ahead of other teams, more into training and fitness and practice before that was a popular thing for women's teams to do," Pezer says. "In terms of strategy, Joyce set the yardstick. We practised regularly, so we had an edge that way.

"In those days Sheila and I were still playing national-calibre softball. Joyce had also been an excellent softball player. Our sweeping, sliding and ability to handle the three draws on Wednesday came from being in good cardiovascular condition. We could hang in there without running out of steam.

"We got off to a slow start in 1971 because early in the week I couldn't find draw weight if my life depended on it. The 1972 Lassie in Saskatoon was our best. We lost our first game to Lee Tobin of Quebec, and that was kind of a wakeup call. Nobody even came close to us after that."

Pezer never even had to throw her last rock in any of the last eight games as Saskatchewan won them all by at least three points.

Pezer's 1973 triumph in Charlottetown was probably her greatest clutch performance. Saskatchewan and Manitoba, scheduled to meet in the last draw, were building up anticipation for a battle of undefeated rinks until the host Islanders knocked off the defending champions 8–7 in Draw 6.

"They just about declared a provincial holiday," Pezer remembers.

Manitoba skip Joan Ingram remained unbeaten, so Saskatchewan would have to win the round-robin finale to force a first-place tie and then beat Manitoba again to retain the Lassie trophy. Pezer stole two in an extra end of the round-robin game with a perfect draw to the button and an equally perfect bump-and-roll behind cover to win 7–5, then took the tiebreaker 6–4.

Pezer, who was born in Melfort and had started throwing rocks as a six-year-old on the two-sheeter her father managed in the village of Meskanaw, quit while she was on top. Already employed in the Psychology Department at the University of Saskatchewan, she resumed her studies to earn her doctorate in Psychology. Later she would develop a specialization in sports psychology and assist elite teams skipped by the likes of Linda Moore and Sherry Anderson. Chances are she found few, if any, curlers with a greater desire to win than she had.

"To give you an idea of how fanatical I was at one time," she says, "here's a thought I had at the '72 Canadian championship in Saskatoon that I'll remember as long as I live. I had to make a shot and I remember the thought going through my head, 'If I have a choice between making this shot and dying right now, or missing this shot and living, then by God I am ready to die.' That's how I felt. It was just a funny little thought. It wasn't even the last shot of the Lassie, it was some time in the middle of the week.

"And okay, I knew I wasn't going to die, but it gives you an idea of how important competition was to me. It was a way of affirming for myself that this was an important thing to do."

Pezer, Rowan, McKee and Morrison were the first women's team to win three straight Canadian titles and McKee achieved legendary status by being a national champion six times. The best single season recorded by any women's team in the pre-Scott era, however, was probably the 1973–74 campaign of Farnham, Saunders, McBeath and Collins. They entered four cash spiels and won them all, played more than 80 games and lost only three, and trampled the field at the 1974 Lassie in Victoria with a 9–0 record.

Saskatoon's reign over women's curling ended in 1975 when Marj Mitchell of Regina won the province and was relegated to runner-up status at the Lassie by Quebec's Tobin. Saskatchewan would not win the Lassie again, but when the CLCA resumed a sponsorless tournament in 1980, Mitchell would be there to take Saskatchewan women's curling to an even higher plateau.

WAITING IN WINNIPEG FOR THE BIG O

It was time. The ice was ready. Some 1,100 spectators in Winnipeg's St. James Civic Centre, most of them women, were ready. The cameras, microphones and crews of the CBC were ready. Three Winnipeg men and four Saskatoon women were ready. Everything was ready for curling's Battle of the Sexes at 1:15 P.M. on Sunday, November 12, 1972, except the skip of the men's team, Canadian and world champion Orest "The Big O" Meleschuk.

Five days earlier, Meleschuk and Canadian women's champion Vera Pezer had staged a cheesy surprise announcement at the news conference publicizing the *CBC Curling Classic* that would be held that week. Pezer stepped to the microphone and issued a challenge to Meleschuk for a game to be held the day after the eight-team men's tournament concluded. Meleschuk accepted. Everyone in the room was caught off guard except for the personnel of the two rinks and the CBC, which had arranged the game beforehand as a bonus attraction for the televised competition. (The *CBC Curling Classic* was a double-knockout affair contested over four days, with each game edited and televised months later as part of a weekly series.)

Tennis's showdown between Billie Jean King and Bobby Riggs was still 10 months in the future. This was something of an original publicity stunt.

"CBC was looking to promote the Classic, so it set up the challenge," Pezer recalls some four decades later. "And Meleschuk and his team grossly underestimated us. I think they were naïve. I can remember being at the reception the night before, and one of his players, it might have been (third Dave) Romano, came up to our lead, Lee Morrison, and asked if we played just draws or if we played takeouts, too. So they didn't have a clue, these people. But they found out."

Saturday's reception was primarily a windup for the teams in the CBC Classic that was won by 1972 Ontario men's champion Eldon Coombe of Ottawa. Coombe had stolen the final from Meleschuk, who—after allowing two in the 10th with hammer and one in the extra end with hammer—got hammered.

So, when game time arrived Sunday afternoon with Meleschuk nowhere in sight, there was cause for worry. Finally, at 1:40 P.M., 25 minutes after the scheduled throw of the first stone, Meleschuk arrived, not so much walking as wafting in to the arena.

"He had a significant hangover," McKee remembers. (Or, as it was put in the *Winnipeg Free Press*, he was "showing obvious effects of an all-night, farewell party for the out-of-city competitors . . .")

At least Meleschuk could focus clearly enough to discern male from female.

"I can't believe this," he said, surveying the spectators. "I thought this was going to be a nice, friendly, sociable game . . . all the Libbers and vultures must be here."

Presumably, Meleschuk did not habitually turn up to "nice, friendly, sociable" games in such a state. No doubt the audience included numerous feminists (however they may be defined) and quite a few "vultures"—members of the curling media who would enjoy seeing Meleschuk, hardly the most popular champion in Brier history, embarrass himself in his own home town.

Sure enough, Meleschuk did start out looking bad, but so did Pezer. Both teams were unable to read the ice for the first four ends, and plenty of shots were missed. Romano's question was answered: yes, the women could make takeouts—not with the same authority as the men but with almost equal effectiveness. By the fifth end, when Pezer stole a point to take a 2–1 lead, it was apparent that Meleschuk, Romano, John Hanesiak and Pat Hailley would not coast to victory. Meleschuk got his game together after the fifth-end break to take one in the sixth and steal one in the eighth. Now he led 3–2 and was threatening to steal again in the ninth.

It might have been at this point, or in a previous end, when the CBC control truck erupted in a great howl of laughter. No one in the arena heard it except commentators Don Chevrier, Don Duguid and Doug Maxwell and a few cameramen tuned in to the truck via their headphones. The skips were wearing microphones—a routine practice today but one that was quite new in '72—and Meleschuk, delighted with how the end was shaping up, had quietly said to Romano: "I've got 'er by the balls now."

Even if Pezer had brought any along with her, Meleschuk was wrong. She executed a delicate tap-

The Canadian women's champions who beat the men's world champions: (from left) Joyce McKee, Lee Morrison, Vera Pezer, Sheila Rowan

back with last rock in the ninth end to tie the game 3–3. Then, with her final delivery of the tenth, she made a dead solid perfect hit-and-roll to lie shot, behind cover, in the top of the four-foot circle. Meleschuk's misfortunes with the hammer revisited him; he wrecked on the guard, and Pezer's team won 4–3.

"Well, that's it," Meleschuk muttered. "Never again. Enough's enough."

Hailley, Meleschuk's lead, saw a parallel with an event that had occurred two months earlier.

"This is just like the Canada–Russia hockey series," Hailley said. "You don't know how good the opposition is until you play 'em."

Suddenly, the quality of Pezer, Rowan, McKee and Morrison—and, by extension, women's curling—had to be acknowledged. Congratulations poured in.

"We were still in Winnipeg the next morning, and I recall getting phone calls from the radio stations in Saskatoon," Pezer says. "The whole curling community in our city, including the men, reacted really well.

"I believe that game had a significant effect on providing exposure for women's curling. Within a couple of years CBC set up a special event for four women's teams; Marj Mitchell (of Regina) won the first one. They put a mixed team in the Classic as well. Those were positive changes."

Pezer, Rowan, McKee and Morrison did not achieve anything like the fame and adulation King did for beating Riggs. It might be worth noting that Riggs, although he had been a Wimbledon and U.S. Open champion in his youth, was a 55-year-old man when King defeated him. Pezer, on the other hand, triumphed over a reigning men's world champion.

"A hung over one, though," she is quick to point out. "That was an equalizer. That added a few years to him."

REGGIE CLEVELAND: START, FINISH AND IN BETWEEN

Reggie Cleveland, Saskatchewan's first truly significant major-league pitcher, had a baseball career that could be neatly divided into four segments: great prospect, stud starter in St. Louis, swing man in Boston, and reliever in Texas and Milwaukee. Cleveland signed with the St. Louis Cardinals at 17 after three years on the Swift Current Indians under player-coach Jack McLeod, himself an excellent pitcher.

"Oh, could he throw!" McLeod says of Cleveland. "No curve at first, just a fastball. Mechanics, we had to work on those. He was a pretty wild kid. Nobody took batting practice against him. His second year we got him throwing kind of a half-assed curve ball, and I said, 'Well, you gotta know with that fastball, if you ever got a change-up, Reg . . .' "

McLeod arranged for a Cardinals scout to watch a game in Swift Current. Although the game was rained out and the pitcher's mound too soaked to use, the scout had Cleveland pitch on flat ground and signed him on the spot.

Reggie Cleveland

Cleveland tore through the minor leagues and was rewarded with late-season call-ups to St. Louis in both 1969 and '70. He made the parent club for good in spring training of 1971, cracking a rotation that featured Hall of Famers Bob Gibson and Steve Carlton, and another star, Jerry Reuss. Cleveland earned his first victory April 26, 1971, in San Francisco when he outpitched the great Juan Marichal in a 2–1 duel.

Although the Cardinals fell short of a title, Cleveland had a satisfying 12–12 record in 34 starts with 148 strikeouts. He was selected the National League's Rookie Pitcher of the Year by *The Sporting News*. His average of six strikeouts per nine innings would gradually decline as the years went by, but Cleveland's control remained excellent; he usually averaged fewer than three walks per nine innings in his 11 major-league campaigns.

There was no sophomore jinx for Cleveland in 1972. True, he posted a losing record of 14–15, but a seven-game winning streak that included three shutouts had him at 11–4 in mid-July. After that, poor run support—the Cardinals scored two or fewer runs in seven of his starts—condemned him to a string of tough losses. Cleveland rebounded with his best season in 1973 (14–10, 3.01 ERA) but was traded to the Boston Red Sox that December.

Exclusively a starter with the Cardinals, Cleveland found himself on a better team but in a worse situation with the Red Sox. Manager Darrell Johnson could not settle on a rotation and used only Luis Tiant and Bill "Spaceman" Lee as regular starters in 1974 and Tiant, Lee and Rick Wise in 1975. Cleveland was one of seven pitchers who were yanked in and out of starting duty. Don Zimmer, who replaced Johnson after the latter was fired during the 1976 season, made more use of Cleveland in the rotation, but his days as an exclusively starting pitcher were through.

There was one great treasure in that period of transition, however. On October 16, 1975, in Cincinnati, Reggie Cleveland became the first Canadian pitcher to start a World Series game. It was Game 5, and the Red Sox gave Cleveland a run to work with in the

SASKATCHEWAN-BORN MAJOR LEAGUE BASEBALL PITCHERS

ED BAHR **Born: October 16, 1919, Rouleau**

Year	Team, League	W	L	G	GS	SV	IP	H	BB	SO	ERA
1946	Pittsburgh NL	8	6	27	14	0	137	128	52	44	2.63
1947	Pittsburgh NL	3	5	19	11	0	83	82	43	25	4.59
	2 seasons	11	11	46	25	0	220	210	95	69	3.78

RALPH BUXTON **Born: June 7, 1914, Weyburn**

Year	Team, League	W	L	G	GS	SV	IP	H	BB	SO	ERA
1938	Philadelphia AL	0	1	5	0	0	9	12	5	9	4.82
1949	New York AL	0	1	14	0	0	27	22	16	14	4.05
	2 seasons	0	2	19	0	0	36	34	21	23	4.25

REGGIE CLEVELAND **Born: May 23, 1948, Swift Current**

Year	Team, League	W	L	G	GS	SV	IP	H	BB	SO	ERA
1969	St. Louis NL	0	0	1	1	0	4	7	1	3	9.00
1970	St. Louis NL	0	4	16	1	0	26	31	18	22	7.62
1971	St. Louis NL	12	12	34	34	0	222	238	53	148	4.01
1972	St. Louis NL	14	15	33	33	0	231	229	60	153	3.94
1973	St. Louis NL	14	10	32	32	0	224	211	61	122	3.01
1974	Boston AL	12	14	41	27	0	221	234	69	103	4.31
1975	Boston AL	13	9	31	20	0	171	173	52	78	4.43
1976	Boston AL	10	9	41	14	2	170	159	61	76	3.07
1977	Boston AL	11	8	36	27	2	190	211	43	85	4.26
1978	Boston–Texas AL	5	8	53	0	12	76	65	23	46	3.08
1979	Milwaukee AL	1	5	29	1	4	55	77	23	22	6.71
1980	Milwaukee AL	11	9	45	13	4	154	150	49	54	3.73
1981	Milwaukee AL	2	3	35	0	1	65	57	30	18	5.15
	13 seasons	105	106	428	203	25	1809	1843	543	930	4.01

DAVE PAGAN **Born: September 15, 1949, Nipawin**

Year	Team, League	W	L	G	GS	SV	IP	H	BB	SO	ERA
1973	New York AL	0	0	4	1	0	13	16	1	9	2.84
1974	New York AL	1	3	16	6	0	49	49	28	39	5.11
1975	New York AL	0	0	13	0	1	31	30	13	18	4.06
1976	N.Y.–Baltimore AL	2	5	27	7	1	70	72	27	47	4.73
1977	Pittsburgh NL	0	0	1	0	0	3	1	0	4	0.00
1977	Seattle AL	1	1	24	4	2	66	86	26	30	6.14
	5 seasons	4	9	85	18	4	232	254	95	147	4.96

ALDON "LEFTY" WILKIE **Born: October 30, 1914, Zealandia**

Year	Team, League	W	L	G	GS	SV	IP	H	BB	SO	ERA
1941	Pittsburgh NL	2	4	26	6	2	79	90	40	16	4.56
1942	Pittsburgh NL	6	7	35	6	1	107	112	37	18	4.19
1946	Pittsburgh NL	0	0	7	0	0	8	13	3	3	10.57
	3 seasons	8	11	68	12	3	194	215	80	37	4.59

first inning. One run was almost never enough against the Big Red Machine, though. Tony Perez homered in the fourth inning and knocked Cleveland out of the box in the sixth with a three-run shot. Cleveland took the loss as Cincinnati won 5–2 and went on to take the Series in seven games.

Early in 1978 Cleveland was dealt to the Texas Rangers, who were desperate for a closer. Cleveland filled the new role capably (5 wins, 12 saves) but was traded again after the season to the Milwaukee Brewers, who had all the starters they needed and Rollie Fingers to finish games. Cleveland's last three seasons—except for a brief turn in the rotation in 1980—were spent in spot relief. He retired before the Brewers qualified for the 1981 post-season.

A lifetime record of 105–106, with no 20-win seasons or other notable accomplishments, is hardly sensational. Cleveland's misfortune, after a dazzling apprenticeship and arrival in the St. Louis organization, was to consistently arrive somewhere at the wrong time: in Boston when the manager couldn't handle a pitching staff, in Texas when he had to take on-the-job training as a closer, and in Milwaukee when the Brewers only needed someone for garbage innings. It is interesting to speculate what he may have done had he been allowed to remain in his natural starting role, but fate denied him that.

DAVE PAGAN: TORN AWAY FROM HIS FASTBALL

Right-hander Dave Pagan, born in Nipawin and raised in Snowden, could hurl a baseball consistently over 90 miles per hour and even close to 100 when healthy—which, unfortunately, was not often.

He was only 14 when he began pitching senior ball. Starting with Snowden and Nipawin, he helped the Prince Albert Bohs win the provincial championship in 1968 and joined the Eston Ramblers at the Canada Games in Halifax the following year.

By 1970 the New York Yankees signed him, and by 1973 he became a frequent traveller on the infamous player shuttle between the Syracuse Chiefs and the Yankees.

Pagan's first major-league victory was an impressive one but also marked the beginning of his downfall. He was given a start against the Kansas City Royals and went all the way in an 8–2 victory, yielding six hits and striking out seven batters. At one point, however, he felt a twinge in his right shoulder. Pagan, flushed with the thrill of mowing down major-league opponents, kept throwing. He even took a two-hit shutout into the sixth inning of his next start against the World Series champion Oakland A's before he left the game with shoulder stiffness. His injury, misdiagnosed as tendinitis, was in fact a torn rotator cuff.

Earlier that season, Baltimore manager Earl Weaver said Pagan had thrown as hard against the Orioles as Nolan Ryan of the California Angels. Those days would come no more.

Pagan added new pitches, but the junk wasn't enough to make up for his lost fastball. He changed teams three times in the 1976 and 1977 seasons, going from the Yankees to the Orioles to the Seattle Mariners to the Pittsburgh Pirates.

In a final burst of power, Pagan threw a complete game on May 20, 1977, beating Oakland 3–0 on six hits, one walk and eight strikeouts for the Mariners' only shutout of the season.

1973–74 REGINA PATS: ENDING THE MEMORIAL CUP DROUGHT

FORTY-FOUR YEARS HAD PASSED SINCE THE REGINA Pats had won the Memorial Cup in 1930. No Saskatchewan team had captured the national junior hockey championship since then, although 12 Western Canada titles had been achieved (seven by Regina, two by Moose Jaw and one each by Saskatoon, Estevan and Weyburn). When the Pats finally broke through in the 1973–74 season, they boasted several stars whose fame would extend beyond their junior exploits: Dennis Sobchuk of Lang, the high-scoring centre who was already committed to a WHA career; defenceman Greg Joly of Calgary, whom the Washington Capitals would make the first overall pick in the 1974 NHL entry draft; and a pair of Moose Jaw products, goaltender Ed Staniowski and Clark Gillies, the hulking left-winger who would enjoy a Hall of Fame career with the New York Islanders.

Coach Bob Turner remembered the turning point of the Pats' championship season occurring at the Ahearne Cup tournament in Sweden over the Christmas–New Year period.

"It solidified the club," Turner, who died in February of 2005, said in a 2003 interview. "We lived together for three weeks and had a lot of hardships. Most of the teams beat us badly. I used to holler sour grapes about reffing before we went there, but boy . . . we were up 3–2 on Sodertalje (of Sweden) going into the third period and were made to play two men short until they got ahead of us."

Sodertalje won 5–3. Regina managed a 5–5 tie with the London (England) Lions and everything else was a humiliation: 5–0, Leksand; 10–5, Moscow Dynamo; 10–2, Helsinki IFK; 8–1, Stockholm IAK; 15–2, Djurgaarden.

"The whole experience brought us closer together," Staniowski said. "We were facing pros who played more hockey than us, against fiercer competition, and we got thrashed."

"But after that," Turner said, "we didn't lose more than four or five games to the end of the regular season."

Regina's 43–14–11 record for 97 points made the Pats runaway winners of the Eastern Division. Sobchuk had 68 goals and 146 in 66 games, silencing speculation that he'd coast through the season after signing a 10-year contract with the WHA's Cincinnati Stingers that would take effect in the autumn of 1974. The deal, signed in August of 1973, made the slender Sobchuk a popular target for opponents, fans, and media.

"I proved my critics wrong, and they had to be quiet," Sobchuk said. "I took a lot of ribbing from my teammates, naturally—like, everyone else had numbers on their skates, and they put dollar signs on mine."

Gillies rarely sought a fight but habitually pulverized would-be conquerors out to make a reputation.

"He wouldn't hit anybody until somebody did something to one of his teammates," Turner said. "He was like a big, friendly bear until you got him mad, but when you got him mad, look out!"

If Gillies was the bear that only a fool would annoy, then Rob Laird was the wolverine just spoiling for a confrontation. Laird was a mere 5-foot-7 and 170 pounds but would tangle with anyone, from the Western Canada Hockey League's meanest heavyweights to other vertically challenged instigators like Terry Ruskowski of the Swift Current Broncos.

"Rob Laird may not have had as much talent as a lot of guys on that team," Ruskowski says, "but he came to play every night. He and I were the same type of player, especially when it came to fighting. We had a great bout in Swift Current, each of us must have thrown a couple of dozen punches. We see each other occasionally, and we still talk about that; we shake our heads and say how stupid we were, but it was one heck of a scrap."

Swift Current was on the verge of delivering a knockout blow to the Pats in the early going of the best-of-seven division final at Regina's Exhibition Stadium. The Broncos, with Ruskowski and Bryan Trottier at centre, won the first game 7–3 and led the second 5–1 after 40 minutes with Ruskowski's right wing, Don Larway, firing a hat trick in each contest.

Pats goaltender Ed Staniowski

Glen Burdon, who centred Regina's second line between Laird and Rick Uhrich, sparked perhaps the greatest comeback in Pats history when his rink-length solo dash produced a goal at 1:51 of the third period. Joly tallied on the power play three minutes later. Uhrich made it 5–4 at 9:01. Burdon tied it at 12:58. Uhrich put Regina ahead at 14:45. Gillies ended the scoring on a power play, with Sobchuk getting his fourth assist of the period, at 19:16. Regina's six unanswered tallies beat the Broncos 7–5.

"I've never witnessed a comeback like that in my life," Ruskowski recalls. "We just couldn't stop them. We could have called 15 time-outs, and we weren't going to stop them. You could see it snowballing. The fans never sat down. It was incredible.

"If we had won that game, it could have been a different story. We beat them one more time (in Game 4) but down deep I think every one of us knew that they were a better team."

Tiger Williams became the focal point of Game 5 when he and Ruskowski led a charge of Broncos players into the crowd at Exhibition Stadium. Williams had just been penalized for holding at 6:50 of the third period with the Broncos trailing 6–2.

"I can take needling from the fans," Williams told the *Leader-Post*, "but I'm not going to take being kicked in the back."

Fifty policemen and 30 minutes were required to restore order. No further penalties were assessed, no more goals were scored, and the Pats ended the series with a 4–1 victory in Swift Current. Regina then swept the Calgary Centennials four straight in the league final, with Burdon winning Game 3 on an overtime end-to-end rush similar to his comeback-igniter against the Broncos. By coincidence, the Calgary Corral, where the Pats won the WCHL title, was also the site of the Memorial Cup.

No longer a best-of-seven series pitting East against West, the Memorial Cup now featured the champions of the Western Canada, Ontario, and Quebec major junior leagues. A single round robin would establish a finalist. The other two teams would play a one-game semi-final, with the winner going on to the sudden-death final. The St. Catharines Black Hawks had gone undefeated through the Ontario playoffs (12 wins, two ties) and dumped the Quebec Remparts 4–1 in the tournament opener.

"St. Catharines had a few decent-sized guys, and they were moving around like they were hot stuff. They thought they'd push us around," Gillies recalled. "One of them (Larry Finck) made the mistake of picking a fight with Robbie Laird 10 seconds into the game and Robbie just destroyed him."

Two minutes later Gillies did the same to Gary McAdam. Intimidation having had its short-lived day, the rest of the night turned into Greg Joly's one-man show.

"It was the closest thing I've seen to Bobby Orr," Turner said that night, and others who were there insist the comparison was valid.

"I never saw a guy handle the puck and dominate a game with his stickhandling and skating like that," Gillies said.

Joly played more than 50 minutes, scored two goals and treated the puck like a private possession as the Pats prevailed 4–0. His performance was so extraordinary that the Washington Capitals used it as the rationale for making him their first pick in that summer's draft. Joly was an NHL bust in more ways than one; his performance fell far short of expectations, and his body fell apart, piece by piece (knee, ankle, wrist).

Regina earned the bye to the final but almost seemed not to show up for the opening faceoff as Quebec led 3–0 after 12 minutes. It was 3–1 when the first intermission arrived, and Turner prepared to fire up his players with some old-fashioned dressing-room inspiration.

"I walk into the dressing room," Turner says. "Sobchuk stands right up and says, 'We don't need you in here, Coach. We're going to win the game.' So I just turn around and walk out. And brother, they poured it on, just went out like gangbusters. Same thing after the second period, I stayed outside the room, spent the time talking to people who were hanging around. All I did the rest of the game was open and close the gate."

The Pats had resolved on their own to skate harder and become the aggressors. Remparts forward Richard Nantais had whipped Laird in the round-robin game and roughed up Sobchuk in the first period of the final. Thirteen minutes into the second period, after the Pats had tied the score 3–3, Nantais tried to re-establish Quebec's physical edge by challenging Gillies to a fight.

"I could hear the whispering on our bench after he pounded on Sobby in the first period: 'Watch out for Nantais, watch out for Nantais'," Turner says. "I went to Gillies and said, 'Clarkie, you get after that guy if he starts anything else.' I hardly ever did that. Well, then Nantais went right after him, and that was the worst thing to do. Gillies just beat the piss out of their tough guy, and you could see their whole team go down."

Uhrich and Sobchuk scored within three minutes of the beating. Sobchuk finished with three goals as the Pats breezed home 7–4. Despite their poor opening period, Regina outshot Quebec 52–31.

Although he discreetly left his players alone in the Memorial Cup final, Turner was no empty suit. If they were able to handle the championship situation themselves, it was because he had made them prepare for it.

"Turner worked them hard," says Norm Fong, then the Pats trainer and now the Saskatchewan Roughriders' equipment manager. "They never had a

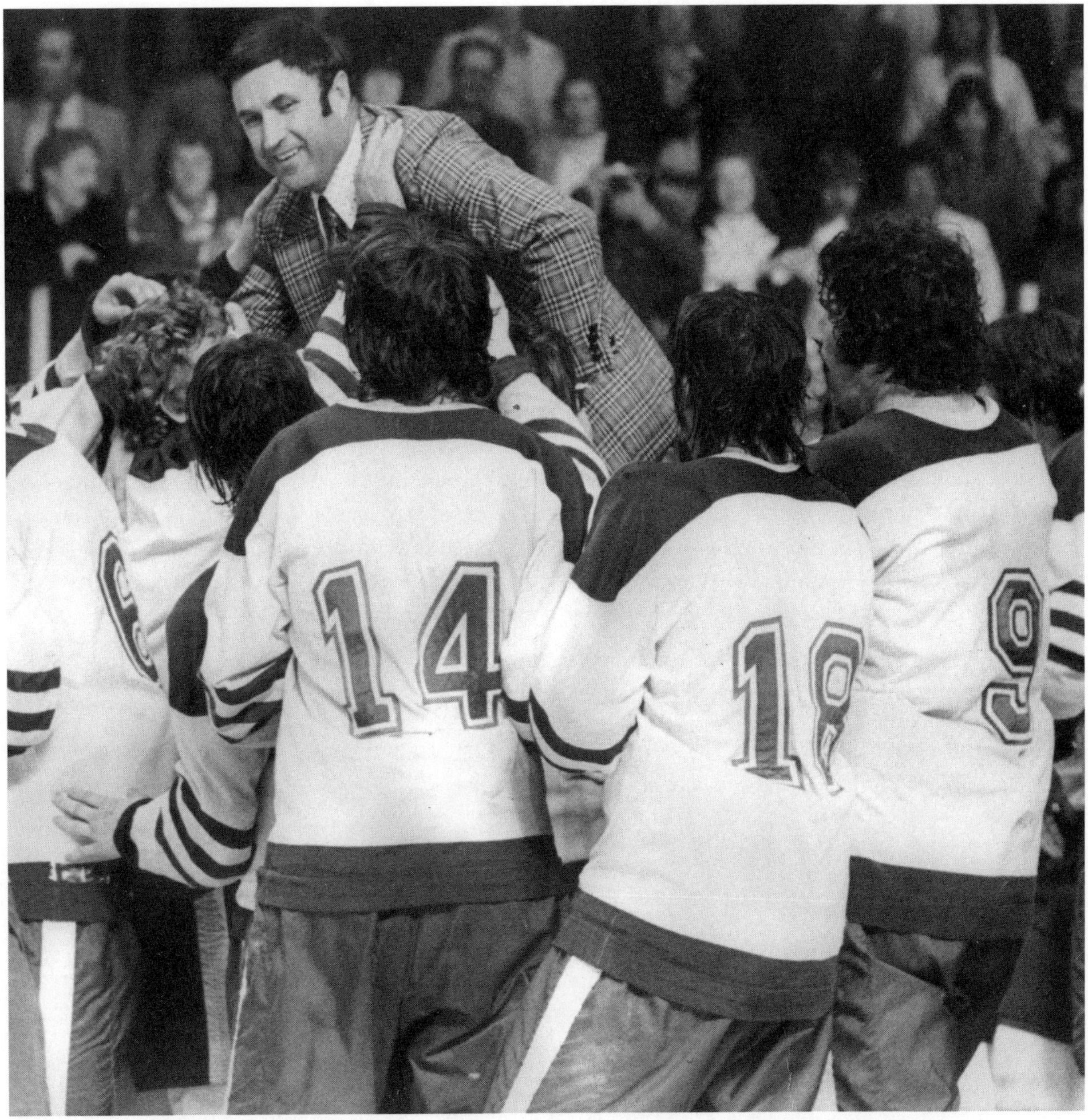
Bob Turner takes a ride after his discreet coaching job in the Memorial Cup final

day off. They were on the ice every day from training camp to the Memorial Cup. There was no such thing as an optional practice."

Turner knew how to keep his players in line, from stars like Sobchuk to grinders like Laird.

"I'd tell them, 'When scouts come to see me, I'll tell them the truth, I'm not going to lie for you. You want to go to the bars and live it up, I'll know about it. Don't think I won't. I know what you're doing. This is too small a town.' "

Not that Turner needed informants to know when his players would party hearty.

"We'd play Friday night," Turner explains, "and practise Saturday morning. There was only a little wall between my office and the dressing room, and I could hear them all in there, bragging to each other about what a great time they'd had after Friday's game. Then we'd get on the ice and I'd say, 'Okay, boys, we're going to *skate* today. It must have been a good party last night. Some of you look like you didn't even get home.'

"And I could hear them saying to each other, *'How did he know?'* "

JIM HUNTER: CRAZY CANUCK

Jim Hunter, luckily for the cyclists of the world, loved to ski. A ski instructor discovered his talent during a family excursion to Whitefish, Montana, when he was 11 years old. A year later, he moved with his mother and siblings to Calgary to develop his skills while his father remained in Shaunavon to run the family dairy farm.

"Talk about sacrifice by your parents," Hunter says. "Mom would get off work early on Friday afternoon and pick me up from school. We'd stop at A&W in Medicine Hat for a hamburger and root beer. When we arrived at the farm, she'd go to sleep, and we'd jump on a piece of equipment and work until 9 or 10 o'clock at night, then all of Saturday until midnight or two in the morning. On Sunday, we'd go to church, have family dinner together and then drive back. We did that 20 to 25 weekends a year for three years."

Then came the day Hunter realized he would inevitably become a world-class athlete.

"I was 14, and I'd been invited to the national team summer camp in Nelson, B.C. I got on my bike and I rode from Calgary to Nelson, 400 miles, in four days. When I showed up, the junior team coach said to me, "It's great you rode your bike up from the bus depot, but you can't ride with the national team."

" 'I didn't ride from the bus depot,' I said.

" 'What? Where did you ride from?'

" 'From Calgary; I did it in four days. Trans-Canada to Banff, then up to Radium, Radium to Cranbrook, Cranbrook to Creston, and then north over the Columbia Ferry and across the bridge into Nelson.'

"He turned to the other coach and said, 'Do we have anybody on the national team who can ride 400 miles in four days?'

" 'No way.'

Jungle Jim Hunter was daring and versatile on the slopes

"Although I was only 14, I knew that day I was better than them. I suddenly realized that those guys were totally beatable. It was only a matter of time before I developed the skills."

Hunter was accomplished both in technical and downhill skiing, something rarely seen in Canada since the national team put all its resources into downhill racing in 1974. At the concurrent Olympic and world championship competition in Sapporo, Japan, in 1972 he had finished third in the combined, which factors individuals' performances in slalom, giant slalom and downhill.

He was also one of the Crazy Canucks, the five men (Hunter, Dave Irwin, Dave Murray, Steve Podborski and Ken Read) who captured international attention when Europeans otherwise monopolized downhill skiing.

"There were three aspects to the nickname," Hunter explains. "There was the insanity with which we approached our training process, the craziness of the physical fitness, and then the abandonment with which we attacked the race course.

"My impact on the Crazy Canucks was to raise that bar of fitness to a new level. For instance, we'd have to go up a mountain pass in a Volkswagen van in first gear; that's all they could get out of it. I'd get out and run seven, eight miles to the top and reach it before the van did. Stories like that became the talk of the tour."

Hunter won eight Canadian titles and, while he never won a World Cup race, is the only Canadian man to be have been ranked in the top 10 of all three major events: slalom, giant slalom and downhill.

ARNOLD BOLDT: HIT THE HEIGHTS

TRACK MEETS ARE SIMULTANEOUSLY EXCITING AND aggravating because so much can be happening at once. What will you watch at this particular moment—the race, the shot put, or the high jump?

By popular demand, officials at the 1976 Olympiad for the Physically Disabled—now commonly known as the Paralympic Games—in Toronto turned their backs on tradition on August 9. All other events were put on hold while the men's amputee high jump was in progress.

Everyone wanted to see Arnold Boldt jump.

Boldt had to be seen to be believed and appreciated. Having no right leg, he would hop several times on his left, spring off the ground—*waaaay* off the ground—and launch his head, torso and leg over the bar. Witnessing this for the first time was like seeing your first knuckleball: "Brain to eyes, reality check!"

After seeing Boldt do this several times, one began to appreciate his unique athleticism. High jumping requires a controlled approach in which horizontal momentum is transferred into vertical lift. Two-legged jumpers could adjust their speed and balance on their approach; Boldt had to be absolutely precise. They could transfer their energy with weight shift through two ankles, two knees and two hips; he couldn't.

Boldt's right leg was amputated just below the hip after a grain auger accident on the family farm near Osler (25 kilometres north of Saskatoon) when he was three years old. He took a liking to the high jump and standing broad jump as a schoolboy and created his own practice facility on the farm. Boldt built a high-jumping bar out of 2x4s, backed by hay bales. (He

Arnold Boldt

even had his own equivalent of an indoor season, when the basement couch served as the landing area.) In his teens, Boldt also played on wheelchair basketball and amputee volleyball teams in Saskatoon.

One way Boldt was like anyone else in 1976 was that he had never heard of the Olympiad for the Physically Disabled. Clued in by Stan Holcomb, a prosthetist and friend, Boldt began training in earnest for the volleyball team, the standing broad jump and the high jump.

Only 18 years old, Boldt stunned onlookers in Toronto with a winning broad jump of 2.96 metres (9 feet 8½ inches), a world record and 32 centimetres beyond the runner-up's best effort. Boldt promised he would set another world record in the high jump three days later, and arrangements were made to stop all other events at that time. When he entered the competition at 1.65 metres, only one other competitor remained in the field. Boldt cleared the height in his warmup suit. The rival couldn't make anything higher than 1.65; Boldt went all the way to 1.86 metres (6 feet 1¼ inches—his own height), delivering the world record and astonishing millions who would see his performance replayed on television.

Indeed, Boldt was the first star of "disabled" sport in Canada. How his performances compared with able-bodied champions was irrelevant. It was obvious, just from watching him, that he was exceptional. (For the record, the men's and women's Olympic champions of 1976 cleared 2.25 and 1.93 metres respectively.) He was inducted into Canada's Sports Hall of Fame in 1977, the first paralympic athlete to achieve that distinction.

Boldt attended the universities of Saskatchewan and Manitoba and competed in regular high jump competition. As a Canadian student-athlete of the time, he dealt with the same financial hardship as most of his peers while improving his performance.

"My best performances came at these meets, probably due to being the right time of year," Boldt said. "I found it difficult to train through the summer for the disabled meets because I had to work. I believe in the theory that if you are an average athlete and you compete against someone better, you will always perform better than if you compete against someone who is not as good as you."

While the notion of Boldt as "an average athlete" is amusing, his competitive university experience did propel him, literally, to new heights. He repeated his Paralympic gold-medal double in 1980 at Arnhem, Netherlands, with a world-record high jump of 1.96 metres. One year later at a meet in Rome, he eclipsed both his standing broad jump and high jump standards with efforts of 2.99 and 2.04 metres (9 feet 9¾ inches and 6 feet 8¼ inches) respectively. He would high-jump 2.08 metres (6 feet 9⅞ inches) indoors in Winnipeg in 1981, surpassing the province's record for able-bodied residents.

Unlike most able-bodied men his height, he could dunk a basketball.

Boldt repeated as Paralympic high jump champion in 1984 (1.95 metres), 1988 (1.94) and 1992 (1.80). He retired from competition in 1994 with five gold medals in the high jump and two in the broad jump from the Paralympic Games. More important, he was the first Canadian "disabled" athlete to achieve public acclaim as someone who stared down the seemingly impossible and made it achievable. Arnold Boldt opened a path that men like Terry Fox and Rick Hansen would widen into a road of unlimited potential.

NOT MANY BOYS NAMED TONY IN RIDERVILLE

After winning the 1966 Grey Cup, the Roughriders embarked on a dizzying decade of regular-season success. They won 108 games, lost only 49 and tied 3. Four times they finished first; on three occasions they tied for first but slipped to second through the tiebreaker process. They outscored their opponents by an average of 90 points a year. They won 14 of 22 playoff games.

And they won zero Grey Cups. The core of the '66 championship team— upgraded and supplanted with talented people like Steve Molnar, Wally Dempsey, Bill "The Undertaker" Baker, Ralph Galloway, Rhett Dawson, Lorne Richardson and Ken McEachern—was constantly denied the ultimate prize, sometimes under the most appalling circumstances.

Defeat wasn't so hard to swallow in the 1967 Grey Cup, when a truly overwhelming Hamilton Tiger-Cats defence inflicted a 24–1 whipping, or in the 1969 title game, when Ottawa's Russ Jackson prevailed 29–11 in a storybook swan song. But 1970 was sup-

Roughriders Roger Goree and Ken McEachern (20) close in on Calgary's Willie Burden

posed to be the Roughriders' year, if ever a year was anyone's year. Saskatchewan went 14–2; no other CFL team won more than nine games. Those 14 victories, a CFL record at the time, were achieved despite injuries to the superstars George Reed and Ron Lancaster. Reed played only 10 games, the last six on a fractured tibia that wasn't discovered until X-rays were taken from unconventional angles. Lancaster suffered with arm trouble so severe that he rarely threw the football in practice after Labour Day, yet he still won the Schenley Award as the CFL's most outstanding player.

Calgary and Saskatchewan split the first two games of the best-of-three Western final, setting up the rubber match at Taylor Field on November 22 in abominable conditions: minus 16 Celsius with 55-kilometre winds that made for a windchill of minus 31 (in Fahrenheit, 35 below). Snow and ice covered the field, rendering yard stripes invisible and causing a controversy that galls Saskatchewan to this day. Players, spectators and even game film suggest that Reed and quarterback Gary Lane—pressed into service after Lancaster suffered broken ribs in Game 2—carried the ball into the end zone in the third quarter.

"I was sitting on the east side," sportscaster Dale Isaac recalls, "freezing my butt off because it was such a bitterly cold day. That was about as cold as I can ever remember it being at a football game. It has to be really cold for Saskatchewan people to say it was 'bitterly' cold. In those days you were a little freer to move around, and I followed the drive to where I was looking right down the goal line. I swear to this day, Gary Lane scored the touchdown. There's no question in my mind that he crossed the goal line with the football. A good upper third of his body was in the end zone with the ball tucked up around his shoulder."

Calgary's Larry Robinson attempted a 32-yard field goal with three seconds remaining and the Stampeders trailing by two points. Given the slick field and the crosswind blowing into his face, the chances of success were slim. Sure enough, the kick was wide—until the wind blew it between the goalposts to give Calgary a 15–14 victory and a berth in the Grey Cup, where it lost 23–10 to the Montreal Alouettes.

"They had to know that we both scored," Reed says. "We should have played in the Grey Cup, no ifs, ands or buts about it. We would have beaten Montreal, I know it, because we handled them that year (29–10). Of all the losses in my career, that hurts the most—that one and the '72 Grey Cup game."

Two years later: better weather, different venue (Hamilton), similar story. Saskatchewan went an uninspired 8–8 but upset Edmonton 8–6 and Winnipeg 27–24 to face the Tiger-Cats for the Grey Cup. Hamilton went ahead 10–0 as Dave Fleming scored a disputed touchdown. (Did he come down with his feet in bounds?) Saskatchewan tied it by half-time with its own disputed touchdown. (Was Tom Campana open in the end zone because Bob Pearce had run a pick play?) The score remained 10–10 as the second half turned into one long battle for field position. Hamilton was pinned back on its own 15 with 90 seconds to go.

Now, of all times, a second-year tight end transformed himself from a decent young player into a CFL legend and the two most painful words in Roughriders history: *Tony Gabriel.* Tiger-Cats rookie quarterback Chuck Ealey connected with Gabriel for gains of 27, 12 and 15 yards. Those three receptions for 54 yards brought Gabriel's game totals to . . . *three receptions for 54 yards.* Saskatchewan head coach Dave Skrein abetted Gabriel's heroics by playing Bill Manchuk at linebacker on the final drive instead of the slower but more experienced first-stringer Wayne Shaw, who had made Gabriel a non-factor by bumping him on the line at every opportunity. Ealey would complete one more pass on the winning drive, to Garney Henley, and 19-year-old Ian Sunter booted a 33-yard field goal on the final play. Hamilton won 13–10.

Then came 1976. Reed had retired but Lancaster won his second Schenley Award with his best passing year ever: 3,869 yards. Saskatchewan's 11–5 record was the best in the league, as were its 427 points scored and 238 points allowed. Eleven players were Western all-stars, six of them all-CFL. Most details of the game have been forgotten. (At least one unjustly so: Roughriders middle linebacker Cleveland Vann made 12 tackles in a tremendous performance.) One image remains permanently fixed in the mind of every Roughrider fan who witnessed it: Tony Gabriel scooting past Roger Goree and Ted Provost to catch Tom Clements' 24-yard touchdown pass in the dying seconds to give Ottawa its 23–20 victory.

A 15-year streak of playoff berths produced one Grey Cup but three heartbreaking near-misses. There would be no near-misses of any kind for a long, long time. Following 1976, the Roughriders would miss the playoffs for 11 straight seasons.

Have you ever noticed how rare it is to find a young man named "Tony" who was born in Saskatchewan?

BRIAN CLAYPOOL: A BRIEF RIDE

Few sports deal in such brief time intervals as bull riding. To register a score the cowboy must stay aboard the bull for a mere eight seconds, although it is probably the most terrifying eight seconds in all of sports, a span in which the competitor tries to control a beast that has the potential to make the rider's next heartbeat his last.

Brian Claypool was born in Lucky Lake in 1953 and grew up in Saskatoon, where his parents operated Claypool's Saddlery. Between the business and his father Ralph's involvement in chuckwagon races, Brian was naturally attracted to rodeo. He showed early promise when, at 13, he topped a field of 98 young cowboys to win the boys' steer riding event at the Calgary Stampede. An avid hockey player and wrestler as well, Claypool won the 1971 provincial 130-pound wrestling championship while attending E.D. Feehan High School and placed fifth at the Canadian Olympic trials in 1972.

Later in '72, just before his 19th birthday, Claypool obtained his Rodeo Cowboys Association card and won the saddle bronc riding and all-around cowboy in the first rodeo he entered as a professional. His next competition featured two rounds of bull riding. He won them both, establishing a reputation as a top-notch bull rider that he would embellish time and again: as the Calgary Stampede winner in 1974 and '76; as Canadian year-end leader from 1974–76; as Canadian champion in '75 and '76; by setting a record for winnings in '75; by qualifying for the

Brian Claypool was a champion bull rider until his death in a plane crash at 25

Canadian Finals Rodeo four straight years (1974–77) and for reaching the biggest show of them all, the National Finals Rodeo, in 1974 and '76.

Claypool was also a good saddle bronc rider and frequently won all-around cowboy honours. He was both consistent and sensational on the bulls, able to win two or three rounds in one rodeo, and frequently the first man to go eight seconds on several previously unconquered bulls.

His generous and supportive relationships with his fellow competitors were recognized at the 1976 Calgary Stampede with the Guy Weadick Award for the cowboy "most symbolic of the western spirit in action."

It was a dazzling, exhilarating career but, like a bull ride, it had a brief and sudden ending. On May 22, 1979, a Piper Cherokee aircraft carrying four cowboys crashed in a California canyon. The victims, en route to rodeos in Inglewood, Calif., and Las Vegas, were two Alberta men along with 20-year-old Lee Coleman of Pierceland and the pilot, Brian Claypool. He was 25 years old.

TERRY PUHL: A LONG RUN IN THE SHOW

Terry Puhl's teenage years coincided with a booming Canadian interest in baseball brought about by the Montreal Expos' entry into the National League in 1969. Televised games made dreams of big-league baseball as realistic as careers in the NHL or CFL, especially for the boys in Melville who were winning provincial championships almost every year.

"We had great players, and we were together for so many years," Puhl recalls. "One tournament that really stands out for me is the Western Canadian in Westlock, Alberta. I think we were 12 or 13, around that age. I pitched the first game, a two-hitter. I remember Maurice Butler, he later played running back with the Regina Rams and some pro ball with the Roughriders, pitched the second game and threw a two-hitter. And then I pitched the third and final game and threw another two-hitter. So we gave up six hits and just blew through that tournament. On the year I think we were 31-and-oh. We never lost a game."

Terry Puhl, age 12

Puhl's first tryout camps were primarily for experience as he would have been too young to sign a contract. He first showed his stuff for the Expos but got the impression the camp was mainly a promotional exercise. Then came the St. Louis Cardinals, who started weeding out prospects with a 60-yard sprint.

"I've often thought since then, how many times in baseball do you ever run 60 yards in a straight line? It never happens," Puhl says. "The Cardinals clearly felt that if you couldn't run, go someplace else, they had no interest in you. That's the way they designed their club."

At 15, Puhl impressed the Cincinnati Reds at their annual camp in Yorkton.

"They showed a lot of interest in me—as a pitcher. They said that if I had been 17 then, they would have signed me. Then when I became 17, they didn't want to sign me. But that's okay. It worked out."

By the time he was 17, Puhl wasn't as overwhelming on the mound as he had been two years earlier. His arm was still strong, however, and he was only one of several batters who made the Melville Elks an overwhelming midget club. As the team's top hurler, his exploits in provincial playdowns included striking out 12 batters in a seven-inning game, a three-hitter, and earning both victories in the best-of-three final against the Viscount Atlases to put the Elks into the first Canadian midget championship in Barrhead, Alta.

Puhl was the winning pitcher in three of Melville's four victories at the nationals, including a long relief performance in the championship final when the Elks came back from a 4–0 first-inning deficit to rout Cardale, Man., 14–8. Puhl was the tournament's most valuable player and top pitcher. Catcher John Maserek, who hit three home runs, and outfielder Ross Mahoney, a pick-up from Regina who led all hitters with a .646 average, joined Puhl on the all-star team.

"Wayne Morgan was the Houston Astros' scout, and he asked me after the tournament if I would consider a pro contract," Puhl remembers. "'I guess I would,' I said. He said, 'Well then, give your arm a bit of a rest, and in two weeks time I'll come in to Melville and put you through a light workout.' Two weeks to the day, I came home from school and there he was, sitting in our kitchen with my parents. He says, 'Come on, let's go out to the field.' He hit me some balls in right field, he ran me, just to see if my arm was okay, to see what I could do and couldn't do. He brought me back into the kitchen and told my parents he wanted to offer me a contract.

"It was Wayne's idea to sign me as an outfielder. He put a good sell-story on me that that's what I should be, based on my talents, and I didn't really argue with him. I said, 'Okay, if that's what you want, that's what I'll do.' I was excited, I just wanted to play pro ball. That's the only thing that was going through my head."

His natural gifts of speed and hand-eye co-ordination, combined with a willingness to take instruction and work, allowed Puhl to became a complete

SASKATCHEWAN-BORN MAJOR LEAGUE BASEBALL PLAYERS (NON-PITCHERS)

JOE "STUBBY" ERAUTT **Born: September 1, 1921, Vibank** **Position: Catcher**

Year	Team, League	G	AB	R	H	2B	3B	HR	RBI	BB	SO	Avg.	SB
1950	Chicago AL	16	18	0	4	0	0	0	1	1	3	.222	0
1951	Chicago AL	16	25	3	4	1	0	0	0	3	2	.160	0
	2 seasons	32	43	3	8	1	0	0	1	4	5	.186	0

TERRY PUHL **Born: July 8, 1956, Melville** **Position: Outfield (1300 games), First Base (4 games)**

Year	Team, League	G	AB	R	H	2B	3B	HR	RBI	BB	SO	Avg.	SB
1977	Houston NL	60	229	40	69	13	5	0	10	30	31	.301	10
1978	Houston NL	149	585	87	169	25	6	3	35	48	46	.289	32
1979	Houston NL	157	600	87	172	22	4	8	49	58	46	.287	30
1980	Houston NL	141	535	75	151	24	5	13	55	60	52	.282	27
1981	Houston NL	96	350	43	88	19	4	3	28	31	49	.251	22
1982	Houston NL	145	507	64	133	17	9	8	50	51	49	.262	17
1983	Houston NL	137	465	66	136	25	7	8	44	36	48	.292	24
1984	Houston NL	132	449	66	135	19	7	9	55	59	45	.301	13
1985	Houston NL	57	194	34	55	14	3	2	23	18	23	.284	6
1986	Houston NL	81	172	17	42	10	0	3	14	15	24	.244	3
1987	Houston NL	90	122	9	28	5	0	2	15	11	16	.230	1
1988	Houston NL	113	234	42	71	7	2	3	19	35	30	.303	22
1989	Houston NL	121	354	41	96	25	4	0	27	45	39	.271	9
1990	Houston NL	37	41	5	12	1	0	0	8	5	7	.293	1
1991	Kansas City AL	15	18	0	4	0	0	0	3	3	2	.222	0
	15 seasons	1531	4855	676	1361	226	56	62	435	505	507	.280	217

ballplayer and reach the major leagues on July 12, 1977, four days after his 21st birthday. He was ideally suited to the Astrodome: fast in the field and on the bases, strong defensively, a solid contact hitter with good gap power. (Ironically, this is also the description of an ideal St. Louis Cardinals outfielder.)

Puhl hit .301 in 60 games as a rookie and followed it with three straight seasons in the .280s. The 1980 campaign was wonderful: Puhl reached double figures in home runs (13) and assists (14) as the Astros won the National League West Division title, the team's first championship in its 19-season history. Puhl was sensational in the NL championship series, going 10-for-19 for a gaudy .526 batting average, but the Philadelphia Phillies won the best-of-five battle 3–2 with the last four games all going into extra innings.

In a harsh twist of fate, Puhl's greatest glory led to his worst disaster. Lacking a power hitter in a ballpark that made fly balls virtually wilt, the Astros decided not to acquire a true longball threat but to transform Puhl into one.

"I always could put the bat on the ball, and drive it to left field and left-centre," says Puhl, a lefthanded batter. "I never did pull the ball well in my youth, and when I started doing it in the big leagues it got me into a lot of trouble.

"It probably would have been best to leave me alone, let me drive the ball to the opposite field and take what you get. All of a sudden it was yank everything, and I really lost my ability to hit the ball the other way."

A few weeks into the 1981 season, Puhl's average was an embarrassing .167. He would finish the strike-shortened campaign at .251, the worst average of his career in full-time play, with a mere three home runs. He would improve only to .262 in 1982.

"I had to actually rebuild my entire swing and understand everything about it so that I could be a productive major-league player again. That was a very difficult time. Fortunately, Denis Menke came into our organization as the hitting instructor. He became a good friend and helped me."

Puhl enjoyed productive seasons in 1983 (.292, eight homers) and '84 (.301, nine homers). Seemingly back on track in what should have been the prime of his career, Puhl was struck down in 1985 by his first severe hamstring injury . . . and his second . . . and his third.

"I blew out my right hamstring rounding first," he recalls. "I tried to come back a little too quick and blew it out again. Then towards the end of the season it got so frustrating I said, 'Okay, I'll try to come back one more time,' and I blew it out the third time. I came back way too quick, and I just couldn't get well. It was probably some time into the 1987 season before it really healed."

Puhl batted over .270 in four of his six seasons as a part-timer with Houston. He signed with the New York Mets as a free agent for the 1991 season but was cut in spring training. He joined the Kansas City Royals for six weeks while George Brett was on the disabled list, then retired from baseball. Since then, he has worked full-time in Houston as a stockbroker and financial advisor, an occupation he began midway through his baseball career.

"I was always known around Houston as 'The Canadian'," Puhl says. "There were a few years when there was a real drought for Canada, at least in the National League. To this day in Houston, people recognize me and say, 'You were from Canada, weren't you?' I guess it was written about so often that it became the focal point of how people related to me.

"A person's values are always evolving along with him. I think I kept a steady head. I don't miss the glamour of the big leagues very much because I'm as comfortable sitting quietly in a chair as I am being around people. It was all very satisfying and enjoyable, though, and I'm thankful to everyone who played a part in helping me have a major-league baseball career."

THE FLAWLESS FIELDER: TERRY PUHL IN HIS OWN WORDS

Terry Puhl holds the major-league record for highest fielding percentage (.993—18 errors in 2,651 chances) by an outfielder who handled at least 1,000 chances in a career. He accomplished this playing virtually all his home games in the Astrodome, which was notorious for making outfielders' lives difficult with its glass ceiling and hard artificial turf. On the road, Puhl had to contend with constantly changing conditions: day games, night games, grass, synthetic surfaces, three time zones and an infinite web of nuances that made his assignment far more complex than it appeared from the bleachers.

I STARTED IN THE ASTROS ORGANIZATION IN 1974 at Covington, Virginia, for a 60-game season; that's all they have in Rookie League. Wayne Morgan signed me as an outfielder, which I had virtually never played before, and I played that whole season in left field. It wasn't that hard an adjustment. Once you'd taken a month of fly balls in spring training, it was like you'd never played any other position. I had an above-average arm, very accurate, and I didn't make mistakes. If the ball was hit up in the air in my direction, you could count on the batter being out. It's just the way I was.

When I got to the big leagues I became better because I got to work with Bill Virdon, who was our manager. Bill was a great centre fielder with the Pittsburgh Pirates—played beside Roberto Clemente for years—and he taught me a lot about how to get yourself in proper position and doing all the little things right. I learned the different hitters, to get good jumps on the ball, receiving the ground ball close to the infield—things that aren't even taught now.

Plus, I worked real hard at it. Bill Virdon killed us in the outfield. He has a legacy of being maybe the greatest fungo hitter in major league history. When you did something wrong mechanically, Bill would stop you and make you do it properly. He wouldn't let you get away with bad technique, so it became a habit. He said, "If you don't hit the cutoff man, you don't play for me." Ask guys who played with me, and the first thing 80 percent of them will say is, "He never missed a cutoff man." That's a reason why I didn't have many errors. A lot of outfield errors are throwing errors, and I always threw the ball through the cutoff, always.

Fielding can be practised. It's a lot of repetition. But then a lot of people take it for granted that if you can play defence, catching a fly ball in Cincinnati is the same as catching a fly ball in San Diego. That's a bunch of hogwash. If you could play the outfield in San Francisco at Candlestick Park, you could play it anywhere. I really had a difficult time in San Francisco with the wind and everything. I got so comfortable in

Houston that I felt I could handle the outfield without a lot of unnecessary stress. It was almost second nature, whereas outfielders coming into the Astrodome viewed it as a real difficult place to play because of dealing with the windows, the day, the night, picking up the ball. There were a lot of things that have nothing to do with just catching a fly ball or any of the fundamentals. Catching on the correct side, hitting the cutoff man, those are very consistent, but the atmospheres that you played in, that's where, as they say, the rubber meets the road.

You couldn't take your eye off the ball when you played in the Astrodome during the day. If you did, you would probably lose it in the windows if you got a bad angle. There was a triangle behind the home plate area that was darkened, but the ball would occasionally get out of that triangle and into those windows. I had one play with Gary Matthews when he played with the Atlanta Braves. I was in centre field, and he hit a ball into left-centre. I was trained to run to a spot and then pick the ball up again—which I did, except I couldn't see the ball. My heart began racing. I was thinking, "Oh gosh, I've lost it in the windows!" The ball actually went out for a home run, and that was one of the few times I was happy to see a home run hit against us.

Terry Puhl

You've got to deal with the lights in every ballpark. They're different in each field, right field versus left field, it's always different from city to city. *(Puhl played 235 games in left field, 343 in centre and 787 in right.)* Going into Philadelphia in right field, you had a tendency to lose the ball in the lights on a semi-line drive. That used to put the fear of God in me. In San Diego, a semi-line drive to *left* field would go directly into the lights. The grass at San Diego had those fancy cross-cut sections so it would look pretty on TV, and a ball would waver as it bounced. You could literally run right past it and not make contact with it. It was a real difficult change in Montreal when they first put the roof on, a completely different ceiling than the one we had in Houston. Atlanta had the Falcons playing football in its stadium, so in September the field would be all chewed up. You really had to concentrate.

I treated my defence separately from the offensive game. I didn't take poor offensive performance out to the field. When I hit the dugout, I was an offensive player; when I got to the field, I had a different job. That was my strength, to be able to differentiate the two. It takes hard work to hit .300; I did that three times. I had five seasons where I fielded 1.000; that happens from good habits and taking pride in what you do defensively.

My best catch was probably off of Mike Scioscia of the Dodgers in the seventh inning of Nolan Ryan's fifth no-hitter. I was playing right field, and we shaded Mike, a left-handed batter, the other way. He hit a line drive into right centre, but I had been moved over that way a little bit and, as I was trained, I just took off to a spot and picked up the ball again when I got there. When I made the catch I was outstretched about a foot and a half off the ground.

Nolan said after the game that he knew he had a no-hitter going, but it was only after that play that he thought he was going to get it, and he did: the first man, and the only one, to throw five no-hitters. Of course, he ended up with seven, but that's the one that broke Sandy Koufax's record. About 10 minutes after the game, Nolan walked by my locker and said, "Hey Terry, nice catch." He still notes to this day that it was.

MOSTLY IN HER OWN WORDS: DIANE JONES KONIHOWSKI

My family moved to Saskatoon from Vancouver when I was five years old. Mom put me in all the sports: gymnastics, swimming, broomball in winter, softball in summer. I thrived on it, and I lucked out because I had very good gym teachers, and I met with success early. When I got to high school, I lucked out again. Bob Adams went to my church, St. Timothy's Anglican. He knew my sister Joanne and I would be coming to his school (Aden Bowman Collegiate), and he took us under his wing.

Bob worked hard with me. He made me feel guilty for missing workouts. I hated running because I was not a natural runner, and I had a bad attitude because of it. It wasn't my height that hampered me. I was 5-foot-7 in Grade 9 and I topped out at 5-11. I just don't think I was blessed with fast-twitch muscles. It took me 14 years to become a comfortable runner.

At the same time I was showing promise in track and field, I was also playing volleyball. We won provincials and went to the first Canada Winter Games in 1967 in Quebec City. Two years later at the Canada Summer Games in Halifax I won Saskatchewan's only gold medal, in pentathlon, and there was a lot of hype around that. At the time, the Canada Games were something new, and I didn't appreciate their value. They're so important because that's the first opportunity, outside of a provincial games where you have a multi-games environment, and that's very different from a one-sport competition or a weekend tournament. Then I went to the Empire Games in Scotland, and that was a village-type atmosphere, and then the Munich Olympics in 1972. Just about every year I attended some sort of Games—Olympic, Commonwealth, Pan-Ams. It's not until you look back and say to yourself, "Where did this all begin?" that you realize the Canada Games played an important part.

The only year I missed out on was 1971. I didn't make the Pan-Am team because I'd put on weight. I was living with a girl friend from Regina, we weren't eating particularly well, and I was up to 180 pounds. I thought, "Whooaa, I really *liked* representing Canada, it's what I want to do, I'm going to have to lose some weight!" In those days we didn't have sports scientists, nutritionists, psychologists . . . you had to figure it out for yourself.

One thing I didn't have to figure out was weight training. Bob Adams introduced me to weightlifting, and I am so thankful to him for teaching me properly. I had really great technique. But I had to desegregate the University of Saskatchewan weight room. I was the first female to use it. The guys told me to leave. Then some of them left because I wouldn't. I remember looking outside; there were no signs saying "Men Only" or "No Females Allowed." I couldn't understand it, but I definitely had invaded these guys' territory. It took them awhile, but they realized I was just an athlete coming in to do her workout. I wasn't there to threaten them. Later they became my workout partners and spotters. I think I taught them good technique. In those days it was just about pumping as much weight as you could, bench-pressing 500 pounds, and it would drive you nuts because their technique was the pits.

I gravitated towards pentathlon because I thrived on variety. I remember not wanting to sit in the stands and watch the bloody track meet, so I did everything, 10 or 11 events. When I competed for the U of S, I would do the pentathlon plus high jump, long jump, shot put and all the relays. In 1975 at the national championships I won the pentathlon with a record score, I broke a 22-year-old record in the shot put, I won the long jump, I won the hurdles and my team won the relay. I was also a good high jumper, behind Debbie Brill for years. Twenty-five years ago I was high-jumping 1.88 metres, and Debbie was clearing 2.01.

Diane Jones placed 10th in the 1972 Olympic pentathlon as a 21-year-old, which automatically made her one of Canada's medal hopes for the 1976 Games in Montreal. Her country, however, was her greatest handicap. She had to train full-time, but she also had to provide for herself. Financial assistance from public sources was ridiculously meagre.

I got one of these "grants-in-aids" of $1,800. That was for an entire year, and it had to go for your university tuition, and that was *it.* Abby Hoffman did a survey of our athletes in 1975, and it said that many of them were living on dog food and stuff like that. Why you'd use dog food when you could buy Kraft Dinner for the same price, I don't know. But it was

Diane Jones training in Saskatoon, early 1970s

very evident that our athletes were in dire need of money. I was training in Santa Barbara with (American pentathlete) Jane Fredericks, and I spoke out about the situation at that time. The Saskatchewan government came through for me and reimbursed my training expenses. I'll never forget that; I wrote a letter of thanks for their support. It was terrific in Santa Barbara because I could work out every day with (American decathlete) Bruce Jenner, Jane and her coach, Sam Adams.

I never had a full-time job when I was competing because I was a student and then training took up too much time. I sold shoes at Eaton's and worked at my dad's bakery during high school, but that was it. Later, in Edmonton, I'd work for a couple of weeks during Klondike Days as a cocktail waitress in a saloon at the Sheraton Cavalier. Remember Miss Kitty in *Gunsmoke*? It was one of those outfits—fishnet stockings, garter belt—but a short skirt, next to nothing. I don't remember having to deal with any crap from drunks or anyone. I'd had a lot of publicity, everybody knew who I was, and there was a lot of respect. And I was good, I was damn good, I'd remember every drink on each order. I got big tips, and I earned good money.

Then I was chosen as the Coin Girl. I was hired for a year before the Olympics to promote the Olympic coins. I had moved to Santa Barbara, but every second weekend I was somewhere in Canada promoting the coins. I gave so much of myself that I blew it for my medal chances. I arrived in Montreal unfocused, and it was so frustrating because the pentathlon medals were up for grabs, but when I dug down I wasn't lean and mean, I had nothing there. There was a distraction involved with Mick Jagger, but that wasn't what hurt me, it was my poor preparation.

We were in the middle of the high jump, my best event in the most important competition of my career, and this young usher is following me around.

"You've got to have this," he says. "It's from Mick Jagger." How the kid got down on the track apron, I don't know, but he's just shaking. Mick's up there watching, making sure he gives me this message. I'm trying to concentrate, but I turn around.

"What do you want?"

"Here, I've got to give you this note. It's from Mick Jagger."

I grabbed it, and put it in my bag. I ended up winning the high jump portion of the pentathlon event, so I was whisked away to the media room. On the way there I meet, of all people, Telly Savalas! He was so gorgeous I didn't even notice he was bald! I talked to that guy for what seemed like 25 minutes, he was so nice. And these people are after me to get to the media room . . .

"Diane, Diane, you gotta go . . ."

"Go away!"

Finally, I did the media thing. Later I got back to my room, emptied my bag and there's the note from Mick inviting me to a party. I called him and said I couldn't do the party. He had to leave the next day, so that was the extent of my contact with him. When (Toronto reporter) Earl McRae wrote the story, I got a ton of mail from angry females: "How could you turn down Mick Jagger?" I don't like the guy, he's a creep, he's too skinny, he's too short, he's got big lips. I wasn't interested in Mick Jagger at all. I didn't even keep the note. Isn't that funny?

Jones was in fourth place with 3,764 points after four events, a mere four points from the bronze medal and only 24 from first place. However, the last event, the 200 metres, was her weakest, and she slipped to sixth place (with 4,582 points) as East Germans swept the medals. After 1976, the pentathlon became a greater test of versatility as the 200 metres, a long sprint, was replaced by the

SOUTHERN SKATERS TAKE A SHINE TO THE LONG BLADES

Brenda Webster

Speed skating took a competitive toehold in the south of the province in the late '70s with the emergence of four world-class competitors.

Cathy Turnbull of Regina won the first of seven national short-track championships in 1976. She hit her peak in 1979–80, setting a world record in the 1,000 metres and winning three gold medals at the world short-track championships. Turnbull was an alternate on the Canadian Olympic speed skating team at Lake Placid in 1980, when short-track was still excluded from the program. She had placed first at the 1979 Canadian junior and 1980 Canadian senior championships.

Craig Webster of Regina joined the national team in 1977 and won two World Cup races in 1979. At the 1980 Olympics he placed 27th in the 1,000 metres, 23rd in the 1,500 and 20th in the 5,000.

Brenda Webster, Craig's sister, showed her versatility as a 15-year-old in 1977 by winning the North American junior championships in both long- and short-track and well as the world junior short-track title. In 1979 she took part in the world, world sprint, world short-track and world junior championships. She placed 19th in the 1,000 metres and 11th in both the 1,500 and 3,000 at Lake Placid in 1980.

Shelley Rhead (Skarvan) of Moose Jaw was only 10 when she won a bronze medal at the 1975 Canadian short-track championships. She won seven gold medals at nationals between 1977 and 1991. Her sixth-place 500-metre showing at Calgary in 1988 marked Saskatchewan's first top-10 finish in an Olympic speed skating event. Rhead also competed in the 500 (19th) and 1,000 (21st) in 1992 at Albertville, France.

800 metres, a middle distance that became a genuine test of endurance when placed at the end of the schedule. The raw strength necessary for sprinting was primarily useful for only one event now: the shot put. Stamina also became vital as the five events were packed into one day instead of spread over two. Jones, who embraced a husband (pro footballer John Konihowski) and a double surname in 1977, reshaped her body for smoother flight and less power.

Dropping the 200 metres was heaven. The pentathlon had been for the really strong, fast female and there wasn't a lot of diversity in the event. I was a far, far better 800-metre runner than I was at 200, and the training for that particular event naturally trimmed you down. You can't afford to carry any extra weight to do a decent 800, so by the time the 1978 Commonwealth Games in Edmonton came around, I was a svelte 140 pounds, down 12 from my Montreal weight. It was the thinnest I'd ever been.

She was the star of the Games, first as the final baton carrier—equivalent to the final Olympic torch bearer—at the opening ceremonies who received a wink from Prince Andrew as she presented the baton to Queen Elizabeth. In competition, she destroyed the pentathlon field with 4,768 points, the best performance in the world that year. She was named Canada's female athlete of 1978, a distinction she also had won in 1975.

I knew that we were going to host the Commonwealth Games, that I'd be living in Edmonton and I would have had all the pressures all over again, but I was a lot smarter than I was for Montreal, a lot more focused. I gave of myself to the media, but it was in small doses, very controlled. I was on a mission. It was all about positioning myself for Moscow, about letting the other athletes around the world know Diane Jones Konihowski scored this, you're going to have to watch out for her. The gold medal was great, but it was all about being Number One in the world that year.

I made a huge breakthrough in 1979 when I went to Madrid with Lyle Sanderson and John. Lyle had been my core coach ever since I'd been at the U of S and he was great. He raked coaches for information when we were in Europe, and we'd talk about what my competitors did in training and watch. We'd go to Madrid to train in the spring because it was really cheap. You could live in this residence that had a

The leaner Diane Jones Konihowski training for the '78 Commonwealth Games

weight room, walk to the track, get three meals a day and have laundry that came back whiter than when you bought it, all for $10 U.S. a day. Fabulous. It was cheaper to train there than any place else, so we went there along with the Brits and Poles and a number of others.

Poland's women hurdlers were 1–2–3 in the world and using different techniques. I was beside myself because the hurdles were my weakest event; I was having real difficulties and wow, here was a new technique. Well, to make a long story short, John could speak a little Ukrainian and so could the Polish coach, and he agreed to help me because he knew who I was and he wanted me to beat the Russians. I could train with him in Poland in the fall, but because the technique and his methods were a secret, he wouldn't let Lyle come along. He would only coach me in private. John couldn't come because he was playing football.

So I went over by myself and spent a miserable six weeks living in Warsaw, where the people were very friendly but nobody spoke English and the food was terrible and there was no hot water in the showers. But I learned more about hurdling from that man in six weeks than I had in 15 years.

From there I went to New Zealand for the winter, and I met a Dr. Brown who did wonders for my back. I had always experienced stiffness in the lumbar region, and he could see that I had great flexibility everywhere but there. It took a lot of treatment, but he fixed me up. I was so loose I could bend over and touch 12 inches *below* my toes. I learned that I could take a day off from training and not suffer, that sometimes it was necessary for healing. I was totally tuned in to my body and in perfect shape. Things just could not possibly have been coming together better for the Olympics in Moscow.

Well, when you're in New Zealand you are so far out of the loop, you don't know what's going on in the world. On April 23, a friend phones me with the bombshell that we're boycotting. I just freaked out from the get-go and spoke out against it. I was pretty pissed off. For the next three days I was on *The Journal, The National*—I was really newsworthy. God, I was a zombie; everybody wanted to talk to me because nobody else was saying anything against it as far as I can remember. My mom phoned in tears: "Oh, you've got to renounce what you're saying, everybody is calling you a communist." My sponsor called from Toronto and asked me to take back everything I'd said.

> **"It was awful. I was going for the gold, I saw it within my reach, and it was just taken away from me."**
>
> –Diane Jones Konihowski

"I can't," I said. "We're still trading with the Russians, and Aeroflot planes are still landing. It's wrong. Why are we boycotting?" It was brainwashing, pure brainwashing. It was the Canadian Olympic Association which said we couldn't go, so I was very disappointed in the COA. Iron Lady Thatcher said no, but the British Olympic committee sent their Olympians anyway. Why all of a sudden did sport become so important in Canada?

It was awful. I was going for the gold, I saw it within my reach, and it was just taken away from me.

Abby Hoffman phoned me in the middle of June. She was director general of Sport Canada.

"Diane," she said, "you have a special invitation from the Organizing Committee to compete in Moscow." To compete as an individual under the Olympic flag.

"Oh my god, Abby . . . I have to think about this."

I couldn't do it. I don't think I would have made it out of the country. Literally. I said no for the safety of my family and friends. So I phoned Abby back and told her I had to turn down the invitation.

"While we were in New Zealand, we had sublet our apartment to a couple of friends," says John Konihowski, "but our names and number were in the Edmonton phone book, and those women were being continually harassed. When Diane was given the chance to compete as an individual, she had reason to be concerned about her family. People would stop her dad or her mom in the street and say, 'Your daughter's supporting the Soviet regime.'

"People who didn't know our home address would send letters to us through the Eskimos. One of them was made up of words clipped from newspapers: COMMUNIST LOVER. I showed it to Dave Cutler and asked him, 'What do you think of this garbage?' I wasn't even thinking at the time; if I was, I would have passed it over to

the police. Dave said, 'Just throw it out; don't even show it to Diane.' That's what I did. I wish now I had kept some of it, but at the time it really got me irritated.

"Then after one game, this player from another team gets in my face and calls me a communist lover. I won't mention his name, but he was a Canadian. Then before one game in Edmonton, a couple of drunks came down the rail and hollered, 'Go home, communist, go home!' It didn't detract from my football, but it wore Diane down quite a bit. I kept a lot of these things from her, but she was still getting harassed in the media, and she was becoming fragile and scared. She had to shut it down. Physically, she could have been ready for Moscow. Mentally, she was a wreck."

The Russians won gold, silver, and bronze. Jane Fredericks and I weren't there; the best in the world weren't there. The Americans held some games in Philadelphia. I won, and the American media acted as if I had won the gold medal and gone to heaven, but it didn't mean anything to me. Two weeks after the Olympics there was a meet in Germany. I beat the Olympic medallists, I beat Jane, I beat them all.

The public backlash against me was intense but short-lived. They didn't hold it against me. For so many years people came up and said, "You were so right, I really admired you for speaking out." I don't think there has ever been one person that has come up to me that was negative.

ALSO IN THIS DECADE

- Frank Boehm of Regina won his second Canadian men's singles 10-pin bowling title in 1970. His first was in 1964.
- Barb Turnbull of Saskatoon, runner-up to Marlene Streit at the Canadian women's amateur golf championship in 1969, joined Streit, Gail Moore and Jocelyn Bourassa to finish fourth at the 1970 world amateur championship in Madrid.
- The first Special Olympics Provincial Summer Games for individuals with mental disabilities were held in Regina in June 1970. There were 250 participants. Special Olympics had grown to accommodate 1,300 athletes across Saskatchewan by the 21st century.
- Larry McGrath of Kindersley won his third Canadian mixed curling title (1967, '68, '71) with Darlene Hill at third and John Gunn at second. Marlene Dorsett played lead for the first two championships and Audrey St. John for the third. McGrath skipped the Saskatchewan men's champions in 1974 and finished second at the Brier.
- Kathy Rollo of Saskatoon placed ninth in women's platform diving at the 1972 Olympics in Munich.
- Boyd Anderson, a left winger born in Carrot River and raised in Wawota, scored five goals in 3 minutes 7 seconds during a Western Canada Hockey League game on October 7, 1972. All five goals came during a five-minute Medicine Hat Tigers power-play that began at 10:04 of the third period in a 10–1 victory over the Flin Flon Bombers. Anderson scored at 10:08, 10:17, 11:50, 12:47 and 13:15.

Barb Turnbull

Harvey Mazinke of Regina and his team of Billy Martin, George Achtymichuk and Dan Klippenstein won the 1973 Brier with a 9–1 record, three wins ahead of the rest of the field. At the world championship in Regina, Mazinke ploughed through the round robin, winning all nine games by a combined score of 84–24, only to lose the final 6–5 in an extra end to Kjell Oscarius of Sweden when TV lights and a warm afternoon turned the ice perplexingly soft.

Light heavyweight (90-kilo) wrestler Terry Paice, born in Whitewood and raised in Moose Jaw, earned the gold medal at the 1974 Commonwealth Games in Christchurch, New Zealand, and bronze at the 1975 Pan-American Games in Mexico City. Paice finished fifth in the 1976 Olympics, the highest of any Canadian wrestler in Montreal.

Robin Hahn of Belle Plaine and Cathy Wedge of Saskatoon shared in Canada's gold medal in the equestrian three-day event at the 1971 Pan-American Games in Cali, Colombia. Hahn, who had placed eighth in the individual three-day standings at the 1968 Olympics, also made the 1976 Olympic team. So did Wedge, despite suffering a broken arm, broken leg, broken collar bone and torn ligaments in both knees in a 1974 spill. They helped Canada finish sixth in Montreal.

Swimmer Martha Nelson of Saskatoon placed 18th of 44 competitors in the women's 200-metre individual medley at the 1972 Olympics in Munich. Four years later in Montreal, Wendy Lee of Regina was 11th of 34 women in the Olympic 400-metre freestyle. Barb Shockey of Saskatoon, an 800-metre bronze medallist at the 1979 Pan-American Games in San Juan, Puerto Rico, was denied her Olympic opportunity by the 1980 boycott.

Joanne McTaggart of Regina enjoyed a superb 1975 track season, briefly holding the world indoor 300-metre record (38.2 seconds) and winning two medals in the relays at the Pan-American Games in Mexico City: gold in the 4x400 and bronze in the 4x100. She was eliminated in the heats of the 200-metre heats and ran the third leg of the 4x100 for the fourth-place Canadian team at the 1976 Olympics in Montreal.

1973 Canadian men's curling champions (clockwise from top left) Billy Martin, Harvey Mazinke, George Achtymichuk and Dan Klippenstein

Saskatoon Imperial 400s won the 1978 Canadian junior men's softball championship by defeating St. John's, Nfld., 6–4 in the final.

University of Saskatchewan Huskiettes won the first of three consecutive Canadian university women's volleyball championships in 1979. Melanie Sanford, Saskatchewan's captain for all three titles and a future national team member, was named the tournament's most valuable player.

Pitcher Rob Guenter of Saskatoon struck out 18 batters in 14 innings as Canada outlasted the United States 1-0 in the gold medal men's softball final of the 1979 Pan American Games in San Juan, Puerto Rico.

WEAR EVER

These pieces of sports history are all on public display (clockwise from top right): Craig Mackay's warmup jacket from the 1948 Olympics (Saskatchewan Sports Hall of Fame and Museum, Regina); 1938 Yorkton Terriers hockey sweater (Yorkton Sports Hall of Fame and Museum); 1914 Saskatoon Quakers baseball jersey (Saskatchewan Baseball Hall of Fame and Museum, Battleford); and Gordie Howe statue (Saskatoon).

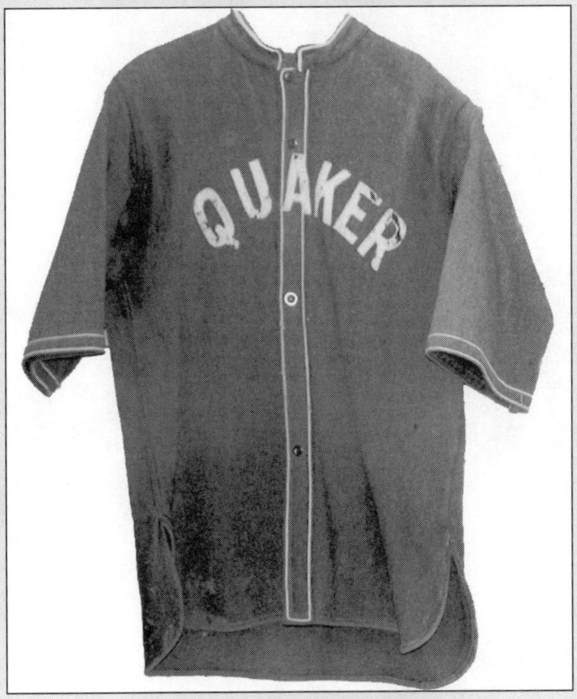

"The whole deal about running with the ball is that you're not supposed to go down unless they make you go down," says Ray Elgaard, whose stubborn resistance to tacklers delighted Saskatchewan football fans.

1980–1989

Shock & Joy

ARRIVALS

April 6, 1982: Lisa Franks, Paralympic athlete, Moose Jaw.
February 27, 1985: Braydon Coburn, hockey player, Shaunavon.
May 10, 1985: Ryan Getzlaf, hockey player, Regina.

DEPARTURES

August 9, 1980: Mel Kerr, baseball player, 77.
March 10, 1981: Eleanor Powley Van Impe, speed skater, 71.
October 16, 1981: Dorothy Walton, badminton player, 72.
December 7, 1982: Harry Jerome, sprinter, 42.
October 18, 1983. Marj Mitchell, curler, 35.
December 6, 1983: Earl McCready, wrestler, 78.
January 19, 1984: Max Bentley, hockey player, 63.
August 19. 1984: Tony Zasada, rower, 23.
November 3, 1984: Stan Obodiac, writer/publicist, 62.
March 16, 1985: Eddie Shore, hockey player and executive, 82.
July 20, 1985: Pat Fletcher, golfer, 69.
February 24, 1986: Tommy Douglas, premier (1944–61), 81.
October 28, 1986: Julien Audette, aviator, 72.
December 30, 1986: hockey players Trent Kresse, 20; Scott Kruger, 19; Chris Mantyka, 19; Brent Ruff, 16.
September 26, 1987: Ethel Catherwood, high jumper, 79.
March 29, 1988: Ed George, marksman, 83.
August 6, 1988: Gordon Garvie, wrestler, 43.
September 7, 1988: Walter Dieter, First Nations politician, 72.
April 10, 1989: George Genereux, trap shooter, 54.

FAME AND FORTUNE—GOOD OR BAD—IS FLEETING. RICK FOLK WON SASKATCHEWAN'S LAST WORLD MEN'S curling championship (to this point) and Marj Mitchell the province's first world women's title. Both would be gone before decade's end, Folk relocated to British Columbia and Mitchell lost to cancer.

A round-robin format vulnerable to abuse that unfolded in Regina's favour in the 1978 WCHL playoffs worked against the Pats in the 1980 Memorial Cup and left the event with egg on its face.

Two pixieish girls, Trudy Treslan and Stacy Singer, made headlines with their championship performances in figure skating and baton twirling, respectively. Lynn Kanuka Williams, all grown up but waif-like in stature, emerged from one of the most controversial collisions in Olympic history to win a medal for Canada.

Back on the hockey rink, the winter of 1986–87 brought sorrow as four Swift Current Broncos were killed in a bus accident and Brad Hornung of the Regina Pats suffered a broken neck that rendered him a quadriplegic. Nevertheless, the Broncos rallied to win the Memorial Cup two years later and Hornung persevered to become a productive person.

Finally, Roger Aldag, the man who personified Rider Pride, was rewarded for his dedication through 11 frustrating seasons by being on the winning side in the greatest Grey Cup game ever played.

RICK FOLK: LAST KING OF THE CORN

ONCE UPON A TIME, THERE WERE CORN BROOMS. Men slapped them on sheets of curling ice with such vigour that *tha-WHACK, tha-WHACK, tha-WHACK* was the distinctive sound of the game, not *"HAAARRRRDDD, HURRY HAAARRRRDDD!"* And oh, did they leave debris! Not occasional bits of hair, not lint, but straw, bits of straw, lengths of straw, straw chaff, little gangs of straw lying in the four-foot circle waiting to pull rocks in to the pot.

"When I was young, I'd listen to the provincial finals on the radio, and part of the fun was listening to the rhythm of the corn brooms," says Rick Folk. "That's something I miss, along with the artistry of sweeping. It was a real art to know how to keep them clean, when to get off the sweep, and when to let the rock try to catch something if possible. Once there was no straw on the ice, the sweepers got really lazy and kept their brushes in the air, assuming they'd never catch anything. Now they keep them down on the ice and rely more on heavy sweeping."

Folk was the best male skip Saskatoon ever produced, the winner of three straight provincial championships (1978–80) as well as Canadian and world champion in 1980. He also skipped a provincial junior champion (1970), five provincial mixed champions (1974–75, '81–83) and two Canadian mixed champions (1974, '83). After moving to British Columbia in 1988, he won four men's titles there (1989, '93–95) along with another Canadian and world crown (1994). His 1978–80 men's rinks changed personnel each year. Jim Wilson replaced Roger Schmidt at lead in 1979 and Ron Mills succeeded Rod Thompson in 1980.

Tom Wilson was a constant presence at second, as he was on all five of Folk's championship mixed teams. The sweeping of the Wilson brothers was vital to the team's success, especially at a time when Canadian curlers were switching *en masse* to push brooms.

"I realize the Richardsons were excellent sweepers, but I never got to play against them," Folk says. "I only watched them, and they were fantastic. In my opinion the Wilsons were the best. In the period when I played, there was no better sweeper than Tom Wilson and not a better pair than Tom and Jim. They swept hard, they swept often and they were smart. Then the brush came in, and almost everybody switched around to it. It was difficult for us because everyone was playing a different game than we were; sooner or later we were in the minority and everybody was thinking, 'Ah, they're just yucchin' up the ice,' but they had really short memories because two or three years before that everybody had straw brooms and no one was complaining then."

Nor was Folk complaining in 1980 when the Brier changed sponsors (from Macdonald Tobacco to Labatt Breweries) and format (from straight round robin to round robin plus playoff). Folk had tied for second place each of the last two years but defeated the champion in the round robin both times,

Rick Folk later in his career (note the brush at right)

Alberta's Ed Lukowich in 1978 at Vancouver and Manitoba's Barry Fry in 1979 at Ottawa. Neither qualified for the 1980 Brier at Calgary, but Folk was not necessarily the man to beat.

"It was a great field," Folk remembers. "Paul Gowsell was the home-town favourite, and then there were Russ Howard from Ontario, Al Hackner from Northern Ontario, Jimmy Ursel from Quebec, and Earle Morris was skipping the Manitoba team with Clare and Garry DeBlonde on it. We knew we'd have to play well all week, but the playoff took a little of the pressure off. You could afford to lose one or two games, and we liked our chances if it came down to a one-game showdown.

"We were excited because Don Lewis was brought in from Regina to be the icemaker, and we knew he'd give us fair ice. Conditions in Vancouver and Ottawa weren't that snappy. It had been really unpredictable in '78 and '79. Vancouver had a huge frost problem; you could only use a two-foot strip down the middle of the sheet, one foot on each side of the centre line. In Ottawa the rocks were really mismatched. Sometimes there was a 30-foot difference between two rocks, and by the time you figured it out it was too late."

Folk and Gowsell provided an interesting contrast, and not because Folk was conservative and clean-cut while Gowsell was unconventional and shaggy. Gowsell was playing his first Brier as if every game was a Monday on the cash spiel circuit he had ruled the last two winters. This might have been fine in past years, where two losses or even one could deny a team the championship, but with the new playoff format the Brier had become more than ever a test of stamina as well as skill. When Gowsell beat Folk 8–4, it raised Alberta's record to 5–1 while Saskatchewan dropped to 5–2. On the last day of the round robin, however, while Folk calmly won his last two games, Gowsell collapsed with losses to last-place Nova Scotia and to Quebec. Saskatchewan won the round robin and the bye to the final with a 9–2 record. Alberta slipped to 8–3, the same as Hackner's Northern Ontario foursome. Hackner prevailed 6–5 in the semi-final.

Folk jumped out to an enormous lead in the final. Mills made a split at the top of the house to set up a three-pointer in the first end. Saskatchewan stole three more in the second when Hackner's sweepers laid off his final draw, only to see it pick up chaff and wreck on a guard. A couple of deuces and steals allowed Hackner to come back within a point, but Folk scored another trey in the ninth to win 10–6. From there, Folk, Mills and the Wilsons went to Moncton and went undefeated at the Air Canada Silver Broom to become world champions, finishing with a 7–6 decision over Kristian Soerum of Norway.

Renowned for his composure, Folk admits to one instance of discomfort: at the 1989 Brier in Saskatoon when he represented B.C. The week proceeded smoothly enough until the next-to-last draw, when he took the ice against Saskatchewan champion Jim Packet of Estevan. Folk's 5–3 victory knocked Packet out of playoff contention; B.C. ended up going all the way to the final, where it lost 3–2 to Alberta's Pat Ryan (who ended up being Folk's third on his 1994 world championship rink).

"That was one of the weirdest feelings I ever had in my life, to be in my home-town at the Brier and see the opposing skip wearing Saskatchewan colours. That felt unreal. I had so many friends and family cheering me on all week, but that game I think they were cheering for Saskatchewan. Too bad we eliminated them, but we needed the win more than they did."

Obviously, it was easier to prevail in Saskatoon as the B.C. champion than to win as the world champion. The most amazing aspect of Folk's 1980 world championship is that he didn't come close to defending it, or his Canadian title, or even his provincial title the following year. As incredible as it seems, Folk failed to qualify out of the Nutana club playdowns in Saskatoon. Extended to 13 games (and losing the toss in 12 of them), Folk's rink was knocked out of the A Event by Gerry Dmytryshyn, the B by Bob Simister, the C by Merv Mann, the D by Murray Eddy and the E by Arvid Lundquist. Outside of Saskatoon, only Mann had any substantial reputation.

Then again, maybe it wasn't so incredible that Folk struggled in club playdowns, considering he was forced to win his last three games to qualify out of the E Event the year before.

"Saskatchewan is unbelievably tough to get out of," Folk says. "It's such a long playoff system, especially if you're in the cities. We'd start our playdowns at the Nutana on January 2, usually with 60 or 70 teams gunning for 8 or 10 spots. That was a lot of curling, and you had to be pretty darn tough because *everybody* knew the ice."

Saskatchewan is so tough to get out of that no one has successfully defended a men's championship since Folk achieved his three-peat of 1978–80. Moreover, his Brier triumph was Saskatchewan's seventh in 26 years. Since then, the province is a woeful 0-for-25, its winning tradition at the Brier nothing more than a memory.

Corn brooms weren't the only things that Rick Folk escorted to their extinction.

MARJ MITCHELL: THE SPIRIT OF WOMEN'S CURLING

Every year the Scott Tournament of Hearts presents the Marj Mitchell Award to the competitor who "best embodies the spirit of curling." In Mitchell's case, this meant excellent shot-making, teamwork, sportsmanship and, as she exemplified in her world championship year of 1980, a fighting spirit that strove for victory even when it seemed beyond her reach.

Mitchell and her Regina Callie team of Nancy Kerr, Shirley McKendry and Wendy Leach arrived at the 1980 Canadian women's curling championship in Edmonton as one of the favourites on the basis of Mitchell's experience as the 1975 national runner-up. That apparent advantage over a largely inexperienced 1980 field evaporated when Saskatchewan lost three of its first four games in a round robin that would send three teams to the playoffs. With experience, however, comes composure. Saskatchewan won five straight, including three nail-biters, to get back in the hunt.

"Monday night (when Saskatchewan was 1–3) you wouldn't have been able to convince me of it, but here we are, still alive," Mitchell said.

One-point leads, deficits, and margins of victory became Saskatchewan's constant companions as the tournament wore on. Ontario's Chris Bodogh snapped Mitchell's streak with a 7–6 decision. Entering the last draw of the round robin, Nova Scotia's 20-year-old Colleen Jones was comfortably in first place at 8–1, with eight teams jam-packed at four or five losses. Newfoundland's Sue Anne Bartlett was in great shape to steal a winning point from Saskatchewan in an extra end until Kerr made like a bulldozer with triple and double takeouts to clear the ice for Mitchell's winning draw in a 5–4 decision. That left Saskatchewan, Alberta, British Columbia and Ontario tied for second with 6–4 records. Mitchell caught a break in her tiebreaker, getting an open draw for three in the first end after Joan Dexter of B.C. threw a first-end takeout between two rocks. Saskatchewan cruised home 7–4. Similar good fortune seemed to unfold in the semi-final when Saskatchewan led 6–1 after five ends, but Ontario fought back and even took the lead before Saskatchewan prevailed 8–7 to reach the final against Nova Scotia.

Marj Mitchell

Mitchell, Leach, McKendry and Kerr wasted no time building a lead in the final, stealing single points in the first, second and third ends and forcing Jones to hit and stick for one against four Saskatchewan counters in the fourth. Mitchell's deuce in the fifth pushed her lead to 5–1. Jones replied with three in the sixth but couldn't mount a threat after that. She rubbed a guard with her final draw, and Mitchell didn't have to throw her last rock for Saskatchewan to win 6–5 and earn the championship. To do so, Mitchell's team had won eight of its last nine games, five of them by a single point, two in an extra end.

"I was surprisingly relaxed through it all," Mitchell said. "There's more pressure when you're winning.

When we lost those three almost immediately, we relaxed. At that point it was do the best we could and see what happens."

Kerr added, "I kind of like it when they write you off. You can sneak up on 'em."

They would have no such luxury at the second world women's curling championship in Perth, Scotland. Now wearing Canada's colours, the team held on for a 9–7 opening decision over Italy, then crushed its next five opponents by a combined score of 65–17. Mitchell lost her undefeated record when Elizabeth Hogstrom of Sweden won 7–6, a result that gave Sweden first place when both teams finished the round robin at 8–1. Canada clobbered Scotland 9–4 in the semi-final to set up a rematch with Hogstrom. Sweden took early control with two in the first end. Canada was flawless from there on, allowing no steals or deuces, biding its time, stealing one in the seventh and taking two in the ninth. Ultimately, the world championship came down to a single point scored in the extra end: Canada 7, Sweden 6.

Winning the national and world championships brought prestige back to the province that hadn't won a women's title since 1974. With Rick Folk going all the way on the men's side, Saskatchewan became the first Canadian province to produce world champions of both genders, and in the same year, too. (Unbelievable as it seems, while Folk's rink was eliminated in Saskatoon club playdowns in 1981, Mitchell's was knocked out at the city level! Marian Mazinke was the skip who bounced Mitchell out of the Regina playdowns.)

Mitchell's defining characteristic was her command of intangibles. She isn't remembered for great shots or strategy but for her demeanour and leadership. That was especially evident in 1980, when her team had plenty of opportunities—sometimes several in one game—to give in to the odds or the pressure.

"As soon as you begin to allow yourself to look for an excuse as to why you aren't going to do well," she once said, "well, you probably won't do well."

An attitude like that can be contagious.

"Marj was able to get the maximum out of us as individuals," McKendry said. "That was her strength as a skip."

Mitchell died of cancer at 35 in October of 1983, only four months after her diagnosis. Despite a short life and curling career, her legacy was enormous. Her team's 1980 championship run put Regina on an equal footing with Saskatoon in women's curling and kept Saskatchewan among the country's elite.

1980 MEMORIAL CUP: EGGING ON MIKE KEENAN

TURNABOUT IS FAIR PLAY, WHAT GOES AROUND comes around, and payback's a bitch.

On April 10, 1978, the Flin Flon Bombers visited Regina for the last game of an ill-conceived three-team round-robin playoff series that also involved the Brandon Wheat Kings, runaway first-place finishers in the Western Canada Hockey League's East Division. Although the Bombers had lost 9–6 the night before in Brandon, they left the ice waving "bye-bye" to the Wheat Kings' fans. Everyone knew that a lopsided Regina victory in the last game could eliminate the powerhouse Wheat Kings and set up a division final between Flin Flon and the Pats. All the Bombers had to do was lose to Regina by at least six goals.

"I remember it well," says Ed Chynoweth, then president of the league. "Brandon had the best team of the three, without a doubt. I got a call from the Wheat Kings' governor wanting to know if I was going to be at the game in Regina to make sure it was going to be run right, and I said, 'No, I'm not going near it. We've dug this hole; I'm prepared for the worst.' The rest is history. The worst came."

Dirk Graham scored four goals as Regina won 10–4. All three teams finished 4–4 but Flin Flon's goals for and against were 46–43, Regina's were 43–44 and Brandon's were 40–42. First-place Brandon was eliminated from the East Division playoffs. (Elsewhere, first-place Lethbridge was eliminated from the Central Division, and first-place Portland was eliminated from the West Division. For unspecified reasons, the league trashed the three-team round-robin playoff format after 1978.)

Two years later, the Pats were not only champions of the league (now the WHL) but hosts for the Memorial Cup tournament that would begin in

Brandon and wind up at the Agridome. Regina and the Peterborough Petes, champions of the Ontario Hockey League, were pegged as co-favourites. The Cornwall Royals of the Quebec Major Junior Hockey League rounded out the three-team field that would play a double round robin to eliminate one team.

Sound familiar? Smell trouble?

Peterborough won its games in Brandon, 5–4 in overtime over the Pats and 8–6 over Cornwall. Regina put itself in serious jeopardy by losing 5–3 to the Royals in Brandon, then 4–3 to the Petes in Regina. Finally, the Pats hammered Cornwall 11–2. Regina ended the round robin with a 1–3 record but had the goal-differential advantage if Cornwall also finished 1–3. That would put the Pats in the sudden-death final, on their home ice, against the Petes. Peterborough could avoid that undesirable scenario simply by not winning the last game of the round robin against Cornwall.

Sound familiar? Smell trouble?

On Friday, May 9, 1980, the turnabout/come-around/payback for April 10, 1978, unfolded before 5,823 spectators, many of them outraged Pats fans who got such a kick out of the Flin Flon flim-flam two years earlier. Peterborough actually held a 4–1 lead halfway through the game. Then Cornwall got a goal before the second period ended and three more before the third period was 10 minutes old.

"At the time I was very upset," admits Bryan Murray, then coach of the Pats and now general manager of the NHL's Ottawa Senators. "Peterborough didn't try to do anything with the puck in the third period. They actually carried the puck back to their own end on a couple of occasions and threw it back deep in the zone. They gave Cornwall second and third chances to be able to score their goals.

"We (the Pats) were responsible for our own fate. We had a 3–0 lead on the Petes in the Agridome, and they came back to beat us. We had our chances. There was a real bitterness in the building for the final game. It was disappointing for all of us—for the city, I'm sure, and for people connected with the hockey team.

"It certainly tainted the Memorial Cup. The format was changed after that so it wouldn't happen again. For those of us on the Pats, it didn't affect our careers, but it did affect our memories of junior hockey."

> **"Peterborough didn't try to do anything with the puck in the third period. They actually carried the puck back to their own end on a couple of occasions."**
>
> –Bryan Murray

One quirky coincidence of the tournament was the parallel roads all three coaches would follow. Within two years, Murray would move on to coaching assignments in the American Hockey League and NHL. So would Cornwall's Doug Carpenter and Peterborough's Mike Keenan, who had already developed the warm and fuzzy persona that would become his trademark.

He was asked if his team had thrown the game.

"I have no comment about tonight's game. We're preparing for Sunday's game," Keenan replied.

He was asked about his team's third-period collapse.

"I have no comment about tonight's game. We're preparing for Sunday's game."

Elsewhere under the stands, the author of this book was having his own surreal interview with Carpenter.

"Did your team play well?"

"No," Carpenter said.

"Are you surprised that you won, then?"

Pause.

"No."

It wasn't as if anyone needed a magnifying glass to read between the lines. The court of public opinion delivered its verdict—Peterborough guilty of larceny—through radio station CKCK, where disc jockey and sportscaster Barry Burns turned his Saturday afternoon music slot into an open-line show devoted to the Memorial Cup, including the aftermath of Friday's game when the Petes were pelted with soft drinks and coins. One caller suggested disrupting Sunday's nationally televised final by throwing eggs on the ice.

Which came first, the chicken or the eggs? A live chicken was thrown towards the Peterborough bench

Sunday. The clean-up crew got nearly as many shifts (16) as Cornwall centre Dale Hawerchuk; that's how often they were called upon to scrape broken eggs from the ice. That didn't include the frequent assaults on the Peterborough bench, where the Plexiglas backing sprayed shell, yolk and egg white all over Keenan and the Petes.

It was 1947 all over again for Regina, with the Pats in place of the Moose Jaw Canucks, the Petes in place of Toronto St. Mike's and eggs instead of whisky bottles.

Whether Regina deserved a comeuppance for the Flin Flon flim-flam is problematical. After all, the Bombers instigated that one. If Keenan and the Petes truly did tank the round-robin finale, however, their theme song quickly became "Instant Karma." Cornwall won the final and the Memorial Cup 3–2 in overtime.

Since the 1980 Memorial Cup, Keenan and Murray have become longtime NHL peers but not friends.

"No, there has been a carryover, pretty much," Murray admits. "Mike and I have had many conversations over time—never about that particular case. I guess things do fade to some extent, but we've never been buddies."

EVAN HARDY FOOTBALL ALUMNI: SOUL MEN

HEAVEN KNOWS THERE HAVE BEEN HUNDREDS OF noteworthy Saskatchewan high school champions in dozens of sports, and yes, it is unfair to single one out, but just how many teams could boast among their alumni an Olympic medallist, a Stanley Cup champion and key players on Grey Cup champions for three different teams within a decade?

In 1979 the Evan Hardy Souls of Saskatoon won their third consecutive 4A football championship, with each final triumph coming at the expense of a different Regina team: 29–6 over Campbell in 1977, 33–9 over O'Neill in 1978 and 54–17 over Thom in 1979. Then their classmates spent the next decade saying, "Hey, check out what Bob, Brian, Larry and Mike did!"

Bob Molle, a massive two-way lineman, was also the 1980 provincial high school heavyweight wrestling champion. He accepted a scholarship from Simon Fraser University in Burnaby, B.C., with the stipulation that he be allowed to both wrestle and play football. Simon Fraser, the only Canadian university offering full athletic scholarships, competed exclusively against American institutions. Facing the best wrestlers to be found in California and the Pacific region, Molle compiled a 134–5 record at SFU while also winning Canadian championships and representing Canada abroad.

Molle finished fifth at the 1983 world championships and earned a bronze medal at the 1983 Pan-American Games in Caracas. He was training for the 1984 Olympics when he suffered a debilitating back injury: a herniated disc with a pinched sciatic nerve. Not only was he in terrible pain, but his left leg was virtually numb. There was no alternative but to have surgery even though the Games in Los Angeles were only three weeks away. The 2½-hour operation left a six-inch incision that would have to heal. Molle received conflicting opinions on the prognosis for his recovery. One doctor told Molle it was up to him; several people said the Olympics were out of the question.

Then Gene Kiniski visited the hospital. Kiniski, whose son Nick also wrestled for SFU, was one of the most colourful professional wrestlers of the 1950s and '60s, a tough customer whose raspy voice made him sound like he'd taken a few too many shots to the throat when he was with the Edmonton Eskimos. Kiniski caught Molle in a pessimistic mood and growled, "Hell, we'll prove them wrong. What do they think we are, average people or what?" Kiniski had pressed the right button on Molle's ego.

"It just kind of clicked right there," Molle said. "We always felt that we were superior to other people. I don't know whether we are or not, but we always took that attitude. He's played pro football and wrestled, so he has a keen idea of what competition is all about and the price you have to pay to keep above the rest.

"Gene made me get up every morning and walk with him through the hospital hallways. After a week, I went right from the hospital to his place. I'd lost 27 pounds, and he fed me."

Darlene Solie learned to play softball in Sedley, refined her game in Regina, and took it to the highest level in Saskatoon. A frequent high school and provincial champion in Regina, she moved to Saskatoon in 1980 to compete in Senior A ball with Saskatoon Harmony Centre and helped that team win a national championship. She also enjoyed seven seasons (1980–86) with the national women's softball team and earned a silver medal at the world championship in 1981.

Solie and Brenda Staniforth of Sedley, at third base and pitcher respectively, were key members of Canada's gold-medal winners at the 1983 Pan-American Games in Caracas. After losing three times to the United States earlier in the tournament, Canada scored twice in the first inning of the final, and Staniforth pitched five strong innings in a 5–4 victory.

Seven other women were from Saskatchewan or playing for teams in the province in 1983: first baseman Ann Tkachuk of Humboldt; outfielder Kathy McCune of Lashburn; outfielder Donna Veale of North Battleford; and outfielder Nancy Brentnell, shortstop Janis Cookson, catcher Shawna Hicks, and pitcher Shan McDonald of Saskatoon.

Darlene Solie

Molle showed up for his first Olympic match on August 8, exactly 21 days after his surgery. His upper-body strength and moves were still excellent; his balance was visibly affected; his endurance was questionable. He pinned his first two opponents and dispatched the third by technical superiority (a 10-point lead) to reach the gold-medal match against an old nemesis, Bruce Baumgartner of the United States. Baumgartner would have been favoured to win under normal circumstances; before a home crowd and against a hobbled opponent, it should have been a mismatch. Through sheer willpower, Molle managed a 2–2 draw through the first period, but Baumgartner discerned his opponent's imbalance and leg weakness. It was all Molle could do to hold the final score to 10–2 and prevent the match from being stopped on technical superiority. Molle's silver medal was as honourable a prize as Baumgartner's gold under the circumstances.

Back at Simon Fraser, Molle became the first player from that school to be named All-American and the first man to win four straight heavyweight titles at the National Association of Intercollegiate Athletics (NAIA) championships. Molle went on to play seven CFL seasons on the offensive line for the Winnipeg Blue Bombers, winning the Grey Cup in 1988 and 1990.

Before Molle won his Grey Cup ring, however, a linebacker from that 1979 Evan Hardy football squad made a major contribution of his own to a Canadian professional champion. He was no longer a linebacker but a centre—on skates. Brian Skrudland had moved on from the Souls to play three years of junior hockey with the Saskatoon Blades, where his talent level was so unimpressive that he was completely bypassed in the NHL draft. Still, his grit moved the Montreal Canadiens to sign him as a free agent.

Skrudland put in two minor-league seasons before joining the Canadiens in 1985–86 along with another rookie, goaltender Patrick Roy, whose inspired play led Montreal all the way to the Stanley Cup final against the Calgary Flames.

The Habs got off to an awful start in Calgary, losing 5–2 and struggling to force the Flames to overtime in the second game. As centre on the checking line, Skrudland won the faceoff to start the fourth period and started a series of passes that ended up with him and Mike McPhee heading into the Calgary zone on a two-on-one break. McPhee faked a slapshot and slid the puck right in front of the net to Skrudland, who redirected the disk over Mike Vernon's shoulder for the fastest goal in NHL overtime history: nine seconds. Montreal won the next three games and the Stanley Cup.

Skrudland played eight seasons in Montreal, 17 in the NHL, never came within a sniff of 20 goals in a season, and was the first captain of the Florida Panthers. After his retirement in 2002, the Blades retired the No. 10 he wore in Saskatoon, a rare honour for a player who had little to offer but a good example.

Larry Wruck was the Souls alumnus who became a professional linebacker; specifically, the Linebacker Who Got Away. After three junior football campaigns with the Saskatoon Hilltops, Wruck attended the Saskatchewan Roughriders' 1983 training camp and made a favourable impression on head coach Joe Faragalli. Unfortunately, Faragalli's neck was being measured for the guillotine by new general manager John Herrera, whose football savvy seemed to consist primarily of flashing the gaudy Super Bowl ring he had received as a member of the 1980 Oakland Raiders (where he was in scouting and public relations).

Faragalli sent Wruck back to the Hilltops but placed his name on a junior protected list; later that year Faragalli was fired. His replacement was Reuben Berry, a man with no CFL experience and, like Herrera, no appreciation for Canadian players. Wruck was virtually ignored at training camp in 1984 and asked to be traded. Herrera obligingly sent him to Edmonton for punter Paul Hickie, who lasted one whole season with the Roughriders.

By the spring of 1985, Herrera was gone from Saskatchewan. So, too, were Bryan Illerbrun, Bob Poley (although they'd come back), Ken Clark, Dwight Edwards, Mike Emery, Greg Fieger, Marshall Hamilton and Gerry Hornett, non-imports all. ("If you lose an American, you can get a pretty good football player down in the States to replace him," Ken Preston, the Roughriders' general manager from 1958–77, said in 1985. "But if you lose a Canadian, it's a bit more difficult—that is, unless you're lucky enough to have a guy like John Herrera somewhere in the league to make deals with.")

Edmonton, which needed luck like Alberta needs more oil, happily took its time grooming Wruck, giving him a few years of reserve and special-teams duty before he became a precious CFL commodity, a starting defensive non-import. Wruck was a Western all-star linebacker by 1989 and would log 12 CFL seasons, all of them with the Eskimos, playing 213 regular-season games and missing only one, and winning Grey Cups in 1987 and 1993. He was a starter in Edmonton when Don Matthews was defensive co-ordinator, when Joe Faragalli was head coach and when Ron Lancaster was head coach, but he wasn't good enough for John Herrera or Reuben Berry—not that Roughrider fans were *bitter* about it. Not much.

Luckily, Souls grad Mike Anderson went the American route and didn't report to the Roughriders until 1985, after he had graduated from San Diego State University. The son of Paul Anderson, a Roughrider himself from 1953–58, Mike stuck around for 12 years as a centre and guard and was one of the men who made life safe for quarterbacks Kent Austin and Tom Burgess when Saskatchewan won the 1989 Grey Cup.

TRUDY TRESLAN: SILENCE IS GOLDEN

Composure is a trait usually acquired through years of exposure to uneasy situations. It is not something expected of a 13-year-old competing in a national championship, particularly when something unforeseen occurs. Trudy Treslan of Beechy (70 kilometres northeast of Swift Current) showed the aplomb of a veteran in 1984 at the Agridome to earn the only gold medal ever won by a Saskatchewan competitor at the Canadian figure skating championships.

Trudy Treslan

Treslan, who had been training in Saskatoon, was the last of 16 skaters in the novice girls section to perform her three-minute long program on the afternoon of January 12. She had skated well in the compulsory program and knew she could finish among the medallists with a strong free skate.

It had gone very nicely, and Treslan was gearing up for her big finish when—BOOP!—her music cut out. There were supposed to be 31 more seconds of music to interpret; instead, the Agridome sound system was silent.

Now, the question was, would Treslan break down along with the sound system? (It's not as if the figure skating community expects its athletes to be stoic. What other sport designates a section of the competition site as the "kiss-and-cry" area?)

"I didn't really know what had happened at first," she told *Leader-Post* reporter Gregg Drinnan. "I tried to keep calm and steady, and to forget about it. It had never happened to me before. I just went over to the referee and asked her if I should keep going from where I left off or just start from the end of my slow part. She said to start from the end of my slow part, so I did."

With the sound restored, Treslan resumed her program and completed it without any major flaws. Her excellent free skate gave her a narrow victory, with 16 ordinals to the runner-up's 17. That night, when the Agridome was filled to capacity for the senior women's competition, Treslan received her gold medal and was showered with dozens of bouquets.

Thrilled but still composed, Trudy Treslan got her father, Roger, to drive her to the nearby Regina General Hospital, where she gave the flowers to patients in the pediatric ward.

STACY SINGER: TWIRLED CHAMPION

"WATCHING THE VIDEOS NOW, I GUESS I probably was the best," Stacy Singer says of the first world baton twirling championship she won in 1985. "I don't know if *I* would have picked me, but they had never seen anyone that young who could do anything like that. They thought I was cute."

Cute? *Cute?* Look at the picture. Eight-year-old Stacy Singer was cute like Shirley Temple, cocker spaniel puppies, baby booties or newly hatched chicks. She was *adorable!*

She was also as single-mindedly driven to succeed as any athlete, probably more than would be healthy for most children her age. Her self-discipline was exceptional, her physical co-ordination and her concentration the product of intense practice.

Sure, Stacy Singer was a pretty little thing, but she went out and earned that junior world title as an eight-year-old in 1985, when the age limit for juniors was 14. Later that limit was bumped up one year and she ruled the world's juniors again in 1988, '89, '90, '91 and '92. Singer added the 1993 senior world crown to her laurels before heeding a doctor's advice to retire from the sport before her body self-destructed.

No one had to push Singer into the sport. In fact, she had to be restrained. Three-year-old Stacy was mesmerized by the way her babysitter twirled the baton and happily watched the older girl practice at the Martin School of Dancing and Baton Twirling in Regina. Stacy asked her sitter's coach, Maureen Johnson, to teach her. Johnson politely told her to come back when she was four years old. She did and three years later was competing at nationals.

"I was up with the older kids after just a couple of years of twirling," Singer says. "It didn't occur to me I was that much younger than everyone else. I thought it was normal to want to succeed."

Baton twirling demands gymnastic and dance skills, the intricate but seemingly effortless throwing and catching of the baton, musical and artistic interpretation, and the execution of compulsory moves. Like any other judged sport, it's not just what you do, it's how you do it.

"When I was really young, I wasn't into technique at all. I didn't care. I wanted to do hard stuff, and I was going to it regardless of what my coach said. She would try to get me to do the easy stuff nicely, but I would go off on my own and do things that were 10 times harder, things that girls at the worlds were doing. So I ended up figuring out the hard stuff and then getting the technique down."

Singer qualified for the 1985 worlds in Frankfurt, West Germany. At this point, success was strictly a matter of accomplishing new and more difficult tricks. At 8, her ambitions were not focused on medals or trophies. For that matter, she wasn't really focused on ambition when she arrived in Frankfurt.

"There was a skating rink beside the gym, and I really liked to go skating with my shoes on. That was my big priority, I wanted to play. I wasn't really concerned about the competition. It didn't cross my mind whether I would win or even come close. During warm-ups a band would play, and I was more interested in playing my baton as if it was an instrument. My coach was embarrassed.

"I didn't realize what was going on, really. I was just going out to do my routine like every other time. I made the finals, which was seven girls, and after we had all performed they announced the finishers from seventh place up. When they announced second place and it wasn't me, the Canadian contingent just went crazy, and they were all hugging me. I didn't understand it. I thought I probably got eighth. I didn't get that I was the only one left.

"When I stepped up on the podium I was sort of passing out. I dropped the trophy and got a dent in it. I was home before I understood exactly what I'd done, but that's a pretty young age to realize what a world championship means."

Singer then learned that raw athleticism would not bring her any more world titles. As she earned bronze medals in 1986 and '87, she realized Johnson was right about the importance of technique.

"She didn't get on my case about it. She was always easy on me because I was so hard on myself it was ridiculous. She'd be hard on all the other kids. When I got the bronze, I was devastated; I thought I was horrible."

Singer applied herself to the finer points of the sport in preparation for the 1988 worlds in Japan.

When the finals arrived, she had perfect form and a perfectly dreadful case of stage fright.

"Right before I went on, I told Coach I don't want to go out there, I don't want to do it. I had worked hard on the routine, and I didn't want to screw it up."

Johnson coaxed her into the gym, and Singer captured her second gold medal. Her pixie-like body was paying a serious price for the achievement, however.

"Some of the ways I trained were probably not healthy because I was so hard on myself. If I missed the catch on a trick, I'd make myself catch it a hundred times. Even if I was in severe pain, I wouldn't stop until I'd finished. I'm not sure how healthy that is, but it's part of the reason why I became good.

"I had knee surgery at age 11, after my second world championship. The bone in the kneecap was actually dying, so they had to drill holes in it for new blood vessels to grow and it got better."

As she recovered from knee surgery, Singer developed mental discipline to prevent nervousness from sabotaging her efforts as it almost had in Japan.

"World championships in Europe and Japan were massive events. In France the fans paint their faces, and the atmosphere is almost like a soccer game. They had to give me a bodyguard there.

"I taught myself to become very introverted for competition. At the hotel, I'd be fine, but once I was in the gym, that was it. It started as soon as I'd walk into the building. I didn't see anyone around me, I didn't notice what was going on. People may have taken that for snobbishness or something. I wouldn't even hear them, I was so in focus. I'd go up there on autopilot."

Stacy Singer, 8, world champion

On autopilot, Singer convincingly won three more world junior titles and, in her first and only attempt, the senior world championship. Then it was time to give it up.

"The doctors weren't sure if my knee problem was caused by my training regimen, but I'm sure it had something to do with it. My hip trouble for sure was from twirling. We do these things called illusions. . . ."

Illusions. Figure skaters do them, too, but they have the advantage of beginning them with a smooth gliding momentum. In an illusion, the athlete keeps one leg—suppose it's the left—straight and immobile while turning her right leg, torso and head in unison in a diagonal orbit. Think of her left leg as the hub of a Ferris wheel, the rest of her as the wheel itself. The illusion is that the athlete's pelvis doesn't explode from centrifugal force.

Question: Who is your favourite baton twirler . . . ever?

Jo-ann: My favourite twirler is Stacey *(sic)* Singer. She was amazing. I still do not think that anyone has matched her technical skills with her baton! Triple illusion catch inside an illusion. . . . How many people can do that?

–Chat-room posting, April 2004, Scottish Baton Twirling Federation web site

"I would try to do four illusions under a throw at the University of Regina gym, where the ceiling is 30 feet high; normally somebody trying that many illusions would toss 50 feet. I was trying to go so fast, I would break all the blood vessels on my face and my eyeballs.

"The pain in my hips started when I was about 14. Finally, a doctor told me, when I was 17, that if I kept going I'd probably end up in a wheelchair by the time I was 25, so that was a pretty good reason to stop competing. The disappointing part is that in baton twirling you can never learn all there is to learn. That's what was so much fun about it. Even when you're at the top, you can still come up with things that are harder, neater or different; that's what I really enjoyed—that and the travel.

"I went to worlds in Germany, Italy, France, Texas, Switzerland, the Netherlands and Japan. We always took a week-long tour afterwards. I was with my best friends, and because most of them were quite a bit older than me, my mom would just say, 'Okay, go.' We had fun; it was great. It gave me the desire to see the world and be adventurous."

Her athletic retirement had the fortunate aspect of allowing her to channel her energy solely on her studies at the U of R, where she was indulging a lifelong interest in biology.

"Even as I child I was interested in animals. In grade school I was always the kid who brought home the duckling or chick that hatched in the classroom. Once I found out about genetics I got more and more interested in that."

Singer achieved her B.Sc. in Biology and continued into graduate studies. She has spent a year in Australia and been the recipient of three NSERC (National Sciences and Engineering Research Council of Canada) grants in pursuit of her Doctorate. Her research specialty is the role of molecular genetics in plant growth and development.

The ends of a baton become blurs when it is twirled by a master.

The electrons of a molecule rotate around their nucleus faster than the eye can follow.

Stacy Singer, 27, peers into a microscope and glimpses the ultimate twirl.

Cute.

ON HER MEDAL: LYNN KANUKA IN HER OWN WORDS

I'M COACHING KIDS NOW, AND A COUPLE OF MY athletes have gone to provincial championships. I can hardly believe that I qualified twice but didn't even go. In Grade 11 my boyfriend's graduation was on the second day of provincials. I wasn't particularly attached to that boy, either; it was more like, I'll go to the grad, and next year I'll go to provincials if I make it. I wasn't that hyped about competing, I guess. Then in my own Grade 12, my graduation at Marian High School fell the same weekend as provincials. It happens to lots of athletes, and they juggle both. I chose not to juggle the track stuff and said, "No, I'm going to my grad." I just wasn't that worried about how far my running was going to take me.

I was at the U of S for just one year, but fantastic things happened there. Back then there was no Field House, and we always talk fondly of those times, how we had so many people in that tiny little gym with the unbelievably sharp banked corners, the system with fast groups and slower groups, the workouts outside as well as inside—a lot of fun. The goal was to do well but to really have a good time doing it. I did well. Still, I was bent on being a doctor, so I studied and worked to get decent marks. Sometimes it was dark and 40 below outside and I was supposed to do a workout, but I had a science lab at 6 o'clock, so there were times when I didn't do the workout.

I said to myself, "You gotta run, you know. You're

It wasn't until Rob Chernoff of Regina crouched in the pool for the men's 200-metre individual medley heats at Los Angeles in 1984 that a Saskatchewan man finally achieved the status of Olympic swimmer.

Chernoff began competitive swimming in Regina when he was eight years old and was setting provincial age-group records by 11. By 1980, when he was 14, Chernoff was in top form, breaking provincial age-group records 63 times and setting a national mark for 14-year-olds in the 100-metre breaststroke.

He moved to Calgary in 1981 to train with national team coach Derek Snelling. Breaststroke continued to be Chernoff's best single discipline, but his all-around skill made him an excellent candidate for the individual medley—equal parts backstroke, breaststroke, butterfly and freestyle. By finishing the 200 IM in 2 minutes 6.69 seconds at the 1984 Olympic trials in Toronto, Chernoff qualified for the Los Angeles Games.

With only a year of international experience behind him, Chernoff did not qualify for the final in Los Angeles. He remained on the national swim team for four more years and represented Canada at the 1985 World University Games in Kobe, Japan, and in 1986 at the Commonwealth Games in Edinburgh and the world swimming championships in Madrid. Chernoff left competitive swimming in 1988. Six of the 107 Saskatchewan age-group records he set were still standing in 2004.

Rob Chernoff

talented, you're letting it go here. Maybe you should go away where it's warm, and you'll run regularly." So I went to the library and looked up all the universities where I thought I would like to go: California, New York, Rhode Island, you name it. I fired off a letter of what I had done to date, and about 10 universities replied and said they'd be interested. I finally chose San Diego State because I wanted to go be a beach girl. Really, that was my motivation. It was, like, "Wow, the beach, man, I've been to Disneyland, I know what it's like there! Really, you're going to pay for my schooling for four years? Yeah!"

I graduated with a B.Sc. in Physical Education. My plans still were to come back and be a doctor, maybe end up in the sports sciences. I had become disgruntled with running and I thought, "Ah, I'm done, it's been a great run, I got all my school paid for, I'm going to go back and I'm going to go back to school." My (then) husband Paul (Williams) influenced me to try for the 1984 Olympics, which were about two years away. He had grander dreams and expectations for his own running and also recognized my talent. He said, "Lynn, don't stop, not now, not yet. If you train and focus, then we've got a shot, we can make the Games."

I had a lot of injuries. All of them were stress fractures, bone problems. I'm a small person, just five feet tall and 100 to 105 pounds. I wear a size 5 shoe; my spikes are smaller, though, like a men's 3½. I think the root cause of my injuries was the stress of large muscles pulling on the sheaths around small bones over time. I had an injury pretty well every year, as long as I ever ran. I had a lot in my shinbones, and mine was the first femoral stress fracture they'd ever seen at the UBC Sports Medicine Clinic. (I was living in Vancouver by then.) I was complaining about my thigh, and everyone just thought it was a deep tissue muscle injury until the bone scan clearly revealed a stress fracture high in the front of the bone. I had them in both legs for some time.

With any kind of bone trauma, you need at least a month or two off your legs; you just can't take the pounding. To be in good shape and face six weeks or more of no running—that's devastating. My coaches and I pioneered water running. I had experimented with regular swimming, but it didn't work; once my legs healed, I would be aerobically fit, but I felt really awkward when I ran. It took a long time to get comfortable again. The idea for running in the water came from injured racehorses—they just tread water, basically, with a running action. Dr. Doug Clement of UBC, one of my coach-doctors, said, "Why don't you try that?" It made sense. Anything that I would have done on land I transferred to the water. You basically use the running action to stay afloat in the deep end of the pool. When the bone is healed, you have a comfortable transfer of fitness because you've kept the running muscles active.

In 1983 I qualified for the world track championships in Helsinki. I was a finalist in the 3,000 metres (placing 10th) and did well enough to think I can do it next year, I could be an Olympic finalist. I was excited to go to Los Angeles because the Canadian team's base camp was actually in San Diego, right where I used to live when I was at school. I couldn't wait to go back there and run all my usual routes. And I had raced on the L.A. Coliseum track against UCLA athletes when I was running, so it was familiar to me. You know, my comfort level was really there.

I won the bronze medal in the women's 3,000-metre final that's mostly remembered for the collision involving Mary Decker and Zola Budd. (*Decker was the American favourite while Budd, a South African who ran barefoot, was competing for Great Britain.*) The fear of taking a fall is very real. It's very physical in there, a lot of bumping and jostling. I had been tripped up and fallen in a race, so it wasn't an unheard of thing to me. It's a wonder more of us didn't fall down in the final because we all had to jump over the collision. A German girl, Brigitte Kraus, went down and never finished, but no one ever talks about her.

Mary went right to the front but wasn't able to get clear; everybody was right there. The collision was a complete accident. Zola had a funny little kick to one side and Mary's other foot came up and hit it. They locked feet and down she (Decker) went. That was it. I was tucked right behind them in fifth or sixth place. When we had run another lap and I saw Mary on the infield, I thought, "Great!" Well, all's fair in the game, right? Actually, nothing unfair was done to her, not in my view. Sometimes these things just happen, you know?

But it took a bit of time to regroup. We were a tightly bunched pack until that happened, and suddenly, *whoosh*, we completely spread out. Everybody lost focus. I remember hearing the sound of the crowd going from this huge, loud happy roar for their potential gold medallist to an awful boo. Do you know what it's like when thousands of people are just going *"RRRRR?"* With 80,000 people in the Coliseum, it sounded horrible. I remember thinking, "This is the Olympic final, and they're booing! This is awful!" A lap or two went by before all of a sudden it clicked on me: "Where am I?" And that's when I looked, and I counted people ahead of me: 1, 2, 3, 4, 5! I was in sixth place, and there were two laps to go, maybe a little more. Then I remember going, "Lynn! Get back, get in the game, get in the game!" So I woke up, and I passed the person in front of me, and I kept counting and thinking, "Wow, I can get the next person!"

Still, I had to stay focused, take one step at a time and not go too quickly. I remember always being taught to just focus on the task at hand and break it down. The first task was to get by the person in front of me. Then, *"DING, DING!"* I heard that bell lap, and it was 1, 2, 3, I was in fourth place. I could see Zola Budd out front. She was dying and I thought, "I'm gonna get her and I'm gonna have a medal!" And that's what happened. She continued to fall back. I don't know where she ended up (seventh), but then I also knew there were other athletes right behind me, and they were close to me, so I had to try really hard to hang on to that bronze medal.

The top four finishers were: Maricica Puica, Romania, 8 minutes 35.96 seconds; Wendy Sly, Great Britain, 8:39.47; Lynn Kanuka, Canada, 8:42.14; and Cindy Bremser, United States, 8:42.78.

I crossed the finish line totally elated. I remember being *so* excited, just incredibly excited. I guess I bent over and caught my breath, and then I raised my head a bit and the first person I saw was Dr. Jack Taunton from the UBC Clinic, a good friend and wonderful mentor. Out of all of that sea of humanity up there, I could see him, arms outstretched, not too far up in the stands. I remember going, "Jack! Jack! Yes! I did it!" And then I looked at him and I went, "Wow, you got a haircut!"

Everyone I knew was excited for me. I don't think at that time I had any awareness of the impact or what that means to people that you're connected to, and I'm always touched by that. People still bring it up. I feel lucky that I have that many friends and family that shared in it with me.

The following year, 1985, I had great success in street races. I won three events in New York, Chicago and San Francisco, and that was so much fun. They had big sponsors for one-mile races down major city streets. There wasn't as much seriousness attached to it, so I loved it. I was thrilled to get paid for what I was doing because I'd have done it anyway.

Lynn Kanuka competing at the 1984 Olympic Games

I think the biggest payday I ever had was $10,000 for a 10K, the L'Eggs mini-marathon in New York one year. I might have got about $5,000 American just to show up, and then I also won the race. Once I ran some more good track races as well, I would get appearance fees anywhere from $800 American up to 5,000 bucks just to show up on the starting line. During my peak years as an athlete there was a lot of attention at that time on middle-distance runners. The mile was a really big event in Europe, and I raced a lot, so I made some good money and got some good sponsorship. I used to work in a running store and as a part-time waitress; I appreciated what I was making.

I won gold in the 3,000 and bronze in the 1,500 at the 1986 Commonwealth Games, and in 1989 I finished third at the world cross-country championships. That is my most memorable athletic moment, even greater than my Olympic medal, and probably the one I'm most proud of. Cross-country running is probably the most well-respected discipline among world-class distance runners. There's not much recognition for it here, but there is in Europe, where it's like the Olympics of middle-distance running.

There was also another Olympics for me, in 1988, but the Ben Johnson scandal and everything else touching on drugs diminished the whole experience. It was just awful to have such a negative force, like a cloud, placed over the Games for everybody. I still appreciate all the things the Olympic movement embodies. It has not tarnished my view of what it means to be an Olympic athlete.

Tony Zasada (left, with Regina Rowing Club teammate Rob Currie) became the first Saskatchewan rower to reach the Olympics, finishing fifth in the coxed pair at the 1984 Summer Games in Los Angeles. Zasada took up the sport in 1977 at the age of 16 and started accumulating prestigious honours in various events within three years. He started with two gold medals in 1980 and three in '81 at the North West International Rowing Association championships, recorded victories at the 1981 and '82 Royal Canadian Henley Regattas and was part of the men's eight that took bronze at the 1983 Pan-American Games in Caracas. It was a tremendous record in a sport that requires many years of experience, but Zasada was denied the opportunity to achieve his potential. On August 19, 1984, only a few weeks after returning from Los Angeles, he was killed by an impaired driver in a head-on automobile collision at the age of 23.

BRAD HORNUNG: LOOKING UP

YOU'RE NOT GOING TO SEE THINGS EYE-TO-EYE with Brad Hornung, not in the physical sense. He's in that wheelchair, you're standing up, and he's all right with that even if you're uncomfortable. He knows you're uncomfortable.

Maybe that's why he has that bumper sticker on the bottom of his chair, away from the eye contact people tend to avoid:

MY OTHER VEHICLE IS A ZAMBONI.

It's okay, you can laugh. A Zamboni is used to clean the ice; Hornung uses this to break the ice.

"You try to use humour to make people feel comfortable," says Hornung, 36 years old and 18 years removed from the accident that left him a quadriplegic. "You just try to be friendly because it's hard for people who have never been around people in wheelchairs. They're scared to say the wrong things.

"The best ones are kids because they'll ask anything. That's really good. They'll come up and push on my head cushion and say, 'What's that?' An adult will never do that. The kids do. You tell them, and they say, 'Okay.' Meanwhile, the parent's going, 'Don't ask.'

"There are a lot of things to laugh about—like people who talk to you very loudly as if being in a wheelchair means you're deaf. That happens a lot."

Brad Hornung could tell you how he gets a good sideline view of Roughriders games from the wheelchair section of Taylor Field. He can talk about politics or current events or, as he did in the summer of 2004, joining the ranks of the unemployed when the Chicago Blackhawks dismissed their whole scouting staff, him included.

"My contract ran out on June 30. Maybe another team will hire me but not until the NHL sorts out its labour situation. Ah, it's part of the job. Happens to everybody."

What happened to Brad Hornung on March 1, 1987, shouldn't happen to anybody. But it does. And to a great many people, the image of Brad Hornung is still the one they saw from their seats in the Agridome or on the front sports page of the next day's *Leader-Post:* prone, immobile, unconscious, his upper body obscured by the careful ministrations of doctors, trainers and the crews of first aid and ambulance attendants methodically going about the grim business of saving his life.

Brad Hornung, January 1986

It was a Western Hockey League game between the Moose Jaw Warriors and the Regina Pats. Seven minutes into the second period Hornung, in his second year with the Pats, charged towards the Warriors goal with teammate Craig Endean on his left side and Moose Jaw captain Troy Edwards trying to force Hornung away from the net. Hornung dished the puck to Endean.

Gregg Drinnan, then Assistant Sports Editor of the *Leader-Post,* gave a dispassionate description of the moment that changed Brad Hornung's life:

As Hornung sped across the goal line, about to cut behind the net, Edwards—with the shaft of his stick—gave him a push in the small of his back. It was not a vicious manoeuvre by any stretch of the imagination . . . it's the kind of play that hasn't been (penalized) for a while now.

It's the type of play that Edwards does a hundred times a season. It's something that Brad Hornung has done to one opponent or another on numerous occasions. The way the game is played today, this type of thing is incidental contact. It's an accepted part of the game.

Jostled in that vulnerable microsecond of weight shift, Hornung tumbled head-first, face-down, into the boards. Everyone in the rink knew instantly by the impact and Hornung's total lack of movement that the situation was serious. Pats co-owner Bill Hicke was seated in a private box far above and away from the play. He had seen Lou Fontinato break his neck when the two were teammates on the Montreal Canadiens in 1962.

"I knew Brad was hurt," Hicke recalls. "I had no doubt that Edwards was not trying to injure him; it was just something that they now allow. I was never hit from behind in 16 years of playing pro hockey, but the game changed. I left the box and got to the ice as fast as I could. When I got there, the doctors had already done a tracheotomy."

Hornung had swallowed his tongue. He had not stopped breathing, but Dr. Rameo Rojas, recognizing the probability of paralysis, slit Hornung's trachea to insert a breathing tube—a decision that almost certainly saved Hornung's life, which hung in the balance before thousands of shocked spectators and thousands more listening on the radio. Hornung was given heart massage on the ice. The teams went to their dressing rooms. Edwards broke down in the Warriors' room. Forty minutes passed before Hornung was stabilized, immobilized and put in an ambulance.

"I can't recall much of it," Hornung says now. "The next morning Dr. (Chris) Ekong explained what happened and what the situation was. It's hard for me to put this, but I kinda knew what he was saying and seemed to take it in stride. Maybe it was the medications. Maybe it was because I woke up on the respirator and with the halo on my head. I had seen a

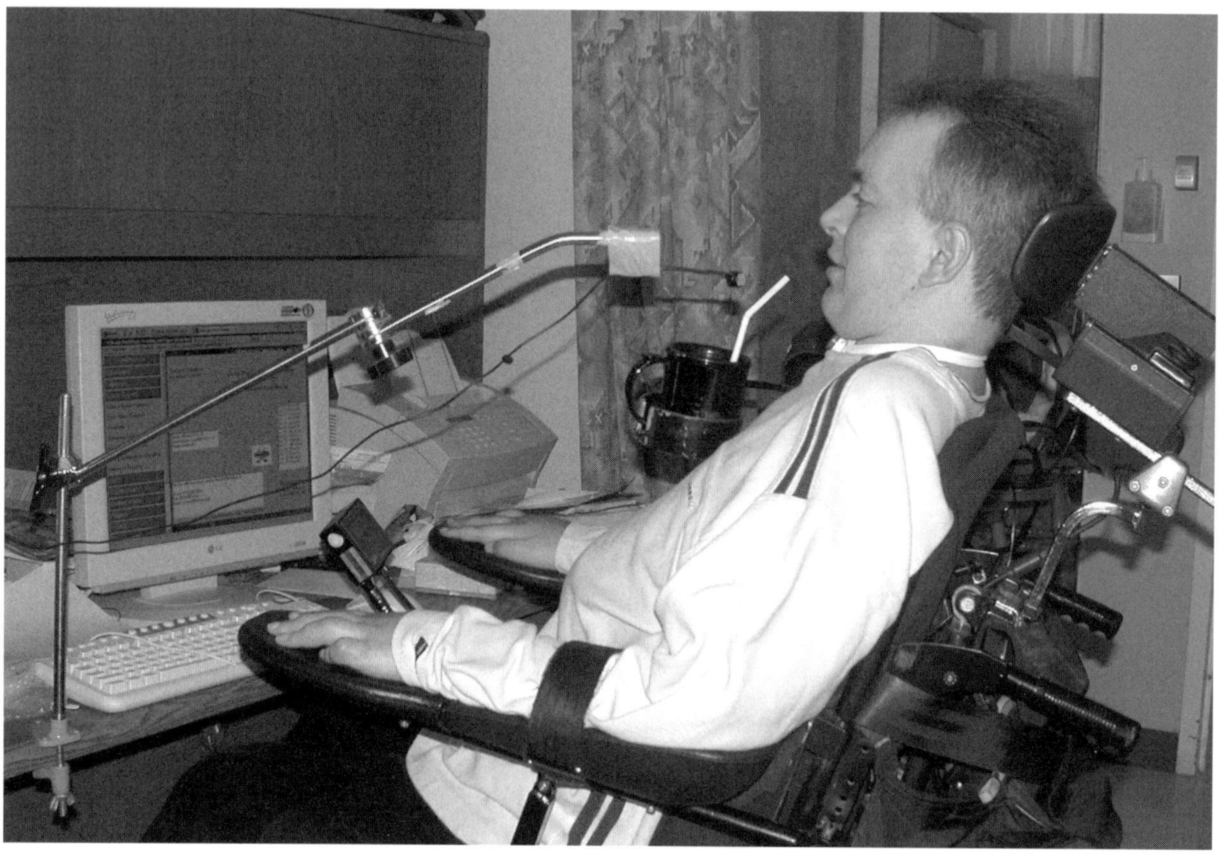

Brad Hornung at work on his voice-activated computer

halo before in a *Sports Illustrated* article about Darryl Stingley. I just don't remember being shocked when they told me that I was paralyzed."

At a media conference on March 3, Dr. Ekong announced that Hornung had suffered the same fate as Stingley, a New England Patriots wide receiver whose neck had been broken in an NFL game. Hornung was paralyzed for life from a burst fracture of the third cervical vertebrae and a crushed spinal cord. He would never walk again, never skate again, never play major-league hockey as his father, Larry, had in the NHL and WHA.

"Brad was too young to be actually graded because he wasn't draftable yet," says Lorne Davis, then and now an Edmonton Oilers scout, "but he had a great chance of making it to the NHL by what I saw of him.

"The only thing he lacked (at 5-foot-10, 175 pounds) was a bit of size and strength, but at 18 you have time to work that out. He definitely had the tools, no doubt about that."

Hornung had 17 goals and 35 points as a rookie and had improved to 32 goals and 66 points in 61 games. Growing taller and more robust was reasonable, given that his father was a 6-foot, 190-pound defenceman. Born in Weyburn, Larry Hornung had played junior in Flin Flon, Moose Jaw and Weyburn, spent 48 games with the NHL's St. Louis Blues, and laboured six seasons in the WHA, mostly with the Winnipeg Jets.

"I had known Larry since we had worked at Billy Lesuk's hockey school out at Fort Qu'Appelle in the '70s," Davis says. "Larry and Billy had been teammates on the Jets. Larry was one of the nicest individuals you could ever meet and respected by everybody. He had been through his own hell. He was an alcoholic, recovered from that a few years after his playing career ended, and then worked with alcoholics to help them recover.

"We were both scouts, and there's a certain closeness among scouts. Larry was at the game when Brad was injured; I'm sure it affected him greatly, but he showed no weakness whatsoever. Neither did Terry, Brad's mother. They handled it so well, I just couldn't believe it."

Father, mother, sister and grandfather all stood toe-to-toe with the emotional agony for Brad's sake.

"They did everything they could to make my life

Terry Simpson

The Prince Albert Raiders won the 1985 Memorial Cup under the guidance of head coach Terry Simpson in only their third WHL season.

Playmaking centre Dan Hodgson had 13 assists in five games at the Memorial Cup tournament that the Raiders completed with a 6–1 whipping of the Shawinigan Cataractes. Hodgson collected 119 and 112 assists respectively in his last two junior seasons.

Prince Albert moved up to the Tier 1 ranks in 1982 after winning seven straight Saskatchewan Junior Hockey League championships. Simpson and the Raiders earned the Centennial Cup as national Tier 2 champions in four of those seven seasons.

the most that it can be," Brad says. "Dad wrote letters to every rehab outfit across North America to get the best info available. There was never a feeling of, 'Oh, you're going to spend the rest of your life in bed watching TV.' There were computers. I could get a van with a lift and travel. It was something to look forward to."

Hornung corrected two mistakes that were made in the wake of his accident. First, Edwards, wracked with guilt, was about to quit hockey. He had read of a football player (perhaps Stingley) who wondered why the man who paralyzed him never took the trouble to contact him afterwards. Edwards was determined to at least extend that courtesy to Hornung. Edwards contacted Pats head coach Doug Sauter, who arranged a brief meeting in Hornung's hospital room on March 5. "Keep playing; don't quit," Hornung told Edwards. If it was forgiveness Edwards needed, he could have it; but with no malice on Edwards' part, Hornung considered forgiveness unnecessary. Edwards returned to the Warriors, finished the season, and played a bit of minor pro hockey before returning to his home town of Raymore to settle down, make a living and play some senior hockey. Sadly, many spectators in out-of-town rinks treated him with a vicious contempt that counterbalanced Hornung's rational compassion.

Larry Hornung

The second mistake was a professional one. Dr. Ekong's prognosis included the pronouncement that Hornung "will never breathe on his own." That would have virtually chained him for life to a respirator, the one aspect of his fate that Hornung detested.

"There was a short period where I didn't know if I was going to be able to get rid of the respirator," he says. "That's what I worked for. My diaphragm wouldn't move well on its own, and I had to teach myself to breathe again. It took some exercise, but after a while my breathing came back."

Hornung completed his high school education in his new home at the Wascana Rehabilitation Centre through two correspondence courses he took with a tutor. Then he enrolled at the University of Regina in English 100, a mandatory class for all students and notoriously difficult for most.

"My final mark was something in the 60s, my worst ever. It wasn't discouraging at all. My goal was just to leave my room, be on campus, get out in the fresh air, be around people. It was a success. I kept at it."

It took nearly seven years to earn his Bachelor's degree in History, a major he selected simply to satisfy his interest. Hornung continued his studies at the University of Regina in Administration, completing two years of courses and then putting in a work term with the Blackhawks for two semesters that spanned the 2000–01 NHL season.

"It was media analysis. Every morning I'd receive all of the day's NHL news on my computer and break it down into different categories: injuries, healthy scratches, unhappy players, those sorts of things, information that might be useful if the team is considering picking up a player on waivers or in a trade.

"I was hoping to break into scouting. I'd been interested in it for a long time. I'd talked with my father and asked him a lot about it, about what you look for in this guy and that guy and how that plays into the draft."

Larry Hornung died of cancer May 8, 2001, only 55 years old. His was not an easy life, but he had faced its difficulties with strength and dignity. Those characteristics, more than his hockey skills, were the qualities passed down from father to son. Brad Hornung soon became a full-time member of the Blackhawks' scouting staff. He correlated all reports from the network of junior scouts, managed the data entry and scouted WHL games at the Agridome, watching from the concourse at the same end of the rink where his playing career ended in 1987, no demons haunting him, no longer isolated, part of a team effort again after more than a decade of pursuing an education for his own sake.

"The thing is, anybody that Brad has had anything to do with, or has touched, has just thought the world

Hornung back in the Agridome, scouting a WHL game during the 2003–04 season

of him," Davis says. "One of the best conversations I had with him is after his dad died. He handled that just the way Larry handled Brad's accident, with a quiet strength and courage.

"It's amazing how happy he is all the time; he never seems depressed whatsoever. Brad's easy to talk to."

Just don't shout at him. The guy's not deaf, you know.

RUEBEN MAYES: A SMALL-TOWN GUY WITH BIG AMBITION

Rueben Mayes took North Battleford with him to New Orleans and keeps it with him in Pullman, Washington.

"A small-town environment gave me a good perspective on things," Mayes says. "You have a chance to think, see what's real effective and what the consequences of your actions will be, and not get caught up in the hype of things. It also helps me find people who give me wisdom and good advice on things I don't know about.

"Being raised in a small town you meet people, older people whom you respect, and you learn to listen to and learn from. I'm very much someone like that. I always like to learn new things."

One of the first things young Rueben learned was that he had inherited some athleticism, particularly running ability.

"My father played baseball and hockey. He was a natural athlete but never at a very competitive level because of his work; he owned an auto repair shop. My mom ran some track when she was young, I think middle distance. I didn't talk about my long-term goals with my parents, but they were always supportive of my sports endeavours."

Mayes showed exceptional promise at North Battleford Comprehensive High School as both a football player and a sprinter. In fact, he still holds the provincial indoor records for the juvenile and junior 50-metre dash at 6.12 and 5.87 seconds respectively. He was the Saskatchewan high school champion at

Rueben Mayes with Washington State

100 metres in 1981 (10.8 seconds, hand-timed) and the 110-metre hurdles and the 100 metres in 1982 (14.42 and 10.87 respectively, electronic).

Canada's national track team beckoned, but Mayes was more interested in football, preferably at an American university. Don Hodgins, his coach on the North Battleford Vikings, sent a videotape of Mayes' football highlights to Hugh Campbell, then at the height of his glory as head coach of the Edmonton Eskimos dynasty.

"Hugh Campbell sent the film to Jim Walden, who was head coach at Washington State, and his staff liked what they saw," Mayes says. "They had filled up all their scholarships at WSU, but then a kid who had committed pulled out. They flew me down and offered me a full scholarship."

Mayes' first two years at Washington State were undistinguished. It would take a lot of improvement to become a starter, let alone a star.

"I think it was just a matter of taking a whole lot of reps (repetitions in practice). Don Hodgins was a great coach, but the American kids have a lot more access to a higher level of competition in high school. When I came to WSU, I was pretty raw. I was very fast and instinctive, but I had to learn a lot about football. It took me awhile to learn about blocking and a greater understanding of the game. I had a real good freshman year. Then as a sophomore I wasn't as focused; I got hurt and only played in six games. When I came back the next fall I was much more focused, back on track on my goal of being an NFL player. The combination of working hard, getting focused and the repetitions worked itself out.

"I never thought I had set my sights too high, not really. I didn't think my time was running out. I just had to work hard, and then it happened."

"It" was the month of October 1984. Mayes was the Cougars' starting tailback beside Calgary-born quarterback Mark Rypien. Washington State was losing a Pacific-10 conference game October 20 at Stanford, trailing 28–7 at halftime and 42–14 10 minutes into the third quarter, when Mayes and Rypien engineered the biggest comeback in Cougar history. Five unanswered touchdowns gave WSU an astonishing 49–42 victory. Mayes had four second-half majors, one on a 53-yard run and another on a 53-yard pass reception. One week later at Oregon, Mayes ran through the Ducks for 357 yards, an NCAA single-game record. His 573 yards in consecutive games was another record (both since broken). Mayes finished the year with 1,632 yards and added 1,236 in 1985 to complete his Washington State playing days with 3,519 yards. He still holds the Cougars' single-game, single-season and career rushing records, no small achievement at a school whose alumni include George Reed.

Still, it wasn't enough to make a satisfactory impression on NFL scouts. Two rounds of the 1986 draft concluded without Mayes' name being called. Auburn's ultra-talented Bo Jackson had been selected first overall, but Mayes didn't consider himself inferior to the other 10 running backs—Keith Byars, John L. Williams, Ronnie Harmon, Reggie Dupard, Neal Anderson, Garry James, Dalton Hilliard, Darryl Clack, Anthony Toney and Kenneth Davis—chosen ahead of him. Nor was he interested that the

Saskatchewan Roughriders had made him the second overall pick in the CFL draft.

"The CFL didn't appeal to me because I wanted to see how I would do against the best of the best. Yeah, I was kind of disappointed on (NFL) Draft Day. I remember telling Marie, who was my girlfriend and is now my wife, that if they don't respect me enough to draft me higher I'm just going to go to law school and be a lawyer. Right after I said that I got a phone call from New Orleans; they had drafted me in the third round. I said, 'Okay, I'm going to give it my best shot.' "

New Orleans didn't have an incumbent halfback, but the job was hardly Mayes' to take. Hilliard was the heir apparent. He was a second-round draft choice, taken 31st overall to Mayes' 57th, and was something of a home-town favourite as a product of Louisiana State University.

"Yeah, Dalton Hilliard was ahead of me, but I came in saying that if I'm going to be here I'm going to play, I'm going to start. Jim Mora (Sr.) had just become the Saints' head coach, and we had a difficult camp in Hammond, Louisiana: hot, humid and very rigorous. I have a genetic defect with my Achilles tendons; they're pretty small, and they bothered me all through college. In training camp they began to get sore, and I had to sit out a couple of games.

"I was very frustrated and upset when I realized that I had to rest my legs, but coach Mora assured me that things were going well, that I'd had a good training camp. I was able to work myself into the lineup. In the first three regular-season games I just got in for a couple of plays here and there. I was very anxious to get out there and produce, but I had to focus on working hard, waiting for my opportunity and trying to make the most of it. That's kind of how I always operated anyway."

Mayes was promoted to the starting lineup in the Saints' fourth game. He showed that he could not only gain yardage but carry a heavy workload, too. His best games reflected that: 24 carries for 172 yards against Tampa Bay; 33 for 157 against New England; 28 for 203 against Miami. At season's end, despite his inactivity in the first three of New Orleans' 16 games, Mayes had piled up 1,353 yards on 286 carries. He was the unanimous choice for Rookie of the Year, made the NFC second all-star team and went to the Pro Bowl.

His rookie season would also be Mayes' high point as

Rueben Mayes

a professional. He lost one game to a players' strike and three to injury in 1987, managed 917 yards on 243 carries, and helped the Saints to a 12–3 record that put them in the playoffs for the first time in their 21-year history.

"I had a knee injury, and that slowed me up. Running back is a very punishing position, especially in the NFL. My body wasn't as durable as I would have liked it to be, but I got the most out of my body!"

Between the knee and his chronic Achilles problems, Mayes was condemned to a steady decline. He slipped to 628 yards in 1988, sat out the entire 1989 campaign, gained 510 yards in 1990, and missed another full season in 1991. Mayes tried to come back with the Seattle Seahawks but ran with the ball just 28 times in 1992 and only once in one game in 1993, when he retired at the age of 30.

Mayes' return to the West Coast afforded him the opportunity to return to Washington State in Pullman and earn a Masters of Business Administration Degree. After seven years of successful fundraising for WSU, he moved to Seattle in March 2004 to become Assistant Dean of External Relations for the University of Washington's School of Business. Within five months, Washington State had lured him back to be director of development of its Office of Undergraduate Education.

Evidently, the high points of Rueben Mayes' second career are still to come.

SWIFT CURRENT BRONCOS: DISASTER, RENEWAL AND SCANDAL

By Saskatchewan standards, the weather in Swift Current barely qualified as blustery on the afternoon of Tuesday, December 30, 1986. The temperature was near 0° Celsius with a 55-kilometre wind and just a light dusting of snow when the Broncos bus left the Centennial Civic Arena shortly after 3:30 P.M. for a Western Hockey League game in Regina against the Pats. Those conditions, however, created a deadly road hazard familiar to prairie drivers: "black ice," a transparent sheen that usually isn't discovered until a vehicle lights upon it.

Only four kilometres east of Swift Current the bus, about to negotiate a long gentle curve, reached the newly formed invisible hazard and skidded sideways to the right. It slid off the highway shoulder and into the ditch. With luck, it would have ground or rolled to an eventual halt, but this was no one's lucky day. Suddenly, the ditch ended. The bus struck an approach—a side road—and toppled on its right side. All the occupants remained inside the bus except for four players who occupied the seats that faced each other at the very back of the bus's right side. The window beside that seat burst open.

Four young men on their way to the hockey game were killed instantly. Trent Kresse, 20, was engaged to be married. He was tied for seventh in the WHL scoring race with 56 points. Scott Kruger, 19, was the man tied with Kresse. He had registered 106 points the previous season for the Prince Albert Raiders despite being only 5-foot-5 and 135 pounds. Scott was the older brother of Trevor Kruger, one of the Broncos' goaltenders. Chris Mantyka, 19, was Swift Current's enforcer or, as he considered himself, his teammates' protector. A season ago, before Swift Current returned to the Tier 1 ranks, Mantyka set an SJHL record with 502 penalty minutes. Brent Ruff, 16, was a rookie intent on following in the NHL footsteps of his older brother, Lindy.

"The incredible thing about it is that there were 25 people in the bus and none of the others had serious injuries," says John Rittinger, then the Broncos' governor. "The rest suffered things like separated shoulders and cuts and bruises. No one was hospitalized more than a day.

"It was just a few minutes until I heard about it. All of them were already at the hospital when I got there. Someone in authority handed me a list of players and told me that four were killed and whoever they were, they weren't on that list. They asked me who was missing, and I was so much in shock myself that I couldn't figure it out even though Mantyka was living with me.

"If it was members of your own family, it couldn't have been worse. Our team was unique in that respect because the city is so small (about 16,000 residents); P.A.'s (39,000) and Moose Jaw's (35,000) teams might be as close to their communities, but it's doubtful. In a city this small, the players knew a lot of people and were close to them. There was no animosity towards the bus driver, Mr. Archibald. The players all called him Archie. They laid no blame at all on him and unanimously wanted him to stay as their driver."

Three days later a memorial service was held at the Civic Centennial Arena.

"It was without a doubt one of toughest experiences I ever had," recalls Ed Chynoweth, then president of the WHL and now president of the Kootenay Ice. "There were 4,000 people at the rink. All the

Trent Kresse

Scott Kruger

Chris Mantyka

Brent Ruff

Broncos captain Kurt Lackten and John Rittinger at the memorial service

players from the Eastern Conference were there, wearing their sweaters over shirts and ties. My son Dean was playing in Medicine Hat at the time, and you couldn't help but ask, "What if it had been him?"

"Looking down at the families, seeing all the players in their sweaters, it was a traumatic experience, but also very moving. We get over it; you wonder if the parents ever do."

The Broncos requested and were granted a three-game hiatus from their schedule.

"Our first game back was in Moose Jaw," Rittinger recalls, "and we informed the Warriors we wanted them to play like it was any regular-season game; don't pussyfoot around with us. And they took us at our word. Theo Fleury, he slashed Peter Soberlak across the back of the knees, just wicked."

(Rittinger acknowledges that this probably was Fleury's way of fulfilling Swift Current's request. Fleury dished out and received so many hacks in the WHL that for him *not* to slash someone would have been a dead giveaway that he was taking it easy on the Broncos.)

"It's hard to say how long the accident affected the city," Rittinger says. "Some individuals were very distraught, but it picked up quickly because the fans felt obliged to support the players. It was important to pick ourselves off the floor. We had been in the WHL until 1974, when the franchise moved to Lethbridge. As it turned out, we got the same franchise back when we re-entered the league in the summer of 1986, but the team we got wasn't very good.

"Some players wouldn't even report here. Who wants to go live in a little place like Swift Current? That's how we got Sheldon Kennedy, in a trade for

Joe Sakic

one of those guys who wouldn't come here. So it wasn't an expansion team we started with but it wasn't much better."

Kennedy courageously revealed himself in 1996 to be the victim of molestation at the hands of Broncos head coach Graham James, thus bringing to light one of Canada's most appalling scandals and well-kept secrets. Back in the '80s, however, all the general public knew was that Kennedy was a gritty, high-scoring right wing and that James was an outstanding, if somewhat eccentric, coach—highly literate, extremely quotable, temperamental and unpredictable. His most outrageous stunt came one night in Swift Current when a succession of Broncos penalties and Medicine Hat power-play goals in the third period turned a runaway victory into an imminent defeat. Outraged at the referee, James threw his tie, shoes, jacket and shirt on the ice before stomping off to the dressing room, his Santa-esque belly jiggling all the way.

When he focused his mind on hockey, James could be brilliant, especially with the talent he had at his disposal. Foremost among the Broncos was Joe Sakic, who recorded 133 and 160 points in his two major junior seasons. Appropriately, he shared the scoring championship his second season with Fleury while fans in two of junior hockey's smallest cities thrilled to one of the most exciting one-on-one rivalries ever presented.

Sakic was an NHL rookie with the Quebec Nordiques by 1988–89, but even without him James made the Broncos an awesome offensive force with a power play that averaged a ludicrous 2½ goals a game. Of the 447 goals they scored in 72 games, 180 came with a man advantage. Swift Current's 111 points were 25 more than any other team in the WHL. The Broncos swept all three of their playoff series in four straight games, outscoring their opponents 83–37.

As Tim Tisdale relates (see *In His Own Words*, p. 284), the Broncos were nearly denied the Memorial Cup by the host Saskatoon Blades. Swift Current defeated the Peterborough Petes 6–4 and the Laval Titan 3–2 in the round robin before falling 5–4 to Saskatoon. Goal differential put the Blades in the national final while the Broncos had to beat Peterborough again, 6–2, in the semi-final.

True, the prospect of a Memorial Cup 28 months after the deadly bus crash made Swift Current sentimental favourites. At the same time, the Blades were overdue for Destiny to smile their way, having never won a WHL title or the Memorial Cup.

Saskatoon held a 3–2 lead after 40 minutes. Kimbi Daniels' third-period tally forced overtime, and Tisdale netted the winner at 3:25 of sudden-death overtime.

Swift Current, the smallest city in Canada with a major junior hockey team, the city that had absorbed the worst disaster in the history of Canadian hockey, had won the Memorial Cup. It was no longer a place that junior players avoided.

"Thanks to the Memorial Cup and our alumni network, it's the opposite," Rittinger says. "It's a good place to play hockey. There's no big-city atmosphere. You get to know all the people, it's easy to visit with

Sheldon Kennedy buzzes the Seattle Thunderbirds' net; the clover above his number 12 bears the numbers of the four Broncos who perished in 1986

the rest of the players, there's no problem getting to the rink, and there's a good education system.

"But initially, it was: 'Swift Current! Why would you want to go there?' Now, when Dan Lambert or Joe Sakic tells you this is the place to play hockey, it's okay."

Swift Current is also the place where no Bronco wears the number 8, 9, 11 or 22 in respect of the memory of Trent Kresse, Scott Kruger, Brent Ruff and Chris Mantyka. Since 1987, the WHL has also commemorated the quartet by awarding its most valuable player the Four Broncos Memorial Trophy.

That remains the visible legacy of the Broncos of the 1980s. The invisible legacy is that left by Graham James. Even though he was coaching in Calgary when he was arrested, Swift Current was the focal point of his pedophilia.

"Graham James was an unbelievable coach; this is my professional opinion," Rittinger says. "I can't say enough about his ability as a coach and in putting that team together.

"It's sad because he's a very intelligent man and was well-liked. That huge flaw in his makeup deprived a lot of people of his talent."

TIM TISDALE: IN HIS OWN WORDS

Fate decreed that Tim Tisdale, who was born in Shaunavon but moved to Swift Current as an infant, would be closest to the signature events of the Swift Current Broncos' history. As a rookie, he was physically closest to the four players who were killed when the team bus crashed on December 30, 1986. In his last junior hockey game on May 13, 1989, he scored the winning goal in overtime as the Broncos won the Memorial Cup.

WEATHER CONDITIONS WEREN'T GREAT. IT WAS snowing, but we didn't think much about it. We went around the corner, and we could tell the bus wasn't going to make it. Everyone sort of grabbed on. The bus went in the ditch, we all bounced, and I guess everyone thought, "Okay, we're in the ditch, we're fine." Then the bus hit the approach, still going at a pretty good speed. Unfortunately, those windows seemed to pop out, and the bus landed on those four guys. I was sitting right in front of them. I looked behind and didn't see anything. Because of that, I felt maybe they'd been thrown from the bus. The last place I thought they'd be is underneath it.

It took a little while for us to realize what had happened. They did a good job getting everybody off the bus as quickly as they could. We were all a little shocked, a little dazed. People passing by stopped immediately; we piled into vehicles and went to hospital as quick as we could. We never had a chance to stand outside and survey what was going on. That was probably for the best; I don't think any of us needed to see that.

Tim Tisdale

Once we got to the hospital and realized there were guys missing, then it started to sink in. It was pretty quiet. We knew they weren't just injured because there was no panic in the hospital; the doctors were mostly standing around. My first reaction was to phone home and tell my parents I'm okay. We tried to get as many guys as we could to do that right away. We knew the story would get out very quickly.

I had an extra burden to deal with because on most of our bus trips I was in those seats, where the guys play cards. For whatever reason, I was late that day, which was very out of character for me. I'm usually very punctual. Whether it was fate or destiny, I don't know, but for some reason I wasn't in that location on the bus. For a long time, I had a feeling of guilt, that it should have been me.

If this accident had happened now, there would have been grief counsellors, people to help you deal with it. Back then, that was unheard of. We handled it our own ways. You had to deal with it yourself or it was going to tear you apart. I'm not saying it was extreme guilt, but it was always there: Why? It was a long time before I even discussed it with my parents. Finally, I used it as motivation, that I was given a second opportunity, a second chance, although I'll never know a reason why.

I never slept on a bus again, not a wink, until I was a pro in the minors. I don't think anyone else on the Broncos had my problem. It's not something we talked about. I just couldn't get comfortable or relaxed enough to fall asleep, which can make things difficult when you travelled the distances we did.

Everyone was wondering how to react. We were all just teenagers. You don't know how to do something; it might be perceived as inappropriate. We had a team meeting the next day, and Gord Green took charge. He stood up in front of everybody and said we had to go on. There was no issue of whether we were going to play or not. We owed it to them, but we owed it to ourselves, too, to go out and perform.

Our first game back, we got a tremendous reception from the Moose Jaw fans and all the people from Swift Current who were there. That's when it kicked in that we wouldn't be forgetting anybody, that this is what we all wanted, this is what they would have wanted. It was positive, so loud, standing ovations from the warm-ups on. I'd never seen that many people in a building just to watch the warm-ups. It's a loud building to begin with, and the atmosphere that night felt like everyone was behind us. I couldn't even tell you how the game ended; it really was irrelevant. The fact that we were playing was all that mattered.

Graham James

We made the playoffs, which was remarkable. It's tough to say that individuals received advantages from what happened, but it was a natural consequence: some guys got playing time who weren't getting it before, and they responded in a positive way. Teenagers generally take stuff for granted, and we were the same way before the crash. Afterwards, we didn't take anything for granted on or off the ice. A special bond formed. Other guys will never have an opportunity to know what that's like . . . well, at least I hope they never will.

So we made the playoffs in '87, and we were a better team in '87–88. Then in 1988–89 we ran away with first place. Yeah, we had a killer power play. We had probably the three most offensive-minded defencemen that I've ever seen play junior hockey at one time—Dan Lambert, Darren Kruger and Bob Wilkie—and I've seen some good ones. All three of them could quarterback the power play. Also, we had so much skill that you had to compete for ice time. On most teams, the power play is set; no matter how bad it is, the same guys are out the next time. We had three lines who could work the power play at any time, and if you didn't perform, you weren't going to get on the ice. The key to our success was that sometimes we competed with ourselves more than we competed against our opponents.

I know we only lost two games at home because we heard about them both times. They stick out in my mind because we were skated so hard the next day. Graham James was demanding; when we didn't play well, there was a punishment. He hated to lose, and that rubbed off on the players.

The bus crash was a source of motivation but one that was definitely unspoken. There really weren't a lot of us left from the bus crash (Lambert, Wilkie, goalie Trevor Kruger, and forwards Tisdale, Peter Soberlak and Sheldon Kennedy). There were a lot of nights when it was fresh in my mind, that I wanted to win for that reason. But we didn't want it to be a rallying point for our team.

When we swept the WHL playoffs in 12 straight games, we were all concerned about overconfidence. You know you're going to lose a game at some stage, and probably the best thing for us was dropping one in the Memorial Cup round robin. The winning streak was off our minds, then. But Saskatoon was the host city, and the Blades were the last team we wanted to play. We had swept them, and quite easily, in the playoffs, but they had the crowd behind them, and they had a month to prepare just for us. I don't think they even bothered worrying about how they'd match up against the other two teams (Peterborough and Laval). I think their focus was totally on how they were going to beat Swift Current. I actually lived with Mike Greenlay, the Blades goalie, when we were teammates in Cape Breton the next season, and he confirmed that was so.

We were nervous for the final game, absolutely. That was the one time I actually heard someone publicly say, "Let's do it for those guys." It was said in the media, and it was said in the dressing room, by whom I don't remember. I didn't say anything, but I thought it was inappropriate, especially when there are two brothers (Darren and Trevor Kruger) of one of the victims sitting in the dressing room. That was a memory we shouldn't be throwing back at them, especially when Trevor is the starting goalie. Plus, it made some of our younger guys think there was more to this than just a hockey game; it put a lot of pressure on them.

I've never sat down and watched the game to this day. Why, I'm not sure; maybe I'm afraid the outcome will be different. I know some people that make it an annual thing. The one thing that sticks in my mind is I made a terrible giveaway in the second period that cost us a goal. Going into overtime, in the dressing room, I felt we had had the game in control until I committed that mistake, and I needed to step up and do something about it.

We were pretty poor the first little bit of OT. Trevor stepped up and made a couple of big saves. Finally, we got it out of our end. I think it was my first shift. We got the puck in deep and forced a turnover, then dominated the puck for 30 or 35 seconds. Wilkie carried it in from blue line to the icing line and passed back to Darren Kruger, which you don't see a lot of, one defenceman dropping the puck back to the other. Our team was offence first; I don't recall defence ever being a major concern of ours. I got cross-checked from behind into Greenlay; I was just getting up, and I saw Darren walking in to the top of circle. We made eye contact. He threw it at the net. I just got a stick on it, and it went inside the post. I saw a video replay later; if I had missed it, Brian Sakic was right behind me, and he would have had the opportunity.

I don't remember much after that point. You're just excited. It definitely is something unique. At that point, we were dead tired. Everyone thinks the celebration lasted forever; we got on the bus, and most of the guys slept all the way home. I didn't. We were just totally drained and exhausted from the whole thing by then.

April 9, 1986: The Moose Jaw Warriors and Regina Pats must play the last game of a round-robin WHL playoff series even though Regina is mathematically eliminated. When Moose Jaw's Theoren Fleury gets a second-period breakaway, he tucks his stick between his legs and flips the puck over Pats goalie Stacy Nickel for his second of three goals. OLE! Moose Jaw wins 9–5.

ON GUARD: ROGER ALDAG IN HIS OWN WORDS

I WAS BORN AND RAISED ON A FARM SOUTH OF GULL Lake. I have a brother, Barry, who also played with the Roughriders, and two sisters, Linda and Doreen. We went to a country school called Aldag School. Aldag was the name of the district; it had nothing to do with our family. It was three miles from our farm, and we basically rode our horses in winter or bikes in spring and fall to get there. We had three horses, and I was the baby, so as a young lad I had to share a horse with one of my sisters until one of them reached Grade 7. Then I got to ride my horse myself. The country school went up to Grade 6; then we'd go to the big city of Gull Lake.

My introduction to football was out on the harvest in the old grain truck with a transistor radio, listening to Ron Lancaster march the team down for another touchdown or for a field goal by Jack Abendschan to win another game. We played nine-man football in high school at Gull Lake. To this day they still compete to be No. 1 or No. 2 in the province pretty much all the time. They had some good coaches at that time. Jerry Elmslie had that program going, and everybody seemed to want to play football. We'd get up to 50 people trying out for the team. I don't think we actually cut anybody. We didn't dress everybody, either. But people were certainly willing to come out to every practice.

Gordon Currie

For a line we'd have a centre, two guards and two ends. Then you'd have a quarterback, a tailback, and two slotbacks. This was played on a regulation Canadian field, so there was a lot of room to move, for sure. I played every position but quarterback, even lugged the mail a little bit. I don't know if I was a dominant player, but playing football seemed like a natural thing for me to do, since my brother played football. I was big then, like about 225 pounds in Grade 9, so I guess I'd better play.

I know the reason I drew so much interest was because of my brother. Barry is eight years older than I am, and I did the same as he did: high school in Gull Lake, on to the Regina Rams and then the Roughriders. Barry was pretty much an offensive lineman all the way through for the Rams, even in high school. Back in those years the Roughriders held a high school evaluation camp at their practice field, which used to be the infield of the old horse racing track. In 1972, my last year of high school, the four-day camp was the May long weekend, the same weekend as our graduation. I missed my grad, which I look back on now and kind of regret, but it was the decision I made. The camp had different coaches from universities, Saskatchewan mainly, and the coaches had their contacts in the States. If they thought you had the potential, they looked for a scholarship for you. I had some opportunities for scholarships, but I was one of those guys who fell in love early and ended up staying home and playing with the Rams.

My position was offensive line, but I also played a lot of defence. I don't mean to blow my own horn, but the first two or three games of the year I started at both offensive centre and defensive end, which I thought was pretty neat.

Gordon Currie was the head coach. He was everything you'd want in a coach and more. Gerry Orban was my offensive line coach and one of the best technique coaches I ever had. They teach you technique in high school, but I relied on my size to get me by. When you get to the next level, everybody is pretty much the same strength-wise. That's when technique takes over; If you don't have it, you're going to get beat. That's the biggest thing that Gerry Orban helped me with, polishing my technique, positioning, weight distribution within my stance, not being too aggressive, being aggressive at the right times, the temperament you have to learn.

Gord Currie was my brother's head coach on the Rams for one year. I hardly knew anything about him, but the first time I ever heard him speak, I thought, "My God, he's the kind of football coach I would love to be around." He had everybody's attention. I guess the biggest thing about Gord Currie was

Roger Aldag after winning one of his Mack Truck Awards (no, not the truck itself)

his concern outside the football team; he wanted to make sure he led us down a path of being good citizens. He was a good listener and gave great advice.

We had a great team my first year with the Rams, 1972, and played the Hamilton Hurricanes up in Saskatoon for the Little Grey Cup. We won the national championship two of the next three years. I tore my rib cartilage and broke some ribs in 1973. I missed four or five games, came back for the playoffs and played nose guard. I remember that final game we played in Ottawa at Lansdowne Park. We won the game 9–0. It was quite a thrill because we had two quarterbacks, Lenny Knoll and Bryan Dimen, out with injuries. General Jack Lichtenwald, who was a defensive back, and hurt himself, had to go in at quarterback in the first quarter, and it was quite a deal to win because our chances were pretty slim then. I know the only touchdown we got was a (94-yard) punt return by Bernie Schmidt. It was a defensive game all the way.

I attended three Rider camps as a junior. They said go there for experience, and it was an experience. It was a *different* experience, as far as abuse on my body was concerned. I hung in there for a while, let's put it that way. Still, I learned what it would take to be a professional. It was an eye-opener just to see how these guys worked out hard and stuff like that, and to learn how much stronger I'd have to become.

I still had junior eligibility in 1976, but at that time CFL teams could keep a couple of guys around on a junior protected list, which they did with me. Larry Bird tore up his knee, and I got to start a couple of games at centre until I trashed an ankle and was put in a cast for the rest of the year. We weren't an all-Canadian offensive line by a long shot; in fact, centre was the only Canadian position. The rest of the line were imports: Ralph Galloway, Mike Dirks, Joe Miller and Sam Holt. I didn't worry about American competition that much. My thinking at the time was that you've got an opportunity to play, and you take advantage of your opportunity. It just so happened I hurt myself, and I didn't last very long.

Next year, 1977, I broke my right wrist on a punt cover in the preseason, and I thought, "Well, what a short career this is." I didn't play any more exhibition games, and then they put me in a playing cast and made me the starting left guard when the regular season began. That's why the fingers on my right hand are all buggered; I can move them, but I can't straighten them because of wearing that damn cast all the time. I broke my scaphoid, it's not like I snapped my whole wrist off, but, oh God, it was a pain in the ass. I wore a fibreglass cast for a couple of seasons, and finally I went to the Wascana Hospital and they made me a leather cast.

By 1979, 1980 we had a very young Canadian line with Bob Poley at centre, Neil Quilter and me as the guards and Gerry Hornett at tackle. Then Don Swafford came after Ralph Galloway left. Ron Lancaster was head coach, and it was about the time when he traded Tom Clements to Hamilton that Ron said, "I'll tell you what, I wouldn't stand behind that offensive line, period." Sure, it was a tough thing to hear, but what can you say? It was very true. I wouldn't want to stand back there, either. In my acceptance speech at the Hall of Fame, I thanked Ron Lancaster for sticking with a young offensive line. He did Tom Clements a favour because he would have got killed here. Tom took a pounding.

It's been said over and over about offensive linemen that the only time you develop is when you develop with each other. You've got to trust each other and

Bobby Jurasin (71), the only rookie who ever beat Roger Aldag in training camp drills

develop an understanding of the game, study the film, read defences, that's where all the experience comes. Offensive line is one of the positions where you play as a team.

The biggest factor in my personal success, I think, was a technique of controlled aggression. There were a lot of times I had to be aggressive, probably more so than anybody else because I was smaller, and that's where my timing and being aggressive at the right time helped me out more than anything as far as that actual initial pop of striking people goes. My initial pop was my best physical weapon, something that I had to have to survive.

(Aldag was asked about occasions in training camp when rookie defensive linemen who had dominated their offensive counterparts would get their true test against Aldag. Despite being several inches shorter than all those cocky hotshots, Aldag habitually left them frustrated, humiliated and suddenly educated as to the quality of a real professional football player.)

I don't remember that, probably because I was always focused just on making the team every year. I know (Bobby) Jurasin made the team on account of me, so that's the other side of looking at it. Because he beat my ass—It worked the other way, eh? It was 1986, I'd won my second Mack Truck Award the year before, and that snotnosed little bastard came in here and whipped my ass one-on-one. He gave me a lot of trouble. I always say if he hadn't beaten me, he wouldn't have made the team, ha-ha! I also say the only reason he gave me lots of trouble is because he's the only defensive lineman I ever played that's shorter than me. He got underneath me, eh? He was good, he was good right from the start.

The Mack Truck Award (as outstanding offensive lineman in the CFL) meant a lot to me. It was voted on by the defensive linemen, so of any individual award that's just a reward for an offensive lineman, that is the one that I would say is the best. The awards and honours (four Mack Trucks, twice the league's top offensive lineman, Hall of Fame, number retired) are all nice, but I still have a problem with any individual award. It sounds kind of pig-headed, but you're only as good as the guy you play beside.

I still say my biggest claim to fame as an offensive lineman is that the last touchdown Ron Lancaster ever scored was a quarterback sneak over my ass in Edmonton (in 1978). To me, that was pretty big. It's something I'll never forget. Lancaster's last touchdown; I love that.

THE 1989 ROUGHRIDERS: MORE THAN JUST THE KICK

FRANCE HAD THE REIGN OF TERROR (1793–94), Saskatchewan had the Reign of Error (1977–87). Heads literally rolled in the first, only virtually in the second, though not fast enough to suit the citizens who rebelled against bad management, bad coaching and bad players. For 11 straight seasons, the Roughriders finished no higher than fourth in the CFL's West Division with a cumulative record of 58–117–4. Fan interest didn't dwindle so much as turn sour.

"We constantly heard what a bunch of bums we were," says placekicker Dave Ridgway, who joined the team in 1982. "We heard garbage like, 'Why don't they dress the Rams and use them instead?' Then there was the old joke about somebody leaving four Rider tickets on his windshield for somebody to take; when he got back to his car, there were eight."

Attendance—and consequently, revenue and the team's bank balance—fell until the Roughriders were on the verge of bankruptcy in 1987. That season a successful campaign was held to sell tickets and keep the franchise from folding. Positive change was not limited to financial matters. Former defensive end Bill Baker, a successful executive at IPSCO, became general manager and hired John Gregory as head coach. Baker talked players into accepting pay cuts and, with Director of Player Personnel Dan Rambo, rebuilt the team into a contender. New quarterbacks Tom Burgess and Kent Austin showed promise and spent three years competing for the No. 1 job. Wide receiver Don Narcisse, defensive tackle James Curry, defensive back Albert Brown and Canadian linebacker Dan Rashovich also came on board in 1987. Jeff Fairholm, a non-import slotback, was taken second overall in the 1988 draft. With his speed, Ray Elgaard's up-the-middle power, and Narcisse's command of the sidelines, the quarterbacks had first-rate targets. Calgary was under the direction of a new head coach, Lary Kuharich, and Saskatchewan was happy to pick up certain Stampeders who were suddenly unwanted: former Roughriders Vince Goldsmith (defensive end) and Bob Poley (offensive tackle) plus defensive back Richie Hall. Another 1988 pickup was former Edmonton fullback Milson Jones.

Even in the worst of times, someone like Joey Walters (making a one-handed TD catch in a 1982 game against B.C.) could make a trip to Taylor Field worthwhile

Veterans held over from the Reign of Error included offensive linemen Roger Aldag, Mike Anderson, Bryan Illerbrun, Ken Moore, Vic Stevenson and Mark Urness; halfback Tim McCray; slotback Elgaard; defensive linemen Gary Lewis and Bobby Jurasin; linebackers Eddie Lowe and Dave Albright; and safety Glen Suitor. With the exception of Jurasin, who used quickness and guile to be a formidable pass rusher, and Suitor, there wasn't much reliance on finesse. Elgaard was unique in his physical approach, treating tacklers like a nuisance, divesting himself of them like a horse shaking off flies.

"The whole deal about running with the ball," says Elgaard, "is that you're not supposed to go down unless they make you go down. I'm shocked that it's even an issue of conversation, that everybody doesn't battle for every inch they can get until they're forced to stop. I'm not going to cast aspersions on any players, but I certainly didn't respect people that went down on their own. You do see guys that look for a place to hide; they make their play and then they just want it to end so they don't get hit. I never thought that was cool.

"If I had been 6 feet and 170 pounds, I might have thought differently about it. I was lucky enough to have a physical presence (6-foot-3, 225 pounds) and skills to break some tackles that other guys maybe couldn't, so that's what I did. I also felt that everything—catching the ball, blocking, running a route away from the play—was an important part of the job. If I had an assignment, I was supposed to do it. But the thing I personally enjoyed doing the most was running with the football. If it took three or four guys to tackle me, I recognized that it was good, that these guys were struggling to get me on the ground. I liked that."

Gregory's first season at the helm resulted in another fourth-place finish, but 1988 brought second place, the Roughriders' first playoff berth in 12 years and, to date, their only post-season game at home since 1976. (Too bad they lost it, 42–18, to B.C.) Burgess passed for more than 2,500 yards and Austin for more than 2,000. Elgaard had his best season for yardage with 1,290 yards, and the rookie Fairholm added 833 to create a deadly 1–2 non-import punch at slotback.

Baker left the team to assume the presidency of the CFL. Al Ford succeeded him as general manager and still had Rambo pulling in talent. Two imports moved right in to the starting defence. Linebacker Tuineau Alipate was a native of Tonga who had starred at Saskatchewan's favourite American university pipeline, Washington State. Tackle Chuck Klingbeil was a university teammate of Jurasin at Northern Michigan State who had been unable to latch on to an NFL team (but would later, with the Miami Dolphins). Little attention was paid to a pair of midseason addi-

Don Narcisse (80) would succeed Ray Elgaard (right) as the CFL's all-time leading receiver after Elgaard's retirement

tions on offence, import receiver Mark Guy and non-import running back Brian Walling, because the season was going so badly.

The Roughriders were struggling to win as many as they lost, and when they did win they sure made it difficult. Austin started the opener at home against Calgary, gave way to Burgess, and the Roughriders rallied from a 26–6 fourth-quarter deficit to win 32–29. Burgess started the next nine games, until Austin came off the bench in Toronto to engineer 19 unanswered fourth-quarter points for a 29–24 triumph. Fans gave up the season for lost on September 30 at Taylor Field when the Roughriders gave away a precious victory and third place to the Lions. Saskatchewan had apparently won 30–26 when B.C.'s Mervyn Fernandez stepped out of bounds as time expired. To the astonishment of all, Suitor hammered Fernandez and was flagged for unnecessary roughness to extend the game. A pass into the end zone drew an interference penalty, and Dunigan sneaked in for a touchdown to make the final score 32–30 and drop the Roughriders to 6–7. Not only was B.C. ahead in the standings and riding the momentum of a gift-wrapped win, but Elgaard and Fairholm were out of commission with knee and ankle injuries respectively.

No hope? No problem! Eight days later in Calgary, Austin set a team regular-season record with 492 yards, matching Ron Lancaster's total in the 1963 playoff Miracle of Taylor Field. Austin's improbable prime target, with 194 yards on six receptions, was Rob Bresciani, a product of the Regina Rams and the U of S, who caught four passes for 49 yards in his other 16 games *combined.* Saskatchewan won the game 39–26, split its next two games, and on October 29 prevailed again in Calgary, this time 34–19 as James Ellingson filled the slotback breach with six catches for 106 yards. The Roughriders finished 9–9 and made the playoffs, while the Lions stunk out October and ended up 8–10.

Nevertheless, Saskatchewan was a clear underdog for the Western semi-final in Calgary. Yes, both Austin and Burgess had passed for 2,500 yards, but neither had established real consistency. The team averaged 30 points per game but allowed 31. Saskatchewan's injury list bordered on the ridiculous: Elgaard was still out, Fairholm and Bresciani were on the limp (forcing third-string quarterback Jeff Bentrim into emergency duty as a slotback), and fullback Milson Jones had a broken hand that made him not much more than a blocker. Curry, Albright and Brown were wounded on defence.

The Roughriders had one unexpected intangible factor in their favour, however: fan support. With no television blackout for the playoff game, only 16,286 spectators paid to get into McMahon Stadium, most of them Saskatchewan expatriates keen on witnessing the Roughriders' first post-season game away from Taylor Field since the 1976 Grey Cup.

"It was practically like a home game for us," Ridgway says. "Lary Kuharich was steaming on the sideline! He made an obscene gesture to the fans behind the Stampeders bench, and it wasn't in response to someone saying something like, 'Kuharich, you're a bum.' It was directed to the fact that the whole section behind his bench was cheering for the Riders!"

Saskatchewan held a 23–9 halftime lead but trailed 26–23 late in the fourth quarter with second down at the Calgary 50-yard line. As the Stampeders unleashed a ferocious blitz at Austin, he slipped the ball on a totally unexpected draw play to Walling, who was in the end zone before anyone even realized he was in the lineup. Ridgway added a late field goal to cement the 33–26 upset.

"You want to talk about unheralded people making big contributions," says Bobby Jurasin, "it wasn't just Walling, it was also James Ellingson throwing a block downfield that took out two guys."

That was nice, but the Roughriders had no chance against the Edmonton Eskimos. All you had to do was ask the Edmonton Eskimos, and if you didn't, they'd tell you. Defensive tackle John Mandarich and several defensive backs told reporters their team, a CFL-record 16–2, was so superior that playing the game was essentially a formality.

"There's no reason why we shouldn't blow them out of the water," Mandarich said of the Roughriders.

"They could talk all they wanted," Aldag says. "If they weren't ready, they should have been, because with the team and coaches we had, we were going to go out there and do battle.

"The turning point came when Dave Albright lumbered in for a touchdown after Eddie Lowe schmucked (Edmonton quarterback) Tracy Ham. For a change the ball bounced our way."

Albright's second-quarter touchdown tied the

With help from Roughrider offensive linemen like Ken Moore (64), Kent Austin's passing in the last three quarters of the 1989 Grey Cup was magnificent

game 10–10 after the Eskimos had grabbed an early 10–0 advantage. Although a few of the Roughriders were playing hurt, they were all in the lineup for the first time in two months. Austin threw a touchdown pass to Elgaard and Saskatchewan went into halftime with a 17–13 lead. When Austin injured a knee, Burgess came on in the second half and connected on scoring tosses to Fairholm and Elgaard. In one of the biggest upsets ever seen in the CFL, the overconfident Eskimos were whipped 32–21.

"Did we lose by 30 points? We didn't? Sorry," said Austin.

"We could have been like Edmonton and gone in there blowing our own horn," says Jurasin. "They thought they were better than they really were. We went into Commonwealth Stadium, and we kicked their ass. We didn't just beat them, we kicked their ass! It wasn't a close game. We physically dominated because we wanted it more than they did."

For Roger Aldag, who had missed the 1976 Grey Cup game as a rookie because of a broken ankle and had battled valiantly throughout the Reign of Error, Game Day brought his opportunity for vindication.

"Toronto wasn't that hyped about the Grey Cup, but we certainly were," he recalls. "One thing that sticks out is the game being at 6 o'clock Toronto time. It was a long day, put it that way. I remember Bob Poley and me getting up fairly early that morning, about 8 o'clock, to have breakfast. We decided that since we're in the Grey Cup, we'll put on suits and look like we're real big shots. So we go down to the hotel dining room, and we're eating, and then we look at each other. *What are we doing all dressed up? We don't even play until 6 o'clock!* So we went back to our rooms, put on our blue jeans and denim shirts, and felt a lot more comfortable.

"Another thing that sticks out is the actual running on to the field, the excitement of the crowd roaring and the defence being introduced. That puts a little chill down your back. Then we go to the coin toss, and the game goes so quick. Like, bang! I remember talking to guys that had played in a lot of Grey Cups, and they said the game will go so fast, you'll wonder where it went. Very true. The before and the after go slower, but the game itself is over awful quick."

Spectators, then, must surely appreciate what separates them from the participants, for the 1989 Grey Cup Game provided viewers with the most extended

Dave Ridgway with the Grey Cup

procession of thrills and drama ever packed into a CFL contest. As soon as it ended, some called it "The Greatest Game Ever Played." Many still do.

Gregory was in a can't-win position for naming his starting quarterback. Would it be Austin (the starter since September) or Burgess (who was great in relief against Edmonton)? It was Austin, and for 16 minutes it looked like a mistake. In four possessions he completed only one of seven passes for 19 yards, had one intercepted, and the Tiger-Cats were ahead 13–1.

From that point on, Kent Austin was in total command. His statistics for the last 44 minutes, when every possession was a crucial one, were staggering: 25-for-34, 455 yards, no interceptions. He generated four touchdowns and two field goals on his next seven possessions while Tiger-Cats quarterback Mike Kerrigan, who had put up 27 first-half points, slowed down in the third quarter.

"It was unbelievable to watch the two quarterbacks play as well as they did," Jurasin says. "The defences were just trying to stop the bleeding. Those guys were *on*. We knew what they were doing, we just couldn't stop it. As the game went on, we started to say whoever gets the ball last is going to win."

When Ridgway's 20-yard field widened the Roughriders' lead to 40–33 with only 1 minute 58 seconds remaining, Kerrigan went into all-out, desperation, hurry-up mode. Hamilton reached the Rider 11-yard line in five plays but then faced third down at the 9. Tiger-Cats wideout Tony Champion, playing with fractured ribs, made a sensational flat-out body-twisting catch of Kerrigan's pass in the end zone to tie the game 40–40.

Indeed, the last team to hold the ball would win. Hamilton's game-tying march consumed only 74 seconds, leaving the Roughriders 44 seconds to receive the kickoff and march into field goal position for the 43–40 triumph. Ridgway would split the uprights from 35 yards for what would simply become known as "The Kick" and receive his share of glory—also, much of Austin's, Mark Guy's, Elgaard's and a host of other Roughriders whose contributions faded in the euphoria that followed the winning play.

"I've always said I was only one of a group of guys that brought the Grey Cup to Saskatchewan," Ridgway admits. "People in the business often say you get too much credit when you win and too much blame when you lose. Kent Austin threw for 474 yards in that game, and he was phenomenal in that last drive.

"I can still tell you every play that led up to the field goal when we got the ball back after Champion's catch. The first pass went incomplete. Then Kent went to Ray, a beautifully thrown ball right over Pete Giftopoulos' head. Ray caught it, hit a guy (Lance Shields) and stepped out of bounds. Then Kent threw up the middle to Mark Guy, who got drilled by two guys but held on. Then Mark Guy again to the sideline. Then kneel down and the field goal team comes on."

Guy, with 100 yards on four catches, was the leading contributor of six receivers that Austin utilized. Narcisse caught five passes for 98 yards, Fairholm two for 97, Elgaard six for 73, the unsung Ellingson five for 64 and McCray five for 64.

"Mark Guy was an unsung hero, no doubt about it," Ridgway says. "James Ellingson made several big catches. Narco, as always, was dead steady. The offensive line gave Kent great protection. One guy that never got any recognition in the media for his contribution was Timmy McCray. When you've got an 83-point game going, there are an awful lot of kickoffs, and Timmy McCray returned the ball (six times) for a lot of yardage (169 yards) you never heard about.

"Yeah, I got way too much credit. But I guarantee you, if I had missed it, I'd have got all the credit for that."

ALSO IN THIS DECADE

■ Barb Danaher (formerly Turnbull) of Saskatoon won her record 10th Saskatchewan women's amateur golf championship in 1983. Danaher won her first in 1962 and four straight from 1971–74. In 1981 and 1985, Joanne Goulet of Regina won a provincial title for the fourth straight decade, adding to those she won in 1952, '57, '58, '60, '61, '64, and '76. With nine championships, she has not matched Danaher. Yet.

■ Nancy Jewitt (-Filteau) of Webb took the silver medal in the women's 72-kilogram judo competition at the 1983 Pan-American Games in Havana. Jewitt was a national champion three times (1981, '83, '84.)

Nancy Jewitt

■ Pitcher Gene McWillie of Saskatoon helped Canada win the gold medal in softball at the '83 Pan-American Games.

■ Goaltender Larry Walker of Maple Ridge, B.C., allowed two goals in 12 shots in a Regina Pats intersquad game on September 7, 1983. He was cut from the team the next day and shifted his athletic energy to baseball. Since then he has hit 368 home runs and posted a career batting average of .314 in 16 major-league seasons.

■ Allison Lang of Saskatoon completed her four-year NCAA basketball career at Oregon in 1984 with averages of 19.2 points and 9.8 rebounds in 117 games and two All-American selections. Lang, 6-foot-2½ and 158 pounds, played on the '84 Canadian team that finished fourth at the Olympics in Los Angeles.

■ Elmer Hazzard of Regina topped a 75-man field to win the tricks competition at the 1985 World Masters water-skiing championships. Hazzard, a 10-time Canadian tricks champion, scored 2,890 points; the runner-up had 2,200.

■ Regina wrestler Ron Moncur won the 48-kilogram wrestling gold medal at the 1986 Commonwealth Games in Edinburgh.

■ Regina curlers Ev Krahn, Twyla Widdifield, Shirley Little and June Kaufman won their third consecutive national and sixth straight provincial senior women's championships in 1987.

■ Gina Smith of Saskatoon earned a bronze medal at the 1988 Olympic Games at Seoul in equestrian team dressage. Smith would also win gold in the same event at the 1991 Pan-American Games in Havana.

■ Cyprian Enweani of Saskatoon placed ninth in the men's 200 metres and ran on the men's 4x100 relay team that finished seventh at the Seoul Olympics.

■ Heather Kuttai of Battleford and Richard Schell of Kerrobert formed two-thirds of Canada's silver-medal team in air pistol shooting at the 1988 Paralympic Games in Seoul. Kuttai also won an individual bronze medal at the 1992 Barcelona Games.

■ Yorkton Regional High School captured the provincial boys volleyball championship at the highest level (4A 1981–88, 5A 1989) nine years in a row, winning 18 of 19 sets in those respective finals.

■ Dean Holoein hit a two-run single in the first inning and pitched the shutout as the Melfort 222s defeated Ontario 2–0 to win the 1989 Canadian junior men's softball championship. The same Melfort team had won the 1986 Canadian midget championship.

Sandra Schmirler, three-time Canadian and world champion, and the only Canadian skip of either gender to win an Olympic gold medal in curling

1990–2004

Ladies First

DEPARTURES

January 23, 1990: Buzz Boll, hockey player, 79.
August 15, 1991: Phil Lederhouse, golfer, 75.
October 2, 1991: Hazen Argue, politician, 70.
January 26, 1993: Ken Goff, boxing coach, 82.
January 26, 1993: Jeanne Sauvé, governor-general, 70.
June 27, 1993: Jim Trifunov, wrestler, 89.
November 11, 1995: Emmett Hall, lawyer/judge, 96.
February 29, 1996: Sinclair Ross, writer, 88.
July 12, 1996: Mike Kartusch, hockey coach/administrator, 88.
July 22, 1996: David Greyeyes-Steele, soccer player, 81.
July 27, 1996: Al Rollins, hockey player, 69.
February 25, 1998: W.O. Mitchell, author, 83.
February 26, 1998: Chuck Sebestyen, gymnastics coach, 71.
January 12, 1999: Doug Wickenheiser, hockey player, 37.
September 27, 1999: Grant Warwick, hockey player, 77.
February 7, 2000: Sid Abel, hockey player, 81.
March 2, 2000: Sandra Schmirler, curler, 36.
July 12, 2001: Gas Eichel, boxer, 89.
September 11, 2001: Garnet (Ace) Bailey, hockey player, 53.
January 9, 2002: Harold "Mush" March, hockey player, 93.
December 16, 2002: Wild Bill Hunter, entrepreneur, 82.
December 18, 2002: Ray Hnatyshyn, governor-general (1990–95), 68.
October 29, 2003: Vern Pettigrew, wrestler, 95.
December 15, 2003: Keith Magnuson, hockey player, 56.
December 17, 2003: Mary Baker, softball/baseball player, 84.
May 1, 2004: Ken Charlton, football player, 84.
February 7, 2005: Bob Turner, hockey player/coach, 71.

GOLDEN HARVESTS OCCUR WHEN WHEAT IS MATURE AND FULLY GROWN. AS SASKATCHEWAN NEARED THE end of its first century, it reaped a golden Olympic harvest. The bounty was uniquely female, a collection of women who had spent decades mastering their sport and achieving greatness on their own terms. Speed skater Catriona Le May Doan was the best sprinter in the world but put greater emphasis on the friendships she made. Hayley Wickenheiser played hockey with boys, became the best female hockey player in the world, and played with men because she wanted to keep improving. Sandra Schmirler, Jan Betker, Joan McCusker and Marcia Gudereit became the embodiment of Everywoman: moms who balanced their domestic lives with their alter egos of curling champions.

They were all Olympic and world champions, role models and celebrities. Schmirler in particular had a radiant charisma the likes of which curling had never enjoyed. Her death, a scant two years after her team's Olympic glory, was like the black night that follows hard upon a spectacular prairie sunset.

CATRIONA LE MAY DOAN: YEARS OF THE CAT

She showed the younger skaters she's a great skater but also has fun and gets more out of it than just results.
–Jeremy Wotherspoon

I want people, first of all, to see my passion for life and for sport and for people then after that to see what I've accomplished.
–Catriona Le May Doan

LIKE THE ROLLING STONES SANG, YOU CAN'T always get what you want, but if you try sometime, you'll find you get what you need. Catriona Le May Doan pays the price of fame, recognized first as a double Olympic gold medallist in speed skating, her smile and figure instantly recognizable to millions of Canadians who watched those powerful haunches propel her, panther-like, around the ovals of Nagano and Salt Lake City. Only those fortunate to spend time with her get to know the gregarious personality, only her family and close friends know her generous nature. The general public has to take it on faith that the persona before the camera is genuine. It is.

"I really don't care what people have or haven't accomplished," Le May Doan says. "That, to me, doesn't make a person. I enjoy meeting kids who say they dream of winning an Olympic gold medal. They might think it will bring something to their lives, whether its monetary reward or fame or whatever. The biggest thing to me is that people see me as the same person now as I was before the Olympic success, a person who enjoys being around people, who enjoys what she does, who enjoys challenging herself."

Le May Doan's specialty was the 500-metre sprint, the shortest event in long-track speed skating. Ironically, achieving success at that short distance involves a long, hard journey of personal sacrifice that is not likely to bring quick rewards. At Salt Lake City in 2002, Le May Doan was 31 years old and had been skating for 22 years; the top seven finishers in the 500 ranged from 27 to 33 years old.

"There are more attractive things to do than practise speed skating," Brenda Webster, a former Olympian, said in a 1987 magazine article while she was coaching Catriona Le May in Saskatoon. "Catriona works hard and has a good attitude. She's very competitive. She's young (16) and she's got very good technique."

At that time, Le May already owned four national juvenile records and had won a silver and a bronze medal in short-track speed skating at the 1987 Canada Winter Games to go along with the bronze she had won as a 12-year-old in 1983. In warmer months, she stood out on a different track, winning five hurdles and sprint gold medals in four years at the provincial high school track and field championships. She even competed in the 1993 Canada Summer Games in heptathlon and relay races at a time when her speed skating career was showing only modest progress.

Le May Doan was 23rd and 18th overall at the 1989 and 1990 world junior speed skating championships and posted similar results at the world sprint championships the next three years. Her Olympic debut in

A teen-aged Catriona Le May tends to her skates

1992 at Albertville, France, produced an encouraging 14th-place finish in the 500 metres, but she fell in the same event in the 1994 Games at Lillehammer, Norway. Through 1995 she had yet to place higher than 10th in any Olympic or world championship event. It wasn't until 1996, at the age of 25, that she broke into the upper echelons of speed skating with five second-place finishes in World Cup events, the No. 3 world ranking at 500 metres, and the gold medal in that distance at the world sprint championships.

"It was a bit of everything coming together," she says. "It takes years of training to develop strength, endurance and technique, and you have to acquire the maturity to apply that training. Training became more enjoyable as I got older. There are so many technical parts I had to work on, and some just took longer to master. I always had a good start and good speed. How you race is definitely something you have to learn. Training is one thing, but to race in competition requires so much discipline and experience."

In addition to her first international triumph, 1996 was also significant for marriage to Alberta cowboy Bart Doan, a part-time rodeo competitor who totally supported Catriona's ongoing quest to find new plateaus of performance. She couldn't be "the best she could be" as long as she sensed there was any untapped potential within her.

"That's pretty much how I view everything," she says. "I saw from a young age that I did have potential and that some success came quite easily. As soon as I achieved one thing, I moved on to the next thing."

A revolution was afoot in speed skating in 1996–97 with the arrival of the clap skate, which allowed the athlete's heel to lift away from the blade. Pioneered by the Dutch, it could save a skater up to half a second over 500 metres, an interval of time that could separate anywhere from two to eight skaters in any given meet. Le May Doan slipped to seventh in the World Cup standings and second at the world sprint championships in the 500 but, with the rest of a determined Canadian team, was hard at work at the Calgary oval in the summer and fall of 1997, mastering the nuances of the clap skate and priming themselves for a season that would peak with the '98 Olympic Games at Nagano, Japan.

"It was a significant time because we'd been doing training races and had been unofficially breaking world records," Le May Doan says, "but we had to wait for the first sanctioned meet of the season for them to count. It was definitely a special week."

Unleashed on official competition on November 22, 1997, "the Cat" became the queen of sprinters. Bonnie Blair of the United States had broken the 39-second barrier with a 38.99 clocking at Calgary in 1994; her 38.69, also in Calgary, had stood as the world record for 32 months. Le May Doan shattered both the record and the 38-second plateau by covering the 500 metres in 37.90 seconds in her first race. In her second race, she recorded precisely the same time. She also set the 1,000-metre world record: 1 minute 16.07 seconds. One week later, she clocked 1:57.87 in the 1,500 to claim that world record.

Le May Doan held the 1,000-metre record for only one day, yielding it to American Chris Witty, but "the Cat" put the 500 mark further out of reach with a 37.71 and a 37.55 in late December at the Olympic trials. She was cleaning up big time on the World Cup circuit and came to Japan as the clear favourite in the 500 and a medal hopeful in the 1,000. Nagano's oval wasn't as fast as Calgary's, so Le May Doan's time of 38.39 seconds in her first of two races was good enough to put her in first place. Her lead was painfully slim, however: Susan Auch of Winnipeg was second at 38.42 and Tomomi Okazaki of Japan third in 38.55. Moreover, Okazaki matched that time in her second run. That left the Canadians digging in to the starting line knowing that they were in a match race for the gold medal—if they went around again at something approaching Olympic-record speed. Le May Doan got off to her customary blazing start, only to find Auch had virtually matched her off the line. Neither woman wilted. Le May Doan crossed first in 38.21 seconds for a combined time of 1:16.60 flat and the gold medal. Auch, the sister of Derrick Auch, Le May Doan's coach, followed in 38.51 and a combined 1:16.93 for the silver.

Later, Le May Doan was 13th in the 1,500 but earned the bronze medal in the 1,000 metres behind Marianne Timmer of the Netherlands and Witty. For the proverbial icing on the cake, Le May Doan won both 500-metre races and the overall title at the world sprint championships and topped the World Cup standings in both the 500 and 1,000, winning seven gold medals and a silver in the short sprint and two of each metal in the 1,000. Returning home, she suddenly discovered herself to be a celebrity with an image slightly askew from reality. Clad in her skin-tight competition suit, perched atop her skates with her flawless posture and her starting-line scowl, she looked like the Cat that Clawed the Calgary Tower.

"The comment I always get is, 'You're a lot smaller than I thought you were,'" says Le May Doan, who stands 5-foot-7 and competed at 140 pounds. "I think people got the idea from TV that I'm a lot bigger and taller. In general, speed skaters are smaller than people think. Even with that, the biggest change in my life has been the adjustment to fame. It is weird having people recognize you everywhere you go across the country."

Her star continued to shine for another four years as she remained the world's dominant female sprinter. She put herself into the record books four more times in 2001 as she gradually lowered her 500-metre world record to 37.22 seconds and nearly matched that at the 2002 Olympics in Salt Lake City when she posted a time of 37.30 in her first run. Within the

Catriona Le May Doan proudly displays her flags and Olympic medals at a Saskatoon reception after her 1998 triumph in Nagano

context of the competition, though, it was 1988 all over again: Monique Enfeldt-Garbrecht of Germany was a scant four one-hundredths of a second behind, and the rest of the field turned the last pairing into a match race. Again, Le May Doan won the race and the gold medal, her final (37.45) and combined (1:14.75) times relegating the German (37.60 and 1:14.91) to silver. There was no medal in the 1,000 on this occasion; her time of 1:14.72 was good enough for only ninth place yet only 48-hundredths of a second from the bronze medal.

As the calendar year wound down, Le May Doan was honoured as Canada's Female Athlete of the Year, as she had been in 1998 and 2001. She was also awarded the Lou Marsh Trophy as Canada's outstanding athlete of either gender, edging professional basketball star Steve Nash of the Dallas Mavericks in a close vote as she became only the second Saskatchewan recipient of the honour (after George Genereux in 1952). However, as Catriona Le May Doan would prefer to be appreciated more for her character than for her accomplishments, perhaps her greatest honour came at the opening ceremonies of the 2002 Winter Games in Salt Lake City when she served as Canada's flag-bearer, a distinction bestowed more for an athlete's personal reputation than his or her competitive record.

Le May Doan will always have a special place in the hearts of Saskatchewan people for her post-race celebrations after winning the 500-metre events in Nagano and Salt Lake City. Most Olympic champions carry their country's flag on their victory laps. Le May Doan waved an enormous Maple Leaf standard but also toted a tiny Saskatchewan flag during her moments of glory.

"My mom carried it with her in Nagano, and I got it from her," she says. "What was most important was to have the big Canadian flag and then the little Saskatchewan flag. My roots are in Saskatchewan, and I wanted to show that I took pride in where I grew up."

Sandra Schmirler and Jan Betker, typically unfazed by competitive pressure

TEAM SCHMIRLER: CANADA'S QUEENS OF HEARTS

"CLOSE, WHOA, WHOA, OFF! CLOSE, CLOSE, eee–yeEESSS, HURRY! COME ON!"

"Whoa, whoa."

Sandra Schmirler's voice, then Jan Betker's, called the sweep for Joan McCusker and Marcia Gudereit at the Canadian Olympic Curling Trials on November 30, 1997. Schmirler's rock, the last of the seventh end of the final game, struck a biter at the corner of the 12-foot circle and ricocheted towards its final target, Shannon Kleibrink's shot rock on the button. It punched Kleibrink's stone out of the house and left Schmirler with three counters in the four-foot.

The Shot.

Schmirler, trailing 4–3 and in serious danger of trailing by two points with three ends to play, made The Shot. It forever remains her defining moment—forever because in the blink of two years after Nagano she was gone, dead of cancer at 36.

Canada's 10 best women's teams, regardless of location (three from Ontario, two apiece from Saskatchewan and Alberta, and one each from B.C., Manitoba and Nova Scotia) had descended on Brandon for the Olympic trials. Schmirler's team, the defending Canadian champion and three-time world titlist, earned a bye into the final with a 7–2 record. Kleibrink's Calgary foursome won the semi-final over Kelley Law of B.C. in a duel of 6–3 teams. Kleibrink, far more accomplished on the cash spiel circuit than in playdowns, took the lead with three points in the sixth end and had shot rock thoroughly buried for a likely steal in the seventh.

"If there was one time when I ever worried a game was getting away from us, this was it, for sure," Betker says. "We weren't panicked but I'm sure we were all thinking, 'if they get another one here, we're all in big trouble.'

"What made it a great shot was the circumstance. In the Brier with top-notch players, you know, you've seen shots like that but never with a trip to the Olympics on the line and with the team in a tough spot. That's what made it so dramatic—and she didn't just make it, she stuck it perfectly."

Back at the hack, McCusker and Gudereit had a different perspective on the prelude to The Shot.

"We were freaking out," McCusker recalls. "I specifically remember thinking to myself, or even saying out loud, 'It's okay, it's okay if they steal one, we'll get two in 8, force them to take one in 9 and we'll get two in 10.' I was being trying to be Little Miss Optimist, but we were in big trouble, we knew that. We'd missed about six shots in a row, and with our team that was unheard of.

"Then Sandra came down and told us that was the shot. I said, 'Can we get one?' And she said, 'Yeah, yeah, oh yeah, we can get clear shot stone.' There was a chance of multiple points, I knew that, but it was such a low percentage. So we went, 'Oh, that's great. We'll give it a chance, then.' Which meant: we need to hit this pretty thin, so we wouldn't start sweeping too early. Sandra said afterwards she had this vision that she was going to make this shot, a powerful kind of feeling that it was not only there but that we were gonna nail this. She was freaked out by it afterwards, actually."

The collective euphoria of the team and 4,966 fans in the Keystone Centre did not subside for a couple of minutes. Kleibrink, far from vanquished, took two on the eighth to tie the score, but Team Schmirler responded with three in the ninth, ran Kleibrink out of rocks in the 10th, and won 9–6.

The Olympics were alternately the thrill of a lifetime and an exercise in emotional torture for the team. McCusker's grandmother passed away just before the team left for Nagano. Gudereit learned of her grandmother's death just before the fourth draw. Betker went through an on-ice crying jag brought on by the anxiety of separation from her infant son. Gudereit got a touch of flu. Betker got a pounding of flu. Fifth Atina Ford had to play the last game at third in Betker's place. Somehow the team got through the round robin with a 6–1 record that produced a semi-final match with fourth-place Great Britain (Scotland, when you get down to it). There Schmirler and her teammates had the competitive scare of their lives. Forced to an extra end by Krista Hay, Schmirler only had to draw full eight-foot to an unguarded house to win. Halfway down the ice, however, it was apparent the draw was heavy. Gudereit and McCusker lifted their brooms and didn't even accompany the rock past the hog line. Canadians everywhere got that same terrible uncertain feeling as when they hit the brakes at an icy intersection and wonder if the car will stop or skid into catastrophe. Schmirler's rock came to rest nudging the back 12-foot, two inches closer to the button than Hay's. Schmirler won 6–5, and her entire country exhaled as one.

Marcia Gudereit and Joan McCusker

Canada's 7–5 victory over Denmark's Helena Blach-Lavrsen was routine—up 5–2 after five ends, up two coming home with hammer—but for its significance as the gold-medal match. In the two Olympics that have included men's and women's curling as fully-fledged medal sports, this still stands as Canada's only gold medal. Coincidentally, the whole country discovered the quartet that had been the pride of Saskatchewan for the last seven years.

"The weather during the Olympics was so bad that they kept cancelling the Alpine skiing events, and the CBC had to fill with curling," Betker remembers. "We were on all the time. Later we were in Toronto for a function, and people were honking their horns at us as we walked down the street. We kind of expect to be recognized in Regina but not in Toronto. That's when we realized, holy smokes, there were a lot of people watching."

Those millions of viewers saw four women who were exceptional in their curling skill and their ability to balance their personal obligations with their professional and competitive endeavours. Otherwise,

Schmirler in 1993, sporting a perm en route to her first Scott Tournament of Hearts title

they were just a pleasant-looking group of young ladies. Therein lay the charm.

"There are so many sports where women are finished by the age of 20," McCusker says. "If you're a competitive gymnast, figure skater, tennis player, track athlete, the height of your competitiveness is over by the age of 20 or shortly afterwards. In curling you aren't even hitting your stride. You haven't matured, you haven't learned enough yet. Very few sports wouldn't dictate your body type. Because of the Olympics, this sport got so much coverage across Canada of four women who look like any other woman, who are not as tiny as a little figure skater or gymnast, or as big as a sumo wrestler, but somewhere in between—a range of body types and body weights, all of us 30-something, all of us with husbands and children and still competitive personalities.

"We found that women across the country identified with us. We were what they would be if they had chosen to dedicate themselves to a sport. We represented women. Men followed us because we were competitive and successful, and because we were just like somebody they work with, or that they married, or a neighbour. People identified with us when we spoke to the media. We didn't give them clichés; we said things like, 'It doesn't really matter because I'm going to go home to my kids tomorrow and make them lunch and I'll be all right.' We didn't give them, 'I'm crushed, this is my whole world.' We strove to be ordinary. It scared us whenever we got close to being treated in an extraordinary way."

Betker was the only one who grew up in Regina. Schmirler was from Biggar, McCusker from a farm near Saltcoats and Gudereit from Moose Jaw. Schmirler (then Peterson) and Betker became teammates as third and second for Kathy Fahlman and won the 1987 provincial championship. That team broke up two years later after Fahlman lost confidence in her shooting and accepted an offer to play third for Michelle Schneider, then the province's reigning champion. Betker and Schmirler formed their own team in 1990–91 and recruited McCusker and Gudereit (then Inglis and Schiml) for the front end.

"We found out pretty quick that we were all keen competitors," Betker says. "We didn't set a goal of winning the province in our very first year, but when we did, it whet our appetites."

Schmirler's crew went to the national championship in its first season, finished in a three-way tie for third at 7–4, beat Alberta's Deb Shermack 6–3 in the first tiebreaker and lost 6–3 to Ontario's Heather Houston in the second. As eager as they were to get back, Schneider blocked the way in 1992 by beating Schmirler in the Saskatchewan final, but Schmirler stormed to the '93 provincial crown with 15 wins in 16 games. At the Scott in Brandon, the Regina women finished first in the round robin with a 9–2 record and got the bye to the final, where they defeated

Manitoba's Maureen Bonar 7–6 on Schmirler's open hit-and-stick in the 10th end.

Good news, Sandra, Jan, Joan and Marcia: you are the new Team Canada. Bad news: you have three weeks, travel time to Geneva included, to figure out the free-guard zone.

Free-guard zone rules, in their simplest state, dictate that a rock that comes to rest in front of the rings (a guard) can't be removed from play until a certain number of rocks have been played. In North America, through 1993, the free-guard zone (FGZ) didn't exist. In the rest of the world, it was there for the first four shots of each end, and that's how the world championships would be played.

Marcia Gudereit

"More than anything it was the strategy that freaked us out," Betker remembers. "Marcia has great draw weight. We knew that all along. She's just a great finesse player, so it was as if the four-rock rule was made for her. The big adjustment was that we had to dramatically change our game plan because we were primarily a hitting team, and you can't play the FGZ that way. On top of that, we'd be playing all these experienced teams like Elizabet Gustafson (Sweden) and Dordi Nordby (Norway) who not only knew the FGZ but were very familiar with the worlds, and that made us really nervous.

"Sandra watched tape after tape after tape of games played under FGZ rules. We watched some together, but she did it primarily on her own. Then we'd dabble with it in club games, asking teams to try it out against us."

McCusker also recalls the transition to the FGZ as difficult.

"It was frightening," McCusker says. "We were the Lean Green Peeling Machine from Saskatchewan. That's how we won our provincial and Canadian championships, but we knew we'd have to change. Randy Woytowich (Callie clubmate and 1991 Brier runner-up with Joan's husband Brian as his third) had experience with the four-rock rule in bonspiels, and he came out to teach us.

"We figured out what we had to do: mainly, control the front of the house. Our first game was against Dordi Nordby, who was a two-time world champion (1990–91). We were up something like 7–2 after five ends, and we didn't think it was enough."

It was enough; Canada won 12–3 and won seven of its nine round-robin games. The surprise leader at 8–1 was Germany's Janet Clews-Strayer, who had grown up in Regina and fashioned a respectable junior curling record: twice Regina Youth Bonspiel champion, fourth at the 1987 junior provincials, bronze medallist at the '87 Canada Winter Games. Married to a Canadian serviceman stationed overseas, she had skipped a rink of native Germans to their national title.

To create, of all things, a final featuring two Saskatchewan-born skips, Schmirler's team would first have to avenge its round-robin loss to Sweden's Gustafson in the semifinal. Done. Canada 10, Sweden 7. Confident that it had the FGZ and the ice down pat, Canada put the pressure on Germany and never relented en route to a 5–3 victory for its world championship.

As an extra benefit, the team had learned and mastered the FGZ, which was introduced in Canada the following season in a three-rock format.

"We had a leg up on everybody because we'd played the four-rock rules," Betker recalls. "The three-rock FGZ seemed a lot more manageable to us, yet it was probably still a big adjustment for everybody else. That year we were incredible. It was probably our best season ever. Our confidence was flying, and we just dominated everything we entered."

They won all four major cash spiels in which they played. As defending national champions, they had the luxury of an automatic berth in the '94 Scott as Team Canada. They topped the round robin at 10–1, their only loss coming against Manitoba's Connie Laliberte, whom they met in the closest game of any of their seven national, world or Olympic finals. Both teams played conservatively. Laliberte registered a deuce in the seventh end to go ahead 3–2. Schmirler blanked the eighth and ninth ends and played the 10th gunning for two points. Gudereit started with two perfect guards. When a Manitoba peel attempt left a rock at the back of the rings, McCusker and Betker drew to the backing. Laliberte's final attempt to freeze was a touch heavy, leaving Schmirler an open hit for three and a 5–3 triumph.

Steady play in Frankfurt produced a second straight world championship: first place in the round robin at 8–1, a sloppy but controlled 10–6 semi-final decision over Germany and a coolly efficient 5–3 final victory over Christine Cannon of Scotland. A three-peat in 1995 was not in the cards. Team Canada finished in a three-way tie for second at 8–3 at the Scott, won a tiebreaker to earn the second seed for the Page playoffs, lost the 1–2 game to Laliberte and finally lost the semi-final to Cathy Borst (King) of Alberta. Laliberte won the final. In a way, the defeat was a blessing for Schmirler and company. Romances were blooming, biological clocks were ticking and there was no hiding it.

Joan McCusker

"We knew everything about each other," McCusker says. "We were the first to know when one of the others was pregnant. We spent that much time together that if somebody didn't order a beer after a game, you knew. *Okay, what's the deal? Are you pregnant?* We knew intimate details about each other's lives, we knew more about the bunch of us than our husbands did. Absolutely."

McCusker took the whole 1995–96 season off except for a best-of-three series against Laliberte's rink that would decide the first berth in the Olympic trials. (Schmirler won the series 2–0.) Betker married longtime boyfriend Frank Macera and kept curling through pregnancy. Gudereit fell ill during the southern playdowns. Schmirler and Betker went to the provincial playdowns with a substitute front end and lost the final to Sherry Scheirich of Saskatoon. Later in 1996, Betker, McCusker and Gudereit would all deliver babies, and Schmirler would marry Shannon England and revert to using her maiden name. (She had been known as Sandra Peterson even after her first marriage ended in divorce in 1993.)

If a change really is as good as a rest, then the team was genuinely refreshed when 1997 playdowns arrived. Sherry Linton of Regina gave them all they could handle in the southern and provincial finals, but Team Schmirler arrived for the Scott in Vancouver full of confidence and good feelings. The skip's surname switch prompted an obvious nickname for the media to exploit: "Schmirler the Curler." She began by clobbering Team Canada's Marilyn Bodogh 9–2, which turned to be Saskatchewan's first-place record at the end of the week. Schmirler faced Alison Goring of Ontario in both the Page 1–2 game and the final, winning them 6–5 and 8–5 respectively, both times coming home with the hammer and running Goring out of rocks. At the worlds in Berne, Switzerland, Team Schmirler (now Team Canada again) topped the round robin at 7–2, beat Denmark 5–2 in the semi-final and rode a five-point fifth end to wallop Nordby 8–4 in the final.

Then came the Olympics, followed by the '98 Scott, where they were bounced in the semi-final. In eight years they had won three Scotts, three world titles and the Olympic gold medals. Their record in national, world and Olympic trials and championships was 102–28: 77–13 when they won a competition, 25–15 when they didn't. All four were famous across Canada, particularly Schmirler, whose on-ice demeanour radiated determination and at all other times was the epitome of down-to-earth charm. Her perfect teeth were only the centrepiece of a smile that twinkled in her eyes and shone from every line in her face.

She endured a difficult pregnancy in the winter of

1998–99 and seemed more relieved than disappointed when she lost the provincial final to Cindy Street of Moose Jaw. Her second daughter, Jenna, was born June 30. (The first, Sara, became noted as "my best delivery" when Schmirler was asked to rate The Shot after the Olympic trials.) Instead of recovering from her pregnancy, Schmirler was plagued by constant back and neck pain, indigestion and weakness. It took doctors nearly two months to achieve a heartbreaking diagnosis of lymphoma.

Schmirler almost died during surgery early in September, and the family had to publicly reveal her condition. She battled with every ounce of energy she could muster. Schmirler honoured a commitment to work as a colour commentator at the Canadian junior curling championships in February 2000, her raspy voice testifying simultaneously to her condition and her fighting spirit. On March 2 she died.

Sandra Schmirler

On March 4, at the Brier in Saskatoon, Betker, McCusker and Gudereit stepped on to the SaskPlace ice and symbolically walked alone down the centre sheet of ice.

"It had been our plan all along to go to Saskatoon," McCusker says. "We were going to be part of the opening ceremonies anyway. So the original idea was, take our families, get hotel rooms, let the kids go watersliding. You have to remember we all had newborns, so we didn't have a lot of time to mourn or grieve.

"The respectful thing to do in a time of mourning is to give the family space. That's not us, though, right? Therefore, we were fair game for media attention, and, truthfully, there were some people who were fairly aggressive and not very nice. It seemed that everything had a double edge to it. In one way it was an inappropriate thing to put up with; on the other hand, by fielding it, you took it away from Shannon, and from Sandra's mom and sisters.

"At the funeral, for example: it was on TSN, and they can't show the family, so who do they show? That was the last thing we wanted—for people to watch us grieve, and you knew that it was there. I had a baby that wasn't even two months old, and I had to get through that, then find her, feed her and carry on."

Rocket Richard's funeral two months later in Montreal was also nationally televised; no surprise there. For Schmirler's death to grip Canada as it did was astonishing as well as monumental.

"When does the funeral of a curler from a small Saskatchewan town get live coverage coast to coast in this country?" wonders CBC sportscaster Brian Williams. "There's always an outpouring of affection when someone dies of a horrific disease or from a horrific death; but what must be remembered is that she was loved, respected and admired long before she was sick. She was a bigger-than-life personality and with her death that huge persona was magnified a million times again.

"She was a champion. She was calm, a leader, authoritative. You had that feeling that if she said you were going to do it, then you were going to do it. And competitive! She looked like she'd slit your throat, she was so competitive, but after it was over, there was that smile and the joy and the pride, the children, the group of them talking about their families back home.

"She was what's good about the Olympics. It was such a magnificent story if it had ended right at Nagano. When she won that gold medal, she was like a new bride. She glowed. You see pride in athletes, you see pride in accomplishment, but with her, with the whole group of them, it was so sincere.

"It's easy to say she was surrounded by good people. There was a reason for it. Good people are drawn to strong, good people."

RAMS vs. HILLTOPS: END OF A BLOOD RIVALRY

WAY BACK IN 1947, THE SASKATOON HILLTOPS junior football team was created. Seven years later, the Regina Rams were formed. The two were naturally drawn to each other, like hydrogen atoms in a nuclear bomb.

The Hilltops and Rams would bring out the best and the worst in each other: hard-fought battles in crisp autumn and bitter winter weather, championships galore, mutual respect and, once in a while, some plain old hatred. Better to undergo root canal without anaesthesia than be on the losing side of a Rams–Hilltops game.

Regina's dominance of junior football was so overwhelming (five national titles in six years, 15 altogether) that after the 1998 season the Rams' executive took on a greater challenge and aligned the team with the University of Regina. The Hilltops took over as the masters of the Canadian junior game with national crowns in 2001, '02 and '03, bringing their tally of Canadian titles to 12. Together, the Rams and Hilltops have won 27 of the last 51 national junior football championships—not that either organization would relish the thought of the two doing anything together.

Some highlights:

1953: Saskatoon quarterback Ron Adam completed 49 of 76 passes for 941 yards in four playoff games. The Hilltops crushed the home-town Vancouver Blue Bombers 50–6 in the Western final and Windsor AKO 34–6 in Saskatoon for the Little Grey Cup.

1966: After six straight provincial high school championships as head coach of Regina's Balfour Redmen, Gord Currie led the Rams to their first national title, 29–14 over Montreal's N.D.G. Maple Leafs. Regina, which had lost 23–0 to the Hilltops in the regular season, whipped Saskatoon 41–17 in the Man–Sask league final.

1969: Regina won the first game of the two-game Man–Sask final 7–3 and led the series 21–10 when the Hilltops recovered a Rams fumble early in the fourth quarter. Doug Rudolph and Gord Remmen scored touchdowns to give Saskatoon a 23–21 triumph. After that, victories of 39–17 over the Edmonton Huskies and 28–7 over the Ottawa Sooners for the Huskies' second straight Canadian title were comparatively easy.

Kurtis Albers (20) and fellow Hilltops celebrate the 1996 PFC championship

1973: Regina's high-powered offence ground to a halt when the Hilltops clobbered quarterbacks Lenny Knoll (broken ankle) and Jack Lichtenwald (sprained ankle, broken toe) in the playoffs. Lichtenwald had to limp off the bench in the first quarter of the national final against the Sooners after Bryan Dimen, the Rams' last quarterback, sustained a broken collarbone. Regina's defence scored a safety and Bernie Schmidt returned a punt 94 yards for a touchdown in an inspired 9–0 triumph.

1976: In Currie's last game as head coach, the Rams scored 30 points in the fourth quarter to beat the Hamilton Hurricanes 45–23 at Taylor Field and win their sixth Canadian championship in 11 years. Knoll went 25-for-40 for 428 yards, with 21 of his completions going to future Roughriders: Gerry Fellner, Greg Fieger and Maurice Butler. Four Rams linemen would also play for Saskatchewan: Roger Aldag, Bob Poley, Gene LaRocque and Kerry Berryman.

1985: Regina went 8–0 in the Prairie Junior Football Conference for the second straight season and had beaten the Hilltops seven straight times in league finals since 1972. Saskatoon's Spero Kokonas intercepted a Rams pass on the Hilltops' 5-yard line, one of eight Regina turnovers, in the dying minutes to preserve a 31–24 upset. Quarterback Tony Gagnon's passing took Saskatoon to the national final, where it thumped Ottawa 29–11.

1997: After losing twice, each time by 18 points, to the unbeaten Hilltops in the regular season, the Rams whipped Saskatoon 46–27 in the PJFC final. Chris Warnecke caught three touchdown passes totalling 175 yards. In the national final at Kelowna against the Okanagan Sun, the Rams were down 20–17 with third-and-10 on the Sun 45 in the final minute of overtime. Jason Clermont took Chad Ehman's short pass, broke two tackles and rambled for 42 yards before being forced out of bounds with 11 seconds to go. Clermont ran three yards for the winning touchdown on the next play.

Dozens of Hilltops and Rams moved on to CFL careers, most of them with the Roughriders, but they would never play with more emotion than they did in their junior days. Sometimes Hilltops–Rams games decided league championships. Sometimes one team spoiled the aspirations of the apparently stronger rival. And sometimes, when they weren't battering each other, they lost—but not often.

Deb McCormick at the 2003 world women's curling championship in Winnipeg

SASKATOON'S AMERICAN WORLD CURLING CHAMPION

Saskatoon-born Deb McCormick added to the list of Saskatchewan expatriates (Ed Lukowich, Rick Folk) to win world curling championships when she prevailed in 2003 at Winnipeg. McCormick, however, was the first to do it for another country, skipping her United States team from Madison, Wis., to a 5–3 decision over Colleen Jones of Canada in the final.

McCormick's family lived in Saskatoon for only a few years and, with a brief stopover in Toronto, moved to Madison in 1978, when she was four years old. Her prairie roots took hold on the ice.

"I don't think I had a choice because my brother and I just grew up at the Madison Curling Club," she says. "Both my parents played in leagues, so I have memories of being down there, sitting on the rocks, pushing each other around, playing hide-and-seek in the locker room, watching them curl, stuff like that, and when we were old enough we joined the junior program. That's all I remember doing in the wintertime is being down at the curling club."

She was a four-time American junior champion (1991–94) under her maiden name of Deb Henry. She competed in the 1998 Olympics as a second, and in the 2001 worlds and 2002 Olympics as a third.

"I still have a lot of family in Canada," she says. "I really feel that Canada is my heritage, and the United States is my home."

CLAYTON GEREIN: MARATHON MAN (THE SEQUEL)

Clayton Gerein and Christoph Etzlstorfer churned their arms furiously towards the finish line, their 41-kilometre wheelchair marathon at the 2000 Paralympic Games in Sydney, Australia, reduced to a short sprint for the gold medal. There could have been only one thought in Gerein's mind:

What, this again?

Four years earlier in Atlanta, Gerein was locked in a similar home-stretch duel with fellow Canadian Brent McMahon, who beat Gerein to the tape in a time of 2 hours 9 minutes 8 seconds. Gerein's time: the same 2:09:08. At least Gerein won gold in the 5,000 metres that year, along with silver in the marathon and bronze in the 1,500. He had also earned gold and other medals in both the 1988 and 1992 Paralympics.

In 2000, the marathon was Gerein's last chance for gold. Bronze had eluded him in the 5,000 by 1.3 seconds. Now he and Etzlstorfer, an Austrian, ended their race in a photo-finish. Their times: Identical 2:03.12s. After studying the photo, the officials declared Gerein the winner.

Gerein, born in North Battleford and a resident of Pilot Butte (10 kilometres east of Regina), has been rolling along as a champion quadriplegic wheelchair racer for nearly two decades. He was a multi-distance standout at the 1988 Paralympics in Seoul, winning the 400, 800 and 5,000 metres, taking silver in the 1,500 and bronze in the marathon. In time he became more proficient at longer distances. He earned four medals in the 1992 Paralympics in Barcelona: gold in marathon, silver in the 5,000 and bronze in the 800 and 1,500. His split-second loss at the Atlanta Games in 1996 was a surprise because he has won that city's Peachtree Road race 11 times. At various times Gerein has held world records in the 400, 800, 1,500 and 5,000 metres in his classification.

Gerein is still going strong. He set a personal best in the marathon with a 1:54:36 in 2001 at Heidelberg, Germany, and since 2003 has recorded new lows in the 800 (2:05.90), 1,500 (3:58.06) and 5,000 (13:06.99). On April 19, 2004, he won the men's quadriplegic portion of the Boston Marathon with a time of 1:55:14 and five months later earned bronze in the marathon at the Athens Paralympics.

HAYLEY WICKENHEISER: THE GORDIE HOWE OF WOMEN'S HOCKEY

As the Canadian public gradually got to know Hayley Wickenheiser, the first hockey name it associated with her was, naturally, Doug Wickenheiser. Sometimes the two are even linked as brother and sister when in fact they were only distant cousins.

"We weren't really close at all when I was growing up," Hayley says. "In fact, I didn't get to meet Doug until three years before he passed away. I grew up knowing I was related to him and that he played in the NHL. I had my own dream to play for the Edmonton Oilers, so it was nice to have a family member with the same last name in the NHL. He was inspirational to my career."

If Hayley Wickenheiser must be associated with a male hockey player, isn't Gordie Howe the obvious comparison? Both were precocious, with Howe breaking into the NHL as an 18-year-old (long after the soldier-athletes had returned home) and Wickenheiser joining Team Canada at the tender age of 15. Both are uncommonly and deceivingly strong. To look at Wickenheiser in casual dress, one would never guess there are 170 pounds packed on that 5-foot-9 figure; in uniform, she is no giant, but no woman is more solid on her skates. Howe was a prolific scorer, a leader by example, and for some time was arguably the greatest player in the history of his sport. Ditto, ditto and . . . well, yeah, ditto. Maybe the comparison will break down in the 2020s because, as of this book's publication, she doesn't have any daughters (just a son) who can grow up to play alongside her.

Wickenheiser's first hockey paragon was neither Doug Wickenheiser nor Gordie Howe. It was her father, Tom Wickenheiser.

"My parents were teachers in Shaunavon. My mom (Marilyn) curled and my dad was involved with minor hockey and also played oldtimers. I enjoyed watching him play and asked Mom if I could start."

A five-year-old girl playing hockey? How would parents react to such an abnormal request?

"Mom said, 'Sure,' and got me a pair of skates, and Dad built an outdoor rink just outside of our house for my younger brother (Ross) and sister (Jane) and myself. That's where I learned how to skate. There was no girl's hockey in town. Most of the time, I was the only girl playing on boys' teams."

That of course, led to problems . . . not for anyone named Wickenheiser but for others who couldn't handle little Johnny being outplayed by a girl.

"Oh yeah, many times. I remember an instance in Eastend when I was probably nine years old. I had to change in my own dressing room by that time, and the Eastend rink was being renovated, so all I had was an open room in the middle of the lobby. The game was getting a little bit rough and out of hand. During the intermission, one of the mothers burst into the room and told me that I shouldn't be on the ice, that I didn't belong with her son and those sorts of things. I was maybe the best player on my team, and he was the best on his team. We were always going at it. I was pretty aggressive, and I didn't back down from anybody, especially at that age. And she was a pretty aggressive mother, so we had a rivalry.

Hayley Wickenheiser

"That's really the only incident that I can vividly remember. For the most part my parents sheltered me from that. My dad coached me until we left Shaunavon, and he was able to keep everybody away so I didn't have to deal with the consequences of being a girl and being that good so young. A lot of parents didn't like that.

"Every single game I knew there would be one or two guys on the other team that wanted to kill me. I felt uncomfortable, stared at. The comments would usually come before I hit the ice. Once I stepped on it, I had the confidence, I knew I would do well. That was my little safety haven, out on the ice."

About the only team that didn't set out to cause Hayley grief was Shaunavon, and not just because her dad was sometimes the coach.

"I knew all the boys, I went to school with them and was best friends with them. I was one of the boys, basically, or at least one of the kids in town, and they were always very good to me. Once I moved to Calgary I found that I could earn my teammates' respect by proving that I could play.

"The worst thing as a teenager was probably guys trying to run you or making comments here and there. It wasn't that bad because I was a good enough player that I had respect from those teams. I could handle the contact as long as it was legal. When they did try to run me, I would try to outskill them. I never really lost my composure. What my dad always told me was: 'Score goals; you know, that will make them even more upset.' That's how I tried to deal with it."

Tom Wickenheiser started an all-girls hockey team in Shaunavon. The age range of 5 to 15 tells all about how competitive it strove to be, but it was a start. Hayley finally got a chance to play some serious all-girls hockey when she was invited to try out for Saskatchewan's 17-and-under team for the 1991 Canada Winter Games, but Marilyn and Tom moved

At Salt Lake City: Team Canada's top gun

to more secure teaching jobs in Calgary in 1990. Hayley ended up with Team Alberta at the Canada Games and recorded six points in three games, including the game-winning goal in the gold-medal game.

Wickenheiser's move to Calgary provided something she had lacked in Saskatchewan: realistic inspiration. Perhaps she dreamed of playing for the Edmonton Oilers, but she was so tiny that even their stickboys would tower over her. Then everything fell in place, thanks to television and a growth spurt.

"I had never heard of women's hockey all the time I lived in Shaunavon. Then, shortly after we moved to Calgary I saw the women's world championship on TV. Right away I knew that's where I wanted to be.

"At the Canada Games I was a skinny little rail. I had always been small for my age until I got to 13, 14 years old. I started to grow, and I got so that when I was invited to the national selection camp in Kitchener I was one of the bigger players."

She was also, at 15, one of the youngest—in fact, the youngest by far, like Mozart surrounded by Haydn and his peers.

"The next youngest players were probably 18 or 19 years old. They called me High-Chair Hayley, that was my nickname. I was nervous, I was excited. I'll never forget meeting veterans like France St. Louis and Stacie Wilson who took me under their wing and gave me so much respect for such a young player. I was always in awe of these players and just felt lucky to be there at 15. I really looked to them for leadership and guidance. Who knows how I would have turned out without them? The veterans really bought into the Canadian way, that it's everybody for your country and for the team. They were very selfless people, and I was lucky—I saw that at 15 years old."

National team coach Shannon Miller, a Melfort product, saw no need to delay. She put Wickenheiser on the Canadian roster. There were some objections raised from the least expected sources.

"My parents didn't want me to play! They actually wanted me to go back for another Canada Games because they thought I was too young, but I knew the national team is what I wanted, and I've stayed with them ever since.

"Shannon believed in me at a young age. She knew that I was a bit of raw talent, had a lot of energy and that I could play if given the right opportunity and guidance along the way."

Miller put Wickenheiser on a line with two of Canada's best players, Wilson and Angela James, but Wickenheiser slid into the boards and tore knee ligaments in her second practice with the team. She returned in time to play one game in the world championship round robin, then take a regular shift and record one assist in the semi-final and final as Canada repeated its 1991 championship performance. On receiving her gold medal, Wickenheiser was 15 years 8 months 5 days old.

While achieving fame as a hockey player, Wickenheiser was also ascending heights on the softball diamond. A capable shortstop, third baseman and outfielder, she made Canada's team for the 1995 world junior championship in Normal, Illinois, and rose all the way to the Olympic team for the 2000 Summer Games at Sydney, Australia. (Another Saskatchewan product, shortstop Jacki Nichol of Saskatoon, was a teammate.) A series of tough losses relegated Canada to eighth place in Sydney, but Wickenheiser earned the distinction of being, before her 22nd birthday, both a Winter and Summer Olympian. The Winter Olympic experience, of course, had come in 1998 at Nagano, Japan, where the hockey team settled for silver medals after a depressing loss to the United States that wouldn't be purged until the next Olympics four years later. (See "How Emerald Lake saved Salt Lake," p. 314.)

Wickenheiser's hockey career came full circle in the 2002–03 hockey season as she reverted to her childhood role of playing against boys—men, actually. She was going to become a trail blazer out of necessity. Women's senior hockey didn't challenge her or force her to improve her skills; the only way to achieve that was by playing with men, preferably in Europe, where the de-emphasis on bodychecking more closely resembled the rules of women's hockey.

"My hope is that someday there's going to be a women's pro league. That's where I'd play if there was one, but there isn't. I just felt I had to do something to rejuvenate myself because I had been with the national team for 10 years and played the same competition all the time. I needed a change. That's why I did it.

"I had trained in the Czech Republic every July and August for years, and I'd had the opportunity to skate with a Division 1 men's team there. The plans for me to try out for a men's team in Finland were in place prior to Salt Lake thanks to a contact I had through a Finnish women's team."

Wickenheiser joined Salamat of the Finnish Second Division in December of 2002, played 23 games and recorded two goals, 10 assists and a plus-6 rating. She usually took a regular shift and was often called on to take key faceoffs. Salamat won promotion to the First Division and everybody was happy—in Finland, anyway.

"The guys on the team were very open and accepting of my presence. They didn't criticize me or come to conclusions too early. There was no controversy in Finland, which surprised me. I knew that in Canada and North America there would be just as many who

Hayley Wickenheiser with Salamat

would criticize it as would support it. I had low expectations as to how I'd be perceived. I guess the Finns hadn't seen a woman play at that level before, and a lot of them probably didn't think that I could really skate and thought it was a big joke. There were probably about 40 media at my first practice, and I could see the surprise on their faces."

That media swarm quickly dissipated when it became apparent, with the matter of gender hidden beneath several layers of clothing and protective gear, that Wickenheiser looked like an ordinary hockey player.

It took some time for Wickenheiser's Salamat experience to bear fruit. The 2003 women's world championship to be held in China was cancelled because of the SARS outbreak. Back in Finland, a new coach had her riding the bench, and she parted ways with the team after 10 games. Wickenheiser relaxed in Calgary with her family for a few months and rejoined Team Canada for the 2004 world championship in Halifax. Her winning goal in the second period of the 2–0 victory over the United States in the gold-medal final was a beauty, a wrist shot from the high slot that froze American goalie Pam Dreyer and found net just under the crossbar.

HOW EMERALD LAKE SAVED SALT LAKE: HAYLEY WICKENHEISER'S OLYMPIC MEMORIES IN HER OWN WORDS

The biggest goal I've ever scored was the tying goal against Finland in the semi-final at the Salt Lake City Olympics in 2002. We have a lot of respect for the Finns. They took us to overtime in the 1997 worlds in Kitchener with almost the same team they had in Salt Lake; a lot of people don't know that. Often in televised games we blow them out, but they're a much better team than most people know.

We went into that game really tight, and they were up 3–2 heading into the third period. We had been outshooting them badly, but their goalie (Tuula Puputti) was standing on her head, which is the scary thing. She was actually that good of a goalie that they could win. We started getting tighter and tighter. Then I scored to tie it up, and I could feel our team relax. Jayna Hefford got one six seconds later, and I knew we had them. We got it together and won 7–3.

That set up the final against the United States, a rematch of the gold-medal game we lost in the 1998 Olympics at Nagano. There were seven or eight of us back from that team who did not want to feel that disappointment again. That feeling was so strong that we were ready to do just about whatever it took to win this game. At the same time, I didn't put as much pressure on myself in Salt Lake as I did in Nagano. Nagano was about trying too hard. We had a stronger team than we had in 1998, pretty much right through. The defence was similar, but the forwards were a lot stronger, and there was no question that Kim St-Pierre was the best women's goalie we'd ever had to that point.

(Team Canada included four Saskatchewan women: forwards Dana Antal of Esterhazy and Kelly Bechard of

Hayley Wickenheiser wearing her favourite necklace

Dana Antal

Sedley, defenceman Colleen Sostorics of Kennedy, and Wickenheiser.)

We had lost eight games in a row to the Americans. What basically had happened in those games is that to prepare for the Olympic Games we had to train so hard physically that at times we were just exhausted. Even in games where we did play great, we just couldn't score. We were wondering what was going on—you have doubts going on all the time—but what kept us believing was our tradition as a team and the knowledge that no matter how bad it got, it would come down to one game, and we could win it. I remember feeling a total calmness stepping on to that ice and personally saying I was going to do my job, play the best that I could play, and I can't worry about anything else. I think every player on the team was thinking like that: If I just do my job, we can win. I would say it was a total team effort that gave us the victory. For the first time that whole season I looked down the bench, and I could say that every single player on our team was there to play and was playing well. That hadn't happened all year long.

We got the early lead, but then it boiled down to the American referee (Stacey Livingston) giving us all those penalties (eight straight minors in 22 minutes) and how we kept our composure while we killed off all those power plays. There are two reasons why we stayed cool. The first is that before we went to the Olympics we went to this retreat in British Columbia called Emerald Lake. One of our exercises was to write down every possible thing that could go wrong at the Olympics, then discuss how we should deal with that situation. We thought of the bus breaking

Kelly Bechard

down, eating bad food, somebody dying in your family during the Games, anything that could happen. One of the things was, bad refereeing in the final game or getting an American ref. How were we going to react to it? We decided that if anybody was at risk of losing their composure at the Olympics, we were going to have a phrase—"Emerald Lake"—to remember what we had talked about.

Colleen Sostorics is overjoyed as she displays her gold medal and bouquet after beating the United States in Salt Lake City

During the final game, we must have said "Emerald Lake" 5,000 times to each other. But it worked! Because every time somebody was going to get anxious or excited, somebody would say, "EmeraldLakeEmeraldLake!" It almost got to the point where it became funny, like: "Are you kidding me? That's another penalty?" "Emerald Lake!" We started laughing about it, and it seemed that we gained composure and the Americans lost it. The second thing, of course, was our coaching staff. They were so calm, and they didn't get riled up. Those were the big reasons why we were able to pull it out.

The Americans scored only once on those eight power plays, early in the second period, and I was able to put us back in the lead a couple of minutes later. I picked up a loose puck at the top of the circle and top-shelfed it. Then Jayna Hefford scored on a breakaway with one second left in the second period, the goal where the puck rolled over the back of the goalie, an incredible goal.

We went in to the dressing room saying we've come this far, we're not going to lose it now. Going into the third period, it was mainly a matter of staying relaxed, doing the right things, and not getting caught up in more penalties. We held them off, basically. I had taken my shifts, killed a lot of penalties, and played on the power play in the first period, but I wasn't tired. None of us were tired. We were running on adrenaline.

I guess I'll always be remembered for going on TV with Don Cherry and saying what I did about the Americans stepping on our flag in their dressing room. I still believe they had a flag in their dressing room. Then they denied it, and I don't think anybody knows what the truth of the matter was in the end, but I was so fired up and so emotional at the moment.

There were other incidents through the course of the Olympics and that whole season when we were such fierce rivals that were signs of disrespect for our team. For example, there was an Olympic Village newspaper that took pictures of a couple of girls on our team. It was posted up in the café, and the Americans came and slashed their faces off the paper and wrote "Canada You Suck," or something like that. They were little gamesmanship things that you do, but there were times when it crossed the line, and I had had enough by the end of the final game.

The flag—we had been told it was in their room through the course of the tournament by security staff at the rink and by Americans that didn't like it. I don't know if they were stepping on it, which some people said was happening. I think they had it in their room as a sign of inspiration or motivation. That was a sign of disrespect; we would never have another nation's flag in our room. I just felt so strongly, and I was so happy that we'd beaten them that, for me, after that game, those were the right things to say at the moment. So I don't regret it at all.

When I look back and see how I was on TV, I'm like, "Oh my God, I can't believe I was so wound up like that," because I'm usually sort of laid back off the ice. I'm a little embarrassed by my reaction, but in the heat of the moment I wouldn't have changed a thing because it was so gratifying and so exciting. My brother and sister up on the side of the bleachers had all the Canadians going crazy, it was great to share it with them at that moment.

I remember Pat Quinn standing on our bench after we won the gold, coming down to congratulate our coaches, and he had tears running down his cheeks. I think that, as a coach himself, he couldn't believe the composure we showed.

We had a genuine bond with the men's team. Guys like Steve Yzerman and Eric Lindros who were at Nagano in '98 were saying, "Way to go, guys, that was awesome." We stayed on the same floor in the village, and we were always crossing paths. As the tournament went on, they'd watch our games, and we'd watch their games. I know that a lot of the men were at our final game cheering for us and were genuinely moved and very inspired by what we did. Having those guys there at the game was special for us, too.

And of course we were there watching them for their gold-medal game against the American men. They seated us for whatever reason beside the women's U.S. team, so when Canada scored we were cheering, and when the Americans scored they were cheering. It just added more fuel to the fire. We didn't wear our medals; we took the high road and handled it with class. Actually, they did too, but every chance we got to cheer was pretty loud.

I knew there was a sense of magnitude about our game because I've had a chance to go coast-to-coast since the Olympics, and everywhere I go everyone tells me where they were or what they were doing, similar to what the 1972 Canada–Soviet series was like.

For women, that was our Stanley Cup, our Mecca. We played with emotion, maybe with an innocence that is lost sometimes in the men's game. Also to have both the men and the women win, that was a boost for Canadians, a special thing. I think that what always make it special is that both of us did it. There will always be the things that live on, like the loonie at centre ice, maybe my comments, Jayna's goal, Mario Lemieux letting the pass go through to Paul Kariya, those things. I was so proud to be a part of that.

ALSO DURING THESE YEARS

- Harness racing driver Ray Remmen of Saskatoon won the 1990 Little Brown Jug with Beach Towel. Remmen had won the 1981 Hambletonian with Shiaway Pat.

- Jeff Thue of Regina earned an Olympic silver medal in heavyweight wrestling at the 1992 Games in Barcelona. Thue was beaten in the gold-medal match by American Bruce Baumgartner, the same man who defeated Bob Molle eight years earlier.

- Brad Watson worked his first game in the NHL on February 5, 1994, joining fellow Reginan Mick McGeough (January 19, 1989) among the league's referees.

- Wrestler Justin Abdou of Moose Jaw won the gold medal in the 82-kilo class at the 1994 Commonwealth Games in Victoria.

- Jason Parker of Yorkton swept all four events in men's speed skating at the 1995 Canada Winter Games in Grande Prairie, Alta. Eight years later in Campbellton-Bathurst, N.B., Melville's Kerry Simpson duplicated Parker's feat in the women's competition.

- The Moose Jaw Diamond Dogs, Regina Cyclones and Saskatoon Riot (later Smokin' Guns) maintained baseball franchises in the independent Prairie League from 1995–97. Saskatoon's first manager was former major-leaguer George Scott. Regina won the PL's first championship. Moose Jaw pulled 75,348 fans (an average of 2,093 per game) into tiny Ross Wells Park; third baseman Shawn Wooten went on to play for the 2002 World Series champion Anaheim Angels.

- Humboldt speed skater Jeremy Wotherspoon captured the silver medal in the men's 500 metres at the 1998 Winter Olympics in Nagano, Japan.

- Paralympic athlete Colette Bourgonje of Saskatoon won silver medals in the 2.5- and 5-kilometre sit-ski races at the 1998 Winter Games in Nagano. Bourgonje had won four bronze medals at Summer Paralympics, doubling in the 100 and 200 metres in Barcelona (1992) and Atlanta (1996)

Cymone Bouchard

Lisa Franks

- The University of Saskatchewan Huskies won their third Canadian university football title in nine seasons by defeating Concordia 24–17. Matt Kellett kicked three field goals and linebacker Trevor Ludtke recovered a fumble in the Concordia end zone with two minutes to go. In 1994, Saskatchewan quarterback Brent Schneider passed for 237 yards as the Huskies overcame a 12–0 halftime deficit to whip St. Francis Xavier 31–12. Saskatchewan's first national title came in 1990 with a 24–21 decision over St. Mary's.

- Heather Dedman scored 24 points to lead the University of Regina Cougars to a 94–85 victory over the University of Alberta Pandas in the 2001 CIS women's basketball national final in Edmonton. Cymone Bouchard of the Cougars was named the tournament's most valuable player with 44 points in three games; she would also be named the top player in the country for the 2003–04 season.

- Howard Weitzel of North Battleford won the 2001 world senior men's horseshoe pitching championship.

Saskatoon rinks pulled off an unprecedented double by sweeping the men's and women's titles at both the Canadian and world junior curling championships in 2003. Celebrating after their triumph in Flims, Switzerland are (left to right, fifth through skip and coach): Tammy Schneider, Chelsey Bell, Janelle Leon, Teejay Surik, Marliese Miller and Bob Miller; Ben Hebert, Kyler Broad, Michael Jantzen, Christopher Haichert, Steve Laycock and Barry Fiendall. Miller went undefeated at the worlds and beat Maureen Brunt of the United States 5–4 for the gold medal. Laycock was 9–2 overall; he edged Emanuel Alberg of Sweden 5–4 in an extra end of the men's final.

Weitzel, a 14-time provincial champion, was Canadian Open champion in 1990.

- Regina curlers Nancy Kerr, Linda Burnham, Kenda Richards and Gertie Pick went 11–0 to win the 2003 world senior women's championship in Winnipeg. Kerr played third on Marj Mitchell's 1980 world championship rink.

- Lisa Franks, a 22-year-old University of Saskatchewan student, won gold medals in the women's T52 200- and 400-metre wheelchair races at the 2004 World Paralympic Games in Athens. She set world records in both events, clocking 1 minute 9.52 seconds in the 400 final and 36.63 seconds in the 200 semi-final. Franks, born and raised in Moose Jaw, had been able-bodied until an arteriovenous malformation left her paralyzed below the waist shortly after her 14th birthday.

- Mark Dacey of Nova Scotia returned to his hometown of Saskatoon to win the 2004 Brier. Dacey scored three in the 10th end of the final to upset Alberta 10–9 and deny Randy Ferbey a fourth consecutive Canadian men's curling championship.

- Forward Ryan Getzlaf of Regina and defenceman Braydon Coburn of Shaunavon were key members of the Team Canada entry that trampled the field at the world junior hockey championship in Grand Forks, N.D., Dec. 25, 2004 through Jan. 4, 2005. Getzlaf poured in three goals and nine assists in six games while Coburn was a solid plus-8 on the blue line.

AFTERWORD

Standing on the Shoulders of Giants

Where better to end this book than with Hayley Wickenheiser and the Shaunavon Badgers? On February 21, 2004, Shaunavon was chosen as the focal point for *Hockey Day in Canada*, the day-long televised celebration of our national sporting passion. Among the celebrities present were Ken Dryden, Wendel Clark, Dick Irvin, Ron MacLean, and the one-man carnival himself, Don Cherry. Fred Sasakamoose, the NHL's first Indian, and Jim Hunter, the original Crazy Canuck of the ski slopes, wandered happily about, sometimes swarmed by the public, sometimes peacefully anonymous. All were enthusiastically welcomed.

Yet among these men of distinction walked one woman with an aura all her own, who could simultaneously tuck her fame in the back pocket of her blue jeans and cast a glow of inspiration from her smile. Like untold thousands, she had moved from Saskatchewan to Alberta in the '80s, but this was still home, and her home still treated her like its own. Two of Shaunavon's native sons, Gary Aldcorn and Rhett Warrener, have played in the NHL. Shaun Van Allen, who grew up there, is a 12-year NHL veteran. Braydon Coburn, the eighth overall pick in the 2003 draft, awaits his turn with the Atlanta Thrashers. Shaunavon (population 1,800 under normal circumstances) has no shortage of hockey heroes.

But Hayley—in this town, there's no need for her surname—is special. You can take the girl out of Saskatchewan, but you can't take Saskatchewan out of the girl. And no, you can't entirely take this girl out of Saskatchewan, not Hayley. Something she had left behind emerged from everyone who greeted her. It was mirrored by the recognition in Hayley's eyes as she renewed acquaintances with the girls and guys of her childhood, with their parents and with her former neighbours. When she popped into the rink she was besieged by media, accommodated them all—she's a charming interview when she doesn't think her flag's been stepped on—and politely broke away to drop the puck for a game between the senior girls' teams of Swift Current and Shaunavon. Hayley spent a period at the bench of each team, encouraging every player after each shift. The girls ranged in age from pre- to mid-teens and were torn between total awe and making an impression. (Can you imagine being any age and having Wayne Gretzky, Bobby Orr or Gordie Howe slap you on the shoulder pads and say, "Nice going out there! Way to skate!" Gasping for breath at the end of a shift was never so convenient.)

After the game the Badgers waited to have their picture taken with Hayley. Television, the ruler of the sports world, wanted a few minutes of her time first. Ten minutes . . . no, 15 . . . 20 . . . the girls waited in the chill outside the rink, rubbing their hands, stamping their feet. At last Hayley arrived, full of apologies.

There she is, and there they are, daughters and younger sisters of the Shaunavon people Hayley had to leave behind in 1990—remnants of her past, fabric of our future.

A century ago Saskatchewan was in its infancy as a province, a broad expanse of geography with a sparse population and harsh climate. Our first great athletes were Indian men who could run great distances rapidly and tirelessly, men from a culture accustomed to the terrain and the necessity of long journeys. The massive settlement of Europeans and Eastern Canadians brought people with a need for structured recreation, for sports that were dominated in the beginning by male individuals, male teams, male leagues. Saskatchewan produced Jim Trifunov, the Saskatoon Crescents, Gordie Howe, the Saskatchewan Roughriders, George Genereux, the North Battleford Beavers, Terry Puhl, Rueben Mayes, curling teams skipped by Garnet Campbell and Ernie Richardson, and the embryo of the junior Western Hockey League.

Along the same time line, women were making their own inroads. To the credit of the athletes, their families and their communities, Saskatchewan became a place where female athletes could succeed—not always with the best of support, facilities or encouragement, but any young woman inclined to excel found a way to

do it. Ethel Catherwood and Phyllis Dewar were like a snowball rolling down a hill, gathering to themselves Bonnie Baker, Diane Jones Konihowski, Stacy Singer, Catriona Le May Doan, curling quartets led by Joyce McKee and Sandra Schmirler, and, of course, Hayley Wickenheiser.

Your sport can be hockey or softball, speed skating or baton twirling, individual or team, indoor or outdoor, winter or summer, popular or obscure. You can be male or female, be part of the crowd or go your own way. You can be city or country, Saskatoon or Shaunavon. You can be anything. Sometimes that's more than anyone dreamed you would be. Sometimes that's the best in the country, even the best on Earth. You live in what sometimes seems like the middle of nowhere in a climate that often feels like an experiment gone haywire, and it doesn't matter because of all these people who went before you and succeeded.

If, as Isaac Newton asserted, we see more clearly because we stand on the shoulders of giants, then the people of Saskatchewan enjoy a wonderful view when they scan their athletic landscape. Out of necessity, our giants leave home to prove their greatness. When we stand on their shoulders, we see that they have conquered the world.

Listen to them, and you'll hear them encouraging you to do it again.

–John Chaput

Appendix: Saskatchewan-Born Players' NHL Career Statistics

Players arranged first in order of birthplace, then by the year they entered the NHL. Goaltenders follow skaters.

Name	Birthdate	Birthplace	Pos	First Ssn	Last Ssn	GP	G	A	P	PM	Teams
James Bedard	Nov. 19, 1927	Admiral	D	1949–50	1950–51	22	1	1	2	8	Chi
Willie Brossart	May 29, 1949	Allan	D	1970–71	1975–76	129	1	14	15	88	Phil, Tor, Wash
Patrick Marleau	Sept. 15, 1979	Aneroid	C	1997–98		558	153	174	327	193	SJ
Hal Picketts	Apr. 22, 1909	Asquith	RW	1933–34	1933–34	48	3	1	4	32	NYA
Clint Smith	Dec. 12, 1913	Assiniboia	C	1936–37	1946–47	483	161	236	397	24	NYR, Chi
Doug MacDonald	Feb. 8, 1969	Assiniboia	LW	1992–93	1994–95	11	1	0	1	2	Buf
Greg Classen	Aug. 24, 1977	Aylsham	C	2000–01		90	7	10	17	48	Nash
Doug Trapp	Nov. 28, 1965	Balcarres	LW	1986–87	1986–87	2	0	0	0	0	Buf
Hub Macey	Apr. 13, 1921	Big River	LW	1941–42	1946–47	30	6	9	15	0	NYR, Mtl
Jim Neilson	Nov. 28, 1940	Big River	D	1962–63	1977–78	1023	69	299	368	904	NYR, Cal, Clev
Barry Pederson	Mar. 13, 1961	Big River	C	1980–81	1991–92	701	238	416	654	472	Bos, Vcr, Pitt, Hart
Marshall Johnston	June 6, 1941	Birch Hills	D	1967–68	1973–74	251	14	52	66	58	MinNS, Cal
Hugh Coflin	Dec. 15, 1928	Blaine Lake	D	1950–51	1950–51	31	0	3	3	33	Chi
Bill Hajt	Nov. 18, 1951	Borden	D	1973–74	1986–87	854	42	202	244	433	Buf
Cliff Koroll	Oct. 1, 1946	Canora	RW	1969–70	1979–80	814	208	254	462	376	Chi
Cam Severson	Jan. 15, 1978	Canora	LW	2002–03		33	3	0	3	58	Ana
Brenden Morrow	Jan. 16, 1979	Carlyle	LW	1999–00		370	97	107	204	573	Dal
Clarke Wilm	Oct. 24, 1976	Central Butte	C	1998–99		395	36	53	89	293	Cgy, Nash, Tor
Lionel Heinrich	Apr. 20, 1934	Churchbridge	LW	1955–56	1955–56	35	1	1	2	33	Det
Kevin Kaminski	Mar. 13, 1969	Churchbridge	C	1988–89	1996–97	139	3	10	13	528	MinNS, Que, Wash
Gord Kluzak	Mar. 4, 1964	Climax	D	1982–83	1990–91	299	25	98	123	543	Bos
Rocky Trottier	Apr. 11, 1964	Climax	RW	1983–84	1984–85	38	6	4	10	2	NJ
Jim Archibald	June 6, 1961	Craik	RW	1984–85	1986–87	16	1	2	3	45	MinNS
Garnet Exelby	Aug. 16, 1981	Craik	D	2002–03		86	1	11	12	175	AtlT
Jeremy Reich	Feb. 11, 1979	Craik	LW	2003–04		9	0	1	1	20	Clmb
Frank Ingram	Sept. 17, 1907	Craven	RW	1929–30	1931–32	101	24	16	40	69	Chi
Morris Mott	May 25, 1946	Creelman	RW	1972–73	1974–75	199	18	32	50	49	Cal
Gerry Ehman	Nov. 3, 1932	Cudworth	RW	1957–58	1970–71	429	96	118	214	100	Bos, Det, Tor, Oak/Cal
Orland Kurtenbach	Sept. 7, 1936	Cudworth	C	1960–61	1973–74	639	119	213	332	628	NYR, Bos, Tor, Vcr
Paul Shmyr	Jan. 18, 1946	Cudworth	D	1968–69	1981–82	343	13	72	85	528	Chi, Cal, MinNS, Hart
Rob Tudor	June 30, 1956	Cupar	RW/C	1978–79	1982–83	28	4	4	8	19	Vcr, StL
Doug Bentley	Sept. 3, 1916	Delisle	LW	1939–40	1953–54	566	219	324	543	217	Chi, NYR
Max Bentley	Mar. 1, 1920	Delisle	C	1940–41	1953–54	646	245	299	544	179	Chi, Tor, NYR
Reg Bentley	May 3, 1914	Delisle	LW	1942–43	1942–43	11	1	2	3	2	Chi
Dick Butler	June 2, 1926	Delisle	RW	1947–48	1947–48	7	2	0	2	0	Chi
Jack Miller	Sept. 16, 1925	Delisle	C	1949–50	1950–51	17	0	0	0	4	Chi
Jim Leavins	July 28, 1960	Dinsmore	D	1985–86	1986–87	41	2	12	14	30	Det, NYR
Les Colwill	Jan. 1, 1935	Divide	RW	1958–59	1958–59	69	7	6	13	16	NYR
Bob Hoffmeyer	July 27, 1955	Dodsland	D	1977–78	1984–85	198	14	52	66	325	Chi, Phil, NJ
Don Gillen	Dec. 24, 1960	Dodsland	RW	1979–80	1981–82	35	2	4	6	22	Phil, Hart
Brad McCrimmon	Mar. 29, 1959	Dodsland	D	1979–80	1996–97	1222	81	322	403	1416	Bos, Phil, Cgy, Det, Hart, Phx
Robin Bartel	May 16, 1961	Drake	D	1985–86	1986–87	41	0	1	1	14	Cgy, Vcr
Fern Flaman	Jan. 25, 1927	Dysart	D	1944–45	1960–61	910	34	174	208	1370	Bos, Tor
Bill Kyle	Dec. 23, 1924	Dysart	C	1949–50	1950–51	3	0	3	3	0	NYR
Gus Kyle	Sept. 11, 1923	Dysart	D	1949–50	1951–52	203	6	20	26	362	NYR, Bos
Frank Mario	Feb. 25, 1921	Esterhazy	C	1941–42	1944–45	53	9	19	28	24	Bos
Chris Herperger	Feb. 24, 1974	Esterhazy	LW	1999–00		169	18	25	43	75	Chi, Ott, AtlT
Al Nicholson	Apr. 26, 1936	Estevan	LW	1955–56	1956–57	19	0	1	1	4	Bos
Blair Atcheynum	Apr. 20, 1969	Estevan	RW	1992–93	2000–01	196	27	33	60	36	Ott, StL, Nash, Chi
Trent Whitfield	June 17, 1977	Estevan	C	1999–00		144	9	11	20	83	Wash, NYR
Vic Myles	Nov. 12, 1915	Fairlight	D	1942–43	1942–43	45	6	9	15	57	NYR
Neil Hawryliw	Nov. 9, 1955	Fielding	RW	1981–82	1981–82	1	0	0	0	0	NYI
Buzz Boll	Mar. 6, 1911	Fillmore	LW	1932–33	1943–44	437	133	130	263	148	Tor, NYA, Bkn, Bos
Fred Gordon	May 6, 1900	Fleming	RW	1926–27	1927–28	81	8	7	15	68	Det, Bos
Gordie Howe	Mar. 31, 1928	Floral	RW	1946–47	1979–80	1767	801	1049	1850	1685	Det, Hart
Dennis Polonich	Dec. 4, 1953	Foam Lake	C/RW	1974–75	1982–83	390	59	82	141	1242	Det
Bernie Federko	May 12, 1956	Foam Lake	C	1976–77	1989–90	1000	369	761	1130	487	StL, Det
Pat Elynuik	Oct. 30, 1967	Foam Lake	RW	1987–88	1995–96	506	154	188	342	459	Wpg, Wash, TB, Ott
Eddie Shore	Nov. 25, 1902	Fort Qu'Appelle	D	1926–27	1939–40	550	105	179	284	1047	Bos, NYA
Frank Waite	Apr. 9, 1905	Fort Qu'Appelle	C	1930–31	1930–31	17	1	3	4	4	NYR
Tom Dewar	June 10, 1913	Frobisher	D	1943–44	1943–44	9	0	2	2	4	NYR
Ralph Nattrass	May 26, 1925	Gainsborough	D	1946–47	1949–50	223	18	38	56	308	Chi
Lew Morrison	Feb. 11, 1948	Gainsborough	RW	1969–70	1977–78	564	39	52	91	107	Phil, AtlF, Wash, Pitt
Ron Greschner	Dec. 22, 1954	Goodsoil	D	1974–75	1989–90	982	179	431	610	1226	NYR
Gord Sherven	Aug. 21, 1963	Gravelbourg	C	1983–84	1987–88	97	13	22	35	33	Edm, MinNS, Hart
Max Sutherland	Feb. 8, 1907	Grenfell	LW	1931–32	1931–32	2	0	0	0	0	Bos
Bryan Hextall (Sr.)	July 31, 1913	Grenfell	RW	1936–37	1947–48	449	187	175	362	227	NYR
Jim McKenzie	Nov. 3, 1969	Gull Lake	LW	1989–90		880	48	52	100	1805	Hart, Dal, Pitt, Wpg, Phx, Ana, Wash, NJ, Nash
Roger Kortko	Feb. 1, 1963	Hafford	C	1984–85	1985–86	79	7	17	24	28	NYI
Jason Herter	Oct. 2, 1970	Hafford	D	1995–96	1995–96	1	0	1	1	0	NYI
Quintin Laing	June 8, 1979	Harris	LW	2003–04		3	0	1	1	0	Chi
Henry Dyck	Sept. 5, 1912	Herbert	C/LW	1943–44	1943–44	1	0	0	0	0	NYR
Grant Jennings	May 5, 1965	Hudson Bay	D	1987–88	1995–96	389	14	43	57	804	Wash, Hart, Pitt, Tor, Buf

Name	Birthdate	Birthplace	Pos	First Ssn	Last Ssn	GP	G	A	P	PM	Teams
Trent Yawney	Sept. 29, 1965	Hudson Bay	D	1987–88	1998–99	593	27	102	129	783	Chi, Cgy, StL
Tony Leswick	Mar. 17, 1923	Humboldt	L/RW	1945–46	1957–58	740	165	159	324	900	NYR, Det, Chi
Ross Lonsberry	Feb. 7, 1947	Humboldt	LW	1966–67	1980–81	968	256	310	566	806	Bos, LA, Phil, Pitt
Jerome Engele	Nov. 26, 1950	Humboldt	D	1975–76	1977–78	100	2	13	15	162	MinNS
Ralph Klassen	Sept. 15, 1955	Humboldt	C	1975–76	1983–84	497	52	93	145	120	Cal, Clev, ColR, StL
Brad Lauer	Oct. 27, 1966	Humboldt	LW	1986–87	1995–96	323	44	67	111	218	NYI, Chi, Ott, Pitt
Brendan Witt	Feb. 20, 1975	Humboldt	D	1995–96		568	19	53	72	894	Wash
Kyle McLaren	June 18, 1977	Humboldt	D	1995–96		514	36	120	192	460	Bos, SJ
Jeff Lank	Mar. 1, 1975	Indian Head	D	1999–00	1999–00	2	0	0	0	2	Phil
Ken Schinkel	Nov. 27, 1932	Jansen	RW	1959–60	1972–73	636	127	198	325	163	NYR, Pitt
Jack Church	May 24, 1915	Kamsack	D	1938–39	1945–46	130	4	19	23	154	Tor, Bkn, Bos
Wayne Smith	Feb. 12, 1943	Kamsack	D	1966–67	1966–67	2	1	1	2	2	Chi
Harold Philipoff	July 14, 1956	Kamsack	LW	1977–78	1979–80	141	26	57	83	267	AtlF, Chi
Tyler Wright	Apr. 6, 1973	Kamsack	C	1992–93		570	77	64	141	803	Edm, Pitt, Clmb
Darcy Hordichuk	Aug. 10, 1980	Kamsack	LW	2000–01		73	1	1	2	276	AtlT, Phx, Fla
Barry Melrose	July 15, 1956	Kelvington	D	1979–80	1985–86	300	10	23	33	728	Wpg, Tor, Det
Wendel Clark	Oct. 25, 1966	Kelvington	LW	1985–86	1999–00	793	330	234	564	1690	Tor, Que, NYI, TB, Det, Chi
Curtis Murphy	Dec. 3, 1975	Kerrobert	D	2002–03		1	0	0	0	0	MinW
Dick Meissner	Jan. 6, 1940	Kindersley	RW	1959–60	1964–65	171	11	15	26	37	Bos, NYR
Barrie Meissner	July 26, 1946	Kindersley	LW	1967–68	1968–69	6	0	1	1	4	MinNS
Dave Lewis	July 3, 1953	Kindersley	D	1973–74	1987–88	1008	36	187	223	953	NYI, LA, NJ, Det
Bob Bourne	June 21, 1954	Kindersley	C	1974–75	1987–88	964	258	324	582	605	NYI, LA
Larry Gloeckner	Jan. 25, 1956	Kindersley	D	1978–79	1978–79	13	0	2	2	6	Det
Greg Paslawski	Aug. 25, 1961	Kindersley	RW	1983–84	1993–94	650	187	185	372	169	Mtl, StL, Wpg, Buf, Que, Phil, Cgy
Jim Mathieson	Jan. 24, 1970	Kindersley	D	1989–90	1989–90	2	0	0	0	4	Wash
Joel Kwiatkowski	Mar. 22, 1977	Kindersley	D	2000–01		149	6	11	18	119	Ott, Wash
Gord Redahl	Aug. 28, 1935	Kinistino	RW	1958–59	1958–59	18	0	1	1	2	Bos
Gordie Nelson	May 10, 1947	Kinistino	D	1969–70	1969–70	3	0	0	0	11	Tor
Glenn Johannesen	Feb. 15, 1962	La Ronge	LW	1985–86	1985–86	2	0	0	0	0	NYI
Lloyd Ailsby	May 11, 1917	Lac Pelletier	D	1951–52	1951–52	3	0	0	0	2	NYR
Tony Hemmerling	May 15, 1914	Landis	LW	1935–36	1936–37	22	3	3	6	4	NYA
Ed Zeniuk	Mar. 8, 1933	Landis	D	1954–55	1954–55	2	0	0	0	0	Det
Gene Sobchuk	Feb. 19, 1951	Lang	LW/C	1973–74	1973–74	1	0	0	0	0	Vcr
Dennis Sobchuk	Jan. 12, 1954	Lang	C	1979–80	1982–83	35	5	6	11	2	Det, Que
Kelly Buchberger	Dec. 2, 1966	Langenburg	RW	1986–87		1182	105	204	309	2297	Edm, AtlT, LA, Phx, Pitt
Bob Baun	Sept. 9, 1936	Lanigan	D	1956–57	1972–73	964	37	187	224	1493	Tor, Oak, Det
Brian Propp	Feb. 15, 1959	Lanigan	LW	1979–80	1993–94	1016	425	579	1004	830	Phil, Bos, MinNS, Hart
Todd Strueby	June 15, 1963	Lanigan	LW	1981–82	1983–84	5	0	1	1	2	Edm
Wade Brookbank	Sept. 29, 1977	Lanigan	D	2003–04		29	2	0	2	133	Nash, Vcr
Dwight Carruthers	Nov. 7, 1944	Lashburn	D	1965–66	1967–68	2	0	0	0	0	Det, Phil
Spence Tatchell	July 16, 1924	Lloydminster	D	1942–43	1942–43	1	0	0	0	0	NYR
Bob Hassard	Mar. 26, 1929	Lloydminster	C	1949–50	1954–55	126	9	28	37	22	Tor, Chi
Larry Leach	June 18, 1936	Lloydminster	C	1958–59	1961–62	126	13	29	42	91	Bos
Barry Gibbs	Sept. 28, 1948	Lloydminster	D	1967–68	1979–80	797	58	224	282	945	Bos, MinNS, AtlF, StL, LA
Garnet Bailey	June 13, 1948	Lloydminster	LW	1968–69	1977–78	568	107	171	278	633	Bos, Det, StL, Wash
Lyle Bradley	July 31, 1943	Lloydminster	C/RW	1973–74	1976–77	6	1	0	1	2	Cal, Clev
Blair Chapman	June 13, 1956	Lloydminster	RW	1976–77	1982–83	402	106	125	231	158	Pitt, StL
Wade Redden	June 12, 1977	Lloydminster	D	1996–97		629	78	208	286	403	Ott
Justin Mapletoft	Jan. 11, 1981	Lloydminster	C	2002–03		38	3	6	9	8	NYI
Ed Cooper	Aug. 28, 1960	Loon Lake	LW	1980–81	1981–82	49	8	7	15	46	ColR
Glen Smith	Mar. 19, 1931	Lucky Lake	RW	1950–51	1950–51	2	0	0	0	0	Chi
Darin Kimble	Nov. 22, 1968	Lucky Lake	RW	1988–89	1994–95	311	23	20	43	1082	Que, StL, Bos, Chi
Beattie Ramsay	Dec. 12, 1895	Lumsden	D	1927–28	1927–28	43	0	2	2	10	Tor
Earl Miller	Sept. 12, 1905	Lumsden	LW	1927–28	1931–32	109	19	14	33	124	Chi, Tor
Duane Rupp	Mar. 29, 1938	MacNutt	D	1962–63	1972–73	374	24	93	117	220	NYR, Tor, MinNS, Pitt
Laurie Boschman	June 4, 1960	Major	C	1979–80	1992–93	1009	229	348	577	2265	Tor, Edm, Wpg, NJ, Ott
Murray Armstrong	Jan. 1, 1916	Manor	C	1937–38	1945–46	270	67	121	188	72	Tor, NYA, Bkn, Det
Gordie Poirier	Oct. 27, 1914	Maple Creek	C	1939–40	1939–40	10	0	0	0	0	Mtl
Barry Dean	Feb. 26, 1955	Maple Creek	LW	1976–77	1978–79	165	25	56	81	146	ColR, Phil
Lynn Powis	July 7, 1949	Maryfield	C	1973–74	1974–75	130	19	33	52	25	Chi, KC
Len Esau	June 3, 1968	Meadow Lake	D	1991–92	1994–95	27	0	10	10	24	Tor, Que, Cgy, Edm
Jeff Friesen	Aug. 5, 1976	Meadow Lake	C	1994–95		770	208	285	493	422	SJ, Ana, NJ
Mike Siklenka	Dec. 18, 1979	Meadow Lake	RW	2002–03		2	0	0	0	0	Phil, NYR
Jeremy Yablonski	Mar. 21, 1980	Meadow Lake	RW	2003–04		1	0	0	0	5	StL
Lorne Henning	Feb. 22, 1952	Melfort	C	1972–73	1980–81	544	73	111	184	102	NYI
Lane Lambert	Nov. 18, 1964	Melfort	RW	1983–84	1988–89	283	58	66	124	521	Det, NYR, Que
Pat MacLeod	June 15, 1969	Melfort	D	1990–91	1995–96	53	5	13	18	14	MinNS, SJ, Dal
Alex Motter	June 20, 1913	Melville	C	1934–35	1942–43	255	39	64	103	135	Bos, Det
Phil Besler	Dec. 9, 1913	Melville	RW	1935–36	1938–39	30	1	4	5	18	Bos, Chi, Det
Sid Abel	Feb. 22, 1918	Melville	C/LW	1938–39	1953–54	612	189	283	472	376	Det, Chi
Arch Wilder	Apr. 30, 1917	Melville	LW	1940–41	1940–41	18	0	2	2	2	Det
Todd McLellan	Oct. 3, 1967	Melville	C	1987–88	1987–88	5	1	1	2	0	NYI
Jarret Stoll	June 25, 1982	Melville	C	2002–03		72	10	12	22	42	Edm
Garth Boesch	Oct. 7, 1920	Milestone	D	1946–47	1949–50	197	9	28	37	205	Tor
Norm Beaudin	Nov. 28, 1941	Montmartre	RW	1967–68	1970–71	25	1	2	3	4	StL, MinNS
Butch McDonald	Nov. 21, 1916	Moose Jaw	LW/C	1939–40	1944–45	66	8	20	28	2	Det, Chi
Norm Larson	Oct. 13, 1920	Moose Jaw	RW	1940–41	1946–47	89	25	18	43	12	NYA, Bkn, NYR

Name	Birthdate	Birthplace	Pos	First Ssn	Last Ssn	GP	G	A	P	PM	Teams
Ken Smith	May 8, 1924	Moose Jaw	LW	1944–45	1950–51	331	78	93	171	49	Bos
Marty Zoborosky	Unknown	Moose Jaw	D	1944–45	1944–45	1	0	0	0	2	Chi
Frank Ashworth	Oct. 16, 1927	Moose Jaw	C	1946–47	1946–47	18	5	4	9	2	Chi
Glen Sonmor	Apr. 22, 1929	Moose Jaw	LW	1953–54	1954–55	28	2	0	2	21	NYR
Norm Johnson	Nov. 27, 1932	Moose Jaw	C	1957–58	1959–60	61	5	20	25	41	Bos, Chi
George Swarbrick	Feb. 16, 1942	Moose Jaw	RW	1967–68	1970–71	132	17	25	42	173	Oak, Pitt, Phil
Jim Wiste	Feb. 18, 1946	Moose Jaw	C	1968–69	1970–71	52	1	10	11	8	Chi, Vcr
Bill Lesuk	Nov. 1, 1946	Moose Jaw	LW	1968–69	1979–80	388	44	63	107	368	Bos, Phil, LA, Wash, Wpg
Larry McIntyre	July 13, 1949	Moose Jaw	D	1969–70	1972–73	41	0	3	3	26	Tor
Don Saleski	Nov. 10, 1949	Moose Jaw	RW	1971–72	1979–80	543	128	125	253	629	Phil, ColR
Clark Gillies	Apr. 7, 1954	Moose Jaw	LW	1974–75	1987–88	958	319	378	697	1023	NYI, Buf
Mike Blaisdell	Jan. 18, 1960	Moose Jaw	RW	1980–81	1988–89	343	70	84	154	166	Det, NYR, Pitt, Tor
Doug Smail	Sept. 2, 1957	Moose Jaw	LW	1980–81	1992–93	845	210	249	459	602	Wpg, MinNS, Que, Ott
John Miner	Aug. 28, 1965	Moose Jaw	D	1987–88	1987–88	14	2	3	5	16	Edm
Brent Gilchrist	Apr. 3, 1967	Moose Jaw	LW	1988–89		792	135	170	305	400	Mtl, Edm, MinNS, Dal, Det, Nash
Bill Lecaine	Mar. 11, 1940	Moose Jaw	LW	1968–69	1968–69	4	0	0	0	0	Pitt
Reed Low	June 21, 1976	Moose Jaw	RW	2000–01		250	3	16	19	694	StL
Chuck Corrigan	May 22, 1916	Moosomin	RW	1937–38	1940–41	19	2	2	4	2	Tor, NYA
Dave Dunn	Aug. 19, 1948	Moosomin	D	1973–74	1975–76	184	14	41	55	313	Vcr, Tor
Dennis Abgrall	Apr. 24, 1953	Moosomin	RW	1975–76	1975–76	13	0	2	2	4	LA
Dave Tippett	Aug. 25, 1961	Moosomin	LW	1983–84	1993–94	721	93	169	262	317	Hart, Wash, Pitt, Phil
Lynn Loyns	Feb. 21, 1981	Naicam	LW	2002–03		33	3	2	5	21	SJ, Cgy
Ed Litzenberger	July 15, 1932	Neudorf	C/RW	1952–53	1963–64	618	178	238	416	283	Mtl, Chi, Det, Tor
Lyndon Byers	Feb. 29, 1964	Nipawin	RW	1983–84	1992–93	279	28	43	71	1081	Bos, SJ
Elmer Lach	Jan. 22, 1918	Nokomis	C	1940–41	1953–54	664	215	408	623	478	Mtl
Doug Horbul	July 27, 1952	Nokomis	LW	1974–75	1974–75	4	1	0	1	2	KC
Lloyd Gronsdahl	May 10, 1921	Norquay	RW	1941–42	1941–42	10	1	2	3	0	Bos
Ed Panagabko	May 17, 1934	Norquay	C	1955–56	1956–57	29	0	3	3	38	Bos
Skip Krake	Oct. 14, 1943	North Battleford	C	1963–64	1970–71	249	23	40	63	182	Bos, LA, Buf
Dale Hoganson	July 8, 1949	North Battleford	D	1969–70	1981–82	343	13	77	90	186	LA, Mtl, Que
Gregg Sheppard	Apr. 23, 1949	North Battleford	C	1972–73	1981–82	657	205	293	498	243	Bos, Pitt
Morris Stefaniw	Jan. 10, 1948	North Battleford	C	1972–73	1972–73	13	1	1	2	2	AtlF
Bernie Lukowich	Mar. 18, 1952	North Battleford	RW	1973–74	1974–75	79	13	15	28	34	Pitt, StL
Ron Delorme	Sept. 3, 1955	North Battleford	C	1976–77	1984–85	524	83	83	166	667	ColR, Vcr
Merlin Malinowski	Sept. 27, 1958	North Battleford	C	1978–79	1983–83	282	54	111	165	121	ColR, NJ, Hart
Bobby Francis	Dec. 5, 1958	North Battleford	C	1982–83	1982–83	14	2	0	2	0	Det
Allan Tuer	July 19, 1963	North Battleford	D	1985–86	1989–90	57	1	1	2	208	LA, MinNS, Hart
Layne Ulmer	Sept. 14, 1980	North Battleford	C	2003–04		1	0	0	0	0	NYR
Jackie Schmidt	Nov. 11, 1924	Odessa	LW	1942–43	1942–43	45	6	7	13	6	Bos
Joe Schmidt	Nov. 5, 1926	Odessa	D	1943–44	1943–44	2	0	0	0	0	Bos
Reg Kerr	Oct. 16, 1957	Oxbow	LW	1977–78	1983–84	263	66	94	160	169	Clev, Chi, Edm
Lindsay Carson	Nov. 21, 1960	Oxbow	C	1981–82	1987–88	373	66	80	146	524	Phil, Hart
Theoren Fleury	June 29, 1968	Oxbow	RW	1988–89	2002–03	1084	455	633	1088	1840	Cgy, ColA, NYR, Chi
Shayne Toporowski	Aug. 6, 1975	Paddockwood	RW	1996–97	1996–97	3	0	0	0	7	Tor
John Rogers	Apr. 10, 1953	Paradise Hill	RW	1973–74	1974–75	14	2	4	6	0	MinNS
Grant Erickson	Apr. 28, 1947	Pierceland	LW	1968–69	1969–70	6	1	0	1	0	Bos, MinNS
Mark Lamb	Aug. 3, 1964	Ponteix	C	1985–86	1995–96	403	46	100	146	291	Cgy, Det, Edm, Ott, Phil, Mtl
Kelly Chase	Oct. 25, 1967	Porcupine Plain	RW	1989–90	1999–00	458	17	36	53	2017	StL, Hart, Tor
Mark Pederson	Jan. 14, 1968	Prelate	LW	1989–90	1993–94	169	35	50	85	77	Mtl, Phil, SJ, Det
Scotty Cameron	Nov. 5, 1921	Prince Albert	C	1942–43	1942–43	35	8	11	19	0	NYR
Rick Wilson	Aug. 10, 1950	Prince Albert	D	1973–74	1976–77	239	6	26	32	165	Mtl, StL, Det
Terry Ruskowski	Dec. 31, 1954	Prince Albert	C	1979–80	1988–89	630	113	313	426	1354	Chi, LA, Pitt, MinNS
Todd Bergen	July 11, 1963	Prince Albert	C	1984–85	1984–85	14	11	5	16	4	Phil
Dale Henry	Sept. 24, 1964	Prince Albert	LW	1984–85	1989–90	132	13	26	39	263	NYI
Dave Manson	Jan. 27, 1967	Prince Albert	D	1986–87	2001–02	1103	102	288	390	2792	Chi, Edm, Wpg, Phx, Mtl, Dal, Tor
Rod Dallman	Jan. 26, 1967	Prince Albert	LW	1987–88	1991–92	6	1	0	1	26	NYI, Phil
Ryan McGill	Feb. 28, 1969	Prince Albert	D	1991–92	1994–95	151	4	15	19	391	Chi, Phil, Edm
Todd Nelson	May 11, 1969	Prince Albert	D	1991–92	1993–94	3	1	0	1	2	Pitt, Wash
Scott Daniels	Sept. 19, 1969	Prince Albert	LW	1992–93	1998–99	149	8	12	20	667	Hart, Phil, NJ
Jeff Nelson	Dec. 18, 1972	Prince Albert	C	1994–95	1998–99	52	3	8	11	20	Wash, Nash
Tavis Hansen	June 17, 1975	Prince Albert	C	1994–95	2000–01	34	2	1	3	16	Wpg, Phx
Denis Pederson	Sept. 10, 1975	Prince Albert	C/RW	1995–96		435	57	71	128	398	NJ, Vcr, Phx, Nash
Joey Tetarenko	Mar. 3, 1978	Prince Albert	RW	2000–01		73	4	1	5	176	Fla, Ott, Caro
Nolan Yonkman	Apr. 1, 1981	Punnichy	D	2001–02		12	1	0	1	4	Wash
Ed Vokes	Unknown, 1904	Quill Lake	LW	1930–31	1930–31	5	0	0	0	0	Chi
Selmar Odelein	Apr. 11, 1966	Quill Lake	D	1985–86	1988–89	18	0	2	2	35	Edm
Lyle Odelein	July 21, 1968	Quill Lake	D	1989–90		1029	50	201	251	2336	Mtl, NJ, Phx, Clmb, Chi, Dal, Fla
Darcy Verot	July 13, 1976	Radville	C	2003–04		37	0	2	2	135	Wash
Barry Nieckar	Dec. 16, 1967	Rama	LW	1992–93	1997–98	8	0	0	0	21	Hart, Cgy, Ana
Bryan Trottier	July 17, 1956	Redvers	C	1975–76	1993–94	1279	524	901	1425	912	NYI, Pitt
Dean Kennedy	Jan. 18, 1963	Redvers	D	1982–83	1994–95	717	26	108	134	1118	LA, NYR, Buf, Wpg, Edm
Bernie Morris	Unknown, 1895	Regina	C/RW	1924–25	1924–25	6	1	0	1	0	Bos
Duke Dukowski	Aug. 30, 1902	Regina	D	1926–27	1933–34	200	16	30	46	172	Chi, NYA, NYR
Walt McCartney	Apr. 26, 1911	Regina	LW	1932–33	1932–33	2	0	0	0	0	Mtl
Don Deacon	June 2, 1913	Regina	LW	1936–37	1939–40	30	6	4	10	6	Det
Joe Carveth	Mar. 21, 1918	Regina	RW	1940–41	1950–51	504	150	189	339	81	Det, Bos, Mtl
Norm Tustin	Jan. 3, 1919	Regina	LW	1941–42	1941–42	18	2	4	6	0	NYR

Name	Birthdate	Birthplace	Pos	First Ssn	Last Ssn	GP	G	A	P	PM	Teams
Grant Warwick	Oct. 11, 1921	Regina	RW	1941–42	1949–50	395	147	142	289	220	NYR, Bos, Mtl
Bob Kirkpatrick	Dec. 1, 1915	Regina	C	1942–43	1942–43	49	12	12	24	6	NYR
Bill Warwick	Nov. 17, 1924	Regina	LW	1942–43	1943–44	14	3	3	6	16	NYR
Alan Rittinger	Jan. 28, 1925	Regina	RW	1943–44	1943–44	19	3	7	10	0	Bos
Gord Buttrey	Mar. 17, 1926	Regina	LW	1943–44	1943–44	10	0	0	0	0	Chi
Art Strobel	Nov. 28, 1922	Regina	LW	1943–44	1943–44	7	0	0	0	0	NYR
Jack Lancien	June 14, 1923	Regina	D	1946–47	1950–51	63	1	5	6	35	NYR
Harry Bell	Oct. 31, 1925	Regina	RW/D	1946–47	1946–47	1	0	1	1	0	NYR
Dunc Fisher	Aug. 30, 1927	Regina	RW	1947–48	1958–59	275	45	70	115	104	NYR, Bos, Det
Al Staley	Sept. 21, 1928	Regina	C	1948–49	1948–49	1	0	1	1	0	NYR
Jack McLeod	Apr. 30, 1930	Regina	RW	1949–50	1954–55	106	14	23	37	12	NYR
Don Smith	May 4, 1929	Regina	LW/C	1949–50	1949–50	11	1	1	2	0	NYR
Paul Masnick	Apr. 14, 1931	Regina	C	1950–51	1957–58	232	18	41	59	139	Mtl, Chi, Tor
Lou Jankowski	June 27, 1931	Regina	C/RW	1950–51	1954–55	127	19	18	37	15	Det, Chi
Bill Folk	July 11, 1927	Regina	D	1951–52	1952–53	12	0	0	0	4	Det
Lorne Davis	July 20, 1930	Regina	RW	1951–52	1959–60	95	8	12	20	20	Mtl, Chi, Det, Bos
Gerry James	Oct. 22, 1934	Regina	RW	1954–55	1959–60	149	14	26	40	257	Tor
Bob Turner	Jan. 31, 1934	Regina	D	1955–56	1962–63	478	19	51	70	307	Mtl, Chi
Murray Balfour	Aug. 24, 1936	Regina	RW	1956–57	1964–65	306	67	90	157	393	Mtl, Chi, Bos
Dale Anderson	Mar. 5, 1932	Regina	D	1956–57	1956–57	13	0	0	0	6	Det
Bill Hicke	Mar. 31, 1938	Regina	RW	1958–59	1971–72	729	168	234	402	395	Mtl, NYR, Oak/Cal, Pitt
Red Berenson	Dec. 8, 1939	Regina	C	1961–62	1977–78	987	261	397	658	305	Mtl, NYR, StL, Det
Terry Harper	Jan. 27, 1940	Regina	D	1962–63	1980–81	1066	35	221	256	1362	Mtl, LA, Det, StL, ColR
Bill Sutherland	Nov. 10, 1934	Regina	C	1962–63	1971–72	250	70	58	128	99	Mtl (playoffs only), Phil, Tor, StL, Det
Garry Peters	Oct. 9, 1942	Regina	C	1964–65	1971–72	311	34	34	68	261	Mtl, NYR, Phil, Bos
Bill Orban	Feb. 20, 1944	Regina	C/LW	1967–68	1969–70	114	8	15	23	67	Chi, MinNS
Ron Snell	Aug. 11, 1948	Regina	RW	1968–69	1969–70	7	3	2	5	6	Pitt
Fran Huck	Dec. 4, 1945	Regina	C	1969–70	1972–73	94	24	30	54	38	Mtl, StL
Curt Bennett	Mar. 27, 1948	Regina	LW	1970–71	1979–80	580	152	182	334	347	StL, NYR, AtlF
Ernie Hicke	Nov. 7, 1947	Regina	LW	1970–71	1977–78	520	132	140	272	407	Cal, AtlF, NYI, MinNS, LA
Larry Wright	Oct. 8, 1951	Regina	C	1971–72	1977–78	106	4	8	12	19	Phil, Cal, Det
Barry Cummins	Jan. 25, 1949	Regina	D	1973–74	1973–74	36	1	2	3	39	Cal
Dwight Bialowas	Sept. 8, 1952	Regina	D	1973–74	1976–77	164	11	46	57	46	AtlF, MinNS
Kim MacDougall	Aug. 29, 1954	Regina	D	1974–75	1974–75	1	0	0	0	0	MinNS
Glen Burdon	Aug. 4, 1954	Regina	C	1974–75	1974–75	11	0	2	2	0	KC
Scott Garland	May 16, 1952	Regina	C	1975–76	1978–79	91	13	24	37	115	Tor, LA
Drew Callander	Aug. 17, 1956	Regina	C/RW	1976–77	1979–80	39	6	2	8	7	Phil, Vcr
Robbie Laird	Dec. 29, 1954	Regina	LW	1979–80	1979–80	1	0	0	0	0	MinNS
Mark Kirton	Feb. 3, 1958	Regina	C	1979–80	1984–85	266	57	56	113	121	Tor, Det, Vcr
Brian Hill	Jan. 12, 1957	Regina	RW	1979–80	1979–80	19	1	1	2	4	Hart
Gord Wappel	July 26, 1958	Regina	D	1979–80	1981–82	20	1	1	2	10	AtlF/Cgy
Rich Preston	May 22, 1952	Regina	RW	1979–80	1986–87	580	127	164	291	348	Chi, NJ
Gerry Minor	Oct. 27, 1958	Regina	C	1979–80	1983–84	140	11	21	32	173	Vcr
Sandy Beadle	July 12, 1960	Regina	LW	1980–81	1980–81	6	1	0	1	2	Wpg
Doug Wickenheiser	Mar. 30, 1961	Regina	C	1980–81	1989–90	556	111	165	276	286	Mtl, StL, Vcr, NYR, Wash
Jim McGeough	Apr. 13, 1963	Regina	C	1981–82	1986–87	57	7	10	17	32	Wash, Pitt
Garth Butcher	Jan. 8, 1963	Regina	D	1981–82	1994–95	897	48	158	206	2302	Vcr, StL, Que, Tor
Taylor Hall	Feb. 20, 1964	Regina	LW	1983–84	1987–88	41	7	9	16	29	Vcr, Bos
Dirk Graham	July 29, 1959	Regina	RW	1983–84	1994–95	772	219	270	489	917	MinNS, Chi
Mark Ferner	Sept. 5, 1965	Regina	D	1986–87	1994–95	91	3	10	13	51	Buf, Wash, Ana, Det
Jock Callander	Apr. 23, 1961	Regina	RW	1987–88	1992–93	109	22	29	51	116	Pitt, TB
Robert Dirk	Aug. 20, 1966	Regina	D	1987–88	1995–96	402	13	29	42	786	StL, Vcr, Chi, Ana, Mtl
Mitch Messier	Aug. 21, 1965	Regina	C	1987–88	1990–91	20	0	2	2	11	MinNS
James Black	Aug. 15, 1969	Regina	LW	1989–90	2000–01	352	58	57	115	84	Hart, MinNS, Dal, Buf, Chi, Wash
Rocky Dundas	Jan. 30, 1967	Regina	RW	1989–90	1989–90	5	0	0	0	14	Tor
Mike Sillinger	June 29, 1971	Regina	C	1990–91		829	164	234	398	507	Det, Ana, Vcr, Phil, TB, Fla, Ott, Clmb, StL
Dave Karpa	May 7, 1971	Regina	D	1991–92		557	18	80	98	1374	Que, Ana, Caro, NYR
Kevin Dahl	Dec. 30, 1968	Regina	D	1992–93	2000–01	187	7	22	29	153	Cgy, Phx, Tor, Clmb
Joby Messier	Mar. 2, 1970	Regina	D	1992–93	1994–95	25	0	4	4	24	NYR
Terry Hollinger	Feb. 24, 1971	Regina	D	1993–94	1994–95	7	0	0	0	2	StL
Chris Snell	May 12, 1971	Regina	D	1993–94	1994–95	34	2	7	9	24	Tor, LA
Jamie Heward	Mar. 30, 1971	Regina	D	1995–96	2001–02	239	25	45	70	116	Tor, Nash, NYI, Clmb
Scott Hartnell	Apr. 18, 1982	Regina	LW	2000–01		331	46	78	124	347	Nash
Chris Armstrong	June 26, 1975	Regina	D	2000–01		7	0	1	1	4	MinW, Ana
Nick Schultz	Aug. 25, 1982	Regina	D	2001–02		206	13	23	36	53	MinW
Dan Focht	Dec. 31, 1977	Regina	D	2001–02		82	2	6	8	145	Phx, Pitt
Garth Murray	Sept. 17, 1982	Regina	LW	2003–04		20	1	0	1	24	NYR
Chris Kunitz	Sept. 26, 1979	Regina	LW	2003–04		21	0	6	6	12	Ana
Art Wiebe	Sept. 28, 1912	Rosthern	D	1932–33	1943–44	414	14	27	41	201	Chi
Jim Hrycuik	Oct. 7, 1949	Rosthern	C	1974–75	1974–75	21	5	5	10	12	Wash
Fred Sasakamoose	Dec. 25, 1933	Sandy Lake Reserve	C	1953–54	1953–54	11	0	0	0	6	Chi
Lloyd Klein	Jan. 13, 1910	Saskatoon	LW	1928–29	1937–38	164	30	24	54	68	Bos, NYA
Jack Leswick	Jan. 1, 1910	Saskatoon	C	1933–34	1933–34	37	1	7	8	16	Chi
Pete Leswick	July 12, 1918	Saskatoon	RW	1936–37	1944–45	3	1	0	1	0	NYA, Bos
Ralph Wycherley	Feb. 26, 1920	Saskatoon	LW	1940–41	1941–42	28	4	7	11	6	NYA, Bkn
Harry Watson	May 6, 1923	Saskatoon	LW	1941–42	1956–57	809	236	207	443	150	Bkn, Det, Tor, Chi
Vic Lynn	Jan. 26, 1925	Saskatoon	LW/D	1942–43	1953–54	327	49	76	125	274	NYR, Det, Mtl, Tor, Bos, Chi

Name	Birthdate	Birthplace	Pos	First Ssn	Last Ssn	GP	G	A	P	PM	Teams
John Harms	Apr. 25, 1925	Saskatoon	RW	1943–44	1944–45	44	5	5	10	21	Chi
Gerry Couture	Aug. 6, 1925	Saskatoon	RW	1944–45	1953–54	385	86	70	156	89	Det, Mtl, Chi
Russ Brayshaw	Jan. 17, 1918	Saskatoon	LW	1944–45	1944–45	43	5	9	14	24	Chi
Pat Lundy	May 31, 1924	Saskatoon	C	1945–46	1950–51	150	37	32	69	31	Det, Chi
Bobby Dawes	Nov. 29, 1924	Saskatoon	D	1946–47	1950–51	32	2	7	9	6	Tor, Mtl
Don Morrison	July 14, 1923	Saskatoon	C	1947–48	1950–51	112	18	28	46	12	Det, Chi
Rod Morrison	Oct. 7, 1925	Saskatoon	RW	1947–48	1947–48	34	8	7	15	4	Det
Vic Howe	Nov. 2, 1929	Saskatoon	RW	1950–51	1954–55	33	3	4	7	10	NYR
Hugh Currie	Oct. 22, 1925	Saskatoon	D	1950–51	1950–51	1	0	0	0	0	Mtl
Jim Hay	May 15, 1931	Saskatoon	D	1952–53	1954–55	75	1	5	6	22	Det
George Senick	Sept. 16, 1929	Saskatoon	LW	1952–53	1952–53	13	2	3	5	8	NYR
Keith Allen	Aug. 21, 1923	Saskatoon	D	1953–54	1954–55	28	0	4	4	8	Det
Bill Hay	Dec. 9, 1935	Saskatoon	C	1959–60	1966–67	506	113	273	386	244	Chi
Ed Van Impe	May 27, 1940	Saskatoon	D	1966–67	1976–77	700	27	126	153	1025	Chi, Phil, Pitt
Ron Boehm	Aug. 14, 1943	Saskatoon	LW	1967–68	1967–68	16	2	1	3	10	Oak
Bob Schmautz	Mar. 28, 1945	Saskatoon	RW	1967–68	1980–81	764	271	286	557	988	Chi, Vcr, Bos, Edm, ColR
Gerry Pinder	Sept. 15, 1948	Saskatoon	LW	1969–70	1971–72	223	55	69	124	135	Chi, Cal
Cliff Schmautz	Mar. 17, 1939	Saskatoon	RW	1970–71	1970–71	56	13	19	32	33	Buf, Phil
Don Kozak	Feb. 2, 1952	Saskatoon	RW	1972–73	1978–79	437	96	86	182	480	LA, Vcr
Larry Sacharuk	Sept. 16, 1952	Saskatoon	D	1972–73	1976–77	151	29	33	62	42	NYR, StL
Rod Norrish	Nov. 27, 1951	Saskatoon	LW	1973–74	1974–75	21	3	3	6	2	MinNS
George Pesut	June 17, 1953	Saskatoon	D	1974–75	1975–76	92	3	22	25	130	Cal
Fred Williams	July 1, 1956	Saskatoon	C	1976–77	1976–77	44	2	5	7	10	Det
Gary Rissling	Aug. 8, 1956	Saskatoon	LW	1978–79	1984–85	221	23	30	53	1008	Wash, Pitt
Bob Stephenson	Feb. 1, 1954	Saskatoon	RW	1979–80	1979–80	18	2	3	5	4	Hart, Tor
Kim Clackson	Feb. 13, 1955	Saskatoon	D	1979–80	1980–81	106	0	8	8	370	Pitt, Que
Brent Ashton	May 18, 1960	Saskatoon	LW	1979–80	1992–93	998	284	345	629	635	Vcr, ColR, NJ, MinNS, Que, Det, Wpg, Bos, Cgy
Darren Veitch	Apr. 24, 1960	Saskatoon	D	1980–81	1990–91	511	48	209	257	296	Wash, Det, Tor
Larry Melnyk	Feb. 21, 1960	Saskatoon	D	1980–81	1989–90	432	11	63	74	686	Bos, Edm, NYR, Vcr
Gord Williams	Apr. 10, 1960	Saskatoon	RW	1981–82	1982–83	2	0	0	0	2	Phil
Moe Lemay	Feb. 18, 1962	Saskatoon	LW	1981–82	1988–89	317	72	94	166	442	Vcr, Edm, Bos, Wpg
Dave Brown	Oct. 12, 1962	Saskatoon	RW	1982–83	1995–96	729	45	52	97	1789	Phil, Edm, SJ
Perry Ganchar	Oct. 28, 1963	Saskatoon	RW	1983–84	1988–89	42	3	7	10	36	StL, Mtl, Pitt
Randy Smith	July 7, 1965	Saskatoon	C	1985–86	1986–87	3	0	0	0	0	MinNS
Todd Ewen	Mar. 22, 1966	Saskatoon	RW	1986–87	1996–97	518	36	40	76	1911	StL, Mtl, Ana, SJ
Mick Vukota	Sept. 14, 1966	Saskatoon	RW	1987–88	1997–98	574	17	29	46	2071	NYI, TB, Mtl
Rich Pilon	Apr. 30, 1968	Saskatoon	D	1988–89	2001–02	631	8	69	77	1745	NYI, NYR, StL
Cam Brown	May 15, 1969	Saskatoon	LW	1990–91	1990–91	1	0	0	0	7	Vcr
Scott Scissons	Oct. 29, 1971	Saskatoon	C	1990–91	1993–94	2	0	0	0	0	NYI
Darren Van Impe	May 18, 1973	Saskatoon	D	1994–95		411	25	90	115	397	Ana, Bos, NYR, Fla, NYI, Clmb
Wade Belak	July 3, 1976	Saskatoon	D/RW	1996–97		275	7	15	22	811	ColA, Cgy, Tor
Chris McAllister	June 16, 1975	Saskatoon	D	1997–98		301	4	17	21	634	Vcr, Tor, Phil, ColA, NYR
Cory Sarich	Aug. 16, 1978	Saskatoon	D	1998–99		373	9	50	59	411	Buf, TB
Jesse Wallin	Mar. 10, 1978	Saskatoon	D	1999–00		49	0	2	2	34	Det
Chris Hajt	July 5, 1978	Saskatoon	D	2000–01		6	0	0	0	2	Edm, Wash
Shayne Endicott	Dec. 21, 1981	Saskatoon	C	2001–02		4	0	1	1	4	Pitt
Ryan Bayda	Dec. 9, 1980	Saskatoon	LW	2002–03		69	7	13	20	38	Caro
Mel Anglestad	Oct. 31, 1971	Saskatoon	LW	2003–04		2	0	0	0	2	Wash
Bert Olmstead	Sept. 4, 1926	Sceptre	LW	1948–49	1961–62	848	181	421	602	884	Chi, Mtl, Tor
Jim O'Neil	Apr. 3, 1913	Semans	C/RW	1933–34	1941–42	156	6	30	36	109	Bos, Mtl
Gary Aldcorn	Mar. 7, 1935	Shaunavon	LW	1956–57	1960–61	226	41	56	97	78	Tor, Det, Bos
Rhett Warrener	Jan. 27, 1976	Shaunavon	D	1995–96		560	16	70	86	757	Fla, Buf, Cgy
Mush Mar.	Oct. 18, 1908	Silton	RW	1928–29	1944–45	759	153	230	383	540	Chi
Morris Lukowich	June 1, 1956	Speers	LW	1979–80	1986–87	582	199	219	418	584	Wpg, Bos, LA
Jeff Odgers	May 31, 1969	Spy Hill	RW	1991–92	2002–03	821	75	70	145	2364	SJ, Bos, ColA, AtlT
Bob Solinger	Dec. 23, 1925	Star City	LW	1951–52	1959–60	99	10	11	21	19	Tor, Det
Lorne Carr	July 2, 1910	Stoughton	RW	1933–34	1945–46	580	204	222	426	132	NYR, NYA, Tor
Greg Hubick	Nov. 12, 1951	Strasbourg	D	1975–76	1979–80	77	6	9	15	10	Tor, Vcr
Hal Laycoe	June 23, 1922	Sutherland	D	1945–46	1955–56	531	25	77	102	292	NYR, Mtl, Bos
Jack Forsey	Nov. 7, 1914	Swift Current	RW	1942–43	1942–43	19	7	9	16	10	Tor
Bill Hogaboam	Sept. 5, 1949	Swift Current	C	1972–73	1979–80	332	80	109	189	100	Atl, Det, MinNS
Darcy Regier	Nov. 27, 1956	Swift Current	D	1977–78	1983–84	26	0	2	2	35	Clev, NYI
Marc Habscheid	Mar. 1, 1963	Swift Current	RW/C	1981–82	1991–92	345	72	91	163	171	Edm, MinNS, Det, Cgy
Jeff Toms	June 4, 1974	Swift Current	LW	1995–96		236	22	33	55	59	TB, Wash, NYI, Pitt, Fla
Trent McCleary	Sept. 8, 1972	Swift Current	RW	1995–96	1999–00	192	8	15	23	134	Ott, Bos, Mtl
Jeff Buchanan	May 23, 1971	Swift Current	D	1998–99	1998–99	6	0	0	0	6	ColA
Darrel Scoville	Oct. 13, 1975	Swift Current	D	1999–00		16	0	1	1	12	Cgy, Clmb
Boyd Kane	Apr. 18, 1978	Swift Current	LW	2003–04		7	0	0	0	7	Phil
Travis Moen	Apr. 6, 1982	Swift Current	LW	2003–04		82	4	2	6	42	Chi
Ted Hampson	Dec. 11, 1936	Togo	C	1959–60	1971–72	676	108	245	353	94	Tor, NYR, Det, Oak/Cal, MinNS
Fred Hucul	Dec. 4, 1931	Tuberose	D	1950–51	1967–68	164	11	30	41	113	Chi, StL
Curtis Brown	Feb. 12, 1976	Unity	C/LW	1994–95		517	100	134	234	324	Buf
Boyd Gordon	Oct. 19, 1983	Unity	RW	2003–04		41	1	5	6	8	Wash
Lulu Denis	June 7, 1928	Vonda	RW	1949–50	1950–51	3	0	1	1	0	Mtl
Keith Magnuson	Apr. 27, 1947	Wadena	D	1969–70	1979–80	589	14	125	139	1442	Chi
Dave Balon	Aug. 2, 1938	Wakaw	LW	1959–60	1972–73	776	192	222	414	607	NYR, Mtl, MinNS, Vcr
Dave Michayluk	May 18, 1962	Wakaw	LW	1981–82	1991–92	14	2	6	8	8	Phil, Pitt (playoffs only w/Pitt)

Name	Birthdate	Birthplace	Pos	First Ssn	Last Ssn	GP	G	A	P	PM	Teams
James Latos	Jan. 4, 1966	Wakaw	RW	1988–89	1988–89	1	0	0	0	0	NYR
Dave Schultz	Oct. 14, 1949	Waldheim	LW	1971–72	1979–80	535	79	121	200	2294	Phil, LA, Pitt, Buf
Brett Clark	Dec. 23, 1976	Wapella	D	1997–98		158	5	6	11	60	Mtl, AtlT, ColA
Paul Meger	Feb. 17, 1929	Watrous	LW	1949–50	1954–55	212	39	52	91	118	Mtl
Max McNab	June 21, 1924	Watson	C	1947–48	1950–51	128	16	19	35	24	Det
Gizzy Hart	June 1, 1902	Weyburn	LW	1926–27	1932–33	104	6	8	14	12	Det, Mtl
Brian Mar.inko	Aug. 2, 1948	Weyburn	C	1970–71	1973–74	47	2	6	8	0	Tor, NYI
Larry Hornung	Nov. 10, 1945	Weyburn	D	1970–71	1971–72	48	2	9	11	10	StL
Walt Ledingham	Oct. 26, 1950	Weyburn	LW	1972–73	1976–77	15	0	2	2	4	Chi, NYI
Larry Giroux	Aug. 28, 1951	Weyburn	D	1973–74	1979–80	274	15	74	89	333	StL, KC, Det, Hart
Tiger Williams	Feb. 3, 1954	Weyburn	LW	1974–75	1987–88	962	241	272	513	3966	Tor, Vcr, Det, LA, Hart
Rick Shinske	May 31, 1955	Weyburn	C	1976–77	1978–79	63	5	16	21	10	Clev, StL
Jim McTaggart	Mar. 31, 1960	Weyburn	D	1980–81	1981–82	71	3	10	13	205	Wash
Rene Chapdelaine	Sept. 27, 1966	Weyburn	D	1990–91	1992–93	32	0	2	2	32	LA
Nick Metz	Feb. 16, 1914	Wilcox	LW	1934–35	1947–48	518	131	119	250	149	Tor
Don Metz	Jan. 10, 1916	Wilcox	RW	1938–39	1948–49	172	20	35	55	42	Tor
Jeff Ulmer	Apr. 27, 1977	Wilcox	RW	2000–01		22	3	0	3	8	NYR
Ralph Keller	Feb. 6, 1936	Wilkie	D	1962–63	1962–63	3	1	0	1	6	NYR
Richard Zemlak	Mar. 3, 1963	Wynyard	RW	1986–87	1991–92	132	2	12	14	587	Que, MinNS, Pitt, Cgy
Peter Schaefer	July 12, 1977	Yellow Grass	LW	1998–99		334	57	70	122	112	Vcr, Ott
Metro Prystai	Nov. 7, 1927	Yorkton	C	1947–48	1957–58	674	151	179	330	231	Chi, Det
Larry Popein	Aug. 11, 1930	Yorkton	C	1954–55	1967–68	449	80	141	221	162	NYR, Oak
Merv Kuryluk	Aug. 10, 1937	Yorkton	LW	1961–62	1961–62	2	0	0	0	0	Chi (playoffs only)
Mike Chernoff	May 13, 1946	Yorkton	LW	1968–69	1968–69	1	0	0	0	0	MinNS
Clayton Pachal	Apr. 21, 1956	Yorkton	C/LW	1976–77	1978–79	35	2	3	5	95	Bos, ColR
Brent Fedyk	Mar. 8, 1967	Yorkton	LW	1987–88	1998–99	470	97	112	209	308	Det, Phil, Dal, NYR

GOALTENDERS

Name	Birthdate	Birthplace	First	Last	GP	W	L	T	Min	GA	SO	Avg	Teams
Earl Robertson	Nov. 24, 1910	Bengough	1936–37	1941–42	190	60	95	34	11820	575	16	2.92	Det (playoffs only), NYA, Bkn
Steve Buzinski	Oct. 15, 1917	Dunblane	1942–43	1942–43	9	2	6	1	560	55	0	5.89	NYR
Harvey Bennett	July 23, 1925	Ettington	1944–45	1944–45	25	10	12	2	1470	103	0	4.20	Bos
Larry Lozinski	Mar. 11, 1958	Hudson Bay	1980–81	1980–81	30	6	11	7	1459	105	0	4.32	Det
Glenn Hall	Oct. 3, 1931	Humboldt	1952–53	1970–71	906	407	326	163	53484	2222	84	2.49	Det, Chi, StL
Tim Cheveldae	Feb. 15, 1968	Melville	1988–89	1996–97	340	149	136	37	19172	1116	10	3.49	Det, Wpg, Bos
Jimmy Franks	Nov. 8, 1914	Melville	1936–37	1943–44	42	12	23	7	2520	181	1	4.31	Det, NYR, Bos
Chico Resch	July 10, 1948	Moose Jaw	1973–74	1986–87	571	231	224	82	32279	1761	26	3.27	NYI, ColR, NJ, Phil
Ed Staniowski	July 7, 1955	Moose Jaw	1975–76	1984–85	219	67	104	21	12075	818	2	4.06	StL, Wpg, Hart
Emile Francis	Sept. 13, 1926	North Battleford	1946–47	1951–52	95	31	52	11	5660	355	1	3.76	Chi, NYR
Bruce Hoffort	Sept. 30, 1966	North Battleford	1989–90	1990–91	9	4	0	3	368	22	0	3.59	Phil
Corey Schwab	Nov. 4, 1970	North Battleford	1995–96		147	42	63	13	7476	360	5	2.89	NJ, TB, Vcr, Tor
Mike Bales	Aug. 6, 1971	Prince Albert	1992–93	1996–97	23	2	15	1	1120	77	0	4.13	Bos, Ott
Johnny Bower	Nov. 8, 1924	Prince Albert	1953–54	1969–70	552	250	195	90	32016	1340	37	2.51	NYR, Tor
Jerome Mrazek	Oct. 15, 1951	Prince Albert	1975–76	1975–76	1	0	0	0	6	1	0	10.00	Phil
Terry Kleisinger	Oct. 10, 1960	Regina	1985–86	1985–86	4	0	2	0	191	14	0	4.40	NYR
Doug Stevenson	Apr. 6, 1924	Regina	1944–45	1945–46	8	2	6	0	480	39	0	4.88	NYR, Chi
Randy Ireland	Apr. 5, 1957	Rosetown	1978–79	1978–79	2	0	0	0	30	3	0	6.00	Buf
Red Almas	Apr. 26, 1924	Saskatoon	1946–47	1952–53	3	0	2	1	180	13	0	4.33	Det, Chi
Dan Ellis	June 19, 1980	Saskatoon	2003–04		1	1	0	0	60	3	0	3.00	Dal
Bert Gardiner	Mar. 25, 1913	Saskatoon	1935–36	1943–44	144	49	68	27	8760	554	4	3.79	NYR, Mtl, Chi, Bos
Dieter Kochan	May 11, 1974	Saskatoon	1999–00		21	1	11	1	849	56	0	3.96	TB, MinW
Jack Norris	Aug. 5, 1942	Saskatoon	1964–65	1970–71	58	20	25	4	3119	202	2	3.89	Bos, Chi, LA
Dave Parro	Apr. 30, 1957	Saskatoon	1980–81	1983–84	77	21	36	10	4015	274	2	4.09	Wash
Chuck Rayner	Aug. 11, 1920	Sutherland	1940–41	1952–53	424	138	208	77	25491	1294	25	3.05	NYA, Bkn, NYR
Al Rollins	Oct. 9, 1926	Vanguard	1949–50	1959–60	430	141	205	83	25723	1192	28	2.78	Tor, Chi, NYR
Ed Dyck	Oct. 29, 1950	Warman	1971–72	1973–74	49	8	28	5	2453	178	1	4.35	Vcr

PHOTO CREDITS

Photo credits are an extension of the copyright page.

David Acoose: 15.

Paul Ahlgren: 319.

Alberta Archives and Saskatchewan Sports Hall of Fame and Museum: 61.

Claus Andersen: 271.

Arlene Antal: 315 (Antal).

Chick Baker: 1 (Baker), 80.

Bogetti-Smith Photography (www.bogetti.com): 318 (Franks).

Garnet Campbell: 1 (Campbells), 118 (2), 120, 195.

Canada's Sports Hall of Fame: 26, 62.

John Chaput: 101, 156, 253 (statue), 274, 277, 303, 305, 306, 309, 318 (Bouchard), 321.

Irene Chernoff: 269.

Doug Cleveland and Swift Current Museum: 230.

Gord Currie: 287.

Joe Daley: 145.

Lorne Davis: 108, 162.

Canada Department of National Defence Library and Archives Canada: 23.

Paul Dojack: 50, 63, 64, 65, 66.

Ron Estay: 213,

F-11 Photographic Design, Saskatoon, and Saskatchewan Sports Hall of Fame and Museum: 229.

Nick Federko: 177.

Sylvia Fedoruk: 5, 113, 198 (McKee), 200.

Terry Harper: 109, 170.

Lyle Helland: 124, 146, 147 (Olmstead), 151, 152, 153, 219, 276.

Bill Hicke: 164, 165, 169.

Hockey Hall of Fame: 140, 189, 190.

Jim Hunter: 236 (2).

Indian Head Rural Sports Hall of Fame: 1 (poster), 59, 95, 107 (Cubans), 314.

Arleene Johnson Noga: 68, 82.

Daisy Junor: 81.

Marv Kereluke: 38 (inset), 172.

Andrew Klaver Photography & Scott Paper Ltd. 1 (Schmirler), 296, 302, 304, 307.

Dale MacMillan: 311.

Alex McFadyen: 31, 73, 84 (Couture), 86, 125 (Worsley), 130 (2), 133, 134, 137, 138, 139, 141 (2), 142, 148, 149 (Lach), 150, 155, 182, 201 (Krekelewitz), 226, 233.

Melville Millionaires Hockey Club: 3, 126.

Moose Jaw Public Library Archives: 14, 36, 56, 83, 136.

North Battleford Sports Museum and Hall of Fame: 67 (Myles), 106 (Tate), 107 (Herron), 178, 206, 216, 217, 218,

Notre Dame, Athol Murray College of: 72, 74, 149 (Irvin), 186, 211.

Herb Pinder Jr.: 221

Prince Albert Historical Society: 1 (Kennedy), 17, 161, 285.

Metro Prystai: 84, 100, 147, 158,

Frank and Margaret Puhl: 224, 245.

Regina City Archives: 38.

Shirley Mullin Rhodes: 103.

Owen Ricker: 144, 159, 171, 187, 188, 191 (2).

Regina *Leader-Post*: 175, 198 (Pickering), 254, 265, 286, 289, 291, 293, 294.

Regina *Leader-Post* & Saskatchewan Sports Hall of Fame and Museum: 181, 192, 208, 272.

RCMP Museum & Saskatchewan Sports Hall of Fame and Museum: 13.

Royal Studios, Regina: 273.

Jussi Salo: 313.

Saskatchewan Archives Board: 12 (RA 3654), 16 (RA 15456), 19 (RB 9640-2), 35 & 46 (RB 4205), 54 & 128 (RD 1587), 92 (SP 1650-1), 98 (SP 889-11), 121 (SP 1560-7), 122 (SP 5190-3), 125 (Gilchrist RB 9532), 167 (RB 10128-3), 168 (RB 4199), 196 (RA 11522), 210 (Shaws RA 20235-2), 246 (SP 6480-11), 249 (SP 1311-4), 290 (SP 18786-1).

Saskatchewan Baseball Hall of Fame: 45, 79 (2), 106 (Francis), 143 (baseball), 242, 253 (Quakers).

Saskatchewan Sports Hall of Fame and Museum: 1 (Decoteau, 1930 Roughriders, Lee) 10, 21, 22, 24, 28, 29, 33, 37, 39, 41, 43, 44, 52, 55, 67 (Chiga-Pettigrew), 87, 88, 89, 91, 94, 96, 97, 104, 105, 110, 117, 119 (2), 123, 129, 131, 143 (Turner), 201 (Vaughn), 203 (2), 204, 205, 207, 209, 210 (McQuarters), 214, 223, 237, 239, 241 (2), 248, 251, 252, 253 (Mackay), 259, 263, 288, 295.

Saskatoon Public Library, Local History Room: 8, 47, 48, 112, 166.

Saskatoon *StarPhoenix*: 1 (Kellett), 7, 85, 185, 257, 275, 282, 299, 301, 308.

Stacy Singer: 267.

Jean Sostorics: 316.

Gene Suignard: 132, 157.

Swift Current Broncos: 280 (4), 281, 283.

Garry Thomas: 312, 315 (Wickenheiser).

John Tisdale: 284.

Mary Trottier and Saskatchewan Sports Hall of Fame and Museum: 173.

Bob Turner: 111, 163, 197, 235.

Wayne Stephenson: 90.

Billy Warwick: 1 (Warwick brothers), 71, 75, 76, 77, 78, 114, 115, 116.

Washington State University: 278, 279.

Joey Weinmeister: 102.

Charlie Wickenheiser: 183.

Yaz's Sports Memorabilia: 135.

Yorkton Sports Hall of Fame and Museum: 1 (Parker), 253 (Terriers).

BIBLIOGRAPHY

Adrahtas, Tom. *Glenn Hall: The Man They Call Mr. Goalie.* Vancouver: Greystone, 2002.

Andrews, Garry. *Huskies, Hounds & Foxes: A glimpse into Saskatchewan's sporting past.* Wynyard, SK: Gnome, 1981.

Archer, John. *Saskatchewan: A History.* Saskatoon: Western Producer Prairie Books, 1980.

Argan, William, with Pam Cowan. *Cornerstones: An Artist's History of the City of Regina.* Regina: Centax, 1995.

Batten, Jack. *The Leafs in Autumn.*Toronto: Macmillan, 1975.

Baun, Bobby, with Anne Logan. *Lowering the Boom: The Bobby Baun Story.* Toronto: Stoddart, 2000.

Best, Dave, ed. *Canada: Our Century in Sport.* Markham, ON: Fitzhenry & Whiteside, 2002.

Bingaman, Sandra. *Spinning into the Spotlight: Figure Skating in Saskatchewan, 1883–1996.* Regina: Saskatchewan Figure Skating Association and Saskatchewan Sports Hall of Fame and Museum, 2000.

Boyd, Denny, and Brian Scrivener. *Legends of Autumn: The Glory Years of Canadian Football.* Vancouver: Greystone, 1997.

Boyle, Mickey. *Ninety Years of Golf: An Illustrated History of Golf in Saskatchewan.* Regina: Centax, 1987.

Brass, Dana. *Twisting and Tumbling Through Saskatchewan: A History of Gymnastics.* Regina: Saskatchewan Gymnastics Association and Saskatchewan Sport Hall of Fame and Museum, 1992.

Browne, Lois. *Girls of Summer: In Their Own League.* Toronto: HarperCollins, 1992.

Carrier, Roch. *Our Life With the Rocket: The Maurice Richard Story*. Trans. Sheila Fishman. Toronto: Viking, 2001.

Coleman, Jim. *Hockey Is Our Game: Canada in the World of International Hockey*. Toronto: Key Porter, 1987.

Conrad, Peter C. *In the Winning Lane: A History of Competitive Swimming in Saskatchewan*. Regina: Swim Saskatchewan, 1990.

Cosentino, Frank, and Glynn Leyshon. *Olympic Gold: Canada's Winners in the Summer Games*. Toronto: Holt, Rinehart and Winston, 1975.

Cowley, Glen. *The Seventh Man: The History of the Kamloops Blazers Franchise*. Kamloops, BC: Rockface, 2000.

Deenshaw, Cleve. *The Commonwealth Games: The First 60 Years 1930–1990*. Victoria: Orca, 1994.

Deenshaw, Cleve. *Olympics 100: Canada at the Summer Games*. Victoria: Orca, 1996.

Dewar, John D. *Basketball: Saskatchewan's Story, 1891–1989*. Regina: Focus, 1989.

Dewar, John M. *Saskatchewan Soccer: A History*.

Diamond, Dan, ed. *Total Hockey*, 2nd ed. Toronto: Total Sports Canada, 2000.

Diamond, Dan, ed. *Total Stanley Cup*. Toronto: Total Sports Canada, 2000.

Etue, Elizabeth, and Megan K. Williams. *On the Edge: Women Making Hockey History*. Toronto: Second Story, 1996.

Falla, Jack, et al. *Quest for the Cup: A History of the Stanley Cup Finals 1893–2001*. Toronto: Key Porter, 2001.

Ferguson, Bob. *Who's Who in Canadian Sport*. Scarborough, ON: Prentice-Hall, 1977.

Ferguson, John, with Stan Fischler and Shirley Fischler. *Thunder and Lightning*. Scarborough, ON: Prentice-Hall, 1989.

Fitkin, Ed. Max Bentley: *Hockey's Dipsy-Doodle Dandy*. Toronto: Baxter/Castle, 1952.

Frayne, Trent. *It's Easy: All You Have To Do Is Win*. Don Mills, ON: Longmans, 1968.

Godbar, Sid. *Go–Vees–Go: The Incredible Saga of the Penticton Vees 1951–55*. Cranbrook, BC: Cranbook Co., 1975.

Gregson, Ian. *Irresistible Force: Disability Sport in Canada*. Victoria: Polestar, 1999.

Hack, Paul, and Dave Shury. *Wheat Province Diamonds: A Story of Saskatchewan Baseball*. Regina: Saskatchewan Baseball Association, 1997.

Howe, Gordie, and Colleen Howe with Tom Delisle. *and . . . Howe!* Traverse City, MI: Power Play Publications, 1995.

Howe, Gordie, with Frank Condron. *Gordie Howe: My Hockey Memories*. Willowdale, ON: Firefly, 1999.

Hughes, Bob. *Regina Rams: A Winning Tradition*. Regina: University of Regina Rams Football Club, 2003.

Humber, William. *Cheering for the Home Team: The Story of Baseball in Canada*. Erin, ON: Boston Mills, 1983.

Humber, William. *Diamonds of the North: A Concise History of Baseball in Canada*. Don Mills, ON: Oxford, 1995.

Hunter, Bill with Bob Weber. *Wild Bill: Bill Hunter's legendary 65 years in Canadian sport*. Calgary: Johnson Gorman, 2000.

Irvin, Dick. *Now Back To You Dick: Two Lifetimes in Hockey*. Toronto: McClelland & Stewart, 1988.

Irvin, Dick. *Behind the Bench: Coaches Talk About Life in the NHL*. Toronto: McClelland & Stewart, 1993.

Irvin, Dick. *Tough Calls: NHL Referees and Linesmen Tell Their Story*. Toronto: McClelland & Stewart, 1997.

Karpan, Robin & Arlene. *Saskatchewan Trivia Challenge*. Saskatoon: Parkland, 2000.

Klein, Jeff Z., and Karl-Eric Reif. *The Hockey Compendium: NHL Facts, Stats, and Stories*. Toronto: McClelland & Stewart, 2001.

Lapp, Richard M. and Alex Macauley. *Local Heroes: A History of the Western Hockey League*. Madeira Park, BC: Harbour, 1993.

Lapp, Richard M., and Alex Macauley. *The Memorial Cup: Canada's National Junior Hockey Championship*. Madeira Park, BC: Harbour, 1997.

Magnuson, Keith, with Robert Bradford. *None Against*. New York: Dodd, Mead & Coompany, 1973.

Marsh, James H., editor-in-chief. *The Canadian Encyclopedia: Year 2000 Edition*. Toronto: McClelland & Stewart, 1999.

McDonell, Chris, selector. *The Game I'll Never Forget*. Toronto: Firefly, 2002.

Nicholls, Ernest A., and Kenneth Leyton-Brown. *Paul Dojack and the Regina Dales 1929–1940: The Formative Years of Junior Football in Western Canada*. Regina: University of Regina, 1997.

O"Brien, Andy. "Those Incredible Vees from Penticton, B.C." *Headline Hockey*. Toronto: Ryerson, 1963. 1–14.

Podneiks, Andrew. *Canada's Olympic Hockey Teams: The Complete History 1920–1998*. Toronto: Doubleday, 1997.

Powers, Ned. *Behind the Sports Headlines*. Saskatoon: The *StarPhoenix*, 1992.

Powers, Ned. *Strikes 'n' Spares: The History of Bowling in Saskatchewan*. Regina: Bowling Federation of Saskatchewan, 1993.

Richardson, Ernie, Joyce McKee and Doug Maxwell. *Curling*. Toronto: Thomas Allen, 1962.

Roxborough, Henry. *Canada at the Olympics*. 3rd ed. McGraw-Toronto: Hill Ryerson, 1975.

Schultz, Dave with Stan Fischler. *The Hammer: Confessions of a Hockey Enforcer*. Toronto: Collins, 1981.

Shearon, Jim. *Canada's Baseball Legends*. Kanata, ON: Malin Head, 1994.

Shury, Dave. "The Rosetown Baseball Riot." *Saskatchewan Historical Baseball Review* 1984, 77–80.

Thiele, Stephen. *Heroes of the Game: A History of the Grey Cup*. Norval, ON: Moulin, 1997.

Thurn, Walter R. *The Famous Bentleys*. New York: Modern Press, 1947.

Weeks, Bob. *The Brier: The History of Canada's Most Celebrated Curling Championship*. Toronto: Macmillan, 1995.

Zawadzki, Edward. *The Ultimate Canadian Sports Trivia Book*. Toronto: Hounslow, 2001.

Zeman, Brenda. *88 Years of Puck-Chasing in Saskatchewan*. Regina: WDS Associates, 1983.

Zeman, Brenda. *To Run with Longboat: Twelve Stories of Indian Athletes in Canada*. Edmonton: GMS Ventures, 1988.

INDEX

PEOPLE

Photographs in bold

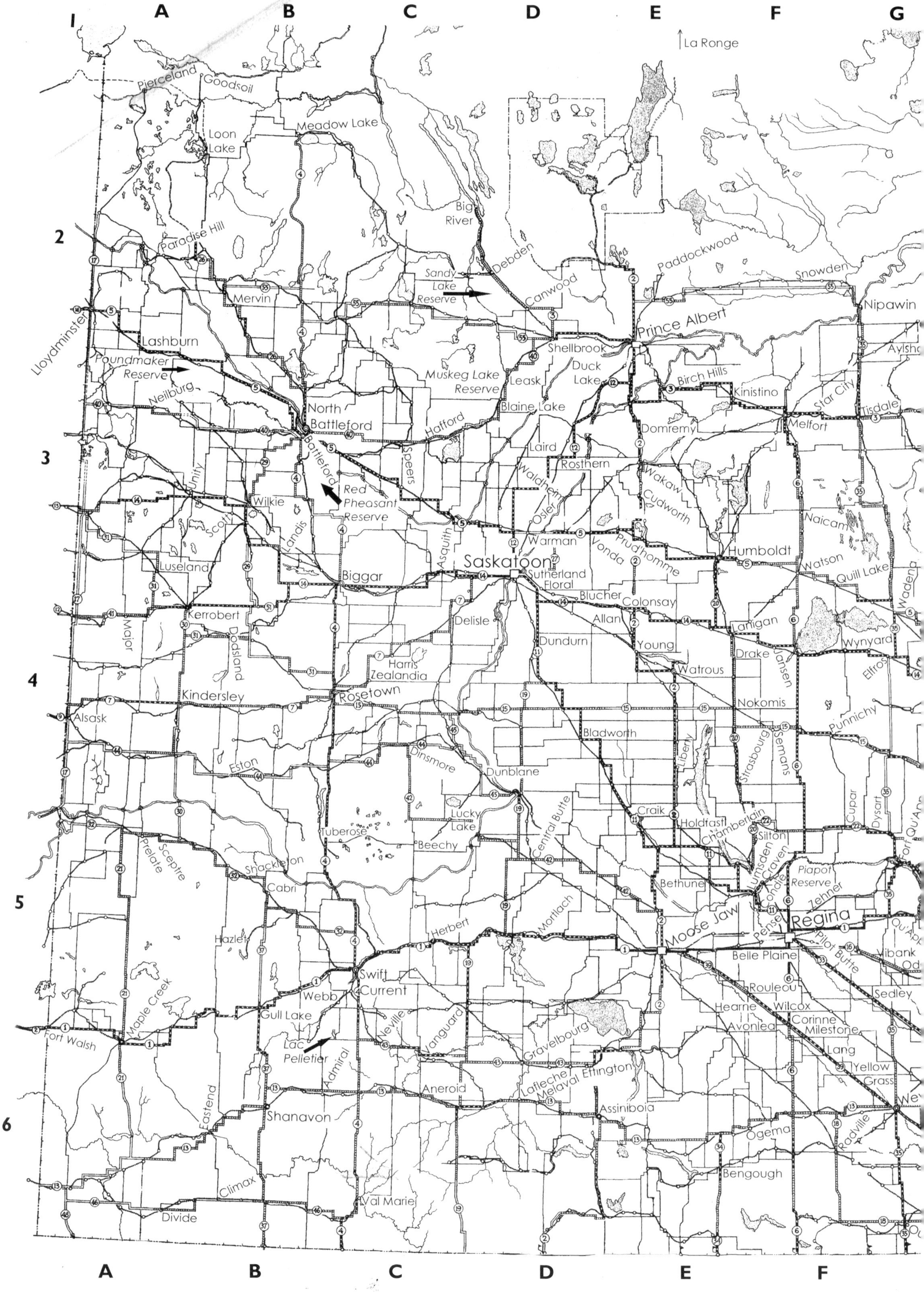
A
B
C
D
E
F
G
1
2
3
4
5
6
La Ronge
Pierceland
Goodsoil
Loon Lake
Meadow Lake
Big River
Paradise Hill
Debden
Paddockwood
Snowden
Sandy Lake Reserve
Canwood
Mervin
Nipawin
Lloydminster
Lashburn
Prince Albert
Shellbrook
Poundmaker Reserve
Duck Lake
Muskeg Lake Reserve
Leask
Birch Hills
Kinistino
Neilburg
Blaine Lake
Star City
Tisdale
North Battleford
Hafford
Domremy
Melfort
Battleford
Laird
Rosthern
Speers
Unity
Waldheim
Wakaw
Red Pheasant Reserve
Cudworth
Wilkie
Osler
Scott
Landis
Asquith
Naicam
Warman
Vonda
Prud'homme
Humboldt
Luseland
Saskatoon
Sutherland
Floral
Watson
Quill Lake
Biggar
Wadena
Blucher
Colonsay
Kerrobert
Allan
Delisle
Lanigan
Major
Dodsland
Dundurn
Young
Wynyard
Drake
Jansen
Harris
Zealandia
Watrous
Elfros
Kindersley
Rosetown
Nokomis
Alsask
Punnichy
Bladworth
Liberty
Strasbourg
Semans
Eston
Dinsmore
Dunblane
Lucky Lake
Central Butte
Cupar
Dysart
Craik
Holdfast
Chamberlain
Silton
Tuberose
Beechy
Prelate
Sceptre
Shackleton
Lumsden
Craven
Piapot Reserve
Cabri
Bethune
Condie
Zehner
Mortlach
Moose Jaw
Pense
Regina
Hazlet
Herbert
Pilot Butte
Belle Plaine
Vibank
Swift Current
Webb
Rouleau
Maple Creek
Gull Lake
Hearne
Wilcox
Sedley
Neville
Vanguard
Avonlea
Corinne
Milestone
Fort Walsh
Lac Pelletier
Gravelbourg
Lang
Admiral
Yellow Grass
Lafleche
Melaval
Ettington
Aneroid
Eastend
Assiniboia
Shanavon
Ogema
Radville
Bengough
Climax
Val Marie
Divide